MW01448093

Beihefte zur Zeitschrift für
Altorientalische und
Biblische Rechtsgeschichte (BZAR)

Herausgegeben von
Eckart Otto und Dominik Markl

Band 22

2019
Harrassowitz Verlag · Wiesbaden

Paradigm Change
in Pentateuchal Research

Edited by Matthias Armgardt,
Benjamin Kilchör and Markus Zehnder

2019
Harrassowitz Verlag · Wiesbaden

Bibliografische Information der Deutschen Nationalbibliothek
Die Deutsche Nationalbibliothek verzeichnet diese Publikation in der Deutschen
Nationalbibliografie; detaillierte bibliografische Daten sind im Internet
über http://dnb.dnb.de abrufbar.

Bibliographic information published by the Deutsche Nationalbibliothek
The Deutsche Nationalbibliothek lists this publication in the Deutsche
Nationalbibliografie; detailed bibliographic data are available in the internet
at http://dnb.dnb.de.

For further information about our publishing program consult our
website http://www.harrassowitz-verlag.de
© Otto Harrassowitz GmbH & Co. KG, Wiesbaden 2019
This work, including all of its parts, is protected by copyright.
Any use beyond the limits of copyright law without the permission
of the publisher is forbidden and subject to penalty. This applies
particularly to reproductions, translations, microfilms and storage
and processing in electronic systems.
Printed on permanent/durable paper.
Printing and binding: Memminger MedienCentrum AG
Printed in Germany
ISSN 1439-619X
ISBN 978-3-447-11170-6

Table of Contents

Preface VII

I. Introductory and Methodological Contributions

Georg Fischer
Time for a Change! 3

Richard E. Averbeck
Reading the Torah in a Better Way 21

Joshua Berman
The Limits of Source Criticism 45

Koert van Bekkum
The Divine Revelation of the Name 59

II. Legal History

Matthias Armgardt
Why a Paradigm Change in Pentateuch Research is Necessary 79

Guido Pfeifer
The Pentateuch Paradigm and Ancient Near Eastern Legal History 93

Benjamin Kilchör
Wellhausen's Five Pillars for the Priority of D over P/H:
Can They Still Be Maintained? 101

Markus Zehnder
Leviticus 26 and Deuteronomy 28 115

III. Torah and Prophets

Eckart Otto
Deuteronomy as the Legal Completion and Prophetic Finale
of the Pentateuch 179

Kenneth Bergland
Jeremiah 34 Originally Composed as a Legal Blend of Leviticus 25
and Deuteronomy 15.. 189

Carsten Vang
The Non-Prophetic Background for the King Law in Deut 17:14–20 207

IV. Dating Issues

Hendrik J. Koorevaar
Steps for Dating the Books of the Pentateuch 227

Lina Petersson
The Linguistic Profile of the Priestly Narrative of the Pentateuch............ 243

Jan Retsö
The Tabernacle and the Dating of P 265

John S. Bergsma
A 'Samaritan' Pentateuch?... 287

Sandra Richter
What's Money Got to Do with It?..................................... 301

Pekka Pitkänen
Reconstruction the Social Contexts of the Priestly and Deuteronomic
Materials in a Non-Wellhausian Setting 323

Index of Ancient Sources 339
Index of Modern Authors 359

Preface

This volume collects papers presented at an international meeting held 16-18 March 2017 in Riehen (Switzerland), together with one additional study that was submitted later (Koorevaar, "Steps for Dating the Books of the Pentateuch"). The title of the meeting was "Paradigm Change in Pentateuchal Research". The implications of the title are twofold. First: It is generally recognised that the old paradigm, classically formulated in Julius Wellhausen´s influential *Prolegomena zur Geschichte Israels* can no longer command a dominant position in the scholarly debate about genesis and structure of the texts that in their fascinating complexity form the Pentateuch. The process that led to the erosion of Wellhausen´s model is in itself complex, and scholarly views on the identity of its shortcomings and weaknesses vary. Second: The title does not prescribe in any way in which direction the search for a new paradigm should proceed. During the conference, however, it became clear that an important element of the new paradigm is the use of empirical methods, in contradistinction to a dominance of subjective criteria and approaches developed in circumstances that are foreign to the cultural world of the ancient Near East.

The scholars who participated at the meeting represent very diverse backgrounds not only in terms of geography (nine countries, three continents), but also in terms of religion/denomination/theological position, and especially in terms of professional specialization: Besides Biblical Studies, also the fields of Assyriology, Legal History, and Linguistics were represented.

The papers read at the meeting had three major focuses, with some papers combining more than one of the respective themes:

1) Some studies address methodological questions. A number of these papers show that Wellhausen´s paradigm is marked, i.a., by the following deficits:
- circular reasoning;
- use of source and redaction criticism in ways that do not begin with observations made in a specific text, but impose preconceived models on the texts;
- neglect of attempts to understand the final text in its literary cohesion;
- lack of empirical backup through comparison with extra-biblical evidence.

All the papers deal with foundational methodological questions, but some do so more explicitly and in more detail than others, while other studies are more focused on the analysis of specific texts (or specific entities of various kinds reflected in texts or material remains).

2) Some studies engage with questions of dating. From about the seventies of the last century, the discussion was dominated by models that related the genesis of the Pentateuch to circles in Jerusalem who were active mostly in the 7th to 5th centuries

BCE. The studies presented at the meeting show, however, that this theory cannot be upheld without serious difficulties.

3) Several contributions deal with the role of P. Some of these studies address the question of the dating of possible P-texts and question the previously dominant model according to which P is exilic or postexilic. In other studies, the distinction between P and non-P as one of the fundamental elements of pentateuchal scholarship is investigated and questioned.

Here is a summary of the articles and their interconnections, arranged in the sequence in which they appear in the main body of this book.

Introductory and Methodological Studies
Georg Fischer's study, "Time for a Change! – Why Pentateuchal Research is in Crisis," serves as the programmatic opening of the volume as a whole. The study pursues two goals: 1. To analyse the roots of the problems in the exegesis of the Torah. 2. To offer alternatives for looking at its texts. In Fischer's analysis, the main reasons for the ongoing problems of Pentateuchal research are rooted in the rationalist approach going back to the Age of Enlightenment; the use of vague terms, fragile and ambiguous criteria, and circular reasoning; the fact that literary genres found in the Torah in many cases do not square with the categories and expectations of modern readers. Furthermore, the fact that it is impossible to reconstruct the (known) sources of texts such as 4Q158 1–2, the Book of Jubilees, and the Temple Scroll – Genesis and Deuteronomy, respectively – shows that there are severe limits to the attempts to reconstruct the assumed sources of Pentateuchal compositions. There are also serious problems related to the priestly writing. Texts ascribed traditionally to P, such as Gen 1:1–2:3; 5:1–32; Exod 1:13–14; 2:23–25; 6:2–8.14–27, are necessary for the coherence of the narrative within their respective contexts and deepen it. In order to overcome the present impasse in pentateuchal studies, Fischer proposes to pursue new (and old) avenues, in a combination of critical research with stimuli from other areas of human expression and art. For example, ancient Egyptian art, as well as some Orthodox icons and modern paintings, are marked by multi-perspectivity. Narrative analyses enable us to perceive Torah texts as being as precisely constructed as rockets or computers; Thomas L. Brodie speaks of "body-like complexity". In all of these texts, separate components come together to form a unity and, as a whole, serve specific purposes. Further comparisons / paradigms for such mixtures of different materials / objects may come from music, architecture, and a reflection on the root of textus, indicating a mesh, or web. Fischer posits that the call for a change in Pentateuchal research will meet with resistance. Yet there will be no progress unless we examine our methods, overcome their inherent weaknesses, and correct them. Pointing to Jeremiah 2:8, Fischer admonishes scholars to find ways to "allow" a biblical text "to be." As can be seen from this overview, Fischer's study is fully located on the level of methodological discussion, without treating a specific biblical text in detail.

This is different in *Richard Averbeck*'s contribution, entitled "Reading the Torah in a Better Way: Unity amid Diversity in Text, Genre, and Compositional History." Here, general methodological considerations are combined with an attempt to find new ways in understanding the patriarchal stories. Averbeck begins with a review of the two dominant theories of the composition of the Pentateuch in the academy today: the (neo-)documentary and the non-documentary (redactional) approaches. It finds them lacking sound rationale and application to the text. What is needed, according to Averbeck, is a radical shift in the reading of the text for its compositional (pre)history. Two points are essential. First, a more generous approach must be taken to the reading of this ancient text, making more allowance for the literary conventions of its ancient authors as opposed to our own modern literary sensitivities. Second, the text needs to be read according to its various literary genres, taking into consideration the genre(s) of its underlying source materials. After addressing general methodological questions, Averbeck turns to the patriarchal narratives in Genesis 12-50. He identifies the pastoral "enclosed nomadism" of the ANE as the underlying cultural context of these chapters. In this context, the identity of the patriarchs can be defined in terms of "enclosed nomadic sheikhs." These kinds of cultures are prone to doing oral "genealogical history", not the kind of history done by (fully developed) nations in the ANE and up into our modern era. Fortunately, useful modern studies of such cultures by cultural anthropologists do exist, for example pertaining to the modern Jordanian Bedouins. Applying this kind of historical and cultural background to our reading of the patriarchal narratives yields important results for our understanding of the compositional (pre)history of Genesis. First, it is unlikely that the genealogies, stories, and promises would have circulated separately in the oral context. They grew and belonged together from the start in genealogical history. This speaks against, for example, separating the supposed P genealogies out from the supposed J, E, or P narratives. Such oral history was most naturally told within a genealogical framework that was supplied as part of the telling of the history. Second, in genealogical historical contexts like that reflected in Genesis, the stories are good and reliable vehicles for carrying true historical memories, even if the story can be told from different perspectives, depending on who was telling them and to whom he was doing the telling. At the core, these are received traditions with longstanding stature. They were carefully preserved and constantly retold. Third, tribal cultures naturally resist writing down their history because of the fluidity with which the traditions needed to be told in variable tribal oral contexts. With regard to the patriarchal traditions in Genesis, like among modern day Bedouins in Jordan, the most natural impetus for the eventual writing down of the oral traditions would have been the need to draw together the genealogical history of the oral patriarchal period in the service of the emerging nation. This speaks against the common historical critical notion of a redaction that did not link the previously independent traditions of the patriarchs and the exodus together until late in the post-exilic period. The oral prehistory was needed as the foundation for the establishment and growth of people as a nation.

The third study of this group is *Joshua Berman*'s "The Limits of Source Criticism: The Flood Narrative in Genesis 6-9". This study focues on one of the methodological pillars of the dominant paradigm, source criticism, as applied specifically to Genesis 6-9. He points out that for a long time, the source-critical division of the Genesis flood account has been celebrated as one of the most important achievements of modern biblical criticism. Berman's study takes a critical look at the source-critical paradigm and examines its hermeneutics. He argues that historical-critical scholarship applies a series of double standards that all work in concert to support the source-critical aims and results. All in all, nine methodological flaws are detected in the source-critical approach to the story: 1. The theory creates the text, rather than the text creating the theory. 2. False doublets are created. 3. The establishment of the putative sources leads to irrational non-sequiturs. 4. A double-stardard for determining doublets is applied. 5. Redactional layers have to be invented to explain inconsistencies or redundancies in the putative sources. 6. The source-critical approach rests on the mistaken assumption that the biblical redactors faithfully preserved their sources. 7. Evidence adduced from cognate materials – particularly from the Mesopotamian version of the flood story contained in Tablet XI of the Gilgamesh epic – that threatens the model's validity is suppressed by simply ignoring it, or otherwise negating the validity of that evidence through unwarranted means. In this context, Berman points out that it is exactly the combined assumed sources of the Genesis account that provide a surprisingly coherent parallel with Tablet XI of the Gilgamesh epic, while none of the isolated sources lead to any such result. This in itself makes the source division highly problematic. 8. Internal evidence is, as a matter of principle and without any good reasons, given priority over external evidence. 9. It is presupposed, again as a matter of principle and without any good reasons, that it is possible to (at least partially) understand the pre-history of the text.

Koert van Bekkum's study is entitled "The Divine Revelation of the Name. Warranted and Unwarranted Confidence in the Literary-Critical Analysis of Exodus 3 and 6." Similar to the two previous articles, more general methodological reflections are combined with the study of a specific set of biblical texts. Van Bekkum notes that since the beginning of Pentateuchal criticism the linguistic and thematic transfer from Genesis to Exodus has been a contested issue. The two stories about the revelation of the divine name to Moses in Exodus 3 and 6 were used to address this problem. The literary tensions in and between both chapters played an important role in the construction of the Older Documentary Hypothesis, later in the definition of a Primary Document that would create a unity between the sources, and finally in the development of the Documentary Hypothesis. Two distinct concepts of how, when and where the divine name was revealed were identified. In this view, Exodus 3 was seen as part of a compilation of the so-called Jahwist and Elohist sources, while Exodus 6 was thought to be a segment of a Priestly source. A recent defence of this model is found in the so-called Neo-Documentarian approach. More recent scholarly work studies both accounts of the revelation of the divine name mostly from a redaction-critical point of view. Exodus 6 is still viewed as "Priestly", but Exodus 3 (and 4) is now defined in many different ways. According to van Bekkum, these new approaches, as well as synchronic readings made significant observations in analysing and interpreting the texts of Exodus 3 and 6 and detected important literary allusions to the book of Genesis. Van Bekkum argues that this situation calls for an evaluation of the criteria that have been used in the diachronic analysis of the texts. Unfortunately, the application of these criteria unnecessarily posits thematic tensions and textual inconsistencies in the stories, often resulting in the fragmentation of the material. Applied in this way, a diachronic approach is not able to do justice to the narrative flow in the transfer from the patriarchal narratives and the Joseph story to the story of the Exodus. The first account of the divine revelation of the name in Exodus 3 reflects explicitly on the discontinuity in the nature of Yhwh and his relation to the patriarchs and Israel, while the consequences of this revelation are highlighted in the second episode in Exodus 6. This clearly indicates that the formal aspects and the content of the texts should not be treated separately and that modern assumptions of what a story should look like should be avoided. The way the text itself reflects on the breaches and discontinuities in the overall narrative of Yhwh's history with Israel might suggest that different types of language and stories in this narrative are not necessarily the result of different sources or editorial strands, but merely different views of realities tied to specific fields of interest and terminology. While they are quite diverse, they are not conceptually inconsistent. A model creating less distance between story and history and paying structural attention to the continuity between the diverse passages and traditions and to the literary configuration of thematic shifts, might be able to offer better answers and provide the opportunity to avoid the fragmentation that is threatening the historical understanding of the Pentateuch under the presuppositions of the old paradigm.

Legal History
The first two studies in this section of the book are written from the viewpoint of ancient Near Eastern and Roman legal history, an adjacent field of research which has great potential in offering a reference or a counterpoint to the discussions on the Pentateuch.

In his essay "Why a Paradigm Change in Pentateuch Research is Necessary. The Perspective of Legal History," *Matthias Armgardt* points out that after two hundred years of work on the basis of de Wette and the more or less modified Wellhausen-paradigm, Pentateuchal research has reached a dead-end. The methodological flaws, among them especially circular reasoning, are obvious. Interestingly, something similar happened to the discipline of the study of Roman Law. After decades of hunting for interpolations in the Corpus Iuris Civilis, about 30 years ago the legal historians became aware that there was something wrong in the methods and assumptions that formed the foundation of their research. Today almost every scholar of Roman Law assumes that the legal texts in the Digest have not been interpolated, unless there is really strong evidence to the contrary. If all the theories about interpolations that scholars in the first decades of the 20th century assumed had been right, the making of the Corpus Iuris Civilis would have taken at least 30 years, not 3 years. Armgardt adds that in the case of the Corpus Iuris Civilis there is no doubt that there were some interpolations, but not as many as have been suspected. Nowadays everybody wonders how it was possible that brilliant scholars could have walked into the trap of arbitrariness and uncontrolled subjectivity in this field of research. Armgardt suggests that a similar turning point has come for Pentateuch research now. A critical analysis of the assumptions and methods this field of research is needed. At the same time, it is clear that the change of a paradigm is never easy. A help in this critical situation is the fact that ground-breaking work has already been done, in particular by Kenneth Kitchen. He, among others, has shown that the right way forward in Pentateuchal studies is to rely on external evidence, especially from the second millennium BCE. Armgardt points out that attempts to show a connection between Deuteronomy and the Vassal Treaties of Esarhaddon or the Law of Gortyn and the Roman Twelve Tables have proven not to be successful. On the other hand, as Armgardt shows, an analysis of the form and the subjects of the treaties in Exodus, Leviticus, and Deuteronomy demonstrates a very strong affinity with extra-biblical material from the second millennium BCE. He also investigates the suretyship of Juda for the return of Benjamin in Genesis 43-44 and points to the strong similarity of this feature with the Old-Babylonian suretyship deeds of the early second millennium BCE, thus again demonstrating the importance of extra-biblical empirical evidence from the second millennium BCE for the historically viable interpretation of the Pentateuch.

A different approach is taken by *Guido Pfeifer*, whose essay is entitled "The Pentateuch Paradigm and Ancient Near Eastern Legal History – a Look back from the Environment." This article is fully devoted to the area of theoretical reflection. Pfeifer looks at the experiences with paradigms, impasses and "new" approaches in ancient Near Eastern legal history. Both legal history in general and ancient Near Eastern legal history in particular were and are determined by various paradigms, sometimes advancing, sometimes hindering cognitive progress. The paradigms dealt with in this article refer to a general framework of the question of whether there was any legal thinking in the ancient Near East. To some extent, this question is "paradigmatic" in addressing the complex relationship between cognitive interests, hermeneutic concepts, and the source material. The late Raymond Westbrook challenged an evolutionistic approach towards cultural and legal history and searched for a new paradigm instead: a paradigm that was even more oriented on the sources and that also took into consideration factors that played a role already before the invention of writing, such as agriculture and urbanization. This could challenge common narratives, among them the one about the origins of science. Pfeifer contends that if we allow ourselves to ask the question of whether there was any legal thinking in the ancient Near East, we must look for hidden traces. Thus, the investigation takes a closer look at the functions of ancient Near Eastern law, at its pre-conditions, and at its role within the texture of the scientific culture of ancient Mesopotamia. By doing so, older and more recent scientific approaches to the intellectual world of the ancient Near East – or paradigms – appear on the scene. What Pentateuchal research and ancient Near Eastern legal history have in common is the ambition to understand the transmitted textual material in a better way. The best way forward is to develop research questions imposed by the source material itself, and to make the hermeneutic concepts used to find answers to these questions as transparent as possible. If the questions are generated with disregard of the sources, there is a risk of anachronistic pre-assumptions. On the other hand, also an examination of texts without any idea of the cognitive interests on the side of the researcher is likely to fail, because sources do not tend to be self-explanatory, even more so when they are investigated isolated from each other. Finally, only transparency of methods and concepts make a scientific discourse possible in the first place, especially beyond the borders of our disciplines. Pfeifer also states that in spite of all efforts, there may be areas of history that remain beyond our reach. Against this background, Pfeifer concludes that it is doubtful whether there is a need or even room for paradigms. The actual challenge might be the refinement of questions and methods that make paradigms obsolete, rather than a paradigm change.

The third of the essays collected in the "Legal History" section is written from the perspective of biblical scholarship, and, like the first one in this group, combines introductory remarks that are of a more general character with observations that deal with specific biblical texts which are relevant for the assessment of the Wellhausenian paradigm. In his essay, *Benjamin Kilchör* addresses the following question: "Wellhausen's Five Pillars for the Priority of D over P/H: Can They Still be Maintained?" Kilchör points out that although the Documentary Hypothesis of Wellhausen has lost much of its convincing power over the last fifty years, Wellhausen's exilic-postexilic dating of P has continued to form a cornerstone of almost all Pentateuch models. The Wellhausenian post-dating of P in regard to D is based on five pillars: 1. the place of worship; 2. sacrifice; 3. the sacred festivals; 4. the priests and Levites; 5. the endowment of the clergy. In his study, Kilchör scrutinizes the two most influential pillars, the place of worship and the relationship between priests and Levites. As far as the place of worship is concerned, Kilchör argues that while Leviticus 17 shows no awareness of any specifics from Deuteronomy 12, the latter chapter presupposes a distinction between the slaughtering of sacrificial and wild animals as we find it in Leviticus 17. With regard to the relationship between priests and Levites, Kilchör mentions that Wellhausen regarded Ezekiel 44 as intermediate piece between D and P. According to this reconstruction, D does not know a distinction between priests and Levites; only Ezekiel would introduce it, and P later presupposes the distinction. Wellhausen's view is, however, no longer accepted in more recent research. Rather, there is a clear trend to see Ezekiel as dependent on P and not the other way round. At the same time, however, instead of questioning Wellhausen's dating of P, redaction criticism is still broadly used as a tool to maintain it. Kilchör argues that since the core of Deuteronomy 12, Ezekiel 44, and also Jeremiah presuppose considerable parts of P-texts, the paradigm that is built around an exilic-postexilic dating of P must be reevaluated in its foundations. As this overview of the article shows, the relationship between Torah and Prophets is also dealt with, besides aspects of legal history.

The last study in the group "Legal History" is *Markus Zehnder's* "Leviticus 26 and Deuteronomy 28: Some Observations on Their Relationship". This study is less directed at addressing methological questions in theory; rather, it aims to practically apply a wide range of methods to a specific set of texts that are important in the assessment of Old Testament legal collections. The three main questions that are addressed in Zehnder's study are the following: 1. How can the structure of the two catalogues of blessings and curses in Leviticus 26 and Deuteronomy 28 be described? 2. How can the relationship between the two catalogues be described? Is one dependent on the other? Is it possible to make any informed suggestions about the date of the catalogues or parts of them? 3. Are there any conclusions that can be drawn from observations on the relationship between the two catalogues as far as the relationship between the major biblical law collections is concerned? These questions are important especially because Deuteronomy 28 is often seen as part of the "Urdeuteronomium," which again is related to the neo-Assyrian period by many scholars, and seen as the main Archimedean point for the reconstruction of the literary history of the Pentateuch, at least the legal material contained in it. These questions are addressed in four different ways. 1. A lexical and structural analysis of the two texts is provided. As far as Leviticus 26 is concerned, the most salient finding is the adversative use of the noun qery, which likely points to an old age of the phrases in which it is used. With respect to Deuteronomy 28, the complexity of the overall structure is remarkable, and clearly distinguishes this text from Leviticus 26. The same goes for the much more detailed references to developments after the implementation of the curses (see Deuteronomy 29-31). In both cases, the observations tend to suggest a chronological post-position of Deuteronomy 28(-31) in comparison to Leviticus 26. 2. The lexical or phraseological / syntactical connections between the two texts are investigated. It turns out that there is considerable thematic overlap, while close lexical or phraseological connections are rare. The detailed observations concerning this part of the investigation do not allow to draw any conclusions. 3. The lexical or phraseological / syntactical connections between Leviticus 26 and Deuteronomy 28 on the one hand and other biblical texts on the other are investigated. This investigation shows that there are a high number of passages in prophetic books that can be shown with a high degree of probability to be dependent on either Leviticus 26 or Deuteronomy 28. Since many of these passages can be dated pre-exilic or early exilic with high confidence, this proves that the corresponding passages in Leviticus 26 and Deuteronomy 28 must be older. Regardless of the question of the direction of dependence between either Leviticus 26 or Deuteronomy 28 on the one hand and other biblical texts on the other, the fact that intertextual links to both catalogues exist indicates that none of the two passages was understood as replacing the other. 4. Observations are adduced concerning the connections, both linguistic and topical, between the two texts and extra-biblical material. This part of the investigation shows that several passages in both texts fit a chronological milieu that pre-dates the neo-Assyrian period. On the other hand, directions of dependence between the biblical and the extra-biblical material can generally not be established with certainty. While Zehnder makes clear that all four avenues are important, it also turns out that not all questions mentioned above can be answered adequately based on the evidence that the four avenues provide, and in some cases only statements of probability with a considerable degree of uncertainty are possible. Zehnder maintains that it is important, in such circumstances, not to press forward answers that are not well founded, or to hide the degree of uncertainty that is connected with some of the more tentative and provisional answers. In his conclusion, Zehnder states that it is likely that Leviticus 26 and Deuteronomy 28 are largely independent compositions. Direct lexical/idiomatic overlap is rare, and can best be explained in terms of a shared dependence on broader curse traditions. However, there are some signs that the author(s) of Deuteronomy 28 might have been familiar with Leviticus 26 or an earlier version of that text. Based on the study of both inner-biblical evidence and extra-biblical comparative material, both catalogues, likely in their entirety, can be dated well before the exile. As in the case of the previous study, not only aspects of legal history, but also the relationship between Torah and Prophets, together with dating issues are dealt with in Zehnder's article as well.

Torah and Prophets
Some of the studies explore the Wellhausenian model from within and identify various aspects that are in need of being addressed. One of these studies is *Eckart Otto's* "Deuteronomy as the Legal Completion and Prophetic Finale of the Pentateuch", the first of three essays that are collected in the "Torah and Prophets" section of the book. Otto's study is devoted to the macrostructure of the Pentateuch and especially Deuteronomy's role in it. He votes for an end of the *captivitas babylonica* of the Book of Deuteronomy which has been more and more detached from the Pentateuch since Julius Wellhausen up to Martin Noth, when the Book of Deuteronomy became part of a Deuteronomistic History from Deuteronomy to 2 Kings and the Pentateuch was amputated to a Tetrateuch or even a Tritoteuch. One of the weaknesses of this view, according to Otto, is that any attempt to correlate the framework of Deuteronomy in Deuteronomy 1-11; 27-34 with any literary layer of the books of the Former Prophets failed. Moreover, the question as to how the Book of Deuteronomy became part of the Pentateuch has not received a satisfactory answer within this model. Against this background, Otto argues that in Deuteronomy 12-26 Moses not only interprets the Sinai-Torah of Exodus but, in the final shape of the Book of Deuteronomy, also the Torah of Leviticus. As an integral part of the Torah, the Book of Deuteronomy is both the legal completion of the Torah, as well as the prophetic finale of all the Pentateuch, and no longer the legal measuring stick for Israel's failed history in the Promised Land. It delivers some hermeneutical keys for the interpretation of all the Torah. The Book of Deuteronomy is situated between Moses' prophe-

cies of doom and salvation in Deuteronomy 4 and the forward-looking chapters Deuteronomy 29-30, portraying Moses as the arch-prophet and the prototype of all prophecy. A special role is also attributed to Deuteronomy 32, a chapter that combines a large number of motives from other parts of the Old Testament canon, with these motives confirming the deuteronomic sealing of the Pentateuch. When the Book of Deuteronomy is understood as the culmination and finale of all the books of the Pentateuch it opens decisive hermeneutical insights into the theology of the Pentateuch as a whole. The return of Deuteronomy to the Torah is, according to Otto, the real paradigm change in the interpretation of the Pentateuch.

A different approach, focusing on one specific passage in the Book of Jeremiah, is found in *Kenneth Bergland's* article, entitled "Jer 34 Originally Composed as a Legal Blend of Lev 25 and Deut 15." Bergland argues that the reuse of Leviticus 25 and Deuteronomy 15 was part of the original composition of Jer 34:8–22, and cannot be removed without collapsing the passage itself. It is therefore not "remixing the language of Zedekiah's proclamation with the Deuteronomic legislation" that brings the author of Jeremiah 34 to the understanding that the "Judean slaves must be—or should have been—released unconditionally and irrevocably" (Chavel, "'Let My People Go!'", p. 81). This thrust in Jeremiah 34 is better explained as an original reuse of Leviticus 25. It appears like a forced neglect when Chavel (like many others) jumps over the possibility of a reuse of Leviticus 25 in the original composition of Jeremiah 34 and insists that "a higher standard not called for in the original Deuteronomic legislation, demanding that the owner recognize his or her slave as a social equal" was the original creation of the author of Jeremiah 34 (Chavel, "'Let My People Go!'", p. 85). Rather, the differences between the justification of manumission in Jer 34:9b and 34:14 are best understood as different strategies of reuse by the same author. Bergland argues that while Jer 34:8–11 shows an alternating and much tighter knit reuse of Leviticus 25 and Deuteronomy 15, Jer 34:12–22 largely relocates Deuteronomy 15 to the prescription to release the slaves in Jer 34:13–14, while Jer 34:15–22 reuses Leviticus 25, primarily in the divine indictment against the people's return of slaves. Against this background, it is reasonable to conclude that the reuse of both Leviticus 25 and Deuteronomy 15 was found in the original composition of Jer 34:8–22. As a conflation of both Leviticus 25 and Deuteronomy 15, Jeremiah 34 would be the youngest of the three. In other words, both Leviticus 25 and Deuteronomy 15 must have been available for the author of Jeremiah 34. Breaking out one of the pieces of Jeremiah by declaring them later redactional insertions would destroy the whole edifice of Jeremiah 34. Bergman's observation have much in common with Zehnder's evaluation of the relationship between various prophetic texts on the one hand and Leviticus 26 and Deuteronomy 28 on the other.

The third study that is devoted to the relationship between Torah and Latter Prophets is *Carsten Vang's* contribution, entitled "The Non-Prophetic Background for the King Law in Deut 17:14–20". Vang's approach is to some degree similar to Bergland's, but reverses the direction of the investigation by beginning with a Pentateuchal passage instead of a prophetic passage, and also takes extra-biblical evidence into consideration. Vang observes that none of the Pentateuch law sections relates any part of their extensive legislation to royal governance. Only in Deut 16:18–18:22 – a section about governance in ancient Israel – do we find regulations for a potential Israelite kingdom (17:14-20). The so-called "King Law" put three restrictions on the king-to-be: He may not provide for himself many horses, many wives and much wealth. These circumscriptions have no parallels in ancient Near Eastern royal ideology. They are also remarkable seen from the perspective of the historical and prophetic writings of the Old Testament which offer a very different view of the king's cultic, social, juridical, and military responsibilities. Contemporary scholarship usually explains the restrictions from two angles. Either Deut 17:1-17 is understood as a Deuteronomic/Deuteronomistic response to the Old Testament prophets' critique of the kings' reliance on military equipment and help from the superpowers. Or the restrictions are interpreted as an allusion to king Solomon's excessive acquisition of horses, foreign women, and wealth. Most scholars therefore date the King Law to the last few decades of the Judahite kingdom or to the exilic or postexilic period. Vang shows that the three restrictions on the king-to-be are not formulated with the prophetic critique of kingship in Judah or Israel in mind. In his view, the restriction against obtaining many horses addresses the issue of luxury horses as a symbol of royal grandness. A martial meaning of the word סוסis not probable here. The constraint on a big harem hardly refers to the issue of political marriages, but rather deals with the temptation to marry many native women which would endanger the Deuteronomic vision of an equal society with no specific class distinction or concentration of power. The restrictions are phrased in a very open and non-specific manner and do not betray any linguistic relation at all to the phraseology in the prophetic writings, where the kings are censured for their reliance on heavy military or political alliances. As far as the connection to Solomon is concerned, Vang concedes that Solomon certainly violates all the restrictions in the King Law. It is, however, a fact that the Deuteronomistic account in 1 Kings 3–11 of Solomon and his reign does not describe him through the lenses of Deut 17:14-20, but explains his downfall from a reflection on the proscription in Deut 7:1-4 against family relations with foreign nations. If the three unusual restrictions on the Israelite king in the King Law neither can be properly explained from historical circumstances in 7th and 6th century Judah, nor from a critical review of the reasons for king Solomon's downfall, it is more natural to see the curtailing of the king's power symbols in the light of the ancient Near Eastern ideals for divinely sanctioned kingship. Israel may opt for a king like the surrounding nations, but they should not import the concomitant notions of royal grandeur. The future king should get his ideals for governance from another source. Vang further argues that the warning not to choose a foreigner as king (Deut 17:15) suggests a context in which the Israelites did not yet have any experience with a royal governance of their own, nor any form of chieftain government or a class of aristocrats. The article contends that the King Law with its restrictions makes best sense in a pre-monarchic context.

Dating Issues
This section is opened by *Hendrik Koorevaar*'s essay, entitled "Steps for Dating the Books of the Pentateuch: a Literary and Historical Canonical Approach". This is one of the contributions that is dealing exclusively with issues of methodology. Koorevaar attempts to give a general, comprehensive overview of factors that need to be considered when dating Pentateuchal books based on biblical textual indications. He begins by underlining that dating the Pentateuch is in fact first and foremost a literary issue. Koorevaar points out that the history of the documentary hypothesis of the Pentateuch has shown that the arguments for the existence of the hypothetical sources (J, E, D, and P) are not, and have never been, tenable. Rather, they were suggestive. Koorevaar concludes that Old Testament scholarship has been put on the wrong track in the past by this hypothesis. Only D as the Mosaic Book of the Law can be clearly identified and reconstructed with the information in the book of Deuteronomy. Koorevaar further observes that from a literary perspective, the series of books beginning with Genesis finishes with Kings. This begs the question in what ways one could talk of a Pentateuch, or a Tetrateuch, Hexateuch. Looking at the Pentateuch, the question arises as to whether it is-a book or a block of books. As a block several literary types characterize the books. Koorevaar argues that Exodus-Leviticus-Numbers is one book, and the Pentateuch therefore a tryptic. This again means that as far as questions of dating are concerned, Genesis, Exodus-Leviticus-Numbers, and Deuteronomy must be studied separately; one should not presuppose the same date for all of them. Even if the results should show that two or more books have to be dated to the same point in time, this does not change the phenomenon that they are different entities from a literary point of view. In the second part of this study, Koorevaar then turns to questions concerning the method of dating. He proposes a historical-canonical approach to address these questions. Five elements need to be observed. 1. Identifying and dating the last-mentioned event in the book. 2. Tracking down all direct or indirect indications or possible indications of the time of the author. In this context, the assumption of *Fortschreibung* is legitimate only when it is clearly formulated as such in its context, as for example in Jeremiah 51:64b with respect to Jeremiah 52. Prophetic utterances (attributed to YHWH) or expectations of people about the future that have not yet been fulfilled, as in Genesis 50:24-26, should not automatically be regarded as *vaticinia post eventu*. Human hope, also human religious hope, is a very normal phenomenon. Post-Josephica in the book of Genesis, pointing to a time *after Joseph*, must be taken seriously as indicators for dating. The question is: How far after him? A further question is: What is the value of the many proposed Post-Mosaica in the Thora, pointing to a time *after Moses*? Genesis 14:14 is discussed by Koorevaar as an example that demonstrates that the study of one text can lead to different positions. The verse mentions the city of Dan. If Dan is the town at the sources of the Jordan, then this is an anachronism (cf. Josh 19:40-48). But if Dan is a town east of the Jordan, as the context indicates, then this is not an anachronism. 3. Identifying the country and the place where the book was

written by its author. 4. Setting up a schematic presentation of all temporal remarks. 5. Trying to discover the ratio or necessity for the proposed date.

The second study in this section is *Lina Petersson*'s "The Linguistic Profile of the Priestly Narrative of the Pentateuch". This is the only study in the volume that is exclusively devoted to linguistics as a means of an empirically-based investigation of the Pentatech. Petersson opens with an overview of the discussion concerning the use of diachronic linguistics for the dating of Old Testament texts in general. She then focuses on the textual corpus that is commonly ascribed to P and addresses the question whether the verbal syntax of the narrative P-sections align with Standard Biblial Hebrew and/or with Late Biblical Hebrew. Having established what the main characteristics of these two phases of Biblical Hebrew in terms of verbal syntax are, she then finds that the verbal syntax in the assumed P-narratives fully fall into the category of Standard Biblical Hebrew. Petersson also points out that this observations cannot be explained in terms of archaising use of language by postexilic authors, because syntax is largely part of the unconscious elements of language and can therefore not be manipulated.

Jan Retsö's essay is on the "The Tabernacle and the Dating of P". Retsö investigates the understanding of the shape of the Tabernacle and its equipment as described in Exodus 25-40. He argues that the object inside the Tabernacle, the *kapporet-'edut-aron*, is something different than what is usually assumed. The text has traditionally been read in light of the description of Solomon's temple. This, however, according to Retsö, has led scholarship astray. Based on a close reading of the text, Retsö comes to the conclusion that Holy of Holies is a canopy standing inside the Tabernacle supported by four columns with a cloth-covering. Inside this canopy stands the *kapporet* which is – contrary to common assumption – a standing plate with two cherubs flanking it, possibly sculptured from the *kapporet* plate itself. The *kapporet* is thus not the lid of a chest, but a standing object, perhaps even with something pictured on it. This kind of sanctuary is called *haman* in later Syro-Palestinian sanctuaries but is mentioned already in Ugaritic texts and later on in Arabia and is archaeologically well documented. The standing plate marks the presence of the deity. The use of this kind of sacrum is vehemently condemned in Old Testament texts from around 600 BCE and onwards, obviously considered pagan. In spite of this the Priestly code describes the central sacrum of early Israel as such an object. This indicates that the description of the sanctuary in P must be earlier than the texts condemning its use, which provides an argument for an early date of the text.

In his study, entitled "A 'Samaritan' Pentateuch? The Implications of the Pro-Northern Tendency of the Common Pentateuch," *John Bergsma* sets out to question the dominating trend within the newer Pentateuchal research which claims that the final redaction of the Pentateuch must be ascribed to postexilic priestly circles in Jerusalem who wanted to promote the legitimacy of the Jerusalem temple by producing their version of the Pentateuch. Bergsma points out that the following facts speak against this Jerusalem-centered view: While Jerusalem (or Zion, or the temple of Jerusalem) is never mentioned explicitly as a cultic place in the Pentateuch, other sites are, with a special weight given to the Shekhem area; Joseph and his descendants are characterized more positively than Judah and his descendants, as can be seen especially in Genesis 48; Joshua is preferred over against Caleb. Such traits give the Pentateuch in its final form a pro-northern character, which would better fit a pro-Samaritan than a pro-Jerusalemite agenda. Moreover, a comparison with the book of Jubilees shows what a pro-Jerusalem Pentateuch would look like. These observations, Bergsma concludes, necessitate a new assessment of the compositional history of the Pentateuch. It is, based on his observations, no longer possible to either claim that the Pentateuch in its final form is a Judean document that "accommodates" some northern traditions, or that the Pentateuch is a "compromise document" between Samarian and Judean interest groups. Bergsma also notes that in fact it does not exhibit any unambiguous evidence of an awareness of a rivalry between Judeans and Samarians/Samaritans that dominated their relationship from about the mid-5th century BCE. This can best be explained if the redaction of the Pentateuch, at least in its larger part, took place in an earlier, likely pre-exilic, period.

As the title of her essay indicates, *Sandra Richter*'s "What's Money Got to Do with It? Economics and the Question of the Provenance of Deuteronomy in the Neo-Babylonian and Persian Periods", focuses on the question of the dating of Deuteronomy as one of the traditional lynchpins of the Wellhausenian paradigm. Richter utilizes the abundant data now available regarding the economic profile of the ancient Near East to consider *Urdeuteronomium* via an economic lens. As many have now demonstrated, the culturally embedded economic realities of biblical literature – forthrightly addressed as an element of narrative or law, alluded to via metaphor or backdrop, or even mistakenly included as anachronism – have much to teach us regarding the provenance of a text. Toward this end, this essay summarizes Richter's past research on the archaeologically reconstructed picture of the economies of the Iron I, IIA, B, and C in ancient Israel, which identifies the diagnostic features of each in rural and urban areas, and moves forward to pursue an in depth investigation of the archaeologically reconstructed economies of the Neo-Babylonian and Persian periods. Juxtaposing the features of these economies to the contents of *Urdeuteronomium*, this essay demonstrates that the writers of *Urdeuteronomium* are writing against the backdrop of a far more functional economy than the "post collapse" society of the highlands after 586 BCE. Whereas the Neo-Babylonian period and the first phase of the Persian period (539-450 BCE) in the Central Hill Country are characterized by massive depopulation and the corresponding collapse of the bêt 'āb, the family farm, kinship networks, and village life, *Urdeuteronomium* is teeming with detailed descriptions of the same in its complex treatment of the laws and lifeways of the people it knows as "Israel". Moreover, whereas the centralized tithe/taxation system that permeates *Urdeuteronomium* assumes a functioning cult site in which the known products of the diversified agriculture and animal husbandry of the villages of the Iron Age are being redistributed via a barter-based, reciprocal economy, archaeology has yet to identify such a site in the hill country during the Neo-Babylonian and early Persian periods. Rather, although a discussion of the current state of research at Tell en-Naṣbeh, Bethel, and Ramat Raḥel is offered, the picture of catastrophic economic decline commencing at the beginning of the Neo-Babylonian period in "Beyond the River" does not begin to shift until the emergence of the Persian Empire. Persia's redeployment of the maritime expertise of the Phoenicians launches economic recovery first and most extensively along the coast and major trade routes. Thus, throughout most of the Persian period, "Beyond the River" may be distinguished into two major economic zones: (1) the large, wealthy urban centers along the Mediterranean coast; and (2) the rural and agricultural lifestyle of the hill country. Of particular interest is that similar to the *pax Assyrica*, the increasingly complex economic system of the Persian Empire is facilitated by the collection and redistribution of a fungible medium of exchange at the local, national, and international level. Whereas in the Assyrian period this medium of exchange was primarily *Hacksilber*, in the Persian period this means of exchange is *coinage* – in particular the gold daric. And although both archaeology and the biblical text demonstrate that many types of coinage were ubiquitous in the Persian economic system, coinage is completely absent from *Urdeuteronomium*. Continuing her discussion of the interpolation of *Hacksilber* in Deut 14:24-26, augmented by the economic anachronisms of the Chronicler (for example David's collection of the golden *daric* for the Jerusalem temple; see, e.g., 1 Chron 29:7), Richter concludes that the economy described and assumed in *Urdeuteronomium* shows no hint of the empire-driven realities of the Persian empire or its means of exchange. The clear implication of this empirical inquiry is that neither the "post collapse" profile of the Neo-Babylonian period nor the empire economy of the Persian period provide a tenable backdrop to *Urdeuteronomium*. Rather the quantifiable economic markers both stated and assumed in *Urdeuteronomium* are best located in the robust village economy of the hill country in the transition period between the Iron I/Iron IIA periods.

The last contribution of this volume is *Pekka Pitkänen*'s "Reconstructiong the Social Contexts of the Priestly and Deuteronomic Materials in a Non-Wellhausenian Setting." This article examines the social setting of the priestly and Deuteronomic materials in Genesis-Joshua. Pitkänen starts with an examination of the current state of Pentateuchal scholarship, arguing that the rejection of the Wellhausenian synthesis does not need to mean rejecting the idea of sources behind the Pentateuch. He then clarifies that the essay is based on the view that the Covenant Code is the oldest source on which P, and especially D build, and that H is a development on P. The essay relies on earlier work by the author according to which Genesis-Joshua is a programmatic and essentially unified document that attests to settler colonialism, the attempt of new arrivals to replace the previous inhabitants of the area. The document was written by two authors who used older sources and worked together, with one author from priestly circles writing Genesis-Numbers and the other from Deuteronomic circles composing Deuteronomy and Joshua. Pitkänen proposes that the priests stand not only behind the composition of P/H, but also D. He also describes Deuteronomy's vision of the Israelite society. This is followed by comments on the date of Genesis-Joshua, with the programmatic nature of the document in the context of settler colonialism and the importance of the role of Shiloh in it, both indicating a premonarchic date prior to the disaster at Aphek and the capture of the ark from Shiloh as depicted in 1 Samuel 4. Thereafter, the essay points out how technologies of writing would have been available for the ancient Israelites already in the late second millennium BCE, despite scholarly prejudices prominent in the West that have been set against such an understanding. Subsequently, comments are made in regard to the correlation of textual evidence and archaeology, keeping the programmatic nature of the documents expressly in view. Pertinent considerations that relate to social hegemony and their implications for the history of early Israel are taken into account as part of this discussion. In the final section of the main body of his essay, Pitkänen postulates the provenance of the Priestly and Deuteronomic legal materials in the following way: the Priestly and Holiness materials were produced by priests, while certain features in the Deuteronomic materials point towards Levites as being behind their composition. Considering that priests are associated with the south and Levites with the north as attested by the list of Levitical towns in particular, Pitkänen posits that the overall composition of Genesis-Joshua is likely to have contributed towards uniting two geographical regions, under the rubric of settling the land of Canaan by the ancient Israelites and promoting Yahwism. A summary with conclusions that reiterates the importance of seeking alternatives to the Wellhausenian synthesis rounds up the article. In terms of methdology, this last contribution will be seen by many as not as far removed from the ruling paradigm as other studies collected in this volume. However, the modification of some of the central building blocks of the Wellhausenian synthesis is far-reaching, and the consideration of empirical data – in this case, primarily writing – is in line with a cause that is shared by many authors in this volume.

As can be seen from the overview of the studies collected in this volume, their authors do not present one single answer to the question what exactly the shape of a new paradigm for Pentateuchal studies looks like. Interestingly, there is a clear line of convergence as far as questions of dating are concerned: In those studies that touch these questions in one way or another, the Pentateuch is seen as rooted in the pre-exilic period.

It is the hope of the editors that the views collected in this volume substantially contribute not only to identify the weaknesses and cracks in the edifice of the old dominant paradigm, but also to point constructively to particular building blocks that will be helpful in the construction and establishment of a new paradigm. We are also confident that this will not only benefit Pentateuchal studies, but biblical studies more generally.

The editors of this volume would like to thank all those who made the conference and the publication of the papers presented at the conference possible. In particular, we would like to mention the Swiss National Science Foundation and the Fonds for Teaching and Research of the United Bible Groups of Switzerland for their financial support of the conference; the STH Basel, which not only made their campus available as a stimulating venue for the meeting, but also provided the necessary printing cost subsidies; the editors of BZAR who kindly accepted the volume for publication in their series; last but not least Genadi Kimbel for his dedicated assistance both in the organization of the meeting as well as in the formatting of this volume.

Konstanz/Basel/Los Angeles, Matthias Armgardt,
December 2018 Benjamin Kilchör
  and Markus Zehnder

I. Introductory and Methodological Contributions

Time for a Change!

Why Pentateuchal Research is in Crisis

Georg Fischer (University of Innsbruck)

Edward L. Greenstein compared the various models for the Pentateuch to the descriptions of different parts of the anatomy of an elephant, each provided by one of *five blind men who are unaware* that the animal is one and the same and that many sinews hold it together.[1] Nearly 20 years later, Georg Aichele and his colleagues have taken up this image for Biblical studies in general and applied it to other approaches, too.[2] One may even go one step further and compare the investigations of the Pentateuch to an elephant that has grown excessively and become so oversized that nobody can handle it.

This is the situation we face today. The *number of publications* in this field outweighs by far what a scholar is able to read; as a result, any new contribution will always be 'deficient', inevitably failing to take into account many other studies which might be relevant to the topic.[3] More fundamentally, there is a *dichotomy in the approaches* to Pentateuchal studies. The opposition between diachronic methodologies and a synchronic access to the texts leads to two 'parallel worlds' whose representatives are often critical and suspicious with respect to positions of the 'other' side, sometimes even hostile or dismissive right from the outset.[4]

A further problem arises in the *frequent changes of position*, occasionally even by the same authors,[5] sometimes going around full circle.[6] These are only a few of

---

1 Greenstein, "Formation," 153.
2 Aichele, Miscall, and Walsh, "Elephant," 387.
3 This makes any publication vulnerable, subject to the criticism of not looking at the entire picture.
4 See, e.g., the objections of Carr, *Reading*, 23–24, against those not dealing with transmission history. The other way round, scholars applying a synchronic approach often do not read diachronic studies.
5 The well-received *Einleitung in das Alte Testament* of E. Zenger *et al*. (Stuttgart: Kohlhammer, nine editions till 2015, the last two edited by C. Frevel) may serve as an example. From the first edition (in 1995) to the fifth (in 2004) the presentation of Pentateuchal research has changed three times. This is quite odd for a book aimed to be a lasting orientation for a wide audience of students and scholars, expecting them to change their mind every five years because of 'newer' insights by the experts.
6 A case in point is the discussion about the end of the Priestly writing (P^g): The option of Noth, *Überlieferungsgeschichte*, 8, to see it in Deut 34, returns 50 years later with Frevel, *Blick* – for an overview of the various positions brought forward meanwhile see Zenger, *Einleitung*, 196–203. Another example of the return of earlier theories is the 'revival' of the documentary hypothesis by B. Schwartz, J. Stackert, J. Baden and others.

the main issues: others are the enormous number of hypotheses to explain the growth of individual texts, and, even more, the Pentateuch as a whole; the fragmentation of fairly small texts into many, often tiny layers and/or editorial processes[7]; the suggestions as to what historical "Sitz im Leben" should be attributed to them; the assumption of redactions, textual developments, and "Fortschreibungs-prozesse" without external data, etc.

How should we tackle this 'elephant'? I will first list some of the promising changes that have occurred in Pentateuchal studies within the last 30 years, and then focus on the reasons for the ongoing problems in this field. Finally, I shall suggest some ways by which the present impasse might be overcome.

Before doing so, I want to clarify some issues, in order to *avoid misunderstandings*:

a) Historical and critical investigations of the Bible *have contributed immensely* to a deeper and more appropriate comprehension of it, and they still do so. I, too, want to see biblical texts with their historical roots and grasp their meaning by reflection and discussion of various interpretations and positions.

b) My criticism (in parts 2 and 3) is not directed, *in principle,* against any form of diachronic investigations. It focusses more on those studies which do not seriously engage with the observations brought in by authors with a synchronic approach. Personally, I see Deuteronomy and the variety of the law codes[8] as one example of texts pointing to diverse origins.

c) The Torah contains many very different texts. My remarks mostly have in view the *narratives in Genesis and Exodus*, as they were the initial reason for distinguishing sources and are still a very disputed field. Nevertheless, some statements are also applicable to other areas, even to prophetic books such as, for example, Jeremiah.

d) Next, I have to admit that the topic is so large that I can *only touch on some of the relevant points*, skipping over much of the important literature. I ask pardon in advance for omitting reference to many major contributions.

e) Finally, the breadth of the topic is such that I can only *present a very general view of it*, not going into very much detail or discussing all aspects of an issue. The examples represent only a selection; obviously there would be many more, and perhaps even more pertinent ones.

---

[7] A relatively recent example is Berner, *Exoduserzählung*. He distinguishes, in Exod 3 alone, twelve different stages of development (103–105).

[8] For a critical investigation of their relationships see Kilchör, *Mosetora*. – I thank him and the other organizers of the conference for the invitation to deliver the keynote speech.

1. Promising changes

(i) There have been a number of developments in recent years that give some cause for hope. The first one is the *reduction of sources*, a sign that exegetes are paying more attention to the bonds that hold the Pentateuch together. Julius Wellhausen suggested a model of four documents, JE, D, and P,[9] and this paradigm has dominated the understanding of the Pentateuch for nearly a century. Erhard Blum has significantly contributed to the topic,[10] by suggesting that there are essentially only two main "Kompositionsschichten," K^D and K^P. This tendency has continued, and in present-day discussion some influential scholars consent in accepting merely one layer, mostly understood as being "P," and distinguished from other material, designated "non-P," the latter being difficult to define more exactly.[11] As a result, we are left with a main stratum and a body of other texts, the status of which – as a whole – escapes identification, as it varies so much in itself.

(ii) The second positive outcome of Pentateuch scholarship in the past decades is the recognition that the originally proposed first layer, J, seen as stemming from early Monarchic times, is, in fact, *quite late*.[12] In the sequence, ever more texts were regarded as being exilic or postexilic, and a majority of exegetes in Europe today view at least the final redaction / version of the Pentateuch as emerging some time in (late) Persian times, maybe with Ezra around 400 BC. This provides a more appropriate historical and social setting for large parts of the Torah, including its laws, in the community of the Second Temple.

(iii) The ongoing disputes about how to explain the Pentateuch and its development have led to another, third, major change. This is the *greater degree of (self-) critical reflection and a humbler stance*[13] towards the outcome of our scholarly endeavours. Even scholars trained in historical-critical research have become more aware of its limits.[14] This leads to a more careful method of proceeding[15] and, in the end, hopefully, to more and longer-lasting results.

---

9 Wellhausen, *Prolegomena*, v. He had precursors in Karl-Heinrich Graf, Abraham Kuenen, and others (cf. Zenger, *Einleitung*, 103–106).
10 Especially relevant is Blum, *Studien*.
11 For a recent discussion about this development around P and its interpretation see the contributions in the collective volume of Hartenstein and Schmid, *Abschied*.
12 One of the first proponents of this position was H. H. Schmid, *Jahwist*. For an early positive evaluation of it see the review of van Seters, "Recent Studies," 667–672, who himself had opted for a similar view a year earlier (idem, *Abraham*).
13 Frevel, in his review of *Abschied von der Priesterschrift?*, 1211, realizes "… vielleicht so etwas wie eine neue Bescheidenheit". Similarly, Marx, "Méthodes," 337, invites "… à un peu d'avantage d'humilité".
14 Some examples are the critique of Seebass in the review of the Genesis commentary of his friend L. Ruppert, 1289: "… unbedingt der Nachweis der Notwendigkeit eines Eingriffs erbracht werden sollte"; the call to caution with regard to "redactions" by Krüger, "Anmerkungen," 62–63. – Even Erhard Blum, in an oral remark towards the end of the Pentateuch

(iv) The aspects mentioned above about the transformation occurring within Pentateuchal studies also show up in a new effort to *combine the two 'opposing' methodological approaches*. The aim of the Herder commentary series, initiated by Erich Zenger, proposing a "diachron reflektierte Synchronie,"[16] has meanwhile (spring 2017) borne fruit in more than 35 volumes, the most recent ones, by Eckart Otto, systematically applying both synchronic and diachronic analyses.[17] Another similar, bilingual project, is the International Exegetical Commentary on the Old Testament / Internationaler Exegetischer Kommentar zum Alten Testament (IECOT / IEKAT), of which several books have already appeared.[18]

These and other developments in Pentateuchal studies are *hopeful signs*. Change is on the way, but slowly, not systematically, and sometimes with regressions.[19] The increased awareness of the continuing problems will lead to further reflection, intensified discussion,[20] and stronger efforts to open new ways, hopefully leading to deeper insights.

2. Reasons for the ongoing problems

2.1 Historical roots

When we try to trace the origins of the present state of research, one can find many reasons for it. Historically, the critical analysis of the Pentateuch started in the time of the Enlightenment ("Aufklärung"), marked by a *rationalist approach* to the Bible, which emphasized human reasoning and the individual over established authorities, traditions, and communities. This attitude gives priority to one's own thinking, set-

---

conference in Jerusalem in May 2014, expressed his dissatisfaction with the state of Pentateuchal research after so many years of investigations by so many people.

15 So Nicholson, *Pentateuch*, 232, recognizes the need for "… a duly cautious use of this criterion" (viz. of the names for God).
16 This is the formulaic expression used in E. Zenger, *Dokumentation* (Freiburg: Herder, n.d.), 3, and more often.
17 E. Otto, *Deuteronomium 1,1–4,43*, and another three volumes on Deut.
18 Utzschneider and Oswald, *Exodus 1–15*; Dietrich, *Nahum – Habakuk – Zefanja*; Redditt, *Sacharja 9–14*, among others. All of them apply, for every unit, in sequence, a synchronic and diachronic perspective.
19 See, e.g., the 'revival' of the "Urkundenhypothese" by B. Schwartz, J. Baden, *et al.* (end of note 6), or Berner, *Exoduserzählung*. Another recent example is Ede, *Josefsgeschichte*; she distinguishes, in Gen 50 alone, more than ten isolated motifs (469–511).
20 The remark of Aichele, Miscall, and Walsh: "… we are intensely aware of the present division within biblical studies and are disturbed by the fact that it is rarely if ever openly discussed" (Aichele *et al.*, "Elephant," 387) is pertinent in this regard.

ting it above what is to be investigated, in this case, God's word in human words.[21] Otto Schwankl, in his essay on the state of biblical research, named this bias of the exegesis, because of its origin, "Gen-Defekt" (genetic defect).[22] This does not mean that we have to leave aside critical reflection, but invites us to see the possible limitations of such investigations and try to overcome them.

Another feature is connected with the historical background of the literarycritical approach, a major objective of which is to detect the *'original' version* of a text. What was 'first' gains priority over later developments which are often suspected of changing the earlier meaning by adding new, sometimes even contrasting, elements. Going back to the roots seems to provide access to the 'authentic' message. This may explain the desire to trace the origin of a biblical text. If it were possible, it would make sense and be laudable; yet there are a number of difficulties, as the following exposition will show.

2.2 General problems

a) Disparate material

The Pentateuch is an agglomeration of various genres, traditions, narrative blocks, collections of laws, etc. What originally may have had separate origins has been *transmitted as a whole*.[23] As this 'unification' process belongs to a period prior to the earliest extant manuscripts, we have no secure access to any phase before the divergent materials were gathered into what now appears as 'scrolls' / 'books' and, in its entirety, as Pentateuch / Torah.[24]

As a result of that, we are left with an *impasse*. In research we need 'differences' as a criterion for establishing another source (e.g. discerning 'P' from its surroundings), yet the text itself – deliberately – presents disparate materials intricately linked, and therefore as *'divergent unity'*, of prose and poetry (Exod 14–15),[25] of law and narration (e.g. Exod 19–24), etc. Trying to separate them, in order to attribute them to various layers, inevitably must lead to an ambiguous procedure which

---

21 I do not say that this is done deliberately; often it may be done un- / subconsciously. However, it influences the *overall access* to the biblical texts, holding modern 'logic' and criteria in greater esteem than what is to be interpreted, thus attributing more authority to one's self than to the Bible. – The remarks by A. Marx and C. Frevel about the need for humility (see note 13) show a growing awareness of this problem and its root.
22 Schwankl, "Fundamentum," 177.
23 Sarna, *Genesis*, xvi, uses for that, with respect to the Book of Genesis, the expression "unified document".
24 Obviously there is a need to go beyond Deuteronomy and the Pentateuch and include the following books (Joshua, etc., up to Kings), too, as many motifs point to them as prolongation or fulfilment.
25 For their inner connections, also in other texts like Deut 32; Judges 5, etc., see especially Watts, *Psalm*.

fails to respect the 'integrated' character of the text.[26] So any proposal to divide it is flawed right from the beginning, as it has to use a measure and a method which are *in contrast* to the investigated object.

b) The optimism about reconstructing earlier versions / traditions

Historical-critical investigations presuppose the *ability* to reconstruct textual developments. Benjamin Ziemer has convincingly shown, using the examples of the Book of Jubilees and the Temple Scroll, that it is impossible to deduce from them what Genesis and Deuteronomy, their respective 'sources', looked like.[27] These are two extant cases, from biblical times, to which we have access and through which we can receive insight into ancient writing procedures. They strongly caution against any assumption that we, today, are able to gain access to earlier forms of biblical texts with any acceptable degree of verisimilitude.[28]

One must conclude, therefore, that there are *two fundamental difficulties* with the literary-critical approach to the Pentateuch. From the point of view of the text, the divergence of the materials brought together in it is so interwoven that it opposes a division into layers or an attribution to earlier traditions. From the point of view of developments in extant, comparably old documents, a reconstruction of previous stages of biblical texts seems excluded – unless we get new, external data, it seems impossible to say anything about the prior textual stages with certainty. We may try to speculate about earlier phases in the genesis of these texts, but such research remains on the level of hypotheses, and has rarely led to acceptable results.

2.3 Obstacles in the path of investigation

Besides the fraught historical origin of Pentateuchal criticism and the general difficulties, there are a number of inherent problems with its methodology.

a) Imprecision of the terminology

As I perceive it, one of the main causes for the lasting troubles in Pentateuchal studies is the *vagueness of the terms* used. We may take as an example some recent publications on "P," the Priestly writing, which is supposed to be the "last stronghold"[29] for those applying historical-critical analyses. The book *Abschied von der*

---

26 Berman, *Inconsistency*, has shown that in a paradigmatic way especially in Part III: "Renewing Pentateuchal Criticism," where he deals with the history of interpretation of Exod 2:1–10 and Gen 6–9 as examples.
27 Ziemer, "Diskussion" – The same seems to be true for the Gilgamesh-epic. The Akkadian version does not allow us to reconstruct its earlier versions, as Hallo, "Das Buch Genesis," 60f, shows.
28 This is not to say that biblical texts did not undergo textual developments; the argument addresses our ability to *responsibly* reconstruct them.
29 Thus in my review of the book *Abschied von der Priesterschrift?*, 105: "letzte Bastion", and

Priesterschrift? (see note 11) shows a disconcerting variety of positions among scholars who are experts in the field. This applies to the extent of the passages attributed to P, to its character, and to its historical setting. As a result, they are all talking about different things, albeit using the same term "P." Furthermore, the language, the themes, and the style[30] of these texts diverge quite a lot. "P" thus seems to be something of a chameleon.[31] In present-day discussion, it can change its appearance, its vocabulary, its main interests – nobody has ever defined it clearly in a way that has found general acceptance. Besides that, the dispute about whether it is a source, or should be seen as connected with editorial processes, displays profound disagreement about how to interpret these texts.

The 'vagueness' applies also, and even more, to the "*Yawhist*."[32] The tendency today to call it "non-P"[33] rather than "J" is an indication of the growing awareness of how the application of this term to the texts subsumed by it is insecure.[34] The discussion about "J" shows similar features to that about P, with a still higher level of divergence. The uncertainty is further increased with respect to the "*Elohist*,"[35] and the labels "D" and "dtr" are similarly open to definitions and understandings.

What is true for the various sources, is even more applicable to the *higher levels of the composition process*. The term "redaction" in particular serves for some of today's exegetes as a kind of 'grab bag', covering almost any intervention by the ancient writers, thus permitting them to explain omissions, additions, changes, etc. Similarly, theoretical concepts like "Fortschreibung", source, tradition, "Ergänzung", "Bearbeitung" are often used without being clearly defined, and without there being any opportunity neither to verify nor to falsify these theories based on external data. This common practice of proposing theories about the genesis of Pentateuch texts is highly speculative, works on a meta$^{2\ (or\ even\ 3)}$-level and is, assuming one agrees with its presuppositions and the general legitimacy of the procedure, unas-

---

similarly Frevel in his review of the same book, 1210: "Fels in der Brandung".

30 One of the few exegetes describing P's style of presentation is McEvenue, *Narrative Style*. However, he concentrates merely on three, and debatable texts, of which two are intertwined with other elements (The Flood Narrative, and the Spy Story in Num 13–14), and the last one, Gen 17, is, even in his eyes, "the least narrative" (177). Indeed, a comparison with Gen 1, the first generally assumed "P"-text, reveals a quite different "style" and theological character, thus raising the question of its connection to the other supposed "P"-texts.
31 G. Fischer, "Need," 66.
32 Ska, "Yahwist." He shows the variety of perceptions of "J" offered over the last two centuries and states at the end the lack of a thorough investigation of "J's style, ... compositional devices and patterns," etc. (23).
33 See Frevel's review (note 13), 1212: "Nicht-P," and similarly many others.
34 This – negative – designation follows logically from what showed up above as "disparate material". It is hard to find a common denominator for all the relevant texts.
35 One of the major defenders of this theory is Graupner, *Elohist*. He sees E's "Kerygma" in the affirmation that the kingly God is *Yahweh* (390), in strange contrast to the preferred use of אלהים in this source.

sailable. It repeatedly puts forward new suggestions which lead to further discussions. This 'play' can continue ad infinitum.

b) The criteria

Traditionally, the major criteria for distinguishing sources fall into three distinct groups: stylistic variations, the different names for God, and duplicate narratives, or repetitions.[36] As has long been recognized, there are problems with all of them, and they have already received extensive criticism. I shall, therefore, give only a brief treatment of the problems.

(i) Different vocabulary and style may be required *according to the topic or intention*. Thus the Song of Moses in Exod 15 is the fitting answer of praise for God's rescue in the chapter before. Some *toledot* in Genesis are needed to bridge long time periods (Gen 5; 11:10–26); other *toledot* serve to show connections among 'relatives' (Gen 10; 11:27–32; 25:12–18; 36) or to introduce narrative blocks (Gen 2:4; 6:9; 25:19; 37:2). Despite their different functions, they are necessary, taken together, for the structuring and understanding of the entire book. An author or composer of a book may have many reasons to vary the language.[37]

(ii) The biblical God has *only one 'name'*, יהוה, as revealed to Moses in Exod 3:14–15. The other expression, אלהים "god(s)", is a common term used to designate beings belonging to the divine sphere. It may be applied to Yhwh, too, in various forms,[38] and the change between 'name' and general noun, with or without article, seems to indicate specific nuances, according to context and speaker.[39] It thus cannot be taken as a criterion for differentiating layers without further arguments.

(iii) Nicholson adduces, as an example of duplicate narratives, the stories about Hagar in Gen 16 and 21. Although he also recognizes differences between them, and discusses at length various options, he suggests, in a rhetorical question, that Gen 21 had an editor who took it from an independent source.[40] It is, however, very hard to see how Gen 21 can be regarded as a kind of 'repetition', being so *dissimilar* from Gen 16. In addition, the expulsion of Hagar and Ishmael is 'needed' for the further development of the narration. In an analogous way, apparent 'duplicates' (e.g. Gen 12:10–20; 20; 26:1–11) serve precise functions within their respective contexts.[41]

---

36 Sic, among many others, Nicholson, *Pentateuch*, 228–237. The latter criterion is often used in a more general way, as 'repetitions'. Brodie, *Genesis*, 5–6, gives a longer list of six "arguments against unity," adding especially "internal contradictions".

37 Besides this, the use of the vocabulary is often not consistent. Frevel, *Blick*, 341f, for example, postulates the end of P^g in Deut 34:8, but is unable to argue for it with specific words. He has to admit that there are "keine präzisen literarkritischen Schnitte und redaktionskritischen Zuweisungen" possible, which is equivalent to a dismissal of the criterion.

38 The dominant use is without article, beginning in Gen 1:1. האלהים "the God" starts with Henoch in Gen 5:22, 24. Both terms are to be understood with reference to Yhwh in most of the cases, yet they are not his 'name', as other divinities may also be designated so.

39 Exod 3–4 is especially relevant in this regard; see G. Fischer, *Jahwe*, 224–228.

40 Nicholson, *Pentateuch*, 232–237.

41 For the texts mentioned see I. Fischer, *Erzeltern*.

To sum up, what had already emerged as a problem in dealing with the "disparate material" (2.2, a) continues here with the main criteria applied in historical-critical research. They all are *subject to intense criticism and are more than ambiguous* when used as reasons for distinguishing sources.

c) Implementation of the research

Besides the general problems and the ambiguity of the criteria, there are also difficulties with the *manner in which the investigations are carried out*. These show up in various ways.

(i) Among the promising changes, I have listed a growing dialogue between the two opposite approaches. The reality, however, is that there is still *widespread negligence* of the 'other' position. This is especially true on the side of the dominant historical-critical scholarship. Major 'synchronic' commentaries on Genesis[42] are, by and large, not taken seriously in present-day discussions and diachronically oriented studies.[43] In contrast, all of the previously mentioned commentaries (see in note 42) discuss the arguments of the historical-critical approach, sometimes at length and in detail.[44] Thus there is an imbalance in dealing with synchronic scholarship by the 'other side'. This is evident in many areas: in the organisation of congresses, the nomination / invitation of speakers, the major publications, etc.[45] As a consequence, the prevailing impression is coined by diachronic positions, and there is little debate or real confrontation with the other side.[46]

---

42 E.g. those of B. Jacob (see note 49 below), U. Cassuto, G. Wenham (Word), V. P. Hamilton (NICOT), N. M. Sarna (JPS; cf. note 23), T. L. Brodie (see above note 36), and others (cf. the studies of Jan P. Fokkelman on Genesis), who are convinced about the 'unity' of the book or reluctant in accepting sources to explain it.

43 See for examples the commentaries of C. Westermann (BK; he knew Jacob's and Cassuto's commentaries), L. Ruppert (FzB) and H. Seebass, as well as recent monographs by W. Bührer (Am Anfang ...), the studies of N. C. Baumgart and E. Bosshard-Nepustil on the Flood Narrative, and many others.

44 B. Jacob dedicates 100 pages at the end of his commentary to it (949–1048).

45 Further examples: Houtman, *Pentateuch*, has proferred the most profound investigation of Pentateuchal theories and arrived at the conclusion that source criticism cannot explain how the Pentateuch came into being (419: "... dass die Quellentheorie keine befriedigende Antwort auf die Frage nach der Entstehung des Pentateuch zu leisten vermag") – as this result is 'unwelcome', his study is seldom quoted and still more rarely accepted. – T. Römer, in his article "Pentateuchforschung" (Wibilex, December 2015, based mainly on the respective part of his *Einleitung* from 2013), refers comprehensively to some main developments of the research, yet bypasses almost completely the synchronic positions for the actual discussion, thus producing a one-sided, biased picture.

46 A common practice is the affirmation of a "consensus," e.g. about the existence of "P," neglecting all the researchers strongly opposing it (see those commenting on Genesis mentioned in note 42). Carr, *Reading*, 43, perceives a "... remarkable level of long-standing consensus." The contributions in the volume *Abschied von der Priesterschrift* (note 11) and Römer (the article quoted in the previous footnote) go into the same direction, not taking seriously the objections

(ii) The recent discussion of two possible 'origin traditions' of Israel, one of the Patriarchs, the other of the Exodus,[47] offers another example of a problematic procedure. In order to be able to separate these traditions, one has to declare all hints at the Exodus in Genesis (e.g. 15:16; 46:4, etc.) as redactional additions. This means that the evidence in the text speaking against the thesis is "neutralized" and ascribed to another layer.[48] Such a practice is *"circular reasoning"*, first sidelining contrasting arguments and then concluding that the proposed theory is correct. This does not exclude the possibility that there may have been two different 'origin traditions', but it shows that proving it with some degree of probability presents a problem.

(iii) The discordant state of Pentateuchal studies offers a great opportunity for an open discussion, to try to clarify the different viewpoints and find out the reasons for them, thus providing a more balanced background for further research. However, often 'schools' proceed on their established path, affirm their hypotheses in a continuing stream of new publications, and *rarely engage seriously* with contrasting positions. As the last 200 years have shown, the field is so disputed that such one-sided perspectives and/or presentations cannot become lasting contributions; they only prolong the present state of dichotomy.

We may thus conclude that the way in which the study of the Pentateuch is proceeding shows wide-ranging deficiencies. The disdain for synchronic interpretations and the sometimes optimistic proposals of new theories, based on weak arguments and without critically cross-checking them, are further roots of the ongoing problems in the field. Instead of propagating a non-existent "consensus," the field of Pentateuchal studies displays a fundamental breach in methodology and an antagonism towards other views. Unless these are addressed seriously and without preconceptions, there will never be a solution.

3. Avenues to pursue, new and old

There can be no way back to pre-critical exegesis. Historical backgrounds and critical investigation have enriched our understanding of the whole Bible enorm-ously. We have to continue along this 'old' and well-trodden path and yet find a way to make Pentateuchal studies *fruitful again*.

In doing so, we have to *overcome the weaknesses* of the literary-critical approaches, especially if they are short on (self-) 'criticism' and rather more specula-

---

to this hypothesis of P, neglecting and denying the contrasting actual state of research.
47 See especially K. Schmid, *Erzväter*.
48 Several authors have therefore criticized the proposed theory, e.g. Krüger, "Anmerkungen," 61f.

tive than 'historical'. With this in mind, I want to address three issues in this final part: first, a closer look at 'P' is clearly necessary; secondly, some comparisons for understanding the Torah may open alternative perspectives to the widely assumed research paradigms of textual developments; and finally, some pointers to potentially rewarding new avenues will be offered.

3.1 Understanding 'P' as the key

Once again, I start by guarding against a possible misunderstanding: I do *not deny the existence of connections, similar interests and motifs* between the texts traditionally ascribed to the "Priestly writing". Some of them have certain characteristics that point to common intentions. Instead, I want to propose that we look at them from another angle, giving more weight to the way in which they relate to their immediate contexts and perceiving them in their specific functions within the whole.

After that clarification, I now share the knowledge and firm conviction gleaned from decades of dealing with Pentateuch studies. As long as one holds firmly to P, assuming its existence in whatever form, whether it be a source, a layer, or a redactional reworking, there will be, in my estimation, *no adequate solution* to the problems of Pentateuchal research. After nearly 200 years of trying in vain to find an answer, based on the assumption of this hypothetical Priestly stratum (in whatever form), we have still not arrived at definitive results, and the impasse because of the fundamental problems underlying this theory has become obvious. Therefore, it is time to attempt to formulate an explanation without it. As a *counter-proposal*,[49] I suggest daring to do away with it altogether!

In the following, I want to present some observations which will demonstrate that *taking 'P' out of the picture* eases the interpretation and can be more convincing:

a) There is widespread acceptance among historical-critical researchers about the attribution of the "*Toledot-formula*" to P. Yet, even in its first instance, in Gen 2:4, one encounters the problem that it has to be taken, as is true for every other occurrence, as the beginning of the next unit[50] which decisively is "non-P." Some other cases of the *toledot*, too, raise questions about their ascription to P, i.e. where they start narrations (e.g. Gen 6:9; 25:19; 37:2). Furthermore, if one were to remove these formulas from the Book of Genesis, many necessary connections and binding motifs would be missing, and it would be hard to understand it.

b) The *genealogy in Exod 6:14–27* is regarded as largely belonging to P. It is framed by a kind of repetition, bringing in Yhwh's address to Moses ordering him to speak to Pharaoh (Exod 6:10–12, 28–30), which is generally attributed to another

---

49 This suggestion is not new. It follows Benno Jacob's position, e.g. in his commentary *Das Buch Genesis* (1048), and others who similarly get along well and in an illuminating way without P.
50 Hieke, *Genealogien*, 49–50; also Jacob, *Genesis*, 71–74.

source. The difference between the verses before the genealogy and after it lies in the argument about Moses' authority over the Israelites. In V 12 Moses sees it as a problem, in V 30 he does not mention it at all. This indicates that his lineage given in V 16–20 is a solution to his missing authority.[51] The individual units of Exod 6:12–30 (viz. V 10–12/13, 14/16–27, 28–30) are strongly interlinked and need each other; it is improbable that they belong to different sources.[52]

c) The two small examples above demonstrate the *'double', ambiguous character* of the so-called 'P'-texts. On the one hand, they are *essential for the structure* of the whole[53] and must not be dismissed. On the other hand, as in the case of the genealogy in Exod 6, they look like *'additions'*. At first sight they do not seem to be necessary, yet they contribute to the inner coherence of the text on a more refined level, and therefore they are definitely needed.[54] This ambiguous appearance of the so-called 'P'-texts may be one reason for the endless debate as to whether they are a source or a redaction.

Instead of that, what is regarded as 'P' *adheres indissolubly* to the surrounding texts.[55] In Exod 1–15, the 'P'-elements form, together with the other units / materials, such a dense fabric that it is impossible to extract them without destroying the narrative.[56] The same holds true for the Book of Genesis; removing what is seen as 'P' would make it fall apart into a series of unconnected pieces, hard to understand in their sense and logic.

An illustration from literature sums up the situation: the famous fairy-tale of Hans Christian Andersen, "*The Emperor's New Clothes*,"[57] describes different perceptions, or rather public statements of perceptions. Instigated by initial pronouncements and intensified by a process of common imagination, the nakedness of the Emperor is declared as "new clothes." The apparent 'naiveté' of a young child sees reality without the preconceptions of adults influenced by public opinion and thus helps others to perceive and express the truth.

---

51 Marx, "généalogie," has shown that very clearly.
52 G. Fischer and Markl, *Exodus*, 98, based on the previous studies: G. Fischer, "Exodus 1–15," and idem, "Keine Priesterschrift," both new in idem, *Anfänge*, 128–137 and 138–167, here 136 respectively 143.
53 This is valid e.g. for Gen 1:1–2:3; 17, the *toledot*-formulas and –texts, Exod 6:2–9, etc. Another problem not discussed here is the thematic orientation attributed to P. Several times it is hard to see explicit 'priestly' interests in the P-texts, cf. Weimar, *Studien*, VII: "Ganz entgegen dem eingebürgerten Namen handelt es sich bei der Priesterschrift um einen wesentlich prophetisch inspirierten, ganz und gar unkultischen, geradezu utopischen Geschichtsentwurf."; this raises the question whether the label 'P' is appropriate at all.
54 For the Flood narrative, see J.A. Berman, *Inconsistency*, 236–268, among others.
55 Marx, "Méthodes," 333: "… les textes sacerdotaux …" collent "à ces autres écrits … et les suivent pas à pas …".
56 G. Fischer, "Exodus 1–15," 161.
57 Originally in Danish: "Keiserens nye Klæder", first published in 1837.

In my view, a similar process is necessary with respect to 'P'. It is a *chimera* leading scholars in a false direction. Instead of giving attention to the many and strong bonds these texts have with their surroundings and which are clearly observable, the hypothesis of the Priestly writing impels scholars to give preference to speculations and interpretations that are highly debatable and have many arguments against them.[58]

3.2 New paradigms

Up to now it is clear that the "paradigm change," referred to in the title of the conference and this book, has *not yet* taken place. Nevertheless, in recent research, there are several developments and tendencies emerging (mentioned in 1 above) which give us reason to hope that this might happen soon. *New models* will play an important role in such a change and it will be necessary to leave behind the paradigm of a successive, reconstructible textual development which has taken place over the centuries, from the earliest stages to the final form.

Thomas L. Brodie, in his commentary on the Book of Genesis (Genesis as Dialogue, 2001, 36), has dealt at length with questions of its unity. In his preface (xiv), he quotes an article of André Chouraqui[59] who compares the construction of Genesis to the precision of *assembling a computer or a rocket*. Brodie himself also uses other comparisons, "body-like complexity" (11) and "pyramid" (80).

All of Brodie's suggestions point in one direction, namely the *deliberate combination of various, even contrasting, elements into one highly functional entity*. The same holds true, on a small scale, for a clockwork mechanism, or, in larger dimensions, for a house. They are both made of different materials, may even originate in distinct times and places; however, in each case, as they are extant now, all the separate components come together to form a unity and, in combination, contribute to the overall formation of the clock and the house, so that each, as a whole, is able to fulfil its function.

In various cultures, there are further models which might help us to understand what the 'different materials / elements / interests' of the Pentateuch aim to communicate. The following examples and comparisons are intended to point to similar phenomena in other areas of inventions, communication, and artistry, in order to get ideas for or insight into *possibly analogous features* in biblical literature. Assuredly,

---

58 The review of *Abschied von der Priesterschrift?* by Frevel uses two images for 'P', which, in combination, – unwittingly – reflect the situation. He speaks of 'P' as "Fels in der Brandung" (= a rock in the surf, 1210) and of the "forschungsgeschichtlich gewichtige[n] Tanker 'Priesterschrift'" (= the tanker ship 'Priestly writing', weighty in the history of research, 1212), thinking that the latter is still afloat; yet, in reality, like the "Exxon Valdez" in Prince William Sound on March 24 of 1989, the tanker 'P' is set on a course to seize up on rocks, break apart and spill its contents.

59 Chouraqui, " Traduction," 455.

there is a difference between the various modes of expression of the human mind. However, they show common features and might help us to perceive biblical texts more accurately.

Let us first have a look at *visual arts*. In Ancient Egypt, artists often presented human figures in a combination of two perspectives, from the front for one eye, shoulder and the upper part of the body, and from the side, as profile, for face, pelvis and feet.[60] Orthodox icons, also, frequently mix different points of view, e.g. depicting buildings with a foreshortening technique, yet not using it for other parts of the icon.[61] In a similar way, modern painters may combine several perspectives.[62]

Music offers further analogies. The concertos of Johann Sebastian Bach or symphonies of Ludwig van Beethoven consist of 'voices' for many different instruments, and may include a choir. The different movements often involve changes of rhythm (3/4, or 4/4 time etc.) and/or key (from major to minor, or reverse), sometimes even within themselves. Likewise, there may be changes of *tempi*, and sound intensity (*piano*, *forte*, …). There are repetitions, or reversions of motifs, contrasting melodies, and occasionally pauses, with no music at all – this kind of 'mixing' on various levels is not a sign of multiple composers, but of one mind creating a piece of art.

Architecture contributes another example of the importance and, at times, necessity of employing several perspectives. In order to construct a building, a ground plan does not suffice. It has to be supplemented by floor plans, roof design, scale drawings, basic specifications for the main components of the building, not to mention details of interior and exterior trims, and so on. Biblical techniques, like the parallelism characteristic of Hebrew poetry, or the combination of 'diptychs',[63] may likewise try to render a more adequate, complete vision of a complex reality, consisting of many aspects. The delicate blend of two units, or even more perspectives, conveys a rich message.

In conclusion, a reflection on the literary character of the Pentateuch, especially on the origin of the word "text", may also be helpful. The Latin root is *textus*, indicating a mesh, texture, netting. The web may be composed of several fabrics, threads going in various directions, and any number of colors.[64] Nevertheless, despite com-

---

60 Brunner-Traut, *Frühformen*. She calls this kind of raffiguration "Aspektive" (5–13, and more often, with conspicuous examples on pp. 35–38).
61 Florenskij, *Perspektive*. The full title renders the main idea of his book: "the reverted perspective".
62 An example is Joan Miró's picture "Personages et chien devant le soleil" from 1949 (in the Kunstmuseum in Basel), showing one figure in upright position, the other figure upside down, and the dog portrayed in yet another direction at the right-hand side, as if he would walk from the bottom to the sky.
63 For this feature in Genesis see especially Brodie, *Genesis*, 16–19, and more often. Many exegetes observe two narrations of creation (Gen 1:1–2:3; 2:4–25), two accounts of sin (Gen 3 and 4), etc.
64 In this, and some other cases above referring to mostly modern comparisons, one may be able to trace back the origins of the individual elements, as information about its sources might be

prising all these different elements, the text / web is *primarily a single entity*, and to take any part away from it would destroy its unity and possibly render it dysfunctional.

3.3 Time for a change

Pentateuchal research, in its prevailing form throughout the last century, resembles calculations where the result / sum cannot be correct. When one realizes this, one has to go back to the start, and check the individual operations, in order to discover the reasons for the false outcome. Similarly, we today have to *examine our methods and possibly correct them*.

There *will be opposition* to that, as the examples of C. Houtman's study (see note 45) or the Genesis commentaries (mentioned in note 42) show. The literary-historical approaches are still dominant, and scholars not willing to play the diachronic 'game' are likely to encounter many difficulties and setbacks, and to find their work ignored or sidelined. Frequently a preference for literary-historical investigation is also the condition for an assignment.

Pentateuchal studies have changed a lot in the past century. The secondary literature has multiplied to such an extent that nobody can read it completely. Several publications are so voluminous – one of the most recent ones, FAT 111, even exceeding 1200 pages – that it is hard to process all the material presented. In addition, the rate of publication of new books and articles has greatly increased. Pentateuchal research has become *like an 'elephant'* which can no longer be handled by a single person.

But this mainstream approach, which has, to a considerable extent, become unfruitful and irresponsible, must change. We might get a hint of this from the terminology used. 'Pentateuchal' research refers by its very name to the "five parts", indicating a "divisive" approach. Instead of that, we should be *serving the Torah*, which in the original means "instruction, teaching," and thus urges us to learn from it by focussing on its contents. A phrase in the Book of Jeremiah might be particularly interesting in this context. Jer 2:8 reads: "… those handling / grasping the Torah do not know me", and is a divine accusation which directs those who study the Pentateuch towards an inner relationship with God, as a precondition for interpreting it correctly.[65] This should be a foundation for our research and for our responsibility

---

available today. This stands in contrast to biblical research where, normally, such access to possible roots is not at our disposal. Valuable exceptions are those cases, where biblical texts draw on earlier ones, like the Books of Chronicles on the Books of Genesis, Samuel and Kings, or the Decalogue in Deut 5 on the one in Exod 20; for the latter see Markl, *Dekalog*, 184f, 209, and more often – I am grateful to him for a critical reading of a first draft of this paper.

65 For Jer 2:8 and its significance see G. Fischer, "Relationship," 900. – התורה in Jer 2:8 refers, with a high probability, to "the Torah," and not simply to some other instruction; it is thus very relevant for all those dealing with the five books of the Pentateuch.

and duty as exegetes to comply with the force of the Torah's messages and to make them accessible to a broad audience.

The Torah still offers *promising fields* for future research. There is no need to sidestep into daring, unfounded speculations. The texts, as they are, contain many indications of responsible groups, their interests and aims, and thus, indirectly, hold clues to their theological, historical and sociological backgrounds. The combinations of different, sometimes even conflicting passages and positions invite complementary interpretations, and investigation into their mutual relationships and their functioning. Repetitions and closely connected wordings ask to be understood in their respective contexts. Studies of these and other similar areas will help to penetrate the dense fog that obscures research of the Torah and lead us to perceive it, in the end, as a huge, beautiful, brightly lit cathedral.[66]

Bibliography

Aichele, George, Miscall, Peter, and Walsh, Richard. "An Elephant in the Room: Historical-Critical and Postmodern Interpretations of the Bible." *JBL* 128 (2009): 383–404.
Berman, Joshua A. *Inconsistency in the Torah. Ancient Literary Convention and the Limits of Source Criticism.* New York: Oxford University Press, 2017.
Berner, Christoph. *Die Exoduserzählung. Das literarische Werden einer Ursprungslegende Israels.* FAT 73. Tübingen: Mohr, 2010.
Blum, Erhard. *Studien zur Komposition des Pentateuch.* BZAW 189. Berlin: de Gruyter, 1990.
Brodie, Thomas L. *Genesis as Dialogue. A Literary, Historical, and Theological Commentary.* New York: Oxford University Press, 2001.
Brunner-Traut, Emma. *Frühformen des Erkennens. Am Beispiel Altägyptens* (Darmstadt: Wissenschaftliche Buchgesellschaft, 1990.
Carr, David M. *Reading the Fractures of Genesis. Historical and Literary Approaches.* Louisville: Westminster John Knox, 1996.
Chouraqui, André. "Une Traduction de la Bible." *Études* 343 (1975): 447–462.
Dietrich, Walter. *Nahum – Habakuk – Zefanja.* IECOT. Stuttgart: Kohlhammer, 2014.

---

[66] Cf. G. Fischer, "Wege aus dem Nebel? Ein Beitrag zur Pentateuchkrise," *BN* 99 (1999): 5–7, new in idem, *Anfänge*, 279–282, esp. 282. Other articles in the same book are also relevant to the topic, besides those mentioned in note 52 above, especially "Zur Genese der Genesis," "Exodus 3–4 'revisited'," and "Zur Lage der Pentateuchforschung". – I am grateful to Mrs. Felicity Stephens for having corrected the English of this article.

Ede, Franziska. *Die Josefsgeschichte. Literarkritische und redaktionsgeschichtliche Untersuchungen zur Entstehung von Gen 37–50.* BZAW 485. Berlin and New York: de Gruyter, 2016.
Fischer, Georg. *Jahwe unser Gott. Sprache, Aufbau und Erzähltechnik in der Berufung des Mose (Ex 3–4).* OBO 91. Fribourg: Universitätsverlag, 1989.
—. "Keine Priesterschrift in Ex 1–15?" *ZKTh* 117 (1995): 203–211.
—. "Exodus 1–15. Eine Erzählung," in *Studies in the Book of Exodus.* Edited by Marc Vervenne. BETL 126. Leuven: Peeters, 1996, 149–178.
—. "Wege aus dem Nebel? Ein Beitrag zur Pentateuchkrise." *BN* 99 (1999): 5–7.
—. "The Need for a New Vision of the Torah," in *A Critical Study of the Pentateuch. An Encounter Between Europe and Africa.* Edited by Eckart Otto and Jurie LeRoux. Altes Testament und Moderne 20. Münster: Lit, 2005, 62–73.
—. *Die Anfänge der Bibel. Studien zu Genesis und Exodus.* SBAB 49. Stuttgart: Katholisches Bibelwerk, 2011.
—. "ותפשי התורה לא ידעוני – The Relationship of the Book of Jeremiah to the Torah," in *The Formation of the Pentateuch. Bridging the Academic Cultures of Europe, Israel, and North America.* Edited by Jan C. Gertz et al. FAT 111. Tübingen: Mohr, 2016, 891–911.
—. Review of *Abschied von der Priesterschrift?*, by Friedhelm Hartenstein and Konrad Schmid. *ZKTh* 138 (2016): 105.
Fischer, Georg and Markl, Dominik. *Das Buch Exodus.* NSK-AT 2. Stuttgart: Katholisches Bibelwerk, 2009.
Fischer, Irmtraud. *Die Erzeltern Israels. Feministisch-theologische Studien zu Genesis 12–36.* BZAW 222. Berlin and New York: de Gruyter, 1994.
Florenskij, Pavel. *Die umgekehrte Perspektive.* Berlin: Mattes & Seitz, 1989.
Frevel, Christian. *Mit Blick auf das Land die Schöpfung erinnern. Zum Ende der Priestergrundschrift.* HBS 23. Freiburg: Herder, 2000.
—. review of *Abschied von der Priesterschrift?*, by Friedhelm Hartenstein and Konrad Schmid. *ThLZ* 141 (2016): 1209–1212.
Graupner, Axel. *Der Elohist. Gegenwart und Wirksamkeit des transzendenten Gottes in der Geschichte.* WMANT 97. Neukirchen: Neukirchener Verlag, 2002.
Greenstein, Edward L. "The Formation of the Biblical Narrative Corpus." *AJS Review* 15 (1990): 151–178.
Hallo, William W. "Das Buch Genesis innerhalb der Literatur des Alten Orients," in תורה *Die Tora. In jüdischer Auslegung. Band I. Bereschit.* Edited by W. Gunther Plaut. Gütersloh: Kaiser, 1999, 59–67.
Hartenstein, Friedhelm, and Schmid, Konrad, eds. *Abschied von der Priesterschrift? Zum Stand der Pentateuchdebatte.* VWGTh 40. Leipzig: Evangelische Verlagsanstalt, 2015.
Hieke, Thomas. *Die Genealogien der Genesis.* HBS 39. Freiburg: Herder, 2003.
Houtman, Cees. *Der Pentateuch. Die Geschichte seiner Erforschung nebst einer Auswertung.* CBET 9. Kampen: Kok Pharos, 1994.
Jacob, Benno. *Das Buch Genesis.* Berlin: Schocken, 1934 = Stuttgart: Calwer Verlag, 2000.
Kilchör, Benjamin. *Mosetora und Jahwetora. Das Verhältnis von Deuteronomium 12–26 zu Exodus, Levitikus und Numeri.* BZAR 21. Wiesbaden: Harrassowitz, 2015.
Krüger, Thomas. "Anmerkungen zur Frage nach den Redaktionen der großen Erzählwerke im Alten Testament," in *Les Dernières Rédactions du Pentateuque, de l'Hexateuque et de l'Enneateuque.* Edited by Thomas Römer and Konrad Schmid. BETL 203. Leuven: Peeters, 2007, 47–66.

Markl, Dominik. *Der Dekalog als Verfassung des Gottesvolkes. Die Brennpunkte einer Rechtshermeneutik des Pentateuch in Ex 19–24 und Dtn 5*. HBS 49. Freiburg: Herder, 2007.
Marx, Alfred. "La généalogie d'Exode vi 14–25." *VT* 45 (1995): 318–336.
—. "Méthodes et modes dans la recherche sur le Pentateuque," *RB* 122 (2015): 321–339.
McEvenue, Sean E. *The Narrative Style of the Priestly Writer*. AnBib 50. Rome: Biblical Institute Press, 1971.
Nicholson, Ernest. *The Pentateuch in the Twentieth Century. The Legacy of Julius Wellhausen*. New York: Clarendon Press, 1998.
Noth, Martin. *Überlieferungsgeschichte des Pentateuch*. Stuttgart: Kohlhammer, 1948.
Otto, Eckart. *Deuteronomium 1,1–4,43*. HThKAT. Freiburg: Herder, 2012.
Redditt, Paul R. *Sacharja 9–14*. IECOT. Stuttgart: Kohlhammer, 2014.
Sarna, Nahum M. *Genesis*. JPS Torah Commentary. Philadelphia: Jewish Publication Society, 1989.
Schmid, Hans H. *Der sogenannte Jahwist. Beobachtungen und Fragen zur Pentateuchforschung*. Zürich: Theologischer Verlag, 1976.
Schmid, Konrad. *Erzväter und Exodus. Untersuchungen zur doppelten Begründung der Ursprünge Israels innerhalb der Geschichtsbücher des Alten Testaments*. WMANT 81. Neukirchen-Vluyn: Neukirchener Verlag, 1999.
Schwankl, Otto. "Fundamentum et anima Theologiae. Zur Lage der biblischen Exegese 50 Jahre nach *Dei Verbum*." *BZ* 60 (2016): 161–181.
Seebass, Horst, review of *Genesis. Ein kritischer und theologischer Kommentar*, by Lothar Ruppert. *ThLZ* 127 (2002): 1287–1289.
Ska, Jean L. "The Yahwist, a Hero with a Thousand Faces. A Chapter in the History of Modern Exegesis," in *Abschied vom Jahwisten. Die Komposition des Hexateuch in der jüngsten Diskussion*. Edited by Jan C. Gertz et al. BZAW 315. Berlin and New York: de Gruyter, 2002, 1–23.
Utzschneider, Helmut and Oswald, Wolfgang. *Exodus 1–15*. IECOT. Stuttgart: Kohlhammer, 2013.
van Seters, John. *Abraham in History and Tradition*. New Haven: Yale University Press, 1975.
—. "Recent Studies in the Pentateuch: A Crisis in Method." *JAOS* 99 (1979): 663–673.
Watts, James W. *Psalm and Story. Inset Hymns in Hebrew Narrative*. JSOTS 139. Sheffield: JSOT Press, 1992.
Weimar, Peter. *Studien zur Priesterschrift*. FAT 56. Tübingen: Mohr, 2008.
Wellhausen, Julius. *Prolegomena zur Geschichte Israels*. Berlin: Georg Reimer, 1899.
Zenger, Erich et al. *Einleitung in das Alte Testament*. Edited by Christian Frevel. 8th ed. Stuttgart: Kohlhammer, 2012.
Ziemer, Benjamin. "Die aktuelle Diskussion zur Redaktionsgeschichte des Pentateuch und die empirische Evidenz nach Qumran." *ZAW* 125 (2013): 383–399.

Reading the Torah in a Better Way

Unity and Diversity in Text, Genre, and Compositional History

Richard E. Averbeck

(Trinity Evangelical Divinity School)

The title of this volume uses the term "paradigm change," referring specifically to the scholarly study of the composition of the Pentateuch. The premise is that the current "paradigm" is so defective that the field needs to shift away from it to something new. The term naturally calls to mind paradigm changes in the natural sciences as described by Thomas Kuhn in his well-known book, *The Structure of Scientific Revolutions*.[1] At a certain point, a field of scientific inquiry comes to a place where a fundamental change is called for because current knowledge and ongoing advances in the field cannot be absorbed into the old paradigm. To borrow a biblical expression, one cannot "put new wine into old wine skins." There are, however, important differences between the natural sciences and biblical studies as disciplines. Biblical studies as a field does not limit itself to one controlling paradigm at a time, but has multiple (and often) conflicting paradigms in play at the same time.[2]

1. Conflicting Paradigms

The most natural place to begin our inquiry is with Julius Wellhausen's "*New* Documentary Hypothesis," often referred to as "source criticism" or "the JEDP theory." This was prevalent and something of a consensus for a time in the academy during the latter part of the 19th century and through much of the 20th century.[3] It was "new" back in the 19th century, since he drew together the results of earlier historical critical documentary source analysis from the 17th and 18th centuries under the early influence of Baruch Spinoza, Richard Simon, and Jean Astruc, among others, as well as later 19th century scholars, who lived just before or during the time of Wellhausen (e.g., Wilhelm de Wette, Karl Heinrich Graf, and Abraham Kuenen). Well-

---

1 Kuhn, *Structure*.
2 See the important distinctions between physical science and social science in Shedinger, "Kuhnian Paradigms".
3 Wellhausen, *Prolegomena*.

hausen thought of "E" (the Elohist) as a supplement to "J" (Yahwist) document, and often referred to "JE." He also accepted de Wette's proposal that "D" was from the time of Josiah or just before. The major contribution Wellhausen made to the Documentary Hypothesis was to move "P" from its position as the early foundational source in the Pentateuch to the very end of the period of composition, thus putting priestly concerns at the end of Israelite history, after the prophets rather than before them.

At the beginning of the 20th century Hermann Gunkel thought of his new form critical approach as going back behind Wellhausen's documentary sources to their oral tradition-historical background. Wellhausen himself resisted thinking that one could go back behind the documents in a way that would meaningfully contribute to understanding the history of Israelite religion. Gunkel responded that Wellhausen was not historical enough because he was too bound to the supposed written documents that underlie the current text, rather than the origin and development of the traditions that lay behind these intermediate documents.[4]

Gerhard von Rad, Martin Noth, and others, took Gunkel's approach forward in the 20th century.[5] Progressively, form critical analysis became the starting point for a new *non*-documentary paradigm of historical critical study of the Pentateuch, combined with tradition history and redaction. This overall method is now often referred to simply as "tradition history" or "redaction criticism."[6] On this view, the underlying traditions built up layer by layer through time until they were redacted together and eventually reached the form in which we have them in the Pentateuch. Under the influence of Rolf Rendtorff,[7] and now carried forward in ever new ways by scholars such as Konrad Schmid and David Carr,[8] this is the predominant method especially in the German academy and, therefore, in Europe overall. An early form of "D" (Deuteronomy) is considered the first actual written compilation of Israel's traditions, produced sometime during the 7th century, followed later by "P" as an exilic and/or post-exilic source document or layer of redaction. John Van Seters agrees, but argues that there was also a late "J" document (much of Genesis, Exodus, and Numbers) that was added in the 6th century as a supplementary prologue to "D." Those who take "P" to be post-exilic sometimes also argue for a post-priestly final redaction of the Pentateuch.[9] Some scholars, especially from the Israeli School initiated by Yehezkel Kaufmann, put "P" in the pre-exilic period, before Deuter-onomy.

---

4   For a brief but very helpful review of the intellectual movements that underlie these movements in late 19th century OT scholarship see Hayes and Prussner, *Old Testament Theology*, 77–90.
5   See the most helpful discussion in McKane, *Studies*, 225–244. See also Campbell and O'Brien, *Sources*, 12–17 and the brief but cogent summary in Hayes and Prussner, *Old Testament Theology*, 126–32.
6   See the helpful discussion in Campbell and O'Brien, *Sources*, 12–17.
7   See, e.g., Rendtorff, *The Old Testament,* and his earlier writings on this topic cited there.
8   Schmid, *Genesis*; Carr, *Formation*.
9   See, e.g., the discussion in Schmid, "Post-Priestly Additions".

The redaction critical approach, however, has not replaced the documentary approach. In recent decades, the latter has once again come forward in the "*Neo*-documentary" revival, referred to as "neo" to avoid confusion with Wellhausen's "new" documentary hypothesis. Neo-documentarians reject some of the outmoded Wellhausenist trappings of the documentary approach, including its historically catastrophic view of second temple Judaism that developed under the influence of "P" and basically put the lively religion of the OT prophets to death. In some ways, however, the neo-documentarians go even further than Wellhausen. This is the case, for example, in their treatment of "E," which to them is a full-fledged source discernible in the current Pentateuch by documentary analysis.[10] They believe that, although the text as it stands is incoherent, preexisting and coherent documents are embedded in it and can be separated out through historical critical documentary analysis of the text. The key indicator of unity in a text is plot consistency, and this is the core issue in their isolation of sources. When the text shows literary contradictions on the level of the plot, historical critical neo-documentary analysis steps in to discern the sources.[11]

In my view, the harsh reality is that this too is destined to become just one more of the multiplying theories leading to even more of the same after that. All agree that critical method in the study of the composition of the Pentateuch has become an increasingly "pluralistic" affair. There is very little agreement between those who hold opposing theories or even between scholars who follow the same basic approach, whether source or redaction as outlined above. As the influential redaction critic Konrad Schmid puts it, scholars "cannot reach consensus on even the fundamental methodological questions, let alone on the reconstruction of the different stages of the text of the Hebrew Bible."[12] The fact of the matter is that none of the "paradigms" currently in place are likely to produce a consensus. They have gone too far beyond the available verifiable data, found problems where there are none, propounded competing theories that they often treat as if they are verified, used them to build up other theoretical constructs that easily collapse when the previous arguments cannot bear the weight, and so on. The multiple, and increasingly multiplying, dissections and reconstructions do not inspire confidence that any of these approaches will ever yield results that can stand the test of time and scrutiny.

---

10 Stackert, *Prophet*, 1–35. Recall that Wellhausen generally referred to JE, not treating E as a separate independent pre-existing source document.
11 Baden, "Why Is the Pentateuch Unreadable?," 250–251.
12 Schmid, *Genesis*, 46, 339.

2. The Question of the Readability of the Hebrew Text as it Stands

In the academic study of the Pentateuch the supposed starting rationale for applying the methods reviewed above is that the text itself is fragmented – it cannot be read as coherent in its current state. There have been numerous recent attempts to make this point.[13] In support of this general tenet, for example, John Barton cites Exod 24:1–17 and asks, "If Moses goes up the mountain in verse 9, how can God tell him to come up in verse 12? Or again, if he goes up in verse 15, how can he go up again in verse 18? Who was with him: …?" and so on.[14] I think of John Barton as an exceptionally good scholar and have learned from his other publications. Moreover, I am fully aware that other scholars also see what he sees here as incoherence. I have responded to it briefly in another place.[15] In my view, this way of reading this particular text is a clear example of the inherent problems with the critical method as it is practiced today, so here is a more expanded response.

Are we really going to require the ancient writer(s) to make a point of saying that Moses, Aaron, Nadab and Abihu, and the elders came down from the mountain after they ate and drank in v. 11? Joshua never went up on that first occasion, according to Exod 24:1–2 and 9–11, and neither did Hur (see v. 14). The following verses make it clear that only Moses and Joshua were supposed to go up on the later occasion. Moreover, v. 12 tells us that, on that occasion, Moses was to go up and "be there" (וֶהְיֵה־שָׁם), whereas his visit along with the Elders and Nadab and Abihu in vv. 9–11 involved only a relatively brief encounter for the purposes of eating the covenant ratification meal in God's presence, as representatives of the nation at large (cf. vv. 1–2).

In v. 14 we learn that the elders were supposed to wait for Moses (and Joshua; "until *we* come back to you"), and that Aaron and Hur would be in charge of adjudicating disputes among the people. Moses had previously been performing this adjudication (Exod 18). This is another indicator that they had come down off the mountain between vv. 11 and 12, and they were to wait there at the foot of the mountain for him to return. Furthermore, on the larger narrative discourse level, Exod 32:1 tells us that, after God gave Moses the two tablets of stone (cf. Exod 24:12 with 31:18), he came down to the people and Aaron at the foot of mountain. Clearly, Aaron, and apparently also Nadab and Abihu and the elders of Israel, had been at the foot of the mountain with the people the whole time, waiting for Moses to come down.

---

13 See, e.g., Barton, "Reading Texts Holistically"; Ska, *Introduction*, 40–95; Brettler, "Coherence"; and most recently Baden, "Why Is the Pentateuch Unreadable?" and Jeffrey Stackert, "Coherence".
14 Barton, "Reading Texts Holistically," 374.
15 See Averbeck, "Pentateuchal Criticism," 167 and the literature cited there.

As for Exod 24:15–18, the Hebrew syntax of the passage does not allow for the simplistic reading suggested by Barton and others. There are not two more trips up the mountain in Exod 24:12–18. A more nuanced rendering follows here (my translation):

> [15] When Moses went up unto the mountain, the cloud covered the mountain. [16] The glory of the LORD settled on Mount Sinai so that the cloud covered it for six days, and then on the seventh day he [the LORD] called unto Moses from the midst of the cloud. [17] Now, the appearance of the glory of the LORD was like a consuming fire on the top of the mountain in the sight of all the Israelites, [18] and Moses entered into the midst of the cloud as he went (further) up, to the top the mountain.

There is only one trip up the mountain in vv. 12–18, not two. The text simply elaborates on what was involved in the ascent: how Moses (and Joshua) went up step by step, how the Lord's glory appeared to the people at the foot of the mountain, and so on. The prepositions and verbal syntax here are consistent with the pattern set in Exod 19–20.[16] Exod 24:12 tells the reader of the Lord's instruction for Moses to come back up on the mountain, v. 13 tells us that Moses and Joshua proceeded to do so, vv. 15–17 highlight the fact that cloud of the Lord's presence covered the mountain as they came up, and v. 18 reports that Moses entered the cloud as he proceeded further up the mountain.

How is any of this unclear? Could not a writer assume that a reader had the intelligence to know that Moses, Aaron, Nadab, Abihu, and the elders came down off the mountain between verses 11 and 12, and that he has simply moved on to the next scene in vv. 12–13, when Moses brings Joshua back up with him? Writers necessarily assume that the readers of their texts (or those who hear them read) bring something to their reading, at least something this obvious and, in fact, indicated in other ways in the narrative. Both ancient and modern writers commonly leave such things to their readers. Totally explicit writing is not possible anyway, and it would not be good writing even if it were possible. So, how are these points so obviously redundant, contradictory, or left as gaps in the text by poor redactors, as Barton argues? The problem is with how the text is being read by the modern reader, not with the text itself or the writer or redactor, or whatever you want to call him. This is just one example of the problem. Unfortunately, there are multitudes of others running rampant through the reading of the text by source and redaction critics.

---

16 For a discussion of these details in reading the Exod 19–20 and 24 narrative(s) see Averbeck, "Pentateuchal Criticism," 159–173.

3. The Problem of Forced Methodology

The current dispute over the connection between the patriarchal and exodus accounts offers a different kind of example for the problem of the conflicting paradigms in the field. According to the Hebrew Bible as it stands, the patriarchal traditions in Genesis are part of the background for what happens in Exodus. There are strong links between the two, from Genesis forward (e.g., Gen 15:12–16; 50:25–26) and from Exodus backward (throughout Exod 1–4). In his book on *Genesis and the Moses Story*, however, the redaction critic, Konrad Schmid, analyses the cross references in Genesis to Exodus and, conversely, those in Exodus to Genesis.[17] He comes to the conclusion that the two sets of traditions are heterogeneous, and that they existed independently until a Priestly (P, late 6th century BCE) or post-Priestly redaction linked them together. At that time, redactors inserted direct literary connections between Genesis and Exodus in Genesis 50:25–26 and Exodus 1. Other important texts that make this connection are Genesis 15; Exodus 3–4; and Joshua 24 (the latter reflecting a Hexateuch principle, rather than a Pentateuch).

One of the major weaknesses in Schmid's approach is the underlying assumption that wherever a particular account of Israelite history begins, that must be the point at which the writer or redactor believed the actual history started. This is necessary to his method. There is little or no consideration given to the possibility that the reason for choosing to start an account at one point or another may have to do with the historiographical point being made rather than with contradictory views of the beginning of Israel's history in the understanding of the composer(s) or redactor(s). Another well-known redaction critic, David Carr notes this methodological problem. He points out that, as Schmid himself has shown, a number of second temple interpretations of history focus exclusively on either the ancestral or exodus traditions, but we know that these interpreters had the whole Pentateuch before them. So "why could not Deuteronomy and/or non-Priestly narrators do the same."[18]

More recently, in his book on Moses as a prophet, Jeffrey Stackert argues, contrary to Schmid, that the earlier sources (Stackert's E and J) show a narrative continuity from the patriarchal and Joseph narratives on into the Exodus narratives, so the patriarchal and exodus stories were linked together early in Israel's history.[19] There was no waiting for P or a post-priestly redactor to combine them. Stackert's approach is documentary, more specifically, ***neo***-documentary, while Schmid's is

---

17 Schmid, *Genesis*. See his own summary on pp. 334–335 and my extensive review of this volume in *RBL* 05/2011.
18 From Carr, Review of *Genesis and the Moses Story* (by Schmid), 583. For a more complete summary and critique of Schmid's overall proposal, see Averbeck, Review of *Genesis and the Moses Story* (by Schmid).
19 Stackert, *Prophet*, 26 n. 84 and 73 n. 7.

documentary regarding P, but redactional for the earlier traditions J, E, and D. So round and round we go again.[20]

It is hard to see how coming to the biblical text in this way is helpful in our reading of it, or in our understanding of its compositional prehistory. A few of those who have practiced such methods are beginning to see the problem they have created for themselves, and are proposing major shifts in the field. David Carr, for instance, puts it this way:

> ... we know far less than we think we do about the formation of these texts. Put another way, I am evermore struck with just how fraught and difficult it is to us to know anything secure and detailed about the undocumented prehistory of any text. The field is littered with the carcasses of dead theories by once-prominent pentateuchal scholars, and I suspect that many theories advanced today will fare no better.[21]

Too many times the scholar's method is given priority over the text; so much so that large or small pieces of the text must be pushed aside in favour of the method. As a result of this methodological "free for all," the field of scholarship as a whole has become so "pluralistic" that it is now "fragmented." There is little hope that those who practice these methods in this way will ever put their textual and methodological "Humpty Dumpty" back together again in any coherent way. It is ironic that these kinds of critical approaches as they are applied today have ended up being far more contradictory between themselves than the Hebrew text could ever be; the same text they label as unreadable, contradictory, and incomprehensible.

4. Reading the Hebrew Text in a Better Way for the Composition of the Torah

The main goal in what follows is to suggest a better way forward in the study of the composition of the Pentateuch, and apply it to the Book of Genesis, especially the patriarchal narratives in Genesis 12–50. There are two major points of method that are essential to breaking away from the troubling tendencies illustrated above. First, the place to begin remains the same – with the reading of the Hebrew text as it stands. The way we read, however, needs to be more generous toward the text and those who composed it, whether we refer to them as authors, compilers, redactors, editors, or whatever. One of these labels might be more pertinent in one place or the other, but the point here is to take a more humble stance as modern scholars toward

---

20 For a review and critique see Averbeck, Review of *A Prophet Like Moses* (by Stackert).
21 Carr, "Data," 106. See also his earlier remarks in Carr, *Formation*, 4–5.

the text and the scribes who composed it. We need to allow them the leeway to collect materials, record traditions, and tell stories in their own ways, even sometimes from different perspectives, since often the same incident can be viewed from differing points of view.

The problem is that there is a distinctly negative bias toward the internal coherence of the Hebrew text built into the way the historical critical method is practiced. It often blurs clear reading. Scholars need to start with a more generous stance toward the text and allow it to testify to its own compositional prehistory without so much extraneous and bias interference. It was written, compiled, or redacted under different conditions and according to ancient conventions that are sometimes quite dissimilar to ours today.[22] What may seem incoherent to us may have been perfectly coherent to them, or perhaps properly conflictual in the sense that, as noted above, one can legitimately look at the same historical reality from different perspectives. I am not suggesting that we should turn a blind eye to problems that actually do exist in the text. On the contrary, if there is a real problem, so be it. It is crucial, however, that we stop seeing problems where there are none. If we let the text have its voice without so much interference, even some of the "fractures" or "seams" we might think we see in it actually resolve themselves in simple and natural ways, and in favor of its coherence.

A second point of method is complementary to this more generous way of reading the text, and essential to it. We need to read the various parts of the text according to their genre, and this includes reading them for their most natural compositional prehistory. This plays an important part in reading for the compositional background of the Book of Genesis in its two major parts: the primeval narratives (Gen 1–11) and the patriarchal narratives (Gen 12–50), respectively. The proto-historical nature of the early chapters of Genesis recalls a number of chronographic, legendary, and mythological compositions extant from the ANE world. Some of these sources take us through a sequence of pre-flood, flood, and post-flood, similar to the sequence in Genesis 1–11, and extend from there into traditions about more recent history, like the patriarch accounts in Genesis 12–50. Although we must take special care to do comparative work according to good comparative methodology (e.g., considering both comparisons and contrasts, propinquity, etc.),[23] the overall scheme of these texts and some of the other patterns and motifs are worthy of serious consideration in our pursuit of the compositional background of the Book of

---

[22] See, e.g., the most recent exposé of the shortcomings of source criticism on this count in Berman, *Inconsistency,* and the literature cited there. David Carr (e.g., in his book *The Formation of the Hebrew Bible*) has made an attempt to draw out some of the most useful considerations in this regard as well.

[23] For the methodology of comparative analysis see, e.g., Averbeck, "Sumer"; Younger, "The 'Contextual Method'," xxxv–xlii, and the literature cited in them.
This essay does not treat the primeval narratives in depth. That will have to wait for another occasion. In the meantime, however, I have found the in depth work in the Master Thesis of one of my students most helpful and stimulating on this topic: Lang, "Imageship".

Genesis. Unfortunately, due to lack of space and time, we will not be able to treat the primeval narratives in any detail here. The spotlight in this essay is on the patriarchal narratives in Genesis 12–50.

The patriarchal narratives focus on the family, clan, and tribal ancestry of ancient Israel, long before the Lord brought them out from slavery in Egypt to make them into their own independent nation (Exodus through Joshua and beyond). These narratives, therefore, are of a different sort than the primeval ones, even though the main structural framing device is the same throughout the book – the sequence of "generations" (*tôlᵉdôt*) formulas running through Genesis (Gen 2:4a; 5:1a; 6:9a; 10:1a; 11:10a; 12:27a; 25:12a, 19a; 36:1a, 10a; 37:2a). The approach to the compositional history of Genesis presented in the following discussion takes these formulas as well as the genealogies and the kinds of stories embedded in and around them to be indicators of the original prehistory of the traditions they contain.

As the text presents itself, the genre of the patriarchal accounts is very dissimilar from that of the primeval narratives introduced briefly above. Genesis 12–50 presents "genealogical history," or perhaps we should use the term "prehistory" since, by its very nature, this kind of historical memory originates in an oral context, not written. Of course, we cannot go back and talk to people who lived in the patriarchal world. We have substantial written ANE sources from that day and even earlier, as noted above, but what if the source material behind the literary composition of Genesis 12–50 was actually developed and passed down through long periods of time in oral form in an oral cultural context?

Cultural anthropologists have produced studies of how these kinds of human cultures and societies work and, in particular, how they preserve and pass down their historical traditions. Again, methodological awareness and limits are essential, but this is also a source of actual verifiable data from human cultures that may help us understand the biblical world and the background of the composition of the biblical text in that world. It is especially significant that some of this material comes from the very ancient cultural world of the Middle East that is still alive today. On the one hand, again, by the nature of the situation, propinquity in time is not possible. We have no live informants from the ANE to tell us their family, clan, and tribal genealogical history. On the other hand, we can claim some level of geographical and cultural propinquity for long standing Middle Eastern traditions studied by cultural anthropologists.[24]

Methodologically, analogues from the ANE and modern cultural anthropology do not control how we read Genesis. They are suggestive, however. The hope is that they will open our minds to the kinds of things that are already there in the text, but easy for us to miss or misunderstand because we are so far removed in time, place, and culture. Our reading of the Hebrew text of Genesis is not constrained by these

---

24 See the methodological considerations treated in Wilson, *Genealogy*, 11–55, which now needs updating and qualification on the basis of more recent work by Shryock, *Nationalism*, and others.

analogues. We must not apply them to the text when the text itself does not clearly call for them. Even then, there are not only comparisons but also contrasts, and Genesis often transforms what we have from the ANE world in both form and function. Moreover, the modern analogues from cultural anthropology are, in fact, modern. They may well provide helpful perspectives in understanding what we have in Genesis, especially when they derive from the Middle East (see above and further below). However, there have been many new developments in the Middle East too, from the ancient days until now, including, but not limited to, the rise of Islam. This calls for caution.

5. Genealogy and Narrative in the Genesis Patriarchal Accounts

The "generations" (*tôl^{e}dôt*) formula and its rather natural background in genealogical history is introduced above. This formula is important not only for the overall structure of the book, but also for discerning the nature of the original source material that lies behind the patriarchal narratives.[25] The primary concern here is not with the historicity of the patriarchs or the patriarchal accounts, but with the nature and history of the sources, compilation, and composition of the genealogies and the narrative accounts embedded in and around them. Nevertheless, the question of the historicity of the patriarchs themselves is a relevant consideration and will arise along the way, especially in so far as it relates to how the ancient Israelites viewed and used these traditions.[26]

The narratives of Genesis 12–50 present the patriarchs as enclosed nomadic pastoral sheikhs whose life and culture was based in family and clan kinship. "Enclosed nomads" were pastoralists constituted and organized on the basis of kinship (whether biologically real or socially constructed), who lived and moved about, often as a powerful force, amid a regional network of tribal groups and urban centres, with which they had various kinds of shifting relationships: filial, political, residential, and sometimes conflictual (even among themselves).[27] Consider, for

---

[25] Here I will be relying upon (but not reviewing every detail of) my previous publication about genealogical history in the patriarchal narratives; Averbeck, "Factors." Further research on oral tradition and genealogical history has pushed this further along.

[26] For the issue the historicity of the patriarchs and the Genesis accounts, see briefly Averbeck," 130–137 and the literature cited there.

[27] With regard to "enclosed nomadism" and the patriarchs, see the very helpful summary of scholarly literature and current status of the discussion, and the proposal made in Fleming, "Mari," 41–48, 56–59, 71–78. For a helpful summary of pastoral nomadism in the ANE see Schwartz, "Pastoral Nomadism," 249–258. See also more recently the collection of essays in Szuchman, *Nomads*, esp. the very stimulating discussion by Porter, "Beyond Dimorphism".

example, the introductory lines of Abram's commission in Gen 12:1 ("go forth from your homeland, your kin, and your father's house"), and the reflections of patriarchal lifestyle in Genesis 12–50 (e.g., the various elements of kinship, pastoralism, and relationships of various sorts with urban centres in Gen 12:6–8; 13:3, 18; 14:13–14; 18:1; 20:1; 21:22–34; 22:19; 23:1–6; 24:1–4; 26:26–33; 29:1–3; 31:17–24; 33:18–34:2; 35:1–8, 16–21; 37:1, 12–17; 46:5–7; 47:1–6).

Pre-existing *literary* sources were sometimes used in the writing of the Bible,[28] but the genealogical structure of Genesis and the historical cultural realities of non-urban pastoral life introduced briefly above lead us to believe that largely oral traditions lie behind the patriarchal narratives.[29] This is not a matter of earlier history versus later history, as if orality is lost in the more sophisticated literary world. Even according to later Israelite traditions – and even when there were kings in Israel – the promises to their patriarchal fathers were of no small significance (see, e.g., Exod 2:24; 3:6; 32:13–14; Lev 26:42; Deut 1:8; 7:7–11; 26:3–5; Josh 24:2–4; 1 Kgs 18:36; 2 Kgs 13:22–23; Ps 105; 1 Chron 29:17–19; 2 Chron 30:6; Neh 9:7–8; etc.). This was where their roots lay, and they knew it.

The reality, therefore, is that the familial, cultural, social, national, and historical consciousness of ancient Israel as it is reflected in the Book of Genesis was based in their genealogical history, including the stories that fill out that history. This is a very different kind of history from that normally produced in an urban based political context, where cities, city-states, and kingships provide much of the framework and substance for the historiography. It should not be thought, however, that one of these kinds of history replaces the other. Both are essential to the history of a people that grows out of one kind of environment and develops into another. The continuity of the "generations" (*tôlᵉdôt*) formula sequence in Ruth 4:18–22, for example, supports the linkage between the two in the Hebrew Bible, from Perez the son of Judah (Gen 38:27–30) to David the renowned king of the later nation of Israel.[30]

In the case of the patriarchs in Genesis, if we are willing to trust what the text tells us about them and how they lived – that is, if we are going to read the text in a reasonably generous way – there are compositional implications. Cultural anthropology provides convincing evidence that "genealogical history" is characteristic of "non-literate societies" that they "recount history" through specified "relations of blood and kin." The genealogies serve as "the basis for recounting stories about" the known individuals in the history of the lineage.[31] By the nature of things we cannot

---

28 For this see Averbeck, "Pentateuchal Criticism," 156–158 and the literature cited there.
29 Person, "Problem of 'Literary Unity'." Person does not treat the genealogies. His purpose is to suggest that, if we take oral tradition seriously, there are certain consequences for source and redaction approaches to the composition of the Bible, since the latter are based largely on literary transmission of traditions. For an earlier critique of the standard literary approaches to composition without due attention to the orality of the ancient Israelite world, see Niditch, *Oral World*.
30 For the details see the helpful discussion in Block, *Judges, Ruth*, 733–737.
31 See the review of some of this material in Averbeck, "Factors," 117–137, briefly summarized

listen in on how this happened in ancient Israel because what we have is written, not oral. We cannot go back to that time and be in the oral moment listening to and questioning informants. Nevertheless, there are still cultures today in which genealogical history is at the core of their historical conception of things. This information needs to be used with due caution, but at the very least it offers cultural analogues that might help us better understand the real world oral background of what we find in the patriarchal narratives. This can help us avoid imposing our modern, western, literate, and literary culture upon them

Modern day Jordan is an example of this, especially the Bedouin culture and its influence even on their modern conception of their history as a nation. It is especially helpful that this material comes from the Middle East and claims great longevity there. Furthermore, culturally, the Bedouin are relatively close to how we understand the enclosed nomadism of the ANE and the patriarchs in Genesis. They live in tents, move their flocks around, have relationships with urban centers in their region, etc. The best source for this that I am aware of is Andrew Shryock's well-researched ethnological study of genealogical history in modern day Jordanian Bedouin culture. There are several important points here that we need to consider in our approach to the patriarch accounts in Genesis; that is, if we are going to read them according to their original oral prehistory.

6. The Original Link between the Genealogies and the Narratives

First, in the oral context, the stories do not develop separately from the genealogies. In his first report of an interview with a Balga tribal leader, Shryock gives an informative example of how this worked among the Jordanian Bedouin:

> ... when I began our interview by asking how he became a Shaykh, he obviously thought the question was premature. "No," he said. "We must bring it all from the beginning. Step by step. In an organized way." He then recited an

---

here. Another important source cited there is Gosden and Lock, "Prehistoric histories," 5. See also the helpful analysis and application of this anthropological information to the Israelites in their ancient Near Eastern context in Cross, "Kinship." I am indebted to my former colleague at Trinity, Dr. Robert Priest, professor of mission and anthropology, for his help in collecting the most useful publications about kinship, genealogy, and genealogical history from the field of cultural anthropology. For a helpful review of kinship studies in cultural anthropology see Peletz, "Kinship Studies".

extensive genealogy of the Slayhat clan and followed it with an account of how the clan's "first ancestor," Abu Silah, arrived at Balga.[32]

Note that the tribal leader could easily recite an extensive genealogy, and immediately attached a story to it that he saw to be essential to his own position as a tribal leader, a "Shaykh." The report goes on to include multiple stories replete with names of important ancestors. Based on his review of data from cultural anthropology, Wilson also observes that "Genealogies at the oral level are apparently not *created* for the purpose of linking pre-existent narratives" (emphasis his).[33] In the oral context, the genealogies and the stories are created and preserved together. The genealogical history of this kind of people gives special meaning to their life. Without it, they are at a loss to explain who they are and what is important to them.

Fifty years ago Claus Westermann already observed this reality in his massive three volume commentary on Genesis. He accepted the standard historical critical division between the JE and P materials in Genesis, as well as the relative dating of P later than JE.[34] He also recognized, however, from an anthropological point of view, that genealogy is a standard part of oral tradition in non-writing kinship groups, where family and clan lineage and the stories that go with it are central to the identity, historical consciousness, and functioning of the group. He, therefore, allowed for the importance of oral tradition combined with genealogy in the kind of society reflected in the patriarchal narratives.[35]

Similarly, but from a quite different point of view, Joel Baden as a neo-documentarian has recently argued forcefully, and I think correctly, in his treatment of the promise texts in Genesis (e.g., Gen 12:1–3; 13:14–17; 15:1–20; etc.), that it makes no sense to separate the patriarchal promises from the stories as later redactions, which is what non-documentary scholars regularly do. To do so is to suppose that "the purportedly originally independent patriarchal traditions" were, in fact, lacking any "theological meaning" to those who preserved them before they were brought together by those who added the promises. No. The narratives would only be meaningful and worthy of preservation "when the promise is an integral part of the story" from the start.[36]

The important point for us here is that the genealogies, the promise passages, and the narratives naturally belong together and support each other. Without one there would be no reason and rationale for the others. Presently, today, redaction critical scholars see a fundamental distinction between P and non-P as basic and essential to their work on the composition of the Pentateuch. Similarly, from a (neo-) documentarian point of view, the genealogies in Genesis are still considered part of the P strand, while the patriarchal stories are variously assigned to J, E, or P (see the

---

32 Shryock, *Nationalism*, 11–12.
33 Wilson, *Genealogy*, 55.
34 Westermann, *Genesis 12–36*, 35.
35 Westermann, *Genesis 12–36*, 37, 44, 54–56.
36 Baden, *Promise*, 55–56.

summary and critique of these theoretical approaches early in this essay). One of the most radical results of reading these texts from a well-informed cultural anthropological point of view is that we must allow for the regular practice in such societies of keeping genealogy and oral tradition together, and that none of this would be preserved without a motivating rationale (i.e., the promises). Normally, in oral genealogical history the stories do *not* develop separately from the genealogies. The fact of the matter is that it is unlikely that the stories themselves would have ever circulated orally without their genealogical frame.[37]

7. The Historical Core of Family, Clan, and Tribal Genealogical History

Second, Shryock forcefully attacks those who argue that "tribal historicity" is not to be taken seriously because it is oral. As he puts it, "tribal history was a *received* tradition [*not* an invented one], a rich canon of memorized stories and poems, most of them demonstrably old" (the bracketed addition is mine).[38] The "tribal mentality" of the Bedouin "is intrinsically historical" even though it has been maintained over the centuries in oral form. Shryock gives verifiable evidence that the same stories are told with the same essential features today as far back as the records that are available from the 18th century. And there are other cultures where the same is also true.[39]

This is not to deny the fact that, among the Jordanian Bedouin, oral presentations of genealogies and the stories of genealogical history will differ. The relationships between kinship groups are often conflictual. One telling of the ancient genealogies and stories may treat others as just a pack of lies. In the oral context the same genealogy or story, therefore, can be told from different points of view because, in fact, there are different perspectives from which a story can be seen and told, and the perspectives could even change with new developments in the ancient day. "The tribal past, in the absence of standard texts, is continually reconstructed in speech. The reconstruction is quite accurate, but it is flexible as well. ... the historical associations ... are extremely responsive to context."[40] The fact of the matter is that within a particular family, clan, and tribal group, one cannot get away with just making up stories. At their core these are received oral traditions with long standing stature, carefully preserved and constantly retold.

---

37 Westermann, *Genesis 12–36*, 37, 44, 54–56.
38 Shryock, *Nationalism*, 23 and 25 with the full argument developed on pp. 20–25.
39 See Averbeck, "Factors," 133–134 and the literature cited there.
40 Shryock, *Nationalism*, 33.

What does this suggest for the oral genealogical prehistory of Israel? We will discuss the move from oral to written form below but, in the meantime, we must observe that, from the point of view of oral genealogical history, what we have in Genesis lacks some of the conflictual features of the Jordanian Bedouin analogy. This is to be expected because Genesis, in fact, is written and captures the traditions that were held in common by one line from Abraham through the sons of Jacob. This family and clan line eventually, over centuries, grew into the tribes of Israel. It would have been different if the stories from the point of view of the secondary lines of descent from the patriarchs were included. Nevertheless, one can still see that the sons and their heirs did indeed vie for position and prominence (see, e.g., Genesis 27, 37, and 48–50), and the Isaac versus Ishmael opposition is renowned from ancient days until now in Genesis versus the Koran (cf. the stories in Genesis 16–17 and 21, and the genealogy in Gen 25:12–18).

It is helpful to consider how the Genesis genealogical history is utilized and expanded to include later clan developments in Exod 6:14–25 for the genealogy of Moses and Aaron, especially Aaron and his sons. This genealogy follows the sequence of the births of Jacob's sons from Reuben to Simeon to Levi in Gen 29:31–34 (cf. Exod 6:14–16). It does not continue with the other sons. Once you get to Levi you need go no further, since this is the tribe from which Moses and Aaron originated, and that is the primary concern in the context. Furthermore, the genealogical growth of the tribe of Levi continues with the clans and families that derive from him (vv. 17–19), and the further growth of the Kohath clan through Amram, Izhar, and Uzziel (vv. 20–22; expanding also on Korah, Izhar's son, cf. Num 16), and especially Amram down to the time of Aaron and Moses (v. 20). It also includes Aaron's wife and their sons (vv. 23), and even his son Eleazar with his wife and their son Phinehas (v. 25; cf. Num 25 and Judg 20:27). It appears that this is a literary reflection of how genealogical history would have worked in the oral context. The genealogy gives the required setting for the story, as in the citation from Shryock's report quoted above.

8. The Transition from Oral to Written Form in the Emergence of the Nation

This brings us to the third point. The Bedouin naturally resist writing down their genealogical history. As Shryock puts it, "This mode of history making is not only textless, it is avowedly *anti-textual* as well."[41] One group is related to one ancestor and the other to another ancestor, so they would want to hear the stories that relate

---

41 Shryock, *Nationalism*, 34.

most closely to them, told in accordance with their particular hoary traditions, and often in conflict with others. The telling of the history would be adjusted for the occasion by those who believed, were responsible for, and would contend for the traditions of the people of their particular tribal, clan, and family in-group. Shryock observes, "It would be wrong to conclude from this fact (as many ethnographers do) that tribal history is not really about the past; more to the point, the past, for tribespeople, is obviously inseparable from the present. History is *now* as it happened *then*."[42] Again, the history is still about the real past.

It is not clear to me how closely the patriarchal genealogical history in its oral stage corresponded to this worldview, but I am convinced that it is much closer than what has been proposed in either the documentary or non-documentary approaches critiqued earlier in this essay. Separating out the supposedly late "P genealogies" from the stories (whether assigned to J, E, or P) embedded in and around them is simply not realistic to the prehistory of this kind of literature. We must keep the genealogies, the stories, and the promises together in their transmission and composition. Moreover, the tribal, clan, and family genealogical material is not limited to what we find attached directly to the *tôlᵉdôt* formulas.

For example, at the end of the Genesis 22 account of the *Aqedah* there is a section of genealogy that follows through on the family branch of Terah still residing in upper Mesopotamia. There is no *tôlᵉdôt* formula here, but Gen 22:20–24 expands what is found in the *tôlᵉdôt* genealogical unit in Gen 11:27–32 by extending it forward to the next two generations from Abraham's brother Nahor and his wife, Milcah. It runs through Bethuel their son, and his daughter Rebekah, who would become the wife of Isaac, the one who had just been spared according to the promises stated clearly in both genealogical contexts (Gen 12:1–3 and 22:15–18). We cannot go into all the details here. The point is that this is important genealogical grounding for what is still to come in the remaining stories about Abraham, Isaac, and Jacob (esp. Gen 24 and 28–32). If the analogy with the Jordanian Bedouin stands, telling the stories would have been combined with reciting the genealogies even in the oral stage.

As for the history of the process of the literary composition of Genesis, it would seem most likely that the impetus for this activity in ancient Israel, like in modern Jordan, was the need to draw together the genealogical history of the patriarchal period in service of the emerging nation. Shryock observes that the oral Bedouin local genealogical history remains alive as long as there are elders alive to tell it, but the younger generations generally consider it passé and favour the political history of the modern state. Nevertheless, the traditional oral foundation is retained, in a stripped down sense, by the way it is written into the modern political history of the emerging Jordanian state in the service of those who are in power or grasping for it.[43] The orality, flexibility, liveliness, and sectarian nature of the ancient family,

---

42 Shryock, *Nationalism*, 35.
43 Shryock, *Nationalism*, 34–37.

clan, and tribal genealogical history is sacrificed in favour of modern political history that offers stability, unity, and access to position and power in the emerging nation state.

If we follow the analogy through into the composition of the Genesis and its relationship to Exodus, Schmid's proposal (outlined and critiqued above), that the patriarchal traditions and the exodus traditions were unconnected until a Priestly (P, late 6th century BCE) or post-Priestly redaction linked them together, is quite unlikely. It runs counter to the most natural compositional reading of the text, which would suggest a historical progression and organic connection between the era of oral genealogical history and the incipient writing of the political history of Israel as an emerging nation. If I understand Shryock correctly, the shift from the ancient to the modern is taking place in relatively quick order in Jordan – over just a couple generations. According to the biblical text, this took place slowly over many generations. The ancient roots in family, clan, and tribal genealogical history were maintained even as they moved toward national unity and political history. It is abundantly clear that the kinds of struggles that come with such a progression from an already existing family, clan, and tribal sense of genealogical history to a newly developing sense of national identity and unity are in full evidence in the text.

For example, the Korah rebellion in Num 16 reveals ongoing internal clan level conflict within the tribe of Levi. On the tribal level, the backdrop for the long term north/south divide between Judah and Ephraim (Israel) is found in Genesis 48, especially vv. 19–20. Moreover, the Book of Judges shows how the various tribes could function according to their own situation with internal variations and conflicts, sometimes in combinations and sometimes individually. The press toward national unity, however, is clearly manifested in the action of the twelve tribe league in Judges 20–21, and in the well-known refrain, "In those days Israel had no king; everyone did as they saw fit" (Judg 17:6 and 21:25; cf. 18:1 and 19:1). Similarly, as noted above, the genealogy in Ruth 4:18–22 continues the pattern of the patriarchal *tôl^edôt* formula from Genesis 38 through to the time of David.

These textual realities have been staring us in the face for a long time, but for me it took the reading of Shryock to see what was there all along. This is how the methodology suggested here is intended to work. The analogy is genre based and powerful as a stimulus to how we should read the Genesis patriarchal narratives from the point of view of the history of their composition. This material was not all invented or linked together compositionally at a later time, but arose naturally out of what was happening in the historical shift from the ancient roots to the emergence of the nation. A few ANE texts also support this kind of reading. The Assyrian King List, for example, begins with a list of "17 kings who lived in tents"; in other words, nomadic kings from around 2000 BC. Some think these may be names of tribes, not persons.[44] In any case, the point is that these people, like the ancient Israelites, had a

---

44 Millard, "Assyrian King Lists (1.135)," 463.

sense of this kind of origin in enclosed nomadic prehistory, although they did not develop it in literary form like Genesis 12–50.

Much more needs to be done to follow through on this approach to the composition of the patriarchal narratives but, in my view, the data and discussion above provides a way of coming at the material that makes the most sense in light of the most natural prehistory of the textual genre as a we have it. Limitations of space will not allow us to follow through on such issues as the Joseph "novella" (Gen 37, 39–48), which reads somewhat differently from the previous patriarchal narratives. It is reminiscent of certain kinds of literary narratives we have from Egypt, especially Sinuhe, which dates to the Middle Kingdom (ca. 2040–1786).[45] One wonders if perhaps this was written as an earlier literary composition and then worked into the literary account of the patriarchs as a pre-existing document at the time when Israel was emerging as a nation delivered from slavery in Egypt, according to the text as we have it. The Egyptian setting and linguistic features of the text makes this all the more likely.

The writer formalized the oral genealogies and used them to provide the literary framework of the patriarchal narratives in the form of the *tôlᵉdôt* formulas, reflecting the important place the genealogies had in the oral context. This was important to the historical consciousness of the emerging nation. The writer also inserted other similar genealogical details in the service of the ancestral stories he preserved, as in Gen 22:20–24 (treated above). It bears repeating here again that, in light of the genre of the patriarchal narratives and data from cultural anthropology discussed above, the most likely time and context for writing down such oral traditions would be when the descendants of the patriarchs through the line from Abraham to Isaac to Jacob and his sons were emerging as a nation.

9. Conclusion

The writer of Genesis also used the *tôlᵉdôt* formulas to frame the primeval narratives in Genesis 1–11 which, moreover, had the effect of binding them forward to the patriarchal narratives in Genesis 12–50. This was intentional, of course, since the theology of the promises in the patriarchal narratives always included blessings to "all the clans of the earth" (Gen 12:3b; cf. 10:32) through Abraham's seed. It is likely, therefore, that the same author composed the two sections of Genesis together, each with the other in mind. The theology must not be relegated to secondary status. This is a large part of what motivated and guided the writer of Genesis. Abraham and his family provide the needed segue from the world history of the primeval narratives to the national history of Israel, all of which is essential to the redemptive

---

45 Lichtheim, "Sinuhe (1.38)," 77–82.

program of God. Compositionally, the genre background of the *tôlᵉdôt* formula belongs to the genealogical history (or prehistory) represented in a literary way in the patriarchal narratives. The one who composed the text used this formula to arrange the primeval narratives as well, thereby organizing and unifying the book as a whole at the same time.

As noted above, the genre background of the primeval narratives is really quite different from the patriarchal accounts. A more detailed treatment of Genesis 1–11, however, will have to wait for another time. Only a few pertinent remarks can be offered here. Basically, Genesis 1–11 situates Israel within its larger ANE common cultural environment, and speaks to Israel from within that world. This was a way to connect with Israel from a larger ANE point of view. After all, the ancient Israelites were ANE people too. In this case, however, we have plenty of extant literary texts from the ancient world that contain some of the same major motifs and patterns that we find in the biblical narratives. It appears that the writer reworked and reshaped the traditions we know from these extant written materials, recast them in ancient Israelite Yahwistic categories, and added other material in the process.

This does not mean that the writer would have needed direct access to these written literary texts in his day in order to compose Genesis 1–11. Many of the traditions would have been widely known in the common cultural oral world of the regular people of that ancient day. For example, they would have known the story of the flood in one form or another.[46] On the literary level, this story surfaces in one of the most widely distributed and well-known literary compositions of the ANE world, the Akkadian Gilgamesh Epic, as well as other compositions. It is also mentioned, for instance, in the Sumerian King List (SKL), which bears the sequence: pre-flood, flood, and then post-flood, like in Genesis 5–11.[47]

Of course, this is a king list, not a genealogy. This fact alone distinguishes the SKL from the genealogies we have in Genesis 5 and 11. Yet, this transformation of the genre makes perfectly good sense when we consider that the writer of Genesis was thinking in terms of family, clan, and tribal traditions, not city-state kingships like we have in Mesopotamia. Ancient Israel had no previous sequence of human kings, but of patriarchs instead. The SKL was composed in its final form in the Isin period (ca. 2000–1800 BC), in retrospect of the long city-state kingship history of the region. This kingship was artificially conceived of as one single monarchy from the beginning, starting in Eridu before the flood. It moved from one city-state to

---

46 The cuneiform culture had spread far and wide across the ANE from at least the middle of the third millennium (see, e.g., Ebla in upper Syria) down into and through the history of Israel. We know that Akkadian was the *lingua franca* of the ANE for perhaps 1500 years. The Amarna letters from the Late Bronze Age show that even small chiefdoms in towns like Jerusalem and Shechem had access to cuneiform scribal culture. Moreover, archaeological excavations have recovered cuneiform literary texts in Canaan dating to the Bronze and Iron ages; see Horowitz, Oshima, and Sanders, *Cuneiform in Canaan*.
47 Glassner, *Mesopotamian Chronicles*, refers to the SKL as "Chronicle of the Single Monarchy."

another, before and then after the flood, until it final came to reside in Isin, according to the SKL.[48]

Different genres require different tactics when we read texts for their compositional history. This is because the underlying source materials are of a different kind. On the one hand, it is largely ANE literary traditions that lie behind the primeval narratives in Genesis 1–11. On the other hand, it is largely oral genealogical history that underlies the patriarchal accounts as we now find them in Genesis 12–50. Probably the most helpful analogues for the compositional history of the patriarchal genealogies, narratives, and promises, therefore, are to be found in the modern ethnographic analyses that cultural anthropologists have produced in their study of oral cultures with ancient roots, especially from the Middle East.

Historically and theologically, through these compositional processes and their yield in the Book of Genesis, the Lord met the emerging ancient Israelite nation where it was in its real world context and took it forward from there into the future he intended. In doing this, he did not leave the rest of the world behind, but from the start intended that through this chosen people he would bring blessing to the whole world (Gen 12:3b, "and all peoples on earth will be blessed through you"). The proto- and pre-history of the emerging nation of Israel that we find in Genesis provided the undergirding for their historical consciousness from the beginning. In terms of methodology in the study of the composition of the Pentateuch, I have tried to show that reading the text in a more generous way, and in light of its inherent genre as a whole and in its parts, offers the best and most realistic access to a units compositional prehistory and the history of the literary compositional process.

Bibliography

Averbeck, Richard E. "Sumer, the Bible, and Comparative Method: Historiography and Temple Building," in *Mesopotamia and the Bible: Comparative Explorations* Edited by Mark W. Chavalas and K. Lawson Younger, Jr. Sheffield: Sheffield Academic Press and Grand Rapids: Baker Academic, 2002, 88–125.
—. "Factors in Reading the Patriarchal Narratives: Literary, Historical, and Theological Dimensions," in *Giving the Sense: Understanding and Using Old Testament Historical Texts*

---

48 For details about the purpose and historical development of the traditions in the SKL, see Steinkeller, *History,* 39–81 and Milstein, *Tracking the Master Scribe,* 42–50 and the literature cited in those places.

(Essays in Honor of Eugene H. Merrill). Edited by David M. Howard, Jr. and Michael A. Grisanti. Grand Rapids: Kregel, 2003, 115–137.

—. Review of *Genesis and the Moses Story: Israel's Dual Origins in the Hebrew Bible*, by Konrad Schmid, *RBL* 05/2011.

—. "Pentateuchal Criticism and the Priestly Torah," in *Do Historical Matters Matter for Faith: A Critical Appraisal of Modern and Post Modern Approaches to the Bible*. Edited by James K. Hoffmeier and Dennis R. Magary. Wheaton, IL: Crossway, 2012, 151–179.

—. Review of *A Prophet Like Moses,* by Jeffrey Stackert, *Themelios* 42 (2017): 520–522.

Baden, Joel S. *The Promise to the Patriarchs*. Oxford: Oxford Univ. Press, 2013.

—. "Why Is the Pentateuch Unreadable? Or, Why Are We Doing This Anyway?" in *The Formation of the Pentateuch. Bridging the Academic Cultures of Europe, Israel, and North America*. Edited by Jan C. Gertz, *et al*. FAT 111. Tübingen: Mohr, 2016, 243–251.

Barton, John. "Reading Texts Holistically: The Foundation of Biblical Criticism" in *Congress Volume Ljublijana 2007*. Edited by André Lemaire. SVT 133. Leiden: Brill, 2010, 367–380.

Berman, Joshua A. *Inconsistency in the Torah: Ancient Literary Convention and the Limits of Source Criticism*. Oxford: Oxford Univ. Press, 2017.

Block, Daniel I. *Judges, Ruth*. NAB 6. Nashville, TN: Broadman & Holman, 1999.

Brettler, Marc Zvi. "The 'Coherence' of Ancient Texts," in *Gazing on the Deep: Ancient Near Eastern and Other Studies in Honor of Tzvi Abusch*. Edited by Jeffrey Stackert *et al*. Bethesda, MD: CDL Press, 2010, 411–419.

Campbell, Anthony F. and O'Brien, Mark A. *Sources of the Pentateuch: Texts, Introductions, Annotations*. Minneapolis, MN: Fortress Press, 1993.

Carr, David M. Review of *Genesis and the Moses Story* in its previous German edition, by Konrad Schmid, *Biblica* 81 (2000): 583.

—. *The Formation of the Hebrew Bible: A New Reconstruction*. New York: Oxford Univ. Press, 2011.

—. "Data to Inform Ongoing Debates about the Formation of the Pentateuch," in *The Formation of the Pentateuch. Bridging the Academic Cultures of Europe, Israel, and North America*. Edited by Jan C. Gertz, *et al*. FAT 111. Tübingen: Mohr, 2016, 87–106.

Cross, Frank Moore. "Kinship and Covenant in Ancient Israel," in *From Epic to Canon: History and Literature in Ancient Israel*. Baltimore: Johns Hopkins Univ., 1998, 3–11.

Fleming, Daniel E. "Mari and the Possibilities of Biblical Memory." *Revue d'Assyriologie* 92 (1998): 41–78.

Glassner, Jean-Jacques. *Mesopotamian Chronicles*. In vol. 19 of *Society of Biblical Literature Writings form the Ancient World*. Edited by Benjamin R. Foster. Atlanta, GA: Society of Biblical Literature, 2004, 117–126.

Gosden, Chris and Lock, Gary. "Prehistoric histories." *World Archaeology* 30 (1998): 2–12.

Hayes, John H. and Prussner, Frederick C. *Old Testament Theology: Its History and Development*. Atlanta: John Knox Press, 1985.

Horowitz, Wayne; Oshima, Takayoshi, and Sanders, Seth L. *Cuneiform in Canaan: Cuneiform Sources form the Land of Israel in Ancient Times*. 2nd edition. University Park, PA: Eisenbrauns, 2018.

Kuhn, Thomas S. *The Structure of Scientific Revolutions*. 2nd edition. Chicago: Univ. of Chicago, 1970.

Lang, Brenden. "When Imageship was Lowered from Heaven: A Study of the Genre and Functions of Genesis 5 in Light of Comparative Literature," *MA thesis at Trinity Evangelical Divinity School*, 2018.

Lichtheim, Miriam. "Sinuhe (1.38)," in *The Context of Scripture, vol. I, Canonical Compositions from the Biblical World*. Edited by William W. Hallo and K. Lawson Younger, Jr. Leiden: Brill, 1997, 77–82.

McKane, William. *Studies in the Patriarchal Narratives*. Edinburgh: The Handel Press, 1979.

Millard, Alan. "Assyrian King Lists (1.135)," in *The Context of Scripture, vol. I, Canonical Compositions from the Biblical World*. Edited by William W. Hallo and K. Lawson Younger, Jr. Leiden: Brill, 1997, 463.

Milstein, Sara J. *Tracking the Master Scribe: Revision through Introduction in Biblical and Mesopotamian Literature*. Oxford: Oxford Univ. Press, 2016, 42–50.

Niditch, Susan. *Oral World and Written Word: Ancient Israelite Literature*. Library of Ancient Israel. Louisville, KY: Westminster John Knox Press, 1996.

Peletz, Michael G. "Kinship Studies in Late Twentieth-Century Anthropology." *Annual Review of Anthropology* 24 (1995): 343–372.

Person, Raymond F., Jr. "The Problem of 'Literary Unity' from the Perspective of the Study of Oral Traditions," in *Empirical Models Challenging Biblical Criticism*. Edited by Raymond F. Person, Jr. and Robert Rezetko. Atlanta: SBL Press, 2016, 217–237.

Porter, Anne. "Beyond Dimorphism: Ideologies and Materialities of Kinship as Time-Space Distanciation," in *Nomads, Tribes, and the State in the Ancient Near East: Cross-Disciplinary Perspectives*. Edited by Jeffrey Szuchman. OIS 5. Chicago: Oriental Institute Press, 2009, 201–225.

Rendtorff, Rolf. *The Old Testament: An Introduction*. Philadelphia: Fortress Press, 1986.

Schmid, Konrad. *Genesis and the Moses Story: Israel's Dual Origins in the Hebrew Bible*. Transl. by James D. Nogalski. Siphrut 3. Winona Lake, IN: Eisenbrauns, 2010.

—. "Post-Priestly Additions in the Pentateuch – A Survey of Scholarship," in *The Formation of the Pentateuch. Bridging the Academic Cultures of Europe, Israel, and North America*. Edited by Jan C. Gertz, et al. FAT 111. Tübingen: Mohr, 2016, 589–604.

Schwartz, Glenn M. "Pastoral Nomadism in Ancient Western Asia," in vol. 1 of *Civilizations of the Ancient Near East*. Edited by Jack M. Sasson. Farmington Hills, MI: Charles Scribner's Sons, 1995, 249–258.

Shedinger, Robert F. "Kuhnian Paradigms and Biblical Scholarship: Is Biblical Studies a Science?" *JBL* 119 (2000): 453–471.

Shryock, Andrew. *Nationalism and the Genealogical Imagination: Oral History and Textual Authority in Tribal Jordan*. Berkeley: University of California Press, 1997.

Ska, Jean-Louis. *Introduction to Reading the Pentateuch*. Transl. Sr. Pascale Dominique. Winona Lake, IN: Eisenbrauns, 2006, 40–95.

Stackert, Jeffrey. *A Prophet Like Moses: Prophecy, Law, and Israelite Religion*. New York: Oxford Univ. Press, 2014.

—. "Pentateuchal Coherence and the Science of Reading," in *The Formation of the Pentateuch. Bridging the Academic Cultures of Europe, Israel, and North America*. Edited by Jan C. Gertz, et al. FAT 111. Tübingen: Mohr, 2016, 253–268.

Steinkeller, Piotr. *History, Texts, and Art in Early Babylonia: Three Essays*. Studies in Ancient Records 15. Boston and Berlin: Walter de Gruyter Inc., 2017, 39–81.

Szuchman, Jeffrey ed., *Nomads, Tribes, and the State in the Ancient Near East: Cross-Disciplinary Perspectives*. OIS 5. Chicago: Oriental Institute Press, 2009.

Wellhausen, Julius. *Prolegomena to the History of Israel*. Edited by D. A. Knight. Atlanta: Scholars Press, 1994 (reprint from the 1885 edition).
Westermann, Claus. *Genesis 12–36: A Commentary*. Transl. by John J. Scullion S.J. Minneapolis, MN: Augsburg Pub. House, 1981.
Wilson, Robert R.. *Genealogy and History in the Biblical World*. New Haven and London: Yale Univ. Press, 1977.
Younger, K. Lawson, Jr., "The 'Contextual Method': Some West Semitic Reflections," in *The Context of Scripture, vol. III, Archival Documents from the Biblical World*. Edited by William W. Hallo and K. Lawson Younger, Jr. Leiden: Brill, 2002, xxxv–xlii.

The Limits of Source Criticism

The Flood Narrative in Genesis 6–9

Joshua Berman (Bar-Ilan University)

In this study I highlight nine methodological flaws in the current practice of source criticism. All of these are well-displayed in what has long been the parade example of the achievements of source-criticism, namely the flood narrative of Genesis 6–9.

1. A Theory that Creates the Text, Instead of the Text Creating the Theory

My first critique of source critical method concerns the relationship between theory and text: should theory stem from the textual data? Or should theory dictate what the text should look like? The impetus to separate the Genesis flood account into two strands has always stemmed from the difficulties the received text presents us. At its best, the theory of two versions stems *from* the text and the difficulties it presents. It is indisputable that the source-critical approach to the flood story well accounts for several of these difficulties, such as the seemingly conflicting numbers of animals to be rescued on the ark (cf. 6:19–20; 7:2–3) and the repeated narrations of Noah's entry into the ark (cf. 7:7; 7:13). Indeed, in a scientific inquiry the data should drive the theory and when scholars point to difficulties in the text and adduce a theory of sources to explain those difficulties they are remaining loyal to this axiom.

However, the source critical approach to the Genesis flood narrative violates this principle at several junctures, when it takes the theory as a given, and uses it—perhaps, *abuses* it would be a better word—to recreate the text, when the received text itself is entirely unproblematic. Consider the source-critical approaches to v. 6:7: "The Lord said, 'I will blot out from the earth, man whom I created, from man to the beasts, to the creeping things, to the birds of the sky, for I regret that I made them." The verse itself is coherent and clear. It functions well as a whole: man is the pinnacle and raison d'être of the universe. If man is to be destroyed there is no point in sustaining the world created for his benefit.[1] Indeed, the fate of all of creation is

---

* This paper is an abridged version of my larger study, "Source Criticism and Its Biases: The Flood Narrative of Genesis 6–9," in my *Inconsistency in the Torah: Ancient Literary Convention*

linked to that of man elsewhere in the flood account as well (8:1, 21; 9:15). There would appear to be no reason to aggressively bisect this verse, assigning parts of it to one source and parts of it to another. And yet this is what critics have increasingly proposed.[2] For these scholars, the words "from man to the beasts to the creeping things to the birds of the sky" (מאדם עד-בהמה עד-רמש ועד עוף השמים) are a later interpolation of P language into the non-P original of the verse.

The motivation for scholars to do so stems from a desire to achieve ideological divide between the two hypothesized sources, P and non-P; lining up seeming doublets and contradictions in parallel columns is insufficient. There must be a fundamental ideological divide between the two accounts that justifies their original composition and preservation as distinct traditions. It is inconceivable that two communities would preserve two separate accounts of the flood if the differences between them were purely of a lexical nature. One of the greatest ideological dividing lines that scholars try to wedge between the two hypothesized versions of the flood concerns the scope of God's wrath. For source critics the P version maintains that God wished to destroy all that he had created while non-P maintained that God wished to annihilate man alone. Moreover, the P version should, ideally, resonate with and echo the language of the account of creation in Genesis 1, long considered a P text. The received version of v. 6:7, however, does not square with the ideological wedge that source-critics hypothesize. Verse 6:7 is found in the midst of the hypothesized non-P version's introduction to the flood story. And yet, the verse calls for the destruction of all of creation—supposedly P's ideology—and even invokes the language of the fifth and sixth days ("from man to the beasts to the creeping things to the birds of the sky") from the account of creation of chapter 1, theorized to be a Priestly chapter.[3] If the entire verse is retained as emanating from hypothesized non-P, a major ideological divide between the two versions is itself, "blotted out," as it were. This would represent a challenge to the source-critical theory, for it would eviscerate the ideological distinction between the two versions, calling into question why two separate versions had been maintained in the first place. It would also challenge the accepted view that the account of creation in Genesis 1 is the exclusive purview of the Priestly source. Excising the catalog of animals from v. 6:7 purchases the source critic the ideological wedge that he needs to legitimate the presence and ideological distinction of the two sources. Note well: here there is no difficulty in the text that gives rise to the theory; rather a difficulty in the theory is then read back into the received text, whose words must now be reassigned in a manner that will conform to the source-critical theory. Critics could have read v. 6:7 and concluded that there is no great ideological divide between the two sources, though that would

---

and the Limits of Source Criticism (New York: Oxford University Press, 2017), 236–268.
1   Cf. Ps 8:5–6.
2   See Carr, *Reading*, 57; Ska, "The Story of the Flood," 1–22; Levinson, "A Post-Priestly Harmonization," 115.
3   See the recent discussion in Levinson, "A Post-Priestly Harmonization," 113–123.

have undercut the very argument for their existence. Critics could have argued that there are indeed doublets and contradictions within the Genesis account that seem to suggest compositional growth, yet without committing themselves to the larger enterprise of identifying two parallel complete versions of the flood. By positing the catalog of animals in 6:7 as a late interpolation of P language into a non-P text, critics choose the one path that will preserve the paradigm of the source-critical approach that there are two separate sources interwoven in the text. The damning evidence of so-called P terminology square in the middle of a so-called non-P passage is not allowed to undercut the hypothesis. Rather, it is "quarantined" under the guise of editorial interpolation, and disallowed rhetorical and hortatory contact with the rest of the passage, lest it contaminate that source's hypothesized ideological purity and distinction from the P source. And thus a perfectly coherent verse is aggressively torn asunder. The needs of the theory—wrongly—are allowed to determine the text.

2. Creating False Doublets

Further, the two-source theory is foisted upon the text in that it creates dichotomies and doublets that are of its own creation and not inherent in the text. Indeed, it is difficult to reconcile the numbers of animals to be rescued as per 6:20 (pairs of all animals) and 7:2–3 (seven of each of the species listed). The divide between the two figures is real and begs explanation. Samuel Loewenstamm has correctly observed, however, that the source-critical approach to the Genesis flood story too easily blurs the line between "real difficulties" and "imaginary difficulties" in the story's structure."[4] To my mind, one such "imaginary" difficulty and contrived doublet concerns the source of the deluge. For source critics, the P version claims that God allowed the waters of the depths and the heavens to flood the earth (7:11; 8:2) whereas the non-P source maintains that the deluge was rainfall (7:4, 12; 8:2).[5] The difference and distinction between the two founts of the deluge are presented as if they are of a kind with the differences between the number of animals taken, that is, mutually exclusive.

Logically, of course, there is no reason why the deluge could not have emanated from both rain clouds and heavenly and earthly wellsprings. There is no contradiction between the two. Moreover, the notion of divine deluge stemming from two founts is a common trope. In fact, consider the sources of the deluge in Tablet XI of the Gilgamesh Epic, both rain and opened dikes (XI:98–103):

---

4   Loewenstamm, "The Flood," 116.
5   See e.g. Carr, *Reading*, 52–55.

> I gazed upon the appearance of the *storm*,
>
> The *storm* was frightful to behold!...
>
> A black cloud rose up from the horizon,
>
> Inside [the cloud] Adad was thundering...
>
> Erregal tore out the *dike* posts,
>
> Ninurta came and brought with him the *dikes*.[6]

Divine deluge that stems from both from cloud rain and from the wellsprings of the earth are a familiar trope in biblical literature (Ps 77:17–18; Prov 3:20). Moreover, the Genesis flood account mentions these two founts together at two junctions (7:11–12; 8:2). However, if we adopt a reading whereby the Genesis flood derived both from cloud rain and from other wellsprings together, it would no longer be possible to bisect the text into two accounts. Source critics *must* ignore the attested trope in Tablet XI of the Gilgamesh Epic and the other biblical sources of divine deluge from rain and from other wellsprings, and create an "imaginary" distinction, in Loewenstamm's words, so that each of the putative versions of the story will have a flood unto itself. When critics separate the founts of the deluge, they do so not because the theory solves a problem in the text; rather a problem in the theory gives rise to an unnecessary and forced distinction in the text.

3. Irrational Non-Sequiturs in the Putative Sources

In addition to creating unnecessary and unwarranted dichotomies, the source critical reading also produces non-sequiturs in the putative sources that it recovers. Consider the MT version v. 7:15–16: "[The animals] came unto Noah, unto the ark, two by two, from all of the living creatures. They were male and female of all creatures, as

---

6 Translated by Benjamin Foster, in Hallo, *Context*, 1:459. Andrew George renders an alternative translation, but one that also demonstrates that the flood in this account stemmed both from rain storms and from dikes:

> There came up from the horizon a black cloud,
> Within it Adad did bellow continually,
> Šullat and Ḫaniš were going at the fore,
> "Throne bearers" travelling over mountain and land.
> Errakal was ripping out the mooring poles;
> Ninurta, going (by), made the weirs overflow.

See George, *Gilgamesh*, 1:709.

God had commanded him. And the Lord closed him in." The final phrase of v. 16, "And the Lord closed him in," follows directly from the previous elements in vv. 13–16. Noah and his family enter the ark, the animals enter the ark, and to conclude, the Lord "shuts the hatch" as it were, and closes Noah in. However, in the putative non-P source, the following text is hypothesized: "(7:10) And after seven days, the waters of the deluge were on the earth. (7:12) The rain was on the earth forty days and forty nights (7:16b) and the Lord shut him in." Source critics splice the text in this fashion, because v. 16b refers to God as YHWH, and thus must be assigned to the non-P source. However, this reading is deficient on two grounds. In the first place, it creates a non-sequitur as it implies that the Lord enclosed the ark only after it had been raining already for forty days and forty nights! Secondly, it removes v. 16b, the notice of the Lord shutting in Noah from the simple context of the verses in which it is organically found in the Genesis text, following the embarking of Noah, his family and the animals.

4. A Double-Standard for Determining Doublets

The great appeal of the source-critical approach was that it supposedly produced two texts that would read cleanly, without the repetitions and doublets that seem to plague a synchronic reading of the Genesis text. However, neither the proposed P text, nor the proposed non-P text achieves this. Consider that within the non-P account we find the following reconstruction (7:12): "And the rain was upon the earth forty days and forty nights. (7:16b) And God sealed him therein. (7:17) And the deluge was forty days upon the earth, and the waters increased and lifted the ark so that it rose above the earth." The note in v. 17a that the deluge was forty days is glaringly superfluous following the exact same claim two verses earlier in the non-P version.

The fact that source critics are willing to overlook this doublet calls into question the criterion of doubling that is the basis for the hypothesis of two strands. The criterion does not seem to be applied rigorously and consistently. Rather, it seems that source critics see doublets when these will fit into the procrustean bed of two separate sources, but overlook doublets when they remain within the hypothesized versions.

5. The Reductive Nature of Source Critical Redaction

Other needless repetitions abound in the flood narrative, such as the extended repeated report of Noah's entry into the ark in the hypothesized P version. Difficulties such as the unnecessary and juxtaposed repetition of the duration of the rain in non-P, and the wholesale repetition of the boarding of the ark in hypothesized P, might have been the types of literary phenomena that could have called into question the very suggestion that we have here two conflated sources. The bisection of the text clearly does *not* provide us with two accounts, each free of repetition and free of incongruities. And yet rather than walking back from the hypothesis, source critics have sought to buttress their hypothesis by resort to a series of redactors, who are the agents responsible for the disruptive passages.[7]

The recourse to redactors and addenda is made solely on the argument that by doing so, we will be able to preserve the integrity of the two sources, purportedly identified in the remaining verses of the narrative.[8] The strategy is reductive. For the source critic, data that complicates the split into two sources is not considered probative in order to disprove the theory. Instead, "bad" data—data that are incongruous with the two-source theory—are isolated from the "good" data, and are assigned to redactors. The theory is thus always sustained. The hermeneutics of the source critical approach take as axiomatic that the scholar has the full capacity to determine the text's compositional history. This strategy of the textual quarantine of inconvenient passages empowers scholars to propose a clean history of the text's composition. However, it would be methodologically more prudent to arrive at the sober conclusion that, in fact, the "bad data" complicates our capacity to account for the present shape of the text.

---

[7] For an opinion in this vein concerning the duration of the flood, see Driver, *of Genesis*, 91; for opinions that 7:8–9 are also the intrusion of a redactor, see discussion in Levinson, "Post-Priestly Harmonization," 121; on the repeated figure of six hundred years as redactional see McEvenue, *Narrative Style*, 52.

[8] Similar "quarantining" of bad data by assigning it to a redactor is exhibited in vv. 7:8–9. Verse 7:2 speaks of a distinction between clean and unclean animals, a distinction which source critics believe is exclusive to the non-P source. However, the narrative of 7:8–9 speaks of pairs of animals boarding the ark, in accordance with the verses assigned to the P source (cf. 6:20). It is unclear therefore how clean and unclean animals (as per the non-P source) and pairs of animals (as per the P source) can be combined in these verses. For a recent discussion of source-critical resolutions, see Levinson, "Post-Priestly Harmonization," 121.

6. The Mistaken Presumption of Preserved Sources

The source-critical approach rests on the foundational assumption that the biblical redactors faithfully preserved their sources and that these sources, therefore, are recoverable by properly analyzing the received, redacted version we have today. However, this assumption is challenged both by contradictions within the source critical approach itself, and by the evidence we now have of editorial practices of scribes in ancient Israel and in the ancient Near East.

The source critical approach rests on an internal contradiction in its claims. Source criticism does not produce two complete stand-alone accounts of the flood when the 14 snippets of hypothesized P and the 13 snippets of Non-P are separated and reconstructed. The P account may be considered a full account, but not so the non-P account, where two omissions are notable. First, it lacks a command to build an ark. Moreover, the non-P account does not report the exit from the ark by Noah and the animals. Source critics are forced to concede that the final redactor does not retain full fidelity to the putative original version of this account but has borrowed from it selectively. Source critics aver that material from an original source may be missing, but what is preserved, is the *ipsissima verba* of the original source and can be recovered. Yet, if the redactor could violate the integral nature of the original version by omitting sections of it, by what right may we assume that he has not supplemented and otherwise altered those putative versions?

Source critics retort that the redactional logic of such conflation lies in the desire to conflate the sources as fully as possible so as to create a relatively seamless whole. But the very fissures highlighted by source criticism undermine that claim. For their theory to account for the unevenness of the flood narrative, source critics must make three claims: 1) that the redactor worked tirelessly to disassemble the original sources and then conflate them, combining a total of 27 snippets, some no longer than a phrase; 2) that the redactor freely omitted material from the non-P source, and yet with no clear explanation of why he would or could do so; 3) that in the end the redactor(s) had free reign to tamper with the text, and yet performed his (their) task in sloppy fashion, or that later accretions are responsible for the unevenness seen in passages such as the accounts of Noah's embarking the ark, discussed earlier. Had both versions been fully preserved, perhaps one could aver that the redactor's need to preserve the wording of both texts in their entirety leads in the end to unevenness in the text. But source critics freely admit that material from non-P is missing in the final version or that non-P was never a full expansion.[9]

The stakes here are enormous. The very enterprise of tracing the history of composition of Hebrew scriptures rests on the assumption that the earlier sources are recoverable solely on the basis of the internal literary evidence within the received

---

9   See discussions in Ska, "The Flood," 1–22; Gertz, "Source Criticism," 169–180.

text, and without supporting textual witnesses or epigraphic evidence. But those putative sources are available only if we assume that redactors and editors never altered or augmented their sources. Were diachronic scholars to concede the possibility that earlier sources had undergone alteration or augmentation, their concession would effectively shut down the quest for the compositional history of the text.[10] Scholars committed to tracing the development of the text, therefore have a vested interest in upholding the axiom that original sources were neither altered nor augmented during redaction.

Source-critics, however, are additionally challenged to demonstrate that the original sources have been preserved in light of what we now know about compositional practices in the ancient Near East. David Carr and Juha Pakkala have amply demonstrated that when ancient writers edited and redacted hallowed texts, they did not display fidelity to their original texts as they incorporated them into new creations. There is not a single documented case of this either within biblical literature—say, Deuteronomy's use of the Covenant Code, or the Chronicler's use of Samuel-Kings—or outside of it. This dramatically weakens the claim of source-critics for such activity in the compositional history of the Genesis flood account. It is, of course, true that a certain literary activity can be sui generis to that culture. Were source critics able to demonstrate that their approach indeed produces two complete strands free of the doublets and inconsistencies identified earlier we could perhaps allow that aggressive conflation was a form of scribal activity found in Israel alone. However, the simple bisection of the received text into two strands still produces hypothesized sources suffering from the same redundancies and inconsistencies that plagued the received text. This, combined with the absence of external control to legitimate the mode of compositional activity it proposes, raises serious questions about the methodological validity of the source-critical approach to the Genesis flood account.

7. Disregard for Mesopotamian Parallels

The source critical approach to the flood narrative is also challenged by evidence from the cognate literature of the ancient Near East, which suggests that the Genesis version of the flood story hews closely to the plot line of its Mesopotamian parallel. In 1978 Gordon Wenham highlighted the common plot structure found in Genesis 6–9 and in the Mesopotamian flood account of Tablet XI of the Gilgamesh Epic.[11]

---

10 See discussion of this point in Zahn, "Empirical Models," 38; Pakkala, *God's Word Omitted*, 14.
11 Wenham, "Coherence," 346–347; Cf. Rendsburg, "Flood Story," 115–127.

He identified seventeen plot elements common to both, that appear in precisely the same order in both traditions:

	Motif	Genesis Flood Account	Gilgamesh Tablet XI
1	Divine decision to destroy mankind	6:6	ll. 14–19
2	Warning to the flood hero	6:13	ll. 20–23
3	Divine command to build ark with dimensions	6:14–21	ll. 24–31
4	Hero complies with command	6:22	ll. 3–85
5	Command to board the ark	7:1–4	ll. 86–88
6	Hero boards the ark with family and animals	7:5–16	ll. 89–93
7	Closing the door of the ark	7:16	l. 93
8	Description of the flood	7:17–24	ll. 96–128
9	Destruction of life	7:21–23	l. 133
10	End of rain, etc.	8:2–3	ll. 129–131
11	Ark grounding on mountain	8:4	ll. 140–144
12	Hero opens window	8:6	l. 135
13	Reconnaissance of the dove and raven	8:6–12	ll. 145–154
14	Hero exits ark	8:15–19	l. 155
15	Hero offers sacrifices	8:20	ll. 155–158
16	Divinity smells sacrifices	8:21–22	ll. 159–161
17	Divinity blesses flood hero	9:1 ff	ll. 189–96

The broad similarity in plot is unmistakable. Neither of the two hypothesized sources, P and non-P comes close to having all of the plot elements that are shared in sequence by MT Genesis 6–9 and Tablet XI of the Gilgamesh Epic. If the two-source theory is correct then, following Gary Rendsburg, "we are supposed to believe that two separate authors wrote two separate accounts of Noah and the flood, and that neither of them included all the elements found in the Gilgamesh epic, but that when the two were interwoven by the redactor, *voila*, the story paralleled the Gilgamesh flood story point by point."[12] How is it that there are six elements in the epic absent from hypothesized P, that just happen to be present in hypothesized non-P? The conclusion from this should be clear. Rather than claiming that the Genesis flood account represents the redaction of two pre-existing sources, we should maintain that the Genesis account represents a significant reworking of a well-known Mesopotamian template. By contrast, the source-critical approach to the Genesis flood account cannot allow that the Genesis text hews closely to the plot of the flood tale in Tablet XI of the Gilgamesh Epic. For if this is allowed then the source critical approach is delegitimated, because this pattern requires one to read the final form of the account, and not its putative sources.

8. Prioritizing Internal Evidence over External Evidence

Although Wenham's study appeared in a prominent journal forty years ago, it has attracted but the scantest attention by source-critics. This is no accident. Claus Westermann's Genesis commentary is one of the most comprehensive expositions of source-critical scholarship to the flood story, one rich with references to the Mesopotamian parallels.[13] His comments about the role of cognate literature in historical-critical scholarship to the Genesis flood account speak volumes. He writes: "The first step in the inquiry into the tradition of the flood narrative must be a comparison of the two accounts contained in Gen 6–9 and an explanation of the way in which they are put together; the comparison must then be extended to the extra-biblical parallels."[14] Note well the hierarchy in Westermann's programmatic statement. Parallels from cognate literature play an important role in historical-critical analysis of biblical literature. But it is a secondary role, one that can only be entertained after the source-critical exercise is first executed on the basis of internal evidence alone. Westermann offers no explanation for this hierarchy; it is assumed as self-justifying. Although later scholars who engage the Mesopotamian parallels do not openly re-

---

12 Rendsburg, "Flood Story," 116.
13 Westermann, *Genesis 1–11*, 384–458.
14 Ibid., 396.

flect on their hermeneutics in the way that Westermann does in this passage, it would appear that the standard practice has been to follow his lead: source-critical conclusions are to be determined exclusively from the data within the text itself. No outside materials can make a claim to inform that discussion.

9. A Foundational Epistemological Error

My final critique of the source-critical approach concerns an epistemological fallacy that has long dominated compositional theory of the Pentateuch in general and the scholarship to this narrative in particular. Consider the following comment by J. A. Emerton in a widely cited study defending the source critical approach to the flood narrative and the difficulties found in that text: "If a scholar thinks he can advance a better, or even an equally satisfactory, explanation, then he may offer it as an improvement on, or substitute for, the hypothesis of a redactor (and if he cannot, he had better refrain from finding fault with it)."[15] I'd like to focus attention on Emerton's parenthetical statement. For Emerton the source-critical approach provides us with a reasonable solution for many of the problems raised by a synchronic reading of the text. Scholars may challenge this approach, however, only if they believe they have "a better, or even an equally satisfactory explanation." For Emerton, we *must* adopt a hypothesis to account for the growth of the text. Note well, however, that the source-critical approach is measured only against other alternative hypotheses. For Emerton, if source-criticism offers a fuller explanation of the data than any other theory, we do not subject it to scrutiny on its own terms. There is no possibility of delegitimizing the source-critical approach unless and until we find an alternative hypothesis to account for the data that is more compelling. This, I would maintain, is a profound methodological flaw. Epistemologically, Emerton – and with him most of those who do compositional history of the text – assumes that scholars have the keys to unlock the difficulties of the text. All that we must do is to choose between the competing hypotheses offered to explain the difficulties within the text. For source critics like Emerton there does not seem to be an option of maintaining that the compositional history of the text might be beyond our reach.

The possibility that our understanding of the pre-history of the text may be partial at best is not entertained. Methodological rigor, however, demands that a hypothesis must withstand scrutiny and stand on its own, regardless of whether competing hypotheses fare worse. It may well be that the hypothesis of two sources explains more textual data than any other hypothesis available to us today. We must reject the two-source hypothesis however, because it collapses under the weight of its own deficiencies, eight of which I have identified here.

---

15 Emerton, "Examination," 402.

Note well: source critics differ whether to assign certain troubling verses or even phrases to the P or non-P strand; they differ on whether the non-P strand should be considered part of a larger J source; they differ as to the chronological priority of one strand over the other; they differ as to whether the two versions have been redacted together, or whether one is derived from the other. Remarkably, though, source-critics are nearly unanimous in their belief that scholars possess the tools to offer a complete accounting of the history of the text. Nearly all source-critical analyses of the Genesis flood narrative account for all of the verses found in Genesis 6–9. The analyses are total in nature. We might have expected that more source-critical scholars would leave chunks of the passage as unresolved problems, or as passages whose provenance is unclear. The fact that source-critics differ with one another on a variety of issues, but claim nearly unanimously that the entire textual puzzle may be solved speaks volumes to the overconfident epistemology that undergirds the source-critical approach.

Conclusions

The arguments presented here lead to the conclusion that the Genesis flood account is a reworking of the Mesopotamian flood tradition as evidenced in Tablet XI of the Gilgamesh Epic. The logic of appropriation and adaptation of a well-known canonical tale is well-understood and requires no special pleading. This interpretation of the text does not mean that the text has no compositional history. It does not deny that this account contains seemingly irreconcilable contradictions and a wide array of doublets. The source-critical approach, however, of two nearly complete versions with various accretions, is not the only avenue available to the historical-critical scholar. Samuel Loewenstamm, for one, rejected the source critical approach, and yet nonetheless identified two traditions concerning the chronology of the story, and two traditions concerning the number of animals Noah was charged to take.[16] The interpretation proposed here does not aim to explain away all of the doublets found in this account. Some may hold that these are due to literary conventions lost to us.[17] Others may admit that there is a compositional history here, but that it is buried in the prehistory of the text. At this point in time, we can see the fissures, but we do not have the capacity to unscramble the egg, as it were. Within this interpretation, the act of interpreting is carried out conservatively—no evidence is avoided, and only what is clear is maintained as such. If aspects of the text defy our capacity to understand them, so be it.

---

16 Loewenstamm, "Flood," 93–121.
17 Cassuto, *Commentary*, 37–39; Rendsburg, *Redaction*, 7–26.

Bibliography

Carr, David M. *Reading the Fractures of Genesis: Historical and Literary Approaches*. Louisville: Westminster John Knox Press, 1996.
Cassuto, Umberto. *A Commentary on the Book of Genesis*. Translated by Israel Abrahams. Jerusalem: Magnes Press, 1961.
Driver, S. R. *The Book of Genesis, with Introduction and Notes*. London: Methuen & Co., 1905.
Emerton, John. "An Examination of Some Attempts to Defend the Unity of the Flood Narrative in Genesis: Part I." *VT* 37 (1987): 401–420.
George, A. R. *The Babylonian Gilgamesh Epic: Introduction, Critical Edition and Cuneiform Texts*. 2 vols. Oxford: Oxford University Press, 2003.
Gertz, Jan Christian. "Source Criticism in the Primeval History of Genesis: An Outdated Paradigm for the Study of the Pentateuch?," in *The Pentateuch*. Edited by Thomas B. Dozeman, Konrad Schmid and Baruch J. Schwartz. FAT 78. Tübingen: Mohr Siebeck, 2011, 169–180.
Hallo, William W., ed., *Context of Scripture*. 3 vols. Leiden: Brill, 2003.
Levinson, Bernard M. "A Post-Priestly Harmonization in the Flood Narrative," in *The Post-Priestly Pentateuch: New Perspectives on its Redactional Development and Theological Profiles*. Edited by Federico Giuntoli and Konrad Schmid. Tübingen: Mohr Siebeck, 2015, 113–123.
Loewenstamm, Samuel. "The Flood," in idem, *Comparative Studies in Biblical and Ancient Oriental Literatures*. Neukirchner: Verlag Butzon & Bercker, 1980, 93–121.
McEvenue, Sean E. *The Narrative Style of the Priestly Writer*. AnBib 50. Rome: Biblical Institute Press, 1971.
Pakkala, Juha. *God's Word Omitted: Omissions in the Transmission of the Hebrew Bible*. FRLANT 251. Göttingen: Vandenhoeck & Ruprecht, 2014.
Rendsburg, Gary A. "The Biblical Flood Story in Light of the Gilgamesh Flood Account," in *Gilgamesh and the World of Assyria*. Edited by Joseph Azize and Noel Weeks. Leuven: Peeters, 2007, 115–127.
—. *The Redaction of Genesis*. Winona Lake: Eisenbrauns, 1986.
Ska, Jean L. "The Story of the Flood: A Priestly Writer and Some Later Editorial Fragments," in idem, *The Exegesis of the Pentateuch: Exegetical Studies and Basic Questions*. Tübingen: Mohr-Siebeck, 2009, 1–22.
Wenham, Gordon J. "The Coherence of the Flood Narrative," *VT* 28 (1978): 336–348.
Westermann, Claus. *Genesis 1–11: A Commentary*. Translated by J.J. Scullion. Minneapolis: Augsburg, 1984.
Zahn, Molly. "Reexamining Empirical Models: The Case of Exodus 13," in *Das Deuteronomium zwischen Pentateuch und deuteronomistischem Geschichtswerk*. Edited by Eckart Otto and Reinhart Achenbach. Göttingen: Vandenhoeck & Ruprecht, 2004, 36–55.

The Divine Revelation of the Name

Warranted and Unwarranted Confidence in the Literary-Critical Analysis of Exodus 3 and 6

Koert van Bekkum

(Evangelical Theological Faculty Leuven /
Theological University Kampen)

1. Introduction

"Why is the Pentateuch incoherent?" According to Joel Baden, this issue is "the driving question of all critical enquiry" into the composition of the biblical Books of Genesis to Deuteronomy, and in his view, the Documentary Hypothesis is its "simplest and best answer."[1] In light of the lively scholarly debate of the last decade, also in this volume, it can safely be argued that the first part of Baden's statement reflects more or less a consensus: most hypotheses regarding the compositional history of biblical books try to offer an explanation of thematic tensions, textual inconsistencies and linguistic patterns as they have been perceived by generations of scholars since Baruch Spinoza (1632–1677) and Isaac de La Peyrère (1596–1676).

The second claim, however, does not represent the general direction in scholarly research. Despite Baden's Neo-Documentarian efforts, the classical literary-critical analysis has been exchanged for redaction- and compositional approaches. After a farewell to the standard characterizations of the Elohist and Yahwist Sources, now even the Priestly Writing is subjected to serious reinterpretation.[2] But what is more important, almost none of these analyses conveys the confident tone and absolute certainty that is characteristic of Baden's writing. Two centuries of literary-critical investigation, new diachronic approaches, synchronic readings offering strikingly coherent views of the text, and empirical models in reconstructing textual development have put the traditional criteria of literary criticism into perspective.[3] Accordingly, Baden's question is rephrased. "Why is the Pentateuch incoherent?" has also

---

[1] Baden, *Composition*, 249. Cf. Baden, "Why is the Pentateuch Unreadable?," 243–252.
[2] Cf. e.g. Volz and Rudolph, *Elohist*; Dozeman and Schmid, *Farewell*; Hartenstein and Schmid, *Abschied*.
[3] See e.g. Carr, *Formation*; Gertz et al., *Formation*, Parts 1 and 2.

become "Why do we perceive the Pentateuch as incoherent?" Ongoing research has made it clear that not only does the complicated compositional history of the literary work of Genesis to 2 Kings and the creation of the canonical entities of the Pentateuch and the Former Prophets play its part, but also the assumptions and background of the scholar him- or herself should be taken into account.

Accordingly, it is no surprise that apart from all kind of new approaches and a lively debate on literary-critical criteria, scholars explicitly call for methodological modesty in diachronic analysis.[4] This, however, has serious consequences and also creates a highly complicated situation. On the one hand, it is impossible to ignore previous research and to act as if it would be possible to start all over again. On the other hand, however, the observations and results of previous generations of scholars should be put into perspective by careful methodological reflections, while also their and our own perspectives deserve consideration. It is only in this way that more common ground can be discovered on the question how to distinguish between warranted and unwarranted confidence in diachronic research.

This chapter contributes to that direction by taking a look at a specific issue, that is, the literary-critical analysis of both accounts of the divine revelation of the Name in Exodus 3 and 6. There are two reasons why this case deserves specific attention.

First, the discrepancies between both passages played an important part in the formulation of the Old and New Documentary Hypothesis. According to Exod 6:2–6, God appeared to the patriarchs as El Shaddai, "God Almighty," but did not tell them his true name, YHWH. In Genesis, God indeed introduced himself to Abraham and Jacob as El Shaddai (Gen 17:1; 35:11, cf. 48:3), while Isaac blesses Jacob in this name (28:3). In Exod 3:1–15 the "God of your fathers" (cf. Gen 31:5, 42; 46:1) also revealed his name YHWH only to Moses, that is, with the enigmatic phrase *'ehyeh ăšer 'ehyeh* (אֶהְיֶה אֲשֶׁר אֶהְיֶה, 3:14). In the book of Genesis, however, Enosh, the third generation of humanity, began to invoke YHWH (Gen 4:26) and characters in Genesis all regularly use this name.

According to the Older Documentary Hypothesis, the accounts of Exod 3 and 6 confirmed the assumption that the differences in the names of God could be used to detect different sources in the book of Genesis. The Documentary Hypothesis distinguished more sharply between these sources on the basis of linguistic differences and distinct concepts of how and when the divine name was revealed and called them sources J, E and P.

The second reason for paying attention to these passages is that they have become an important battle ground in the recent redaction-critical and compositional analysis of the Pentateuch.[5] This model takes a completely different point of depar-

---

4　Berman, "Challenge," 1–25. See also the debate in *JBL* 133 (2014): 648–681. For a similar call from the perspective of an evaluation of the cultural-historical roots of historical criticism, see also Hahn and Wiker, *Politicizing*; Morrow, *Three Skeptics*; Berman, *Inconsistency*.
5　Michael Pietsch therefore characterizes Exod 3–4 as "Paradigma für eine Überprüfung des

ture, that is, the observation of Rolf Rendtorff that the theme of the promise of land to the ancestors, which was central to the formation of the book of Genesis, is nearly absent in the book of Exodus. Exod 3–4 and 6, however, include several references and allusions to both the patriarchal narratives and the story of the Exodus. Accordingly, a complicated discussion takes place on the nature and date of these chapters and of the supposed late literary connection between Genesis and Exodus. Scholars also disagree which of the two accounts of the divine revelation of the Name contains the original text.[6] Despite these conflicting views, however, it is still generally assumed that Exod 3 and 6 present conflicting accounts.

The following two sections highlight the most important elements in these two scholarly debates. A fourth section takes a look at the basic literary-critical criteria that have been used and a fifth investigates the meaning of Exod 3 and 6 in the development of the plot in the transition from Genesis to Exodus. It will turn out that that these criteria not only unnecessarily increase the thematic tensions and textual inconsistencies in the stories, but are also often self-defeating and result in fragmentation. A final section offers some suggestions as to how methodologically modest literary-historical reconstructions can still make use of valuable observations in previous research.[7]

2. From the Old to the New Documentary Hypothesis

Early modern historical research into the composition of the Pentateuch started with one vital question: Did Moses write the Pentateuch?[8] In order to defend a more

---

jüngsten Konsenses in der Pentateuchforschung." Pietsch, "Berufung," 155.
6 As outlined in section 3, Exod 3 is viewed as a late pre-exilic pre-Priestly basic text (Dozeman; Carr; Römer; Pietsch), an editorial text (Levin) or historiographical chapter (Van Seters) by a late Yahwist, or as a post-exilic deuteronomistic (Blum) or post-Priestly compositional passage reinterpreting Exodus 6 (Otto; Schmid; Gertz; Achenbach). Over against this debate maintains Ludwig Schmidt that Exod 3 still confirms that the source-documents J and E indeed exist. Schmidt, "Berufung".
7 I refrain from discussing the historical and theological backgrounds of the diverse solutions, although it cannot be denied that they play a significant part in the debate. Vriezen's opinion, for instance, that Exod 3:14 is E, but at the same time might reflect Moses' most important discovery, that is, the nature of God's transcendence – a discovery that has become foundational for Israel's faith –, is deeply influenced by his theological convictions. In a similar way, Achenbach's interpretation of the divine Name as a transforming entity connecting a plurality of meanings and stimulating historical research and self-criticism reflects the both secular and religious plural context of the West at the beginning of the 21st Century. Vriezen, "'Ehje ašer ʿehje," 510–511; Achenbach, "Ich bin der ich bin," 90–91.
8 Cf. Spinoza, *Theological-Political Treatise*, 119–125.

traditional point of view against the criticism of, for instance, Spinoza, the French physician Jean Astruc argued that Moses had access to old accounts. One of Astruc's main arguments was the alternation between God's names "Jehovah" and "Elohim" and the lack of this alternation from Exod 3 onwards, where Moses no longer depends on tradition, but gives an eyewitness account. Astruc also discussed differences in content between Exod 3 and 6, but only does so in order to make it clear they cannot be used as an argument against his source criticism.[9] Johann Gottfried Eichhorn took up Astruc's main argument in his *Einleitung in das Alte Testament* (1823). In his view, however, Exod 3 and the following chapters were written by an anonymous author, because Moses' father in law is not called Reüel, but Jethro.[10]

Interesting reflections, both on the use of literary-critical criteria and the function of Exod 3 and 6 in the composition of the Pentateuch, were offered by Hermann Hupfeld in 1853. He strongly disagreed with authors defending the Mosaic authorship and the unity of the Pentateuch. Nevertheless, this criticism had shown that there is a plan behind the composition, creating unity between the sources that had been used. According to Hupfeld, the plan underlying this so-called *Urschrift* or Primary Document consisted of four periods:

(1) from the creation to the beginning of the flood (Gen 1:1–2:5*; 9:28–29);
(2) from the flood to Abraham (Gen 6:9–11:26*);
(3) from the elected fathers to Israel in Egypt (Gen 11:27–Exod 1:1–7; 2:23–25*);
(4) from the deliverance from Egypt to the division of the land of Canaan (Exod 6:2–9; 12:37, 40–41, 51; 13:20; 15:22–23a, 27; 16:1; 17:1; 19:1–2; 20:1–17; 21:1–23:19; 24:3–8).

According to this scheme, God revealed himself during the third phase as El Shaddai (Gen 16:3, 15–16).[11] With regard to the fourth period, Hupfeld made use of a proposal of Wilhelm de Wette, who had argued that it is important to distinguish between the pre-Mosaic and Mosaic period, because of the fact that the "theocratic legal history" starts with the divine revelation of YHWH's name. In De Wette's opinion, Exod 6 was just a superfluous repetition of Exod 3.[12] Hupfeld, however, presented an alternative. In his view, Astruc had been apologetic and had therefore missed the crucial point. The remark in Exod 2:23–25* and in particular Exod 6:2 as a further explanation of Exod 3 had been written by the author of the Primary Document in order to take away any doubt on this issue: while Elohim had been the

---

9 Astruc, *Conjectures*, 9–18, 140–142, 387–395. Cf. Smend, "Jean Astruc," 166–167; Gertz, "Jean Astruc," 195
10 Eichhorn, *Einleitung*, Bd. 3, 178, 248–251.
11 Hupfeld, *Quellen*, 77–86.
12 De Wette, *Kritik*, 54–55, 177.

usual name for God in the narratives describing the free communion with God in the time of the patriarchs, now the name of YHWH characterizes the theocracy of the Mosaic period.[13]

Hupfeld was not entirely clear to what extent the Primary Document in the first chapters of Exodus includes earlier material and comments on it.[14] Therefore, scholars extensively discussed the nature of the diverse sources in these chapters. August Knobel and Theodor Nöldeke limited the *Grundschrift* or Primary Document in the Moses tradition to Exod 1:1–7, 2:23–25 and 6:2–7:7, with the exception of the reference to the patriarchs in 6:8.[15] In addition, Nöldeke argued that Moses and Aaron apparently had not been mentioned before and that the genealogy in Exod 6:14–27 was a later addition based on Gen 46:9–26.[16]

Knobel and August Dillmann also offered more precise descriptions of the specific characteristics of the Primary Document[17] and presented detailed linguistic arguments for their view that many stories, including for instance Exod 3, had been written by a "Jehovist", who had blended the sources J and E. Their evidence included, for instance, the name Jethro (3:1 against 2:18) and the use of the name Elohim (3:1, 4, 6, 11–15), the designations "mountain of God" and "Horeb" (3:2, but see 4:27), the term "sight" (הַמַּרְאֶה, 3:3), the address "Moses, Moses" (3:4), the phrase "God of your fathers" (3:6), the verb for "meeting God" (נִקְרָה, 3:18), the verb "to go" (עלה, 3:19), the explanation of the name YHWH (3:13–15), the sign (3:12), the elders who will accompany Moses to the king (3:16, 18), and the mention of the Egyptian treasures (3:21–22).

According to Dillmann, the name YHWH in 3:2, 4, 7, 8, 17 (not so much in 15, 16, 18), and the "clothing" (וּשְׂמָלֹת, 3:22) show that a redactor created a unity with J, which had a parallel account. But in his view, most material in 3:15–22 originally belonged to the Elohist source, just like chapter 5, while he ascribed Exod 4 to J.[18]

The rest is history. First, Colenso raised the idea that later scribes and editors of the Pentateuch did not take 6:2–9 seriously, because it was entirely fictional.[19] Then, after most material of the Primary Document was renamed as the Priestly Writing and was dated after the exile, Julius Wellhausen and Abraham Kuenen formulated their summaries of the New Documentary Hypothesis. This resulted in a more precise definition of the P-profile of Exod 6, while the problem of the blended nature of Exod 3:1–6:1 was avoided by maintaining that it was composed by the Jehovist.[20]

---

13 Hupfeld, *Quellen*, 87–88.
14 Cf. Kaiser, "Heir," 221–222.
15 Knobel, *Exodus und Leviticus*, viii, x–xi; Nöldeke, *Untersuchungen*, 36.
16 Nöldeke, *Untersuchungen zur Kritik*, 37.
17 Knobel, *Exodus und Leviticus*, xi, xviii; Dillmann, *Exodus und Leviticus*, 22–23.
18 Dillmann, *Exodus und Leviticus*, 23.
19 Colenso, *Critical Examination of the Pentateuch*, Part 5, 69–71.
20 Wellhausen, "Composition," 531–532 (= *Composition des Hexateuchs*, 61–62); Wellhausen, *Prolegomena*, 329–330, 338; Kuenen, *Historisch-critisch onderzoek*^{2}, 60–1, 70–1. With regard to the P–profile of 6:2–4, 5–9, Kuenen, *Historisch-critisch onderzoek*, 61, noted that these pas-

With regard to one crucial issue, however, they disagreed. Both Wellhausen and Kuenen observed that in 6:2, Moses appears as already known to the reader. In order to solve this problem, Wellhausen placed the genealogy of 6:13–25 before this verse. Kuenen, however, also observed problems in 2:25 and 6:2–9 and a doublet in 6:10–12 and 6:29–30. Therefore he proposed that a later editor reworked 6:2, wrote 6:6 on the base of the terminology from book of Ezekiel, and also inserted the genealogy.[21]

So at face value, the Documentary Hypothesis formulated an apprehensible consensus. At the same time, it is clear that it remained very hard to offer a comprehensive explanation of all the evidence. The blending of elements in Exod 3 that were supposed to be J and E remained a contested issue, because the chapter itself offers a fairly consistent narrative.[22] In addition, it was hard to define the exact extent of the P-fragment in Exod 6, and to offer a convincing explanation as to how this was integrated into the present context.

3. Compositional Approaches

It is most interesting to see how the recent compositional reflections addressing the question for the connection between the books of Genesis and Exodus deal with these issues. In these studies, there is an increasing tendency, following the analysis of Martin Noth, to take at least 3:1–4:18 as one unity.[23] As mentioned above, the observation of Rolf Rendtorff that, from a thematic point of view, the connection between Genesis and Exodus is very weak, is also taken as a point of departure.[24] Accordingly, scholars started to explore the option that originally the ancestral tradition, with its supposed story of an autochthonous origin of Israel and inclusive image of God, and the Exodus tradition with its non-indigenous narrative and exclusive image of God, were totally separated.[25] The primary method in this enterprise was not to look for literary sources, but to study "larger units" in order to discover

---

sages are closely connected to Gen 17; 35:9–15 in its use of "Elohim," "El Shaddai," "the land in which you are a stranger," the promise, the prediction, and the change of the name, while the typical features of the Elohim-passages are missing. In his view, the perspective of Exod 3 is much broader and also includes the settlement in Canaan (3:8, 17).

21 Wellhausen, "Composition," 532 (= *Composition des Hexateuchs*, 62; Kuenen, *Historisch-critisch onderzoek*, 70–71, 318–319.
22 For the Neo-Documentarian reflections in this regard, still distinguishing J and E-sources in Exod 3–4, see Baden, *Composition*, 74–75, 120–121, 126.
23 Noth, *Überlieferungsgeschichte*, 221; idem, *Exodus*. ATD, 19–21. Noth still maintains that the passage contains elements of both J and E.
24 Rendtorff, *Problem*, 85–90.
25 Cf. Schmid, *Old Testament*, 161–162.

compositional passages bridging the gap between Genesis and Exodus. This resulted in the conclusion that these passages were at the earliest written during the exilic period, because the standard dates of D and P still functioned as chronological anchors.

In this debate, nobody doubts the priestly nature of Exod 6. With regard to Exod 3, however, the views differ significantly. Exploring Rendtorff's view, Erhard Blum first characterized Exod 3–4 as a post-exilic deuteronomistic, but still pre-Priestly compositional unit (Blum).[26] John Van Seters and Christoph Levin in their turn opted for an editorial text or a historiographical chapter from Yahwist origin.[27] More popular became the hypothesis by Konrad Schmid and Reinhard Achenbach that Exodus 3 and 4 are to be viewed as a post-Priestly compositional passage reinterpreting Exodus 6.[28] In response to this idea Blum modified his solution and agreed that Exod 4 is post-Priestly.[29] Levin, however, insisted that Exod 3 connects the Genesis stories to the Plague narrative, as is in his view evident from no less than eight phrases and linguistic features that also occur frequently in the primeval history and the history of the patriarchs.[30] Similar connections with passages in Genesis led Thomas Dozeman and David Carr to the conclusion that the Moses story of Exod 3 and 4 can be defined as a late pre-exilic pre-Priestly basic text with post-Priestly additions.[31] Thomas Römer agrees with this point of view and even tries to date the first version of the story to the 7th century BCE, when Israel became acquainted with the Assyrian adoption-legend of Sargon, the founder of the Assyrian Empire.[32] At the same time, he maintains that the P-version of Moses should be understood as a source, not a compositional layer.[33]

4. Literary Arguments

It is enlightening to take a more detailed look at some of the arguments in this debate and at the methodological considerations they provoke.

---

26 Blum, *Studien*, 20–28.
27 Levin, *Jahwist*, 326–333; Van Seters, *Life of Moses*, 46–47.
28 Otto, "Nachpriesterliche Pentateuchredaktion," 101–111; Schmid, *Erzväter*, 73; idem, "Literary Gap," 31–42; idem, *Old Testament: A Literary History*, 82–83; Achenbach, "Ich bin der Ich bin," 73–88.
29 Blum, "Erzväter," 123–140; idem, "Genesis," 91–96.
30 Levin, "Redactional Link," 137–141.
31 Dozeman, "Commission of Moses," 115–126; Carr, "Pre-Priestly Narrative Connections," 165–179.
32 Römer, "Exodus 3–4;" Römer, "Revelation".
33 Römer, "Von Moses Berufung".

First, it is clear that there is a literary connection between Exod 2:23a and 4:19. But how is this to be interpreted? Is this a doublet implying that Exod 3–4 is an insertion into an existing continuous exodus narrative, or is it more natural to interpret these verses as editorial remarks, structuring one and the same story?[34] The same question can be asked with regard to the resumption of 6:10–12 in 6:29–30. A literary transition does not always indicate an editorial shift, even if there is also a change in the terminology and concept of the text, or a thematic transfer. This also applies to the alternation of names in Exod, the book of "names" (שמות), for instance, of Jethro and Reuel, Moses' father in law. The use of a different name can often be explained by reasons of style and content. So instead of viewing them as indications of diachronic development, it is also possible to interpret them as part of a consistent pattern in the story.[35]

Another striking issue is the P-like features in Exodus 3 and 4, such as the "crying out" of 2:23 in 3:7 and 9, and the attestation of Israel's refusal to listen in 4:1, which is also presupposed in Exod 6. Does this definitely imply that the passage as a whole is post-P? Are these elements later additions? Or is it also possible that one and the same composer uses two different thematic and linguistic traditions? In particular the relation to the passages in Genesis make it very hard to make a decision in this respect. Exod 3 is clearly related to Gen 46:1–4, which in turn can be connected to the travel commands in Gen 12:1–2; 26:2–3; 31:3. These texts are often assigned to different layers. But they "represent a remarkably cohesive and balanced system leading from the patriarchs outside of Egypt to the stay in Egypt and the trip back out."[36] In turn, Exod 6 contains allusions to Gen 17 and 35:9–15, and other passages. A detailed look at them in the context of the overall framework of the book of Genesis shows that it is hard to maintain that both books were only related to one another on a secondary level. In this way, the present debate underlines that defending the view that the P-like material once was a source on its own is not without problems, for the passages fit appropriately in their present context.[37]

This observation is also important for another issue, that is, the relationship between Exod 6:2–8 and several texts in the book of Ezekiel. In a careful essay on the terminological and thematic connections between Exod 6:8 and Ezek 20:5–6, Johan Lust convincingly argues that a literary dependency seems plausible. The direction of this dependency, however, cannot be decided on the basis of the evidence itself, although there is a tendency to favour the priority of Exod 6.[38] Accordingly, it is evident that the assumptions regarding the existence, nature, and date of P significantly influence the ways in which this observation is explained. At the same time, it

---

34 Cf. Pietsch, "Berufung," 160.
35 Fischer, "Exodus 1–15," 162–163.
36 Carr, "Pre-Priestly Narrative Connections," 165–166. For the observation that the "JE"-story of Exod 3–4 comprises references to the patriarchal narratives, see e.g. Stackert, *Prophet Like Moses*, 36–69.
37 Cf. Ska, "Quelques remarques," 100–105; Van Seters, *Life of Moses*, 103.
38 Lust, "Exodus 6:2–8".

has to be noted that the expression "I swore" in 6:8 is most likely to be understood as an allusion to both Gen 50:24 and Exod 3:20.[39]

A third literary-critical criterion regards the presupposition of scholars that the omission of certain elements in a text or the use of a specific formula betrays a different source or redaction. It is, for instance, stated that Exod 3 relocates the story of Exod 6. Geography, however, is just not an issue in this passage.[40] Another example is Rendtorff's claim that Exod 3 knows nothing of the promise to the fathers as formulated in, for example, Gen 15 and 50:24. But this statement can only be substantiated if the shorter formula of Exod 3:8 summarizing precisely these promises is interpreted as a later addition. Yet, this is unlikely, because in the context of the narrative logic of Genesis – 2 Kings the mention of the pre-Israelite nations in this verse merely indicates that another step is taken in the process of the fulfilment of the promised land.[41]

In a similar way, it has been argued that Exod 6 simply presupposed that Moses was not mentioned before. Others admitted that this is not the case.[42] Nevertheless, the solutions presented to this problem are more focused on creating an ongoing pre-Priestly source connecting Genesis to Exodus than on obtaining a clear understanding of the present text.[43]

Needless to say, 6:2–9 adds a new, particular element to the dialogue between YHWH and Moses. The passage not only repeats the history of Israel, but also reveals what is contained in the name YHWH in reaction to a question. It indeed cannot immediately be attached to 2:25,[44] but addresses a specific issue raised in the previous chapters, as can be observed by the use of terminology that is also prominent in Exod 5. YHWH's answer to Moses, for instance, is that he will act with an "outstretched arm" (6:1, 6), so that people will "know" him (6:3, 7). This clearly interacts with pharaoh's "not knowing" in 5:2. Apparently, it is important that both Egypt and Israel learn who YHWH is.[45] In this way, the passage does not offer a complete revelation of the name, but reformulates this revelation with a specific goal in mind.[46] After Moses' request has been rejected by the pharaoh and his good rela-

---

39 Fischer, "Exodus 1–15," 165.
40 Thus Schmid, *Old Testament. A Literary History*, 82. For the relation between phrase אֶרֶץ מְגֻרֵיהֶם in Exod 6:4 and the patriarchal narratives, see Awabdi, *Immigrants*, 130–133, 159.
41 Cf. Moberly, *Old Testament*, 11–12; Van Bekkum, *From Conquest to Coexistence*, 129.
42 See note 17 and 20 above, cf. Römer, "Von Moses Berufung," 145.
43 Cf. Römer, "Elusive Yahwist," 26–27.
44 Fischer, "Keine Priesterschrift," 208.
45 Ska , "Quelques remarques," 102–105, who also mentions the verbs נצל (5:23; 6:6) and עבד (5:9, 11 15, 16, 18, 21; 6:5–6), and סבלת (5:4–5; 6:7). In addition Fischer, "Keine Priesterschrift," 207, mentions close textual relations between Exod 6:6 and 12:12; 15:12–16, cf. 7:5, 17; 8:9, 27; 11:4, 8.
46 Dozeman, "Commission of Moses," 115–157. An enumeration of expressions linking Exod 3 and 6 is offered by Fischer, *Jahwe unser Gott*, 223–224. The textual elements connecting Exod 6:2–9 to the book of Genesis and to the Holiness Code, see Tucker, *Holiness Composition*, 73–77.

tions with Israel have ended, God assures him that he will prove himself to be Israel's deliverer despite this resistance; and again, this is precisely what is expressed in the name YHWH.

5. Exodus 3 and 6 at the Crossroads of the Patriarchs and Moses

This brings us to the question to what extent both revelations can be characterized as a doublet. Römer's main argument for his idea that Exod 6 is part of a source, not a redaction, is that if that were the case, one would expect that the perspective of the redactor would have been woven into the present narrative of Exod 3. This argument, however, is not conclusive. What if, as is admitted by, for instance Kuenen and Dozeman, the scope of Exod 3 is indeed much broader and includes Moses' installation as a prophet, a ritual that is normally attached to a divine revelation, and the promise of Israel's settlement in Canaan (3:8, 17)?

In this context, it is most interesting to take a look at the literary function of the passages from the perspective of more synchronic analyses of Exod 3 and 6.[47] Moses meets God for the first time. In this encounter not only does the God of the patriarchs reveal his Name, but the description of this self-revelation also turns out to be foundational for many aspects of the following story and for the way the God of the fathers will be venerated. For the first time (a) the mountain of God is mentioned, in language highlighting (b) God's holiness, and (c) depicting the calling of a prophet. At the same time, YHWH's self-revelation to Moses anticipates also (d) God's encounter with Israel and (e) contains catechetical instruction. In this way, the chapter introduces many characteristics of YHWH himself and of his relation to Israel which were still missing in the story of Gen 12 – Exod 2.[48]

From the perspective of diachronic analysis, this is a very important observation. De Wette, Hupfeld, and Rendtorff rightly paid attention to the conceptual and linguistic transfer from Genesis to Exodus. But now it turns out that this transfer is deeply rooted in the narrative as a whole. The major shift is already prepared in the book of Genesis; the story in Exod 3 about YHWH's self-revelation at the mountain of God reflects explicitly on this discontinuity; and its further consequences for Israel and the pharaoh are highlighted in the dialogue between YHWH and Moses in Exod 6. YHWH's self-revelation in the paranomastic phrase 'ehyeh ăšer 'ehyeh in Exod 3:14 can be interpreted as the ultimate expression of this episode of transition in the relation between Israel and its God. While the paranomastic construction

---

47 For the following paragraphs, cf. Houtman, *Exodus*, 306–310, 315–361, 470–475; Fischer, *Jahwe*, 99–171; Fischer, "Exodus 1–15," 152–155, 163, 165; Moberly, *Old Testament*, 13–67.
48 Cf. Moberly, *Old Testament*, 13–26; Fischer, *Jahwe*, 201–204.

signifies the intensity of his concrete involvement in Israel's misery in Egypt, the verb *hyh* denotes the very nature of his existence and also indicates his hiddenness. The fact that the exact meaning of a paranomastic phrase always has to be determined in the context, illustrates precisely what is at stake in these and the following chapters: in the Exodus from Egypt and his revelation at Sinai God will reveal his Name and truly prove that his Name is YHWH (cf. Exod 33:19; 34:6–7).[49]

As a result, it can be concluded that the hypothesis of post-Priestly textual blocks connecting traditions and stories and creating unity rightly takes a look at the "larger units" in the books of Genesis and Exodus, for it can be observed that there is a plan behind the composition of the Pentateuch. On the base of the literary-historical consideration of Exod 3 and 6, however, it cannot be argued convincingly that these chapters are inconsistent and that the traditions of the patriarchs and the Exodus were originally separated.

6. Towards an Alternative

The main question, then, is how to use the results of the previous sections in improving the search for the compositional history of the Pentateuch. The recent empirical study of documented cases of transmission history in the Ancient Near East offers an important series of methodological constraints in this respect. The assumption, for instance, of oral stages of transmission that would later be superseded by written stages, does not reflect the historical reality of an oral-literary continuum. The criterion of vocabulary and style has turned out to be untrustworthy. It is also essential to be cautious in creating sources, because these more often reflect our own scholarly assumptions than historical reality. Finally, it is dangerous to posit too many stages of transmission or editorial activity.[50] In addition, the history of the analysis of Exod 3 and 6 makes it clear that the formal aspects and the content of these stories should not be treated separately and that all too specific and modern views of what a story should look like have to be avoided.

When these constraints are taken into account, what criteria can be used in studying the making of the Pentateuch? This is a very difficult question. But a first im-

---

49 Thus already Vriezen, "'Ehje ašer 'ehje." Cf. Fischer, *Jahwe*, 147–154; Achenbach, "Ich bin der ich bin," 84–86; Peels, *Traag tot toorn*, 16–23; Dohmen, *Exodus 1–18*, 156–165. Consequently, both the immediate and the larger context make the translation "What does it matter who I am?," suggesting that God's reaction avoids to answer the question for his Name, highly unlikely. Thus e.g. Enns, *Exodus*, 100–107, cf. Houtman, *Exodus*, 103–104, 348. For a diachronic explanation of the fact that Exod 3:14–15 indeed prepares Exod 6:2–13, see Gertz, *Tradition*, 294–298.
50 Cf. Carr, *Formation*, 13–149. Yet, Berner, *Exoduserzählung*, 67–105, 153–66, distinguishes eleven compositional stages in Exod 3 and four in Exod 6.

portant observation is that on the one hand some major differences can be observed in language, phraseology, and concept between Exod 3 and 6. This might betray its history of composition. The narratological unity and terminological overlap, however, does not justify the conclusion that the chapters present two versions of one and the same story.

In addition, one should be very careful in using only linguistic features. This also regards the use of the designations YHWH and Elohim in the book of Genesis, as is illustrated by Blum's literary-critical analysis of the patriarchal narratives from this point of view.[51]

So even if the text of both Exod 3 and 6 implies that the patriarchs only knew God by the name El Shaddai – and I think these chapters do so –, it is still hard to use this as a criterion to detect passages in Genesis that are related to this concept. For the assumption that these texts accordingly would not use the name YHWH is ours, and not that of the scribes.[52] Both passages merely stress the identity of the God of the patriarchs and the God of Moses. Why would we forbid scribes, who according to their texts perceived the revelation at Sinai and fulfilment of the promise of the land as the definite substantiation of God's identity, to call this God by his very name?

Within this line of thought, I am inclined to think that the great contribution of Hermann Hupfeld was not, as Wellhausen argued, that he made a distinction between two Elohist sources (nowadays called E and P^g). It was his intuition that there is a *plan* behind the composition of Genesis, or, as I would propose as a working hypothesis, of the Enneateuch, a plan with a P-like framework from Genesis to Numbers and a dominant undertone of a deuteronomistic historiographic tradition from Exodus to 2 Kings.[53] Both compositional strands and their underlying stories, legal traditions, and other material are integrated by a network of connections, sometimes in very natural, sometimes in more uneven ways.

In order to overcome the difficulties in the use of linguistic features in this debate, it might also be wise to be cautious and approach the dominant "P"- and "D"-language or the "J"-stories not so much as the result of different sources or editorial strands stemming from diverse theological schools, but as various "colligatory concepts" or "narrative substances." That is, they should be treated as different views of reality tied to specific fields of interest and terminology, creating cohesion and consistency in providing a proposal on how to view reality. Moreover, it should be recognized that these different views are not necessarily conceptually and theologically inconsistent.[54]

---

51 Blum, *Komposition*, 471–475.
52 Cf. Moberly, *Old Testament*, 36–78; Holwerda, *Historia revelationis*, 242–248. For different solutions taking Exod 3 and 6 as complementary chapters, see e.g. Hood, "I Appeared".
53 Cf. Averbeck, "Reading the Torah," 30–38; Van Bekkum, *From Conquest to Coexistence*, 412–416; Van Bekkum, "Geography." For the early date of P-language, see Petersson, "The Linguistic Profile".
54 The terms "colligatory concept" and "narrative substances" are used in the philosophy of his-

Finally, it can be considered that from the perspective of the content of Exod 3 and 6, it is not astonishing that the overall narrative of Genesis to 2 Kings sometimes has to bridge great breaches and irregularities, for the God of this narrative is told to do things that no human being is able to conceive. According to the scribes, a transcending and transforming power drives the content of the narrative. In this perception of history, it is as part of the overall story that decisive steps in creating new realities as in Exod 3 and 6 take place.

In the short term, this line of thought does not result in concrete proposals about the historical growth of the Pentateuch. But it might offer a better explanation of the fact that Exod 3 and 6 are part of a network of connections that create a narrative unit with great diversity and incredible historical depth, from which it is hard to extract sources.

For whatever can be said, it is clear that the connection between the books of Genesis and Exodus and the identity of the God of the patriarchs and of Moses are essential elements in the literary work of Genesis to 2 Kings. Untying these traditions is not without risk. If the traditions of the fathers, the patriarchs and the Exodus, and possibly many more, were originally separated and not part of the same story – "pearls hung on the same scarlet thread," as Wellhausen called them[55] – the question is not only when, but also *why* they were connected. Why did they tell a story in which originally not two, but twelve tribes coming from Egypt revered the same deity as the patriarchs?

For Martin Noth, the first who distinguished the traditions of Genesis, Exodus, and Sinai systematically, his hypothesis of an ancient Israelite *Zwölfstammenbund* was a great help in explaining why the Pentateuchal traditions were tied together.[56] This theoretical construct, however, has disappeared from the scene. Moreover, since the 1990s it has become highly contested whether the kings David and Solomon ever claimed or ruled territories outside Judah and Jerusalem and historians time and again highlight that the territorial kingdoms of Israel and Judah did not differ much from their neighbours with regard to culture and religion. Accordingly, it has become much harder to find tradition-historical reasons for the connection between the supposed separate traditions and foundation myths. At the same time, the idea of Israel's unity is so deeply rooted in the Hebrew Scriptures that it is hardly convincing that this is only the result of cultural and religious influence by refugees on the run for the late 8th Century BCE Neo-Assyrian armies.[57] Accordingly, additional hypotheses have to be formulated explaining why the Judean authors in 7th

---

tory and were introduced by Ankersmit, Narrative Logic.
55 Wellhausen, *Prolegomena*, 330: "Es ist als ob P der rote Faden sei, an dem die Perlen von JE aufgereiht werden".
56 Noth, *Überlieferungsgeschichte*, 277.
57 Thus e.g. Schmid, *Old Testament*, 80, 160; Römer, "Revelation," 310, 314.

century Jerusalem, in exile, or in the Persian Province Yehud believed that the diverse traditions belonged together.

For many taking part in the debate regarding the compositional history of Genesis – Deuteronomy or Genesis – 2 Kings, this remains a problematic issue. A model creating less distance between story and history,[58] paying structural attention to the continuity between the diverse passages and traditions[59] and to the literary configuration of thematic shifts, being more cautious in detecting many stages of transmission in the present text, might be able to offer better answers and provide the opportunity to avoid the fragmentation that is now threatening the historical understanding of the Pentateuch and the Enneateuch.

Bibliography

Achenbach, Reinhard. "'Ich bin, der ich bin!' (Exodus 3,14). Zum Wandel der Gottesvorstellungen in der Geschichte Israels und zur theologischen Bedeutung seiner Kanonisierung im Pentateuch," in *Berührungspunkte. Studien zur Sozial- und Religionsgeschichte Israels und seiner Umwelt. Festschrift für Rainer Albertz zu seinem 65. Geburtstag*. Edited by Ingo Kottsieper et al. Ugarit Verlag, 2008, 73–95.

Albertz, Rainer. "Noncontinuous Literary Sources Taken Up in the Book of Exodus," in *The Formation of the Pentateuch*. Edited by Jan C. Gertz, *et al*. FAT 111. Tübingen: Mohr, 2016, 609–617.

Ankersmit, Frank R. *Narrative Logic. A Semantic Analysis of the Historian's Language*. Martinus Nijhoff Philosophy Library 7. Den Haag–Boston–London: Nijhoff, 1983.

Arnold, Bill T. "Reexamining the 'Fathers' in Deuteronomy's Framework," in *Torah and Traditions. Papers Read at the Sixteenth Joint Meeting of the Society for Old Testament Study and the Oudtestamentisch Werkgezelschap, Edinburgh 2015*. Edited by Klaas Spronk and Hans Barstad. OTS 70. Leiden–Boston: Brill, 2017, 10–41.

Astruc, Jean. *Conjectures sur la Genèse*. Edited by Pierre Gibert. Paris: Noêsis, 1999 [1753].

---

58 The often assumed distance between story and history in Exodus and Sinai narratives is put into perspective by Hoffmeier, "Exodus," and in the stories of conquest and settlement and of the early monarchy by Van Bekkum, *From Conquest to Coexistence*; "How the Might Have Fallen".

59 Both the thematic diversity and literary continuity, e.g., between the patriarchs and the "fathers" in Deut is highlighted by Arnold, "Reexamining the 'Fathers,'" between the laws in Deut and Exod, Lev and Num by Kilchör, *Mosetora*, and between the Priestly texts and the Holiness Code by Tucker, *Holiness Composition*.

Averbeck, Richard. "Reading the Torah in a Better Way. Unity and Diversity in Text, Genre, and Compositional History," in *Paradigm Change in Pentateuchal Research*. Edited by Matthias Armgardt, Benjamin Kilchör and Markus Zehnder. BZAR 22. Wiesbaden: Harrassowitz, 2019, 21–43.

Awabdi, Mark A. *Immigrants and Innovative Law: Deuteronomy's Theological and Social Vision for the גר*. FAT II, 67. Tübingen: Mohr Siebeck, 2014.

Baden, Joel S. *The Composition of the Pentateuch: Renewing the Documentary Hypothesis*. New Haven: Yale University Press, 2012.

—. "Why is the Pentateuch Unreadable? or, Why Are We Doing This Anyway?," in *The Formation of the Pentateuch*. Edited by Jan C. Gertz, *et al.* FAT 111. Tübingen: Mohr, 2016, 243–252.

Bekkum, Koert van. *From Conquest to Coexistence. Ideology and Antiquarian Intent in the Historiography of Israel's Settlement in Canaan*. Culture and History of the Ancient Near East 45. Leiden–Boston: Brill, 2011.

—. "Geography in Num 33 and 34 and the Challenge of Pentateuchal Theory," in *Torah and Traditions. Papers Read at the Sixteenth Joint Meeting of the Society for Old Testament Study and the Oudtestamentisch Werkgezelschap, Edinburgh 2015*. Edited by Klaas Spronk and Hans Barstad. OTS 70. Leiden–Boston: Brill, 2017, 93–117.

—. "How the Mighty Have Fallen. Sola Scriptura and the Historical Debate on David as a Southern Levantine Warlord," in *Sola Scriptura. Biblical and Theological Perspectives on Scripture, Authority, and Hermeneutics*. Edited by Hans Burger, Arnold Huijgen and Eric Peels. Studies in Reformed Theology, 32. Leiden–Boston, 2017, 159–181.

Berman, Joshua A. "Empirical Models of Textual Growth: A Challenge for the Historical-Critical Tradition." *JHS* 16 (2016): 1–25.

—. *Inconsistency in the Torah. Ancient Literary Convention and the Limits of Source Criticism*. Oxford: Oxford University Press, 2017.

Berner, Christoph. *Die Exoduserzählung*. FAT 73, Tübingen: Mohr Siebeck, 2010.

Blum, Erhard. *Studien zur Komposition der Pentateuch*. BZAW 189. Berlin: Walter de Gruyter, 1990.

—. "Die literarische Verbindung von Erzvätern und Exodus: Ein Gespräch mit neueren Endredaktionshypothesen," in *Abschied vom Jahwisten. Die Komposition des Hexateuch in der jüngsten Diskussion*. Edited by Jan C. Gertz, Konrad Schmid, and Markus Witte. BZAW 315. Berlin–New York: Walter de Gruyter, 2002, 119–156.

—. "The Literary Connection between the Books of Genesis and Exodus and the End of the Book of Joshua," in *A Farewell to the Yahwist? The Composition of the Pentateuch in Recent European Interpretation*. Edited by Thomas B. Dozeman and Konrad Schmid. SBL.SS 34. Atlanta: Society of Biblical Literature 2006, 89–106.

Carr, David M. *The Formation of the Hebrew Bible. A New Reconstruction*. Oxford–New York: Oxford University Press, 2011.

—. "What Is Required to Identify Pre-Priestly Narrative Connections between Genesis and Exodus? Some General Reflections and Specific Cases," in *A Farewell to the Yahwist? The Composition of the Pentateuch in Recent European Interpretation*. Edited by Thomas B. Dozeman and Konrad Schmid. SBL SS 34. Atlanta: Society of Biblical Literature 2006, 159–180.

Colenso, John William. *The Pentateuch and the Book of Joshua Critically Examined. Part V*. London: Longmans, Green and Co., 1865.

Dillmann, August. *Die Bücher Exodus und Leviticus*. Kurzgefasstes Exegetisches Handbuch zum Alten Testament. Leipzig: Hirzel, 1880.

Dohmen, Christoph. *Exodus 1–18*. HThKAT. Freiburg im Breisgau: Herder, 2015.

Dozeman, Thomas B. "The Commission of Moses and the Book of Genesis," in *A Farewell to the Yahwist? The Composition of the Pentateuch in Recent European Interpretation*. Edited by Thomas B. Dozeman and Konrad Schmid. SBL.SS 34, Atlanta: SBL, 2006, 107–129.

Dozeman, Thomas B., and Konrad Schmid, eds. *A Farewell to the Yahwist? The Composition of the Pentateuch in Recent European Interpretation*. SBL.SS 34. Atlanta: Society of Biblical Literature 2006.

Eichhorn, Johann Gottfried. *Einleitung in das Alte Testament. Dritter Band*. Göttingen: Carl Eduard von Rosenbusch, 1823.

Enns, Peter. *Exodus*. The NIV Application Commentary Series. Grand Rapids: Zondervan, 2000.

Fischer, Georg. *Jahwe unser Gott. Sprache, Aufbau und Erzähtechnik in der Berufung des Mose (Ex 3–4)*. OBO 91. Fribourg: Universitätsverlag, Göttingen: Vandenhoeck & Ruprecht, 1989.

—. "Keine Priesterschrift in Exod 1–15?" *ZKTh* 117 (1995): 203–211

—. "Exodus 1–15. Eine Erzählung," in *Studies in the Book of Exodus*. Edited by Marc Vervenne. BETL 126. Leuven: Peeters, 1996, 149–178.

Gertz, Jan C. *Tradition und Redaktion in der Exoduserzählung*. FRLANT 186. Göttingen: Vandenhoeck und Ruprecht, 2000.

—. "Jean Astruc and Source Criticism," in *Sacred Conjectures. The Context and Legacy of Robert Lowth and Jean Astruc*. LBHOTS 457. Edited by John Jarick. New York–Londen: T&T Clark, 2007, 190–203.

Gertz, Jan C., Bernard M. Levinson, Dalit Rom-Shiloni, and Konrad Schmid, eds. *The Formation of the Pentateuch. Bridging the Academic Cultures of Europe, Israel, and North America*. FAT 111. Tübingen: Mohr Siebeck 2016.

Hahn, Scott, and Wiker, Benjamin. *Politicizing the Bible. The Roots of Historical Criticism and the Secularization of Scripture, 1300–1700*. New York: Crossroad Publishing Company, 2013.

Hartenstein, Friedhelm, and Konrad Schmid, eds. *Abschied von der Priesterschrift? Zum Stand der Pentateuchdebatte*. Veröffentlichungen der Wissenschaftlichen Gesellschaft für Theologie 40. Leipzig: Evangelische Verlagsanstalt, 2015.

Hoffmeier, James K. "The Exodus and Wilderness Narratives," in *Ancient Israel's History. An Introduction to Issues and Sources*. Edited by Bill T. Arnold and Richard S. Hess. Grand Rapids: Baker Academic, 2014, 46–90.

Holwerda, Benno. *Historia revelationis Veteris Testamenti*. Kampen: Copiëerinrichting Van den Berg, 1954.

Hood, Jared C. "I Appeared as El Shaddai: Intertextual Interplay in Exodus 6:3," *Westminster Theological Journal* 76 (2014): 167–188.

Houtman, Cees. *Exodus: Volume 1*. HCOT. Leuven: Peeters, 1993.

Hupfeld, Hermann. *Die Quellen der Genesis und die Art ihrer Zusammensetzung*. Berlin: Wiegandt und Grieben, 1853.

Kaiser, Otto. "An Heir of Astruc in a Remote German University: Hermann Hupfeld and the 'New Documentary Hypothesis'," in *Sacred Conjectures. The Context and Legacy of*

Robert Lowth and Jean Astruc. LHBOTS 457. Edited by John Jarick. New York–Londen: T&T Clark, 2007, 221–248.

Kilchör, Benjamin. *Mosetora und Jahwetora. Das Verhältnis von Deuteronomium 12–26 zu Exodus, Levitikus und Numeri*. BZAR 21. Wiesbaden: Harrassowitz, 2015.

Knobel, August. *Die Bücher Exodus und Leviticus*. Kurzgefasstes Exegetisches Handbuch zum Alten Testament. Leipzig: Hirzel, 1857.

Kuenen, Abraham. *Historisch critisch onderzoek naar het ontstaan en de verzameling van de Boeken des Ouden Verbonds. Tweede, geheel omgewerkte uitgave. Eerste deel. De Thora en de historische boeken des Ouden Verbonds*. Leiden: J.C. Matthes, 1887.

Levin, Christoph. *Der Jahwist*. FRLANT 157. Göttingen: Vandenhoeck & Ruprecht, 1993.

—. "The Yahwist and the Redactional Link between Genesis and Exodus," in *A Farewell to the Yahwist? The Composition of the Pentateuch in Recent European Interpretation*. Edited by Thomas B. Dozeman and Konrad Schmid. SBL.SS 34. Atlanta: Society of Biblical Literature 2006, 131–141.

Lust, Johan. "Exodus 6,2–8 and Ezekiel," in *Studies in the Book of Exodus. Redaction—Reception—Interpretation*. Edited by Marc Vervenne. BEThL 126. Leuven: University Press – Peeters, 1996, 209–224.

Moberly, R.W.L. *The Old Testament of the Old Testament. Patriarchal Narratives and Mosaic Yahwism*. Minneapolis: Fortress Press, 1992.

Morrow, Jeffrey L. *Three Skeptics and the Bible: La Peyrere, Hobbes, Spinoza, and the Reception of Modern Biblical Criticism*. Eugene: Wipf and Stock Publishers, 2016.

Nöldeke, Theodor. *Untersuchungen zur Kritik des Alten Testaments*. Kiel: Schwers'sche Buchhandlung, 1869.

Noth, Martin. *Überlieferungsgeschichte des Pentateuch*. Stuttgart: Kohlhammer, 1948.

—. *Das zweite Buch Mose: Exodus*. ATD 5. Göttingen: Vandenhoeck & Ruprecht, 1959.

Otto, Eckart. "Die nachpriesterliche Pentateuchredaktion im Buch Exodus," in *Studies in the Book of Exodus. Redaction—Reception—Interpretation*. Edited by Marc Vervenne. BEThL 126. Leuven: University Press – Peeters, 1996, 61–111.

Peels, H.G.L. *Traag tot toorn. Een onderbelicht aspect van het oudtestmentisch godsbeeld*. Apeldoornse studies 58. Apeldoorn: Theologische Universiteit, 2011.

Petersson, Lina. "The Linguistic Profile of the Priestly Narrative of the Pentateuch," in *Paradigm Change in Pentateuchal Research*. Edited by Matthias Armgardt, Benjamin Kilchör and Markus Zehnder. BZAR 22. Wiesbaden: Harrassowitz, 2019, 243–264.

Pietsch, Michael. "Abschied vom Jahwisten? Die Berufung des Mose in der jüngeren Pentateuchforschung." *ThLZ* 139 (2014): 151–166.

Rendtorff, Rolf. *Das überlieferungsgeschichtliche Problem des Pentateuch*. BZAW 147. Berlin: Walter de Gruyter, 1977.

Römer, Thomas C. "The Elusive Yahwist: A Short History of Research," in *A Farewell to the Yahwist? The Composition of the Pentateuch in Recent European Interpretation*. Edited by Thomas B. Dozeman and Konrad Schmid. SBL.SS 34. Atlanta: Society of Biblical Literature 2006, 9–27.

—. "Exodus 3–4 und die aktuelle Pentateuchdiskussion," in *The Interpretation of Exodus. Studies in Honour of Cees Houtman*. Edited by Riemer Roukema. Contributions to Biblical Exegesis and Theology 44. Leuven: Peeters, 2006, 65–79.

—. "The Revelation of the Divine Name to Moses and the Construction of a Memory About the Origins of the Encounter Between Yhwh and Israel," in *Israel's Exodus in Trans-*

disciplinary Perspective. Text, Archaeology, Culture, and Geoscience. Edited by Thomas E. Levy, Thomas Schneider, and William H.C. Propp. Cham: Springer, 2015, 305–315.

—. "Von Moses Berufung zur Spaltung des Meers. Überlegungen zur priesterschriftlichen Version der Exoduserzählung," in *Abschied von der Priesterschrift? Zum Stand der Pentateuchdebatte*. Edited by Freidhelm Hartenstein and Konrad Schmid. Veröffentlichungen der Wissenschaftlichen Gesellschaft für Theologie 40. Leipzig: Evangelische Verlagsanstalt, 2015, 134–160.

Schmid, Konrad. *Erzväter und Exodus. Untersuchungen zur doppelten Begründung der Geschichte Israels innerhalb die Geschichtsbüchern der Alten Testaments*. WMANT 81. Neukirchen-Vluyn: Neukirchener, 1999.

—. "The So-Called Yahwist and the Literary Gap between Genesis and Exodus," in *A Farewell to the Yahwist? The Composition of the Pentateuch in Recent European Interpretation*. Edited by Thomas B. Dozeman and Konrad Schmid. SBL.SS 34. Atlanta: Society of Biblical Literature 2006, 29–50.

—. *The Old Testament. A Literary History*. Minneapolis: Fortress Press, 2012.

Schmidt, Ludwig, "Die Berufung des Mose in Exodus 3 als Beispiel für Jahwist (J) und Elohist (E)," *ZAW* 126 (2014): 339–357.

Ska, Jean Louis. "Quelques remarques sur Pg et la dernière rédaction du Pentateuque," in *Le Pentateuque en question*. Edited by Albert de Pury. Geneva: Labor et Fides, 1989, 95–125.

Smend, Rudolf. "Jean Astruc. A Physician as a Biblical Scholar," in *Sacred Conjectures. The Context and Legacy of Robert Lowth and Jean Astruc*. Edited by John Jarick. LBHOTS 457. New York–Londen: T&T Clark, 2007, 157–173.

Spinoza, Benedict de. *Theological-Political Treatise*. Edited by Jonathan Israel. Translated by Michael Silverthorne and Jonathan Israel. Cambridge Texts in the History of Philosophy. Cambridge: Cambridge University Press, 2007

Stackert, Jeffrey. *A Prophet Like Moses*. New York: Oxford University Press, 2014.

Tucker, Paavo. *The Holiness Composition in the Book of Exodus*. FAT II, 88. Tübingen: Mohr Siebeck, 2017.

Van Seters, John. *The Life of Moses. The Yahwist as Historian in Exodus and Numbers*. Louisville: Westminster/John Knox Press, 1994.

Volz, Paul, and Rudolph, Wilhelm. *Der Elohist als Erzähler: Ein Irrweg der Pentateuchkritik? An der Genesis erläutert*. BZAW 63. Giessen: Töpelmann, 1933.

Vriezen. Th.C. "'Ehje ašer 'ehje," in *Festschrift A. Bertholet*. Edited by W. Baumgartner and O. Eissfeldt. Tübingen: J.C.B. Mohr, 1950, 498–512.

Wellhausen, Julius. "Die Composition des Hexateuchs," *Jahrbuch für Deutsche Theologie* 21 (1876): 392–450, 531–602; 22 (1877): 407–499. Repr. in *Die Composition des Hexateuchs und der Historischen Bücher des Alten Testaments*, Berlin: Walter de Gruyter, [4]1963, 1–208.

—. *Prolegomena zur Geschichte Israels*, Berlin: Reimer, [6]1905.

Wette, Wilhelm Leberecht Martin de. *Kritik der Israelitischen Geschichte. Erster Theil: Kritiek der Mosäischen Geschichte*. Halle: Schimmelpfenning, 1807.

II. Legal History

Why a Paradigm Change in Pentateuch Research is Necessary

The Perspective of Legal History

Matthias Armgardt (University of Konstanz)

1. Introduction

Concerning Pentateuch research, Eckart Otto has recently posed the question: "What went wrong in the last two hundred years ...?"[1] Of course it is of greatest importance when somebody who belongs to the most important Pentateuch researchers asks such a fundamental question. And indeed, after two hundred years of work on the basis of de Wette and the more or less modified Wellhausen-Hypothesis Pentateuch research seems to be deadlocked.

As a legal historian, I would like to draw your attention to the fact that something similar has happened to the scholarship of Roman Law. After decades of hunting interpolations of the classical Roman Law in the Corpus Iuris Civilis, about 30 years ago the legal historians became aware that there was something wrong in the foundations or, to be more precise, in the methods and assumptions. Today, almost every scholar of Roman Law assumes that the legal texts in the Digest have not been interpolated unless there is really strong evidence for the contrary. If all interpolations that were assumed by the scholars in the beginning of the 20th century had been true, the making of the Corpus Iuris would have taken at least 30 years, not 3 years. And I want to add that in the case of the Corpus Iuris we are sure that there were some (!) interpolations, but not as many as it had been presumed. Nowadays everybody asks themselves how such brilliant scholars could have fallen into the trap of arbitrariness and uncontrolled subjectivity in this field of research.

In my opinion, a similar turning point has come for Pentateuch research now. A critical analysis of the assumptions and the methods is now of highest importance. A change of the Paradigm is never easy. It requires strong encouragement. This is why this conference is important in my eyes. For this reason I am glad that several non-theologians have contributed to this volume to support this change that is absolutely necessary in my opinion. Unfortunately, Prof. Kitchen from Liverpool could not

---

1   Otto, *Tora*, 2.

come to our conference. But I am going to mention some important results of his painstaking research later.

In the second part of this contribution, I would like to make some remarks on the law in the Pentateuch from the perspective of a legal historian. I will especially focus on a legal topic in the book of Genesis: the suretyship of Juda for the return of Benjamin.

2. Methods and Assumptions

I would like to start with methods in historical research. The crucial point is how to avoid circularity in argumentation leading to arbitrariness of the results. Theologians and historians often use models containing unproven assumptions. These models are then used to "correct" the sources, for example to assume processes of edition and redaction. This is very dangerous, because unproven assumptions hidden in the model cannot be evaluated stronger than the source itself. This would be wrong consideration of evidence!

Every historical source is a piece of evidence. Of course, evidence can be wrong and misleading. But we need counterevidence for a successful argumentation against every source. Unproven assumptions and hypotheses are not counterevidence. In the contrary, they have to be based on independent strong evidence themselves and it has to be carefully shown that the counterevidence is stronger or more probable than the source we want to correct. If this task is not fulfilled, fundamental standards of scientific argumentation are violated.

A very important part of the right argumentation is the adequate treatment of the question of burden of proof. Whoever argues against a statement stated by a historical source has to carry the burden of proof. Only if he manages to show that the counterevidence he presents implies a stronger historical probability, a modification of the source is justified. Additionally, I want to defend a basic rule stated by the legal historian Gerhard Otte: If we want to argue against a source without presenting a source supporting our view, we violate basic standards of rational argumentation. This would be speculation, not science.

I want to conclude these short remarks about methods with some hints about the importance of evidence or counterevidence coming from external sources, i.e. sources being independent of the source I want to argue for or against. Every modification of a historical source by assuming a process of redaction leading to modifications of the content of the source *without* having an independent source contradicting the source to be modified and supporting my assumed correction of it, violates fundamental standards of correct consideration of evidence and of rational argumentation. Therefore, evidence or counterevidence coming from independent external sources is of highest importance for rational historical argumentation. Only sufficient external evidence avoids circular and therefore void argumentation. Additionally, it is not enough that the independent counterevidence simply shows that the contrary is possible, but moreover that it is true or at least highly probable.

3. External Evidence of the First Millennium Concerning the Law Codes of the Pentateuch?

In the following I want to analyze two famous attempts to show that a considerable redaction of the Pentateuch took place in the middle of the first millennium. Of course such a redaction is possible. But the question is whether it can be proven that such a redaction is more probable than the contrary.

3.1 Curse Lists of Deuteronomy and the Treaty of Esarhaddon

A lot of Pentateuch scholars follow Frankena[2] who already in 1965 thought that the curse lists we find in the Neo-Assyrian Vassal-Treaty concluded in 672[3] between Esarhaddon and the Medes, which was edited first by Wiseman in 1958, have been transferred to the curse list of Deuteronomy (Deut 13:2–10 and 28:20–44). When I compared Deuteronomy 28 and VTE for the first time I was rather disappointed because of the low rate of coincidence. As everybody knows Kitchen showed that there are curse lists of the second millennium fitting much better with the curse list of Deut 28.

Let me sum up Kitchen's results: Between Deut 28 and VTE are only 7 coincidences and two times the sequence is changed. Kitchen found 15 coincidences with curse lists from the early second millennium (ten of them stem from the Codex Hammurapi) and six coincidences with curse lists from the late second millennium. All in all, Kitchen presented evidence showing 40 references of Deuteronomy 28 with treaties earlier than Esarhaddon.[4] Thus, Frankena's hypothesis has been refuted by comparison with external sources, i.e. the historical probability of his hypothesis is not strong enough to argue against Deut 28. Kitchen comes to the conclusion:

> Thus, it is nowadays impractical to try to establish any special relationship between [Deuteronomy] and Esarhaddon's [VTE] (or any other Neo-Assyr-

---

2 Frankena, "Vassal Treaties." Cf. Kitchen and Lawrence, *Treaty*, vol. III, 230 (n. 25).
3 Kitchen and Lawrence, *Treaty*, vol. I, 963–1004 (especially 984–990).
4 Kitchen and Lawrence, *Treaty*, vol. III, 230–233 (especially 232).

ian document of this class), and entirely inappropriate to hark back to Frenkena's well-meant but misleading study.[5]

3.2 Deuteronomy – Solon/Gortyn – 12 Tables

Burckhardt, Seybold and von Ungern-Sternberg have recently presented an interdisciplinary comparison of Deuteronomy, the Law of Gortyn and the Roman Twelve-Tables.[6] The fundamental idea behind this comparison was that Deuteronomy was made or at least significantly modified by King Josiah (639–609).[7] But in my opinion the results of this research project show that the assumption of a modification of Deuteronomy by Josiah is not justified at all. Seybold and von Ungern-Sternberg tried to defend the idea of a step by step increase of Deuteronomy and of countless modifications of the text in theological-homiletic, redactional and historical respect.[8] They did not offer any evidence for these assumed editions. At the end of the day, they had to admit that there is no evidence for a direct contact of Deuteronomy and Solon's Law of Gortyn.[9]

But the volume is worth reading, because we find evidence against the hypothesis of an edition in times of Josiah. First of all, the authors have to admit that in Deuteronomy the central place is never named Jerusalem.[10] They do not have any explanation for that. This is a strong indicator that Jerusalem was not the capital when the text was written. Second, the critical contribution of the ancient historian Raaflaub who attacks the fundamental ideas of Seybold and von Ungern-Sternberg draws the attention to the fact that in Deuteronomy 17 the lack of and the limitation of royal prerogatives cannot be explained by the hypothesis of an edition in times of Josiah. No hint for royal privileges concerning the courts or the army can be found in Deuteronomy. It is not credible that King Josiah tried to build up his empire and his power by making a law code like Deuteronomy that strongly limits his royal rights.[11]

Thus, firstly, there is no evidence for a modification of Deuteronomy by Josiah; secondly, there is even counterevidence against the hypothesis of an edition of Deuteronomy by Josiah.

Let me add the perspective of legal history: Deuteronomy is not a legal code at all. Its content is much too weak for that. We only find some additions to the Covenant Code. These additions are supposed to be for the time at the end of the hiking

---

5 Kitchen and Lawrence, *Treaty*, vol. III, 232.
6 Burckhardt, Seybold and von Ungern-Sternberg, *Gesetzgebung*. Cf. my review in SZ Rom 131 (2014): 429–433.
7 Burckhardt, Seybold and von Ungern-Sternberg, *Gesetzgebung*, 11–16; 105ff.
8 Burckhardt, Seybold and von Ungern-Sternberg, *Gesetzgebung*, 106.
9 Burckhardt, Seybold and von Ungern-Sternberg, *Gesetzgebung*, 56.
10 Burckhardt, Seybold and von Ungern-Sternberg, *Gesetzgebung*, 121.
11 Burckhardt, Seybold and von Ungern-Sternberg, *Gesetzgebung*, 180f.

through the desert, like the command to establish special cities of asylum in the near future when cities shall be founded. This shows the ex-ante perspective of the nomads in the desert. There is no hint for an important modification of Deuteronomy by Josiah.

4. Evidence for the Origin of the Pentateuch in the Second Millennium

Let me come now to evidence for the origin of the Pentateuch in the second millennium.

4.1 Structure of Treaties

As Kitchen has pointed out, the structure of international treaties significantly changed through the second and first millennium. This offers the possibility to compare the structure of the treaties in the Pentateuch with the seven different structures of the different periods (from middle of the third millennium to the late first millennium).[12]

First of all, we have to take into consideration that we do not find the texts of the treaties themselves in the Pentateuch, but only texts containing *reports*[13] of the treaties with references to their content. Firstly, we have the report of the covenant at Sinai (Exod 20:1–25:9; 34:8–28; 35:1–19; Lev 11–15; 18–20; 24–27), secondly, we have the renewal of the covenant at Moab (Deut 1:1–32:47) and then the report of the covenant with Joshua (Josh 24,1–28). In spite of the fact that especially the report of the Sinai covenant is interrupted five times, we get an impression of the structure of the covenant itself by the report. This is important for the external comparison with other treaties of the different periods.

As Kitchen has shown by making use of colored chronograms, the covenants of the Pentateuch and Joshua have the structure being usual for period V (from about 1400 to 1200 BC). We know the usual structure for this period due to many examples especially of Hittite treaties.[14] The structure of treaties from other periods significantly differs from the treaties of the fifth period.

Of course, it is not impossible that the three reports of the biblical covenants were written later, but this is not probable at all and whoever wants to defend such a

---
12 Kitchen and Lawrence, *Treaty*, vol. II, 268.
13 Kitchen, *Reliability*, 370.
14 Kitchen, *Reliability*, 372.

hypothesis has to bring strong evidence for that, because he has to carry the burden of proof.

4.2 Content of Covenants: Subject Analogues

Kitchen presents further evidence for the origin of the law codes in the second millennium. If we compare the content of the report of the Sinai Covenant (Exod–Lev) and the Moab Covenant (Deut) with all temporarily available treaties of the second and first millennium, we see how deeply the Pentateuch is rooted in the second millennium. Kitchen made a table about the subject analogues and showed that for the Sinai Covenant there are 82 analogues from the second millennium and only 2 of the first, and for the Moab Covenant there are 43 analogues from the second millennium and only 5 from the first.[15] If we take this into account, there is not much reason to assume a groundbreaking edition of the covenant reports in the first millennium. Whoever wants to argue for an edition and modification in the first millennium has to explain why almost the whole content of the biblical covenants comes from the second millennium.

EXOD–LEV		DEUT	
3rd millennium	13	3rd millennium	5
Early 2nd millennium	33	Early 2nd millennium	18
Mid. 2nd millennium	16	Mid. 2nd millennium	7
Late 2nd millennium	20	Late 2nd millennium	13
1st millennium	2	1st millennium	5

As a legal historian, I would like to make some remarks on the *goring ox*. As Jackson[16] has shown, the rules for the goring ox in the Covenant Code are very subtle. He made a comparison with the rules for the goring ox in the CH and the CE and showed that we find in the Covenant Code all topics of the CH and/or of CE and also original rules.

---

15 Kitchen and Lawrence, *Treaty*, vol. III, 256.
16 Jackson, *Wisdom Laws*, 280ff. (especially 286).

Topic	CE	CH	Exod 21
Non-vicious ox kills "man"		250	v.28
Vicious ox kills "man"	54		v.29–30
Vicious ox kills son		251	v.31
Vicious ox kills slave	55	252	v.32
Non-vicious ox kills ox	53		v.35
Vicious ox kills ox			v.36

This is striking and we get the impression that the writer of the Covenant Code was very acquainted with the rules of CH and CE – maybe by direct knowledge, or maybe by exact knowledge of the Mesopotamian Common Law of the second millennium. Prof. Otto wrote a whole book about the relation of CE and the Covenant Code worth being carefully studied by legal historians.[17]

As the late legal historian Reuven Yaron mentioned the very close parallel between CE 53 and Exod 21:35 is really striking: the sharing of the avail and of the dead ox. We have to take into consideration that as far as we know the CE has not been transmitted for hundreds of years like the CH. Thus it is probable that there was a strong tradition of Near Eastern Common Law in the second millennium.

From the perspective of legal history, the following question comes up: Why do we find such incredibly detailed rules for the goring ox in the Covenant Code whereas other legal topics are not so important? Typically the legislator develops rules according to the social and economic needs. I have the impression that the rules for the goring ox were very important in the desert. After the settlement in Canaan these rules became less important when every peasant received his piece of ground where he could make firm fences avoiding accidents with goring oxen. But this was not possible as long as the Israelites were nomads and accidents with goring oxen were much more probable during that time.

5. Narratives in Genesis and the Old-Babylonian Law of the Second Millennium: The Suretyship of Juda

Since several Pentateuch researchers admit nowadays that the law codes of the Pentateuch, especially the Covenant Code, have very old roots going back to the second millennium, I want to draw your attention now to one legal issue in the narrative of

---

17 Otto, *Rechtsgeschichte*.

Genesis: the suretyship (sometimes guarantee, in German "Bürgschaft") of Judah in Gen 43:4–8 and 44:32–33.

Gen 43:3–8 reports that the sons of Jacob had to go to Egypt to buy cereals because of a famine. Josef forced them to bring Benjamin to Egypt who had stayed with his father Jacob in Canaan. Since Jacob did not agree with his youngest son Benjamin accompanying his brothers to Egypt, Judah gave his father Jacob a suretyship for him.

Gen 43:9

אָנֹכִי אֶעֶרְבֶנּוּ מִיָּדִי תְּבַקְשֶׁנּוּ אִם־לֹא הֲבִיאֹתִיו אֵלֶיךָ וְהִצַּגְתִּיו לְפָנֶיךָ וְחָטָאתִי לְךָ כָּל־הַיָּמִים:

I will be surety for him (אֶעֶרְבֶנּוּ); of my hand shalt thou require him (תְּבַקְשֶׁנּוּ); if I bring him not unto thee, and set him before thee, then let me bear the blame (חָטָאתִי) forever.

Later, Josef puts Benjamin under suspicion of theft and wants to take him as his slave. In this situation Judah offers himself to become Josef's slave instead of Benjamin by saying to Josef:

Gen 44:32–33

כִּי עַבְדְּךָ עָרַב אֶת־הַנַּעַר מֵעִם אָבִי לֵאמֹר אִם־לֹא אֲבִיאֶנּוּ אֵלֶיךָ וְחָטָאתִי לְאָבִי כָּל־הַיָּמִים:

וְעַתָּה יֵשֶׁב־נָא עַבְדְּךָ תַּחַת הַנַּעַר עֶבֶד לַאדֹנִי וְהַנַּעַר יַעַל עִם־אֶחָיו:

For thy servant became surety (עָרַב) for the lad unto my father, saying: If I bring him not unto thee, then shall I bear the blame to my father forever.

Now therefore, let thy servant, I pray thee, abide instead of the lad a bondman to my lord; and let the lad go up with his brethren.

According to Mark's commentary of suretyship in Biblical Law,[18] Juda stands surety for Benjamin in the relation to Josef. But this is not an adequate juridical interpretation. For the reconstruction of the suretyship we have to take the Old-Babylonian suretyship into consideration and this will show how closely the legal institute of suretyship in Genesis is linked with the Old-Babylonian Common Law.

Firstly, we have to read together verses 43:9 and 44:32 both containing עָרַב (to stand surety). The idea to interpret אֶעֶרְבֶנּוּ in verse 43:9 as a future suretyship of Judah for Benjamin in relation to Josef in case of Benjamin being captured is wrong. This becomes evident if we read 44:32, because according to this verse, Judah says

---

18 Mark, Bürgen/Bürgschaft, 4.1.1., with wrong reference to Ebach, *Genesis 37–50*, 321.

to Josef that he already stood surety for his brother Benjamin in relation to his father Jacob. Judah says explicitly: עָרַב אֶת־הַנַּעַר מֵעִם אָבִי

In Gen 44:33 Judah offers himself to become a slave instead of Benjamin, but in this verse עָרַב is not mentioned at all.

The problems of the exegesis arise, because the concept of suretyship in Genesis is completely different from suretyship in modern and Roman law. For modern and Roman suretyship, we need three independent persons, the creditor, the debtor and the surety. The suretyship secures a claim of the creditor against the debtor. The surety concludes a contract with the creditor to secure the claim of the creditor against the debtor.

Whereas in modern civil law and in Roman law a claim of a creditor against a debtor to be secured is necessary for suretyship, this is not true for the Old-Babylonian Law. According to Babylonian Law two uncommon constructions can be found:

First, Koschaker/Ungnad[19] and San Nicolò[20] have shown that Babylonian suretyship sometimes has the character of a guarantee. The guarantor promised a success whose occurrence lay beyond his own power. Koschaker showed that there were Old-Babylonian sureties without any separate claim to be secured. These were independent self-reliant guarantees.[21]

Second, there were self-suretyships strengthening an obligation of the surety. In the case of self-suretyship, the surety and the debtor were one and the same person. The reason for this double legal act seems to lie in the fact that according to Old Babylonian law, an obligation or debt (Schuld) was not as closely linked with liability (Haftung) as in classical Roman Law or today's law. Thus it was not in vain to strengthen the obligation by an additional self-suretyship of the debtor.[22]

The question whether the suretyship of Juda is an independent guarantee or a self-suretyship strengthening an obligation is not easy to answer. In Gen 43:9 there are two verbs: ערב and בקש. It is possible that both verbs simply stand for the same legal act: then the suretyship would have the character of an independent guarantee.

But we cannot exclude the second possibility, that בקש stands for an additional obligation of Juda to bring Benjamin back to his father. That בקש can have such a juridical meaning is supported by the talk between Jacob and Laban in Gen 31:39. In this context בקש means the damages Jacob had to pay for lost animals because of the herding contract he concluded with Laban.

Thus, I cannot present a clear answer concerning the dogmatic construction, but luckily this does not seem to be necessary. More important and illuminating is the comparison with the Old-Babylonian suretyship law. We know of Old-Babylonian

---

19 Koschaker and Ungnad, *Hammurabi's Gesetz*, 20.
20 San Nicolò, "Bürgschaft," 78–79.
21 Koschaker and Ungnad, *Hammurabi's Gesetz*, Nr. 1470ff and p.20; San Nicolò, "Bürgschaft," 79.
22 Koschaker, *Bürgschaftsrecht*, 109.

suretyship exclusively by deeds. Neither in CH nor in CE can we find rules for suretyship. This has a parallel in the Pentateuch: suretyship is not mentioned in the law codes of the Pentateuch but only in Genesis.

In Old-Babylonian deeds we find suretyship having the character of guarantees for a slave not being captured by the enemy. Let me present a deed that has been translated into German by Koschaker and Ungnad (EG 22):

> 1 gewisser Šamaš-rabi, Sklave des Balmu-namḫe, – bei Balmu-namḫe, seinem Eigentümer, haben sich der Schneider Ḫâsirum, der Schneider Gimil-Amurrim, Ḫunâbatum, dessen Ehefrau, und Ibḳu-Amurrim für ihn verbürgt. Sucht er den Palast, einen Mächtigen, das Frauenhaus auf, entkommt er, flieht er, nimmt ihn ein Feind (gefangen), tötet ihn ein Löwe, so werden der Schneider Ḫâsirum, der Schneider Gimil-Amurrim, Ḫunâbatum, dessen Ehefrau, und Ibḳu-Amurrim 1 Mine Silber darwägen.[23]

> For Šamaš-rabi slave of Balmu-namḫe, - in relation to Balmu-namḫe, his owner, the tailor Ḫâsirum, the tailor Gimil-Amurrim, Ḫunâbatum, his wife, and Ibḳu-Amurrim stood surety. If he goes to the palace of a mighty one, if he goes to the women's refuge, if he escapes, if he escapes, *if he is captured by an enemy*, if he is killed by a Lion, the tailor Ḫâsirum, the tailor Gimil-Amurrim, Ḫunâbatum, his wife, and Ibḳu-Amurrim will pay one Mine of Silver.[24]

The deed stems from the time of Rîm-Sin of Larsa (about 1822–1763 BC). According to Koschaker/Ungnad the context of this deed is the following:

Balmu-namḫe is the owner of a slave. Probably the slave owed Balmu-namḫe money, could not pay his debts and became his slave. The sureties are his relatives and tailors he is working for to earn some money.

The similarity between the deed's case and the suretyship in Genesis is striking. When Judah stood suretyship in relation to Jacob for Benjamin's return, the risk was that Benjamin would be captured in Egypt like Simeon. The situation is analogue in the deed:

The relation of the owner Balmu-namḫe to the slave in the deed and the relation of the father Jacob to his son Benjamin in Genesis are similar. In the deed the tailor takes the slave with him, in Genesis Juda takes Benjamin with him. In both cases the slave or Benjamin are in danger to be captured by an enemy. In both cases he who takes the slave or son with him stands surety for the return of the slave or son. Whether there is an additional obligation of the tailor towards the owner or of Juda towards Jacob remains an open question and seems to be unimportant for the validity of the suretyship. Thus, the suretyship can be a guarantee or a self-suretyship adding the liability to the obligation to return the slave or son.

---

23 Quoted from Koschaker and Ungnad, *Hammurabi's Gesetz*, 26.
24 Koschaker and Ungnad, *Hammurabi's Gesetz*, 26.

Therefore, the suretyship of Genesis perfectly suits to the suretyships of Old Babylonian law.

The later development of suretyship in Jewish law shows that there are important differences between the old suretyship law in Genesis and the later developments. If we compare the concept of surety in Genesis with that in Proverbs, we can see an important contrast.

If we read for example Proverbs 27:13, we see the typical three-persons-relationship of the modern suretyship:

Prov 27:13

קַח־בִּגְדוֹ כִּי־עָרַב זָר וּבְעַד נָכְרִיָּה חַבְלֵהוּ

Take his garment that is surety for a stranger; and hold him in pledge that is surety for a foreign woman.

The advice is given to the creditor. His debtor is a stranger or a foreign woman and the creditor shall go to the surety to get the money back he gave to the debtor as a credit. This is the typical three-person-relationship of Roman law and modern law. We find this concept of suretyship in Proverbs 6:1–5, too. The exegesis of these verses is more complex, but it is clear that we have a creditor, a debtor and a surety.

The Talmudic Law refers to this kind of suretyship, too. Already in the Mishnah and in the Tosefta we find the typical situation that a creditor gives a debtor a credit and the surety presents himself as a security for the credit being repaid.

Thus, in the biblical sources of the first millennium BC and in the Talmudic Law the concept of suretyship significantly differs from that in Genesis. This is strong evidence against the assumption that the narratives of Genesis could have been written in the first millennium. If this had been true, the concept of suretyship in Genesis would have been totally different and more like those we find in the Proverbs or Sirach.

Additionally, we have evidence from the development of suretyship within the Babylonian Law supporting our result. As already Koschaker has pointed out, the self-suretyship of the debtor himself, as we find it in the Old Babylonian Law came to an end very early in the Neo-Babylonian period.[25] His explanation for the disappearance of the self-suretyship of the debtor strengthening his own obligation is still very convincing. According to Koschaker, the distinction between debt/obligation (Schuld) and liability (Haftung) being characteristic for the Old-Babylonian Law[26] disappeared quite early in the Neo-Babylonian period. Full liability of the debtor became part of his obligation *ipso iure*. First, the self-suretyship disappeared when a "dare" was owed, because of the congruence of obligation and liability, later on it

---

25 Koschaker, *Bürgschaftsrecht*, 143–146 (especially 145); Petschow, "Bürgschaftsrecht," 243.
26 Koschaker, *Bürgschaftsrecht*, 108–109.

disappeared even in cases of incongruence when a "facere" was owed.[27] Thus, a strengthening of the obligation by a self-suretyship of the debtor himself became redundant.[28] In addition to that, the guarantee ("Erfüllungsübernahme") became an independent obligation and it was not called "suretyship" anymore.[29]

Thus, the suretyship in Genesis perfectly goes together with the Old-Babylonian-suretyship-deeds, whereas during the Neo-Babylonian period the Babylonian suretyship law significantly changed. There is no serious reason to assume that the Josef-narrative was not written in the early second millennium.

6. Conclusions

On the one hand, the tries to show a connection between Deuteronomy and the Vassal Treaties of Esarhaddon or the Law of Gortyn and the Roman twelve tables were not successful.

On the other hand, an analysis of the structure and the subjects of the treaties in Exod, Lev and Deut show a very strong affinity with the second millennium. Additionally, the suretyship of Juda in Genesis has very strong similarity to the Old-Babylonian suretyship deeds of the early second millennium.

Therefore, I think it is time to give up the models and prejudices of the 19th century and to start with a historical reconstruction of the Pentateuch within the framework of external evidence of the second millennium.

Of course, later redactions and changes are possible. But whoever wants to argue for that has to present very strong evidence because he has the burden of proof. Theories about what could have happened are not sufficient at all.

---

27 Koschaker, *Bürgschaftsrecht*, 145–146.
28 Koschaker, *Bürgschaftsrecht*, 144–145.
29 Koschaker, *Bürgschaftsrecht*, 106–107, concerning BV 74 (20th year of Darius).

Bibliography

Armgardt, Matthias. Review of *Die Tora – Studien zum Pentateuch. Gesammelte Aufsätze*, by Eckart Otto. *SZ Rom* 128 (2011): 497–499.
—. Review of *Gesetzgebung in antiken Gesellschaften*, by Leonhard Burckhardt, Klaus Seybold, and Jürgen von Ungern-Sternberg. *SZ Rom* 131 (2014): 429–433.
—. "Zur Entwicklung der Bürgschaft im Jüdischen Recht," in *Der Bürge einst und jetzt. Festschrift für Alfons Bürge*. Edited by Ulrike Babusiaux, Peter Nobel and Johannes Platschek. Zürich: Schulthess, 2017, 3–20.
Burckhardt, Leonhard, Klaus Seybold, and Jürgen von Ungern-Sternberg, eds. *Gesetzgebung in antiken Gesellschaften*. Beiträge zur Altertumskunde 247. Berlin: de Gruyter, 2007.
Ebach, Jürgen. *Genesis 37–50*. HThKAT. Freiburg i. Br.: Herder, 2007.
Frankena, Rintije. "The Vassal Treaties of Esarhaddon and the Dating of Deuteronomy." *OTS* 14 (1965): 122–154.
Jackson, Bernard S., *Wisdom Laws – A Study of the Mishpatim of Exodus 21:1–22:16*. New York: Oxford University Press, 2006.
Kitchen, Kenneth A. *On the Reliability of the Old Testament*. Grand Rapids MI: Eerdmans, 2003.
Kitchen, Kenneth A. and Paul Lawrence. *Treaty, Law and Covenant in the Ancient Near East*. 3 vols. Wiesbaden: Harrassowitz, 2012.
Koschaker, Paul. *Babylonisch-assyrisches Bürgschaftsrecht. Ein Beitrag zur Lehre von Schuld und Haftung*. Leibzig: B.G. Teubner, 1911. Repr. Aalen: Scientia, 1966.
Koschaker, Paul and Arthur Ungnad. *Hammurabi's Gesetz. Bd. VI: Übersetzte Urkunden mit Rechtserläuterungen*. Leipzig: E. Pfeiffer, 1923.
Mark, Martin. Art. Bürgen/Bürgschaft. In: *Das Wissenschaftliche Bibellexikon im Internet* (www.wibilex.de), 2014.
Otto, Eckart. *Rechtsgeschichte der Redaktionen im Kodex Ešnunna und im "Bundesbuch". Eine redaktionsgeschichtliche und rechtsvergleichende Studie zu altbabylonischen und altisraelitischen Rechtsüberlieferungen*, Fribourg: Universitätsverlag, 1989.
—. *Die Tora – Studien zum Pentateuch. Gesammelte Aufsätze*. BZAR 9. Wiesbaden: Harrassowitz, 2009.
Petschow, Herbert. "Zum neubabylonischen Bürgschaftsrecht." *ZA* 53 (1959): 241–247.
San Nicolò, Marian. "Bürgschaft," *RLA* (1938): 77–80.

The Pentateuch Paradigm and Ancient Near Eastern Legal History

A Look Back from the Environment

Guido Pfeifer (Goethe University of Frankfurt)

1. Introduction

A contribution to this volume on Paradigm Change in Pentateuchal Research from the viewpoint of Ancient Near Eastern legal history offers an interdisciplinary perspective from a shorter or longer distance or – alluding to a well-known text edition series – a look back from the environment of the Old Testament. The possible benefit of this perspective seems to be obvious regarding the many impressive examples of comparative studies as well on legal institutions as on the tradition of the textual material as such.[1]

But since the declared aim of the conference is "to explore whether a fundamental paradigm change can overcome the current impasse of old models and open new approaches" this paper will not focus on a comparison of another detail. It rather reports from the experience with paradigms, impasses and "new" approaches in an adjacent field of research which might offer a reference or a counterpoint to the discussion on the Pentateuch. Both, legal history in general and Ancient Near Eastern legal history in peculiar were and are determined by various paradigms, sometimes to the better, sometimes to the worse of cognitive progress. The probably most prominent example can be seen in the discussion of the character of the so-called law collections[2] which will *not* be in the center of the following reflections, although it seems impossible not to touch on it at least. Instead, the paradigms dealt with in the following refer to an even more general framework of the question if there was any legal thinking in the Ancient Near East.[3] To some extent, this might even show up as "paradigmatic" for the complex relation between cognitive interests, hermeneutic concepts and the potential of the source material which constitutes the actual problem of our research.

---

1 See e.g. Otto, *Rechtsgeschichte*.
2 For an overview over the discussion of the Laws of Hammurabi see Charpin, *Writing*, 71–82.
3 Pfeifer, "Wissen," 263–266.

Not little of Mesopotamia's fascination is derived from its primaries or "firsts" – the first cities, the first schools, the first weekend, the first beer and, as some might say, the first legal order.[4] The underlying tone of this perspective reveals a clear teleological comprehension of history with a vanishing point in the modern world. It's "only" the departure to a better end that we all live in. In one of his last papers, published in 2010, the late Raymond Westbrook challenged this meant to be overcome evolutionistic approach towards cultural and legal history and asked for a new paradigm instead; a paradigm even more oriented on the sources and with turning points on our minds that took place before the invention of writing, such as agriculture and urbanization.[5]

But Westbrook's caveat may not only inspire us to change certain directions of thought, but also to challenge common narratives, among them the one about the origins of science. Here, Mesopotamia is believed not to have been the first, but the communis opinio ascribes the invention of science to the Greek – and the invention of the legal profession to the Romans.[6] What is left for Mesopotamia is method and practice, the solution of technical and practical problems.[7] However, if we allow ourselves to ask the question if there was any legal thinking in the Ancient Near East we must look for hidden traces. Even though many of the following aspects may seem to be manifest, we take a closer look at the functions of Ancient Near Eastern law, at its pre-conditions and at its role within the texture of the scientific culture of Mesopotamia. By doing so, even more, older and more recent scientific approaches to the intellectual world of the Ancient Near East – or paradigms – will appear on the scene.

2. Functions of Ancient Near Eastern law

The functions of Ancient Near Eastern law concern the framing effect of the legal order in general, the phenomenological manifestations of the legal order and the effect of law as a discipline. According to Max Weber the ideal legal order provides foreseeable rules and their enforcement in an authoritative way; for him this matter of fact makes the legal order the decisive factor of the economic system.[8] This holds true, if we look at the earliest sales contracts from the middle of the 3rd millennium.[9] The documentation of a transaction facilitates the proof of its validity in case of a

---

4 Cf. DER SPIEGEL Geschichte, Edition 2/2016, "Mesopotamien. Aufbruch in die Zivilisation".
5 Westbrook, "Early History," 1–13.
6 Pfeifer, "Wissen," 263–266.
7 Cancik-Kirschbaum, "Gegenstand und Methode," 13–21.
8 Weber, *Wirtschaft und Gesellschaft*, 11–17; see also Pfeifer, "Character," 261.
9 Wilcke, *Early Ancient Near Eastern Law*, 76–109

conflict and thus the resolution of the conflict by legal means. But the allocative function of law can be generalized: More recent sociological approaches stress the reduction of complexity by the legal order, even though it may produce a complexity of its own.[10] However, we should know these ex ante considerations may enrich our linguistic tool box, but they should not lead to pre-assumptions, when we look at the sources. What do we find there?

Apart from private and official letters we find lexical lists, contracts and litigation documents and the so-called law collections.[11] Legal lexical lists as lexical lists in general gathered technical terms and entire text modules in Sumerian and Akkadian language. They counted as parts of the education in the scribal schools and demarked the basis of other literary genres. A prominent example is the series *ana ittišu*, an Old Babylonian text from the city of Nippur, delivered as a copy in the famous library of the Assyrian king Assurbanipal.[12] The technical terms and text modules return in texts from the legal practice, as they are often referred to, namely contracts and litigation documents, products of trained scribes based on lexical lists. There we can identify e.g. the standard interest rates for barley and silver as also shown in the series *ana ittišu*.[13] As mentioned before, the main purpose of these texts is the documentation of transactions which could be used as piece of evidence in case of litigation. As such, they could also be regarded as records of individual legal relationships and show "normal" cases. In contrast to that, problematic cases were object of litigation procedures which were also documented, but without any legal reasoning. Again, their main purpose lies in the documentation of the results of such procedures providing evidence for further conflicts. The most prominent records of Ancient Near Eastern Legal History are of course the so-called law collections. They share the background of scribal schools and seem to reflect legal practice (i.e. cases) as well as legal custom on a more abstract level. Again, several sections e.g. of the Laws of Eshnunna and the Laws of Hammurabi concern general tariffs and interest rates, but also problematic cases and modifications of general rules.[14] The normative character of the law collections is still discussed.[15] The context of the scribal schools might even indicate the character of compendia,[16] on which judges could have been trained, but regarding the official character and the way at least the Laws of Hammurabi were also presented as inscriptions it becomes quite clear that this could be just one in a bundle of aspects. Returning to the functions of law it seems obvious that a main factor is the liability of legal relationships which were

---

10 Luhmann, "Komplexität," 3–35.
11 For the following see Pfeifer (2018) 6–12.
12 Edition and translation by Landsberger (1937).
13 Pfeifer, "Recht," 8.
14 Pfeifer, "Recht," 9–11.
15 See above fn. 2.
16 Johnson, *Compendia*, 289–315.

documented and could be used as evidence and thus made the basis of economic activities.[17]

3. Pre-conditions of Ancient Near Eastern law

As the functions of Ancient Near Eastern law reveal little to nothing of legal thinking we should consider its pre-conditions in our research for hidden traces. The delivered texts show as such a broad spectrum of institutions and protagonists, e.g. various councils of judges or the existence of scribal schools,[18] but they give us only the results, not the details of the making. Therefore, we must face the lack of background information about the origin and functioning of the texts. This becomes obvious, when we return to the genres for a second time.

The technical coherence of the texts is manifest in the use of technical terms and text modules as we have already seen. But if we ask for their inner cohesion we may hardly get an answer. The arrangement of the lexical lists is only partly, but not completely reproducible for us: Sometimes we seem to recognize principles, such as a series of acronyms, but there is no compulsory consequence to that. Contracts show normal cases and litigation documents the results of procedures, as mentioned above, but no legal reasoning. Also within the legal rules of the law collections there is no reasoning to be found, but mere causality in the form of protasis and apodosis or matters of facts and legal consequences – a structure we also know from future-telling omina and medical texts.[19] An identification of further systematical structures that goes beyond the work of Herbert Petschow[20] is still a desideratum as Eckart Otto has shown,[21] even though we can assume a certain extent of a legal-theoretical reflection and a legal-dogmatic direction of thought as a background of the law collections. Nevertheless, we are confronted with a certain theoretical deficiency of Ancient Near Eastern law. There are a very small number of school texts which could be defined as "problem literature" with some reasoning in them, as Hans Neumann has shown.[22] Dominique Charpin examined recently a letter from the official correspondence of Samsuiluna, the son of Hammurabi, which shows the deduction of an abstract rule from a concrete case.[23] But after all, we get the impression that the common narrative must be confirmed: Theory belongs to Greece, Mesopotamia gets away with method.

---

17 Pfeifer, "Recht," 11.
18 Pfeifer, "Judicial Authority".
19 Pfeifer, "Recht," 12.17.
20 E.g. Petschow, "Systematik," 146–172.
21 Otto, "Rechtssätze," 63–77.
22 Neumann, "Bemerkungen," 159–170.
23 Charpin, *Writing*, 73.

4. Law in the texture of Ancient Near Eastern scientific culture

Maybe the contextualization of law with other genres of written knowledge could provide further insights. But these are as such not less influenced by specific scientific approaches towards the Ancient Near Eastern intellectual world.

Benno Landsberger evolved in a paper published in 1926 and often referred to, the problem of the conceivability of Sumerian and Babylonian thinking and shaped the term "Eigenbegrifflichkeit" of the Babylonian world for this phenomenon.[24] He aimed for nothing less than to make the semantics of the – obviously specialized – Sumerian and Babylonian terminology accessible; a task we are still working on. Wolfram von Soden developed from that basis the idea of the Sumerian "Listenwissenschaft" which he explained with the Sumerian will to order, whereas according to him the (Semitic) Babylonian people imitated this pattern only insufficiently.[25] Von Sodens approach from 1936 is, due to its obvious racist impact, not very common today.

More recent approaches that deal with epistemic structures are characterized by a strong emancipatory tendency to liberate the history of science from the "Classical" (i.e. Greek-Roman) paradigm. But the proposed models show a very disparate range: Dietz Otto Edzard tried to explain the lexical lists as works of art.[26] Jim Ritter offers a model of rational practice, in which textual procedures, as well in mathematical problem texts as in the law collections, come close to algorithms used in modern computer programming.[27] Markus Hilgert adopted the post-structuralist pattern of a rhizome for the lexical lists.[28] But all of these models seem either anachronistic and/or rather limited in their explanatory effect. Most appealing seems a concept which Claus Wilcke offered with "Das geistige Erfassen der Welt", in which e.g. lexical lists mark the attempt to inventory the world and make it manageable.[29] Law and the legal order would fit well to such an intellectual infrastructure of the Mesopotamian world.

But the benefit of law may be as well independent of its ranking as a scientific discipline.[30] There is no doubt that Ancient Near Eastern law is characterized by interdependencies with other intellectual infrastructures, such as divination or medicine. The linguistic structure of the omina is identical with the one of legal rules in

---

24 Landsberger, "Eigenbegrifflichkeit," 355–372.
25 Von Soden, "Leistung," 411–464.509–557.
26 Edzard, "Listen," 17–26.
27 Ritter, "Reading Strasbourg," 177–200.
28 Hilgert, "Listenwissenschaft," 277–309.
29 Wilcke, "Recht," 209–244.
30 Even though it must be admitted that it would be very nice to verify a legal science "avant la lettre".

the law collections: The If-Then-construction reveals a consequent casuistic view of the world which allows no contingency. If we consider the fact that legal terminology is also used in rituals dealing with unfavorable auguries we could however come close to the idea that Ancient Near Eastern law provided a normative order (in an untechnical sense) of some referential character for other disciplines.[31] But the idea that law is a normative order among others is nothing more than a notional concept and throws us back to the beginning.

5. Conclusion

The topic of these reflections may seem quite distant from the actual discussion of the understanding of the Pentateuch. However, what we have in common is the ambition to understand the delivered text material in a better way. According to that, there seems to be no alternative to developing questions of research from the source material itself and make the hermeneutic concepts used to find answers to these questions as transparent as possible.[32] For, if the questions are generated with disregard of the sources the risk of anachronistic pre-assumptions is apparent as already mentioned. But also, the examination of texts as such without any idea of the cognitive interests is likely to fail, because sources do not tend to be self-explanatory, even more so if they are regarded isolated from each other. Finally, transparency of methods and concepts make a scientific discourse possible at all, especially beyond the borders of our disciplines. And yet, to borrow an insight from Joshua Berman: Yes, there might be a history that remains beyond our reach.[33] If, after all and against this background, there is a need or even room for paradigms should be doubted seriously. The actual challenge might be recognized in the refinement of questions and methods that make paradigms obsolete rather than a paradigm change.

Raymond Westbrook stressed the dependency of legal historical research from the choice of the point of view, claiming that depending on whether we tend more to philosophy or to history we will be allowed or forced to speculate.[34] Maybe, an alternative perspective is that towards gravitational waves: We have good reasons to assume that also in the ancient Near East there has been some sort of legal thinking to make the legal order work, but our instruments of comprehension are still too inefficient to take notice clearly.

---

31 Pfeifer, "Recht," 12–14.
32 Cf. Also Ernst, "Epistemologie," 256–259.
33 Berman, "Flood Narrative," 56.
34 Westbrook, "Early History," 13.

Bibliography

Berman, Joshua. "The Limits of Source Criticism. The Flood Narrative in Genesis 6–9," in *Paradigm Change in Pentateuchal Research*. Edited by Matthias Armgardt, Benjamin Kilchör and Markus Zehnder. BZAR 22. Wiesbaden: Harrassowitz, 2019, 45–57.

Cancik-Kirschbaum, Eva. "Gegenstand und Methode: Sprachliche Erkenntnistechniken in der keilschriftlichen Überlieferung Mesopotamiens," in *Writings of Early Scholars in the Ancient Near East, Egypt Rome and Greece*. Edited by A. Imhausen and T. Pommerening. Berlin/New York: De Gruyter 2010, 13–45.

Charpin, Dominique. *Writing, Law and Kingship in Old Babylonian Mesopotamia*. Chicago: Univ. of Chicago Press 2010.

Edzard, Dietz Otto. "Die altmesopotamischen lexikalischen Listen – verkannte Kunstwerke?" in *Das geistige Erfassen der Welt im alten Orient. Sprache, Religion, Kultur und Gesellschaft*. Edited by C. Wilcke. Wiesbaden: Harrassowitz 2007, 17–26.

Ernst, Wolfgang. "Zur Epistemologie rechtsgeschichtlicher Forschung," *Rechtsgeschichte* 23 (2015): 256–259.

Hilgert, Markus. "Von ,Listenwissenschaft' und ,epistemischen Dingen'. Konzeptuelle Annäherungen an altorientalische Wissenspraktiken." *Zeitschrift für allgemeine Wissenschaftstheorie* 40 (2009): 277–309.

Johnson, J. Cale, ed., *In the Wake of the Compendia. Infrastrucural Contexts and the Licensing of Empiricism in Ancient and Medieval Mesopotamia (= Science, Technology and Medicine in Ancient Cultures Vol. 3)*. Boston/Berlin: de Gruyter, 2015.

Landsberger, Benno. "Die Eigenbegrifflichkeit der babylonischen Welt." *Islamica* 2 (1926): 355–372 (Repr. Darmstadt 1965).

—. *Die Serie ana ittišu (MSL 1)*, Roma: Pontificum Inst. Biblicum 1937.

Luhmann, Niklas. „Zur Komplexität von Entscheidungssituationen." *Soziale Systeme* 15 (2009): 3–35.

Neumann, Hans. "Bemerkungen zu einigen Aspekten babylonischen Rechtsdenkens im Spannungsfeld von Theorie und Praxis," in *Babylon. Wissenskultur in Orient und Okzident*. Edited by E. Cancik-Kirschbaum, M.van Ess and J. Marzahn. Berlin/Boston: De Gruyter 2011, 159–170.

Otto, Eckart. *Altorientalische und biblische Rechtsgeschichte. Gesammelte Studien*. Wiesbaden: Harrassowitz 2008.

—. "Nach welchen Gesichtspunkten wurden Rechtssätze in keilschriftlichen und biblischen Rechtssammlungen zusammengestellt? Zur Redaktionsgeschichte keilschriftlicher und biblischer Rechtssatzsammlungen." *ZAR* 18 (2012): 63–77.

Petschow, Herbert. "Zur Systematik und Gesetzestechnik im Codex Hammurabi," *Zeitschrift für Assyriologie und vorderasiatische Archäologie* 57 (NF 23, 1965): 146–172.

Pfeifer, Guido. "Judicial Authority in backlit Perspective: Judges in the Old Babylonian Period." *forum historiae iuris* 2010. No pages. Cited 25 May 2018. Online: https://forhistiur.de/2010-08-pfeifer/?l=en.

—. "Vom Wissen und Schaffen des Rechts im Alten Orient." *Rechtsgeschichte* 19 (2011): 263–266.

—. "The Character of Ancient Near Eastern Economy: Response to Christophe Pébarthe," in *Symposion 2011. Akten der Gesellschaft für Griechische und Hellenistische Rechtsge-

schichte. Edited by G. Thür et al. Wien: Verlag der Österreichischen Akademie der Wissenschaften 2012, 261–266.

—. "Neues aus der Alten Welt (IV). Wirtschaft, Recht und Gerechtigkeit im alten Mesopotamien." *Merkur* 68, no. 7 (July 2014): 631–637.

—. "Das Recht im Kontext normativer Ordnungen der Welt des Alten Orients." *Zeitschrift der Savigny-Stiftung für Rechtsgeschichte, Romanistische Abteilung* 135 (2018): 1–20.

Ritter, Jim. "Reading Strasbourg 368: A Thrice-Told Tale," in *History of Science, History of Text (Boston Studies in the Philosophy of Science 238)*. Edited by K. Chemla. Heidelberg: Springer 2005, 177–200.

Von Soden, Wolfram. "Leistung und Grenze sumerischer und babylonischer Wissenschaft." *Die Welt als Geschichte* 2 (1936): 411–464; 509–557 (Repr. Darmstadt 1965).

Weber, Max. *Wirtschaft und Gesellschaft. Grundriss der verstehenden Soziologie*. 5th ed. Tübingen: Mohr Siebeck, 1980.

Westbrook, Raymond. "The Early History of Law: A Theoretical Essay." *Zeitschrift der Savigny-Stiftung für Rechtsgeschichte, Romanistische Abteilung* 127 (2010): 1–13.

Wilcke, Claus. *Early Ancient Near Eastern Law. A History of its Beginnings. The Early Dynastic and Sargonic Periods*. München: Verlag der Bayerischen Akademie der Wissenschaften, 2003.

—. „Das Recht: Grundlage des sozialen und politischen Diskurses im alten Orient," in *Das geistige Erfassen der Welt im alten Orient. Sprache, Religion, Kultur und Gesellschaft*. Edited by C. Wilcke, Wiesbaden: Harrassowitz 2007, 209–244.

Wellhausen's Five Pillars for the Priority of D over P/H: Can They Still Be Maintained?

Benjamin Kilchör

(Staatsunabhängige Theologische Hochschule Basel)

> Finally, it must also be said that the common dating of the 'priestly' sections, be they narrative or legal, to the exilic or post-exilic period, likewise rests on conjecture and the consensus of scholars, but not on unambiguous criteria.[1]

At first glance it might seem a bit awkward that I am critiquing a book that is almost 150 years old: The *Prolegomena zur Geschichte Israels* of Julius Wellhausen, first published in 1878. Over the past one hundred and fifty years of Pentateuchal research, the state of the question has changed significantly. While it is true that some Neo-Documentarians in the United States come quite close to the Documentary Hypothesis as represented by Wellhausen;[2] nonetheless, in continental Europe, Rolf Rendtorff's book *Das überlieferungsgeschichtliche Problem des Pentateuch* (1976) initiated the demise of the dominance of Wellhausen's Documentary hypothesis. The Elohist died quickly and easily, and although some scholars still defend the Jahwist,[3] they do so in a completely different setting than that suggested by Wellhausen.

Nonetheless, the reason why I still would argue that the current paradigm in Pentateuchal research is rooted in Wellhausen's *Prolegomena* is because the distinctive element in Wellhausen's concept is the relationship between D and P, in which the origins of D are dated to the 7th century BC, while the origins of P are dated to the exilic or post-exilic period (6th/5th century BC). Of course, Wellhausen was not the first who postdated P with regard to D; scholars like George, Graf, and Kuenen had already done so.[4] However, Wellhausen presented such a convincing overall picture that P—until then regarded by most scholars as the oldest source within the Pentateuch—has ever since been regarded as the product of an exilic or post-exilic school with later additions and redactions.

---

1 Rendtorff, *Problem*, 203.
2 E.g. Baden, *Redaction*; idem., *Composition*; Stackert, *Prophet*.
3 E.g. Levin, *Jahwist*; Van Seters, *Prologue*; idem., *Life of Moses*; for the discussion see also Gertz / Schmid, *Abschied*.
4 See Houtman, *Pentateuch*, 98–114.

As persuasive as Wellhausen's overall picture is, we must acknowledge two weaknesses: first, that Wellhausen hardly looked at the textual evidence in detail; and, second, that the attractiveness of his overall picture was so great that scholars afterwards tended just to work within in this paradigm without critically questioning some of its basic assumptions.

Wellhausen's reconstruction of the dating of the Pentateuchal sources and of Israel's religious history is erected on five pillars:[5] 1. The Place of Worship; 2. Sacrifice; 3. The Sacred Feasts; 4. The Priests and the Levites; 5. The Endowment of the Clergy. Although I think that none of these pillars confirms the post-dating of P with regard to D, here I can only focus on two pillars due to limited space. The two I have chosen to address have been the most influential in convincing scholars of the posteriority of P: The Place of Worship and the Priests and the Levites.

Before I delve into the texts, let me briefly explain why this issue is important also from a theological point of view: The Pentateuch explicitly distinguishes between the Torah given by YHWH in Exodus, Leviticus and Numbers, and the exposition of this Torah by Moses in Deuteronomy (cf. Deut 1:5).[6] As I showed in my dissertation, both P and non-P legislative material is closely interwoven in Deuteronomy's exposition. In the legal hermeneutics of a synchronic reading of the Torah, therefore, not only the Covenant Code but also the P/H texts constitute the background of the Deuteronomic Law. On the other hand, the result of Wellhausen's postdating of P is a legislative chaos in the diachronic study of the Pentateuch, whereby the "priestly" parts (including H) of the Torah given by YHWH are not only regarded as written in response to the Mosaic exposition in Deuteronomy, but they are also placed in front of Deuteronomy in literary sequence. Therefore, the 'naïve' reader reads Deuteronomy as the Mosaic exposition of the P/H legislation, which is precisely contrary to the intention of both legal corpora.[7] My contention, however, is that Wellhausen's postdating in incorrect, and we can only recover a reasonable theology of the Mosaic exposition of YHWH's Torah that distinguishes between the words of YHWH and their exposition by Moses if the texts are interpreted in their right order also in diachronic terms. The same is true, as I will briefly

---

5   Wellhausen, *Prolegomena*, 1–162.
6   Cf. Kilchör, *Mosetora*, 1–30.
7   Nihan, *Priestly Torah*, 554 (n.614) gets to the point when he argues that in the work of Eckart Otto there is a contradiction between his synchronic reading of the Pentateuch (to which I agree in large parts) and his diachronic analysis: "When Otto states, e.g. that ‚alles kommt in der Fabel des Pentateuch darauf an, dass die von Mose gegebene Toraauslegung (Dtn 1,5) identisch ist mit der von Gott gegebenen Tora' […], how should this be concretely understood when contradictory laws in H and D are compared? The idea that Deut 12 could be read, for example, as a commentary on Lev 17 […] seems hard to believe. To be sure, this interpretation is historically correct in the case of the relationship of D to the CC. *But this is not the case with H* since, as argued here (and already by Otto himself!) the relationship goes in the opposite direction, with H representing the exegesis of D." In other words: the synchronic analysis of Otto would be fine if, for example, Deut 12 could be read as a commentary on Lev 17. While Nihan rejects this possibility, this is exactly what I try to do.

show below, with regard to Prophets like Jeremiah and Ezekiel, who are clearly influenced by "priestly" material of the Pentateuch: to uphold Wellhausen's paradigm, the priestly influences must be regarded as later redactions. Therefore, the late dating of P not only affects an integrated reading of Deuteronomy but also of other texts within the Old Testament. Of course, I cannot simply claim that priestly texts should be regarded as older because this would be convenient for a synchronic reading of Biblical texts. Therefore, I want to demonstrate my claim by close exegetical analysis of the respective texts.

1. The Place of Worship[8]

It is well known that already for de Wette, the law regarding the centralization of the place of worship in Deut 12 played an important role for the Josianic dating of Deuteronomy.[9] There has been much discussion of the relationship between the centralization law in Deut 12 and the altar law of Exod 20:24–26, which was interpreted by de Wette and Wellhausen as permitting multiple sanctuaries.[10] However, for the question of the relationship between D and P/H, Lev 17 is much more important than Exod 20:24–26.

According to Wellhausen, the main difference between D and P with regard to the place of worship is that D requires the centralization of worship in a single sanctuary, while P presupposes the actual centralization and projects it back to the Mosaic time by the fiction of the tabernacle, which never existed in fact. Wellhausen rejected Dillmann's objection that Lev 17 still regards every slaughter in terms of sacrifice, while Deut 12 develops the concept of centralization one step further by rendering profane any slaughter outside the central sanctuary.[11] According to Wellhausen, the intention of Lev 17 is "simply and solely to secure the exclusive legitimation of the one lawful place of sacrifice."[12] He imagines that Deuteronomy's profanation of local slaughtering failed: slaughtering and sacrifice were so strongly connected to each other that the common man did not understand this previously unknown distinction between profane and sacred act. Therefore, when he slaugh-

---

[8] Cf. Wellhausen, *Prolegomena*, 1–52.
[9] See the introduction, edition, and translation by Mathys, *de Wettes Dissertatio*, 170–211 (esp. the footnote on pp. 201–202).
[10] See e.g. Joosten, "Syntax"; Kilchör, "בכל המקום"; idem. *Mosetora*, 72–95; idem. "An jedem Ort"; Levinson, *Deuteronomy*, 23–52; Paul, *Het Archimedisch Punt*; Pitkänen, *Central Sanctuary*, 25–110; Reuter, *Kultzentralisation*, 121–156; Schaper, "Schriftauslegung", 111–132.
[11] Wellhausen, *Prolegomena*, 51–52.
[12] Ibid. 51.

tered at home, he still observed, half-consciously perhaps, the old sacred sacrificial ritual.[13]

If we just look to the overall concepts of Lev 17 and Deut 12, as Wellhausen does, it is possible to explain the legal development in either direction: Lev 17 might be the attempt to adjust some problems that arose from the profane slaughtering in Deut 12; or Deut 12 can be read as the attempt to solve the problem of the long distance to the sanctuary if slaughtering is carried out as Lev 17 commands. However, if we look more closely at the texts, I do not think that both directions are equally viable.

First, it is just not true that it is the sole or even the main intention of Lev 17 to secure the exclusive legitimation of the central sanctuary. I do not think that centralization is even an issue in Lev 17 at all. Rather, the focus of the whole chapter is laid on dealing with blood:[14]

> Lev 17:3–4   If anyone of the house of Israel kills an ox or a lamb or a goat in the camp, or kills it outside the camp, and does not bring it to the entrance of the tent of meeting to offer it as a gift to the Lord in front of the tabernacle of the Lord, bloodguilt shall be imputed to that man. He has shed blood, and that man shall be cut off from among his people.

The core of the law therefore deals with blood and bloodguilt. Verses 10–12 explicate that the main issue is the consumption of blood – the concept of centralization plays no role at all. According to vv. 10–12, consumption of blood is forbidden because "the life of the flesh is in the blood." This leads to vv. 13–14, where the question arises, what does one do with blood of wild animals, which are permitted for human consumption but are not sacrificial animals? The answer is that their blood should be poured out and covered with earth. In short, the main focus of Lev 17 is not on the exclusive legitimation of the central sanctuary but rather on the prohibition of the consumption of blood. While the blood and the fat of sacrificial animals belong to the altar (17:6; cf. Lev 3:17), the blood of wild animals should be poured out and covered with earth (17:13). If Lev 17 had been written to adjust the failed distinction of profane and sacral slaughtering as formulated in Deut 12 with the goal to defend the exclusive legitimation of the central sanctuary, we would expect a much more explicit reference to centralization.[15] Furthermore, the rules regarding profane slaughtering of wild animals, where the blood is poured out and covered with earth, show that Wellhausen is wrong to suggest that Lev 17 was writ-

---

13 Cf. Otto, *Deuteronomium 12,1–23,15*, 1162: "Diese Forschungsposition hat sich bis heute durchgesetzt und wird zuletzt von A. Cholewiński (*Heiligkeitsgesetz*, 1976, 149–178) und C. Nihan (*Tora*, 2007, 402–430) vertreten."
14 Cf. Pitkänen, *Central Sanctuary*, 80–81; Schwartz, "Prohibitions", 37–42; idem., "'Profane' Slaughter", 16.
15 Cf. Schwartz, "'Profane' Slaughter", 23: "The law does not *prohibit* profane slaughter, because in the priestly view *there is no such thing as profane slaughter.*"

ten because the common man was not able to distinguish between a religious and a profane act. In the case of profane slaughtering, one could just point the common man to the rules as they are given with respect to wild animals in Lev 17:13–14. If the common man can understand how to slaughter wild animals, he could just apply the slaughtering of wild animals to the slaughtering of ox, lamb, and goat.

This is indeed what we find in Deut 12, and this leads me to the second point. Deut 12 presupposes the distinction of the sacral slaughtering of sacrificial animals and the profane slaughtering of wild animals, just as we find it in Lev 17. While the handling of blood is the main distinction according to Lev 17 (the blood of sacrificial animals belongs to the altar, the blood of wild animals belongs to the earth; in both cases it must not be eaten), there is a second, more implicit distinction: With regard to sacrificial animals, not only the blood but also the fat must not be eaten and belongs to the altar (17:6), as is stated in Lev 3:1–17. With regard to wild animals, the prohibition of consumption of blood is repeated (17:13–14), yet without a prohibition of the consumption of fat. In other words, while the consumption of blood is forbidden in general on the basis that the life of every creature is in its blood, the consumption of fat is not forbidden *per se*. The fat should be burned on the altar as a pleasing aroma for the Lord only in case of sacrificial slaughtering (Lev 3:16; 17:6).

The distinction between sacrificial and profane slaughtering of sacrificial animals is introduced for the first time in Deut 12:13–19. Most scholars regard these verses as the oldest core of Deut 12, dating to the seventh century and belonging to Josiah's reform. The law is "mainly concerned with the practical consequences of the centralization law ('profane' slaughtering)."[16] After the centralization law (Deut 12:13–14), the profane slaughtering of sacrificial animals is permitted by the following words:

> Deut 12:15a   However, you may slaughter and eat meat within any of your towns, as much as you desire, according to the blessing of the Lord your God that he has given you.

Of course, if such an innovation is introduced, certain questions arise: If previously the blood and fat of sacrificial animals have always been brought to the altar, what shall we do with them both from now on? Deuteronomy 12:15b answers this question generally:

> Deut 12:15b   The clean and the unclean may eat of it, as of the gazelle and as of the deer.

---

16 Römer, *Deuteronomistic History*, 60. Cf. Otto, *Deuteronomium 12,1–23,15,* 1150: "Es kristallisiert sich als Konsens auch in der neueren Forschung heraus, dass Dtn 12,13–(18).19 literaturhistorischer Kern des Kapitels aus spätvorexilischer Zeit ist, wie es schon die ältere Forschung vertrat."

This brief note presupposes the knowledge of a "profane" slaughtering of wild animals like gazelle and deer as we find it in Lev 17:13–14. Moreover, the explicit mention that both the clean and the unclean may eat of it not only resembles the priestly concept of clean and unclean in general, but also the explicit mention in Lev 17:13 that "anyone of the house of Israel, or of the strangers who sojourn among them," who slaughters a wild animal is forbidden to eat its blood. Deut 12:16 gives a short explanation of what it means to eat of sacrificial animals as of the gazelle and as of the deer:

> Deut 12:16   Only the blood you must not eat; you shall pour it out on the earth like water.

Deuteronomy here refers precisely to the distinction between the slaughtering of sacrificial animals and wild animals as we find it in Lev 17. First, the word רק ("only") signals a limitation of the prohibition, which should most likely be interpreted in terms of a permission to eat the fat, as a comparison with Lev 3:17b (cf. Lev 17:14) shows:[17]

> Deut 12:16a   רק הדם לא תאכלו
>
> Lev 3:17b   כל חלב וכל דם לא תאכלו

Lev 3:17b specifies that in case of sacrificial slaughtering of cattle, sheep, and goats, both the fat and the blood must not be eaten; whereas Deut 12:15–16 introduces a profane slaughtering whereby the fat is allowed for consumption as in the case of the slaughtering of wild animals. This answers the question with regard to the fat. But what about the blood? This question is answered in Deut 12:16b again with reference to Lev 17:13–14: "You shall pour it out (שפך) on the earth (ארץ) like water." This corresponds to what Lev 17:13 states regarding the blood of wild animals: "You shall poor it out (שפך) and cover it with dust (עפר)."

In sum, postdating P/H over against D with regard to centralization of worship only makes sense in the "big-picture-view" as we find it presented in Wellhausen's model. When the key texts (Lev 17 and Deut 12) are examined more closely, however, we do not find any hint that Lev 17 was written to reverse and prohibit the profane slaughtering of Deut 12 because the common man was not able to understand the distinction between the religious and the profane act, as Wellhausen claimed. On the other hand, the innovation of profane slaughtering of sacrificial animals in Deut 12:15–16 is clearly formulated in terms of the distinction between sacrificial slaughtering of sacrificial animals and profane slaughtering of wild animals as we find it in Lev 17. The rules for wild animals of Lev 17:13–14 are applied to the profane slaughtering of sacrificial animals in Deut 12:15–16.

---

17 Cf. Kilchör, *Mosetora*, 84–86.

2. The Priests and the Levites

Wellhausen starts his chapter on the priests and the Levites[18] with Ezek 44.[19] According to him, Ezek 44 degrades all the Levites who formerly (before Josiah's reform) have served as priests at the high places to servants of the priests of Jerusalem, the Zadokites. Wellhausen interprets Ezek 44 as an intermediate stage between Deuteronomy – in which all the Levites are priests, and P – in which the Levites are distinguished from priests from the beginning (Num 3) and never had priestly rights.

The issue of priests and Levites is quite complex. I just want to point to a few fundamental problems with Wellhausen's overall picture.

First, most scholars today reject the thesis that Ezek 44 has something to do with the Josianic reform and that the Levites in Ezek 44 are former priests of the high places.[20]

Second, and even more important, scholars since Hartmut Gese have agreed that the (post-) priestly text Num 18 antedates Ezek 44 at least on a traditio-historical level.[21] In other words: The distinction of P between priests and Levites is presupposed in Ezek 44. This has led most scholars to regard those texts in Ezek 40–48 that deal with Zadokites and Levites as later additions from the Persian or even Hellenistic period.

To consider the issue more broadly, we may say that Wellhausen regarded Ezekiel in general as an intermediate stage between D and P. However, recent studies in the book of Ezekiel have shown that Ezekiel refers to priestly texts throughout his book.[22] Given the fact that it was a central argument for Wellhausen that Ezekiel both chronologically and conceptually links D with P, it is surprising that the discovery that Ezekiel presupposes P at many places has not result in a rejection of

---

18 Wellhausen, *Prolegomena*, 115–145.
19 Ibid., 116–121.
20 While Wellhausen's model was almost canonical for nearly a hundred years, the situation changed with regard to Ezekiel 44 with the habilitation dissertation of Antonius H. J. Gunneweg, who pointed to the fact that Ezek 44 does not blame the Levites for having sacrificed at the high places (*Leviten*, 203). Since Gunneweg, most scholars reject the model of Wellhausen for a couple of reasons (see short overviews on recent research in Rudnig, *Heilig*, 291–294 and Konkel, *Architektonik*, 304–308; more recently see also Samuel, *Von Priestern zum Patriarchen*, 367; MacDonald, *Priestly Rule*, 4–10). A recent exception is Schaper, *Priester*, 122–129, who basically still works with Wellhausen's model.
21 See Konkel, *Architektonik*, 308: "Überblickt man die Forschung, so fällt auf, dass eine direkte Abhängigkeit von Ez 44,10-16 von P heute nicht mehr angenommen wird. Unabhängig davon, ob Ez 44 exilisch oder nachexilisch, ob P insgesamt oder in Teilen vorexilisch, exilisch oder nachexilisch datiert wird: Alle Positionen seit Gese kommen darin überein, dass Ez 44,10-16 zumindest traditionsgeschichtlich eine inhaltliche Weiterentwicklung dessen darstellt, was in Num 18 kodifiziert ist".
22 E.g. Levitt Kohn, *New Heart*; Lyons, *Law*. See already Klostermann, "Ezechiel"; Hurvitz, *Linguistic Study*.

Wellhausen's paradigm.[23] Rather, it has led to diachronic hypotheses, which regard all the texts with priestly influence in Ezekiel as later additions. In his review on Daniel Block's commentary on Ezekiel, Michael Konkel formulates three remarks with regard to Block's holistic approach. The first remark is very revealing (my translation):

> The vote for the authenticity of the entire book of Ezekiel not only depends on the analysis of the text itself, but is related to a larger theoretical frame. B. assumes in the sense of the Kaufmann-school an early dating of Old Testament texts, especially the priestly source. Thus it is possible for him to see in Ezekiel the recipient of a large part of Old Testament literature [...], who himself revised his texts to a great extent. On the other hand, the model of *Fortschreibung* is related to the framework of a late dating of the priestly source. It is precisely the references to P, H, the Dtr literature, and the other prophetic books, which then force the diachronic equalization.[24]

In other words, the diachronic models of the composition of the book of Ezekiel are driven by Wellhausen's paradigm, especially his exilic dating of the priestly source. Therefore, allusions to priestly texts in the book of Ezekiel can only be regarded as additions of a later redactional stage.

Incidentally, in the last years, Dalit Rom-Shiloni has published several articles where she shows that not only Ezekiel but also Jeremiah uses priestly traditions throughout the book, both in poetical and prose texts.[25] Recently, in her main paper at the IOSOT 2016 in Stellenbosch with the title "The Forest and the Trees: The Place of Pentateuchal Materials in Prophecy of the Late Seventh / Early Sixth Centuries BCE,"[26] she concluded that the allusions to priestly texts of the Pentateuch are so widely spread throughout Jeremiah and such a fundamental part of several texts, that they cannot be explained just as a result of post-priestly redactions. Georg Fischer, though differing in dating questions and dating altogether later than Rom-Shiloni, agrees that Jeremiah presupposes all the books of the Torah, including texts commonly ascribed to P.[27]

---

23 A quite awkward example is Samuel, *Von Priestern zum Patriarchen*, 367–369, who first agrees to reject the three main persuppositions of Wellhausen's interpretation of Ezek 44 and even adds another argument against Wellhausen (p.367), just to conclude that Wellhausen's model is still valid in its core (p. 369).
24 Konkel, Review of D.I. Block, 298: "Das Votum für die Authentizität des ganzen Ezechielbuches ist nicht nur abhängig von der Analyse des Ezechieltexts selbst, sondern steht innerhalb eines grösseren Theorierahmens. So ist es ihm möglich, in Ezechiel den *Rezipienten* eines Grossteils der atl Literatur zu sehen [...], der selbst in grösserem Umfang seine Texte überarbeitete. Dem gegenüber steht das Fortschreibungsmodell im Rahmen einer Spätdatierung der Priesterschrift. Gerade die Bezüge zu P, H, der dtr Literatur und den anderen Prophetenbüchern sind es, welche dann die diachrone Entzerrung erzwingen".
25 E.g. Rom-Shiloni, "Actualization"; idem., "Allusions"; idem., "A Non-Deuteronomic Phrase".
26 Published now as Rom-Shiloni, "Forest".
27 Fischer, "Relationship"; idem., "New Understanding," 30–31.

Now, back to Wellhausen and his theory about the priests and the Levites: Not only was he wrong in regarding Ezekiel as an intermediate stage between D and P with respect to the distinction of priests and Levites, but also his explanations with regard to Deuteronomy are very problematic in several respects. According to Wellhausen, in Deuteronomy the Levites are priests, what is expressed by the formula "the priests, the Levites." Only after the demotion of the priests which served at the high places before the centralization by Josiah, as required in Ezek 44, did P change the formula by a *waw* so that the distinction became clear: "the priests *and* the Levites."[28]

However, as Antonius H. Gunneweg showed, the identification of priests and Levites by Deuteronomy's formula "the priests, the Levites" is untenable in all texts in question.[29] The insight that this formula already presupposes a distinction (and would be redundant otherwise) is generally accepted today. For most scholars this did not mean, however, that Wellhausen's late dating of the priestly texts with this distinction was obsolete. Gunneweg, for example, did not question the postdating of P at all, but rather employed this chronological suggestion as the basis for outline a more complex history of the relationship between priests and Levites. In his view, Deuteronomy tried to identify formerly different groups in the sense that all Levites should be priests and all priests should be Levites; while P rejects priestly claims of Levites, but gives them other subordinated responsibilities instead.[30]

However, the context in which the formula "the priests, the Levites" occurs in Deut 24:8–9 is very interesting and relevant to this discussion:

> Deut 24:8–9   Take care in case of leprous disease, to be very careful to do according to all that *the priests, the Levites*, shall direct you. As I commanded them, so you shall be careful to do. Remember what the Lord your God did to Miriam on the way as you came out of Egypt.

Deuteronomy here refers back to what God commanded to "the priests, the Levites," and also to what God did to Miriam. These are clearly references to priestly texts, namely to Lev 13–14 (laws about leprosy) and to Num 12 (Miriam's leprosy). We have here an example where Deuteronomy's formula, which was so important for Wellhausen's theory, is used in a context where it clearly refers to priestly texts. Some scholars have tried to avoid this conclusion by suggesting that Deut 24:8–9 does not refer to the priestly texts but rather to older sources which were used by P later on.[31] But this is obviously an *ad hoc* argument to avoid acknowledging that the evidence does not fit the theory. It is more honest, in my view, to suggest that Deut

---

28 Wellhausen, *Prolegomena*, 140.
29 Gunneweg, *Leviten*, 119.
30 Cf. Gunneweg, *Leviten*, 219–225.
31 E.g. Skweres, *Rückverweise*, 194;

24:8 is a later addition[32] in which the formula has a unique function unlike its usage in the rest of Deuteronomy, as Harald Samuel proposed.[33] But is this really a credible solution? It seems unlikely. Like the proposal that Deut 24:8 refers to older sources not preserved to us but used by P, Samuel's proposal of a unique function for the formula is just a makeshift solution intended to defend Wellhausen's paradigm.

Finally, we may note that in Deut 18:1–8 we find a distinction between priests (vv. 3–5) and Levites (vv. 6–8), whereby priests are addressed in terms of "sons", while Levites are addressed in terms of "brothers". This is exactly the distinction formulated in Num 18:1–2 with priests as the sons of Aaron and Levites as Aaron's brothers.[34] Again, this distinction in Deut 18:1–8 is sometimes ascribed to a later redactor.[35] This is another example of a phenomenon that we observe time and time again: Wellhausen's paradigm is defended by ascribing to a later redactor everything that does not fit the 6th/5th century dating of P, be it in Deuteronomy, be it in Ezekiel (or in Joshua, in Kings, in Jeremiah, etc.).

3. Conclusion

I tried to show that the two most influential of Wellhausen's five pillars for the postdating of P to D do not stand up under close scrutiny of the relevant texts. However, in the history of biblical scholarship since Wellhausen, observations which call into question the pillars of Wellhausen's paradigm have not resulted in a fundamental reassessment of the paradigm, but rather in increasingly sophisticated methods to immunize Wellhausen's model against every substantive critique, especially by using redactional criticism to explain away all textual data that does not fit. In my view, the evidence against the dating of P on the basis of the arguments of Graf-Kuenen-Wellhausen has become so strong that we should seriously ask if the whole program of Pentateuchal research for the last 150 years has been on the wrong track. It might be necessary that we go back to the point where Pentateuchal research committed itself to the Wellhausen paradigm with regard to the dating of P. Indeed, I would suggest that the exilic/post-exilic dating of P—one of the last elements in Pentateuchal research that remains unquestioned with only few exceptions[36]—is one

---

32 Cf. Otto, *Deuteronomium 23,16–34,12*, 1828f.
33 Samuel, *Von Priestern zum Patriarchen*, 146.
34 Kilchör, *Mosetora*, 215–220.
35 E.g. Otto, *Deuteronomium 12,1–23,15*, 1491.
36 Cf. especially scholars like Yehezkel Kaufmann, Avi Hurvitz, Menahem Haran, Moshe Weinfeld, Jacob Milgrom, Israel Knohl, who are related to the so-called Kaufmann-school. However, there has never been a serious discussion of their arguments, as the somewhat polemical (yet with well-founded polemics) study of Thomas M. Krapf, *Priesterschrift*, shows.

of the main reasons why Pentateuchal research has reached an impasse. As long as every model is forced to fit 6th/5th century dating of P, all the other texts of the Pentateuch (and the Old Testament in general) cannot find their right place.

Bibliography

Baden, Joel. *J, E, and the Redaction of the Pentateuch*. FAT 68. Tübingen: Mohr Siebeck, 2007.
—. *The Composition of the Pentateuch: Renewing the Documentary Hypothesis*. New Haven: Yale University Press, 2012.
Cholewiński, Alfred. *Heiligkeitsgesetz und Deuteronomium*. AnBib 35. Rom: Biblical Institute, 1976.
Fischer, Georg. "ותפשי התורה לא ידעוני – The Relationship of the Book of Jeremiah to the Torah," in *The Formation of the Pentateuch: Bridging the Academic Cultures of Europe, Israel, and North America*, ed. Jan C. Gertz et all. (FAT 111; Tübingen: Mohr Siebeck, 2016), 891–911.
—. "A New Understanding of the Book of Jeremiah. A Response to Robert R. Wilson," in *Jeremiah's Scriptures. Production, Reception, Interaction, and Transformation*, ed. Hindy Najman and Konrad Schmid (SJSJ 173; Brill: Leiden, 2017), 22–43.
Gertz, Jan C. and Schmid, Konrad (eds.). *Abschied vom Jahwisten: Die Komposition des Hexateuch in der jüngeren Diskussion*. BZAW 315. Berlin: de Gruyter, 2002.
Gunneweg, Anton H. J. *Leviten und Priester. Hauptlinien der Traditionsbildung und Geschichte des israelitisch-jüdischen Kultpersonals*. FRLANT 89. Göttingen: Vandenhoeck & Ruprecht, 1965.
Houtman, Cees. *Der Pentateuch. Die Geschichte seiner Erforschung neben einer Auswertung*. Kampen: Kok Pharos, 1994.
Hurvitz, Avi. *A Linguistic Study of the Relationship between the Priestly Source and the Book of Ezekiel: A New Approach to an Old Problem*. CRB 20. Paris: Gabalda, 1982.
Joosten, Jan. "The Syntax of Exodus 20:24b. Remarks on a Recent Article by Benjamin Kilchör." *BN* 159 (2013): 3–8.
Kilchör, Benjamin. "בכל המקום (Ex 20,24b) – Gottes Gegenwart auf dem Sinai." BN 154 (2012): 89–102.
—. *Mosetora und Jahwetora. Das Verhältnis von Deuteronomium 12–26 zu Exodus, Levitikus und Numeri*, BZAR 21. Wiesbaden: Harrassowitz, 2015.
—. "'An jedem Ort' oder 'am ganzen Ort' (Ex 20,24b)? Eine Antwort an Jan Joosten." *BN* 165 (2015): 3–17.
Klostermann, August. "Ezechiel und das Heiligkeitsgesetz," in idem., *Der Pentateuch: Beiträge zu seinem Verständnis und seiner Entstehungsgeschichte*. Leipzig: Deichert, 1893.

Konkel, Michael. *Architektonik des Heiligen. Studien zur zweiten Tempelvision Ezechiels (Ez 40–48)*. BBB 129. Berlin: Philo, 2001.
—. Review of D.I. Block, *The Book of Ezekiel: Chapters 25–48. BZ* 44 (2000): 296–298.
Krapf, Thomas M. *Die Priesterschrift und die vorexilische Zeit. Yehezkel Kaufmanns vernachlässigter Beitrag zur Geschichte der biblischen Religion*. OBO 119, Göttingen: Vandenhoeck & Ruprecht, 1992.
Levin, Christoph. *Der Jahwist*. FRLANT 157. Göttingen: Vandenhoeck & Ruprecht, 1993.
Levinson, Bernard M. *Deuteronomy and the Hermeneutics of Legal Innovation*. New York/Oxford: Oxford University Press, 1997.
Levitt Kohn, Risa. *A New Heart and a New Soul. Ezekiel, the Exile and the Torah*. JSOTS 358. London: Sheffield Academic Press, 2002.
Lyons, Michael A. *From Law to Prophecy: Ezekiel's Use of the Holiness Code*. LHBOTS 507. New York: T&T Clark, 2009.
MacDonald, Nathan. *Priestly Rule. Polemic and Biblical Interpretation in Ezekiel 44*. BZAW 476. Göttingen: de Gruyter, 2015.
Mathys, Hans-Peter. "Wilhelm Martin Leberecht de Wettes *Dissertatio critico-exegetica* von 1805," in *Biblische Theologie und historisches Denken. Wissenschaftliche Studien aus Anlass der 50. Wiederkehr der Basler Promotion von Rudolf Smend*, ed. Martin Kessler and Martin Wallraff (SGWB 5, Basel: Schwabe Verlag, 2008), 170–211.
Nihan, Christophe. *From Priestly Torah to Pentateuch. A Study in the Composition of the Book of Leviticus*. FAT II/25, Tübingen: Mohr Siebeck, 2007.
Otto, Eckart. *Deuteronomium 12,1–23,15*. HThKAT. Freiburg i. Br.: Herder, 2016.
—. *Deuteronomium 23,16–34,12*. HThKAT. Freiburg i. Br.: Herder, 2016.
Paul, Mart-Jan. *Het Archimedisch Punt van de Pentateuchkritiek. Een historisch en exegetisch onderzoek naar de verhouding en de reformatie van koning Josia (2 Kon 22–23)*. 's-Gravenhage: Uitgeverij Boekencentrum, 1988.
Pitkänen, Pekka. *Central Sanctuary and Centralization of Worship in Ancient Israel. From the Settlement to the Building of Solomon's Temple*. GDNES 5. Piscataway: Gorgias Press, 2003.
Rendtorff, Rolf. *Das überlieferungsgeschichtliche Problem des Pentateuch*. BZAW 147. Berlin: de Gruyter, 1976.
—. *The Problem of the Process of Transmission in the Pentateuch*. JSOTS 89. Sheffield: Sheffield Academic Press, 1990.
Reuter, Eleonore. *Kultzentralisation. Entstehung und Theologie von Dtn 12*. BBB 87, Frankfurt a.M.: Anton Hain, 1993.
Rom-Shiloni, Dalit. "Actualization of Pentateuchal Legal Traditions in Jeremiah. More on the Riddle of Authorship." *ZAR* 15 (2009): 254–281.
—. "'How can you say, 'I am not defiled'' (Jer 2:20–25): Allusions to Priestly Legal Traditions in the Poetry of Jeremiah." *JBL* 133 (2014): 757–775.
—. "'On the Day I Freed Them From the Land of Egypt': A Non-Deuteronomic Phrase within Jeremiah's Covenant Conception." *VT* 65 (2015): 621–647.
—. "The Forest and the Trees: The Place of Pentateuchal Materials in Prophecy as of the Late Seventh / Early Sixth Centuries BCE," in *IOSOT XXII, Congress Volume Stellenbosch 2016*, ed. L. C. Jonker, G. R. Kotze, and Ch. M. Maier (Leiden: Brill, 2017), 56–92.
Römer, Thomas. *The So-Called Deuteronomistic History. A Sociological, Historical and Literary Introduction*. New York: t&t clark, 2007.

Rudnig, Thilo A. *Heilig und Profan. Redaktionskritische Studien zu Ez 40–48*. BZAW 2000. Berlin: de Gruyter, 2000.
Samuel, Harald. *Von Priestern zum Patriarchen. Levi und die Leviten im Alten Testament*. BZAW 448. Berlin: de Gruyter, 2014.
Schaper, Joachim. "Schriftauslegung und Schriftwerdung im alten Israel. Eine vergleichende Exegese von Ex 20,24–26 und Dtn 12,13–19." *ZAR* 5 (1999): 111–132.
—. *Priester und Leviten im achämenidischen Juda. Studien zur Kult- und Sozialgeschichte Israels in persischer Zeit*. FAT 31. Tübingen: Mohr Siebeck, 2000.
Schwartz, Baruch J. "The Prohibitions Concerning the 'Eating' of Blood in Leviticus 17," in *Priesthood and Cult in Ancient Israel*, ed. Gary A. Anderson and Saul M. Olyan (JSOTS 125; Sheffield: JSOT Press, 1991), 34–66.
—. "'Profane' Slaughter and the Integrity of the Priestly Code." *HUCA* 67 (1996): 15–42.
Skweres, Dieter E. *Die Rückverweise im Buch Deuteronomium*. AnBib 79. Rome: Biblical Institute Press, 1979.
Stackert, Jeffrey. *A Prophet Like Moses: Prophecy, Law, and Israelite Religion*. New York/Oxford: Oxford University Press, 2014.
Van Seters, John. *Prologue to history: the Yahwist as historian in Genesis*. Louisville: Westminster John Knox Press, 1992.
—. *The life of Moses: the Yahwist as historian in Exodus-Numbers*. Louisville: Westminster John Knox Press, 1994.
Wellhausen, Julius. *Prolegomena zur Geschichte Israels*. 6th ed. Berlin: Georg Reimer, 1905.

Leviticus 26 and Deuteronomy 28

Some Observations on Their Relationship

Markus Zehnder (Biola University / Ansgar Teologiske Høgskole / Evangelical Theological Faculty Leuven)

1. Introduction: Questions and Methods

The three main questions that will be addressed in this study are the following:
1. How can the structure of the two catalogues of blessings and curses be described?
2. How can the relationship between the two catalogues be described? Can one of the two catalogues be demonstrated to be earlier than the other? Is one dependent on the other? Is it possible to make any informed suggestions about the date of the catalogues or parts of them?
3. Are there any conclusions that can be drawn from observations on the relationship between the two catalogues as far as the relationship between the major biblical law collections is concerned?

These questions are important especially because Deuteronomy 28 is often seen as part of the "Urdeuteronomium," which again is related to the neo-Assyrian period by many scholars, and seen as the main Archimedean point for the reconstruction of the literary history of the Pentateuch, at least the legal material contained in it.[1]

It is not possible to answer these questions globally; rather, they are in need of refinement.
- Are we talking about the redactional final compositions of Leviticus 26 and Deuteronomy 28?
- Are we talking about single units within the compositions? One cannot *presuppose* that the compositions are a literary unit, nor can one *presuppose* that they are not. This means that one must make a difference between different passages within Leviticus 26 on the one hand, and within Deuteronomy 28 on the other.
- Additionally, it is clear that Deuteronomy 29–31 contains many elements that are topically parallel to the latter passages of Leviticus 26, beginning

---

1 See, e.g., van der Toorn, *Scribal Culture*, 151–152, 155.

ca. in v. 39. This means that these chapters also have to be taken into consideration.

"Earlier" and "later" does not necessarily include an assertion of direct dependence; this will need to be established based on specific observations, and the possibilities of both texts being related to a broader common tradition or their commonalities not being intentional need to be considered.[2]

Because of the breadth of the questions and the length of the two catalogues, there are many aspects that can only be treated briefly or not at all.

In terms of *methodology*, the study will pursue four avenues:
1. Lexical and structural analysis of the two texts (Leviticus 26 and Deuteronomy 28).
2. Study of the lexical or phraseological / syntactical connections between the two texts.
3. Study of the lexical or phraseological / syntactical connections between Leviticus 26 and Deuteronomy 28 on the one hand and other biblical texts on the other.
4. Observations concerning the connections, both linguistic and topical, between the two texts and extra-biblical material.

As far links and parallels with both biblical and extra-biblical texts are concerned, it is neither necessary nor possible in the present context to try to cover all possible cases of such contacts, nor to analyse the exact nature or function of the links in detail. It is also beyond the scope of this study to investigate further types of relationships between the relevant texts that are not manifest on the lexical or phraseological / syntactical level, with some exceptions as far as extra-biblical texts are concerned where a clear thematic overlap is evident. Rather, the main goal is to use linguistically recognizable links and parallels to provide a clearer image of the differences between Leviticus 26 and Deuteronomy 28 and especially to investigate whether such links provide insights into the chronological milieu in which the two texts fit best, regardless of the existence or absence of dependence, or insights that allow the recognition of relationships of possible literary dependence, which again would enable us to assess proposals concerning the relative dating of the two texts.

Because of this special focus, parallels with texts that are part of literary works that can hardly be used to assess with any specificity the dating of either Leviticus 26 or Deuteronomy 28, such as the Deuteronomistic history or Psalms and Proverbs, will not be investigated. Rather, the main focus will primarily be on prophetic texts that might be pre-exilic or early exilic. As far as such texts are concerned, it has to be borne in mind that in terms of addressing the possible direction of dependence, it is in principle difficult to postulate that specific legal regulations are dependent on

---

2 Together with other possible types of relationship for which the term "dependence" would not be appropriate. Also models that reckon with the possibility of mutual influence have to be taken into account.

"prophetic statements of accusation and judgment."[3] This is related to the fact that "prophets served as mediators between biblical law and the actions of their own contemporary audience."[4] Their accusations are based on the addressees' misdeeds, and it would be difficult to propose any other object of the infractions than the laws that are collected in the Pentateuchal law collections.[5]

On the other hand, both in the cases of links between Leviticus 26 and Deuteronomy 28 on the one hand and prophetic texts on the other, as well as other possible cases of literary connections, more specific criteria concerning the possible direction of dependence – if dependence is the likely explanation – have to be applied on an individual case base.[6]

As the investigation will show, all four avenues are important. At the same time, it will also become clear that not all questions can be answered adequately based on the evidence that the four avenues provide, and in some cases only statements of probability with a considerable degree of uncertainty are possible. This is, however, not surprising, since as in any historical investigation, the available evidence is limited. It is important, in such circumstances, not to press forward answers that are not well founded, or to disguise the degree of uncertainty that is connected with some of the more tentative and provisional answers.

2. General Observations

2.1 Only Two Fully Developed Catalogues of Blessings and Curses

There are only two fully developed catalogues of blessings and curses (or promises and menaces) in the Hebrew Bible.

What does this mean? Does it mean that there are not three major law collections (Covenant Collection; Priestly Collection, including the so-called Holiness Code;[7] Deuteronomic Laws) on exactly the same level?

It might be argued that there is a short blessing at the end of the Covenant Collection as well, in Exod 23:25–26, together with warnings in the context. Interest-

---

3 Lyons, "How Have We Changed?," 1064.
4 Ganzel and Levitt Kohn, "Ezekiel's Prophetic Message," 1077. They also mention Y. Kaufmann's observation that the Pentateuchal laws in no instance (explicitly) refer to the prophets.
5 This does not mean that the respective laws must be formulated in exactly the same way as they are found in the extant Pentateuch and are already part of the extant Pentateuch.
6 For tentative identifications of such criteria see, e.g., Lyons, *Law*, 56–109; Zehnder, "Observations," 193.
7 The question of the relationship between the so-called Holiness Code in Leviticus 17–26 and the (other) Priestly laws does not need to be addressed further at this point.

ingly, there is an analogue to this in Exod 34:10–17, though without explicit reference to a blessing. In fact, Exod 23:20–33 is often understood as a blessing and curse section that concludes the Covenant Collection.[8] However, curses are all but missing, and the passage deals with a specific topic, the conquest of the land. This connects the passage with Exod 34:10–16; Num 33:50–55; and Deuteronomy 7, more than with Leviticus 26 and Deuteronomy 28.

It seems to be (more) plausible to understand Exod 24:1–11 as a sealing of the Covenant Collection with an *implicit* type of blessing and curse in the ritual described there. However, since this is only implicit, we are left again with Leviticus 26 and Deuteronomy 28 as the only *explicit* / "real" blessing and curse (or promise and menace) sections concluding a major collection of legal material.

The fact that Leviticus 26 constitutes the first extended explicit section of blessings and curses (or promises and menaces) in some way closing a law collection, parallel to the one found in Deuteronomy 28, has implications for the understanding of the structure of the biblical law collections: The division between Deuteronomy and the preceding law collections in Exodus through Numbers is more accentuated than the division between the (Priestly) laws in Leviticus (and Numbers) and the Covenant Collection. This squares well with the observation that the literary boundary markers are stronger at the transition of Numbers / Deuteronomy (and Genesis / Exodus) than within the complex Exodus through Numbers.[9]

2.2 The Terms "Blessing" and "Curse"

The terms "blessing" and "curse" are not used in Leviticus 26, as opposed to the situation in Deuteronomy 28. This is an observation that needs to be kept in mind, even if there seems to be no simple answers as to the exact meaning of this fact.[10]

2.3 Intertextual Links between Leviticus 26 / Deuteronomy 28 and Other Texts in the Hebrew Bible

In other parts of the Hebrew Bible, a good number of intertextual links with both Leviticus 26 and Deuteronomy 28 can be found. Regardless of the question of the direction of dependence between either Leviticus 26 or Deuteronomy 28 on the one hand and other biblical texts on the other, this indicates that none of the two passages was understood as *replacing* the other.[11]

---

8 So Balentine, *Leviticus*, 198; Wenham, *Leviticus*, 327.
9 See Koorevaar, "The Books of Exodus - Leviticus – Numbers," 423–453.
10 Cf., e.g., Zehnder, "Structural Complexity," 503, footnote 1.
11 This is especially evident if one takes into consideration that intertextual links can be detected with texts that are so late that there can be no doubt about both Leviticus 26 and Deuteronomy

2.4 The Delimitation of the Relevant Material in Deuteronomy

As far as Deuteronomy is concerned, one must take into consideration the chapters following Deut 28 because blessing and curse are also dealt with in chs. 29–30 (/31), pointing to a sequence of divine punishment and reestablishment of God's people after the punishment that is in important ways similar to the developments described in Lev 26, including those passages that follow the menaces proper in Lev 26.

3. The Promise/Blessing Section in Leviticus 26

3.1 Structure and Possible Dependence

The promise/blessing section in Leviticus 26 is well structured. There are no obvious signs of dependence on other sources (neither structurally nor lexically).[12]

The promise/blessing section in Leviticus 26 is structured in a way that makes the dwelling of God with his people, the intimate community between God and his people, the ultimate goal and climax of the promises.[13] This is different from what is found in ordinary blessing sections that are attached to treaty texts. Perhaps this is one reason why there is also a lexical difference between Lev 26:3–13 and such texts, insofar as the word "blessing" is not used in Leviticus 26.

3.2 Close Connections with Ezekiel and Genesis 17

There are close connections between the promise/blessing section in Leviticus 26 and Ezekiel;[14] also linguistic links with Genesis 17 can be found.

---

28 predating them. Two random examples are the link between Lev 26:30 and 2 Chr 14:4; 34:4, 7 through the shared use of the rare noun חמן ('incense altar'), and the quotation of Lev 26:12 in 2 Cor 6:16.

12 See, e.g., Hartley, *Leviticus*, 456.

13 A detailed analysis of Lev 26:3–13 by the present writer that proves the point is in preparation.

14 See, e.g., Grünwaldt, *Heiligkeitsgesetz*, 349; Hieke, *Levitikus,* 1065–1066; Milgrom, *Leviticus 23–27*, 2348–2363; Wenham, *Leviticus*, 330. Some scholars also mention parallels with P (see, e.g., Grünwaldt, *Heiligkeitsgesetz*, 353). Since the nature of the relationship between H and P is a matter of debate, and since the discussion of the dating of P is not settled, this question will not be pursued in the present context.

As Lyons notes, most scholars agree that the type of commonalities between Leviticus and Ezekiel is such that it can be explained only in terms of some kind of literary dependence – which is true both for the promise and menace sections of Leviticus 26; see Lyons, "How Have We Changed?," 1055.

Verses 3 and 13 (frame): very close parallel of v. 3 with Ezek 11:20a (while Ezek 11:20b is parallel to v. 12b)[15] as well as Ezek 36:27b, and of v. 13 with Ezek 34:27b.
Verses 4–5: close connections with Ezek 34:26–27; 25:19; 28:26; 36:30.[16]
Verses 6–8: close connections with Ezek 34:25, 28.[17]
Verses 9–10: close connections with Gen 17:6–7, 19–21; Ezek 36:11;[18] elements of vv. 9 and 11 are combined in Ezek 37:26.
Verses 11–12: close connections with Ezek 34:30–31; 36:28; 37:23, 26–27.[19]

There are also close connections with Leviticus 25 (v. 5 with Lev 25:19; v. 10 with Lev 25:22).[20]

If it is more likely that Leviticus 26 is known to Ezekiel than the other way around, the larger part of the promise section in Leviticus 26 can be said to be pre-exilic.

Elaborated arguments for this direction of dependence are found, for example, in Milgrom's commentary on Leviticus. Milgrom claims that Ezekiel uses Leviticus 26 to describe the future restoration. As the most outstanding examples he identifies Ezek 34:24–28; 36:9–11; 37:26–27.[21] With respect to the first passage, Milgrom states: "Thus the mixed metaphors, changes of subject, stylistic inversions, and explanatory expansions make it amply clear that Ezekiel has reworked the blessings of Lev 26:3–13."[22]

With respect to the third passage, he assumes that "Ezekiel follows with the adoption formula of Lev 26:12, but ... he drops the anthropomorphic verb *wĕehithallaktî* ... for YHWH. Similarly, Ezekiel omits the anthropomorphic *wĕlō'-tigʻal napšî 'etkem* ... 'my soul will not abhor you' (v. 11b)."[23]

In a concluding, summarizing remark, Milgrom states: "It is Ezekiel who exhibits expansions, omissions, and reformulations, all of which lead to the conclusion that Ezekiel is the borrower."[24]

---

15 Cf. Häner, *Nachwirken*, 280–281.
16 See, e.g., Gerstenberger, *Das dritte Buch Mose*, 372.
17 See, e.g., Gerstenberger, *Das dritte Buch Mose*, 373.
18 See, e.g., Hieke, *Levitikus*, 1069.
19 See, e.g., Hartley, *Leviticus*, 463.
20 So also, e.g., Grünwaldt, *Heiligkeitsgesetz*, 368.
21 Milgrom, *Leviticus 23–27*, 2348–2352.
22 Milgrom, *Leviticus 23–27*, 2349.
23 Milgrom, *Leviticus 23–27*, 2351.
24 Milgrom, *Leviticus 23–27*, 2351. Hartley concurs, basing his assessment on the observation that such links are not only found in the promise section of Leviticus 26, but also in the menace section, and that it is not only Ezekiel, but also a number of other (especially prophetic) texts in the Hebrew Bible that show such links. He states that it is "more likely that Lev 26 was a source used by Ezekiel and the other prophets, for a single source can be drawn on by a variety of authors over a couple of centuries more readily than that source can come into existence by pulling material from such a diversity of sources" (Hartley, *Leviticus*, 460).

Some additional observations concerning the relationship of Leviticus 26 and Ezek 34:24–28 can be adduced that support the assumption that Ezekiel draws on Leviticus 26:

a) Ezekiel 34:24–30 stands out against the rest of the chapter by not containing the catch-words רעה and צאן; this renders some probability to the assumption that this passage has its own background, different from the rest of the chapter. This would mean that the chapter is composite and not a literary unity.

b) While Lev 26:6 talks about YHWH putting "peace" in the land, in the sense of outward security, related to the absence of foreign invaders and harmful beasts, Ezek 34:25 uses the expression "covenant of peace," which presupposes a concept of שלום that goes far beyond what is found in Lev 26:6, a state of an all-encompassing positive relationship between God and his people.

c) Also, the plural of גשם ("rain") is attested only 5 times in the Hebrew Bible, and only in Leviticus 26 and Ezekiel 34 in those parts called *Torah* and *Nevi'im*, with Ezekiel having the other attestations of the noun in the singular (while Leviticus has no other attestations). This suggests that גשם (sg.) is a common noun form in Ezekiel, while גשמים (pl.) is not. One can also argue that the unexpected shift from גשם (sg.) in the first phrase of Ezek 34:26, which closely resembles Lev 26:4a except for the number of the noun "rain", to גשמי ברכה (pl.) in the explanatory phrase in Ezek 34:26 shows that Ezekiel is dependent on Leviticus 26.[25]

d) Both Ezekiel 34 and 37 contain temporal markers that show that the new state of affairs will last forever (לא עוד ;לעולם ;עד־עולם; see Ezek 34:10, 22, 28; 37:22, 25–26, 28). This goes beyond what is found in Leviticus 26 and clearly marks the more developed, definitive version.[26]

e) As far as Ezek 34:27a is concerned, which is parallel to Lev 26:4b, the difference of the sequence of "land / produce" and "trees / fruit" against the background of Seidel's Law likely points to Ezekiel 34 being dependent on Leviticus 26, because it is the latter that has the more natural order.[27]

f) In the case of Ezek 34:27b and Lev 26:13, the connection of the Israelites' status as slaves with their stay in Egypt, as attested in Lev 26:13, is much more traditional and frequent than the general reference to their status as slaves owned by wholly unspecified people, as attested in Ezek 34:27. As is very often the case, experiences from the Exodus are used as a paradigm for the future redemption of Israel.[28]

A different view is taken by Grünwaldt, who argues for a dependence of Lev 26:4–6, 13 on Ezek 34:25–30 (see *Heiligkeitsgesetz*, 350–351). However, he simply enumerates the differences between the two texts, without presenting any compelling argument for the proposed direction of dependence.

25 Thus Lyons, *Law*, 64.
26 Cf. Häner, *Nachwirken*, 457.
27 Cf. Lyons, *Law*, 71.
28 Cf. Lyons, *Law*, 107.

g) The same line of dependence is evident in Ezek 34:30–31, which contains elements found in Lev 26:12. The ordinary covenant formula "I will be your God, you will be my people", as attested in Lev 26:12, is split up in Ezekiel 34 in way that is not attested anywhere else, and that is obviously influenced by the literary context that speaks of YHWH as the pastor of his flock, Israel.

h) In the case of Ezek 37:27, one can observe that two syntactically unconnected elements from Lev 26:11–12 (v. 11: משכני; v. 12: "I will be your [→ their] God", "you [→ they] will be my people") are combined, which is likely a sign for Ezekiel 37 being dependent on Leviticus 26. That there is a direct (intentional) connection at all is established by the fact nowhere else do the two elements appear together, and nowhere else in the Latter Prophets does משכן refer to God's dwelling.[29]

i) An argument can also be made for Ezek 11:20 being dependent on Lev 26:3, 12, and not the other way around: The passage that precedes Ezek 11:20, Ezek 11:17–19, makes clear that when the Israelites return to their country, YHWH himself will change their hearts (v. 19), so that they will be able to walk in his ordinances. This goes far beyond the conditional formulations of the promise section of Leviticus 26. It would not be possible to explain why an earlier, much more far-reaching and confident concept was dropped and exchanged with the if-clauses found in Leviticus 26.[30] The same holds true for the parallel between Ezek 36:27 and Lev 26:3;[31] again, in Ezekiel 36, the keeping of the commands is envisioned as a consequence of YHWH's previous changing their hearts through his spirit.

j) Moreover, in Ezekiel 36 (see vv. 23, 26), the salvation of Israel has its goal in YHWH's demonstrating to the nations who he is.[32] Such a universal perspective is likely later than the narrower one found in Leviticus 26.

On a more general level, it may be observed that in those cases in which passages of the promise/blessing section of Leviticus 26 – together with elements of Lev 26:(39/)40–45 – find linguistic analogues in Ezekiel in the context of his description of the future, Ezekiel departs from the conditional framework of Leviticus 26, which reflects the traditional blessing sections attached to law corpora and treaties, and uses them in an unconditional way, with the hope for the future restoration being unilaterally grounded in YHWH's own actions.[33] It may be argued that this clearly marks a later stage in the theological application of such materials.

Thus, it is likely that the blessing section of Leviticus 26 is pre-Ezekiel. It is, however, not possible based on the observations adduced so far to assess how far it goes back in time.

---

29 See Lyons, *Law*, 71.
30 Cf. Häner, *Nachwirken*, 281.
31 Cf. Häner, *Nachwirken*, 454.
32 The same perspective is also present in Ezek 37:28, which concludes with the promise that YHWH will again be Israel's God and Israel his people.
33 See, e.g., Lyons, *Law*, 149–150.

Since the dependence of Ezekiel on Leviticus 26 affects most of the blessing/promise section, not just isolated parts, it is likely that the whole section predates Ezekiel.

It also gives support to the assumption that the blessing/promise section of Leviticus for the most part is a literary unity and not composed of various independent pieces at a late redactional stage.

3.3 Connections with Other Texts in the Hebrew Bible

Connections between the promise/blessing section of Leviticus 26 and other texts in the Hebrew Bible are also found. Here are two salient examples:

a) Zechariah 8:12 is close to Lev 26:4: Leviticus 26:4bα is almost verbatim parallel to Zech 8:12aγ, while Lev 26:4bβ is parallel to Zech 8:12aβ, with just עץ השדה of Leviticus 26 being replaced by גפן in Zechariah 8.

b) The juxtaposition of נתן and גשם, as attested in Lev 26:4, is not only found in Ezek 34:26, but also in Jer 5:24, and besides these passages only in two more instances in the Hebrew Bible.

3.4 Overlap between Lev 26:9, 12–13 and Exod 6:4, 7

There is an interesting overlap between Lev 26:9, 12–13 and Exod 6:4, 7.[34] Three elements are shared, to a high degree verbatim:

a) God's declaration that he has "established his covenant" (הקימתי את־בריתי) "with you/them" (אתם / אתכם);

b) the description of the mutual relationship as YHWH being their god and Israel being his people;

c) and the self-description of YHWH as "I am the Lord who has brought you out of … Egypt".

This correspondence forms a kind of *inclusio* that binds together the beginning and the completion of the Exodus. It can be argued that also Deut 28:66, which mentions the ships going back to Egypt, also direct the reader's attention to the beginning of the Exodus. However, the relationship to the Exodus is not as intimate as it is in the case of Leviticus 26. The fact that Leviticus 26 is more explicitly related to the beginning of the Exodus might be taken as a hint to its preceding Deuteronomy 28. This is, however, of course not the only possible interpretation of the literary features described here.

---

34 This is also observed by Hieke, *Levitikus*, 1069.

4. The Blessing Section in Deuteronomy 28

4.1 The Structure of the Blessing Section in Deut 28:1–14: General Observations

The blessing section in Deut 28:1–14 is well structured.[35] However, in this case, as opposed to Leviticus 26, we are dealing with a more complex two-part structure, and the second part seems to be composite.[36] The higher degree of complexity that distinguishes Deut 28:1–14 from Lev 26:3–13 may point to the Deuteronomic text representing a later stage.

The fact that a climax such as the one found in Lev 26:11–12 is missing in Deut 28:1–14 speaks against a simple borrowing. The use of מטר in Deuteronomy 28 (v. 12) as opposed to גשם in Leviticus 26 (v. 4) also speaks against a direct dependence of the two texts.

In addition, and more generally, there are no signs of a dependence of Deut 28:1–14 on any other biblical text, neither structurally nor lexically.[37]

4.2 The Structure of the Blessing Section in Deut 28:1–14: Details

The blessing section of Deuteronomy 28 is framed by vv. 1–2 and 13b–14, containing elements of repetition. The main body consists of two main parts: vv. 3–6 and vv. 7–13a.[38]

Alternatively, it is possible to detect a chiastic structure that covers vv. 3–13a, organized topically:[39]

> A // A´ economic success (v. 3a // v. 12b–13a);
> B // B´ fertility of soil (v. 3b // v. 12a);
> C // C´ fertility of humans and animals (v. 4 // v. 11);
> D // D´ abundant food (v. 5 // v. 8);
> E // E´ military success (v. 6 // v. 7).

However, in this reconstruction of the structure of the blessing section vv. 9–10 are not covered, and the clear phraseological identity between vv. 3 and 6 with the repetition of ברוך in the same verse is not reflected. Also, the topical identification is highly disputable in several cases.

---

35 It also has to be noted that there are clear parallels with Deut 7:13; see Zehnder, "Fluch und Segen," 193–194. It seems that Deuteronomy 7 is dependent on Deuteronomy 28.
36 For a similar assessment see Tigay, *Deuteronomy*, 258–259.
37 At least not beyond isolated lexical items. Cf., e.g., Craigie, *Deuteronomy*, 335–338.
38 For a similar assessment see, e.g., Finsterbusch, *Deuteronomium*, 164.
39 See Tigay, *Deuteronomy*, 490.

The first part (vv. 3–6) consists of a series of four sentences beginning with the formula "blessed shall be ...". The framing verses 3 and 6 both contain the phrase ברוך אתה, forming an *inclusio*. In the second part of the blessing section, there are two if-clauses, as opposed to the situation in Leviticus 26:

v. 9: the Lord will establish you as a holy people
>**if** you keep the commandments

v. 13–14: the Lord makes you the head,
>**if** you listen

Also this distinction between Leviticus 26 and Deuteronomy 28 may suggest that the latter text is the more recent one.

There is a further observation that points in the same direction. The blessing section of Deuteronomy 28 exhibits a strong reflection on the relative position of the addressees to other peoples (vv. 1, 10 and 12). This reflection on the peoples is not found to the same degree in Leviticus 26.[40]

Also the reference to cities in Deut 28:3 and storehouses in Deut 28:8, both without parallel in Leviticus 26, may be interpreted as pointing to (imagined) life conditions that are "later" than those reflected in the promise section of Leviticus 26.

On the other hand, the use of words that occur otherwise only in the context of the Exodus story could tentatively be interpreted as pointing to a relatively high age.[41]

5. The Menace/Curse Section Proper in Lev 26:14–33

5.1 Clear Structure and Close Connection with Promise Section

The curse/menace section proper in Lev 26:14–33 exhibits a five-part structure: Verses 14–17; verses 18–20; verses 21–22; verses 23–26; verses 28–33.

The menace/curse section is structurally a coherent whole, reflecting a steady process of intensification.

Not only is there a process of intensification, but it is also remarkable that the menaces are not simple curses – the words "curse" or "cursed" are not used; rather, they have the purpose to call the people back to obedience to God's laws. There is, as in the promise section, a clear theological outlook of this section. It is not a simple prediction of disaster, but a call to the people to change their ways so that the

---

40 As observed also by, e.g., Cholewinski, *Heiligkeitsgesetz*, 311.
41 Examples are שגר ("offspring"; see Deut 28:4 and Exod 13:12; only two more attestations in Deuteronomy 28 and one more in Deuteronomy 7) and משארת ("kneading trough"; see Deut 28:5 and Exod 7:28; 12:34; only one more attestation in Deuteronomy 28). See also the blessings in Exod 23:25–27.

disaster will not take place at all, thus an explicitly educational text.[42] This is different from what is found in ordinary curse sections related to laws, treaties and loyalty oaths in the ancient Near East. As in the case of the promise section, this specific character may be one of the reasons way the words "curse" or "cursed" are not used.

This specific character also makes the sequel after the menace section and proper look more naturally connected with the preceding segments than it would otherwise be the case. The whole section beginning in v. 14 and ending in v. 45 depicts an almost natural, very well conceivable process: The first attempts to correct the people's ways by exacting ever severer punishments fail; but in the end, they do succeed, and God's original and ultimate purpose, to restore community between him and his people, is attained.[43]

There are close connections with the preceding promises/blessings:[44]

Menaces / Curses, Lev 26:14–33	Correspondences in Promises/ Blessings, Lev 26:3–13
16 / 19–20 / 26	→ 4–5 / 10
17 / 25	→ 9
22 / 25	→ 6
30	→ 11
33	→ 5
(36)	(→ 7)

The clear structure of the curse/menace section proper in Lev 26:14–33 and the close connection with the promise section make it unlikely that the section as a whole or large parts of it are dependent on another text or consist of several literary layers.[45] This does, however, not exclude that traditional, pre-existing material has been used in this section.

5.2 Some Signs of Possible Literary Disturbances

a) Leviticus 26:16: Grammatically, בהלה and קדחת / שחפת are not parallel; the first noun or the two latter nouns could in theory be secondary insertions. Incidentally, the two latter nouns are attested only here and in Deuteronomy 28.

---

42 See, e.g., Gerstenberger, *Das dritte Buch Mose*, 395; Grünwaldt, *Heiligkeitsgesetz*, 356; Hieke, *Levitikus*, 1077; Noordtzij, *Leviticus*, 266.
43 For a similar assessment see Lyons, *Law*, 32.
44 Cf., e.g., Balentine, *Leviticus*, 199–200; Levine, *Leviticus*, 276.
45 For an analysis of the structure of the menace section of Lev 26 see Zehnder, "Structural Complexity," especially 506–508, 524. Gerstenberger, on the other hand, is an example of those who assume that the menace section proper has undergone several revisions (see *Das dritte Buch Mose*, 375, 378). For arguments for the literary unity of Lev 26:3–45 as a whole see, e.g., Grünwaldt, *Heiligkeitsgesetz*, 115–121.

b) Leviticus 26:19: The sequence of two *waw*-perfect verbs with YHWH as subject is remarkable. The element "sky like iron and earth like bronze" could theoretically be secondary. It could also be misplaced, because it makes more sense in connection with v. 20b. On the other hand, vv. 19–20 could be understood as an artfully arranged segment in which 19a parallels 20a and 19b parallels 20b.

c) Leviticus 26:29: The syntax of this verse is exceptional in its context because in this case the subject is in the second person plural, not in the first person singular.

Also, this verse (describing cannibalism as a consequence of extreme famine) could be interpreted as a summary of a longer version such as the one found in Deut 28:53–57. On the other hand, the Deuteronomic version could be explained as an expansion of the version in Leviticus 26; however, the change in person in Leviticus 26 is not explained if this line of argument is followed.

5.3 Parallels of the Menace/Curse Section in Leviticus 26 with Extra-Biblical Texts

There are (relatively) close parallels between Leviticus 26 and (mostly Aramaic) texts from the Syrian-Levantine area dating to the 9th–8th centuries.

a) Leviticus 26:26 ("When I break your staff of bread, ten women will bake your bread in one oven, and they will bring back your bread in rationed amounts, so that you will eat and not be satisfied") finds a clear parallel in the bilingual treaty of Tell Fekheriyeh, dated to the 9th century BCE, where the following passage is found:[46]

> "And let one hundred women bake bread in an oven, but not fill it".[47]

> "One hundred women bakers shall not fill an oven."[48]

The same formula is also found in the Bukan inscription, dating to around 700 BCE:

> "May seven women bake in one oven and not fill it".[49]

The fact that Lev 26:26 does not show the same numbers associated with the baking women either in Tell Fekheriyeh or in Bukan very likely shows that the biblical text is not directly dependent on either of the two. The number 100 would have been attractive to copy because of the higher degree of dramatization of the situation, and the number seven would have fitted the menace/curse section of Leviticus 26 very well because of the importance of the number seven in that section. Since a

---

46 The parallel is also observed by Cathcart, "Curses," 144; Levine, *Leviticus*, 278.
47 Kaufman, "Reflections," 163; (l. 22 of the Aramaic version).
48 Kaufman, "Reflections," 163 (ll. 35–36 of the Akkadian version). The oven is also mentioned in Esarhaddon's succession treaty (§ 47, 443).
49 Baranowski, "Curses," 187.

direct literary dependence from the extra-biblical parallels can be excluded, it is at least possible that the biblical version predates both Aramaic inscriptions.

b) There is some overlap between Lev 26:31 ("I will not smell your soothing aromas") and the following passage of the treaty of Tell Fekheriyeh:[50]

> "Whoever removes my name from the vessels of the Temple of Hadad my lord, may Hadad my lord not accept his food and his water from his hand; may Sola my lady not accept his food and his water from his hand".[51]

> "Whoever removes my name from the vessels of the Temple of Adad my lord, Adad my lord shall not accept his food and his water; Shala my lady shall not accept his food and his water."[52]

c) There are also parallels with the Sefire treaty between Bar-Ga'yah and the king of Arpad, dating to the 8th century BCE. Sf I A 30 talks about the sending (*šlḥ*) of wild animals against Arpad, similar to what is found in Lev 26:22 (where also the verb שלח is used):

> "May the gods send every sort of devourer against Arpad and against its people."[53]

Also Sf II A 9 mentions wild animals:

> "[… and may] the mouth of a lion [eat] and the mouth of [a …] and the mouth of a panther."[54]

d) In Sf I A 32, finally, mention is made of Arpad being turned into a hill of ruins (*tēl*), in close correspondence with Lev 26:31 (חרבה):

> "And may Arpad become a mound to [house the desert animal]."[55]

e) There are two possible parallels with the Balaam inscription of Deir 'Alla, Comb. II, dating to the 8th century.

Line 10 contains the catch-word "hate" (*sn'*), in accordance with Lev 26:17:

> "You will cover with one piece of clothing. Be it that you are hated (or: that you hate) oh men, be it that you ...."[56]

Line 12 uses the motif of the sighing in the heart, which is found also in Lev 26:36:

---

50 This is also observed by Levine, *Leviticus*, 278.
51 Kaufman, "Reflections," 162 (ll. 17–18 of the Aramaic version).
52 Kaufman, "Reflections," 162 (ll. 26–30 of the Akkadian version).
53 Fitzmyer, *Sefire*, 44–45.
54 Fitzmyer, *Sefire*, 122–123.
55 Fitzmyer, *Sefire*, 44–45.
56 Hoftijzer and van der Kooij, *Aramaic Texts*, 174; Crawford, *Blessing*, 131.

"(he/they will say) in (his/their) heart: who is sighing, is a blinded one sighing in his heart?"[57]

It needs to be stressed, however, that in both these cases the correspondences are very vague – which of course can hardly be otherwise given the fragmentary textual preservation of the Balaam inscription(s).

f) The motif of the eating of one´s own children, attested in Lev 26:29, also appears, i.a., in EST[58] ll. 448–450, 547–550, 570–572,[59] as well as in the Annals of Ashurbanipal. It is already attested in the treaty between Ashur-Nerari V of Assyria and the king of Arpad:

"[M]ay they eat the flesh of their sons and daughters, and may it taste as good to them as the flesh of spring lambs."[60]

g) Mention of the deity's dwelling / cultic installations in the curse, as we find it in Lev 26:30–31, is also found in extra-biblical material, for example in the epilogue to the Laws of Lipit-Ishtar xxii 34–52:

"May [...] the god Enlil [...] revoke the gift of the lofty Ekur temple. May the god Utu, judge of heaven and earth, remove the august word. ...".[61]

These parallels, especially those mentioned under 1–4, speak against a late date (exilic or post-exilic) of the curse/menace section of Leviticus 26 as a whole.

6. Close Connections between the Menaces/Curses in Leviticus 26 and Ezek 14:12–23 and Related Observations

6.1 Lexical and Phraseological Correspondences between Leviticus 26 and Ezek 14:12–23

a) חיה and שכל pi, together with the shared motif of the desolation of the land because of the wild animals (Lev 26:22; Ezek 14:15);[62]
b) שבר + ל + מטה־לחם (Lev 26:26; Ezek 14:13);[63]

---

57 Hoftijzer and van der Kooij, *Aramaic Texts*, 180; Crawford, *Blessing*, 132.
58 EST: Esarhaddon's Succession Treaty.
59 See Parpola and Watanabe, *Neo-Assyrian Treaties*, 46 (§47, ll. 448–450), 52 (§69, ll. 547–550), 53 (§76, ll. 570–572).
60 Parpola and Watanabe, *Neo-Assyrian Treaties*, 11, rev. IV 10–11.
61 Roth, *Law Collections*, 34–35.
62 See also Grünwaldt, *Heiligkeitsgesetz*, 358.
63 So also Gerstenberger, *Das dritte Buch Mose*, 383; Grünwaldt, *Heiligkeitsgesetz*, 359; Hartley, *Leviticus*, 466; Levine, *Leviticus*, 281; Wenham, *Leviticus*, 332.

c) שממה (Lev 26:33; Ezek 14:15–16);
d) בוא hi + חרב + על (Lev 26:25; Ezek 14:17);[64]
e) שלח + דבר (Lev 26:25; Ezek 14:19, 21).

As far as the question of the direction of a possible dependence is concerned:

The sequence "breaking the rod of bread" – "famine" in Ezek 14:13 can be explained as a short-hand reference to Lev 26:26 and 29, where these punishments are described in more detail. In addition, the noun לחם with the suffix of the second person plural masculine appears already in Lev 26:5, which makes its appearance in Lev 26:26 well motivated.

In the case of the correspondence between Lev 26:22 and Ezek 14:15, it can be observed that the latter text clarifies the unexplained relationship between the devastation brought about by the wild animals and the desolation of the roads in Lev 26:22, by inserting the causative preposition מפני, making it clear that the desolation of the land is not some further punishment, but the direct consequence of the devastation brought about by the wild animals.[65]

There is a lexical connection with Ezekiel 14 also in the following section of Leviticus 26: the combination of the verb מעל (act faithlessly) and the noun מעל (unfaithful act) appears both in Lev 26:40 and Ezek 14:13.

This supports the assumption that the menace section in Leviticus 26 forms a coherent whole also after the menaces/curses proper end.[66]

To the degree that Ezekiel can be shown to be dependent on Leviticus 26 and not the other way around, there is further proof that larger parts of Leviticus 26 must be pre-Ezekelian.

6.2 Further Lexical and Phraseological Connections between Leviticus 26 and Ezekiel

a) Apart from Job 31:13, only Lev 26:15, 43 and Ezek 5:6 and 20:13, 16, 24 combine the verb מאס (reject) with משפט or חקה as a direct object.[67]

b) Lev 26:19 has the construct גאון עז (pride of power). The exact same construct with the same pronominal suffix attached to עז is found only in Ezek 24:21,[68] while

---

64 So also Levine, *Leviticus*, 280–281. As opposed to the view taken here, Levine opines that this correspondence, together with other similar cases such as the construct מטה־לחם, is a sign of Leviticus being dependent on Ezekiel. The same phrase, always with YHWH in the role of the subject and his people or their land as the entity at the receiving end of the action, is also found in Ezek 6:3; 11:8; 29:8; 33:2–3. The first two are even closer to Lev 26:25 by showing the exact same form of the preposition (עליכם).
65 Thus also Lyons, *Law*, 83. Grünwaldt (*Heiligkeitsgesetz*, 358), however, without presenting specific reasons, implies that Lev 26:22 is dependent on Ezekiel (and Exod 23:29).
66 For more details see Zehnder, "Structural Complexity," 511–524.
67 See also Häner, *Nachwirken*, 155.

the construct with other pronominal suffixes attached to עז is also found in Ezek 30:6, 18; 33:28.[69] There are no further attestations of this construct in the Hebrew Bible.

c) Only in Lev 26:22 and Ezek 5:17 do we find instances where a form of the verb שלח, with YHWH in the role of the subject in the first person singular, is followed by חיה (among other nouns) in the role of the direct object. Similarly, in Ezek 14:21, the same two elements are found, but in reversed order.[70]

d) Leviticus 26:22 is also linked to Ezek 5:17 and 14:15 by the sequence of references to wild animals (חיה) and the topic of ravaging expressed by the verb שכל. Again, this sequence is found only in the three verses mentioned.[71]

e) Lev 26:22 is connected with Ezek 14:21 not only by the combination of חיה and שלח, but also by a combination of the verb כרת hi with בהמה as direct object. In this case, the direction of dependence is quite obvious: the phrase להכרית ממנו אדם ובהמה, as attested in Ezek 14:21, can be explained as a shortening of the more complex sentence והכריתה את־בהמתכם והמעיתה אתכם ונשמו דרכיכם, while there would be no clear and easy explanation for a possible expansion in Lev 26:22.

f) Leviticus 26:26 is linked to Ezek 4:16, 5:15 and 14:13 through the common use of the phrase "to break the staff of bread," in all cases with YHWH as subject, only attested once more, in Ps 105:16. Both in Lev 26:26 and Ezek 4:16, the phrase is followed by a phrase that juxtaposes לחם and במשקל to further underline the severity of the lack of sufficient food.[72] A similar combination of מאכל and במשקל is attested in Ezek 4:10. The fact that Ezekiel varies the exact wording of the description of the want of food[73] and expands it with a reference to the want of water, suggest that he is dependent on Leviticus 26 and not the other way around.[74]

The connection between Ezek 4:16 with Leviticus 26 is further strengthened by the shared use of the phrase עון + ב + מקק (see Lev 26:39), only found one more time, in Ezek 24:23.[75]

---

68 For details see Häner, *Nachwirken*, 288; cf. also Gerstenberger, *Das dritte Buch Mose*, 379; Levine, *Leviticus*, 186, 280. As opposed to Häner, Levine, without giving specific reasons, assumes that the parallel formulation points to Leviticus 26 being dependent on Ezekiel.
69 See also Grünwaldt, *Heiligkeitsgesetz*, 357; he assumes that Leviticus 26 is dependent on Ezekiel.
70 See also Hieke, *Levitikus*, 1079. Häner presents a list of further links between Ezek 5:8–17 and Lev 26 (see *Nachwirken*, 156).
71 Cf. Hartley, *Leviticus*, 465.
72 Cf. also Häner, *Nachwirken*, 156; Hieke, *Levitikus*, 1081; Levine, *Leviticus*, 187.
73 A third version is found in Ezek 12:18–19.
74 Thus Lyons, *Law*, 91.
75 Cf. Gerstenberger, *Das dritte Buch Mose*, 390; Hieke, *Levitikus*, 1088; Levine, *Leviticus*, 279. Based on such linguistic connections, Levine assumes a dependence of Leviticus 26 on Ezekiel, without providing any specific arguments for this view. The verb מקק is also attested in a similar context in Ezek 33:10. Without providing specific arguments, Grünwaldt (*Das Heiligkeitsgesetz*, 361–362, 372) assumes that Lev 26:39 is dependent on Ezek 33:10. However, the fact that the following verse, Ezek 33:11, culminates in a call for return (root שוב) shows

The fact that Ezek 4:16–17 can easily be explained as combining two distant passages in Leviticus 26 suggests that Ezekiel 4 is dependent on Leviticus 26 and not the other way around; and it also suggests that the passages in Leviticus 26 following the menace section proper were seen as an integral part of that chapter. The direction of dependence between Ezek 4:16–17 and Leviticus 26 can also be established by observing that Ezekiel 4 omits the reference to the "sins of the fathers," which is in line with Ezekiel's rejection of the notion of an intergenerational retribution. The same applies for the assessment of the relationship between Ezek 24:23 and Lev 26:39.[76]

g) There are a number of (at times close) links between Lev 26:30–31 and Ezek 6:3–6.[77] Among them, we note the destruction of the במות, the destruction of המניכם (your incense altars), the heaping up of the dead bodies (פגר) before גלוליכם (your idols), and the connection of their towns (עיר) with some realization of the root חרב.

In this case, the direction of dependence can clearly be established: In Ezek 6:3, the addressees are introduced as "mountains," while later in the passage "your bones" (v. 5) and "your dwelling places" (v. 6) are mentioned, presupposing human addressees, as in Leviticus 26.[78]

h) Leviticus 26:32 is closely related to Ezek 27:35, by the shared combination of the masculine plural construct of the verb ישב with a form of the verb שמם followed by the preposition על, expressing the state of terror that characterizes those who witness the punishment of the people of God.

i) The verb ריק hi (Lev 26:33) does not occur in Exodus–Numbers anywhere else, except for Exod 15:9.[79] Most attestations are found in Ezekiel (five times); three out of five attestations (Ezek 5:2, 12; 12:14) are in phraseological contexts that are very close to Lev 26:33, by having the verb ריק followed by אחר with a personal suffix and being used in a syntagmatic relationship with the noun חרב.[80]

In the case of Lev 26:33 and Ezek 5:2, 12 there is a clear hint at the direction of dependence: Ezekiel replaces the locution בגוים as the indicator of the destination of the divinely caused scattering of his people in Lev 26:33, expressed by the verb זרה,

---

that Ezekiel goes beyond the horizon of Leviticus 26, which suggests the inverted direction of dependence.

76 See also Lyons, *Law*, 62, 85.
77 See also Grünwaldt, *Heiligkeitsgesetz*, 360, 370 (postulating, without arguments, a dependence of Leviticus 26 from Ezekiel 6); Hartley, *Leviticus*, 467; Hieke, *Levitikus*, 1083 (postulating, without arguments, a dependence of Leviticus 26 from Ezekiel 6); Levine, *Leviticus*, 188–189 (claiming that Leviticus 26 paraphrases Ezekiel 6); Lyons, *Law*, 63; Wenham, *Leviticus*, 332. Häner (*Nachwirken*, 157) notes links between the whole passage Ezek 6:1–14 and Leviticus 26.
78 See Lyons, *Law*, 63 (with additional arguments supporting the direction of dependence from Leviticus 26 to Ezekiel 6).
79 Cf. Gerstenberger, *Das dritte Buch Mose*, 387; Levine, *Leviticus*, 189, 280. For Levine, this correspondence is a sign of Leviticus 26 being dependent on Ezekiel.
80 The other two occurrences are Ezek 28:7; 30:11.

with the locution לרוח, in accordance with the context of Ezekiel 5 which talks about a sign act in which, i.a., the prophet's hair is cast into the wind.[81]

j) Leviticus 26:33 and Ezek 19:7 share two phrases, the combination of עיר + root חרב (nominal in Lev 26:33, verbal in Ezek 19:7) on the one hand, and ארץ + root שמם (nominal in Lev 26:33, verbal in Ezek 19:7) on the other. It can be observed that both phrases are absolutely indispensable in Lev 26:33 to describe the completeness of the destruction brought about by God's judgment against his people, whereas in Ezek 19:7 we are dealing with a poetic, exaggerating image of the Judean king's power for a limited period of time, in every respect much more dispensable and random than in Leviticus 26, and therefore most likely secondary.

k) Ezekiel 36:33–35 contains two elements found in Lev 26:33: the description of the cities of God's people as חרבה, and the combination of the land of God's people with the root שמם (nominal in Lev 26:33, verbal in Ezek 36:34–35). The fact that the variant in Ezekiel is more elaborated and turned into an element of the description of the positive reversal of the state of the people of God, speaks to the Ezekelian version being dependent on Leviticus 26 rather than the other way around.[82]

Besides specific observations on the relationship between individual passages in Ezekiel and the menace/curse section of Leviticus 26, there is a more general aspect that helps to decide the question of the direction of dependence: While the menace section in Leviticus 26 is divided up in a serious of five paragraphs with the built-in expectation (and therefore, possibility) of a change of course on the side of the people, no such breaks are found in the Ezekelian passages that announce God's judgment on his people, for example in Ezekiel 5–7, where most lexical and phraseological / syntactical links with the menace/curse section of Leviticus 26 are found. In Ezekiel, the punishment is imminent (or actual), and no delay is possible any more. Had Leviticus 26 been dependent on Ezekiel, it would not be possible to explain why in Leviticus 26 all of a sudden the concept of Ezekiel is so drastically changed and the possibility of an avoidance of the judgment is opened up.[83]

There is a further observation that likely points the same way: While in Leviticus 26 there is an expectation that a change of mind among (later generations of) the exiles will – probably in a causative way – be followed by YHWH remembering the covenant with the fathers, such an expectation is replaced in Ezekiel by a more pessimistic view: The change of mind will occur only when YHWH has initiated the new salvation for his people; and his initiative is no longer motivated by any claim of relationship with the fathers, but the beneficiaries are only like foundlings not deserving anything.[84]

---

81 See Lyons, *Law*, 84.
82 See Lyons, *Law*, 100–101. The relevant verses in Ezekiel 36 may also be dependent on other passages within the book of Ezekiel itself (see Lyons, *Law*, 141).
83 Cf., e.g, Häner, *Nachwirken*, 158; Lyons, *Law*, 149–150.
84 Cf. Häner, *Nachwirken*, 289. The relevant texts in Ezekiel are especially Ezek 16:59–63; 20:40–

6.3 Connections between the Menace/Curse Section of Leviticus 26 and Other Parts of the Hebrew Bible outside of Ezekiel

a) The connection between eating and not being satisfied, as found in Lev 26:26, also occurs in Isa 9:19, Hos 4:10, and Mic 6:14. In the case of the latter, there is more overlap with the futility curses of Deuteronomy 28 than with Leviticus 26. In any event, it seems difficult to make a case for a direct dependence of either Isa 9:19, Hos 4:10 or Mic 6:14 on Lev 26:26 or the other way around. But the thematic parallel indicates that the motif that surfaces in Lev 26:26 is well attested in biblical texts that are very likely pre-exilic, perhaps dating to the 8th century BCE, which indirectly supports the case for a pre-exilic date of the menace section of Leviticus 26, especially since there is no later biblical attestation of the motif.

b) The phrase ולא אריח בריח ניחחכם in Lev 26:31b shows partial overlap with Amos 5:21–22,[85] where God's rejection of his people's cultic offerings is also expressed with לא אריח, a phrase that is found nowhere else in the Hebrew Bible. It looks as if Amos has expanded the compact formulation of Lev 26:31b, in the process breaking up the connection between the verb רוח and the noun ריח, deleting the latter. Again, this connection suggests a date in the 8th century BCE as the *terminus ante quem* for Leviticus 26.

c) The noun חמן ('incense altar'), used in Lev 26:30, is attested nowhere else in the Pentateuch. However, the majority of attestations are found in 2 Chronicles.[86] It may well be that this points to 2 Chronicles using Leviticus 26.

In the same verse (Lev 26:30) the verb שמד is used with במה as its direct object. Such a construction is only found again in Num 33:52 and Hos 10:8. It may be, then, that Hosea is again using a passage from Leviticus 26; but no certain proof can be given for this assumption.

d) The verb געל (+ נפש) appears once in the promise section and four times in the menace section proper and the subsequent passages in Leviticus 26. The repeated use of this verb is at the center of an artful play between God's loathing or not loathing and the people's loathing.

Outside of Leviticus 26, the verb occurs only four times in the Hebrew Bible, and only once more with נפש as the subject, in Jer 14:19. As far as the relationship between the latter verse and Leviticus 26 is concerned, it can be said that there is no reason to assume that Leviticus 26 has borrowed the phrase from Jer 14:19.[87] The role of the phrase is so central to Leviticus 26 that it is difficult to see it as a secondary, imported element. Moreover, the opposite direction of dependence would make good sense: The text in Jeremiah 14 takes up this central element of Leviticus 26 in an interrogative sentence and asks, whether now the time of blessing is over and the

---

44; 24:15–27.
85 This is also observed by Cathcart, "Curses," 142–143.
86 See 2 Chr 14:4; 34:4, 7.
87 *Pace* Levine (*Leviticus*, 280), who makes this claim without giving any specific reason.

time of curse has arrived. The assumption of a conscious intertextual relationship between Jeremiah 14 and Leviticus 26 is supported by the observation that the participle of כלה pi found in Lev 26:16 also occurs in Jer 14:12, and only one more time in the Hebrew Bible. However, because of the different syntagmatic contexts and the fact that the verse Jer 14:12 is not part of the same passage as Jer 14:19, caution against too confident conclusions in in place here. On the other hand, the combination of חרב and דבר as found in Jer 14:12 again finds a parallel in Lev 26:25.

6.4 The Use of the *Leitwort* קרי

The use of the *Leitwort* קרי in the menace/curse section proper of Leviticus 26 and the following verses in the same chapter with the meaning "enmity" may point to an early date of the (kernel of the) chapter, because this noun in his cognate form with exactly the same meaning is attested in Ugaritic texts only,[88] while it is not used in other parts of the Hebrew Bible and reappears in later Hebrew with a different meaning.

6.5 Connections to the "Holiness Code"

The linguistic connections between the menaces/curses of Leviticus 26 and the (rest of the) so-called Holiness Code in Leviticus 17–26 are not particularly strong. There are, however, many relationships to the preceding promise/blessing section, and some to Leviticus 25.[89]

The only remarkable lexical bridge between Leviticus 26 and priestly texts, including the "Holiness Code," is the noun ניחוח (soothing) in Lev 26:31. This noun occurs 45 times in the Hebrew Bible; 16 attestations are found in Leviticus (four of them in Lev 17–26), and 18 in Numbers.

The list of lexical peculiarities that distinguish Lev 26:14–33(/45) from other texts in the immediate and wider context is much longer than the list of similarities.

---

88 Cf. Hieke, *Levitikus*, 1079. In Akkadian, there is no cognate.
89 See, e.g., the importance of the number seven and the repeated use of the root שבת, or the combination of the nouns בהמה and חיה. Leviticus 25 also shows strong lexical and phraseological links with the promise/blessing section of Leviticus 26.

7. The Curse Section(s) in Deut 28:15–68

7.1 Complex Structure of the Curse Section in Deuteronomy 28

The curse section in Deuteronomy 28 is considerably more complex than the menace/curse section proper in Leviticus 26.

Four major parts can be identified:[90]

Part 1, Verses 16–19

This part consists of a sequence of four ארור-sentences in relatively close (negative) parallelism to the four ברוך-sentences in the preceding blessing section. However, the sequence of elements two and three is reversed.

The close connection between the blessings and the curses in vv. 16–19 make the verses of this part look "original".

Part 2, Verses 20–47

This part can be subdivided into (at least) two subsections, with v. 29 functioning as a pivot; the subsections are syntactically and topically interwoven with each other.

The opening consists of a series of sentences structured by the sequence imperfect + YHWH as subject: vv. 20–22, 25, 27–28. This pattern is again taken up in vv. 35–36.[91]

Verses 20–22 and 24 are connected by the shared description of the punishment with the use of עד indicating the catastrophic consequences.

Syntactically, v. 23 (heavens to bronze, earth to iron) does not fit in the context. Verse 25 is related to v. 7 in the blessing section.

Deut 28:29 is structurally multifunctional: It is an expansion of v. 28, as v. 26 is to v. 25, and it forms an *inclusio* with v. 26 *and* with v. 34. Both vv. 26 and 29 open with a form of the qal perfect consecutive of היה, and close with ואין + participle. They frame two sentences that begin with יככה יהוה. The second part of the verse reads like a general summary of despair and disaster.

Verses 30–33 form a group of futility curses, opening with the identification of the affected members of the household. Mostly, the first noun functions as the direct object, while the addressee is in the role of the subject. The futility curses continue in vv. 38–42; they all refer to the situation *inside* the Promised Land.

---

90 For a similar structuring see, e.g., Finsterbusch, *Deuteronomium*, 164–165; Tigay, *Deuteronomy*, 257, 261–274 (both, however, treat parts 1 and 2 as one part). Critical scholarship normally assumes that the various parts of the curse section can be attributed to different authors from different periods, with at least the later parts presupposing the Babylonian exile (see, e.g., Finsterbusch, *Deuteronomium*, 164–165; cf. also Wenham, *Deuteronomy*, 340; Tigay, *Deuteronomy*, 489, 491).

91 Verse 37 is an extension of v. 36.

Deut 28:34 is on the one hand an expansion of v. 33; at the same time, it serves as an introduction to the second part of the list that begins in vv. 20–25, extending to vv. 36/37.

Deut 28:35, with the repetition of the phrase לא־תוכל להרפא found in v. 27, creates a kind of *inclusio* of the passage ranging from Deut 28:27–35.

Deut 28:37, in its turn, is on the one hand an expansion of v. 36; at the same time, there are connections to the introduction and the end of the first part of the futility curses, והיית, as in vv. 29 and 33–34.

Verses 43–44 constitute the second last element. These verses take up the topic of the *ger*. This corresponds to the end of the second catalogue of blessings in vv. 12–13.

The last element is formed by the concluding formulations in vv. 45–47.[92]

It is also possible to argue for a coherent chiastic structure that covers vv. 23–42:[93]
A // A´ agricultural disaster (vv. 23–24 // vv. 38–42);
B // B´ defeat or exile leading to becoming a byword (vv. 25–26 // v. 36–37);
C // C´ inflammation (v. 27 // v. 35);
D // D´ madness (v. 28–29a // v. 34);
E // E´ constantly abused (v. 29b // v. 33b);
F oppression (vv. 30–33a).

While v. 41 does not fit into this pattern, and while syntactical repetitions are not accounted for, such an arrangement makes very good sense in terms of topical coherence.

The following parts show only minimal connections with the blessing section, and no clear links with Leviticus 26 either. This may be a hint at their literarily being detached from the two previous parts, as some kind of (later?) expansions. However, this is not certain.[94]

Part 3, Verses 48–57

The topic of this part is the situation in the Promised Land under foreign occupation. The theme of the eating of one's own children is the one that is most elaborated (vv. 53–57).

Verse 48 is a summarizing opening that presents the other side of the coin of v. 47.

---

92 For Tigay, the dividing line goes between v. 44 and v. 45 (see *Deuteronomy*, 267–268, 491–492). Verse 45 is interpreted by him as a hinge joinging vv. 46–57 with vv. 15–44, with the double function of concluding the section in vv. 15–44 and introducing the new section in vv. 46–57 (see *Deuteronomy*, 268, 492).
93 See Tigay, *Deuteronomy*, 491.
94 Cf. the elaborate and helpful discussion of the question whether the last two segments are original or not in Tigay, *Deuteronomy*, 491–492.

Verse 51 exhibits the last clear reference to the blessings; it is, however, somewhat redundant.[95]

Part 4, Verses 58–68

Verse 58 clearly marks the opening of a new paragraph. Verses 59–68 are structured by the sequence *waw*-perfect + YHWH which is repeated three times (vv. 59, 64, 68). There is also an *inclusio* by the double use of מצרים in vv. 60 and 68. Verse 63 marks the transition to the situation in the diaspora. Verse 64 refers back to v. 36, while v. 67 refers back to v. 34.

The most salient special features of this final part are:

a) It presents a kind of an overall retrospective view.

b) In vv. 58 and 61, "writing" and "book" are mentioned. This may imply that the primary focus here is on later generations who will be familiar with the curses not through Mosaic oral communication,[96] but only in written form.

c) The language is heavily "Deuteronomic", even more than in the previous parts.

The first two features could be interpreted as indicating that this part is a later addition. Features one and three could be interpreted in a source-critical way: As opposed to the previous parts, where the material is partly drawn from pre-existing traditions, in the last part it is more or less exclusively the Deuteronomic author himself who adds his concluding, summarizing remarks.

In addition, we also note that verses 62–64 are closely parallel with Deut 4:26–28:[97]

Deut 4		Deut 28	
V. 25	When you become the father of children and children's children and have remained long in the land, and act corruptly, and make an idol in the form of anything, and do that which is evil in the sight of the LORD your God so as to provoke Him to anger,		
V. 26	I call heaven and earth to witness against you today, that you shall surely perish quickly from the land where you are going over the Jordan to pos-	V. 63	And it shall come about that as the LORD delighted over you to prosper you, and multiply you, so the LORD will delight over you to make you perish

---

95 It looks like a case of "recycling".
96 Which is presupposed by the formulation of the text.
97 Translation NASB 1977.

	sess it. You shall not live long on it, but shall be utterly destroyed.		and destroy you; and you shall be torn from the land where you are entering to possess it.
V. 27a	And the LORD will scatter you among the peoples	V. 64a	Moreover, the LORD will scatter you among all peoples, from one end of the earth to the other end of the earth;
v. 27b	and you shall be left few in number among the nations, where the LORD shall drive you.	V. 62	Then you shall be left few in number, whereas you were as the stars of heaven for multitude, because you did not obey the LORD your God.
V. 28	And there you will serve gods, the work of man's hands, wood and stone, which neither see nor hear nor eat nor smell.	V. 64b	and there you shall serve other gods, wood and stone, which you or your fathers have not known.

It is possible to assume that Deuteronomy 4 draws on Deuteronomy 28. This makes especially sense when Deuteronomy 4 as a whole is understood as a late compilation of various elements of Deuteronomy – which is obviously a defensible view.[98] Alternatively, one could also assume that an identical (late?) author is responsible for both passages. Or it could be surmised that the author of the fourth part of Deuteronomy 28 uses material found in Deuteronomy 4. This possibility cannot be rejected out of hand, especially because of the fact that Deuteronomy 4 does not contain the phrase "from one end of the earth to the other end of the earth," which makes it possible to interpret the situation envisaged in Deut 4:26–27 as one in which the Israelites are scattered among the peoples and nations of Canaan only.[99]

What is new in Deuteronomy 28 is that the phrase "few in numbers" is now unequivocally related to the situation in the diaspora.

7.2 Signs of Possible Literary Disturbances in Deut 28:15–68

Overall, most of the language in the curse section of Deuteronomy 28 is quite Deuteronomic or Deuteronomistic, which gives the impression that for the larger part this section is "authentic."[100] There are, however, some possible disturbances:

a) Deut 28:23 does not fit the context in terms of phraseology. On the other hand, the content of the verse connects well with the following verse.

---

98 Otto ("Gesetzbuch," 132) assumes that Deut 4:23–31 is the work of late authors of the Persian period.
99 Thus also Craigie, *Deuteronomy*, 140.
100 For details see Zehnder, "Fluch und Segen," 201–205.

b) Deut 28:37 might be seen as being in tension with v. 36 insofar as v. 36 mentions a גוי as the place where the Israelites are led to, while v. 37 talks about עמים. However, this shift may also be interpreted as reflecting poetical parallelism, in which semantically related terms are exchanged, combined with a shift in number.[101]

7.3 Overlap with Other Biblical Texts Outside of Leviticus 26

a) *Deut 28:21 and Jer 14:12; Ezek 5:12; 6:12:* In these four verses, and nowhere else in the Hebrew Bible, is there a combination of the noun דבר *deber* and the verb כלה *klh* pi.

b) *Deut 28:25, 37 and Jer 24:9:*[102] In this case, Jer 24:9 seems to combine elements of two verses in Deuteronomy 28: Jer 24:9a is parallel to Deut 28:25b (the addressees as a terror to all the kingdoms of the earth), while Jer 24:9b is parallel to Deut 28:37 (the addressees as a horror, proverb, and taunt among all the places or peoples where they will be driven). The combination has the effect to intensify the impression of horror, which is likely the goal of this literary strategy.[103]

c) *Deut 28:27, 35 and Jer 19:11 / Hos 5:13:* The phrase לא־תוכל להרפא is found exclusively in Deut 28:27, 35 on the one hand and Jer 19:11 (לא־יוכל להרפה) on the other. A similar phrase is found in Hos 5:13, with לרפא instead of להרפא.

d) *Deut 26:33 and Hos 5:11:* In both cases, the verb רצץ is used, as well as עשוק and the phrase הלך אחר.

e) *Deut 28:38–40 and Mic 6:15:* Both texts speak about the mismatch between sowing (in both cases using the root זרע) and ingathering, and the failure of the crops of olive and wine. There seems to be no clear evidence for a dependence in one or the other direction.

f) *Deut 28:48 and Jer 28:14:* Another case of an exclusive relationship is attested here. In both cases, YHWH is said to lay (literally, "give", נתן) a yoke of iron (על ברזל) on the neck (צואר) of the people. As far as the question of dependence is concerned, Fischer observes that "[t]he international extension of the object [in Jer 28:14] may be a sign of a process of deliberate reworking and widening".[104]

g) *Deut 28:49 and Jer 5:15:* In a further instance of an exclusive parallel, both verses speak of a nation from afar (גוי מרחוק), whose language is not understandable to the addressees. In this case, it is possible to identify a clear line of dependence: While Deut 28:49 uses a somewhat cryptic phrase, גוי אשר לא־תשמע לשנו, Jer 5:15 is much clearer: a people whose language you do not know, nor can you "understand"

---

101 For similar parallelisms of גוי and עם see, e.g., Deut 4:6(–8); 32:21; Josh 3:14–17; 4:1–2; Ezek 36:15; Ps 96:3, 10; 106:34–35.
102 As far as the connections with passages in the book of Jeremiah are concerned, Fischer notes that "no other chapter of the Hebrew Bible has more links to Jer than Deut 28," and that this relationship is particularly condensed in Jeremiah 29–32 (Georg Fischer, "Fulfilment," 46).
103 See Fischer, "Fulfilment," 48.
104 Fischer, "Fulfilment," 47.

(תשמע) what they say. Thus, it appears that Jeremiah clarifies what is elliptic in Deuteronomy.

h) *Deut 28:51 and Jer 31:12 / Hos 2:10, 24:* The sequence of דגן, תירוש and יצהר is attested in both verses. A relative majority of attestations of this triad is found in Deuteronomy, with five more attestations in addition to Deut 28:51, while it only appears once in the book of Jeremiah. Therefore, it is likely that the attestation in Jer 31:12 is dependent on the one in Deut 28:51. The same triad is also attested in Hos 2:10, 24.

The list shows that there are a number of instances where Jeremianic texts can be shown to be dependent on Deuteronomy 28, which tendentially supports a pre-exilic dating for the latter.[105] Some parallels with texts from 8th century prophets further corroborate this assumption.

7.4 Overlap with Esarhaddon's Succession Treaty (EST) and Other Extra-Biblical Texts

a) There is some overlap with EST; however, this is less decisive and exclusive than is sometimes claimed.[106] There are also connections with other extra-biblical texts, as the following paragraphs show.

b) In Deut 28:38–39, we find a sequence of locusts and worms damaging the agricultural produce of the land. The same sequence appears in the curse section of the Aramaic treaty between Bar-Ga'yah and the King of Arpad:[107]

> "For seven years may the locust devour (Arpad), and for seven years may the worm eat."[108]

c) The same passage in Deuteronomy 28 (more specifically, Deut 28:38) speaks about the fact that the cursed people will carry seed into the fields but gather little. A close parallel is found in the treaty document of Tell Fekheriyeh from about 830 BCE:

> "And let him sow but not harvest. And let him sow one thousand barley (measures) and let him recover a paris from it."[109]

> "Let him plough – let him not harvest. Let him plough one thousand – let him recover one BAN."[110]

---

105 Unless, of course, one assumes a post-exilic date for the traditions preserved in all the relevant verses of Jeremiah.
106 For details see Zehnder, "Building on Stone?," 351–374, 511–516.
107 This is also observed by Cathcart, "The Curses", 147–148.
108 Fitzmyer, *Sefire*, 44–45, Sf I 27.
109 Kaufman, "Reflections," 163 (ll. 18–19 of the Aramaic version).
110 Ibid., ll. 30–32 of the Akkadian version.

d) The last two lines of the Akkadian version of the Tell Fekheriyeh inscription show some overlap with Deut 28:21–22, 27, 59–61 by mentioning a series of plagues and illnesses that will fall on the recipients of the curse:

"Headache, plague, sleeplessness will not be cut off from his land."[111]

e) There is a clear thematic connection between Deut 29:22 ("all its land is brimstone and salt, a burning waste, unsown and unproductive, and no grass grows in it") and a line of the Sefire treaty:[112]

"May Hadad sow in them salt and weeds".[113]

There are also parallels with Hittite vassal oaths, as the following paragraphs show.

f) The unusual sequence of curse – blessing – curse, as attested to in Deuteronomy 27–28, is also found at the end of the treaty between Shattiwaza of Mittanni and Shuppiluliuma I of Hatti.[114]

g) The sequence of field and vineyard as domains being affected by the curse, as found in Deut 28:38 and 51, is attested frequently in the Hittite vassal treaties, but not otherwise.[115]

h) One of the *kudurrus* of Merodach-Baladan I of Babylonia (first half of the 12th century BCE) has a curse that comes close to what is found in Deut 29:22 ("all its land is brimstone and salt, a burning waste, unsown and unproductive, and no grass grows in it"):

"Adad, der Deichgraf des Himmels und der Erde, möge Salpeter seine Felder unbrauchbar machen lassen und (sie) Getreide entbehren lassen; er möge keine Vegetation wachsen lassen."[116]

i) There are also close thematic parallels with the Code of Hammurabi (CH). The following table shows the overlap between Deuteronomy 28, Leviticus 26, EST and CH:[117]

Deut 28	Lev 26	EST	CH
v. 15	**v. 14–15**		**XLIX 18–28**
But it shall come about,	But if you do not		(But) should that

---

111 Kaufman, "Reflections," 163 (ll. 37–38 of the Akkadian version).
112 This is also observed by Cathcart, "The Curses," 150.
113 Fitzmyer, *Sefire*, 46–47, Sf I A 36.
114 See Beckman, *Hittite Diplomatic Texts*, 52–54.
115 See Beckman, *Hittite Diplomatic Texts*, 17, 33 (and in reversed order on p. 92). See also the sequence "prosperity in the country, fertility of man, cattle, sheep, grain (and) wine" in KUB xv ii 23–24 (see Pritchard, *Ancient Near Eastern Texts*, 353).
116 Borger, "Grenzsteinurkunden, 15 (SB 33, Kol. III, 11′–15′).
117 The translation of the biblical passages is from NASB 1977; for EST, see text and translation in Parpola and Watanabe, *Neo-Assyrian Treaties*; for CH, see text and translation in Roth, *Law Collections*, 133–140.

if you will not obey the LORD your God, to observe to do all His commandments and His statutes with which I charge you today, that all these curses shall come upon you and overtake you.	obey Me and do not carry out all these commandments, if, instead, you reject My statutes, and if your soul abhors My ordinances so as not to carry out all My commandments, *and so break My covenant*,		man not heed my pronouncements, ... and should he slight my curses and not fear the curses of the gods, and thus overturn the judgments that I rendered **LI 84–91** May the god Enlil ... curse him with these curses and may they swiftly overtake him.
v. 21–22, 27 The LORD will make the pestilence cling to you until He has consumed you from the land, where you are entering to possess it. The LORD will smite you with consumption and with fever and with inflammation and with fiery heat and with the sword and with blight and with mildew, and they shall pursue you until you perish. ... The LORD will smite you with the boils of Egypt and with tumors and with the scab and with the itch, from which you cannot be healed.	**v. 25, 16** I will also bring upon you a sword which will execute vengeance for the covenant; and when you gather together into your cities, I will send pestilence among you, so that you shall be delivered into enemy hands. ... I will appoint over you a sudden terror, consumption and fever that shall waste away the eyes and cause the soul to pine away; also, you shall sow your seed uselessly, for your enemies shall eat it up.	**§ 38A–39** May Anu ... let disease, exhaustion, malaria, sleeplessness, worries and ill health rain upon all your houses. May Sin, the brightness of heaven and earth, clothe you with leprosy and forbid your entering into the presence of the gods of king.	**LI 50–69** May the goddess Ninkarrak ... cause a grievous malady to break out upon his limbs, an evil demonic disease, a serious carbuncle which cannot be soothed, which a physician cannot diagnose, which he cannot ease with bandages, which, like the bite of death, cannot be expunged.
v. 23 And the heaven which is over your head shall be bronze, and the earth which is under you, iron.	**v. 19** And I will also break down your pride of power; I will also make your sky like iron and your earth like bronze.	**§ 63** May all the gods that are [mentioned by name] in th[is] treaty tables make the ground as narrow as a brick for you. May they make your ground like iron (so that) nothing can sprout from it.	
v. 24 The LORD will make		**§ 64** Just as rain does	**L 64–71** May the god Adad ...

the rain of your land powder and dust; from heaven it shall come down on you until you are destroyed.		not fall from a brazen heaven so may rain and dew not come upon your fields and your meadows; instead of dew may burning coals rain on your land.	deprive him of the benefits of rain from heaven and flood from the springs.
v. 25 The LORD will cause you to be defeated before your enemies; you shall go out one way against them, but you shall flee seven ways before them, and you shall be an example of terror to all the kingdoms of the earth.	**v. 17** And I will set My face against you so that you shall be struck down before your enemies; and those who hate you shall rule over you, and you shall flee when no one is pursuing you.		**L 81–91** May the god Zababa … smash his weapon upon the field of battle; may he turn day into night for him, and make his enemy triumph over him.
v. 26 And your carcasses shall be food to all birds of the sky and to the beasts of the earth, and there shall be no one to frighten them away.	**v. 22** And I will let loose among you the beasts of the field, which shall bereave you of your children and destroy your cattle and reduce your number so that your roads lie deserted.	**§ 41** May Ninurta … fell you with his fierce arrow; may he fill the plain with your blood and feed your flesh to the eagle and the vulture. **§ 59** May Palil, the fore[most] lord, let eagles and vultures [eat your f]lesh.	
v. 28–29 The LORD will smite you with madness and with blindness and with bewilderment of heart; and you shall grope at noon, as the blind man gropes in darkness, and you shall not prosper in your ways; but you shall only be oppressed and robbed continually, with none to save you.	**v. 16a** I will appoint over you a sudden terror, consumption and fever that shall waste away the eyes and cause the soul to pine away;	**§ 40** May he (i.e., Shamash) remove your eyesight. Walk about in darkness!	**XLIX 68–72** May he (i.e., Enlil) cast as his fate a reign of groaning, of few days, of years of famine, of darkness without illumination, and of sudden death. **L 2–6** May he (i.e., Ea) deprive him of all understanding and wisdom, and may he lead him into confusion.
v. 30 You shall betroth a wife, but another man	**v. 16b** also, you shall sow your seed uselessly,	**§ 42** May Venus … before your eyes	

shall violate her; you shall build a house, but you shall not live in it; you shall plant a vineyard, but you shall not use its fruit.	for your enemies shall eat it up.	make your wives lie in the lap of your enemy; may your sons not take possession of your house, but a strange enemy divide your goods.	
v. 32 Your sons and your daughters shall be given to another people, while your eyes shall look on and yearn for them continually; but there shall be nothing you can do.			**XLIX 53–54, 74, 80** May Enlil, the lord, the determiner of destinies . . . order . . . the dispersion of his people.
v. 41 You shall have sons and daughters but they shall not be yours, for they shall go into captivity.			
v. 64 Moreover, the LORD will scatter you among all peoples, from one end of the earth to the other end of the earth; and there you shall serve other gods, wood and stone, which you or your fathers have not known.			
v. 36 The LORD will bring you and your king, whom you shall set over you, to a nation which neither you nor your fathers have known, and there you shall serve other gods, wood and stone.	**v. 33** You, however, I will scatter among the nations and will draw out a sword after you, as your land becomes desolate and your cities become waste.		**LI 19–23** May she (i.e., Ishtar) deliver him into the hands of his enemies, and may she lead him bound captive to the land of his enemy.
v. 45 So all these curses shall come on you and pursue you and overtake you until you are destroyed, because you would not obey the LORD your God by			**LI 84–91** May Enlil, by his word which cannot be altered, curse him with these curses, and may they come upon him quickly!

keeping His commandments and His statutes which He commanded you.			
v. 48 Therefore you shall serve your enemies whom the LORD shall send against you, in hunger, in thirst, in nakedness, and in the lack of all things; and He will put an iron yoke on your neck until He has destroyed you.			**XLIX 53–54, 66–67, 80** May Enlil, the lord, the determiner of destinies . . . determine . . . years of famine.
v. 53–57 Then you shall eat the offspring of your own body, the flesh of your sons and of your daughters whom the LORD your God has given you, during the siege and the distress by which your enemy shall oppress you. The man who is refined and very delicate among you shall be hostile toward his brother and toward the wife he cherishes and toward the rest of his children who remain, so that he will not give even one of them any of the flesh of his children which he shall eat, since he has nothing else left, during the siege and the distress by which your enemy shall oppress you in all your towns. The refined and delicate woman among you, who would not venture to set the sole of her foot on the ground for delicateness and refinement, shall be	**v. 29** Further, you shall eat the flesh of your sons and the flesh of your daughters you shall eat.	**§ 47** . . . Instead of grain may your sons and your daughters grind your bones . . . In your hunger eat the flesh of your sons. In want and famine may one man eat the flesh of another; may one man clothe himself in another's skin; may dogs and swine eat your flesh. **§ 69** Just as [thi]s ewe has been cut open and the flesh of [her] young has been placed in her mouth, may they make you eat in your hunger the flesh of your brothers, your sons and your daughters.	

| hostile toward the husband she cherishes and toward her son and daughter, and toward her afterbirth which issues from between her legs and toward her children whom she bears; for she shall eat them secretly for lack of anything *else,* during the siege and the distress by which your enemy shall oppress you in your towns. | | | |

It is worth noting that those elements that occur both in Deuteronomy 28 and Leviticus 26 also have a correspondence in either EST or CH (and only rarely in both). Overall, parallels with CH are slightly more frequent than parallels with EST.

j) The motif of foreign enemies eating up the produce of the land, as attested in Deut 28:33, is found frequently, i.a., in the Babylonian omen series Šumma Izbu.[118]

All these parallels make it highly probable that many elements in the curse section of Deuteronomy 28 are not just pre-exilic, but reflect very old ancient Near Eastern curse traditions.

8. Relationship between the Curses/Menaces in Deuteronomy 28 and Leviticus 26

8.1 Substantial Thematic Connections, But Little Lexical Overlap

The thematic connections between Leviticus 26 and Deuteronomy 28 are substantial,[119] but close lexical overlap is rare.[120] This is inconclusive when it comes to assess the question of a direct literary relationship.

The list of topics dealt with in the curse/menace sections of Leviticus 26 and Deuteronomy 28 combined contains about 90 elements. About half of the elements found in Leviticus 26 have close parallels in Deuteronomy 28,[121] while the others

---

118 See Leichty, *Omen Series*, e.g. 41 (Tablet 1 94).
119 See, e.g., Fischer, "A Need for Hope?," 379.
120 Thus also Levine, *Leviticus*, 277.
121 As far as the five menace sections proper in Leviticus 26 are concerned, the following items can be mentioned: consumption and fever (Lev 26:16); seed is sown, but the enemies eat the

have no direct counterpart in Deuteronomy 28. What is not found in Deuteronomy 28 is primarily the announcement of the destruction of non-yahwistic cultic installations and the theological topos of the making up of the missed sabbaths.[122]

The high degree of shared topical elements in Leviticus 26 and Deuteronomy 28 could be interpreted as pointing to a specific Israelite/biblical curse tradition, or to a dependence on a broader ancient Near Eastern curse tradition. It would also be natural to assume that EST as well drew from this tradition.

The two options do not exclude one another. The large amount of connections of the biblical texts as well as EST both with the epilogue of CH, Babylonian and Assyrian curse texts of the 2nd millennium and Aramaic curses of the 9th and 8th centuries give support to the latter option.

8.2 Some Clear Cases of Linguistic Overlap

a) The two sicknesses mentioned in Lev 26:16 (שחפת and קדחת, parallel to Deut 28:22);[123]

b) the sequence מדיבת נפש + מכלות עינים in the same verse, Lev 26:16 (parallel to דאבון נפש + כליון עינים in Deut 28:65);

c) the comparison of sky and earth with iron and bronze in Lev 26:19b (parallel in Deut 28:23, though with reversed identification).[124] Lev 26:19 uses נחשה for "bronze", whereas Deut 28:23 has נחשת. The latter is the common word in the Hebrew Bible. This could point to a temporal sequence Leviticus 26 – Deuteronomy 28, with the latter "normalizing" the antiquated language of the former. Apart from this, in the case of the parallels between Lev 26:19 and Deut 28:23, the differences make it unlikely that there is direct dependence in either direction; rather, the alternative assumption that both texts, and also the related version found in EST (§ 63), take up independently a common tradition, is preferable.[125] This model also explains

---

produce (Lev 26:16); being struck down by the enemies and fleeing before them (Lev 26:17); sky like iron and earth like bronze (Lev 26:19); pestilence (Lev 26:25); eating the flesh of the children (Lev 26:29); desolation of the land and settling of foreigners in it (Lev 26:32); scattering among the nations (Lev 26:33).

122 The two elements (the first directly, the second indirectly) are also noted by, e.g., Cholewinski, *Heiligkeitsgesetz*, 312. In addition, also the "breaking of the pride of power" (Lev 26:19), land and trees not yielding their produce (Lev 26:20), wild beasts killing humans and domestic animals (Lev 26: 22), breaking the "staff of bread" and eathing without being satisfied (Lev 26:26) are elements not found in Deuteronomy 28.

123 See also, e.g., Levine, *Leviticus*, 185, 278. Grünwaldt (*Das Heiligkeitsgesetz*, 355) takes it for granted that Lev 26:16 is dependent on Deut 28:22.

124 See also Levine, *Leviticus*, 186, 278.

125 Thus also Milgrom, *Leviticus 23–27*, 2309. Grünwaldt (*Heiligkeitsgesetz*, 357), however, assumes that Leviticus 26 is dependent on Deuteronomy 28, without providing any compelling argument.

best why neither the vocabulary nor the simile are attested anywhere else in the Hebrew Bible.

Interestingly, in both verses of Leviticus 26 that have close linguistic parallels in Deuteronomy 28, there are features that can at least theoretically be interpreted in terms of linguistic disturbances on the side of the version of Leviticus 26. However, on the side of Deuteronomy 28 this is true for v. 23 as well.

One could also argue that the fact that the closest parallels in Deuteronomy 28 to Leviticus 26 appear side by side, points to them being dependent on Leviticus 26. A scenario is easily conceivable in which the author(s) of the curse section(s) in Deuteronomy 28 have split up topics that were found in Lev 26:16 and added to them further elements. If one would give preference to the opposite direction of dependence and assume that Lev 26:16 were dependent on Deut 28:65, it would be difficult to explain why the nominal constructs were replaced by verbal phrases. The scenario proposed here is all the more plausible since it can often be observed in the Deuteronomic law collection that material from earlier law collections was used in this way.[126] However, a common dependence on traditional material cannot be ruled out either.

8.3 Further Instances of Minor Lexical Overlap

a) Both in Lev 26:17 and Deut 28:25 the flight before the enemies is described with the verb נגף.[127] The verb is typical neither of Leviticus or the Holiness Code nor of Deuteronomy. One instance could be dependent on the other, with the direction of dependence being unclear;[128] or both could be dependent on a common tradition; or both could be original in both places.

b) Both Lev 26:6 and Deut 28:26 use of the phrase ואין מחריד. The verb חרד is not found in any other passage either in Leviticus or the Holiness Code or in Deuteronomy, so that it is not possible to argue that the phrase is more naturally at home in one of the two texts.

8.4 Turn of Focus to the Situation in Exile

A turn of the focus to the situation in exile towards the end of the curse sections is found both in Leviticus 26 and in Deuteronomy 28. In both cases, the description of

---

126 See Zehnder, "Observations," 204, 210, 212, 227–229.
127 Thus also Levine, *Leviticus*, 185, 278.
128 Grünwaldt (*Heiligkeitsgesetz*, 355) postulates that Lev 26:17 is dependent on Deut 28:25, because of the motif (in its inverted form) being attested also in Deut 28:7. However, it is questionable whether this argument is strong enough to decide the case.

the situation in exile is not very precise, and both focus on the aspect of fear. The only (possible) precise element, the ships sailing back to Egypt in Deut 28:68, cannot be related to specific historical circumstances in a straightforward way.[129]

8.5 Why Leviticus 26 Cannot be Assumed to Be Late and Dependent on Deuteronomy 28

It cannot be *presupposed* that the menaces/curses of Leviticus 26 are late and dependent on Deuteronomy 28. Several reasons speak against such a presupposition:

a) The individual menaces of Leviticus 26 are contextually meaningful, including those that are closely parallel to Deuteronomy 28 (and in one case also to EST).

b) There are no hints that Leviticus 26 looks like a simple abbreviation of Deuteronomy 28; the chapter as a whole, including the menace section proper, is too well structured in itself.

c) The shift in identification of "sky" and "earth" in their metaphorical relationship with bronze and iron, which distinguishes Lev 26:19 from Deut 28:23, does not fit with the assumption of a direct dependence of the version found in Leviticus 26 on the the version found in Deuteronomy 28, even if one cannot exclude such an explanation *a priori* either.

8.6 The Curse Section of Deuteronomy 28 Is More Complex than Its Counterpart in Leviticus 26

This observation in itself might point to Deuteronomy 28 being later than Leviticus 26, but it is not conclusive.

As mentioned above, most of the language in the curse section of Deuteronomy 28 is very Deuteronomic or Deuteronomistic, which does not indicate a broad or strong dependence on Leviticus 26.

---

[129] If in fact "ships" are mentioned in the verse. Craigie suggests that "in ships" must really be rendered as "in ease, casually" (*Deuteronomy*, 352–353). Tigay mentions that the phrase, with a slight revocalisation, can also be interpreted in the sense of "in mourning, in a lamentful condition" (*Deuteronomy*, 273).

8.7 The Curse Section of Deuteronomy 28 is Linguistically More Closely Related to the Rest of Deuteronomy than Leviticus 26 is to the Rest of Leviticus or the Holiness Code

It can be observed that the curse section of Deuteronomy 28 is linguistically more closely related to the rest of Deuteronomy than Leviticus 26 is to the rest of Leviticus or the Holiness Code.[130]

This could be interpreted as supporting the view that Leviticus 26 is the closing not only of a postulated Holiness Code, but of something bigger, most likely the corpus of texts related to the Sinaitic covenant, perhaps even the "middle piece" of the Pentateuch consisting of Exodus-Leviticus-Numbers as a whole, as possible candidates.[131] Together with the observation that Leviticus 26 has a number of parallels with other curse texts outside the Bible, this could point to the curses in Leviticus 26 being heavily influenced by common ancient Near Eastern curse traditions.[132]

The curses in Deuteronomy 28, on the other hand, could perhaps be relatively more independent, because in their case connections with extra-biblical curse traditions are rather sporadic only, while there is a thorough linguistic connection with Deuteronomy.

8.8 Compact Formulation in Leviticus 26 vs. Elaborate and Repetitive Formulation in Deuteronomy 28

In several instances, when Deuteronomy 28 and Leviticus 26 deal with the same topics, Leviticus 26 provides the shorter variant, while there is repetition and elaboration in Deuteronomy 28, with the repetition and elaboration taking place in more than one passage within Deuteronomy 28. This seems to suggest some kind of dependence of Deuteronomy 28 on Leviticus 26.

Examples are the following four topics:

Illness	Lev 26:16	→ Deut 28:22, 27–28, 59–61
Enemies	Lev 26:17	→ Deut 28:25–26, 30–33, 48–52
Drought	Lev 26:19–20	→ Deut 28:23–24, 40
Deportation	Lev 26:33a	→ Deut 28:36–37, 63–68

---

130 For the linguistic embedding of Deuteronomy 28 in the context of the book of Deuteronomy see Zehnder, "Fluch und Segen," 201–205.
131 Or in theory something smaller, for example just the unit of Leviticus 25–26.
132 Thus (following Reventlow) Hillers, *Treaty-Curses,* 40.

8.9 Theological Development

Deuteronomy 28:63 talks about God's "joy" to destroy (אבד hi) and ruin (שמד hi) his people. It might be argued that this goes beyond what is found in Leviticus 26.

8.10 In Some Cases Prophetic Texts Exhibit Connections to Both Leviticus 26 and Deuteronomy 28 at the Same Time

a) *Isaiah 65:23*: In this verse, which is part of an oracle that promises to the future positive turn of the state of the people of God in which the deprived conditions of the past will be reversed, there is a lexical connection with Lev 26:16, 20 via the shared used of the expression לריק, and with Lev 26:16 via the shared use of the noun בהלה. At the same time, via the shared use of the noun זרע with the meaning "descendants," there is also a connection with Deut 28:46, 59.

b) *Jeremiah 7:33–34*: The first verse, stating that the corpses of the people of God will be food for the birds of heaven and the beast of the earth, is more or less identical with Deut 28:26b, including the added concluding formula ואין מחריד (which is also found in Lev 26:6aβ). Except for the concluding formula, the relationship between the two verses is exclusive.[133] The next verse begins with the verb שבת hi in the first person singular with YHWH as subject, just as in Lev 26:6, where the verb is also preceded immediately by the formula ואין מחריד. Verse 34 is also related to Leviticus 26 via the noun חרבה, which appears both in Lev 26:31 and 33.

c) *Jeremiah 9:15*: This verse is related to Deut 28:64 (and partially 30:3) via the shared use of the verb פוץ hi with YHWH as subject and his people as the object of the scattering; via ב + עמים / גוים as the indication of the location of the scattering; and via the phrase "which you and your fathers did not know." The link with Lev 26:33 is established through the shared motif of YHWH sending the sword behind his people (הריקתי in Lev 26:33, שלחתי in Jer 9:15).

d) *Jeremiah 11:10*: The construct phrase עונת אבתם appears in this exact form only in Jer 11:10 and Lev 26:39. The phrase "to follow after other gods to serve them", on the other hand, is well attested in Deuteronomy, including Deut 28 (vv. 14, 36; see also Deut 29:25). The concluding phrase "to break the covenant" is attested in Lev 26:15, 44 on the one hand and Deut 31:16, 20 on the other, with the specific formulation attested in Deut 31:16 coming closest to the one found in Jer 11:10.

e) *Jeremiah 19:7–9*: Jeremiah 19:7 has several lexical links with Leviticus 26. The combination of the verb נפל with the nouns חרב and איב is also found in Lev 26:7 and 36, with just one further attestation in the whole of the Hebrew Bible. The second part of Jer 19:7 is closely parallel to Deut 28:26a (the bodies of the addressees

---

133   See also Fischer, "Fulfilment," 45–46.

as food for the birds of heaven and the beasts of the earth), with three further attestations of quasi identical phrases in Jeremiah (Jer 7:33; 16:4; 34:20), and nowhere else. In the following verse, Jer 19:8, the noun שמה (horror) is shared with Deut 28:37. The verb שמם in the same verse is one of the key words of Leviticus 26 (vv. 22, 31, 32, 34, 35, 43). Jeremiah 19:9 goes on with the prediction that the addressees will eat their sons and daughters, just as in Lev 26:29 and Deut 28:53, 55, with the formulation in Lev 26:29 being closest to the one in Jeremiah 19. In the same verse, the noun מצוק is used, which is one of the key words of Deuteronomy 28 (vv. 53, 55, 57), and only used two more times outside of the two contexts (1 Sam 22:2; Ps 119:143). An additional indication of Jeremiah 19 being dependent on Leviticus 26 and Deuteronomy 28 is that only Jer 19:9 has God directly causing the eating of the children, which "looks like an aggravation of the more neutral and theologically less offensive statement"[134] in Leviticus 26 and Deuteronomy 28.

f) *Jeremiah 34:17, 20*: In this passage, which is an oracle of doom against the Jerusalemites shortly before the destruction of the city at the hands of the Babylonians, lexical and thematic overlaps are found in v. 17 with Lev 26:25–26 via the shared sequence of חרב and דבר, followed by the theme of hunger (expressed briefly in Jer 34:17 with the noun רעב, and at more length in Lev 26:26).[135] At the same time, Jer 34:20b is practically identical with Deut 28:26a (their bodies as food for the birds of heaven and the beasts of the earth), as is the case with Jer 19:7b.[136]

g) *Ezekiel 4:17*: The combination of מקק and עון is also found in Lev 26:39 (and only one more time, as seen above, in Ezek 24:23), while the expression composed of the verb חסר with the objects לחם ומים finds a close analogue in Deut 28:48, which mentions רעב, צמה, and חסר כל.

h) *Hosea 4:9–10*: Hosea 4:9 uses the noun מעלל to describe the misdeeds of God's people that he will punish on them, as in Deut 28:20. The following verse Hos 4:10, as noted earlier, combines the verbs אכל and שבע to describe a situation in which there is not enough food to be satisfied, as in Lev 26:16.

i) *Amos 4:6–11*:[137] In its overall structure, the passage seems to be parallel with Lev 26:14–33, by presupposing that YHWH sends punishments, in five stages, in order to provoke a positive reaction from the side of his people, while the latter stubbornly refuses to listen.[138] Also the rhetorical structure of YHWH speaking in

---

134 Fischer, "Fulfilment," 47.
135 Cf. Hieke, *Levitikus*, 1080. Additionally, the noun רעב is also attested in Deut 28:48.
136 See Fischer, "Fulfilment;" Bergsma, *Jubilee*, 167–168.
137 A thorough discussion of the relationship between Leviticus 26 and Amos 4:6–12 is provided by Kessler, "Patterns," 943–984. With some right, he makes a distinction in principle between Deuteronomy 28 on the one hand as a text representing the group of "[l]onger series of [descriptive] maledictions functioning as threats and deterrents," and Leviticus 26 and Amos 4 as representatives of the group of "[l]onger series of incrementally applied [descriptive] maledictions intended to produce change and/or repentance" ("Patterns," 953).
138 So also, e.g., Kessler, "Patterns," 957; Levine, *Leviticus*, 276. However, according to Kessler ("Patterns," 969), there is a difference between the two texts in that only Leviticus 26 has the

the first person singular, addressing his people in the second person plural, is parallel. The fact that the people's reaction is expressed with the verb שוב in Amos 4 (vv. 6, 8, 9, 10, 11), as opposed to Leviticus 26, may be taken as a hint to Leviticus 26 preceding Amos 4.[139] The noun לחם in Amos 4:6 is parallel to Lev 26:5, 26, while absent from Deuteronomy 28. The same is true for the noun גשם (Amos 4:7 // Lev 26:4), and for the sequence שבע + לא (Amos 4:8 // Lev 26:26).[140] One can also point to the importance of the phrase ונתתי in Amos 4:6 (with גם אני inserted between ו and נתתי) and Lev 26:17, 19, 30–31.[141] On the other hand, the combination of נכה hi with שדפון (blight) and ירקון (mildew) connects Amos 4:9 with Deut 28:22. A juxtaposition of, among others, כרם and זית and their produce being eaten by either locusts or worms connects Amos 4:9 with Deut 28:39–40. The combination of שלח and דבר, as attested in Amos 4:10, is also found in Lev 26:25, while the connection between plague or disease and Egypt as attested in the same verse in Amos 4 is also found in Deut 28:27, 60. The connection between מהפכה and סדם is found both in Amos 4:11 and Deut 29:22.

Prophetic texts such as these are most naturally explained as combining pre-existing elements found in Leviticus 26 and Deuteronomy 28.[142] All other explanations,

---

whole nation in view and at the same time lacks the gaps between the calamities that are typical of Amos 4. Against this it can be argued both of these claims are not convincing. The same is true for Kessler's contention that the plagues of Leviticus 26 reach a more horrific level than those in Amos 4 (see "Patterns," 972).

If one assumes that Amos 4:6–11 is an exilic text, as proposed, e.g., by Gerstenberger (*Das dritte Buch Mose*, 377), it does not function as a proof for an early date of Leviticus 26 or Deuteronomy 28 even if Leviticus 26 or Deuteronomy 28 could be shown to be source texts used in Amos 4. Gerstenberger, however, does not give any reasons for his late dating of the passage. For an exilic dating of Amos 4 see also Jeremias, *Amos*, 70–72. Stuart, on the other hand, belongs to those who assume a pre-exilic (likely 8th century) dating; see Stuart, *Hosea–Jonah*, 337. Grünwaldt, without giving specific reasons, argues that at least the "Plagensteigerungsschema" was taken over by the author of Leviticus 26 (see *Heiligkeitsgesetz*, 356). Kessler, while assuming that there is "some real literary relationship" between Leviticus 26 and Amos 4 ("Patterns," 975), tends to see the later layers of Leviticus 26 (broadly identified as consisting of vv. 34–35, 40–45) as being written later than Amos 4, while both the earlier layers of Leviticus 26 and Amos 4 "creatively reconfigured the traditional stock of ancient Near Eastern curse vocabulary for use within various theological streams" (see "Patterns," 977–983, citation from p. 983).

139 This is of course only true if one assumes that שוב represents a later development in the conception of the response expected by the people than the one presented in Leviticus 26.

140 Kessler ("Patterns," 962) points to close and encompassing topical parallels between Amos 4 and Leviticus 26: The famine of Amos 4:6 has its parallel in Lev 26:20, 26; the drought of Amos 4:7 has its parallel in Lev 26:19; YHWH's smiting in Amos 4:9 has its parallel in Lev 26:24; the plague of pestilence in Amos 4:10 has its parallel in Lev 26:25; the raging of the sword in Amos 4:11 has its parallel in Lev 26:25, 33.

141 Also the promise section of Leviticus 26 uses ונתתי: Lev 26:4, 6, 11.

142 For a general discription of the phenomenon of harmonization / coordination / combination / collation / conflation / blend see Rom-Shiloni, "Compositional Harmonization," 913–942.

implying some kind of dependence of either Leviticus 26 or Deuteronomy 28 (or both) on the prophetic texts, are much more complicated. Generally, conflation is a sign for the conflating text being later than the sources.[143] In terms of dating, the Jeremianic texts likely indicate a *terminus ad quem* for both catalogues in late pre-exilic times.

The combination of elements both from Leviticus 26 and Deuteronomy 28 again shows that none of the two catalogues replaced (or was meant to replace) the other.

8.11 Most Elements of Both Catalogues Reflect Common Ancient Near Eastern *Topoi*

Practically all elements of both catalogues reflect common ancient Near Eastern *topoi*, even where there is no exact phraseological overlap between the biblical and the extra-biblical texts. This can be gleaned from a comparison between the biblical texts and, e.g., the omen series Šumma Izbu which was mentioned already above. The latter mentions frequently the following topics that also appear in Leviticus 26 and Deuteronomy 28: lack of rain;[144] famine;[145] pestilence;[146] plague;[147] madness and confusion;[148] war and defeat in battle;[149] enemies taking possession of the land's produce;[150] the land being laid waste and scattered;[151] desecration of shrines;[152]

For her assessment of the literary combinations of Priestly and Deuteronomic texts in Jeremiah see pp. 920–941. She thinks that the Jeremianic examples show a familiarity "with pentateuchal materials in their preliminary stages, ... not with a written and redacted book of the Torah" ("Compositional Harmonization," 922); these materials were already seen as authoritative (see "Compositional Harmonization," 941). Whether one leans more to the first or the second option as far as the question of the literary stage of the pre-texts is concerned is of no consequence for the present investigation.

Kessler misses this point in the case of Amos 4:6–11 by not taking into account the overlap between Amos 4 and Deuteronomy 28(–29). For him, the absence of key theological concepts of Leviticus 26 in Amos 4 speaks to the possibility of the latter using the former (see "Patterns," 976–978). However, there is no rule that compels the borrower to use the same theological framework as found in the source text and thereby go beyond the eclectic reference to only some of the elements contained in the source text.

143 See, e.g., Lyons, *Law*, 66.
144 See, e.g., Leichty, *Omen Series*, 51 (Tablet II 59′).
145 See, e.g., Leichty, *Omen Series*, 50 (Tablet II 48′).
146 See, e.g., Leichty, *Omen Series*, 46 (Tablet II 6).
147 See, e.g., Leichty, *Omen Series*, 81 (Tablet V 90)
148 See, e.g., Leichty, *Omen Series*, 46 (Tablet II 3); 58 (Tablet III 39).
149 See, e.g., Leichty, *Omen Series*, 57 (Tablet III 38); 109 (Tablet VIII 73′).
150 See, e.g., Leichty, *Omen Series*, 123 (Tablet X 26′).
151 See, e.g., Leichty, *Omen Series*, 48 (Tablet II 27); 54 (Tablet III 13).
152 See, e.g., Leichty, *Omen Series*, 47 (Tablet II 19).

exile.[153] Similar observations can be made with respect to the promise/blessing sections.[154]

On the other hand, there are *topoi* common in the ancient Near East that are lacking in Leviticus 26 and Deuteronomy 28, such as descriptions of what happens to the enemy or his land, internal strife or revolts, including conflicts between various social groups, and a specific focus on the king and his house. The last two of these differences suggest that the biblical texts reflect a background in which kingship and a marked social stratification where not yet – or no longer – found. While the lack of any developed reflection of kingship might point both to an early and a post-exilic setting, the last point primarily fits an early, pre-monarchic setting.

9. The Passages Following the Curse/Menace Section Proper in Leviticus 26

9.1 Structural Observations

The main fivefold curse cycle proper ends in v. 33; but soft breaks start already at the transition from v. 31 to v. 32. After that we find a series of further developments ("after-thoughts"), arranged in a very sophisticated manner, forming a logical and temporal sequence, with its beginning marked with the אז of v. 34.[155] The main blocks are:

34–35	the land (ארץ תרצה);
36–38(/39)	the exiles' vanishing existence;
(39/)40–41	positive change in the exiles' minds and hearts (הם ירצו);
	41a *flashback*: God's anger, expulsion (הלך בקרי);
42–45	God's remembrance of the covenant
	43 *flashback*: the land, the exiles' repenting (הם ירצו ארץ תרצה).[156]

---

153   See, e.g., Leichty, *Omen Series*, 174 (Tablet XVIII 5).
154   The element of (food) abundance is found, e.g., in Leichty, *Omen Series*, 79 (Tablet V 61–62); for peace see, e.g., Leichty, *Omen Series*, 112 (Tablet VIII 100′); for victory see, e.g., Leichty, *Oment Series*, 116 (Tablet IX 20′).
155   For details see Zehnder, "Structural Complexity," 503–530; for another recent explanation of the passage see Fischer, "A Need for Hope?," 370–378.
156   There are many different views on the structure of these passages. Hieke, for example, proposes a chiastic structure of vv. 42–45, with v. 44aα as the center (which looks quite awkward; see Hieke, *Levitikus*, 1091). Grünwaldt (*Heiligkeitsgesetz*, 114–121) argues for the literary unity of vv. 34–45.

The line of developments described in these verses makes sense, though it is often suggestive and open to different structural interpretations and to different interpretations as far as the meaning of crucial verbs (and sometimes other words) is concerned. One might also argue that the sophistication borders on an excessive amount of complexity, which in turn could be understood as a hint to the involvement of different hands composing the text. But this is not a necessary conclusion.[157]

9.2 The Question of the Literary Unity of Lev 26:14–45

To judge from the contents alone, it seems impossible to determine with absolute certainty whether vv. 34–45 belong to the preceding sequence of menaces/curses. However, the close linguistic relations between the latter and the former make this assumption plausible, though not absolutely certain.

The plausibility of the assumption of literary unity is enhanced by the observations adduced in the following paragraph.

9.3 Passages in Ezekiel Drawing Both on the Menace/Curse Section Proper and the Subsequent Passages

The fact that several passages in Ezekiel seem to draw simultaneously on both the menace/curse section proper of Leviticus 26 and the passage starting with vv. 34 and 39/40 gives the impression that for the author(s) of those Ezekelian texts, Leviticus 26 was accessible as a unified whole. The impression of unity is also present if the direction of dependence is reversed. However, the direction goes very likely from Leviticus 26 to Ezekiel, because the latter seems to apply the technique called "splitting and recombination," a technique which can also be observed, i.a., in Deuteronomy or Deutero-Isaiah.[158]

Here are the most salient examples:

a) *Ezekiel 4:16–17*: The two following elements are combined:[159] שבר מטה־לחם, as in Lev 26:26; נמקו בעונם, as in Lev 26:39.

b) *Ezekiel 15:7–8*: The tree following elements are combined: פני + נתתי + preposition *beth*, as in Lev 26:17 (and nowhere else in the Hebrew Bible); combina-

---

157 Most critical scholars argue for a composite nature of Leviticus 26, with different (exilic and postexilic) authors being responsible for the passages following the menace/curse section proper; see, e.g., Levine, *Leviticus*, 275–281.
158 For Deuteronomy see Zehnder, "Literary and Other Observations," especially 204, 210, 212, 227–229; for Deutero-Isaiah see Sommer, *Prophet*, 68–69 (and passim).
159 Both of them are not exclusive to the two passages, but very rare (the combination of מקק and עון, in fact, is only found one more time, in Ezek 24:23).

tion of the verb מעל with the noun מעל, as in Lev 26:40; combination of ארץ and שממה, as in Lev 26:33.

c) *Ezekiel 16:59–63*:[160] The five following elements are combined: להפר ברית, as in Lev 26:15, 44; זכרתי את־בריתי, as in Lev 26:42, 45;[161] בריתי followed by כי אני יהוה, as in Lev 26:44; the contrast הפר – הקים, as in Lev 26:9 and 15; הקימותי אני את־בריתי אתך, as in Lev 26:9.

In this case, it can be assumed without problems that Ezekiel 16 is dependent on Leviticus 26: Ezekiel refers back to Leviticus 26, including the latter's hope passage, and adds (in v. 63) the explicit element of כפר, which is missing in Leviticus 26, and identifies (in v. 60) the new ברית as a ברית עולם. If it is postulated that the dependence goes the other way around, one would need to explain why Leviticus 26 takes away these elements from Ezekiel 16. Moreover, Ezek 16:61, 63 add the element of "shame" as a result of YHWH's remembering his people, which in turn is related to the situation of the foundling in Ezek 16:3–5. This element is linked to an important theological difference between Ezekiel 16 and Leviticus 26: While in the latter a process is described in which an acknowledgment of guilt precedes YHWH's remembrance of the covenant, in Ezekiel 16 it is only the beginning salvation brought about by YHWH that leads to a process of contrition and acknowledgment of guilt on the side of his people.[162] This concept is more drastic and goes beyond what is found in Leviticus 26.

Besides chapter 16, the specific Ezekelian concept of the future restoration is also expressed in Ezek 11:14–21; 20:33–44; 28:25–26; 34:11–16, 23–31; 36:8–15, 32–38; 37. In many cases, there are linguistic links with Lev 26:39–43. However, the concept in Ezekiel is different from the one presented in Leviticus 26, by depicting the people as basically incorrigible, and restoration (therefore) not being contingent on the people's repentance, but on God's initiative alone.[163]

d) *Ezekiel 18:17–20*: The two following elements are combined: Keyword עון, as in Lev 26:39, 40, 41, 43; combination of משפט and חקה, as in Lev 26:15, 43.

Again, a line of dependence leading from Leviticus 26 to Ezekiel 18 is more natural than the reversed one. Ezekiel 18 deletes the connection to the guilt of the fathers that is found in Leviticus 26, and uses the topic of the addressees' guilt as part of the process that leads to the call for repentance / turning around (שוב, vv. 21 and 23),[164] which in its explicitness goes beyond what is found in Leviticus 26.

e) *Ezekiel 20:8–9*: The four following elements are combined: חמה, as in Lev 26:28; גלול, as in Lev 26:30; יצא hi + preposition *min* + ארץ + מצרים, as in Lev 26:45; לעיני הגוים, as in Lev 26:45.

---

160 Cf. also Häner, *Nachwirken*, 283–284; Hieke, *Levitikus*, 1094; Levine, *Leviticus*, 184, 191.
161 See also Ganzel and Levitt Kohn, "Ezekiel's Prophetic Message," 1082. The combination of ברית + hi פרר and ברית + זכר is also found in Jer 14:21.
162 See Häner, *Nachwirken*, 284. The same situation as in Ezekiel 16 is also found in Ezek 20:30–44 (see especially v. 43).
163 See Lyons, *Law*, 86–88.
164 See Häner, *Nachwirken*, 285.

There is a clear sign of the secondary nature of the passage in Ezekiel in that the phrase "the nations among whom they lived" in Ezek 20:9 does not fit the immediate context that deals with the Israelites' still living in Egypt, not among the nations.

f) *Ezekiel 22:15–16*: The two following elements are combined: זרה בגוים, as in Lev 26:33; לעיני הגוים combined with אני יהוה, as in Lev 26:45.

g) *Ezekiel 24:21–24*: The six following elements are combined: מקדש as in Lev 26:31; גאון עזכם as in Lev 26:19; sequence of חרב and נפל, as in Lev 26:7, 8, 36; combination of אכל and לחם, as in Lev 26:5, 26; מקק בעונות, as in Lev 26:39; כי אני יהוה, as in Lev 26:44.

h) *Ezekiel 25:7*: The two following elements are combined: כרת hi as in Lev 26:22; אבד as in Lev 26:38 (with change from qal to hi).

9.4 Relatively Undeveloped Character of the Description of the New Hope in Leviticus 26

In the passage(s) describing the new hope in Leviticus 26, there is no explicit mention of a repentance of the people manifest in outward acts, or of a return of the exiles to the land, or of a forgiveness of their sins (though this may be *implied* in ירצו את־עונם), or of the institution of a "new" (let alone everlasting) covenant.

This looks "old," and older than what is described in Deuteronomy 29–31. It is much less than what we find in a whole range of prophetic oracles concerning the restitution of Israel after the judgment.

9.5 Reference to Leviticus 26 in Late Texts

There are two prime examples for the reference to passages from Leviticus 26 following after the menace/curse section proper in late texts:

a) The phrase תרצה הארץ את־שבתתיה (Lev 26:34, similar v. 43) is found outside of Leviticus 26 only in 2 Chr 36:21. Remarkably, however, it is connected in this passage with Jeremiah, even though the same phrase is not found in Jeremiah. Rather, in Jeremiah the reference is to the 70 years of exile (Jer 25:11; 29:10), or three generations of exile (Jer 27:7). The author of 2 Chr 36:21, then, seems to combine Leviticus 26 and Jeremiah.[165]

b) The phrase והתודו את־עונם ואת־עון אבתם (Lev 26:40) has a close analogue in Neh 9:2, even if the wording is not exactly parallel. As in the case of 2 Chr 36:21, nothing stands in the way to assume that the author of Nehemiah 9 may have used a much older text. However, how much older cannot be deduced with precision.

---

165 So also, e.g., Hieke, *Levitikus*, 1086.

In any event, these observations show that Leviticus 26, including the passages following the menace/curse section proper – similarly to the case of Deuteronomy 28 – was known in late biblical periods.

9.6 The Widespread Attestation of the Concept of Salvation after Catastrophe

The eventual salvation of a remnant after a far-ranging catastrophe as part of God's judgment is not a new phenomenon in the broader biblical canonical context. The stories of Noah's family or Lot's family can be mentioned as prime examples, and within the Exodus tradition episodes like God's punishment after the adoration of the golden calf also point in the same direction.[166] Even more importantly, this motif is attested early and broadly in ancient Near Eastern literature, from the Sumerian period onward.[167] All of this makes the latter parts of Leviticus 26 look quite "natural" after the menace/curse section proper.

10. Deuteronomy 29ff.

The themes of blessing and curse, and a renewal of the relationship between God and his people after the implementation of the curses, in parallel with Leviticus 26, are found in Deuteronomy after the end of chapter 28.

10.1 The Sequence of Events in Deuteronomy 29–30(/31/32)

Deuteronomy 28–30(/31/32) forms a meaningful sequence of events, in many respects comparable to what is found in Leviticus 26.[168]

a) In Deut 29:18–20, reference is made to "the words of this curse," "all the curse that is written in this book", and "all the curses of the covenant that is written in the book of this law". This is a new perspective, in which the curses are (described as) contained in a written ברית, in the book of the תורה.

---

166 For further examples see, e.g., Hasel, *Remnant*, 389–393.
167 See Hasel, *Remnant*, 382–385.
168 In critical scholarship references to the future beyond the establishment of the covenant at Moab, as they are found in Deuteronomy 29–31/32, are usually understood to be reflections of events that are located in the present or in the past for the real historical addressees after the exile; see, e.g., Ehrenreich, "Tora," 216.

b) From Deut 29:21 onward, an era is envisioned in which the plagues and illnesses have become reality in the land, during the time of the דור האחרון.

c) Verse 26 of the same chapter makes explicitly clear that the desolate condition of the land is the result of the application of "the curse that is written in this book" (הקללה הכתובה בספר הזה).

d) The next verse (Deut 29:27) says that the Lord has expelled them, "as it is this day." Here, then, the perspective is clearly related to a later period.

As in the curse section of Deuteronomy 28, there is a sequence "in the country – in the exile." But otherwise, there are no clear lexical connections. The exception is the identification of the main cause for the punishments, the Israelites' going after אלהים אחרים.[169] Details about the situation in exile that would show familiarity with it are missing. Also, the perspective seems to be from someone living in the land. At this point, in terms of the identification of a *terminus ad quem* for the fomulations of these passages, we are not led further down the chronological line than the mid-sixth century.

e) There is a further change in Deut 30:1 with the introduction of the addressees in the second person singular. The line of events that is unfolded opens with the particle כי, which exhibits certainty about what is to come. This is, firstly, certainty about the implementation of the curses (קללה). The Israelites will sit בכל־הגוים; that is the starting point. But already in this verse, there is mention of שוב (turn), related to לבב (heart).

f) The motif of שוב is taken up in the next verse, Deut 30:2: ושבת עד־יהוה ... (*waw*-consecutive): if you turn to the Lord (?); or: (then) you will return to the Lord, and listen to his voice.

g) The motif of שוב is also found in the following verse, Deut 30:3: Also the Lord will turn (שׁב), and gather you from all the peoples.

h) Deuteronomy 30:5 adds: He will bring you to the land that your fathers possessed. The implication here is that the returnees are a later generation.

i) Deuteronomy 30:6 says: He will circumcise your heart; [with the consequence that] you will love him from all your heart.[170]

k) Deuteronomy 30:7 mentions another aspect: He will put the curses on the enemies.

l) After that, there is a somewhat new beginning in Deut 30:8: ואתה תשוב: and you, now, turn around, and listen to the voice of the Lord. Verses 2 and 8 are closely parallel, which is an important clue for the reconstruction of the structure of the passages under investigation.

m) The next verse (Deut 30:9), mentions a new blessing, directly related to Deut 28:4 and 28:63 (שוש).

n) From Deut 30:11 onward, there is a return back to the "now" of Moses and the people gathering in the plains of Moab.

---

169 See Deut 28:14, 36, 64: Deut 29:25. The phrase is again attested in Deut 30:17; 31:18, 20.
170 Cf. Deut 6:5; 10:12 (and v. 16: מול); 11:13.

o) This changes again in Deut 31:16 and the following verses, where the camera (figuratively speaking) turns to the future: The people will leave the Lord; he will hide his face from them, and they will perish. But then, they will ask themselves whether their calamities are not a consequence of the Lord forsaking them? But the Lord will keep his face hidden from them. Verse 19: Now therefore, write this song for yourselves, and teach it to the sons of Israel.

p) Positive notions of God's relationship with his people are found again in chapter 32 (vv. 36, 39, 43).[171] This means that the dark outlook of Deut 31:16–18 is not the last word. Rather, in various ways the Song of Moses goes beyond the prophecy of doom and contains a number of elements that point to a salvation of a rest of the people.[172]

10.2 Close Parallels with Deuteronomy 4

The same sequence as in Deuteronomy 28–30(/31) also occurs in Deut 4:25–31:[173]

a) *Deuteronomy 4:25*: When you become the father of children and children's children and have remained long in the land, and act corruptly, and make an idol in the form of anything, and do that which is evil in the sight of the Lord your God so as to provoke Him to anger,

b) *Deuteronomy 4:26*: I call heaven and earth to witness against you today, that you shall surely perish quickly from the land where you are going over the Jordan to possess it. You shall not live long on it, but shall be utterly destroyed.

c) *Deuteronomy 4:27*: And the Lord will scatter you among the peoples, and you shall be left few in number among the nations, where the Lord shall drive you.

d) *Deuteronomy 4:28*: And there you will serve gods, the work of man's hands, wood and stone, which neither see nor hear nor eat nor smell.

e) *Deuteronomy 4:29*: But from there you (pl.) will seek the Lord your God, and you (sg.) will find Him if you search for Him with all your heart and all your soul.

The first of the two sentences begins with a *waw*-consecutive; a conditional understanding of the clause is not warranted.

f) *Deuteronomy 4:30*: When you are in distress and all these things have come upon you, in the latter days (באחרית הימים), you will return (שוב) to the Lord your God and listen to His voice.

---

171   There is no explicit mention of the exile (or the return from exile). But the exile is presupposed by the frame.

172   See Otto, "Gesetzbuch," 136.

173   This relationship is also noted, e.g., by Tigay, *Deuteronomy*, 53–54. See also Otto, "Gesetzbuch," 134. For him, Deut 29:21–27 is a repetition of the announcement of the breach of the covenant and the consequent anger of God in Deut 4:23–28, while Deut 30:1–10 is a repetition of the announcement of the salvation of a rest of the people after the catastrophe of the exile in Deut 4:25–31.

The translations are from NASB 1977.

Again, there is clearly no condition here. We also note that Deut 4:30 is parallel to Deut 30:2, 8.

g) Deuteronomy 4:31: For (כי) the Lord your God is a compassionate God; He will not fail you nor destroy you nor forget the covenant with your fathers which He swore to them.

There are a number of lexical / phraseological connections between Deuteronomy 4 and Deuteronomy (28/)29–31.[174] However, Deut 4:29 contains an important element not found in Deuteronomy 28–31: "seek the Lord" (דרש). In view of the importance of this concept in the message of the prophets, one might consider whether this is a hint at Deuteronomy 4 reflecting potentially later developments where Deuteronomy 28–31 are more conservative. The statement that YHWH will "not forget the covenant" (v. 31) connects Deuteronomy 4 with Leviticus 26. The temporal location of Deuteronomy 4 is indicated in v. 30: באחרית הימים.

Deuteronomy 4:25–31 shows that at the time of the writing of this passage, the developments described in Deuteronomy 28–30/31 were seen as a coherent series of events. If one assumes that Deuteronomy 4 precedes Deuteronomy 28–30/31 chronologically, then this can be identified as the one big source text for parts of the changes visible in Deuteronomy 28ff. as compared to Leviticus 26.[175]

The concept of "return" (root שוב) manifest in Deuteronomy 4 and 30, is different from the one manifest in prophetic texts, insofar as it is envisaged only as occurring after the punishment in Deuteronomy, while there are calls to "return" in prophetic texts that aim at preventing the punishment from happening.[176] This difference likely points to the respective texts in Deuteronomy predating the message of the prophets.

However, the possibility remains that both Deut 4:29–31 as well as Deut 30:1–10 may be interpolations from exilic times.[177] On the other hand, the observations adduced below as well as the interpretation of Lev 26:14–45 as a coherent whole show that such a view is not to be taken for granted and would need further evidence to be entertained.

---

174 To name only a few random examples: The verb שחת hi appears both in Deut 4:25 and 31:29; the same is true for the verb כעס hi. The sequence of the qal infinitive absolute followed by a qal imperfect of the root אבד is found both in Deut 4:26 and 30:18. Both in Deut 4:27, 28:64 and 30:3 the Lord is said to scatter (פוץ hi) or have scattered his people.
175 Cf. Fischer, "A Need for Hope?," 384: "Unless one supposes literary operations in both passages, it is more probable that Deut 28–30 develops the program laid down in Deut 4, and thus also [as in Lev 26] corresponds to an original plan".
176 See Tigay, *Deuteronomy*, 54.
177 Thus, e.g., Tigay, *Deuteronomy*, 432.

10.3 Close Parallels between Deuteronomy 29–30(/32) and Jeremiah 29; 30; 32

a) *Jeremiah 29:13–14*: Jeremiah 29:13 is very closely parallel to Deut 4:29, while Jer 29:14 is parallel to Deut 30:3–4.[178]

What is the likely direction of dependence (if any)? The following assumption seems to be the most natural: Jeremiah 29:13–14 combined Deut 4:29 and Deut 30:3–4.[179] The hope indicated in these texts is projected in Jeremiah 29 on the period of the future return from Babylon. There are additional pieces of evidence that point in the same direction: That Jer 29:13 is likely dependent on Deut 4:29 can be deduced from the fact that the phrase בכל־לבבך is frequent in Deuteronomy, but only attested once in Jeremiah. Also, לבב is the typical noun for "heart" in Deuteronomy, while Jeremiah normally uses לב.[180] On the other hand, we note that the verb בקש, while found often in Jeremiah, is only attested one more time in Deuteronomy apart from Deut 4:29 (in Deut 13:11). As far as Jer 29:14 is concerned, it is easier to explain this verse as a simplification of a syntactically more complicated passage in Deut 30:3–4, streamlining and eliminating seemingly unnecessary elements like ורחמך in Deut 30:3. It can also be observed that Jer 29:10–14, as opposed to the immediate literary contexts of Deut 4:29 and 30:3–4, makes a somewhat composite impression. For example, the doubling of the mention of YHWH bringing back his people in v. 10 and v. 14 can well be accounted for by the latter verse being dependent on another source. There is a further aspect that is worth mentioning: At the beginning of the passage of which Jer 29:13–14 is a part, in v. 10, reference is made to a previous word of YHWH. This previous word cannot be identified with Jer 25:11–14, because in this passage it is only mentioned that after 70 years YHWH will punish Babylon, but nothing is said about the bringing back of the people – as opposed to what we find in Jer 29:13–14. Thus, the likely candidate for the previous word is Deuteronomy 4 or 28.

All of this means that the *terminus ante quem* for Deuteronomy 4 and 30 is Jeremiah's letter to the exiles as attested in Jeremiah 29.

b) *Jeremiah 30*: As far as Jer 30 is concerned, we note the following links with both Deuteronomy 28–31 as well as Leviticus 26:

Jeremiah 30	Shared element	Leviticus 26	Deuteronomy 28–31
30:3	שוב שבות,[181]		30:3–5

---

178 Thus also Fischer, *Jeremia 26–52*, 99–100.
179 Cf. Vanoni, "Anspielungen," 385, 387–389. He argues for the dependence of Jer 29:13 on Deut 4:29, but leaves the case of Jer 29:14 open.
180 Thus also Vanoni, "Anspielungen," 387.
181 Also in Jer 30:18.

			(exclusive link)
	and ארץ + ירש + אבות		
30:5	פחד		28:66–67
30:6	ירקון		28:22
30:7	ישע (also 30:11)		28:29, 31
30:8	צואר + על		28:48[182]
30:8	עבד (with foreigners as object)		28:48
30:9	עבד (with YHWH as object)		28:47; with אלהים אחרים as object: 28:14, 36, 64; 30:17
30:10	אל־תירא and אל־תחת		31:8
30:10	מושיע		28:29, 31
30:10	שבי (also 30:16)		28:41
30:10	שוב		28:31, 60, 68; 30:1–3, 8–10
30:10	אין מחריד	26:6	28:26
30:11	פוץ		28:64; 30:3
30:11	יסר	26:18, 23, 28	
30:12	מכה (also 30:14, 17)	26:21	28:59, 61; 29:21
30:13	רפואה, (and רפא in 30:17)		28:27, 35 (רפא)[183]
30:14	נכה	26:24	28:22, 27, 28, 35; 29:6
30:14	עון (and 30:15)	26:39–41, 43	
30:15	חטאת	26:18, 21, 24, 28	
30:17	נדח		30:1, 4, 17
30:18	רחם		30:3
30:18	ישב	26:5, 32, 35	28:30; 29:15; 30:20
30:19	רבה	26:9	28:63; 30:5, 16
30:19	מעט	26:22	
30:22	לעם + ל, לאלהים + ל		29:12
30:23	חמה	26:28	29:22, 27
30:24	אחרית הימים		31:29

What is the likely direction of dependence (if any)? This is difficult to assess in general. The *prima facie* impression is: Jeremiah heavily relies on Deuteronomy 28–

---

[182] In this case, it is possible that Jer 30:8 is not directly dependent on Deut 28:48, but on Isa 10:27 (see, e.g., Fischer, *Jeremia 26–52*, 126).

[183] See also Fischer, *Jeremia 26–52*, 129–130.

31, but also draws on Leviticus 26 here and there. Tendentially, it follows even the sequence of passages found in the two source texts.

Exemplary investigations can also point to a dependence of Jeremiah on Deuteronomy, as the two following examples show:

- Jeremiah 30:3 may be simplifying the double attestation of ירש in Deut 30:5.
- The iron yoke "given" on Israel's neck in Deut 28:48 is removed from it in Jer 30:8, with a simplifying omission of "iron"; also, in Jer 30:8 it is removed for good, which goes beyond the formulation in Deut 28:48. In this case, the opposite direction of dependence is all but impossible.

c) *Jeremiah 32:36–44*: As far as Jer 32:36–44 is concerned, we note the following links with both Deuteronomy 28–31 as well as Leviticus 26:

Jeremiah 32	Shared element	Leviticus 26	Deuteronomy 28–31
32:36	חרב	26:25, 33, 36, 37	28:22
32:36	רעב		28:48
32:36	דבר	26:25	28:21
32:37	קבץ		30:3, 4
32:37	נדח		30:1, 4, 17
32:37	קצף + חמה + אף		29:27;[184] 29:22: אף + חמה
32:37	שוב hi		28:60, 68; 30:1
32:37	בטח + ישב	26:5	
32:39	לב + נתן		28:65; 29:3
32:40	to give into the heart, יראה or s.th. else		30:6
32:41	יטב hi / שוש + על + יטב טוב		28:63; 30:9 (exclusive parallel; יטב hi also in 30:5)[185]
32:43	שממה	26:33	
32:44	שוב שבות		30:3

What is the likely direction of dependence (if any) in this case? The remarks made concerning Jeremiah 30 also apply here. Exemplary investigations can again point to a dependence of Jeremiah on Deuteronomy; the following two cases demonstrate this:

---

184 Only one further attestation, Jer 21:5. See also Fischer, *Jeremia 26–52*, 211–212.
185 Cf. also Fischer, *Jeremia 26–52*, 213; Fischer, "Fulfilment," 45.

- Jeremiah 32:40 mentions יראתי (the fear of me) that the Lord is going to put into his people's hearts, while Deut 30:6 is more drastic and more anthropomorphic with its expectation of the heart surgery that removes the spiritual foreskin from his people's hearts. In addition, the hope of Jer 32:40 is put in the context of a ברית עולם, which is very likely a more developed concept.
- Jeremiah 32:36–37 looks like a kind of concise summary of related elements spread over different parts of Deuteronomy 28 (and possibly Leviticus 26) in the case of v. 36, and Deuteronomy 29 and 30 in the case of v. 37.

As in the case of Deuteronomy 4, the picture emerging from observing the linguistic connections between Jeremiah 29, 30 and 32 with Deuteronomy is that at the time of the writing of the Jeremianic passages, the developments described in Deut 28–30 were seen as a coherent series of events. Especially both Jeremiah 30 and Jer 32:36–44 show close phraseological and lexical links not only with different parts of the curse section in Deuteronomy 28, but also with subsequent passages in Deuteronomy 29 and 30, in isolated instances also with Deuteronomy 31.

On the other hand, we note that an important Jeremianic text dealing with the hope for change in the future, Jeremiah 33, shows a considerable distance to both Leviticus 26 and Deuteronomy 28–31.

10.4 Other Prophetic Texts with Close Links to Deuteronomy 28–31

There are also other prophetic texts that are closely linked to the Deuteronomic passages in question.

An example is Ezek 20:8–9, which shares the sequence of שקוץ and גלול with Deut 29:16. At the same time, there are links with Lev 26:28, 30, 45 (as mentioned above). This indicates that the sequence of curse/menace and new hope beyond the implementation of the curses as found in Leviticus 26 and Deuteronomy 28–31 predates Ezekiel.[186]

---

186 See the argument adduced above for Leviticus 26 predating Ezekiel 20:9.

11. The New Hope in Leviticus 26 and Deuteronomy 29ff. Compared

11.1 Less Developed Stage of Expectations in Leviticus 26

In the passage(s) describing the new hope in Leviticus 26, there is no explicit mention of a repentance of the people manifest in outward acts, or of a return of the exiles to the land, or of a forgiveness of their sins (though this may be *implied* in ירצו את־עונם), or of the institution of a "new" (let alone everlasting) covenant.

This looks "old"; and this is clearly less than what we find in the final chapters of the book of Deuteronomy following Deuteronomy 28,[187] and much less than what we find in many of the prophetic oracles concerning the restitution of Israel after the judgment.

Specifically, it is impossible to assume that the unsolved problem of the circumcision of the heart in Lev 26:41 comes later than God's circumcising the heart of his people in Deut 30:6.[188]

Also the (other) concrete actions in Deuteronomy 30 from God's side on behalf of his people, including the passing of the curses from Israel to the nations (v. 7), culminating in bringing his people back to the land and blessing them even beyond the measure of the fathers (v. 5), go far beyond the promises in Leviticus 26 that focus on God's "remembering" of the covenant.

Moreover, God's restoration of his people is said to be motived by his compassion (רחם pi, Deut 30:3), a word which is not found in Leviticus 26 or in the Priestly writings (or the Holiness Code) at all.[189]

11.2 Complex Chronology in Deuteronomy 29–32

While it is fair to say that Lev 26:34–45 is complex in terms of chronology by dividing the depiction of the future in at least two distinct steps and by breaking up the chronological line with two flashbacks, complexity is in some ways even enhanced in Deuteronomy 29–32 by shifting between various stages of the future and the

---

[187] Where, for example, the root שוב plays an important role.
[188] So also Fischer, "A Need for Hope?," 381–383. In Jer 4:4, there is a call to the addressees to circumcise their hearts, as in Deut 10:16. The announcement that YHWH will circumcise the heart of his people goes beyond all calls to follow God's commands by solving the problem as to how obedience to these commands will last and is no longer endangered by the people's rebellious heart. This expectation comes close to Ezek 36:24–28 and Jer 31:31–34. See also Ehrenreich, "Tora," 220–221; Otto, "Gesetzbuch," 135.
[189] Cf. Ehrenreich, "Tora," 222.

present of the time of Moses.[190] In addition, more chronological precision is provided in the sense that it is made clear that the implementation of the curses will begin only/right after Moses.

11.3 Absence of Hints at Writing in Leviticus 26

Deuteronomy – together with (parts of) Exodus – mention "writing." Writing and "book" are mentioned also in those chapters in Deuteronomy that are under investigation in this study: Deuteronomy 28:58, 61; 29:20–21, 27. On the other hand, there is no mention of writing with respect to the Priestly *torot*.

This is certainly an important difference. In terms of date, this difference might point to Deuteronomy 28–29 (and by extension 28–31) being later than Leviticus 26 – though other explanations of this observation are not excluded.

12. General Observations

References to both blessing and curse are repeated throughout the book of Deuteronomy;[191] there is even a ("second") curse list in Deuteronomy 27. In the Priestly material, including the Holiness Code, the situation looks different: Blessing and curse (in the form of promise and menace) are concentrated just in one chapter.

As with other topics, the most natural explanation seems to be that Deuteronomy builds on earlier materials/concepts and elaborates them.[192]

12.1 Reception History

The picture that emerges concerning the reception history of Leviticus 26 and Deuteronomy 28(–30/31) is: These texts were known in later times, but drawn upon in explicit ways not on a very large scale, with the exception of passages in Jeremiah and Ezekiel, which makes them appear relatively remote in time, and therefore relatively old.

The fact that *both* texts were known and "used" in later times very likely shows that they were meant to be complementary (that is, the alternative, possibly later, version was not meant to replace the other one).

---

190 Whether this time is only imagined (as is usually assumed in critical scholarship) or not, does not matter for the present analysis.
191 See, e.g., 11:26, 29; 30:1, 19.
192 For this principle see Kilchör, *Mosetora*; Zehnder, "Observations," passim.

12.2 Lack of Overlap with the Descriptions of the Catastrophes of 722 and 586

The curse/meance texts of both Leviticus 26 and Deuteronomy 28 are remote from the biblical descriptions of the catastrophes of 722 and 586:
- The destruction of the temple or the capital is not mentioned.
- The hint at a deterioration in the situation of the exiles found both in Leviticus 26 and Deuteronomy 28 has no counterpart in biblical descriptions of the exile.
- The mention of a forced deportation on ships to Egypt as (perhaps) found in Deut 28:68 is not supported by any biblical reports of the fate of the exiles.
- The description of the eating of their own children found both in Leviticus 26 and Deuteronomy 28 has no parallel in the biblical reports about the catastrophes of 722 and 586.
- The same is true for the motif of "fear" that plays an important role both in Leviticus 26 and especially in Deuteronomy 28.
- While the verb שמד is central in the description of YHWH's punishment of his people in Deuteronomy 28, it is not attested in the biblical reports of the catastrophes of 722 and 586.[193]
- The noun דבר (pestilence), which is attested both in Lev 26:25 and Deut 28:21 as an important part of the calamities that will befall a disobedient people, is broadly used in Jeremiah and Ezekiel, but not in the descriptions of the catastrophes of 722 and 586.
- In 2 Kings 17:21, the main reason for the catastrophe of 722 is described with the phrase חטא hi + חטאה גדולה. In contrast to this, the root חטא does not appear at all in either Leviticus 26 or Deuteronomy 28; in Leviticus 26, it is rather the noun עון that is focused on.
- We also note that an important element in prophetic and Deuteronomistic descriptions of the circumstances that led to the exile regularly include the element "they did not listen to the prophets"; this is absent both in Leviticus 26 and Deuteronomy 28.

The combination of a lack of overlap between the description of the catastrophes of 722 and 586 by the Deuteronomistic writers and the two menace/curse catalogues in Leviticus 26 and Deuteronomy 28 on the one hand, and the special density of intertextual links between these two catalogues and passages in Jeremiah and Ezekiel on the other, is best and most naturally explained by the assumption that both catalogues were written some time before the exile and used by Jeremiah and Ezekiel when the catastrophe of 586 drew nearer or had just happened, as the frame of

---

[193] For further observations concerning the differences between Leviticus 26 and especially Deuteronomy 28 on the one hand and biblical descriptions of the catastrophes of 722 and 586 on the other see Zehnder, "Fluch und Segen," 208–209.

reference that made this event understandable as the coming into force of the menaces/curses of the covenant between YHWH and his people. Since the two catalogues were not modeled on the actual happenings of either 722 and 586, they were also applicable to other historical circumstances, both earlier and later, as the biblical references to these texts outside of Jeremiah and Ezekiel confirm.[194]

13. Conclusion

The main results of the study can be summarized in the following way:

1. The most salient finding provided by the lexical and structural analysis of Leviticus 26 is the adversative use of the noun *qery*, which likely points to an old age of the phrases in which it is used. With respect to Deuteronomy 28, the complexity of the overall structure is remarkable, and clearly distinguishes this text from Leviticus 26. The same goes for the much more detailed references to developments after the implementation of the curses (see Deuteronomy 29-31). In both cases, the observations tend to suggest a chronological post-position of Deuteronomy 28(-31) in comparison to Leviticus 26.

2. The investigation of the lexical and phraseological / syntactical connections between the two texts shows that there is considerable *thematic* overlap, while at the same time close *lexical* or *phraseological* connections are rare. The detailed observations concerning this part of the investigation do not allow to draw any clear and detailed conclusions in terms of possible literary dependency between the two passages or chronological sequence.

3. The investigation of the lexical or phraseological / syntactical connections between Leviticus 26 and Deuteronomy 28 on the one hand and other biblical texts on the other shows that there is a high number of passages in prophetic books that can be shown with a high degree of probability to be dependent on either Leviticus 26 or Deuteronomy 28. Since many of these passages can be dated pre-exilic or early exilic with high confidence, this provides positive evidence for the claim that

---

[194] One can also raise the question whether Deuteronomy 28(–31) reflects events that took place between Leviticus 26 and Deuteronomy 28 according to the canonical sequence of texts and events. If this were the case, this could be used as an argument for the sequence Leviticus 26 – Deuteronomy 28(–31). While the limitations of space prevent us from looking at the question in detail, it can be said that there are in fact a number of lexical links between Numbers and Deuteronomy 28–31. However, none of these are exclusive in nature, which makes it impossible to base conclusive arguments on such observations. Moreover, there are cases that further demonstrate the limits of this approach and the results it provides, cases in which there are close lexical links between the descriptions of incidents taking place between Leviticus 26 and Deuteronomy 28 on the one hand and passages not in Deuteronomy 28, but in Leviticus 26, on the other, such as the use of the verbs מאס and נקם and of the noun פגר.

the corresponding passages in Leviticus 26 and Deuteronomy 28 must be older. Regardless of the question of the direction of dependence between either Leviticus 26 or Deuteronomy 28 on the one hand and other biblical texts on the other, the fact that intertextual links to both catalogues exist indicates that none of the two passages was understood as *replacing* the other.

4. As far as connections, both linguistic and topical, between the two passages and extra-biblical material is concerned, it turns out that several passages in both texts fit a chronological milieu that pre-dates the neo-Assyrian period. On the other hand, directions of dependence between the biblical and the extra-biblical material can generally not be established with certainty.

For many of the questions concerning the relationship of Leviticus 26 and Deuteronomy 28(-31), only tentative answers can be given, often with a considerable degree of uncertainty. Broadly speaking, it is likely that Leviticus 26 and Deuteronomy 28(-31) are largely independent compositions. Direct lexical/idiomatic overlap is rare, and can best be explained in terms of a shared dependence on broader curse traditions. However, there are some signs that the author(s) of Deuteronomy 28 might have been familiar with Leviticus 26 or an earlier version of that text. Based on the study of both inner-biblical evidence and extra-biblical comparative material, both catalogues, likely in their entirety, can be dated well before the exile.

Bibliography

Balentine, Samuel E. *Leviticus*. Interpretation; Louisville, KY: John Knox Press, 2002.
Baranowski, Krysztof J. "The Old Aramaic and Biblical Curses." *Liber annuus* 62 (2012): 173–201.
Beckman, Gary. Hittite Diplomatic Texts. SBL Writings from the Ancient World 7. Atlanta, GA: Scholars Press, 1999.
Bergsma, John S. *The Jubilee from Leviticus to Qumran: A History of Interpretation*. Supplements to Vetus Testamentum 115. Leiden: Brill, 2007.
Borger, Rykle. "Vier Grenzsteinurkunden Merodachbaladans I. von Babylonien." *Archiv für Orientforschung* 23 (1970): 1–26.
Cathcart, Kevin J. "The Curses in Old Aramaic Inscriptions," in *Targumic and Cognate Studies*. Edited by K.J. Cathcart and M. Maher. JSOT.S 230. Sheffield: Sheffield Academic Press, 1996, 140–152.
Cholewinski, Alfred. *Heiligkeitsgesetz und Deuteronomium*. Analecta Biblica 66. Rome: Biblical Institute Press, 1976.
Craigie, Peter C. *The Book of Deuteronomy*. NICOT. Grand Rapids, MI: Eerdmans, 1976.

Crawford, Timothy G. *Blessing and Curse in Syro-Palestinian Inscriptions of the Iron Age*. New York, NY: Peter Lang, 1992.

Ehrenreich, Ernst. "Tora zwischen Scheitern und Neubeginn," in *Deuteronomium – Tora für eine neue Generation*. Edited by Georg Fischer, Dominik Markl, and Simone Paganini. BZAR 17. Wiesbaden: Harrassowitz Verlag, 2011, 213–226.

Finsterbusch, Karin. *Deuteronomium – Eine Einführung*. Göttingen: Vandenhoeck & Ruprecht, 2012.

Fischer, Georg. "A Need for Hope? A Comparison between the Dynamics in Leviticus 26 and Deuteronomy 28–30," in *Current Issues in Priestly and Related Literature: The Legacy of Jacob Milgrom and Beyond*. Edited by R.E. Gane and A. Taggar-Cohen. Atlanta, GA: SBL Press, 2015, 369–385.

—. "Fulfilment and Reversal: The Curses of Deuteronomy 28 as a Foil for the Book of Jeremiah." *Semitica et Classica* 5 (2012): 43–49.

—. *Jeremia 26–52*. HThKAT. Freiburg / Basel / Wien: Herder, 2005.

Fitzmyer, Joseph A. *The Aramaic Inscriptions of Sefire*. Biblica et orientalia 19A. Rome: Pontificio Instituto Biblio, 1995.

Ganzel, Tova and Risa Levitt Kohn, "Ezekiel's Prophetic Message in Light of Leviticus 26," in *The Formation of the Pentateuch*. Edited by Jan C. Gertz, et al. FAT 111. Tübingen: Mohr Siebeck, 2016, 1075–1084.

Gerstenberger, Erhard S. *Das dritte Buch Mose: Leviticus*. ATD 6. Göttingen: Vandenhoeck & Ruprecht, 1993.

Grünwaldt, Klaus. *Das Heiligkeitsgesetz Leviticus 17–26*. BZAW 271. Berlin / New York, NY: de Gruyter, 1999.

Häner, Tobias. *Bleibendes Nachwirken des Exils: Eine Untersuchung zur kanonischen Endgestalt des Ezechielbuches*. HBS 78. Freiburg: Herder, 2014.

Hartley, John E. *Leviticus*. WBC. Dallas, TX: Word Books, 1992.

Hasel, Gerhard F. *The Remnant*. Berrien Springs, MI: Andrews University Press, 1974.

Hieke, Thomas. *Levitikus, Zweiter Teilband: 16–27*. HThKAT. Freiburg i.Br.: Herder, 2014.

Hillers, Delbert R. *Treaty-Curses and the Old Testament Prophets*. Rome: Pontificio Instituto Biblico, 1964.

Hoftijzer, Jacob and G. van der Kooij (eds). *Aramaic Texts from Deir 'Alla*. Leiden: Brill, 1976.

Jeremias, Jörg. *The Book of Amos* (trans. D.W. Stott). OTL. Louisville, KY: Westminster John Knox, 1998.

Kaufman, Stephen A. "Reflections on the Assyrian-Aramaic Bilingual from Tell Fakhariyeh." *Maarav* 3 (1982): 137–175.

Kessler, John. "Patterns of Descriptive Curse Formulae in the Hebrew Bible, with Special Attention to Leviticus 26 and Amos 4:6–12," in *The Formation of the Pentateuch*. Edited by Jan C. Gertz, et al. FAT 111. Tübingen: Mohr Siebeck, 2016, 943–984.

Kilchör, Benjamin. *Mosetora und Jahwetora – Das Verhältnis von Deuteronomium 12–26 zu Exodus, Levitikus und Numeri*. BZAR 21. Wiesbaden: Harrassowitz Verlag, 2015.

Koorevaar, Hendrik. "The Books of Exodus - Leviticus - Numbers and the Macro-Structural Problem of the Pentateuch," *The Books of Leviticus and Numbers*. Edited by Thomas Römer. BETL 215; Leuven: Peeters, 2008, 423–453.

Leichty, Erle. *The Omen Series Šumma Izbu*. Locust Valley, NY: J.J. Augusti Publisher, 1970.

Levine, Baruch A. *Leviticus*. The JPS Torah Commentary; Philadelphia, PA / New York, NY / Jerusalem: The Jewish Publication Society, 1989.

Lyons, Michael A. *From Law to Prophecy – Ezekiel's Use of the Holiness Code*. LBHOTS 507. London / New York, NY: T & T Clark International, 2009.

—. "How Have We Changed? Older and Newer Arguments about the Relationship between Ezekiel and the Holiness Code," in *The Formation of the Pentateuch*. Edited by Jan C. Gertz, et al. FAT 111. Tübingen: Mohr Siebeck, 2016, 1055–1074.

Milgrom, Jacob. *Leviticus 23–27*. The Anchor Bible 3B. New York, NY: Doubleday, 2001.

Noordtzij, Arie. *Leviticus* (trans. R. Togtman). Bible Student's Commentary. Grand Rapids, MI: Zondervan, 1982.

Otto, Eckart. "Vom Gesetzbuch zum Buch der Prophetie des Mose als Schlussstein der Tora. Das Deuteronomium," in *Aspekte der Bibel*. Edited by H.-J. Simm. Freiburg i. Br.: Herder, 2017, 124–137.

Parpola, Simo and Kazuko Watanabe (eds). *Neo-Assyrian Treaties and Loyalty Oaths* SAA II. Helsinki: Helsinki University Press, 1988.

Pritchard, James B (ed). *Ancient Near Eastern Texts Relating to the Old Testament* (3rd edition). Princeton, NJ: Princeton University Press, 1969.

Rom-Shiloni, Dalit. "Compositional Harmonization – Priestly and Deuteronomic References in the Book of Jeremiah – An Earlier Stage of a Recognized Interpretive Technique," in *The Formation of the Pentateuch*. Edited by Jan C. Gertz, et al. FAT 111. Tübingen: Mohr Siebeck, 2016, 913–942.

Roth, Martha T. *Law Collections from Mesopotamia and Asia Minor*. SBL Writings from the Ancient World 6. Atlanta, GA: Scholars Press, 1997.

Sommer, Benjamin D. *A Prophet Reads Scripture: Allusion in Isaiah 40–66*. Palo Alto, CA: Stanford University Press, 1998.

Stuart, Douglas. *Hosea–Jonah*. WBC. Waco, TX: Word Books, 1987.

Tigay, Jeffrey H. *Deuteronomy*. The JPS Torah Commentary. Philadelphia, PA / Jerusalem, 1996.

van der Toorn, Karel. *Scribal Culture and the Making of the Hebrew Bible*. Cambridge, MA: Harvard University Press, 2007.

Vanoni, Gottfried. "Anspielungen und Zitate innerhalb der hebräischen Bibel," in *Jeremia und die 'deuteronomistische Bewegung'*. Edited by W. Gross. BBB 98. Weinheim: Beltz Athenäum, 1995, 383–395.

Wenham, Gordon J. *The Book of Leviticus*. NICOT. Grand Rapids, MI: Eerdmans, 1979.

Zehnder, Markus. "Building on Stone? Deuteronomy and Esarhaddon's Loyalty Oaths (Part 1)." *BBR* 19 (2009): 341–374; "Building on Stone? Deuteronomy and Esarhaddon's Loyalty Oaths (Part 2). *BBR* 19 (2009): 511–535.

—. "Fluch und Segen im Buch Deuteronomium," *Deuteronomium – Tora für eine neue Generation*. Edited by Georg Fischer, Dominik Markl, and Simone Paganini. BZAR 17. Wiesbaden: Harrassowitz Verlag, 2011, 193–211.

—. "Literary and Other Observations on Passages Dealing with Foreigners in the Book of Deuteronomy," in *Sepher Torath Mosheh*. Edited by Daniel I. Block and Richard Schulz, Peabody, MA: Hendrickson, 2017, 192–231.

—. "Structural Complexity, Semantic Ambiguity, and the Question of Literary Integrity: A New Reading of Leviticus 26,14–45," in *Nächstenliebe und Gottesfurcht – Beiträge aus alttestamentlicher, semitistischer und altorientalistischer Wissenschaft für Hans-Peter*

Mathys zum 65. Geburtstag. Edited by H. Jenni, M. Saur. Münster: Ugarit Verlag, 2016, 503–530.

III. Torah and Prophets

Deuteronomy as the Legal Completion and Prophetic Finale of the Pentateuch

Eckart Otto (University of Munich)

My experience of the last forty years in the field of Old Testament scholarship has been one of continuous paradigm-change in the interpretation of the Pentateuch, in an effort to overcome Wellhausen's source-critical model of a Yahwist and Elohist preceding a priestly source (P).[1] The Yahwist—and with him the Elohist—have had to leave the scene,[2] and even the hypothesis of P as a source has been intensively criticized.[3] In this paper I argue for a different kind of a paradigm change in Pentateuchal research: to interpret the Book of Deuteronomy once again in the context of the *Pentateuch* and as an integral part of it, as was done in the nineteenth century (e.g. by W.M.L. de Wette);[4] rather than as a part of the *Deuteronomistic History* from Deuteronomy to 2 Kings, whatever its shape may be.[5] In my opinion, this is a most important paradigm change in the interpretation of the Pentateuch, because it means the end of a *captivitas babylonica* for the Book of Deuteronomy, and so also for the Pentateuch as a whole. Martin Noth—and his many followers still today—amputated the Pentateuch to a Tetrateuch whose conclusions were lost, since Deuteronomy was conceptualized as part of the Deuteronomistic History and its redaction.[6] But if we give Deuteronomy back to the Pentateuch, and no longer conceptualize it merely as the legal measuring-stick for Israel's failed history from its entrance into Promised Land (Joshua) to the Babylonian catastrophe of Judah and Jerusalem

---

[1] This paper preserves the character of the oral lecture as it was given at the conference. For a survey of the history of Pentateuch-research in the twentieth century see Otto, "Pentateuch," 682–690.

[2] See Gertz, Schmid and Witte, *Abschied*; Dozeman and Schmid, *Farewell*. The exegetical progress in overcoming the Wellhausen-paradigm is also provoking some exegetical retrogression, in this case by the so called neo-documentarists, who intend to renew and revive the paradigm of the sources of Yahwist, Elohist, and P but without a Yehovist, as it was already outlined in the nineteenth century by Hupfeld, *Quellen*; cf. Baden, *J, E, and the Redaction*; id. "Why is the Pentateuch Unreadable?," 243–251. For Hupfeld's source-critical theory of the Pentateuch, which was basic for Wellhausen, cf. Otto, "Grundzüge," 76–77

[3] See Hartenstein and Schmid, *Abschied*; cf. Frevel in his review of this book, 305–312.

[4] See de Wette, *Beiträge*, 168–179.182–185; cf. Otto, "Grundzüge," 69–72. For de Wette and his meaning for our contemporary understanding of the Pentateuch cf. also Otto, "A Hidden Truth," 19–27.

[5] The beginning of a Deuteronomistic History cannot be found in Deut 1–3 but in 1 Sam 1; pace Noth and many of his followers. See Otto, "Forschungsgeschichtliche Standortbestimmung der Literaturgeschichte," 284–297.

[6] See Noth, *Überlieferungsgeschichtliche Studien*, 43–266; id., *Überlieferungsgeschichte*.

(2 Kings 25),[7] then we have to raise the question: What is the place and function(s) of Deuteronomy within the Pentateuch?

1. The Book of Deuteronomy as Moses' Interpretation of Sinai-*Torah* in Exodus and Leviticus

The superscription of Deuteronomy in Deut 1:1–5 provides us with an important key to answer the question for Deuteronomy's function within the Pentateuch: *be'ebær hajjarden be'areæṣ mô'āb hô'îl mošæh be'er 'æt hattorah hazzo't le'mor* "beyond the Jordan in the land of Moab, Moses began to expound this *torah* (and said)."[8] *B'r* (Piel) in Deut 1:5 is a *verbum dicendi*, so taken together with the following *le'mor* it means "to explain/expound," comparable to Akkadian *bâru* (D-stem) as found, for example, in the *burru*-formula in Babylonian trial records. This superscription in Deut 1:5 defines Deuteronomy's function within the Pentateuch as Moses' interpretation of the *torah*, i.e. of the Sinai-*torah* in Exodus and Leviticus. The legal sections of Deuteronomy in Deut 12–26 and Deut 27 constitute Moses' interpretation of the Sinai-*torah* for a new generation in the land of Moab. Some examples will suffice to show that in Deuteronomy several parts of the Sinai-*torah* were re-interpreted by Moses' through an exegetical process.

For example, the asylum-legislation of the Covenant Code in Exod 21:12–14[9] is revised in Deut 19:1–13.[10] The place of asylum will no longer be the altar of a sanctuary as in Exod 20:24, but rather six towns of asylum in the Promised Land. The principle guiding Moses' hermeneutical process is the reality of the new situation in which the second generation will be living in the Promised Land, in contrast to the first generation who wandered through the desert. We find the characteristic sequence of the pronouns *'ašær* in Exod 21:13 and *kî* in Exod 21:14 also in Deut 19:4 and Deut 19:11, indicating a direct literary connection between these texts, in which Deut 19 is the adopting text. Moses' interpretation of the asylum-legislation in the Sinai-*torah* has the legal-hermeneutical function of actualizing and supplementing the Covenant Code for Israel's life in the Promised Land.[11]

---

7 See Otto, *Das Deuteronomium*; id., "Integration," 331–341.
8 For exegetical details see Otto, *Deuteronomium 1,1–4,43*, 298–328; cf. id., "Mose," 273–284.
9 For the literary and legal history of Exod 21,12–14 see Otto, *Wandel*, 31–34.; id., *Theologische Ethik*, 32–39.
10 For exegetical details see Otto, *Deuteronomium 12,1–23,15*, 1504–1550.
11 See Otto, *Deuteronomium 12,1–23,15*, 1093–1108; id., "The Pre-exilic Deuteronomy," 112–122; Kilchör, *Mosetora*, 14–18; Berman, "Supersessionist," 201–221; pace Levinson, *Deuteronomy*; for a review of this study see Otto, "Biblische Rechtsgeschichte," 5–14.

Deuteronomy as the Legal Completion and Prophetic Finale of the Pentateuch 181

But it is not just the Covenant Code that Moses interprets in Deuteronomy. The priestly legislation of Leviticus is also part of the Sinai-*torah*, and it, too, is re-interpreted, as we can see by the reception of Lev 11 in Deut 14.[12] The literary relation between these texts has been a matter of an intensive discussion in the last decades, but there is—for most scholars, at least—no doubt of a direct literary relation between them. The theory that they were both dependent on a no-longer-extant third text (most recently proposed by C. Nihan)[13] is unconvincing, because it is simply not necessary to postulate a hypothetical source document. The list of clean and unclean animals in Lev 11:2–23 is taken up in Deut 14:4–20 and supplemented by a list of unclean birds. The key to understanding the re-interpretation of Lev 11 in Deut 14 is the law of Deut 12, which is, indeed, the hermeneutical key not only for Deut 14, but for the entire Deuteronomic Code (Deut 12–26). When we analyse Deuteronomy's laws of sacrificial offerings at the elected *maqôm* and of slaughtering animals in the *šeʿarîm*, we can recognize that, in Deut 14, the main accent lies on the terrestrial animals, which are the most important for the Book of Deuteronomy as a whole. For these animals, Deuteronomy provides two criteria of distinction between clean and unclean, and then supplements with a list of examples of both categories. For the aquatic animals, two criteria are given, but no list of examples; and for birds, no criteria, but simply a list of unclean species. The Masoretic version of this list is more complex than that in the Septuagint, because the Masoretic list was an addition to the Masoretic text of Deut 14 after the original reception of Lev 11 in Deut 14— which lacked this list. Thus, we have to recognize two stages of reception of Lev 11 in Deut 14. The first reception of Lev 11 in Deut 14 was guided by Deut 12 as a hermeneutical key, the second one by the idea of adjusting Deut 14 again to Lev 11.

The hermeneutical principle of adjusting earlier legislation in light of Deut 12 is also valid in many other cases of a reception of the Sinai-*torah* in Deuteronomy; for example, in the reception of Exod 23:1–3, 6–8 in Deut 19:15–21;[14] of Exod 23:4–5 in Deut 22:1–4;[15] of Lev 19:19 in Deut 22:9–11;[16] of Lev 19:29 in Deut 23:18–19;[17] of Lev 19:35–36 in Deut 25:13–16;[18] of Lev 18:23 and 20:15–16 in Deut 27:21; of Lev 20:17 in Deut 27:22; and of Lev 20:14 in Deut 27:23.[19] Thus, Moses' interpretation of the Sinai-*torah* in the Book of Deuteronomy includes not only the legal sen-

---

12 For exegetical details see Otto, *Deuteronomium 12,1–23,15*, 1273–1319. For the dependency of Deuteronomy on Leviticus, cf. Kilchör, *Mosetora*, 97–108.
13 See Nihan, *Priestly Torah*, 283–299 (cf. my review of this book, 470–479); id., "The Laws," 401–432.
14 See Otto, *Deuteronomium 12,1–23,15*, 1525–1626.1539–1549.
15 See Otto, *Deuteronomium 12,1–23,15*, 1684–1686.1694–1696.
16 See Otto, *Deuteronomium 12,1–23,15*, 1686–1688; 1701–1704.
17 See Otto, *Deuteronomium 23,16–34,12*, 1783.1790–1792.
18 See Otto, *Deuteronomium 23,16–34,12*, 1832.1859–1860.
19 See Otto, *Deuteronomium 23,16–34,12*, 1934–1935.1950–1956.

tences of the Covenant Code but also *torot* of the Sinai-pericope in the Book of Leviticus.[20]

2. The Book of Deuteronomy as the Finale and Completion of the Pentateuch

When the Book of Deuteronomy is understood as the culmination and finale of all the books of the Pentateuch, it delivers decisive hermeneutical keys for the interpretation of the Torah as a whole. The superscription in Deut 1:1–5 defines Deuteronomy as interpretation of the Sinai-*torah* through Moses' scribal erudition. The post-script of its promulgation on Moses' last day in Moab provides some criteria concerning how to understand the hermeneutics of the relationship between Deuteronomy as part of the Pentateuch, and its addressees living later on in the Promised Land. For example, one of the peculiar narrative motifs in the framework of the Book of Deuteronomy is Moses' premature death after being allowed to see the Promised Land, but not to enter it.[21] The narrative of the Pentateuch itself does not offer a convincing explanation for why Moses has to die before crossing the river Jordan. Numbers 20 asserts that Moses and Aaron failed at Meribah and thus were censured by YHWH. But on the other hand, the epitaph of the Pentateuch in Deut 34:10–12 attributes to Moses the "signs and wonders that YHWH sent him to perform in the land of Egypt against Pharaoh and all his entire land and all the mighty deeds and all the terrifying displays of power that Moses performed in the sight of all Israel," and Deut 29:1–2 attributes these same miracles to YHWH.[22] Thus we can see that the epitaph of the Pentateuch places Moses almost on par with YHWH, who knows Moses face to face. Therefore, a sin or failure of Moses could not be the reason for his premature death, and must be only a secondary explanation for not allowing him to cross the Jordan after he had written down the *torah*. Rather, we will see that this theological tension—that God's arch-prophet has to die a premature death—was intentionally embraced by the authors of Deuteronomy in order to develop the hermeneutical theory of Deuteronomy as Moses' scribal interpretation of the Sinai-*torah*.

In the Book of Deuteronomy, several roles and functions are combined in Moses' person. He is the mediator of the divine revelation of the *torah* at Sinai, the

---

20 See Otto, "Forschungsgeschichtliche Standortbestimmung der Literatur- und Rechtsgeschichte," 1112–1116, with a discussion of the different approaches in Cholewiński, *Heiligkeitsgesetz*; Braulik, "dekalogische Redaktion," 147–182; id., "Weitere Beobachtungen," 183–223 and Kilchör, *Mosetora*.
21 Cf. Otto, "Moses," 137–149.
22 For exegetical details see Otto, *Deuteronomium 23,16–34,12*, 2284–2285.

interpreter of this *torah* in the land of Moab, and the leader of Israel on their way from Egypt to Moab.[23] After Moses' death, the role of leadership was given to Joshua in Deut 31:1–8,[24] but the role of mediator of divine revelation was assumed by the written *torah* itself, which Moses had interpreted and committed to writing in the Book of Deuteronomy. And this is the decisive hermeneutical key for Moses' premature death: Moses had to die, so that the transcribed *torah* could assume Moses' function of mediating the divine will to the generations of addressees of the *torah* in the Promised Land. So one can say Moses had to die, so that he could be resurrected in the transcribed *torah* as the mediator of the divine revelation.[25] Moses' role and function as scribal interpreter and exegete of the *torah* in the Book of Deuteronomy was assumed by the priests and elders (Deut 31:9–10), who became responsible for the exegetical interpretation of the written *torah* in the Promised Land.[26] Moses established himself as the model scribe by his transcription of his interpretation of the Sinai-*torah* in the Book of Deuteronomy. Thus, the chapters Deut 29–34 have a decisive function for the hermeneutics not only of the book of Deuteronomy but of all the Pentateuch. We can conclude that the Book of Deuteronomy was intended to be the completion of entirety of the Pentateuch.

3. The Prophetic Conclusion of the Pentateuch in the Book of Deuteronomy

There remains one function of Moses which we have not yet addressed, namely Moses' prophetic role, as it is described in Deut 18.[27] The most decisive, characteristic feature of the Book of Deuteronomy is to be not only a legal book consisting of *torah*, but also a prophetic book[28] that paints Moses as a prophet on the plains of Moab predicting Israel's Babylonian exile, as in Deut 4:25–31:[29]

> When you have had children and children's children and become complacent in the land, if you act corruptly by making an idol in the form of anything, thus doing what is evil in the sight of YHWH, your God, and provoking him to anger, I call heaven and earth to witness against you today, that you will soon utterly perish from the land that you are crossing the Jordan to occupy;

---

23 Cf. Fischer, "Mosebild," 84–121.
24 For exegetical details see Otto, *Deuteronomium 23,16–34,12*, 2100–2103.2106–2111.
25 See Otto, "Theologie," 141–148.
26 For exegetical details see Otto, *Deuteronomium 23,16–34,12*, 2111–2120.
27 For the analysis of Deut 16,18–18,22 see the exegetical details in Otto, *Deuteronomium 12,1–23,15*, 1417–1503.
28 See Otto, "Gesetzbuch," 124–137.
29 For exegetical details see Otto, *Deuteronomium 1,1–4,43*, 568–581.

> you will not live long on it, but will be utterly destroyed. YHWH will scatter you among the nations; only a few of you will be left among the nations where YHWH will lead you. There you will serve other gods made by human hands, objects of wood and stone that neither see, nor hear, not eat, nor smell. From there you will seek YHWH your God, and find him if you search after him with all your heart and being. In your distress, when all these things have happened to you in time to come, you will return to YHWH your God and heed him. Because YHWH your God is a merciful God, he will neither abandon you nor destroy you, he will not forget the covenant with your ancestors that he swore to them.

After Moses mediates the making of YHWH's covenant with Israel on the plains of Moab in Deut 29:1–14, another Mosaic oracle of doom and salvation follows in Deut 29:15–30:20.[30] This oracle speaks directly to the addressees of Deuteronomy, and culminates in Moses' announcement of the circumcision of the heart of Israel in Deut 30:6, which is the prophetic culmination of all the *torah* of the Pentateuch, summarized in a prophecy of salvation:

> When the next generation, your children, will grow up after you, and the foreigner who arrives from a distant land, sees the plagues of the land and the diseases by which YHWH has made it sick, and that the land has become burning sulfur and salt, that is not being sown or bearing crops or even grass like the overthrow of Sodom and Gomorrah, Admah and Seboim, which YHWH overthrew in his furious anger, then all peoples will ask: Why did YHWH do this to this land? What is the meaning of such frenzied, furious anger? Then people will answer: It is because they abandoned the covenant of YHWH, the God of their fathers, which he had made with them when he brought them out of Egypt... When the time arrives that all these things have come upon you, both the blessings and the curses, which I have presented to you, and you are among the peoples to which YHWH your God has driven you, than, at last, you will begin to think about what has happened to you and you will return to YHWH your God and listen to what he has said, which will be exactly what I am ordering you to do today, you and your children, with all your heart and all your being, then YHWH will reverse your turning away...YHWH your God will circumcise your hearts and the hearts of your children so that you will love YHWH your God with all your heart and all your being and you will live. (Deut 29:21–24; 30:1–3.6)

The Book of Deuteronomy is situated between these prophecies of doom and prophecies of salvation. This leads to the question of the relationship of the Pentateuch to the prophetic books in the canon of the Hebrew Bible. Deuteronomy, the

---

[30] For exegetical details and the theological profile of these chapters in the context of the Book of Deuteronomy and the Pentateuch see Otto, *Deuteronomium 23,16–34,12*, 2022–2077.

finale and completion of all the Pentateuch, gives an answer to this question. The answer is found in Deut 34:10–12, the epitaph of the Pentateuch,[31] and it is most important not only for the interpretation of the Pentateuch itself but for the whole canon of the Hebrew Bible:

> Never since has there arisen a prophet in Israel like Moses, whom YHWH knew face to face.

Thus, Deuteronomy portrays Moses as the chief prophet and archetype or model for all the prophets in the Hebrew Bible, yet this role is connected with his function as mediator of the *torah* and as its interpreter. This means that the prophets after Moses will be bound to the *torah*, and their prophecies will be interpretations of the *torah* in the new and changing situations of Israel's life in the Promised Land and in the diaspora.

The theological dynamic of the Book of Deuteronomy is interwoven not only with the Pentateuch but with the whole canon of the Hebrew Bible. The Pentateuch seems to end in a tragedy for Moses and a catastrophe for Israel. In Moses' oracles in Deut 4 and Deut 29–30, prophecies of doom are followed by prophecies of salvation. In Deut 31:16–21 YHWH begins to speak directly to Moses and announces only doom for the people of Israel:

> YHWH said to Moses: Soon you will lie down with your ancestors. Then this people will begin to prostitute themselves to foreign gods in their midst, the gods of the land into which they are going. When they are with those gods, they will abandon me, breaking my covenant that I have made with them. Then my anger will flare up, and I will abandon them and hide my face from them. They will be devoured, and many calamities and trouble will come upon them. Then they will ask: Have not these calamities come upon us because our God is not here with us? But I shall be hiding my face from them because of all the evil they will have done in turning to other gods. (Deut 31:16–18)

After YHWH's announcement of doom, no salvation follows, contrary to Moses' oracles in Deut 4 and Deut 29–30. The addressees of Deuteronomy could rightly ask the question, Is Moses really a true prophet? After all, YHWH only confirms Moses' prophecies of doom but not those of salvation. This dramatic tension in the theology of the final chapters of the Pentateuch demands a solution, which in this case is not to be found merely by a historical-critical excursion into the literary history of these chapters. The solution is given in *the text itself,* in the divine revelation contained in Moses' song (Deut 32).[32] This song weaves together quotations or allusions to the Psalms (especially the Asaph-psalms), Proverbs, and the *corpus propheticum*, espe-

---

31 For the exegetical details and the theological profile of Deut 34 see Otto, *Deuteronomium 23,16–34,12,* 2261–2286.
32 See Otto, *Deuteronomium 23,16–34,12,* 2130–2203; id., "Singing Moses," 169–180.

cially to the Book of Isaiah. One can read this song as an amphibology, with the text of the song in the foreground, and the alluded and quoted texts of the prophets, psalms and proverbs in the background. Even in the first part of the song, which speaks of judgment on Israel, the background texts are hinting at the coming salvation for Israel and doom for the nations, which is affirmed explicitly in the second part of the song. Here we have the explanation for the strange fact that God only confirms Moses' prophecies of doom but not of salvation: All the scripture – *torah*, prophets, psalms and proverbs – confirms Israel's salvation in Moses' song as the completion and finale of the Pentateuch. *Torah*, prophets, psalms and proverbs now speak all together as the word of God announcing Israel's salvation after all its doom. Thus, when we recognize the theological function of the Book of Deuteronomy as the conclusion of the Pentateuch which simultaneously connects the Pentateuch to the rest of the emerging canon of the Hebrew Bible, we arrive at a new paradigm for interpreting the Pentateuch and the Hebrew Bible that goes far beyond the source-critical model of Julius Wellhausen.

Bibliography

Baden, Joel S. *J, E, and the Redaction of the Pentateuch*, FAT 68. Tübingen: Mohr Siebeck, 2009.
—. "Why is the Pentateuch Unreadable? – Or, Why Are We Doing This Anyway?," in *The Formation of the Pentateuch. Bridging the Academic Cultures of Europe, Israel, and North America*. Edited by Jan C. Gertz et al. FAT 111. Tübingen: Mohr Siebeck, 2016, 243–251.
Berman, Joshua. "Supersessionist or Complementary? Reassessing Legal Revision in the Pentateuchal Law Corpora." *JBL* 135 (2016): 201–221 (= id., *Inconsistency in the Torah. Ancient Literary Convention and the Limits of Source Criticism*. New York: Oxford University, 2017, 171–191).
Braulik, Georg. "Die dekalogische Redaktion der deuteronomischen Gesetze. Ihre Abhängigkeit von Lev 19 am Beispiel von Deuteronomium 22,1–12; 24,10–22 und 25,13–13," in *Studien zum Buch Deuteronomium*. Edited by Gerhard Dautzenberg and Norbert Lohfink. SBAB 24. Stuttgart: Katholisches Bibelwerk, 1997, 147–182.
—. "Weitere Beobachtungen zur Beziehung zwischen Heiligkeitsgesetz und Deuteronomium 19–25," in *Studien zum Buch Deuteronomium*. Edited by Gerhard Dautzenberg and Norbert Lohfink. SBAB 24. Stuttgart: Katholisches Bibelwerk, 1997, 183–223.
Cholewiński, Alfred. *Heiligkeitsgesetz und Deuteronomium. Eine vergleichende Studie*. AnBib 66. Rom: Analecta Biblica Dissertatione, 1976.

De Wette, Wilhelm M. L. *Beiträge zur Einleitung in das Alte Testament, vol. I: Kritischer Versuch über die Glaubwürdigkeit der Bücher der Chronik mit Hinsicht auf die Geschichte der Mosaischen Bücher und die Gesetzgebung.* Halle: Schimmelpfennig, 1806.

Dozeman, Thomas B., and Konrad Schmid, eds. *A Farewell to the Yahwist? The Composition of the Pentateuch in Recent European Interpretation.* SBL Symposium Ser. 34. Atlanta: Society of Biblical Literature, 2006.

Fischer, Georg. "Das Mosebild der Hebräischen Bibel," in *Mose. Ägypten und das Alte Testament.* Edited by Eckart Otto. SBS 189. Stuttgart: Katholisches Bibelwerk, 2000, 84–121.

Frevel, Christian. Review of *Abschied von der Priesterschrift?* by Friedhelm Hartenstein and Konrad Schmid. *ZAR* 22 (2016): 305–312.

Gertz, Jan C., Konrad Schmid and Markus Witte, eds. *Abschied vom Jahwisten. Die Komposition des Hexateuch in der jüngsten Diskussion*, BZAW 315. Berlin/New York: De Gruyter, 2002.

Hartenstein, Friedhelm, and Konrad Schmid, eds. *Abschied von der Priesterschrift? Zum Stand der Pentateuchdebatte.* VWGTh 40. Leipzig: Evangelische Verlagsanstalt, 2015.

Hupfeld, Hermann. *Die Quellen der Genesis und die Art ihrer Zusammensetzung. Von neuem untersucht.* Berlin: Wiegandt und Grieben, 1853.

Kilchör, Benjamin. *Mosetora und Jahwetora. Das Verhältnis von Deuteronomium 12–26 zu Exodus, Levitikus und Numeri.* BZAR 21. Wiesbaden: Harrassowitz, 2015.

Levinson, Bernard M. *Deuteronomy and the Hermeneutics of Legal Innovations.* New York: Oxford University Press, 1997.

Nihan, Christophe. *From Priestly Torah to Pentateuch. A Study in the Composition of the Book of Leviticus.* FAT II 25. Tübingen: Mohr Siebeck, 2007.

—. "The Laws about Clean and Unclean Animals in Leviticus and Deuteronomy and their Place in the Formation of the Pentateuch," in *The Pentateuch. International Perspectives on Current Research.* Edited by Thomas B. Dozeman et al. FAT 78. Tübingen: Mohr Siebeck, 2011, 401–432.

Noth, Martin. *Überlieferungsgeschichte des Pentateuch.* Stuttgart: Kohlhammer, 1948.

—. *Überlieferungsgeschichtliche Studien. Die sammelnden und bearbeitenden Geschichtswerke im Alten Testament.* Vol. 1. SKG.G 18. Halle: Niemeyer, 1943. Repr. Tübingen: Niemeyer, 1957.

Otto, Eckart. "A Hidden Truth Behind the Text or the Truth of the Text. At a Turning Point of Biblical Scholarship Two Hundred Years after De Wette's Dissertatio critico exegetica," in *South African Perspectives on the Pentateuch Between Synchrony and Diachrony.* Edited by Jurie Le Roux and Eckart Otto. LHBOTS 463. New York/London: T&T Clark, 2007, 19–27 (= id., *Die Tora. Studien zum Pentateuch. Gesammelte Aufsätze.* BZAR 9. Wiesbaden: Harrassowitz, 2009, 1–8).

—. "Biblische Rechtsgeschichte als Fortschreibungsgeschichte." *BiOr* 56 (1999): 5–14 (= id. *Altorientalische und Biblische Rechtsgeschichte. Gesammelte Studien.* BZAR 8. Wiesbaden: Harrassowitz, 2008, 496–506).

—. *Das Deuteronomium im Pentateuch und Hexateuch. Studien zur Literaturgeschichte von Pentateuch und Hexateuch im Lichte des Deuteronomiumrahmens.* FAT 30. Tübingen: Mohr Siebeck, 2000.

—. "Die Theologie des Buches Deuteronomium," in *"Vom Leben umfangen." Ägypten, das Alte Testament und das Gespräch der Religionen. Gedenkschrift für Manfred Görg.* Edited by Stefan J. Wimmer and Georg Gafus. ÄAT 80. Münster: Ugarit, 2014, 141–148.

—. *Deuteronomium 1,1–4,43*. HThKAT. Freiburg: Herder, 2012.
—. *Deuteronomium 12,1–23,15*. HThKAT. Freiburg: Herder, 2016.
—. *Deuteronomium 23,16–34,12*. HThKAT. Freiburg: Herder, 2017.
—. "Forschungsgeschichtliche Standortbestimmung der Literaturgeschichte der Ersten Moserede," in *Deuteronomium 1,1–4,43* by id. HThKAT. Freiburg: Herder, 2012, 284–297.
—. "Forschungsgeschichtliche Standortbestimmung der Literatur- und Rechtsgeschichte der Gebotspromulgation Dtn 12–26 in der Zweiten Moserede," in *Deuteronomium 12,1–23,15* by id. HThKAT. Freiburg: Herder, 2016, 1112–1116.
—. "Grundzüge der Deuteronomiumsforschung und der gegenwärtige Forschungsstand," in *Deuteronomium 1,1–4,43* by id. HThKAT. Freiburg: Herder, 2012, 33–230.
—. "Mose, der erste Schriftgelehrte. Deuteronomium 1,5 in der Fabel des Pentateuch," in *L'Écrit et l'Esprit. Études d'histoire du texte et de théologie bibliques En Hommage a Adrian Schenker*. Edited by Dieter Böhler, Innocent Himbaza and Philippe Hugo. OBO 214. Fribourg: Academic Press/Göttingen: Vandenhoeck & Ruprecht, 2005, 273–284 (=id., *Die Tora. Studien zum Pentateuch. Gesammelte Aufsätze*. BZAR 9. Wiesbaden: Harrassowitz, 2009, 461–469).
—. "Moses. The Suffering Prophet in Deuteronomy and Psalm 90–92," in *Propheten der Epochen/Prophets during the Epochs: Festschrift für István Karasszon zum 60. Geburtstag/Studies in Hounour of István Karasszon*. Edited by Viktor K. Nagy and László S. Egeresi. AOAT 426. Münster: Ugarit, 2015, 137–149.
—. "Pentateuch." *RPP* 9:682–690 (= *RGG*[4] 11:1089–1102).
—. review of *From Priestly Torah to Pentateuch. A Study in the Composition of the Book of Leviticus,* by Christophe Nihan. *ThR* 74 (2009): 470–479.
—. "Singing Moses: His Farewell Song in Deuteronomy 32," in *Psalmody and Poetry in Old Testament Ethics*. Edited by Dirk J. Human. LHBOTS 572. New York/London: T & T Clark, 2012, 169–180.
—. "The Integration of the Post-Exilic Book of Deuteronomy into the Post-Priestly Pentateuch," in *The Post-Priestly Pentateuch. New Perspectives on its Redactional Development and Theological Profiles*. Edited by Federico Giuntoli and Konrad Schmid. FS Jean-Louis Ska. FAT 101. Tübingen: Mohr Siebeck, 2015, 331–341.
—. *Theologische Ethik des Alten Testaments*. Theologische Wissenschaft 3/2. Stuttgart: Kohlhammer, 1994.
—. "The Pre-exilic Deuteronomy as a Revision of the Covenant Code," in *Kontinuum und Proprium. Studien zur Sozial- und Rechtsgeschichte des Alten Orients und des Alten Testaments* by id. Orientalia Biblica et Christiana 8. Wiesbaden: Harrassowitz, 1996, 112–122.
—. "Vom Gesetzbuch zum Buch der Prophetie des Mose als Schlussstein der Tora. Das Deuteronomium," in *Aspekte der Bibel. Themen, Figuren, Motive*. Edited by Hans-Joachim Simm. Freiburg/Basel/Wien: Herder, 2017, 124–137.
—. *Wandel der Rechtsbegründungen in der Gesellschaftsgeschichte des antiken Israel. Eine Rechtsgeschichte des „Bundesbuches" Ex XX 22 – XXIII 13*. StudBib 3. Leiden/New York: Brill, 1988.

Jeremiah 34 Originally Composed as a Legal Blend of Leviticus 25 and Deuteronomy 15

Kenneth Bergland (Andrews University)

Introduction[1]

Since the days of Wellhausen, Jer 34 has occupied center stage in the question of the chronological relation between the prophets and the Pentateuch, and more specifically the formation of the Pentateuch. For Wellhausen, "Jeremiah (xxxiv. 14) has not the faintest idea that the emancipation of the slaves must according to 'law' take place in the fiftieth year."[2] In other words, the author of Jer 34:14 does not have "the faintest idea" about Lev 25. Wellhausen saw the order of composition as Exod 21, Deut 15, Jer 34, and finally Lev 25. Since Jer 34 is used to date the so-called P source, this chapter according to Levinson has assumed the position of "an 'Archimedean point' in the relative dating of the Pentateuchal sources."[3] A key question that will be raised in the following is therefore whether Jer 34 shows traces of influence from Lev 25 or not, and if so, whether Lev 25 should be seen as a later redaction or part of the original composition of Jer 34.[4] Generally, those admitting reuse

---

1 This essay is based on the chapter "Manumission Instructions in Exod 21:2–11; Lev 25:10,39–46; Deut 15:12-18, and Jer 34:8–22" in my dissertation *Reading as a Disclosure of the Thoughts of the Heart: Proto-Halakhic Reuse and Appropriation between Torah and the Prophets* (Ph.D. diss., Andrews University, 2018), 229–334.
2 Wellhausen, *Prolegomena*, 120.
3 Levinson, "Zedekiah's Release of Slaves," 319. For a brief history of scholarship on Jer 34 see his pp. 313–318.
4 For representative scholars seeing traces of Lev 25 in Jer 34 as representing a later redaction see Chavel, "'Let My People Go!';" Maier, *Jeremia*, 249–281. And for representative scholars seeing Lev 25 as part of an original composition of Jer 34, see Fischer, *Jeremia 26–52*, 242–261; Bergsma, *Jubilee*, 160–170; Levinson, "Zedekiah's Release," 313–327. Some have claimed that Jer 34:8–22 does not belong to the original Jeremianic composition. Others have found the passage to be appropriate to Jeremianic tradition. Some see the initial prologue and longer sermon in Jer 34:8–22 as a Deuteronomistic supplement to a historical source, possibly a royal annal. For a discussion on the compositional history of Jer 34:8–22 see Cardellini, *'Sklaven'-Gesetze*, 313–315, 318–319; Holladay, *Jeremiah 2*, 238; Lundbom, *Jeremiah 21–36*, 557–558; Levinson, "Zedekiah's Release," 315–318. Lundbom writes: "The main difference between vv 8–11 and 12–22 is that the former is narrative and the latter a cluster of divine oracles, and nothing precludes both of them being written up at the same time" (Lundbom,

of Lev 25 in Jer 34 see it as a later redactional layer. Present discussion on Jer 34 therefore centers around identifying the *ipsissima verba* of the prophet and later deuteronomistic, possibly also priestly, redaction of the chapter. Levinson sums up present scholarship on Jer 34 as follows:

> Thus, the various positions on Jer 34 seem to move within a single universe. The redactional issues are defined in terms of a single question: which verses are Jeremianic, and which are Deuteronomistic. The assumption is that Deuteronomy and its literary history are the only relevant considerations. All of the important challenges or modifications still move within this model and confirm its assumptions. The problem with these approaches is that they do not work. They explain away the evidence that most challenges their own explanatory model, and relegate the material that does not fit the model into problems of syntax, text-criticism or secondary expansion.[5]

In the first part of this essay I will briefly review the arguments for seeing a reuse of both Lev 25 and Deut 15 in Jer 34. Since the latter is commonly more accepted, I will begin there. A main question is, however, whether the reuse of Lev 25 and Deut 15 should be identified as a redactional layer or part of the original composition of Jer 34. I will contend that there is a reuse of both Lev 25 and Deut 15 in Jer 34, and that this reuse cannot be separated from the original composition of Jer 34 without collapsing the passage itself. I will argue that Jer 34 presents a sophisticated blend of Lev 25 and Deut 15, challenging several assumptions within the discussion on the relation between the prophets and the Pentateuch, as well as the formation of the Pentateuch itself.

My concern in the following is not the question of absolute dating, but relative chronology. In other words, I am here not concerned with the question of whether Jer 34 should be seen as a pre-exilic, exilic, or post-exilic text, even if I have not found anything in this chapter to preclude a composition close to the mentioned events.[6] The commonly accepted assumption that a legal blend of passages from

---

Jeremiah 21–36, 558). More generally, Fischer has argued that the book of Jeremiah should be seen as a complex unified composition" (Fischer, *Jeremia 1–25*, 73).

5 Levinson, "Zedekiah's Release," 318.
6 Levinson has recently argued that Jer 34 reused Lev 25 and Deut 15 in its original composition, but questions whether Jer 34 should be seen as "a reliable historical witness to the circumstances leading to the destruction of Jerusalem at the hands of the Babylonian army," and prefers to date that chapter to "scribal exegetical activity in the Persian period" (Levinson, "Zedekiah's Release," 325). To me, diachronic linguistics seems to provide significant aid in the periodization of biblical texts. Relevant for the present discussion is Hurvitz' argument for Leviticus belonging to Classical Biblical Hebrew (CBH) (Hurvitz, *Linguistic Study*) and Hornkohl's argument that MT Jer belong to Transitional Biblical Hebrew (TBH) (Hornkohl, *Ancient Hebrew Periodization*). For a general discussion on the significance of diachronic linguistics for the formation of the Pentateuch, see Joosten, *Verbal System*, esp. pp. 377–410; Joosten, "Diachronic Linguistics".

Lev–Num and Deut necessarily needs to be late,[7] building as it does on a paradigm of the formation of the Pentateuch, cannot be presupposed here where that paradigm itself is up for question. The contribution of this essay to the question of the formation of the Pentateuch is therefore indirect. By clarifying the question of direction of dependence between specific passages in the Pentateuch and the prophets, we establish the relative chronology between these literary corpora. And by arguing for the priority of the Pentateuch and it being reused in the prophets, we challenge Wellhausen's romantic idea of the originality of the prophets.[8]

1. Deut 15:12–18 and Jer 34:8–22

In the following I will briefly summarize the main arguments for seeing Jer 34:8–22 as reusing and being dependent upon Deut 15:12–18.

1.1 A Case for Reuse

1.1.1 Uniqueness

Between Exod 21:2–11, Deut 15:12–18 and Jer 34:8–22 we find several unique parallels in the HB.[9] First, the combination of the root עבד + שֵׁשׁ שָׁנִים is only found in Exod 21:2; Deut 15:12, 18; and Jer 34:14.[10] Second, it is only in Exod 21:2, 7–8; Deut 15:12; and Jer 34:9, 14 we find the combination of the lexemes עִבְרִי + מכר. While מכר + עִבְרִי are used at different points in Exod 21:2, 7–8, only in Deut 15:12 and Jer 34:14 are they used within the same verse. Further, the lexical set אָח + מכר + עִבְרִי is found in relative proximity only in Deut 15:12 and Jer 34:14. The lexical set עִבְרִי + אָח + מכר therefore indicates reuse between Deut 15 and Jer 34, rather than between Exod 21 and Jer 34. Third, the phrase הָעִבְרִי וְהָעִבְרִיָּה in Jer 34:9 reminds of

---

7 Cf. Carr, *Formation*, 29–31, 34, 40–48, 66–71, 90–98, 303, 347–49; Rom-Shiloni, "Compositional Harmonization," 915.
8 Cf. Wellhausen, *Prolegomena*, 397–399. Fishbane commented: "A primary factor in Wellhausen's multi-levelled argument was that if in fact the law came first, one would hardly expect the occurrence of prophecy at all" (Fishbane, *Biblical Interpretation*, 292).
9 In my approach to the discussion of reuse and direction of dependence I have found the lists of what I prefer to call indicators of reuse and direction of dependence proposed by Michael Lyons and William Tooman helpful (Lyons, *From Law to Prophecy*, 59–75; Tooman, *Gog of Magog*, 26–34).
10 A question is the precise time of the release. Exod 21:2–11 and Deut 15:12–18 both advocate a six-year service (שֵׁשׁ שָׁנִים + עבד) and release in the seventh year. Jer 34:14, however, speaks of the beginning of the manumission at the end of the seven years (מִקֵּץ שֶׁבַע שָׁנִים), a phrase parallel to Deut 15:1. This is a well-known question, and it is not possible to enter the debate here.

הָעִבְרִי אוֹ הָעִבְרִיָּה in Deut 15:12. It is only within these two verses in the HB that we find the coupled gender-use of עִבְרִי. Fourth, the lexical set מֵעִמָּךְ + חָפְשִׁי + שלח is again unique to Deut 15:12–13, 18 and Jer 34:14.

1.1.2 Distinctiveness

First, the term עִבְרִי is found 34 times in the HB.[11] However, the use of the lexeme in a legal context in relation to the manumission of slaves is distinct to Exod 21:2; Deut 15:12; Jer 34:9, 14. Second, the combination אָח + עִבְרִי is only found in Exod 2:11; Deut 15:11–12; Jer 34:9, 14.[12] Exod 2:11 is found in the context of Moses seeing a "Hebrew man from his brothers" (אִישׁ־עִבְרִי מֵאֶחָיו) being beaten by an Egyptian, and the combination אָח + עִבְרִי used for how to relate to a Hebrew being one's own slave is therefore distinct to Deut 15:11–12 and Jer 34:9, 14.

1.1.3 Availability of Options

While the technical term for release in Exod 21:2–11; Lev 25:41–42; and Deut 15:16 is יצא, variously combined with חָפְשִׁי and/or חִנָּם, in the passages here under study only Deut 15:12–13, 18 and Jer 34:9–11, 14, 16 prefer the combination שלח + חָפְשִׁי when speaking of the release of slaves.[13]

1.1.4 Thematic Correspondence

First, the differentiated treatment of the Hebrew male and female slave, as found in Exod 21:2–11, is not reflected in Jer 34:8–22. Like Deut 15:12–18, Jer 34:8–22 advocates a similar treatment of the Hebrew male and female slave. Second, there is a thematic parallel between Lev 25:42; Deut 15:15; and Jer 34:13 regarding the exodus from Egypt as rationale for the manumission, something not found in Exod 21.[14]

1.1.5 Multiplicity

The case for reuse between Deut 15:12–15 and Jer 34:8–22 appears to be much stronger than that between Exod 21:2–11 and Jer 34:8–22. Further, all the parallels

---

11 Gen 14:13; 39:14, 17; 40:15; 41:12; 43:32; Exod 1:15–16, 19; 2:6–7, 11, 13; 3:18; 5:3; 7:16; 9:1, 13; 10:3; 21:2; Deut 15:12; 1 Sam 4:6, 9; 13:3, 7, 19; 14:11, 21; 29:3; Jer 34:9, 14; Jonah 1:9.
12 Cf. אָח in Lev 25:39; Deut 15:12; Jer 34:9, 14, 17.
13 Cf. Exod 21:26–27; Deut 15:12–13, 18; Isa 58:6; Jer 34:9–11, 14, 16; Job 39:3, 5.
14 Cf. Bergsma, *Jubilee*, 163. The reference to the exit from slavery and the house of slavery in Jer 34:13 (אָנֹכִי כָּרַתִּי בְרִית אֶת־אֲבוֹתֵיכֶם בְּיוֹם הוֹצִאִי אוֹתָם מֵאֶרֶץ מִצְרַיִם מִבֵּית עֲבָדִים לֵאמֹר) parallels the motivation clauses in Lev 25:42 and Deut 15:15. Here הוֹצֵאִי אוֹתָם מֵאֶרֶץ מִצְרַיִם in Jer 34:13 seems closer to אֲשֶׁר־הוֹצֵאתִי אֹתָם מֵאֶרֶץ מִצְרַיִם in Lev 25:42, than עֶבֶד הָיִיתָ בְּאֶרֶץ מִצְרַיִם in Deut 15:15. But is seems difficult to determine with a satisfactory degree of certainty what passage Jer 34:13 might be reusing the formulation from, or if it might even be combining from various sources, even if there are strong parallels to Deut 29:24. It may be an indication of a frozen formulation having its roots in the Torah-tradition. In any case, it is an appropriate locution in the context of Jer 34 speaking of the release of slaves. Cf. Fischer, *Jeremia 26–52*, 255.

between Exod 21:2–11 and Jer 34:8–22 seem to be best explained as parallels between Deut 15:12–18 and Jer 34:8–22, at points where Exod 21:2–11 and Deut 15:12–18 are parallel as well. Together with the stronger evidence for reuse between Deut 15 and Jer 34 it is therefore no reason to claim a reuse between Exod 21:2–11 and Jer 34:8–22.[15]

1.2 Direction of Dependence

1.2.1 Reference to a Source

Significantly, Jer 34:14 is introduced as a quotation, with YHWH in Jer 34:13 referring back to his previous instruction. It therefore seems reasonable to take Jer 34:14 as the borrowing text and Deut 15:12 as the source text.[16]

1.2.2 Integration

First, while Deut 15:12 consistently refers to the addressee in 2ms, consistent with its surrounding syntax, Jer 34:14 on its side, however, is more mixed. It has the 2mpl (תְּשַׁלְּחוּ) altered to the 3ms (אָחִיו), but when coming to the parallels uses 2ms like Deut 15:12 to refer to the addressee (מֵעִמָּךְ, וְשִׁלַּחְתּוֹ, וַעֲבָדְךָ, לְךָ). When the parallels with Deut 15:12 cease, Jer 34:14 reverts to 2mpl again (אֲבוֹתֵיכֶם), more appropriate for its general syntax. At the point where Jer 34:14 claims to quote the previous instruction, it therefore seems to presuppose a *Vorlage* referring to the addressee in the 2ms as we find it in Deut 15:12, except for the phrase אִישׁ אֶת־אָחִיו הָעִבְרִי.[17]

---

15 Contra Lundbom, *Jeremiah 21–36*, 563 and Levinson, "Zedekiah's Release," 323n. The use of עֶבֶד in Jer 34 might also reflect the contemporary practice in the days of Zedekiah's release, where the Judahites were kept as regular slaves. This accords with the nominal form of עֶבֶד not being used in the quote in 34:14, therefore showing no sign of amalgamation with Exod 21. Sarna finds the parallels between Jer 34 and Deut 15 to lead to "inescapable conclusions." And he sums up: "In the aggregate they exclude any possibility of the direct dependence of the events of Jer. 34 upon Ex. 21:1–11" (Sarna, "Zedekiah's Emancipation, 145).

16 If the author of Jer 34:14 was reusing Deut 15:12, what reason may he have had for eliminating the reference to the female slave found in Deut 15:12? It seems reasonable to take the elimination in 34:14 simply as a short-hand reference to Hebrew male and female slaves, elliptically referring back to either 34:9 or Deut 15:12. For a similar reading see Levinson, "Zedekiah's Release," 320–321n, contra Chavel, "'Let My People Go!'," 86–87.

17 It therefore seems unnecessary to postulate, as Chavel does, that "Jer 34.14 reflects a previous version of Deut. 15.12" (Chavel, "'Let My People Go!'," 78. Cf. 81). It seems that it is the introduction of אִישׁ in אִישׁ אֶת־אָחִיו הָעִבְרִי of Jer 34:14 that determines the 3ms suffix of אָחִיו. Cf. Cardellini, *'Sklaven'-Gesetze*, 317. Chavel might be correct in claiming that Jer 34:14's אֶת־אִישׁ אָחִיו, as a modification of Deut 15:12 reading simply אָחִיךָ, shows influence from and rework the formulation אִישׁ אֶת־עַבְדּוֹ וְאִישׁ אֶת־שִׁפְחָתוֹ in 34:10 (Chavel, "'Let My People Go!'," 80).
This is therefore a case where PNG-shifts indicate reuse by Jeremiah. Jer 34:14 adapts the person and number to accommodate the syntactic form given in Deut 15:12. For similar points see Sarna, "Zedekiah's Emancipation," 147; Holladay, *Jeremiah 26–52*, 241; Fischer, *Jeremia 26–52*, 255. Contra Glanz' claim that in the book of Jeremiah "the insertion of foreign text ma-

Second, we notice a difference between the singular חָפְשִׁי in Deut 15 and plural חָפְשִׁים in Jer 34. Of all the uses of חָפְשִׁי in the HB (Exod 21:2, 5, 26–27; Deut 15:12–13, 18; 1 Sam 17:25; Isa 58:6; Jer 34:9–11, 14, 16; Ps 88:6; Job 3:19; 39:5) it is found as a plural only in Isa 58:6; Jer 34:9–11, 16. The plural form is used consistently in Jer 34:9–11, 16 for the gender inclusive focus of the passage.[18] We find the only occurrence of the singular חָפְשִׁי in Jer 34 in v. 14, exactly where we find the closest parallels to Deut 15:12.[19]

1.2.3 Lexical Dependence

Both Deut 15 and Jer 34 speak of the Hebrew (הָעִבְרִי and הָעִבְרִיָּה) slave. In the entire book of Jeremiah only Jer 34:9, 14 use הָעִבְרִי and/or הָעִבְרִיָּה.[20] Otherwise the lexeme יהודי is preferred in the book, attested in 34:9 as well.[21] The same is the case with Deut 15:12, only here do we find הָעִבְרִי and/or הָעִבְרִיָּה in the book. But if we go with those scholars seeing Deut 15:12–18 as reusing Exod 21:2–11, this might find a simple solution. In Exodus עִבְרִי is attested 14 times.[22] So given (1) that Deut 15:12–18 reuses Exod 21:2–11, and this explains the occurrence of הָעִבְרִי and הָעִבְרִיָּה in Deut 15:12, (2) that there are no convincing reasons that Jer 34 is reusing Exod 21:2–11 directly, and (3) that the book of Jeremiah otherwise prefers the term יהודי over עִבְרִי, a reasonable reading seems to be that Deut 15 borrowed עִבְרִי from Exod 21, and Jer 34 again borrowed it from Deut 15.

2. Lev 25:10, 39–46 and Jer 34,8–22

Given the general consensus that there is reuse of Deut 15:12 in Jer 34:14, while we at the same time observe a clear reworking of the order and meaning of the former in the latter, we should be sensitive to the possibility that Jer 34 might also choose to reuse Lev 25 creatively. As argued below, there is sufficient evidence to claim that Lev 25 was reused in the original composition of Jer 34. But again, we witness a sophisticated form of reuse that cannot be restricted to a direct quotation as such.

---

terial is not responsible for causing PNG shifts" (Glanz, *Participant-Reference Shifts*, 217). For PNG shifts in LXX 41:8–22 see Hornkohl, *Language*, 119.

18 Contrast Deut 15:12 which also has the gender inclusive focus, but nevertheless formulates itself so as to take the singular חָפְשִׁי.
19 Again, a PNG-shift seems to indicate reuse, where the use of the singular of חָפְשִׁי in 34:14 seems to strengthen the claim that this verse is quoting from Deut 15:12.
20 Cf. Hornkohl, *Language*, 306, 312.
21 Cf. Jer 32:12; 34:9; 38:19; 40:11–12; 41:3; 43:9; 44:1; 52:28, 30.
22 Exod 1:15–16, 19; 2:6–7, 11, 13; 3:18; 5:3; 7:16; 9:1, 13; 10:3; 21:2.

2.1 A Case for Reuse

2.1.1 Uniqueness

First, the lexical set שׁוּב + דְּרוֹר + קרא is unique to Lev 25:10, 13; Jer 34:8, 11, 15–17, 22.[23] This also gives a basis for comparing the key term שׁוּב in Lev 25:10, 13, 27–28, 41, 51–52 with the occurrences of the same term in Jer 34:11, 15–16, 22.

2.1.2 Thematic Correspondence

First, the most striking case of thematic correspondence between Lev 25 and Jer 34 may be seen in the absolute abolition of Hebrew slaves.[24] Lev 25:39–46 legitimizes a differentiated treatment of Israelites and non-Israelites, but both Lev 25 and Jer 34 share the absolute ban on enslavement of Israelites/Judahites. This is not found in Deut 15.[25] While Jer 34:14 seems to be reusing Deut 15:12, advocating a release of all dependent Hebrews in the seventh year, Jer 34 nevertheless seems conceptually to be framed around the banishment of slavery of Hebrews altogether found in Lev 25.

Second, it is possible to see a link between the talionic element in Lev 26 and Jer 34. It is true that Deuteronomy and Leviticus formulate themselves in terms of faithfulness to the entire covenant. Nevertheless, Jer 34, and v. 17 in particular, seems to ground its talionic discourse on the implications formulated in Lev 26:25–26 if the manumission instructions in Lev 25 is rejected, as already pointed out by Bergsma.[26] Even if only חֶרֶב and דֶּבֶר are parallel, the thematic link between the hun-

---

[23] An objection to the claim that Jer 34 reuses Lev 25 might be that Jer 34 does not reuse the key term יוֹבֵל from Lev 25. On the possibility that "the term יובל had fallen out of general use" by the time we come to Ezekiel (and Jeremiah), see Bergsma, *Jubilee*, 61. See also p. 164n.

[24] In Lev 25 it is expressed negatively as לֹא־תַעֲבֹד בּוֹ עֲבֹדַת עָבֶד in v. 39, לֹא יִמָּכְרוּ מִמְכֶּרֶת עָבֶד in v. 42, וּבְאַחֵיכֶם בְּנֵי־יִשְׂרָאֵל אִישׁ בְּאָחִיו לֹא־תִרְדֶּה בוֹ בְּפָרֶךְ in v. 46, and positively as כְּשָׂכִיר כְּתוֹשָׁב יִהְיֶה עִמָּךְ in v. 40. A similar norm is expressed twice in Jer 34, with לְבִלְתִּי עֲבָד־בָּם בִּיהוּדִי אָחִיהוּ אִישׁ in Jer 34:9 and לְבִלְתִּי עֲבָד־בָּם עוֹד in 34:10.

[25] As Levinson correctly has pointed out, Deut 15 avoids using עֶבֶד for the Hebrew subservient except for permanent indenture in the phrase עֶבֶד עוֹלָם (Levinson, "Zedekiah's Release," 323). But this restriction is nevertheless different form the absolute abolishment of Israelites/Judaites that we find in Lev 25 and Jer 34.

[26] Bergsma, *Jubilee*, 167. Levinson argues that the talionic element is a *novum* in Jer 34 (Levinson, "Zedekiah's Release," 324). Even if I agree with Levinson in that Jer 34 contains original elements, the link to its sources might be closer in the talionic aspect as well, than he seems to admit. What we see here is that the author of Jer 34:17, 20 has drawn locutions from both Lev 26:25–26 and Deut 28:25–26 in both verses. In Jer 34:17, חֶרֶב, דֶּבֶר, and רָעָב parallel Lev 26:25–26, having חֶרֶב, דֶּבֶר, followed by the theme of famine, in the same order in both verses. Further, Jer 34:17 also appears to borrow the locution of being made a horror for the kingdoms of the earth (לְזַעֲוָה לְכֹל מַמְלְכוֹת הָאָרֶץ) from Deut 28:25. Likewise, Jer 34:20 seems to intertwine the curse formulas from Lev 26 and Deut 28. The phrase וְהָיְתָה נִבְלָתָם לְמַאֲכָל לְעוֹף הַשָּׁמַיִם וּלְבֶהֱמַת הָאָרֶץ in Jer 34:20 parallels וְהָיְתָה נִבְלָתְךָ לְמַאֲכָל לְכָל־עוֹף הַשָּׁמַיִם וְאֵין מַחֲרִיד in Deut 28:26, and given the likely reuse of Lev 26:25–26 in its entirety in Jer 34:17, it also seems reasonable to take the idea of being given into the hands of the enemy (אֹיֵב + בְּיַד + נתן) twice used

ger of Lev 26:26 and רָעָב in Jer 34:17 is clear. They are further found in the same order in both passages. The combination of חֶרֶב, דֶּבֶר, and רָעָב is found predominantly in Jeremiah and Ezekiel.[27] The words are usually given in the order רָעָב, חֶרֶב, and דֶּבֶר in the book of Jeremiah, except in 21:7 and 34:17. Only in 34:17 does it parallel the order found in Lev 26:25–26. Jer 34:17 therefore seems to formulate the sanction against breach of the manumission instruction in Lev 25:39–46 in terms of the curses of Lev 26:25–26.[28] The specific *novum* of Jer 34 is therefore more limited to the talionic punishment being formulated in terms of the שׁוּב + דְּרוֹר + קרא of Lev 25:10 and the curses of Lev 26:25–26.

2.2 Direction of Dependence

2.2.1 Reference to a Source

While the father's neglect to give heed to YHWH's instructions (וְלֹא־שָׁמְעוּ אֲבוֹתֵיכֶם אֵלַי וְלֹא הִטּוּ אֶת־אָזְנָם) in Jer 34:14 is presented as a neglect of the instruction in Deut 15:12–18, Jeremiah's contemporaries in Jer 34:17 are presented as neglecting to give heed to a release instruction strikingly similar to the one found in Lev 25:39–46 (לֹא־שְׁמַעְתֶּם אֵלַי לִקְרֹא דְרוֹר).[29]

2.2.2 Modification

First, even if Chavel sees elements from Lev 25 redacted into Jer 34 at a later stage, his discussion of לְבִלְתִּי עֲבָד־בָּם בִּיהוּדִי אָחִיהוּ אִישׁ in Jer 34:9 claims a sophisticated reworking and conflation of the beginning and end of Lev 25:39–46.[30] He argues that the author of Jer 34:9 reworked Lev 25:39, 46 by drawing from both the beginning and end of the slave release in Lev 25:39–46. If so it would illustrate the sophisticated scribal techniques used to compose Jer 34. Even if I must admit that it requires some goodwill to be able to follow the argument, the syntactic analogy between לְבִלְתִּי עֲבָד־בָּם in Jer 34:9 and לֹא־תַעֲבֹד בּוֹ in Lev 25:39, and the double reversal of בִּיהוּדִי אָחִיהוּ אִישׁ in Jer 34:9, placing אָח at center to produce the phrase, is difficult to ignore. Levinson writes: "The syntactically difficult formulation of Jer 34:9b, לבלתי עבד־בם ביהודי אחיהו איש, represents an exegetical précis of the beginning and end of the manumission law of the Holiness Code, summarizing and integrating its key

---

in Jer 34:20–21 as borrowed from the same locution in Lev 26:25.

27 Jer 14:12; 21:7, 9; 24:10; 27:8, 13; 29:17–18; 32:24, 36; 34:17; 38:2; 42:17, 22; 44:13; Ezek 5:12, 17; 6:11–12; 7:15; 12:16; 14:21; 1 Chr 21:12; 2 Chr 20:9. For discussions on how Ezekiel reuses Lev 26:25–26 see Lyons, *From Law to Prophecy*, 69, 72, 78–79, 82, 91, 94, 100, 113, 117–18, 120–21, 144, 150, 162–63, 183–184.
28 Cf. Miller, "Sin and Judgment," 611.
29 Cf. Fried and Freedman, "Jubilee," 2258.
30 Chavel, "'Let My People Go!'," 91–92.

components. This précis places Jer 34 in the reception history of the Holiness Code, not the other way around."[31]

2.2.3 Conceptual Dependence

As seen above, it is reasonable to see קרא + דְּרוֹר as linked to Lev 25:10. In Jer 34:8c we find the phrase לִקְרֹא לָהֶם דְּרוֹר ("to proclaim a release to them"). The prepositional phrase לָהֶם does not have a referent here. If we go to Lev 25:10, however, we find the clause וּקְרָאתֶם דְּרוֹר בָּאָרֶץ לְכָל־יֹשְׁבֶיהָ ("and they shall proclaim a release in the land to all those dwelling in her"). It may thus be that the prepositional phrase לָהֶם in Jer 34:8 reflects influence from לְכָל־יֹשְׁבֶיהָ in Lev 25:10.[32]

2.2.4 Word-Play

As mentioned, the lexical set קרא + דְּרוֹר + שׁוּב is unique to Lev 25:10; Jer 34:15–17. In Lev 25:10, 41 קרא + דְּרוֹר is used for the proclamation of release and שׁוּב for the return to one's own and ancestral property. In Jer 34:8 קרא + דְּרוֹר has the expected meaning of proclaiming a release. However, already in its first use in our passage, in 34:11, שׁוּב is given an unexpected meaning. We expect that the slaves will return (שׁוּב) home to their inheritance property. But instead שׁוּב is used twice in the following two clauses in 34:11 with other meanings. We find both their masters changing their mind (וַיָּשׁוּבוּ אַחֲרֵי־כֵן) and forcing the slaves to return to slavery again (וַיָּשִׁבוּ אֶת־הָעֲבָדִים וְאֶת־הַשְּׁפָחוֹת). Instead of the expected meaning "return (שׁוּב) home to their inheritance property" based on Lev 25, the lexeme שׁוּב in 34:11 is used in the sense of "change one's mind (שׁוּב)" and "forced re-enslavement (שׁוּב)." Isolated each usage does not seem significant, but as we continue reading it is difficult to avoid the impression that there is an intentional wordplay here.[33]

Jer 34:15 describes how the people had repented (שׁוּב) from their fathers' sins and done what was right in proclaiming a release. But then 34:16 reverts to the theme of their turning back (שׁוּב) from their right actions. With this subversion of שׁוּב in regards to the release, YHWH then declares in 34:17 that he will subvert the meaning of קרא + דְּרוֹר. He will release them to the sword, pestilence, and famine, formulated in terms of the covenantal curses of Lev 26:25–26, as pointed out above. And since the masters returned their slaves, YHWH declares that he will also subvert שׁוּב by surprisingly returning the enemies of the people back upon the city. It is a divine creative reading of Torah, taking its meaning in the opposite direction. Given that the lexical set קרא + דְּרוֹר + שׁוּב is unique to Lev 25 and Jer 34, and that Lev 25 uses them in a plain sense while Jer 34 subverts the meaning of קרא + דְּרוֹר, strengthening the claim that the multiple meanings of שׁוּב is also an intentional play, indicate that Jer 34 is the borrowing text.

---

31 Levinson, "Zedekiah's Release," 323.
32 I am indebted to Carsten Vang for pointing out this possible link.
33 For others who have recognized this wordplay see Fried and Freedman, "Jubilee, 165–168.

3. Jer 34 as an Original Legal Blend of Lev 25 and Deut 15

Having argued and concluded that there is reuse of both Lev 25 and Deut 15 in Jer 34, we can then move to the final and main point of this paper, namely that the reuse of Lev 25 and Deut 15 appear to be part of the original composition of Jer 34:8–22.[34] If we juxtapose the relevant three passages, with terminological parallels as discussed above between Jer 34 and Lev 25 underlined, terminological parallels between Jer 34 and Deut 15 double underlined, and conceptual parallels between Jer 34 and Lev 25 in italics, we get the following:

Lev 25:10, 39–46	Jer 34:8–22
10 וקדשתם את שנת החמשים שנה וקראתם דרור בארץ לכל־ישביה יובל הוא תהיה לכם ושבתם איש אל־אחזתו ואיש אל־משפחתו תשבו: . . . 39 וכי־ימוך אחיך עמך ונמכר־לך לא־תעבד בו עבדת עבד: 40 כשכיר כתושב יהיה עמך עד־שנת היבל יעבד עמך: 41 ויצא מעמך הוא ובניו עמו ושב אל־משפחתו ואל־אחזת אבתיו ישוב: 42 כי־עבדי הם אשר־הוצאתי אתם מארץ מצרים לא ימכרו ממכרת עבד: . . . 46 והתנחלתם אתם לבניכם אחריכם לרשת אחזה לעלם בהם תעבדו ובאחיכם בני־ישראל איש באחיו לא־תרדה בו בפרך: ס	8 הדבר אשר־היה אל־ירמיהו מאת יהוה אחרי כרת המלך צדקיהו ברית את־כל־העם אשר בירושלם לקרא להם דרור: 9 לשלח איש את־עבדו ואיש את־שפחתו העברי והעבריה חפשים לבלתי עבד־בם ביהודי אחיהו איש: 10 וישמעו כל־השרים וכל־העם אשר־באו בברית לשלח איש את־עבדו ואיש את־שפחתו חפשים לבלתי עבד־בם עוד וישמעו וישלחו: 11 וישובו אחרי־כן וישבו את־העבדים ואת־השפחות אשר שלחו חפשים ויכבשום לעבדים ולשפחות: 13 . . . ס כה־אמר יהוה אלהי ישראל אנכי כרתי ברית את־אבותיכם ביום הוציא אותם מארץ מצרים[35] מבית עבדים לאמר: 14 מקץ שבע שנים[36] תשלחו איש את־אחיו העברי אשר־ימכר לך ועבדך שש שנים ושלחתו חפשי מעמך ולא־שמעו אבותיכם אלי ולא הטו את־אזנם: 15 ותשבו אתם היום ותעשו את־הישר בעיני לקרא דרור איש לרעהו ותכרתו ברית לפני בבית אשר־נקרא שמי עליו: 16 ותשבו ותחללו את־שמי[37] ותשבו איש את־עבדו ואיש את־שפחתו אשר־שלחתם חפשים לנפשם ותכבשו אתם להיות לכם לעבדים ולשפחות: ס 17 לכן כה־אמר יהוה אתם לא־שמעתם אלי לקרא דרור איש לאחיו ואיש לרעהו הנני קרא לכם דרור נאם־יהוה אל־החרב אל־הדבר ואל־הרעב[38] ונתתי אתכם לזועה לכל ממלכות הארץ: . . . 20 ונתתי אותם ביד איביהם
Deut 15:12–18	
12 כי־ימכר לך אחיך העברי או העבריה ועבדך שש שנים ובשנה השביעת תשלחנו חפשי מעמך: 13 וכי־תשלחנו חפשי מעמך לא תשלחנו ריקם: . . . 15 וזכרת כי עבד היית בארץ מצרים ויפדך יהוה אלהיך על־כן אנכי מצוך את־הדבר הזה היום: 16 והיה כי־יאמר אליך לא אצא מעמך כי אהבך ואת־ביתך כי־טוב לו עמך: 17 ולקחת את־המרצע ונתתה באזנו ובדלת והיה לך עבד	

---

34 Cf. Bergsma, *Jubilee*, 164–165.
35 Cf. the discussion above on מֵאֶרֶץ מִצְרַיִם מִבֵּית עֲבָדִים.
36 From Deut 15:1.
37 For a discussion of וַתְּחַלְּלוּ אֶת־שְׁמִי in Jer 34:16 as a reuse of a locution from Leviticus see Bergsma, *Jubilee*, 167).
38 For the triad חֶרֶב, דֶּבֶר, and רָעָב as a reuse of the covenant curses in Lev 26–25–26 see above.

עולם ואף לאמתך תעשה־כן: ¹⁸ לא־יקשה בעינך ב<u>שלחך</u> אתו <u>חפשי מעמך</u> כי משנה שכר שכיר <u>עבדך שש שנים</u> וברכך יהוה אלהיך בכל אשר תעשה: פ	וביד מבקשי נפשם <u>והיתה נבלתם למאכל לעוף השמים ולבהמת הארץ</u>³⁹... ²² הנני <u>מצוה</u> נאם־ יהוה והשבתים אל־העיר הזאת ונלחמו עליה ולכדוה ושרפה באש ואת־ערי יהודה אתן שממה מאין ישב: פ

Given that modern commentators easily see the tension between Lev 25 and Deut 15, it would be folly to claim that the author of Jer 34 did not. Rather, the formulations in Jer 34 seem to be studied negotiations between the two. The initial description of Zedekiah's covenant with the people is introduced with a locution from Lev 25 (לִקְרֹא לָהֶם דְּרוֹר, v. 8c), then it is elaborated in locutions from Deut 15 (לְשַׁלַּח אִישׁ אֶת־עַבְדּוֹ וְאִישׁ אֶת־שִׁפְחָתוֹ הָעִבְרִי וְהָעִבְרִיָּה חָפְשִׁים, v. 9a), and finally conceptually formulated in harmony with the ban on enslaving Israelites from Lev 25 (לְבִלְתִּי עֲבָד־ בָּם בִּיהוּדִי אָחִיהוּ אִישׁ, v. 9b). The people's response in 34:10 is similarly intertwining elements from both Lev 25 and Deut 15. The repeated phrase in 34:10c, לְבִלְתִּי עֲבָד־בָּם עוֹד, is conceptually close to Lev 25. Otherwise the verse reads according to the diction of Deut 15 (וַיִּשְׁמְעוּ כָל־הַשָּׂרִים וְכָל־הָעָם אֲשֶׁר־בָּאוּ בַבְּרִית לְשַׁלַּח אִישׁ אֶת־עַבְדּוֹ וְאִישׁ אֶת־ שִׁפְחָתוֹ חָפְשִׁים... וַיִּשְׁמְעוּ וַיְשַׁלֵּחוּ). Finally, the people's reversal in 34:11 seems to be a combination of a play on the verb שוב from Lev 25 and the locution שלח + חָפְשִׁי in Deut 15.

A question is if any or all of the clauses with parallels to Lev 25 or Deut 15 could be removed from Jer 34:8–11, and still leave the passage meaningful? I suggest that this may be a test to see whether the two passages were reused in the original composition of Jer 34 or not. Based on the analysis above, which has shown that each clause in 34:8c–11 contain likely reuse of either Lev 25 or Deut 15, removing the clauses with reuse from either would leave us only with הַדָּבָר אֲשֶׁר־הָיָה אֶל־יִרְמְיָהוּ מֵאֵת יְהוָה אַחֲרֵי כְּרֹת הַמֶּלֶךְ צִדְקִיָּהוּ בְּרִית אֶת־כָּל־הָעָם אֲשֶׁר בִּירוּשָׁלִַם ("The word that came to Jeremiah from YHWH after the king Zedekiah made a covenant with all the people that were in Jerusalem"). First, we could ask whether some of the elements in 34:8c–11 could have been in an original composition without reusing either Lev 25 or Deut 15? We would immediately be confronted with the need to explain how Jer 34:8–11 could be seen as original in regard to the use of such terminology or conception. As argued above, it seems most reasonable to see them as reuse of Lev 25 and Deut 15 in Jer 34, and not the other way around. Second, it would leave us entirely ignorant about the occasion, purpose, content and implementation of Zedekiah's covenant. Third, it is not clear that it would have contained the description of the people's reversal in 34:11, and would therefore have been a deficient introduction to the divine indictment in 34:12–22. And if it was originally not an introduction to 34:12–22 it would be unclear why it was included at all in Jer 34. Fourth, since it would not be a meaningful literary unit in itself, but only function as a prologue to the divine indictment (34:12–22), which reuses elements from both Lev 25 and Deut 15, it

---

39 For how וְהָיְתָה נִבְלָתָם לְמַאֲכָל לְעוֹף הַשָּׁמַיִם וּלְבֶהֱמַת הָאָרֶץ is an exact parallel and likely reuse of the covenant curses in Deut 28:26 see the discussion above.

would undermine the basis for removing such elements from 34:8–11 in the first place. It therefore seems reasonable to assume that there was at least a reuse of either Lev 25 or Deut 15 in the original composition of Jer 34:8–11.

If the clauses with parallels to Lev 25 are removed, לִקְרֹא לָהֶם דְּרוֹר ("to proclaim among them a release") in 34:8c, לְבִלְתִּי עֲבָד־בָּם בִּיהוּדִי אָחִיהוּ אִישׁ ("that none enslave his brother among Judeans") in 34:9b, לְבִלְתִּי עֲבָד־בָּם עוֹד ("that none enslave again among them") in 34:10c, and the possible play on שׁוב from Lev 25 in 34:11a–b we would be left with the Deuteronomic content of the covenant, reading

הַדָּבָר אֲשֶׁר־הָיָה אֶל־יִרְמְיָהוּ מֵאֵת יְהוָה אַחֲרֵי כְּרֹת הַמֶּלֶךְ צִדְקִיָּהוּ בְּרִית אֶת־כָּל־הָעָם אֲשֶׁר בִּירוּשָׁלָ͏ִם . . . לְשַׁלַּח אִישׁ אֶת־עַבְדּוֹ וְאִישׁ אֶת־שִׁפְחָתוֹ הָעִבְרִי וְהָעִבְרִיָּה חָפְשִׁים . . . וַיִּשְׁמְעוּ כָל־הַשָּׂרִים וְכָל־הָעָם אֲשֶׁר־בָּאוּ בַבְּרִית לְשַׁלַּח אִישׁ אֶת־עַבְדּוֹ וְאִישׁ אֶת־שִׁפְחָתוֹ חָפְשִׁים . . . וַיִּשְׁמְעוּ וַיְשַׁלֵּחוּ . . . אֲשֶׁר שִׁלְּחוּ חָפְשִׁים וַיִּכְבְּשׁוּם לַעֲבָדִים וְלִשְׁפָחוֹת:

> The word that came to Jeremiah from YHWH after king Zedekiah made a covenant with all the people who were in Jerusalem . . . each one to send his slave and his maidservant, Hebrew male or female, free. . . . And all the officials and all the people, who had entered the covenant that each one send his slave and his maidservant free, heard . . . They heard and sent away. . . . who they sent away. And they subjected them to slaves and maidservants.

Taken in this way the passage would read procedurally well. But in Deut 15:12–13, 18 שׁלח + חָפְשִׁי follows an occasion, namely the six-year service. In this light, if the release in Jer 34:8–9 was based on Deut 15, it would have removed the occasion given in Deut 15 and instead rooted it in the royal edict. The secondary or dependent character of שׁלח + חָפְשִׁי in Deut 15 would thus be uprooted from its textual roots and transplanted into political soil. This is of course possible, given that Jer 34:8–11 as it now stands anyway grounds the Deuteronomic locution שׁלח + חָפְשִׁי in the royal edict and proclamation of release (לִקְרֹא לָהֶם דְּרוֹר). The present form of the text, however, invites us to seeing Jer 34:8–11 as an active reworking of both Lev 25 and Deut 15. Denying this, and removing the elements parallel to Lev 25, would nevertheless highlight the discrepancy between 34:9 and 34:14. While the occasion in 34:9 would be the royal edict, in 34:14 it would be the seven-year release from Deut 15. We would anyway somehow have to reconcile this discrepancy. And if this is admitted, then the likelihood of Jer 34:8–11 also reworking and incorporating Lev 25 increases. Further, the proximity of וּקְרָאתֶם דְּרוֹר in Lev 25:10 and קָרָא שְׁמִטָּה in Deut 15:2 rather lead us to believe that the author of Jer 34 was actively reworking and conflating Lev 25 and Deut 15, through the לִקְרֹא לָהֶם דְּרוֹר (Jer 34:8c), echoing the locution from Lev 25:10, and which is immediately defined by Jer 34:9a in terms of Deut 15 (לְשַׁלַּח אִישׁ אֶת־עַבְדּוֹ וְאִישׁ אֶת־שִׁפְחָתוֹ הָעִבְרִי וְהָעִבְרִיָּה חָפְשִׁים). The infinite construct of לִקְרֹא (34:8c) and לְשַׁלַּח (34:9a) also invite the two to be co-read. The major issue with the removal of elements from Lev 25 would be seen in 34:11. As argued above, it is likely that as the text now reads there is a play in 34:11a–b (וַיָּשׁוּבוּ אַחֲרֵי־כֵן וַיָּשִׁבוּ . . . אֶת־הָעֲבָדִים וְאֶת־הַשְּׁפָחוֹת) on שׁוב from Lev 25. Either one would have to deny such a wordplay or 34:11 becomes incomprehensible without it. The syntax of the verse would have been disrupted, leaving אֲשֶׁר שִׁלְּחוּ חָפְשִׁים hanging in the air. Re-enslavement is not prohibited according to Deut 15. Since Jer 34:8–11 formulates the problems with the re-enslavement in terms of Lev 25, without the clauses reusing Lev 25 we would therefore remain ignorant about what the problem with the re-enslavement was in the first place. Removing the clauses containing reuse of Lev 25 in Jer 34:8–11, would thus leave 34:8–11 a conundrum. It would neither function well as an introduction to the divine indictment in 34:12–22.[40] The reuse of Lev 25 in Jer 34:8–11 therefore seems original to the composition of these verses.

If the clauses with parallels to Deut 15 are removed, לְשַׁלַּח אִישׁ אֶת־עַבְדּוֹ וְאִישׁ אֶת־שִׁפְחָתוֹ הָעִבְרִי וְהָעִבְרִיָּה חָפְשִׁים ("to send his slave and his maidservant, Hebrew male or female, free") in 34:9a, לְשַׁלַּח אִישׁ אֶת־עַבְדּוֹ וְאִישׁ אֶת־שִׁפְחָתוֹ חָפְשִׁים ("to send each his slave and his maidservant free") in 34:10c, וַיִּשְׁמְעוּ וַיְשַׁלֵּחוּ ("and they heard and they sent off") in 34:10d–e, and אֲשֶׁר שִׁלְּחוּ חָפְשִׁים ("who they sent free") in 34:11c the passage would read

הַדָּבָר אֲשֶׁר־הָיָה אֶל־יִרְמְיָהוּ מֵאֵת יְהוָה אַחֲרֵי כְּרֹת הַמֶּלֶךְ צִדְקִיָּהוּ בְּרִית אֶת־כָּל־הָעָם אֲשֶׁר בִּירוּשָׁלִַם לִקְרֹא לָהֶם דְּרוֹר . . . לְבִלְתִּי עֲבָד־בָּם בִּיהוּדִי אִישׁ׃ וַיִּשְׁמְעוּ כָל־הַשָּׂרִים וְכָל־הָעָם אֲשֶׁר־בָּאוּ בַבְּרִית . . . לְבִלְתִּי עֲבָד־בָּם עוֹד . . . וַיָּשׁוּבוּ אַחֲרֵי־כֵן וַיָּשִׁבוּ אֶת־הָעֲבָדִים וְאֶת־הַשְּׁפָחוֹת . . . וַיִּכְבְּשׁוּם לַעֲבָדִים וְלִשְׁפָחוֹת׃

> The word that came to Jeremiah from YHWH after the king Zedekiah made a covenant with all the people who were in Jerusalem to proclaim a release . . . that none enslave his brother among Judeans. . . . And all the officials and all the people, who had entered the covenant   . . . , heard . . . that none enslave among them again. But afterward they turned around and returned the slaves and maidservant . . . . And they subjected them to slaves and maidservants.

The problem with this formulation is that it presupposes that the reader knows that דְּרוֹר means a release of present slaves. This could be solved by claiming that this is a reuse of Lev 25, and that the reader would immediately recognize the release from there.[41] Both לְבִלְתִּי עֲבָד־בָּם בִּיהוּדִי אָחִיו אִישׁ and לְבִלְתִּי עֲבָד־בָּם עוֹד seem to function as absolute prohibitions, namely prohibiting taking or holding Judahite slaves *per se*. Again, this could be taken as an imperative to release present slaves. But since no actual release of slaves is described, the return of the slaves in 34:11

---

40 Levinson criticizes traditional literary criticism of Jer 34: "Absent the judgment oracle, the whole rationale for the inclusion of the account of the manumission and its reversal in the book of Jeremiah collapses. In other words, the very fact that a preexilic Jeremianic condemnation of the events narrated in the account cannot be clearly identified within the passage should begin to raise questions altogether about the rationale for the inclusion of such an incident in Jeremiah" (Levinson, "Zedekiah's Release," 319).

41 It could also be explained as a common ANE knowledge that דְּרוֹר means a release of present slaves, something that may be a reasonable assumption. Cf. Weinfeld, *Social Justice*.

therefore comes somewhat surprising. It could be understood as a lacuna in the text, a well-known phenomena in biblical narrative,[42] but it would simultaneously leave us with a feeling that something essential is missing. Otherwise, we notice that reading Jer 34:8–11 as originally a reuse of Lev 25 without the elements of Deut 15 actually works better than the reverse.[43] On textual grounds, given the text as we have it, it is therefore no reason to prefer a reuse of Deut 15 over that of a reuse of Lev 25 in the original composition of Jer 34:8–11.

Proceeding to the divine indictment in 34:12–22 we find a similar challenge in removing either the elements parallel to Lev 25 or Deut 15 there. Here the reuse of Lev 15 and Deut 15 is attested more in separate sections. Even if a verse like 34:14 contain a significant concentration of reuse from Deut 15, the intertwining of elements from Lev 25 and Deut 15 is not as condensed as in 34:8–11. As in Jer 34:8–11, again we find that the prescription to release the slaves in Jer 34:13–14 is predominantly formulated in terms of Deut 15, with no clear elements from Lev 15. On the other side, the description of and indictment against the return of the slaves in Jer 34:15–22 is largely formulated in terms of Lev 25 (Jer 34:15–22), with elements from Deut 15 taking a secondary role. Jer 34:8–11 and 34:12–22 therefore utilize consistent and distinct approaches to reusing Lev 25 and Deut 15, Jer 34:8–11 intertwining the two tightly while 34:12–22 keeps them more or less apart in separate sections. And since 34:8–11 and 34:12–22 are interdependent, with 34:8–11 providing the narrative setting and 34:12–22 the divine indictment, it would seem most reasonable to conclude that the same author wrote 34:8–22, but reused Lev 25 and Deut 15 differently in 34:8–11 as compared to 34:12–22.[44] And just as in 34:8–11, it would create disruption removing either the reuse of Lev 25 or Deut 15 in 34:12–22.

---

42 Cf. e.g. Auerbach, *Mimesis*, 3–23.

43 While the people's release of the slaves in 34:10 could be read nicely without the element parallel to Lev 25 (וַיִּשְׁמְעוּ כָל־הַשָּׂרִים וְכָל־הָעָם אֲשֶׁר־בָּאוּ בַבְּרִית לְשַׁלַּח אִישׁ אֶת־עַבְדּוֹ וְאִישׁ אֶת־שִׁפְחָתוֹ חָפְשִׁים . . . וַיִּשְׁמְעוּ וַיְשַׁלֵּחוּ), likewise the people's return of the slaves in 34:11 could be read nicely without the element parallel to Deut 15 (וַיָּשׁוּבוּ אַחֲרֵי־כֵן וַיָּשִׁבוּ אֶת־הָעֲבָדִים וְאֶת־הַשְּׁפָחוֹת . . . וַיִּכְבְּשׁוּם לַעֲבָדִים וְלִשְׁפָחוֹת). But the narrative itself would be severely compromised by a removal of either the parallels to Deut 15 in 34:10 or the parallels to Lev 25 in 34:11. I therefore suggest that both the reuse of Lev 25 and Deut 15 should be seen as original to the composition of Jer 34:8–11.

It is also possible to imagine that elements were omitted from earlier compositions, but as Pakkala has pointed out, this would place any project trying to reconstruct the original composition in jeopardy (Pakkala, *God's Word*).

44 This observation counters Chavel's claim, of seeing 34:9 and 34:14 as representing different redactional layers (Chavel, "'Let My People Go!'," 92). Since Lev 25 and Deut 15 are reused in more separate sections in Jer 34:12–22, in contrast to the closer intertwining of the two in 34:8–11, we simply would expect 34:14 to be a purer quote while 34:9 more intermixed—just as we find it. "The two distinct justifications for manumission in Jer 34:9b and 14," as Levinson puts it, should therefore rather be seen as Jer 34 performing "an exegetical harmonization of the legal sources of the Pentateuch" (Levinson, "Zedekiah's Release," 323; see also p. 322), even if I am not able to follow him in seeing a reuse of the universal manumission from Lev 25:39–46 in Jer 34:14.

Summary

The above evidence lead to the conclusion that the reuse of Lev 25 and Deut 15 was part of the original composition of Jer 34:8–22, and cannot be removed without collapsing the passage itself. It is therefore not "remixing the language of Zedekiah's proclamation with the Deuteronomic legislation" that brings the author of Jer 34 to the understanding that the "Judean slaves must be—or should have been—released unconditionally and irrevocably."[45] This thrust in Jer 34 is better explained as an original reuse of Lev 25. It appears like a forced neglect when Chavel jumps over the possibility of a reuse of Lev 25 in the original composition of Jer 34 and insists that "a higher standard not called for in the original Deuteronomic legislation, demanding that the owner recognize his or her slave as a social equal" was the original creation of the author of Jer 34.[46] As argued above, the differences between the justification of manumission in 34:9b and 34:14 is best understood as different strategies of reuse by the same author. While 34:8–11 shows an alternating and much tighter knit reuse of Lev 25 and Deut 15, 34:12–22 largely relocate Deut 15 to the prescription to release in Jer 34:13–14, while 34:15–22 reuses Lev 25 more in the divine indictment against the people's return of slaves.

Given the above discussion it therefore seems reasonable to conclude that the reuse of both Lev 25 and Deut 15 was found in the original composition of Jer 34:8–22. And as a conflation of both Lev 25 and Deut 15, Jer 34 would be the youngest of the three. I can therefore concur with Levinson as he writes:

> The chapter truly becomes intelligible only once it is recognized that its author knew the Pentateuchal legal sources and exploited them to craft a brilliant exegetical homily on the cause of the Babylonian exile. His *halakic midrash* justifies the exile as punishment for covenantal transgression, for breach of Torah, now meaning an exegetical blend of the manumission laws of Deuteronomy and the Holiness Code. The chapter is a theodicy, one that presupposes not only the formation of the Pentateuch, but a sophisticated process of hermeneutics.[47]

And again: "In other words, this text is a *response* to the legal sources of the Pentateuch, not a *transition point* between them."[48]

---

45 Chavel, "'Let My People Go!'," 81.
46 Chavel, "'Let My People Go!'," 85.
47 Levinson, "Zedekiah's Release," 314–15.
48 Levinson, "Zedekiah's Release," 319.

Bibliography

Auerbach, Erich. *Mimesis: The Representation of Reality in Western Literature.* Translated by Willard R. Trask. Princeton, N.J.: Princeton University Press, 2013.

Bergsma, John S. *The Jubilee from Leviticus to Qumran: A History of Interpretation.* VTS 115. Leiden: Brill, 2007.

Cardellini, Innocenzo. *Die biblischen 'Sklaven'-Gesetze im Lichte des keilschriftlichen Sklavenrechts: Ein Beitrag zur Tradition, Überlieferung und Redaktion der alttestamentlichen Rechtstexte.* BBB 55. Bonn: Peter Hanstein, 1981.

Carr, David M. *The Formation of the Hebrew Bible: A New Reconstruction.* Oxford: Oxford University Press, 2011.

Chavel, Simeon. "'Let My People Go!' Emancipation, Revelation, and Scribal Activity in Jeremiah 34.8–14." *JSOT* 76 (1997): 71–95.

Fischer, Georg. *Jeremia 1–25.* HThKAT. Freiburg: Herder, 2005.

—. *Jeremia 26–52.* HThKAT. Freiburg: Herder, 2005.

Fishbane, Michael. *Biblical Interpretation in Ancient Israel.* Oxford: Oxford University Press, 1988.

Fried, Lisbeth S. and David N. Freedman. "Was the Jubilee Observed in Preexilic Judah?" in Milgrom, Jacob. *Leviticus 23–27: A New Translation with Introduction and Commentary.* AB 3B. New York: Doubleday, 2001, 2257–2270.

Glanz, Oliver. *Understanding Participant-Reference Shifts in the Book of Jeremiah: A Study of Exegetical Method and Its Consequences for the Interpretation of Referential Incoherence.* SSN 60. Leiden: Brill, 2013.

Holladay, William L. *Jeremiah 2: A Commentary on the Book of the Prophet Jeremiah, Chapters 26–52.* Hermeneia. Minneapolis: Fortress, 1989.

Hornkohl, Aaron D. *Ancient Hebrew Periodization and the Language of the Book of Jeremiah: The Case for a Sixth-Century Date of Composition.* Leiden: Brill, 2014.

Hurvitz, Avi. *A Linguistic Study of the Relationship between the Priestly Source and the Book of Ezekiel: A New Approach to an Old Problem.* Paris: Gabalda, 1982.

Joosten, Jan. "Diachronic Linguistics and the Date of the Pentateuch," in *The Formation of the Pentateuch.* Edited by Jan C. Gertz, Bernard M. Levinson, Dalit Rom-Shiloni, and Konrad Schmid. FAT 111. Tübingen: Mohr Siebeck, 2016, 327–344.

—. *The Verbal System of Biblical Hebrew: A New Synthesis Elaborated on the Basis of Classical Prose.* JBS 10. Jerusalem: Simor, 2012.

Levinson, Bernard M. "Zedekiah's Release of Slaves as the Babylonians Besiege Jerusalem: Jeremiah 34 and the formation of the Pentateuch," in *The Fall of Jerusalem and the Rise of the Torah.* Edited by Peter Dubovsky, Dominik Markl, and Jean-Pierre Sonnet. FAT 107. Tübingen: Mohr Siebeck, 2016, 313–327.

Lundbom, Jack R. *Jeremiah 21–36: A New Translation with Introduction and Commentary.* AB 21B. New York: Doubleday, 2004.

Lyons, Michael A. *From Law to Prophecy: Ezekiel's use of the Holiness Code.* LHBOTS 507. London: T&T Clark, 2009.

Maier, Christl. *Jeremia als Lehrer der Tora: Soziale Gebote des Deuteronomiums in Fortschreibungen des Jeremiabuches.* FRLANT 196. Göttingen: Vandenhoeck and Ruprecht, 2002.

Miller, P. D. "Sin and Judgment in Jeremiah 34:17–19." *JBL* 103 (1984): 611–23.

Pakkala, Juha. *God's Word Omitted: Omissions in the Transmission of the Hebrew Bible.* FRLANT 251. Göttingen: Vandenhoeck and Ruprecht, 2013.

Rom-Shiloni, Dalit. "Compositional Harmonization: Priestly and Deuteronomic References in the Book of Jeremiah – An earlier Stage of a Recognized Interpretive Technique," in *The Formation of the Pentateuch*. Edited by Jan C. Gertz, Bernard M. Levinson, Dalit Rom-Shiloni, and Konrad Schmid. *FAT* 111. Tübingen: Mohr Siebeck, 2016, 913–942.

Sarna, Nahum. "Zedekiah's Emancipation of Slaves and the Sabbatical Year," in *Orient and Occident: Essays Presented to Cyrus H. Gordon on the Occasion of his Sixty-fifth Birthday*. Edited by Jr. Harry A. Hoffner. Neukirchen-Vluyn: Neukirchener, 1973.

Tooman, William A. *Gog of Magog: Reuse of Scripture and Compositional Technique in Ezekiel 38–39.* FAT II, 52. Tübingen: Mohr Siebeck, 2011.

Weinfeld, Moshe. *Social Justice in Ancient Israel and in the Ancient Near East.* Jerusalem: Magnes, 1995.

Wellhausen, Julius. *Prolegomena to the History of Israel.* Translated by J. Sutherland Black, and Allan Menzies. Edinburgh: Adam & Charles Black, 1885.

The Non-Prophetic Background for the King Law in Deut 17:14–20

Carsten Vang

(Lutheran School of Theology Aarhus / University of South Africa)

The King Law in Deut 17:14–20[1] contains many peculiar traits. The law shows a fundamentally positive attitude to the very possibility of an Israelite kingship, but it gives no indications of the king's responsibilities and powers, despite the fact that the regulation appears within the section in Deut 12–26 that deals with the legal, societal, and religious offices in Israel (16:18–18:22).[2] In the ancient Near Eastern context, there were some clear and consistent concepts about the king's divinely appointed role and responsibilities. In the words of Gary Knoppers, the royal ideology in the ancient Near East embraced ideals of "health, security, continuity, proficient rule, prosperity, and justice."[3] The king is expected to deal righteously in all legal affairs.[4] However, Deut 17:14–20 is surprisingly silent about the Israelite king's relevance and importance for the national and spiritual welfare of his people. The presentation of the monarchy given here is also markedly different from the portrayal of kingship in the Books of Samuel and Kings. It deprives the Israelite king of any elevated position above his people. And it puts three sets of significant restrictions on the king in vv. 16–17: He must not acquire many horses, many wives and much wealth. It is these restrictions that make the King Law so radical compared with ancient Near Eastern conceptions and practice[5] and also compared with certain other Old Testament texts on divine kingship.[6]

In this article, I would like to explore the literary and historical background for these remarkable restrictions. Scholars have often explained the exceptional restraints in Deut 17:16–17 as a reflection of the prophetic critique of kingship in

---

1 All references are to the Hebrew Bible.
2 Cf. to this section McConville, *God*, 74–98; Lohfink, "Distribution," 336–352; Rüterswörden, *Gemeinschaft*; Vogt, *Deuteronomic Theology*, 204–226.
3 Knoppers, "Deuteronomist," 330.
4 Cf. the Babylonian *Fürstenspiegel* "Advice to a Prince" (W. G. Lambert, *Babylonian Wisdom Literature* [Oxford: Clarendon, 1960], 110–116).
5 McConville, *Deuteronomy*, 283; cf. also Knoppers, "Deuteronomist," 329–330. Vogt, *Deuteronomic Theology*, 218, ascertains: "[N]owhere in the ANE is the power of the king limited by a written document, as the power of the Israelite king is limited by the regulations in Deuteronomy".
6 E.g. Ps 72; 2 Sam 7:11–16; 1 Chr 28:5; 29:23.

ancient Judah and Israel. Scholars see the restrictions as an effect of a) the Old Testament prophets and their attacks on the kings and the crown for their confidence in military equipment, international treaties, and wealth; and b) the negative historical experience with the tendency of the kings in Israel, esp. king Solomon, to pursue their own selfish interests and accumulate enormous economic resources at the expense of the society as such. Deut 17:14–20 is very often interpreted as a Deuteronomic/Deuteronomistic[7] *reaction* to some negative experiences with the kingship in ancient Israel. For that reason, the King Law as such or at least the threefold restraint have been dated to the 7th century BC[8], to the exile[9], or to the postexilic period.[10] A few scholars have dated the King Law to the inauguration of the monarchy in Israel.[11]

This article will argue that there appears to be no connection on the literary level between the King Law and the prophetic criticism of the reliance on military power and international treaties. Even if an intertextual reading of this passage instinctively evokes the description in 1 Kgs 10–11 of Solomon's great abundance of horses, wives, and wealth, nothing in the phrasing of Deut 17:16–17 suggests that these restrictions were formed with king Solomon in particular as a backdrop. The King Law cannot be taken as an indication that essential parts of Deuteronomy or the Pentateuch are dependent on the Prophets. A more plausible background to the King Law should perhaps be sought in pre-monarchic circles in ancient Israel. It appears to stem from a period where Israel has not yet any direct experience with monarchy as governmental system but would be tempted to adopt the value systems of ancient Near Eastern kingship together with the very notion of royal government.

1. A prophetic background to the restrictions on the king in Deut 17:16–17?

One could argue that the prohibition against the king obtaining many horses in some way reflects the general prophetic critique of Judah's tendency to rely on horses and military alliances with foreign powers rather than trusting the Lord. This is a domi-

---

7 The scholarly terms "Deuteronomic" and "Deuteronomistic" are often used somewhat ambiguously. In this article, I use the term "Deuteronomic" for texts being found in the book of Deuteronomy and "Deuteronomistic" for the so-called "school" that is supposed to have edited many texts in the Old Testament.
8 E.g. Dutcher-Walls, "Circumscription," 615–616; Nelson, *Deuteronomy*, 8 and 223; Wazana, "Law of the King," 177 and 185.
9 E.g. Lohfink, "Distribution," 345–46; Otto, *Deuteronomium 12,1–23,15*, 1481.
10 E.g. Ebach, *Das Fremde*, 246; Hagedorn, *Between Moses and Plato*, 142; Römer, "La loi du roi," 110.
11 E.g. Halpern, *Constitution*, 227–229.

nant understanding in many studies on the King Law.[12] The juxtaposition of the nouns סוּס and מִצְרַיִם and the notion of emissaries sent to Egypt in v. 16 supports this interpretation (cf. Isa 31:1–3), just as the prophets often stigmatize Israel's confidence in political treaties with the great powers.[13]

On second thought, however, the probability of this interpretation does not appear likely. First, it should not be overlooked that the wisdom material also contains explicit warnings against relying excessively on horses, chariots and other military equipment.[14] The sceptical attitude towards relying on horses is not restricted to Deuteronomy and the prophets, but seems to be valid for several parts of the Old Testament.[15]

The main problem with this approach, however, is of a methodological nature. Many exegetes have fallen into the trap of interpreting Deut 17:16 in the light of the prophetical utterances about reliance on military strength and international support and in the next step to define the question of affinity and dependence from the very same texts, from which the Deuteronomic phrases have been elucidated. The meaning of the curious prohibition that the king neither multiplies his stock of horses, nor forces (groups of) his people into Egypt in order to obtain many horses, is often derived from the prophetic condemnations of Israel's reliance on military power.[16] סוּסִים and סוּס are just like that understood as war horses.[17] For that reason, many scholars here interpret סוּס as a figure term for military equipment, and martial terms

---

[12] Thus Labuschagne, *Deuteronomium*, 124; Maier, "Grundlage," 227; Mayes, *Deuteronomy*, 273; Otto, *Deuteronomium 12,1–23,15*, 1484–1485; Seitz, *Redaktionsgeschichtliche Studien*, 234–235; Zobel, *Prophetie*, 129–130. 146–147. — Zobel is followed by Graupner (A. Graupner and H.-J. Fabry, "שׁוּב *šûb*," *ThWAT* 7: 1154). Cf. also García López, "Le roi d'Israël," 292, and Rüterswörden, *Gemeinschaft*, 110–111. — Some interpreters have suggested a trajectory from specific prophetical utterances, like Hos 10:13b (Wolff, *Dodekapropheton*, 243) or Jer 22:13–17 (Ben-Baraq, "הארות לרקע ולזמנו," 39–42). According to Reimer, "Return," 227–228, Deut 17:16aβ–b might reflect the situation described in Ez 17:15.
Halpern, *Constitution*, 230, reverses the direction of influence, considering it a "fact that Isa 30:2; 31:1 refer directly to the prohibitions in Deut 17:16; so does Ezek 17:15." Wright, *Deuteronomy*, 212, likewise claims that the aversion to any "return to Egypt" in Deut 17:16 has resulted in echoes in the prophetic attacks on Israel's tendency to rely on many horses and on Egypt. None of them provide any arguments for their contentions.

[13] Besides the biblical references in the preceding note, see Hos 14:4; Isa 2:7–9; 30:1–7.15–16; 31:1–3; Ez 29:16.

[14] Cf. Ps 20:8; 33:16–17; 147:10–11; Prov 21:31. The horse is even termed a "lie" (שֶׁקֶר) in Ps 33:17, being unable to save a person or a king.

[15] For that reason, Weinfeld, *Deuteronomy*, 281, holds that Deut 17:16 is connected with the wisdom tradition in Israel.

[16] See e.g. Maier, "Grundlage," 227–228. Zobel, *Prophetie*, 121–130.146, provides a detailed discussion of the prophetic anti-treaty and anti-סוּס texts. However, apart from a literary-critical investigation of Deut 17:14–20 (pp. 112–119), he does not analyse the meaning of vv. 16–17, but assumes without further ado and without examination that these verses have similar content and business as the prophetic texts mentioned above.

[17] Joshua Berman, "Constitution," 224.

like רֶכֶב "chariot" or פָּרָשׁ "horseman" are considered implied in the very expression סוּס in Deut 17:16.[18]

However, each passage should be interpreted on its own terms, *before* one proceeds to a comparison of the passages in question and to a discussion of the possible lines of dependence. Deut 17:16 should first be seen in its own direct and more distant context in Deuteronomy before dealing with the question of possible relations to the prophetic critique of the national policy of cooperation.

The immediate context for the three restrictions laid upon the king in vv. 16–17 is the notion in vv. 14–15 that on one hand Israel may have a king like the surrounding nations, but on the other hand they should not elect a foreigner as their leading figure. Deuteronomy certainly has an explicit anti-Canaanite bias (cf. 6:14; 18:9–14). In spite of that, Israel receives permission to import the very idea of kingship from the neighbouring nations, but not all its underlying notions and concepts. The restrictive רַק in v. 16aα means that even if Israel complies with the command to make only one of their אָחִים their king (vv. 15b.20aα), their very conception of kingship should differ from that of their neighbours. The three reservations put on the king therefore seem to be directed against the prevailing kingship ideology in Israel's context. They may choose a king like the nations, but his priorities and values should be different from those of the other kings. The prohibitions imposed upon the king in vv. 16–17 do not forbid horses, polygamy and wealth as such, but only the increase of them. V. 16 therefore has in mind those instances, where the Israelite king might be tempted to follow the prevailing understanding of the surrounding world in concerning the attainment of many horses.

The subjects of an ancient Near Eastern king could often determine their king's prestige and glory on the basis of his possessions of these very items: horses, wives, and treasures. From at least the 15th century BC and onward, the horse was widely used both as a visual token of a king's grandeur, power, and prestige and as an efficient tool of war together with chariots.[19] The kings used to send each other gifts of precious horses and chariots as tokens of friendship and homage (cf. 1 Kgs 10:25). Various ancient sources describe the preciously decorated horses and chariots of the kings. The horse and chariot were fit for a king to display his royal status. And one Assyrian text from the time of Adad-Nirari II (911–881 BC) portrays the treasures of a prince, including his horses and chariots, as "befitting his royalty."[20]

Old Testament texts show a similar understanding of horses as being an appropriate symbol of royalty. When David's sons Absalom and Adonijah began to dis-

---

18 E.g. Albertz, "A Possible *Terminus ad Quem*," 280; Braulik, *Deuteronomium II*, 128; Labuschagne, *Deuteronomium*, 124; McConville, "King," 276; Otto, *Deuteronomium 12,1–23,15*, 1485; Tigay, *Deuteronomy*, 167; Vogt, *Deuteronomic Theology*, 216; Wazana, "Law of the King," 183. — Zobel, *Prophetie*, 128, contends that "die enge Verbindung von König und Militärwesen" found in Hos 10:13–15, is demonstrable also in Deut 17:16.
19 I am here building on Ikeda, "Solomon's Trade," 216–218.221–227, and Stendebach, "סוּס *sûs*," *ThWAT* 6: 784–785.
20 See the references in Ikeda, "Solomon's Trade," 221–222.

play their aspirations for kingship they provided for themselves מֶרְכָּבָה וְסוּסִים (2 Sam 15:1; 1 Kgs 1:5). Isaiah predicted that the royal steward Shebna would lose all the precious chariots he had acquired as token of his status (Is 22:18). Samuel warns the people requesting a king that if they get a king "like the nations", this king inevitably will draw attention to himself through taking young people to attend בְּמֶרְכַּבְתּוֹ וּבְפָרָשָׁיו (1 Sam 8:11). When the Persian prime minister Haman is asked to name an exceptional symbol of royal honour to be bestowed upon a subject, he, among other things, emphasizes the honour of riding one of the king's own horses (Esth 6:8–11). Of course, Solomon provided for himself a huge number of horses (1 Kgs 5:6; 10:26). Thus the horse with its accessories of chariot and ostentatious decorations was a wide-spread symbol in the ancient Near East of a king's glory and position. In many areas it was considered an item of status.[21]

It is true that the horse and chariot were a very efficient and much-feared tool in wars.[22] But the tri-partite composition of horses, wives, and wealth in Deut 17:16–17 suggests that סוסים here are not primarily thought of from a military standpoint. A linguistic detail in Deut 17:16–17 seems to imply that many horses, wives, and much silver and gold first and foremost were thought of as belonging to the king as person and not to his "office" as military leader and royal shepherd for his people. Three times in vv. 16–17, the repeated verb רבה hifil has the *lamed of interest* "multiply for himself" to emphasize the person, to the benefit of whom the multiplication will take place. The multiplication of horses, etc., takes place in the context of the king's own personal interest, grandeur, and gain, but not, or only indirectly, to the benefit of his people.[23] Only in 17:16aβ the *lamed of interest* is not found.[24] This tiny difference might indicate that by sending (some of) his people back to Egypt the king may be acting not only in his own interest, but because of an urgent military emergency situation.

Deut 17:16 advises the people electing the king that the he may not improve his own status vis-a-vis his people by multiplying horses for himself.[25] Seen in this light, the possible affinity to the prophetic condemnations appears only slender. Actually, apart from the very common words מֶלֶךְ, סוס and the proper name מִצְרָיִם, there are no shared words or locutions between Deut 17:16 and the "anti-coopera-

---

21 Unlike the mule and the donkey, the Egyptians considered the horse as belonging to the royal and the aristocratic class (L. Störck, "Pferd," *LÄ* 4: 1010).
22 Cf. Cantrell, *Horsemen*.
23 Wherever רבה hifil is used with the *lamed of interest*, it indicates how the subject does a certain act to the multiplied benefit of himself, cf. Jer 2:22 תַּרְבִּי־לָךְ בֹּרִית "use much soap for yourself," or Prov 22:16 לוֹ לְהַרְבּוֹת דָּל עֹשֵׁק "oppressing the poor to increase his own property." For רבה qal with the *lamed of interest*, cf. Deut 8:13 and Prov 4:10.
24 Most versions (LXX, Syr., Tg. Onq., (Tg. Ps.-J.?). Tg. Neof.; also 11Q19 56:17) read לו in v. 16b; but it is not necessarily the case that לו should be implicit in MT (thus Bernard Grossfeld, *The Targum Onqelos to Deuteronomy*, ArBib 9 [Edinburgh: T&T Clark, 1988], 57). SP and Vulg. support the MT (cf. *BHQ*).
25 Cf. Stendebach, "סוס *sûs*," 790: "Vor allem aber wird dem König der Verzicht auf die Arroganz herscherlicher Macht abverlangt ... Denn Pferde und Wagen sind Attribute königlicher Macht".

tion" texts of the prophets. It leaps to the eye that the word סוס stands isolated in Deut 17:16, without any of the terms usually appearing in its lexical field all over the Old Testament.[26] Unlike Deut 11:4 and 20:1, where the context makes clear that סוס refers to martial horses, nothing in Deut 17:14–20 suggests that we should envisage סוס in terms of warhorses. Deut 17:14–20 likewise lacks the dominating terms in the anti-cooperation oracles of the prophets, like בָּטַח or הוֹשִׁיעַ. On the other hand, the Deuteronomic phrase הַרְבָּה (ל) סוּס is found only in Deut 17:16 in the Old Testament. The very open and non-specific wording of 17:16–17 should not be overlooked or dismissed. All three restrictions are phrased in very general terms.

There is nothing in the King Law to suggest that we should understand the notion of "many horses" for the king in a context of military preparations or a policy of cooperation with foreign powers. In Isa 31:1 and Ezek 17:15 the role of Egypt is to provide military assistance by sending a contingent of its horses, chariots, and auxiliary troops.[27] In Deut 17:16, however, Egypt only functions as the most obvious place for horse breeding.[28] Only if one interprets Deut 17:16 in the light of Isa 31:1 and similar passages, does the restriction apparently betray a thematic affinity to the prophetic agenda. But methodologically it is alarming first to derive the meaning of Deut 17:16 from Isa 31 and other prophetic "anti-cooperation" texts, and afterwards define the direction of dependence and its nature from the very same texts.

2. No horses from Egypt

The proscription against obtaining too many horses is extended by v. 16aβ, which says the king may not bring his people back to Egypt in order to acquire many horses לֹא־יָשִׁיב אֶת־הָעָם מִצְרַיְמָה לְמַעַן הַרְבּוֹת סוּס. The reason given for this proscription is expressed through the quotation of a particular statement from YHWH (v. 16b).[29]

---

[26] E.g. סוס and רֶכֶב "chariot" (e.g. Exod 14:9.23; 15:19; Deut 11:4; 20:1; Josh 11:4; Isa 31:1; Zech 9:10); סוס and the verb רָכַב "ride" (e.g. Exod 15:1; Isa 36:8; Hos 14:4); סוס and פָּרָשׁ "horseman" (e.g. Exod 14:9.23; 15:19; 1 Kgs 5:6; Isa 31:1; Hos 1:7); סוס and מֶרְכָּבָה "chariot" (e.g. Josh 11:6.9; 2 Sam 15:1; Isa 2:7; Mic 5:9); or סוס combined with מִלְחָמָה (e.g. Deut 20:1; Prov 21:31; Jer 6:23; Hos 1:7).

[27] Cf. also 2 Kgs 18:24 and Jer 37:5–10.

[28] From the end of the Late Bronze Age, Egypt was known as a place of breeding of the most outstanding chariot horses (Ikeda, "Solomon's Trade," 228–229; cf. Solomon's import of horses from Egypt, 1 Kgs 10:28–29). In the Neo-Assyrian kingdom, big horses imported from Egypt and Nubia were especially appreciated from the days of Tiglath-pileser III (see Dalley, "Foreign Chariotry," 43–47, for references).

[29] The reference for the statement אָמַר יהוה in v. 16b is ambiguous; but Exod 14:13 may provide a possible background for the quotation (Lundbom, *Deuteronomy*, 540; Tigay, *Deuteronomy*, 167). – Lohfink, "Hos. xi 5," 226–228, has suggested that the divine word in v. 16b refers to the prophetic utterance in Hos 11:5a. He is followed by, e.g., Wazana, "Law of the King," 182; Zo-

This extension is often interpreted as a reference to the political endeavours in 7th and 6th century Judah to secure military support from Egypt in times of military crisis. Scholars have discussed whether this prohibition against sending people to Egypt refers to fellow Israelites trading in order to get horses from Egypt[30], or whether it refers to selling Israelites into slavery in exchange for horses.[31] Alternatively it may refer to an offer from the Judean king of auxiliary troops to the Egyptian pharaoh in order to get military support in return.[32] In a recent study, R. Albertz argues that the prohibition in Deut 17:16aβ-b reflects a particular historical situation, namely the military campaign of the Egyptian Psammetichus II against Nubia in 593–92 BC and his endeavours to let Judah into his anti-Babylonian league.[33]

The great variety of scholarly proposals about the precise historical setting that gave rise to the prohibition against sending the people to Egypt indicates in my eyes how tenuous and speculative the proposals are. Like the language of 17:16aα, that of 17:16aβ-b is very general and non-specific. The proscription refers to the king's עַם, but does this term refer to his army, his royal servants or his people at large? The verb being used for the movement to Egypt is the ambiguous שוב in hifil. The only specific term in the restriction is the country of destination, מִצְרַיִם.

The Deuteronomic phrase הֵשִׁיב עַם מִצְרַיְמָה (or הֵשִׁיב עַם אֶל מִצְרַיִם) is never found outside Deuteronomy.[34] No part of this phrase (apart from the toponym itself) reappears in the prophetic anti-cooperation texts. Here שוב hifil is never used in the context of sending emissaries to Egypt or approaching the Egyptian court for military support. The prophetic texts use verbs like יָרַד "go down," עָלָה "go to," or שָׁלַח "send" (Hos 5:13; 8:9; Isa 30:2; 31:1; Ezek 17:15; cf. 2 Kgs 18:4). The Judean king sends מַלְאָכִים "envoys" and similar to Egypt (Isa 30:4; Ezek 17:15), and he receives מַלְאָכִים from the neighbouring countries in order to form an anti-Babylonian coalition (Jer 27:3). On the linguistic level, there is only very slender connection between Deut 17:16aβ-b and the prophetic critique of the diplomatic affairs in 8th – 6th century Judah. In addition, there is no known historical situation in the Egyptian-Judean relationship from the 8th to the 6th century where the phrase הֵשִׁיב עַם מִצְרַיְמָה would make sense.

On the other hand, the use of שוב hifil with עַם as direct object matches Deuteronomy's strong exodus-orientation very well. In the rhetoric of Deuteronomy,

---

bel, *Prophetie*, 144–146. However, the fact that the shared words (שׁוּב אֶל אֶרֶץ מִצְרַיִם) are not restricted to this parallel and that Hos 11:5 differs much in content from Deut 17:16, means that Hos 11:5 does not seem a probable background oracle.
30 E.g. Lundbom, *Deuteronomy*, 540; Mayes, *Deuteronomy*, 272; Nelson, *Deuteronomy*, 224; Zobel, *Prophetie*, 147.
31 E.g. Gerbrandt, *Kingship*, 111.
32 E.g. Nelson, *Deuteronomy*, 224; Reimer, "Return," 227–228; Tigay, *Deuteronomy*, 167.
33 Albertz, "Fresh Look," 282–290. – Römer, "La loi du roi," 107–108, objects, however, that Jews were used as auxiliary troops many times in the Persian and Greek periods.
34 The phrase only appears in Deut 17:16 and 28:68. A similar construction with שוב qal is found only in Exod 13:17.

Israel has left Egypt only a generation ago (cf. 17:14 and 18:9). A warning to the potential king that he may not do anything to his people that might endanger its status as a liberated people fits the overall perspective of the Deuteronomic admonitions. In sum, the restriction in 17:16aβ-b is probably not a response to a particular political situation in Judah, but a theological warning that a future king may not look for horses in Egypt even if the most prestigious horses that would enhance his royal status could easily be found there. The king-to-be may not take any initiatives that will reverse the exodus for any part of his people.[35]

3. Many wives and much wealth

Next, Deut 17:17 severely restricts the king from obtaining a sizable harem and accumulating wealth.

Scholars have often interpreted the proscription against many wives in Deut 17 as a Deuteronomic warning against international marriages.[36] Political marriages were often used in the ancient Near Eastern political system to strengthen the ties between two countries or to seal an understanding of peace between them. However, taking a foreign princess into a king's harem could easily entail the recognition of her homeland's god(s) (cf. 1 Kgs 16:31–32). The Deuteronomistic authors of the Books of Kings obviously censures King Solomon for his apostasy because of his many foreign wives (1 Kgs 11:1–11; cf. Neh 13:26).

Yet we may question whether it is proper to read this proscription against taking many wives as a warning against *foreign* marriages. It leaps to the eye that Deut 17:17a is phrased without using at all the ordinary term for "foreign wives" like נָשִׁים נָכְרִיּוֹת.[37] While Israel is admonished in v. 15 not to elect an אִישׁ נָכְרִי "a foreigner" as their first king, and while Deuteronomy often refers to the unprotected status of the נָכְרִי compared with the citizens (14:21; 15:3; 23:21), the restriction in v. 17a does not use the qualification נָכְרִי. Therefore, the interpreter should not read this qualification into the proscription against many wives in v. 17.

Tigay notes that the proscription in Deut 17:17 against many wives might have another background, namely that a big harem might detract the king from his duties.[38] Prov 31:3 also warns a king against being obsessed with many women. Tigay adduces a parallel from ancient Mari. In a letter to his son, the king of Mari, the Assyrian king Shamshi-Adad I (ca. 1809–1776 BC) condemns him for failing his

---

35 Thus rightly McConville, *Deuteronomy*, 294; Otto, *Deuteronomium 12,1–23,15*, 1485.
36 E.g. Albertz, "Fresh Look," 280; Lundbom, *Deuteronomy*, 541; Nelson, *Deuteronomy*, 224; Nicholson, *Deuteronomy*, 110.
37 1 Kgs 11:1.8; Ezra 10:2.10–11.14.17–18.44; Neh 13:26–27.
38 Tigay, *Deuteronomy*, 167; cf. Nelson, *Deuteronomy*, 224.

royal duties as chief of army because of his preference of spending time with women.[39]

To all appearances, the proscription against taking many wives rather applies to marrying many women from within the covenant people. When a family gets a daughter adopted into the king's family through marriage, the societal and economic status of that family would be raised considerably. A class of beneficiary noblemen would be the result.[40] The fact that Deuteronomy contains no references to court officials (שָׂרִים) in its legislation about the community[41] means that it imagines a society having no particular classes.[42] The limitations on the king's ubiquitous prestige symbols should be seen in with the context of Deuteronomy's vision for an egalitarian power structure.[43]

The king may not set himself apart from his fellow citizens (17:20aα), and he should not take any initiatives that might endanger his dependence on the instructions of God (17:20aβ). Where the shared ideal for an ancient Near Eastern divine king would entail many horses, many wives, and much wealth as ciphers for the king's glory and divine approval, the preferences for the Israelite king go in a totally another direction. In respect of the values of kingship, Deut 17:16–20 is indeed counter-cultural. If we read the restrictions on the king in Deut 17:16–17 without having any knowledge of the prophetic critique of the nation's trust in military strength, political alliances, and much silver and gold, probably no one would have thought in that direction.

4. The historical experience with Solomon's great affluence as a background?

If a prophetic background for the restraints on the king is not probable, another historical background appears to be more feasible. Many scholars suppose that the warning in Deut 17:16–17 against the royal acquisition of many horses, many wives, and much wealth has the negative experiences with king Solomon's reign as its backdrop. Weinfeld contends that "Solomon's sins are echoed in this law."[44] Many scholars share this understanding, and they often express themselves with great

---

39 Tigay, *Deuteronomy*, 168, and Dossin, *Correspondance*, no. 69 rev.
40 Berman, "Constitution," 531; Dutcher-Walls, "Circumscription," 608–609.
41 Robson, "Composition," 50. In Deuteronomy, the שָׂרִים are appointed to ad-hoc tasks.
42 Even the שׁוֹפְטִים (judges) and the שֹׁטְרִים (officials) do not constitute a particular class in Deuteronomy, since both groups are appointed at the local level and not by any central authority (16:18), and since every Israelite may be eligible for these offices. In Deuteronomy, the שׁוֹפְטִים and שֹׁטְרִים belong to the people, not to the king.
43 See Berman, "Constitution".
44 Weinfeld, *Deuteronomy*, 168.

assurance on the matter.[45] Jack Lundbom uses Solomon alone as his basis of explanation for the restrictions in Deut 17:16–17. What the King Law warns against is "precisely what Solomon went to do."[46]

Gary Knoppers, however, has demonstrated how the Deuteronomistic description of king Solomon's reign in 1 Kgs 3–11 in many aspects differs profoundly from the Deuteronomic ideal in Deut 17 of the divinely chosen king who subscribes to the ideal of fearing the Lord rather than seeking the royal status symbols of the surrounding nations.[47] The author describes Solomon's immense wealth and remarkable wisdom as God's faithful fulfilment of his promises to the king at his inauguration (1 Kgs 3:13). Solomon's extensive trade with horses is depicted in a neutral manner in Kings (10:28–29), as an example of his great income and the great respect he enjoys in his own time. The first part of Solomon's long and prosperous reign makes the people of Israel at last experience the Deuteronomic promise of rest in the land (5:5; cf. Deut 12:8).

The Deuteronomistic author certainly censures Solomon for his many foreign wives in 1 Kgs 11:1–9, a critique that evokes Deut 17:17a. However, a close reading of 1 Kgs 11 shows that this passage does not reuse any phrase from Deut 17:17. The only shared words are the plural word נָשִׁים and the noun לֵבָב/לֵב.[48] In spite of the fact that the Book of Kings so often quotes from Deuteronomy and compares the politics of the kings in Israel and Judah to the ideals in Deuteronomy, it comes as a surprise that to all appearance 1 Kgs 11 does not formulate its critique of Solomon on the lexical basis of the restrictions in the King Law.[49] Instead, the author alludes to Deut

---

45 Brueggemann, *Deuteronomy*, 185: "There is no doubt, yet again, that Solomon is indeed the model here"; Clements, *Deuteronomy*, 31: "Clearly only Solomon can have been in mind in such a specification"; Labuschagne, *Deuteronomium*, 123–125; Sweeney, "Critique," 611: "Deut 17:14–20 presupposes Solomon as the royal antitype or the model of royal misbehavior." Cf. also Braulik, *Deut 16,18–34,12*, 129; Hagedorn, *Between Moses and Plato*, 143; Nicholson, *Deuteronomy,* 109–110; Römer, "La loi du roi," 106–107.
46 Lundbom, *Deuteronomy*, 540.
47 Knoppers, "Deuteronomist," 337–344.
48 The phrase נָטָה לֵבָב (hifil) in 1 Kgs 11:2–4 is often taken as a close parallel to the סוּר לֵבָב of Deut 17:17a (e.g. Brettler, "Structure," 90; Römer, "La loi du roi," 106). It should not be overlooked, however, that the two phrases differ as to their sense. While נָטָה לֵבָב (hifil) carries the sense "turn one's heart in a particular direction" and therefore it may have both a positive (1 Kgs 8:58) and a negative connotation (1 Kgs 11:2–4), the Deuteronomic term סוּר לֵבָב exclusively carries the connotation of turning aside from something given. In 1 Kgs 11, it is the foreign wives who are the subject of the leading astray. In Deut 17:17 the king's heart is the subject (Wazana, "Law of the King," 181). The term נָטָה לֵבָב (hifil) does not appear to be an allusive reformulation of וְלֹא יָסוּר לְבָבוֹ in Deut 17:17a.
49 From this meagre pool of isolated, shared words in 1 Kgs 11:1–9 and Deut 17:17, many scholars contend that 1 Kings 11 alludes to the King Law, e.g. Berman, "Law Code," 338–344; Brettler, "Structure"; Wray Beal, *1 and 2 Kings*, 170. – However, the occurrence of two isolated nouns in common cannot support the impulse to find a conscious allusion to a Deuteronomic pretext. In order to have an author intended allusion in a text, the shared words must appear in a similar syntactical construction, see Vang, "Prophet," 283.

7:2–4 by means of a quotation formula (אָמַר־יְהוָה) and by rephrasing the ban on intermarriage with the seven nations in Canaan into a proscription against engagement with the neighbouring nations. For the Deuteronomistic author, the problem with King Solomon is not the great number of his wives *per se*, but rather the *foreign* origin of his many wives. For that reason, Deut 7:2–4 was more appropriate for the author of Kings as the basis of critique rather than the King Law.

Even if the King Law restrictions apparently were not framed from knowledge of Solomon's excesses in wealth, horses and women, it is evident that the king blatantly violates the Deuteronomic proscription, and the question naturally arises whether the authors of 1 Kings 3–11 make any allusion to Deut 17:16–17 in their otherwise neutral description of the king's great wealth, his many horses, and his many foreign wives and concubines in 1 Kgs 9:26–11:9.[50] However, apart from very common words like זָהָב, כֶּסֶף, סוּס, and לֵבָב + נָשִׁים, there are no shared locutions between Deut 17:16–17 and 1 Kgs 9:26–11:9.[51] In addition, the order of presentation in 1 Kgs 3–11 differs from Deut 17:16–17.[52] While 1 Kings first describes Solomon's great wealth in many details and with many examples (1 Kgs 10:21.27), then his many horses and chariots (1 Kgs 10:26. 28–29), and at the end his many wives (1 Kgs 11), the King Law has many horses, many wives and much silver and gold in that sequence. The topical order is different. One reason for the fact that the Book of Kings seemingly leaves Deut 17:14–20 out of account in its castigation of Solomon's kingship may be that the Deuteronomistic authors present David's rule and example as the ideal for divine kingship in Israel. A critique of Solomon from Deut 17:16–17 would also entail a critique of his father David for his many wives (cf. 2 Sam 5:13–16; 1 Chr 3:5–9). In addition, in Solomon's inaugural dream God had promised him great wealth and tremendous honour (1 Kgs 3:10–14). Solomon's great abundance of horses and prosperity is stated as a token of God's faithfulness to his promise. An allusional reference to the restrictions in Deut 17:16–17 would destroy this understanding.

In a recent study, Nili Wazana rightly argues that Deut 17:16–17 cannot be seen as an echo of Solomon's excesses. Due to the significant differences between the phrasing of the King Law and the description of Solomon's reign in 1 Kings 9–11, "it is impossible" to trace a polemic in Deut 17 against particular kings in Israel.[53] Instead, Wazana argues that the idea of many horses, much wealth and many wives are characteristic symbols of great empires, esp. the Neo-Assyrian empire. The three-fold restraint on the king should be seen as a warning against building an em-

---

50 Berman, "Law Code," 342–344, argues that 1 Kings 9:26–11:13 does not allude only to the three restrictions of Deut 17:16–17, but to the whole section 17:14–20, including the promise in v. 20.
51 The common Deuteronomic locution כֶּסֶף וְזָהָב (cf. Deut 7:25; 8:13; 17:17; 29:16) does not appear in 1 Kgs 3–11 at all.
52 Against Weinfeld, *Deuteronomy*, 168 n. 4.
53 Wazana, "Law of the King," 182.

pire in tune with the waning Assyrian hegemony in the second part of the 7th century BC.

Wazana's proposal, however, is open to critique. We have argued above that the prohibition against obtaining many horses should not be interpreted as a restraint on creating an army with chariot forces, and that the proscription against taking many women does not firstly refer to diplomatic marriages. In addition, there is no allusion to Assyria or the Assyrian hegemony in the whole book of Deuteronomy, a fact that Wazana readily acknowledges.[54] The restraints on the Israelite king in Deut 17:16–17 may apply to many periods and to several different cases of divinely approved kingship in the Ancient Near East. Finally, in the wake of Assyria's political collapse in the late 7th century BC, Judah was not able to have any imperial ambitions.

5. The restrictions in their Deuteronomic context

While a background in the political milieu of the 7th cententury BC or the postexilic period seems difficult to maintain, the three circumscriptions on the king's glory and power symbols in Deut 17:16–17 make much sense in the light of Deuteronomy's overall aim. Joshua Berman has shown that Deuteronomy advocates an egalitarian society where no tribe, class or person should have absolute power.[55] It argues for a collective power strategy in society where the people as a collective body is responsible for justice and where the powers of the various offices are curtailed in order not to endanger the egalitarian vision. The primary requisite for the future king is that he should be "one from your brothers" (17:15). In principle, any Israelite male would be eligible for this duty. The three-fold restriction seeks to prevent kingship in Israel from jeopardizing the idea of an egalitarian brotherhood. While the king is supposed to have royal power (he will "sit on his throne," 17:18) and have a hereditary kingship (17:20), he should avoid pursuing royal glory symbols that would lead him to consider himself elevated above his people (17:20). The danger that the king's heart may turn away (v. 17) is coached in the same language as the risk that every Israelite is facing (4:9; 11:16), and the temptation of the king to self-overestimation (v. 20) is identical with the warning raised to every Israelite in 8:14. The king should be the exemplary law-abiding Israelite (v. 18–19). The proscriptions against royal

---

54 It should be admitted that many scholars find traces of literary influence from Neo-Assyrian treaty curses on the curses in Deut 28 (e.g. Weinfeld, *Deuteronomy*, 116–129; Eckart Otto, *Deuteronomium 12–34*, 1994–1997. In a recent study, K. Lawson Younger and Neil A. Huddleston thoroughly examine the issue and refute the popular theory of a trajectory from Assyrian curse traditions into Deut 28: Lawson Younger and Huddleston, "Challenges," 84–104. A Deuteronomic dependence on Assyrian curse themes and phraseology appears difficult to substantiate.

55 See Berman, "Constitution"; idem., *Created Equal*, 53–80.

interest in many horses, many wives, and much wealth will ensure that the kings support the idea of an egalitarian power structure instead of undermining it.

The injunction in 17:15 that Israel must not choose a אִישׁ נָכְרִי (a "foreigner") as king is puzzling and has caused much debate.[56] This restriction is enigmatic, since Israel and Judah to all appearance never were governed by a king of foreign extraction, nor were tempted to elect a foreigner as their king. Nicholson has suggested that the reference to the אִישׁ נָכְרִי in 17:15 may be an allusion to the experiences with the long-lasting hegemony of the Neo-Assyrian great kings. The injunction against a "foreigner" may therefore be a veiled reference to the Assyrian Great King.[57]

However, after decades of Assyrian oppressive hegemony, it would have been unnecessary to warn against a choosing a foreigner as a king, especially when a native dynastic lineage is available. The Assyrian supremacy was imposed on the Israelite and Judean kingdoms by brutal military force, and there was no incident of public choice of the Assyrian Great King.

V. 15 does not refer to circumstances where a foreign power threatens to impose a vassal king of an external origin on Israel.[58] In addition, the term אִישׁ נָכְרִי implies that the candidate is not of a mixed descent, like Abimelek (Judg 9:6), but comes from a foreign people. The verse presupposes that the people as a collective body are in a position of being able to designate a qualified person as their new king. The people are here given the full authority to elect the king (שׂוֹם תָּשִׂים עָלֶיךָ מֶלֶךְ), of course, after due divine appointment. To all appearance this injunction does not reflect a particular historical situation, but addresses the situation where Israel is without a royal power structure but considers a major shift in the prevailing management system. V. 15 gives best meaning in a pre-monarchic setting when Israel was tempted to adopt the idea of royal power structure from outside, but had no ruling families yet or chieftain rule who might qualify for royal power.

6. Conclusion

The restrictions on the king in Deut 17:16–17 are phrased in terms so generic that no particular Israelite king seems to be in view. The circumscription of the powers of the king is in total keeping with Deuteronomy's emphasis on civil leadership[59] and the call for an egalitarian power structure. The background for the restrictions on the

---

56 See Nicholson, "'Do Not Dare'," 46–47, for an overview (= Nicholson, *Deuteronomy*, 117–118).
57 Nicholson, "'Do Not Dare'," 58–61. He is followed by, e.g., Albertz, "A Fresh Look," n. 38; Wazana, "Law of the King," 179.
58 Against e.g. Nelson, *Deuteronomy*, 223.
59 Johnston, "Civil Leadership," 148.

king is probably not the prophetic critique of the royalty in Israel and Judah, nor the Deuteronomistic denouncement of Solomon's excessive acquisition of horses, wealth, and foreign spouses, but rather the overall ancient Near Eastern ideal about royal status and power symbols. This is in total keeping with the egalitarian power structure espoused by the book.

This, of course, tells us nothing about the date of the King Law, only that neither the prophetic critique nor Solomon's abundance appear to have motivated the restrictions. The section could still be late because of other indicators. However, a provenance of the King Law with its restrictions in the exilic or postexilic period does not appear obvious. The very unusual delimitations of the royal power symbols appear more sensible in a context where a non-Israelite pretender to the future throne could be an option. When the Israelite tribal leaders finally went to Samuel to ask for a king "like the nations" to fight their wars (1 Sam 8:5.19–20), a king of foreign descent apparently was no longer an option despite the obvious dissatisfaction with the current Israelite leadership (8:2–5). It seemed self-evident now that a future king should come from the midst of the people, since the elders approached the old prophet and asked him to launch the process to appoint a king. Deut 17:15 in particular and the restraints in King Law in general make best sense against the backdrop of a pre-monarchic background.

Bibliography

Albertz, Rainer. "A Possible *Terminus ad Quem* for the Deuteronomistic Legislation – A Fresh Look at Deut 17:16," in *Homeland and Exile: Biblical and Ancient Near Eastern Studies in Honour of Bustenay Oded*. Edited by Gershon Galil, Mark Geller, and Alan Millard. VTSup 130. Leiden: Brill, 2009, 271–296.

Ben-Baraq, Zafrirah. "(כ–יד :יז 'דב) "חוק המלך" של ולזמנו לרקע הארות [The Religious-Prophetic Background of the 'Law of the King' in Deut 17:14–20]." *Shnaton* 1 (1975): 33–44.

Berman, Joshua. "Constitution, Class, and the Book of Deuteronomy." *Hebraic Political Studies* 1 (2006): 523–548.

—. *Created Equal: How the Bible Broke with Ancient Political Thought*. Oxford: Oxford University Press, 2008.

—. "Law Code as Plot Template in Biblical Narrative (1 Kings 9.26–11.13; Joshua 2.9–13)." *JSOT* 40.3 (2016): 337–49.

Botterweck, G. Johannes, Heinz-Josef Fabry, and Helmer Ringgren, eds. *Theologisches Wörterbuch zum Alten Testament*. 10 vols. Stuttgart: Kohlhammer, 1973–2015.

Braulik, Georg. *Deuteronomium II. 16,18–34,12*. NEchtB. Würzburg: Echter, 1992.

Brettler, Marc. "The Structure of 1 Kings 1–11." *JSOT* 49 (1991): 87–97.
Brueggemann, Walter. *Deuteronomy*. AOTC. Nashville: Abingdon, 2001.
Cantrell, Deborah O'Daniel. *The Horsemen of Israel: Horses and Chariotry in Monarchic Israel (Ninth-Eighth Centuries B.C.E.)*. History, Archaeology, and Culture of the Levant 1. Winona Lake, IN: Eisenbrauns, 2011.
Clements, R. E. *Deuteronomy*. OTG. Sheffield: JSOT Press, 1989.
Dalley, S. "Foreign Chariotry and Cavalry in the Armies of Tiglath-Pileser III and Sargon II," *Iraq* 47 (1985): 31–48.
Dossin, Georges. *Correspondance de Šamši-Addu et de ses fils, transcrite et traduite par Georges Dossin*. ARMT 1. Paris: Imprimerie Nationale, 1950.
Dutcher-Walls, Patricia. "The Circumscription of the King: Deuteronomy 17:16–17 in Its Ancient Social Context." *JBL* 121 (2002): 601–616.
Ebach, Ruth. *Das Fremde und das Eigene: Die Fremdendarstellungen des Deuteronomiums im Kontext israelitischer Identitätskonstruktionen*. BZAW 471. Berlin: de Gruyter, 2014.
García López, Felix. "Le roi d'Israël: Dt 17,14–20," in *Das Deuteronomium: Entstehung, Gestalt und Botschaft*. Edited by N. Lohfink. BETL 68. Leuven: Leuven University Press, 1985, 277–297.
Gerbrandt, Gerald E. *Kingship According to the Deuteronomistic History*. SBLDS 87. Atlanta: Scholars Press, 1986.
Grossfeld, Bernard. *The Targum Onqelos to Deuteronomy*. ArBib 9. Edinburgh: T&T Clark, 1988.
Hagedorn, Anselm C. *Between Moses and Plato: Individual and Society in Deuteronomy and Ancient Greek Law*. FRLANT 204. Göttingen: Vandenhoeck & Ruprecht, 2004.
Halpern, Baruch. *The Constitution of the Monarchy in Israel*. HSM 25. Chico: Scholars Press, 1981.
Helck, Wolfgang, Eberhard Otto, and Wolfhart Westendorf, eds. *Lexikon der Ägyptologie*. 7 vols. Wiesbaden: Harrassowitz, 1975–1992.
Ikeda, Yutaka. "Solomon's Trade in Horses and Chariots in Its International Setting," in *Studies in the Period of David and Solomon and Other Essays*. Edited by Tomoo Ishida. Tokio: Yamakawa-Shuppansha, 1982, 215–238.
Johnston, Philip S. "Civil Leadership in Deuteronomy," in *Interpreting Deuteronomy: Issues and Approaches*. Edited by David G. Firth and Philip S. Johnston. Downers Grove, IL: InterVarsity Press, 2012, 139–156.
Knoppers, Gary N. "The Deuteronomist and the Deuteronomic Law of the King: A Reexamination of a Relationship." *ZAW* 108 (1996): 329–346.
Labuschagne, C. J. *Deuteronomium: Deel 2*. POuT. Nijkerk: G. F. Callenbach, 1990.
Lohfink, Norbert. "Hos. xi 5 als Bezugstext von Dtn. xvii 16." *VT* 31 (1981): 226–228.
—. "Distribution of the Functions of Power: The Laws Concerning Public Offices in Deuteronomy 16:18–18:22," in *A Song of Power and the Power of Song: Essays on the Book of Deuteronomy*. Edited by Duane L. Christensen. Sources for Biblical and Theological Study 3. Winona Lake: Eisenbrauns, 1993, 336–52. [Translated by Ronald Walls of "Die Sicherung der Wirksamkeit des Gotteswortes durch das Prinzip der Schriftlichkeit der Tora und durch das Prinzip der Gewaltenteilung nach den Ämtergesetzen des Buches Deuteronomium (Dt 16,18–18,22)," in *Testimonium Veritati: Philosophische und Theologische Studien zu kirchlichen Fragen der Gegenwart. Festschrift Bischof Wilhelm Kempf*. Edited by H. Wolter. Frankfurter theologische Studien 7. Frankfurt am Main: Knecht,

1971, 143–155. – The English version first appeared as pages 55–75 in Norbert Lohfink. *Great Themes from the Old Testament*. Chicago: Franciscan Herald Press, 1981].

Lundbom, Jack R. *Deuteronomy: A Commentary*. Grand Rapids: Eerdmans, 2013.

Maier, Johann. "Grundlage und Anwendung des Verbots der Rückkehr nach Ägypten," in *Antikes Judentum und frühes Christentum: Festschrift für Hartmut Stegemann zum 65. Geburtstag*. Edited by Bernd Kollmann, Wolfgang Reinbold, and Annette Steudel. BZNV 97. Berlin: de Gruyter, 1997, 225–244.

Mayes, A. D. H. *Deuteronomy*. The New Century Bible Commentary. Grand Rapids: Eerdmans, 1979.

McConville, J. Gordon. "King and Messiah in Deuteronomy and the Deuteronomistic History," in *King and Messiah in Israel and the Ancient Near East: Proceedings of the Oxford Old Testament Seminar*. Edited by John Day. JSOTSup 270. Sheffield: Sheffield Academic, 1998, 271–295.

—. *Deuteronomy*. ApOTC 5. Leicester: Apollos, 2002.

—. *God and Earthly Power: An Old Testament Political Theology: Genesis–Kings*. LBHOTS 454. London: T&T Clark, 2006.

Nelson, Richard D. *Deuteronomy: A Commentary*. OTL. Louisville: Westminster John Knox, 2002.

Nicholson, Ernest. "'Do Not Dare to Set a Foreigner over You': The King in Deuteronomy and 'The Great King'." *ZAW* 118 (2006): 46–61.

—. *Deuteronomy and the Judaean Diaspora*. Oxford: Oxford University Press, 2014.

Otto, Eckart. *Deuteronomium 12–34. Erster Teilband: 12,1–23,15*. HThKAT. Freiburg: Herder, 2016.

—. *Deuteronomium 12–34. Zweiter Teilband: 23,16–34,12*. HThKAT. Freiburg: Herder, 2017.

Reimer, David J. "Concerning Return to Egypt: Deuteronomy xvii 16 and xxviii 68 Reconsidered," in *Studies in the Pentateuch*. Edited by J. A. Emerton. VTSup 41. Leiden: Brill, 1990, 217–229.

Robson, James. "The Literary Composition of Deuteronomy," in *Interpreting Deuteronomy: Issues and Approaches*. Edited by David G. Firth and Philip S. Johnston. Downers Grove, IL: InterVarsity Press, 2012, 19–59.

Römer, Thomas. "La loi du roi en Deutéronome 17 et ses fonctions," in *Loi et Justice dans la Littérature du Proche-Orient ancien*. Edited by Olivier Artus. BZABR 20. Wiesbaden: Harrassowitz, 2013, 99–111.

Rüterswörden, Udo. *Von der politischen Gemeinschaft zur Gemeinde: Studien zu Dt 16,18–18,22*. BBB 65. Frankfurt am Main: Athenäum, 1987.

Seitz, Gottfried. *Redaktionsgeschichtliche Studien zum Deuteronomium*. BWA(N)T 93. Stuttgart: Kohlhammer, 1971.

Sweeney, Marwin A. "The Critique of Solomon in the Josianic Edition of the Deuteronomistic History." *JBL* 114 (1995): 609–622.

Tigay, Jeffrey H. *Deuteronomy* דברים. The JPS Torah Commentary. Philadelphia: Jewish Publication Society of America, 1996.

Vang, Carsten. "When a Prophet Quotes Moses: On the Relationship between the Book of Hosea and Deuteronomy," in *Sepher Torath Mosheh: Studies in the Composition and Interpretation of Deuteronomy*. Edited by Daniel I. Block and Richard L. Schultz. Peabody, MA: Hendrickson, 2017, 277–303.

Vogt, Peter T. *Deuteronomic Theology and the Significance of Torah: A Reappraisal*. Winona Lake, IN: Eisenbrauns, 2006.

Wazana, Nili. "The Law of the King (Deuteronomy 17:14–20) in the Light of Empire and Destruction," in *The Fall of Jerusalem and the Rise of the Torah*. Edited by Peter Dubovský, Dominik Markl and Jean-Pierre Sonnet. FAT 107. Tübingen: Mohr Siebeck, 2016, 169–194.

Weinfeld, Moshe. *Deuteronomy and the Deuteronomic School*. Oxford: Oxford University Press, 1972.

Wolff, Hans Walter. *Dodekapropheton 1. Hosea*. 4th ed. BKAT 14/1. Neukirchen-Vluyn: Neukirchener Verlag, 1990.

Wray Beal, Lissa M. *1 and 2 Kings*. ApOTC 9. Nottingham: Apollos, 2014.

Wright, Christopher J. H. *Deuteronomy*. New International Biblical Commentary. Peabody, MA: Hendrickson, 1996.

Younger, K. Lawson, and Neil A. Huddleston. "Challenges to the Use of Ancient Near Eastern Treaty Forms for Dating and Interpreting Deuteronomy," in *Sepher Torath Mosheh: Studies in the Composition and Interpretation of Deuteronomy*. Edited by Daniel I. Block and Richard L. Schultz. Peabody, MA: Hendrickson, 2017, 78–109.

Zobel, Konstantin. *Prophetie und Deuteronomium: Die Rezeption prophetischer Theologie durch das Deuteronomium*. BZAW 199. Berlin: de Gruyter, 1992.

IV. Dating Issues

Steps for Dating the Books of the Pentateuch

A Literary and Historical Canonical Approach

Hendrik J. Koorevaar

(Evangelical Theological Faculty Leuven)

1. Introduction

When dealing with *Paradigm Change in Pentateuchal Research* regarding the dating of the Pentateuch, the following three key issues or questions should be clearly distinguished.

1. Is the Pentateuch a book or a block of books? If the Pentateuch is a book that was designed as a single literary entity, then we can inquire about the dating of the whole Pentateuch all at once. Then the inner divisions of the Pentateuch are no more significant than the chapter divisions. If, however, the Pentateuch is a literary block with five different books, then those books could have been written at different times, so first, the dating of the books would have to be studied separately.

2. Did tradition correctly keep the size of the Pentateuch? OT research in the 19th and 20th century has suggested that the Pentateuch was originally part of larger literary units, until the Jewish tradition established the Pentateuch borders definitively: Tetrateuch, Hexateuch or Henneateuch. If true, this has significant implications for dating the Pentateuch. For example, if there originally was a Henneateuch, then a lot more material needs to be examined. In such a case, the question of the significance of inner divisions would also need to be raised.

3. Method of dating. When it comes to dating the Pentateuch, OT research has mainly followed suggestions from the 18th and 19th century. This has led to the following results that differ from the witness of the Pentateuch itself.

a. The hypothetical but allegedly original sources, J, E, and P were found to transcend the borders of the Pentateuch, which were viewed as secondary and as introduced later. This complicates the issue whether the borders of the Pentateuch are original.[1]

---

[1] This is visible, for example, in one variant of the documentary hypothesis which is used in the context of dealing with Genesis in Römer, Macchi, and Nihan, *Einleitung*, 176–232. There, the book Genesis is not dealt with as a whole, but in three distinct parts. Genesis 1–11: Die Urgeschichte (Christophe Uehlinger), Genesis 12–36: Die Erzelterngeschichten (Albert de Pury), Genesis 37–50: Der »Josef-Roman« (Christophe Uehlinger). No integrated treatment of the

b. The various dates assigned to these sources differed strongly from the witnesses in these sources and, therefore, in the books of the Pentateuch themselves.

In OT research, these three key issues were consciously or unconsciously connected. Distinguishing these issues well is essential, so that researchers can contribute to the dating of the Pentateuch from different angles.

2. The issue of blocks and books

2.1 The Pentateuch and the question of the extent of a larger or smaller block

In OT research, other blocks of OT material have been suggested besides the Torah block. Four blocks have been influential. For each of the last three blocks, I will mention a scholar that defended that view.

a. The Pentateuch. Genesis – Deuteronomy. This block of five books forms the foundation of the whole canon in Judaism.

b. The Hexateuch. Genesis – Joshua. This idea is part of the (new) documentary hypothesis (Wellhausen). Von Rad thought that the Pentateuch was not closed off for theological reasons.[2] Multiple promises were made to the Patriarchs. All these promises are fulfilled in the Pentateuch, except for the promise of the possession of Canaan. That promise is only fulfilled in the book of Joshua. That is why Joshua has to be part of the collection, so that the pattern of promise – fulfilment is completed. Von Rad also held that the hypothetical sources J, E and P in Genesis – Numbers can also be found in the book Joshua.

c. The Tetrateuch and the Deuteronomistic History Work. Genesis – Numbers + Deuteronomy – Kings. According to Noth, the sources J, E and P can only be found in Genesis – Numbers.[3] Deuteronomy starts a totally different literary work. Deuteronomy is the introduction to Joshua – Kings, which he calls 'The Deuteronomistic History Work' (DtrH). According to him, these two large literary works were later combined.

d. The Henneateuch. Genesis – Kings. Houtman views Genesis – Kings as one big historical work, that was written at once as a final, literary composition.[4]

---

whole of Genesis is offered. This is at odds with the function of the eleven Toledot-formulas that are found in all 'three' parts of Genesis and that divide the book into twelve parts. See Koorevaar, " Aufbau," 203–217.
2 Von Rad, *Problem,* 87–100.
3 Noth, *Überlieferungsgeschichtliche Studien,* 3–110. I. Das Deuteronomistische Werk (Dtr).
4 Houtman, *Pentateuch,* § 114. He refers in § 19 to Spinoza, B., *Tractatus Theologico-Politicus.* Hamburg (Amsterdam) 1670, chapter 8–10. Spinoza had (first?) held the view, that the books

An important idea behind the Hexateuch view was the idea that all the promises had to be fulfilled before the collection could have been written or closed. This idea would have to be rejected by those who hold to the Henneateuch view, since in the book Kings the promise of return from exile is not fulfilled. So, this idea, that all the relevant promises need to be fulfilled before a book or block of books could be written, should be questioned.

We might ask how the Pentateuch came to be the only block known to Judaism, if one of these other blocks was the original collection. Researchers have explained this as a later development in Judaism, fueled by a desire to separate the teaching of Yhwh and Moses from the other books.

This seems to be correct. The Jewish tradition calls the block Joshua – Kings the Former Prophets. But this name does little justice to the books and may have been introduced to solve some other problem.

Joshua – Kings are no prophetic books and they do not contain the characteristic of prophetic history writing with a special interest in prophets. In the book of Joshua, no prophets are even mentioned, and only a few in Judges. Furthermore, the border between Deuteronomy and Joshua cannot have the function of a block border. The beginning of Joshua is clearly connected to the end of Deuteronomy and presents the book Joshua as a continuation.

According to Steinberg, the difference in the demarcation between the first two parts of the Hebrew canon is caused by a literary canon structure based on descending value.[5] The *Torah* has the first rank. The *Nevi'im* and the *Ketuvim* both have the second rank. He displays that graphically as follows:

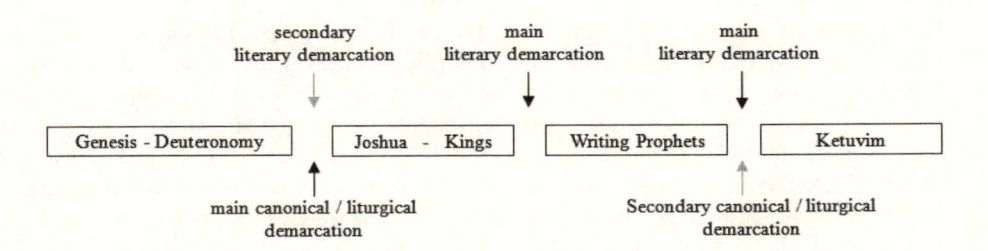

	secondary literary demarcation	main literary demarcation	main literary demarcation
Genesis - Deuteronomy	Joshua - Kings	Writing Prophets	Ketuvim
main canonical / liturgical demarcation		Secondary canonical / liturgical demarcation	

Steinberg was not convinced by various attempts to defend the division of the canon in the three parts *Torah, Nevi'im* and *Ketuvim* with literary arguments. From a literary point of view, he thinks the Writing Prophets had to have originally been an independent unit.

The idea of an original Henneateuch is thus an attractive perspective for OT research, including research on the Pentateuch. Is the Henneateuch a single literary

---

Genesis – Kings were once one work that was created by Ezra to describe the time from creation to the downfall of Jerusalem.

5 Steinberg, *Ketuvim*, 116–117, 'abstufende Wertschätzung' ... 'kanonische Abstufung'.

entity? If so, then someone wrote a huge book. Or are the internal divisions of the Henneateuch more significant than chapter divisions; and does the Henneateuch consist of separate books?

2.2 The book phenomenon and the question of book borders inside of a block

2.2.1 What is a book?

According to Barton, our concept of a book consists of two ideas.[6] One is physical and the other is metaphysical. While discussing the question of whether Leviticus is a separate book or not Kathryn Gutzwiller writes the following.

> [T]he word 'book' ... refers to a physical entity, to pages bound in a volume, but a book is also an intellectual concept, which is composed to be read as an integrated unit. While the physical entity and the intellectual construct normally correspond, this is not always the case, so that we may have a long book published in two or more volumes, each a 'book' in a physical sense. A similar situation prevailed in the ancient world.[7]

Then she goes on to deal with the βίβλος phenomenon during the 6th – 2nd centuries BC in Greece. She mentions a papyrus from the 2nd century BC which contains Homer's two books written on one scroll.

2.2.2 The Henneateuch as closed or open serial model

Researchers who accept the Henneateuch (or DtrH) view hold different positions.[8] Most think it is one great design. For some, book borders are of secondary importance, but for others they are very important. In an overview study of the books of DtrH, McConville makes clear the independent and individual character of each book. But he still holds to the unity of the DtrH.[9] If the Henneateuch is a metaphysical unity and the book borders are important, then we could call this a closed serial model. But what if there are arguments for the view that one of the books is a closed metaphysical unity, which was already written (long) before the exile to Babylon? And what if this could be demonstrated for more books than one? Then Genesis – Kings would be a series of books written at different times that sought consciously to continue each other. We can call this an *open serial model*.

The background of the open serial model could be the following. In Lev 26 and Deut 28–30 blessings or curses are promised to Israel in the land of Canaan. Blessings, if the people follow the ways of Yhwh, and curses if Israel disobeys. The final

---

6   Barton, "What Is a Book?," 1–14.
7   Gutzwiller, "Comments," 37.
8   For an overview see Koorevaar, "book of Joshua," 219–232.
9   McConville, *Old Testament*, 3–13.

curse is exile. In this way Deuteronomy presents itself as an open book that expects to be continued. The writers of Joshua – Kings see themselves as legitimate propagators of the instruction of Yhwh and Moses, who point to blessings and curses after an important phase in the history of Israel in Canaan has been completed. They would have built on Moses' (Deuteronomic) Book of the Law, that was preserved next to the Ark of the Covenant in the sanctuary of Yhwh (Deut 31:24–26) and that makes up most of the later book of Deuteronomy. The priests – the Levites had to take care of this Book of the Law (Deut 17:17–18).

The other books of the Torah were all anonymous. Even though Exodus – Leviticus – Numbers and Deuteronomy contain a lot of Mosaic material, these books are anonymous. The anonymous writers of the Torah wanted to indicate that not they, but others, such as Yhwh and Moses, were the main characters of these books. The writers of Joshua – Kings continued the practice of these Levite priests by writing anonymously. They also had a subordinate role. That is why they also wanted to remain anonymous. They wanted to make sure they would remain in a subordinate role, and I think that they succeeded at that. In a sense, they practiced the word *Fortschreibung*.

2.2.3 Exodus – Leviticus – Numbers as metaphysical unity

In OT research, Ex 19:1–Num 10:10 has been labelled as the Siniai pericope, which wiped out the book borders of Exodus and Leviticus. There are multiple indicators that indicate that the three 'books' were originally one literary work.[10]

Content-related observations

a) Exodus/Leviticus incision. Exodus ends with the erection of the Tent of Meeting in Ex 40 and the Cloud covering the Tent and the glory of Yhwh filling the Tent (Ex 40:34). Moses cannot enter אֶל־ *in* the Tent because of the glory of Yhwh (Ex 40:35). Lev 1:1 continues Exodus perfectly by picking up were Ex 40:34–35 left off. Lev 1:1 tells us that Yhwh speaks מִ *out of* the (recently erected) Tent of Meeting to Moses. So, Moses was not inside but *outside* of the Tent. Why was Moses not inside of the Tent? Aaron and his sons were not yet consecrated as priests. That happens in Lev 8–10. Only after the consecration Moses and Aaron entered the Tent (Lev 9:23–24). The incision made between Exodus and Leviticus is unfortunate in light of the double task given to Moses on Mount Sinai by Yhwh. He was to build the Dwelling place of Yhwh (Ex 25:9) and to consecrate priests for it (Ex 28:1). These two form an inseparable unity, but the second is only completed in Lev 10.

b) Leviticus/Numbers incision. Leviticus ends with: "These are the commandments, that Yhwh gave Moses for the Israelites on Mount Sinai" (Lev 27:34). Numbers begins with "Yhwh spoke to Moses in the wilderness of Sinai desert in the Tent of Meeting on the first day of the second month in the second year after they had come out of the land of Egypt" (Num 1:1). This incision is just as significant as the

---

10 Koorevaar, "Books of Exodus – Leviticus – Numbers," 423–453.

incision between Lev 24 and Lev 25. Lev 25–27 about "The law on the land of God" is inserted text, that is characterized by a phrase about Yhwh speaking to Moses on Mount Sinai (Lev 25:1, 26:46 and 27:34). After this piece, the writer returns in Num 1:1 to where he left of in Lev 24. He has to mention there that God speaks to Moses in the *Wilderness of Sinai* in the Tent of Meeting, because otherwise his audience would think this was taking place on *Mount Sinai*. Moreover, he has to give a detailed time-indication there, because the revelation on Mount Sinai in Lev 25–27 took place at least half a year earlier.

Grammatical observations

Both Leviticus as well Numbers begin with a waw consecutivum: וַיִּקְרָא *and He called* in Lev 1:1 and וַיְדַבֵּר *and He said* in Num 1:1. In both cases Yhwh speaks to Moses. The writer uses the waw consecutivum to indicate that in Lev 1:1 and Num 1:1 he is continuing what he wrote earlier. It is grammatically incorrect to start a new literary work with a waw consecutivum. It is true that the books Joshua, Judges, Samuel, Ezekiel, Jonah, Ruth and Esther start with the consecutive phrase וַיְהִי *and he was (there)*. But this is a literary style for starting a work, in which the original consecutive function has been lost. In these cases, the phrase has become independent. However, in Lev 1:1 and Num 1:1 the waw consecutivum is connected to other verbs and not the verb היה *to be*. No other books in the Hebrew Bible start with a waw consecutivum connected to a verb other than היה.

The macrostructural problem of the Pentateuch is that this block does not consist of only one book or five books, but three books.[11] The Torah is not a Pentateuch, but a Triptych. The weak borders between Exodus – Leviticus – Numbers may have led people to believe that all the book borders within the *whole* Pentateuch are secondary, and so a fog was laid on the Pentateuch. Nevertheless, in OT research it has often been acknowledged that Genesis is an independent literary work.[12] That is also the case for Deuteronomy. The Torah opens with Genesis as book about the beginning. That is followed by Exodus – Leviticus – Numbers, a monumental central panel, the Yhwh-Torah. It closes with Deuteronomy, the Moses-Torah.[13]

2.2.4 Genesis – Kings as the Seven Fold

Because Exodus – Leviticus – Numbers are metaphysically one book, the block Genesis – Kings is not a Henneateuch (nine books), but a block of seven books. What name is suited for this canonical block? There are multiple candidates. Freedman calls Genesis – Kings 'the great primary history'.[14] In light of the strong priestly interest for the central sanctuary in this block, also in Joshua – Kings, we could call

---

11 Koorevaar, "Torah".
12 Koorevaar, " Aufbau," 203–217.
13 For the terminology of Yhwh-Torah and Moses-Torah, see Kilchör, *Mosetora*, 3–11.
14 Freedman, "Deuteronomic History," 226.

it the Priest canon. If we want to put the number seven in the name, then the Hebrew dualis שְׁבָעָתַיִם *šiḇ'tayim, Seven Fold* could be used.

We can divide the Seven Fold into two sub-blocks: the Triptych of Genesis – Deuteronomy as the Revealed Law (תורה נגלה) and the אַרְבַּעָתַיִם *'arba'tayim, Four Fold* of Joshua – Kings as the Demonstrated Law (תורה נראה). 3 + 4 = 7.

In the past, the research on the origin of this complex of books had a wrong starting point: the whole. It was assumed that this complex of a total overarching unity was written and closed at one point in time, although the material it contained might have been developed over a long period of time. This assumption was already found in the Jewish tradition on the Pentateuch. It was later (unconsciously) adopted by adherents of the documentary hypothesis about the Pentateuch. We should start from the other end. If we want to study the origin of the Seven Fold complex, we need to start with each separate book. Is it possible that two or more books were written at the same time? To consider this possibility is good, but this should not be assumed to be true. It should rather be a conclusion based on a comparison of the results of the dating of the separate books.

3. The issue of dating

3.1 The historical-critical approach to the OT: an evaluative reflection

For the sake of dating the books of the Pentateuch correctly, another reflection on our dating methods is important. In the past two centuries, an important stream of OT research has suggested all kinds of methods for identifying and dating sources that yielded results which differed from, and contradicted, the witness of the Pentateuch itself. This was called historical criticism. That term was used to present this approach as correct and scientific. But is that correct? What is historical criticism? Is there something as healthy and unhealthy historical criticism, legitimate and illegitimate? A good, balanced way to evaluate historical criticism is to distinguish different layers in the historical-critical approach. OT historical criticism can be compared to a broad river, which is fed by the following three streams.

1) The task of historical criticism. Historical criticism is a scientific approach to the whole of human history. The OT provides valuable information on the history of Israel and the Ancient Near East. The task of historical criticism is to collect and order all the historical data. Its goal is to present the best possible historical picture of what has happened. This is an important and valuable task.

2) The ideology of historical criticism. Ernst Troeltsch formulated three pillars of this ideology: criticism, correlation and analogy.[15] Criticism: every source should be

---

15 Benckert,"Troeltsch, Ernst," 1044–1047.

viewed with suspicion. Correlation: every event has a cause in this physical world which needs to be discovered. Analogy: whatever happened in the past must also be able to happen today. The last two pillars indicate that the ideology of historical criticism is secular and is a child of the 18th century Enlightenment. It holds to a *closed* three-dimensional worldview, which rejects the possibility of acts of a transcendent God in this material world. Historical criticism is in essence an atheistic ideology and inappropriate to do justice to many witnesses in the OT.[16]

3) Historical-critical hypotheses about the OT from the past. During the 18th – 20th century many different historical-critical hypotheses were proposed about the origin and history of the OT which contradicted the historical claims of the OT. The OT was full of idealized projections from later periods onto the past and would be largely historical fiction. But are these hypotheses true? Were they based on research carried out correctly? Since the 70s of the 20th century it has become clear that the foundations of the documentary hypothesis about the Hexateuch are untenable. This hypothesis no longer has the air of factuality. It seems that in this case historical criticism was illegitimately applied.

3.2 A historical-canonical approach to the OT: some principles

This approach focusses on *all* the historical claims of the OT, irrespective of whether the events reported correspond to our daily experiences. Besides human actions, it maps out also God's actions on the same historical level. A researcher that uses this approach to the OT, respects the object of his or her research. This approach holds to an *open* three-dimensional worldview. God created the three-dimensional world, open to His involvement. The reality of the three dimensions is not denied, but is freed from a wrong absolutism. A correctly used historical-*canonical* approach is completely compatible with a legitimate historical-*critical* approach.

It aims to collect all historical information, which is also the first task of historical criticism, and it takes the historical information of the OT as the starting point. There are reasons for that. The OT books are the object of our study and their witness about history and their origin are our first source for understanding these books in their historical context. That is how these books want to be understood.

A historical-canonical approach does not guarantee that researchers who use this approach will make no mistakes. After all, they can also start to speculate when relevant data from the OT and other literature is absent or unclear. Frequently, ideas or propositions which do not have the support of the explicit witness of the OT are labeled as canonical. Maybe these ideas do not contradict the OT data, but that does not make it evident that they are correct. We should distinguish between what is clearly canonically witnessed, and proposals which can be correct within the canonical framework. Those proposals need not be correct.

---

16 See Long, "Historiography," 145–166.

3.3 A historical-canonical approach: steps for dating

What steps can we take to discover the origin of a book and especially its date of completion? The following five steps can be taken in dating all OT books. They are especially valuable for dating historically orientated books, such as Genesis – Kings. I have used these steps in dating Genesis, and I will refer to this study a few times.[17] Such steps may have been suggested before. That is not to say that all five steps are mentioned, or have been put forward in the same order or have been presented in way they have been formulated below.

1) *Identifying and dating the last-mentioned event in the book*
In Genesis, for example, this is the death of Joseph and placing him in a coffin (Gen 50:26). This is also the last verse. It is possible that it was the death of Joseph that led to the writing of Genesis. In that case, Genesis' last event and the time in which it was written almost coincide. Although this is possible, compelling arguments should be offered for this idea. The writer of Genesis could have lived much later and have ended Genesis with the death of Joseph for theological reasons. After all, Joseph does make an important faith statement.

2) *Tracking down all direct or indirect indications or possible indications of the time of the author.*
Although the OT authors rarely tell us about themselves, they often indicate, consciously or unconsciously, in which time they are living. These indications can include all kinds of explanatory and elaborative remarks. This brings us to the next issue.

OT research has often labeled these remarks as redactional or editorial remarks. In the discussion of the authorship of OT books, the following terms have been used: writer, author, redactor, editor, Fortschreiber, Weiterschreiber, completer, compilator and glossator. A host of related adjectives have also been used. These terms are problematic. They can be confusing and can very easily be used inappropriately in research on OT books, which can lead to incorrect conclusions.

Literary science and the world of publishing use the same or similar terms, in the present as well as in the past. There are even differences between terms such as redactor and editor.[18] The risk regarding biblical sciences as literary science is that the terminology and its content could be influenced by the terminology and processes regarding the formation of books and writings out of the world of publishing. These ideas could influence our view of how OT books came into existence.

In the past, terms such as redactional or editorial remarks were automatically used in OT research to label remarks of someone else than the (original) author. These are later adaptions, upgrades or updates. Researchers of the past were mostly

---

17 Koorevaar, " Bedeutung," 219–239.
18 https://de.wikipedia.org/wiki/Redakteur#Literatur; https://de.wikipedia.org/wiki/Edition.

negative about such later additions. Now researchers mostly view them very positively.[19] But irrespective of whether researchers view these additions as positive or negative, we should ask if it is true that a lot of material was added to the work of the original author. Have we analyzed the development of a book correctly? Have we paid enough attention to the original author and the different ways in which he could have written a book? A book may consist of the contribution of the author, his story, the sources he used to write his story as well as all kinds additional remarks he made. Explanatory or elaborative remarks could have been written by the author himself. We should not therefore simply assume that these are remarks of an editor or redactor.

The issue of *Fortschreibung* (continued writing) is related to this. This is about the possibility of later insertions in or additions to a completed work. It has been argued that the person behind such adaptions would have felt connected to the original author and would have wanted to add to the work in the spirit of the original author and would have wanted his adaptions to have the authority of the author and would therefore have wanted to hide his contribution to the work.

In the past decades, a broad stream of OT research has been convinced that such adaptions were made, especially to the books of the Writing Prophets. Are they right? And are we justified in thinking that we can detect such additions, despite the effort of the *Fortschreiber* to hide his contribution? Is the detection of such 'hidden' additions objective?

We should be open to the possibility of later additions to a OT book by a *Fortschreiber*; but it should be clear that such additions can be detected, and the book should indicate that *Fortschreibung* has taken place. For example, Jeremiah chapter 52 was clearly written by someone else than Jeremiah. This is indicated by Jer 51:64b. עַד־הֵנָּה דִּבְרֵי יִרְמְיָהוּ *Thus far the words of Jeremiah.* Jer 52 is therefore *Fortschreibung* and it is not only that but also *legitimate Fortschreibung* that distinguishes itself from the text before it. Assuming the idea of hidden *Fortschreibung* in the OT is true, how would the *Fortschreiber* of Jeremiah 52 view this? I think he would view this as *illegitimate Fortschreibung* as opposed to his own *legitimate* form of *Fortschreibung*. He clearly indicates his own contribution and does not usurp the position of the original author.

But the issue is more complex. Maybe what has been labeled *Fortschreibung*, actually is text written by the original author. Manfred Dreytza has dealt with this issue.[20] So, terms such as (later) redaction and *Weiterschreibung* are inadequate terms for referring to explanatory and elaborative remarks in an OT book. They could be remarks of the author and might or might not show signs of being written in his time.

Another topic that might be related to dating a book is prophetic utterances (of Yhwh) or expectations of people about the future that have not yet been fulfilled.

---

19 See Leuenberger,"Redaktoren".
20 Dreytza, „Prophetische Prophetenauslegung?," 51–64.

For example, at the end of Genesis Joseph says to his brothers: "I am about to die; God will surely visit you and lead you out of this land to the land, that He promised on oath to Abraham, Isaac and Jacob. And Joseph took an oath of the sons of Israel and said: God will surely visit you and you shall carry up my bones from here." And the book ends thus: "And Joseph died at the age of one hundred and ten years and they embalmed him and he was put in a coffin in Egypt." (50:24–26). This saying of Joseph is based on, among other passages, Gen 15:13–16, 46:1–4. How useful is the idea of vaticinia post eventu (prophetic sayings after the event) here? If that idea is applied to this case, then Genesis can only have been written after the Israelites left Egypt and took Joseph's bones with them (Ex 13:19) and buried his bones in Canaan (Joshua 24:32).

Then Genesis could only have been written in the time of Joshua, at the earliest. However, the idea of vaticinia post eventu clashes with common human experience. It assumes that people do not have hopeful expectations about the future, or at least do not express these expectations or write them down. This is falsified by every (written) expression of human hope.

Joseph's hope is based on what Yhwh told his ancestors about the future, which his ancestors understood to be about the future and not about their own time. That is why prophetic sayings in a book with expectations about the future are not suited for dating that book. They are open expressions of hope about the future. An author can mention the future expectations of a person in his book. In the case of the book of Genesis, the writer even ends with this expectation, and he wants to emphasize the importance of an expectation about the future. That does not rule out the possibility that this expectation was already fulfilled when Genesis was written. That is possible. But this idea should be supported by passages that clearly indicate the writer lived after the burial of Joseph's remains in Canaan. Later readers might know that the expectation has been fulfilled, if they know the content of the book of Joshua. But they will still read the end of Genesis as an expectation about the future. Should later readers and also current readers not know these books, then they read the book in the same way as the first readers, should that expectation not yet be realised in their time.

Every remark in a text that is viewed as an indicator of the time in which the writer wrote should be studied carefully. It is possible, after all, that the detecting of such an indicator was correct, but that the proposed date is not compulsive and an alternative date is also possible. In several books of the OT this step can be an extensive task involving a lot of details. In the case of Genesis, the Post-Josephica are important, which are remarks pointing to a time *after* Joseph. These remarks should be called Post-Josephica and not Post-Mosaica. That term is linked to the time of Moses and issues about the authorship of Moses. In the past, it has been hotly debated whether or not these remarks are Post-Mosaica. By calling these remarks Post-Josephica a researcher does not have to choose a side in that debate, and is free to date Genesis to any time after Joseph.

I will give an example that demonstrates that the study of one text can lead to different positions. In Gen 14:14 Abraham follows his enemies to the place Dan. The reader who knows the OT will automatically understand this to refer to the city at the sources of the Jordan, in the northeast of Canaan. That city was called Dan after the tribe of Dan conquered that area (Joshua 19:40–48, Judges 18:27–29). Before that, the city was called Lesem/Laïs. The book of Genesis must have been written *after* that time. This is seen as a clear example of an anachronism. This anachronism is referred to as a justification for the view that Genesis came into existence in the context of the Hexateuch.[21] It is also possible to accept Dan as an anachronism, but that the author, who lived several centuries after the occupation of Canaan by Israel, used Mosaic sources.[22]

However, is the text really referring to the city at the sources of the Jordan or is it referring to the place with the same name in northern Gilead? That has been suggested several times.[23] That would have major implications for the dating of Genesis. If the entry of the Israelites into Canaan is dated to 1400 BC, then the tribe Dan moved to northern Canaan around 1370 BC. If the entry of the Israelites is dated to 1220 BC, then the tribe of Dan moved north around 1190 BC. If the city in question is Dan in Canaan, then the book of Genesis was written after that time (post quem). If, however, the place in question is Dan in Gilead, then the book of Genesis was written *before* that time (ad quem), as it was not necessary for the author to make a remark distinguishing this Dan in northern Gilead from Dan in Canaan.[24]

Another idea, is that the name of Dan is a later revision of an already existing text. It is an update and can regularly be observed with names of towns. Also, other revisions in the text can happen in order to keep up with semantic developments in the Hebrew language. For Garrett the name of Dan belongs to the Post-Mosaic redaction.[25] We can ask two questions.

1. How likely is it that the proposal of a later update was inspired by the idea of Mosaic authorship of the book of Genesis?

2. Does the text in Gen 14:14 itself give any indications that the name of Dan is an update? In Genesis 14 there are indeed several local upgrades: 'Bela, which is Zoar'(14:2,8), 'the valley of Siddim, which is the salt sea' (14:3), "Enmishpat, which is Kadesh" (14:7), and 'the valley of Shaveh, which is the king's dale.' (14:17). This is not the case, however, with Dan. "It seems extremely improbable

---

21 Millard, „Genesis," (4.2. Hypothesen zur Entstehung des Buches, 4.2.1. Einzelne Beobachtungen). „Bereits vor der Aufklärung war beispielsweise der Anachronismus in Gen 12,6 'Die Kanaanäer waren damals (!) im Land' aufgefallen. Offensichtlich weiß der Verfasser der Bemerkung von einer Zeit, in der die Kanaanäer nicht mehr im verheißenen Land lebten. Deswegen kann die Notiz frühestens aus der Zeit der Landnahme stammen".
22 Aalders, *Oud-Testamentische Kanoniek*, 128–129.
23 Möller, *Einheit*, 93–96.
24 Compare 1 Sam 24:2 (Dan) with 1 Sam 24:6 (Dan-Jaan).
25 Garrett, *Rethinking Genesis*, 86. He presents a paragraph 'The Post-Mosaic Redaction', 85–86, in chapter '3. Mosaic Authorship and Historical Reliability', 51–87.

that the analogy of the entire chapter, which on this interpretation would require 'Laish, the same is Dan,' should be violate in this one instance without any intimation of it, the original name being discarded, and the recent one not added to it by way of explanation but substituted for it."[26] This underlines the necessity to show clear indications in the text itself or in the context, if a scholar suggests a later addition to a text or an update. Such a proposal must have an irrefutable character.[27]

Bela, which is Zoar, in 14:8 for instance, meets this condition. For Dan in 14:14, without any further information, this cannot be said.

It is possible for two researchers using a historical-canonical approach to disagree on the dating of Genesis and to date the book to times centuries apart. However, deviating dates cannot be correct at the same time.

3) *Identifying the country and the place where the book was written by its author*
First, we should try to identify the country in which the book was written. After that, we should look at whether there are indications that a book was written in a specific place. The location of the author may seem irrelevant for dating a book, but identifying it can contribute to the dating of a book, especially if different dates are possible. In such a case, we might ask the following question: Which date is most plausible in light of the location of the author?

4) *Making a schematic presentation of all temporal remarks*
Some remarks might be related to long periods of time, while others might be connected to brief periods of time or even specific moments in time. There is a real possibility that one dating of a book is plausible or even certain in light of all the different and sometimes overlapping indications of time found in the book. Making a schematic overview of all the temporal remarks found in a book can help us arrive at such a dating.

5) *Trying to discover the ratio or necessity for the proposed date*
We should ask why a book was supposedly written at the specific time in question and not earlier or later. What was so important that the author needed to write the book then? What reason(s) did the author have for writing the book? What motive caused the composition? This last step is important, because a mere date has little value. We should evaluate proposed reasons critically. But an implausible reason is possible to give for writing in support of the correct dating.

---

[26] Green, *Unity*, 201–202.
[27] Green, *Unity*, 201, points to an interesting peculiarity in 14:7. "In one instance he uses a name current in his own time proleptically, perhaps for the reason that no other expressed his meaning so exactly. Thus he says (vs. 5–7) that the invaders smote the Rephaim, and Zuzim, and Emim, and Horites, and Amorites, and 'the country of the Amalekites.' His meaning is here carefully guarded by the altered form of expression. They smote not the Amalekites, who derived their name from the grandson of Esau (xxxvi. 12), and accordingly were not in existence in the time of Abram, but the region subsequently occupied by them."

4. Perspective

What can we now expect about the dating of the Pentateuch and what can we expect about it in light of this programmatic proposal?

We can expect that in the future the documentary hypothesis, to which most OT researchers adhered to in the past, will attract a number of OT researchers. Even the classical form of the hypothesis, which was introduced by Wellhausen and which had four sources, will probably have its adherents and defenders in the future. Again and again, the hypothesis will be revised, and these adaptions will be seen as improvements. The quest to find its correct form will continue and the polyphony of proposals will grow. There will also be new efforts, like the idea of a D-stream and a P-stream, to save at least some aspects of the hypothesis. After all, it could not have been completely wrong, could it? Many researchers cannot or do not want to imagine that the great documentary hypothesis, which was defended for two centuries by so many scholars, might have been completely wrong. But it is difficult to escape that conclusion if one reads Houtman's informative overview work on this topic.[28]

What are the chances of the historical-canonical approach proposed here succeeding in gaining a significant number of adherents? Will it not sound revolutionary to researchers that may be dissatisfied by the documentary hypothesis, but are still heavily influenced by it? But how new is this proposal really?

Maybe the way in which it was presented here is new. But many researchers have used one or more of the steps mentioned here and have made valuable contributions. They had a minority position in OT scholarship and their contributions are often not known any more. Nevertheless, many of these researchers, some of which were Jews and others were Christians, have made valuable observations, and these observations can be used in the future. At the same time, stimulations can go out to do new investigations and to deliver new contributions and discoveries, by the streamlined formulation in this proposal, both in finding new details and in drawing new conclusions out of them.

---

28 Houtman, *Pentateuch*.

Bibliography

Aalders, G. Ch. *Oud-Testamentische Kanoniek.* Kampen: J. H. Kok, 1952.
Barton, John. "What Is a Book? Modern Exegesis and the Literary Conventions of Ancient Israel," in *Intertextuality in Ugarit and Israel: Papers Read at the Tenth Joint Meeting of the Society for Old Testament Study and het Oudtestamentisch Werkgezelschap in Nederland en België Held at Oxford, 1997.* Edited by J. C. De Moor. OTS 40. Leiden: E. J. Brill, 1998, 1–14.
Benckert, H. "Troeltsch, Ernst," in *Die Religion in Geschichte und Gegenwart. Handwörterbuch für Theologie und Religionswissenschaft 6.* Edited by Kurt Galling. Tübingen: J. C. B. Mohr (Paul Siebeck), 1986³, 1044–1047.
Dreytza, Manfred. „Prophetische Prophetenauslegung?," in *Christus – die Quelle unserer Erkenntnis: Festschrift zum 25jährigen Jubiläum der Studienarbeit Krelingen.* Edited by Manfred Dreytza. Walsrode: Geistliches Rüstzentrum Krelingen, 1998, 51–64.
Freedman, David Noel. „Deuteronomic History," in *Interpreter's Dictionary of the Bible, Supplementary Volume.* Edited by George A. Butterick. Nashville: Abington, 1976, 226–228.
Garrett, Duane. *Rethinking Genesis: The Sources and Authorship of the First Book of the Pentateuch.* Grand Rapids: Baker Book House, 1991.
Green, William Henry. *The Unity of the Book of Genesis.* New York, London: Charles Scribner's Sons, 1895. (Grand Rapids: Baker Book House, 1979).
Gutzwiller, Kathryn. "Comments on Rolf Rendtorff," in *Reading Leviticus: A Conversation with Mary Douglas.* Edited by John F.A. Sawyer. JSOTS 227. Sheffield: Sheffield Academic Press, 1996, 36–39.
Houtman, C. *Der Pentateuch: Die Geschichte seiner Erforschung neben einer Auswertung.* Contributions to Biblical Exegesis & Theology 9. Kampen: Kok Pharos, 1994.
Kilchör, Benjamin. *Mosetora und Jahwetora. Das Verhältnis von Deuteronomium 12–26 zu Exodus, Levitikus und Numeri.* BZAR 21. Wiesbaden: Harrassowitz, 2015.
Koorevaar, Hendrik J. "The Torah as One, Three or Five Books: An Introduction to the Macro-Structural Problem of the Pentateuch," *Hiphil* 3 (2006). Cited 17 July 2017. Online: http://www.see-j.net/index.php/hiphil/article/view/28.
—. "The Books of Exodus – Leviticus – Numbers and the Macro-Structural Problem of the Pentateuch," in *The Books of Leviticus and Numbers.* Edited by Thomas Römer. BETL 215. Leuven: Peeters, 2008, 423–453.
—. "The book of Joshua and the hypothesis of the Deuteronomistic History: Indications for an open serial model," in *The Book of Joshua.* Edited by Ed Noort. BETL 250. Leuven: Peeters, 2012, 219–232.
—. "Der Aufbau des Buches Genesis und die literarisch-theologische Bedeutung des Entwicklungsansatzes," in: *Genesis, Schöpfung und Evolution. Beiträge zur Auslegung und Bedeutung des ersten Buches der Bibel.* Edited by Reinhard Junker. Holzgerlingen: Hänssler Verlag, 2015, 2016², 203–217.
—. "Die Bedeutung der Post-Josephica für eine Datierung des Buches Genesis," in *Genesis, Schöpfung und Evolution. Beiträge zur Auslegung und Bedeutung des ersten Buches der Bibel.* Edited by Reinhard Junker. Holzgerlingen: Hänssler Verlag, 2015, 2016², 219–239.
Leuenberger, Martin. "Redaktoren," in *Das wissenschaftliche Lexikon im Internet.* No pages. Cited 18 July 2017. Online: www.wibilex.de, Stuttgart: Deutsche Bibelgesellschaft, 2007.

Long, V. Philips. "Historiography of the Old Testament," in *The Face of Old Testament Studies: A Survey of Contemporary Approaches*. Edited by David W. Baker, Bill T. Arnold. Grand Rapids: Baker Books, 1999, 145–166.

McConville, J. Gordon. "The Old Testament Historical Books in Modern Scholarship," *Themelios* 22/3 (1997): 3–13.

Millard, Matthias. „Genesis," in *Das wissenschaftliche Lexikon im Internet*. No pages. Cited 16 July 2017. Online: www.wibilex.de, Stuttgart: Deutsche Bibelgesellschaft, 2006.

Möller, Wilhelm. *Die Einheit und Echtheit der 5 Bücher Mosis. Abriss einer Einleitung in den Pentateuch in Auseinandersetzung mit D. Sellins Einleitung in das Alte Testament*. Veröffentlichungen des Bibelbundes 40. Bad Salzuflen: Selbstverlag des Bibelbundes, 1931.

Noth, Martin. *Überlieferungsgeschichtliche Studien, Erster Teil, Die sammelnden und bearbeitenden Geschichtswerke im Alten Testament*. Darmstadt: Wissenschaftliche Buchgesellschaft, (1943) 1963.

Römer, Thomas, Jean-Daniel Macchi, Christophe Nihan, eds., *Einleitung in das Alte Testament. Die Bücher der Hebräischen Bibel und die alttestamentlichen Schriften der katholischen, protestantischen und orthodoxen Kirchen*. Zürich: TVZ Theologischer Verlag, 2013.

Steinberg, Julius. *Die Ketuvim – Ihr Aufbau und ihre Botschaft*. BBB 152. Hamburg: Philo, 2006.

Von Rad, Gerhard. *Das formgeschichtliche Problem des Hexateuch*. BWANT 4. Stuttgart: W. Kohlhammer, 1938.

The Linguistic Profile of the Priestly Narrative of the Pentateuch

Lina Petersson (Uppsala University)

In this paper I present some of the main contributions of my forthcoming PhD thesis: *Syntax of the Verb in the Priestly Narrative of the Pentateuch – A Diachronic Study*.[1] The aim of this thesis is to determine which stage in the linguistic development of Biblical Hebrew is reflected in the syntax of the verb in the Priestly (P) narrative.[2] In other words, I aim to answer the question whether the verbal syntax in the P narrative corresponds to Late Biblical Hebrew (LBH) usage, or Standard Biblical Hebrew (SBH) usage. Following the introductory overview of previous research, the paper is focused on some central aspects of the theoretical framework and the methodology of my investigation.[3]

1. Introduction to the field of research

A starting point for the systematic study of what would subsequently be termed Late Biblical Hebrew can be found in Samuel R. Driver's introduction to the Old Testa-

---

Author's note: I am grateful for all the comments, discussions, and encouragement from the organizers and participants at the conference in Basel 2017. I would also like to thank Jan Retsö and Paul Hocking for corrections and suggestions in preparation of this paper.

1 Petersson, *Syntax* (forthcoming).
2 The corpus of the P narrative, as delimited in my study, includes the following passages: *Genesis* **1**:1–2:4a; **6**:9–22; **7**:6, 11, 13–16a, 17a, 18–21, 24; **8**:1–2a, 3b–5, 13a, 14–19; **9**:1–17, 28–29; **11**:27, 31–32; **12**:4b–5; **13**:6, 11b–12a; **16**:1a, 3, 15–16; **17**; **19**:29; **21**:1b, 2b–5; **23**; **25**:7–11a, 19–20; **26**:34–35; **27**:46; **28**:1–9; **29**:24, 28b–29; **30**:4a; **31**:18b; **33**:18a; **35**:9–13, 15, 22b–29; **36**:6–8; **37**:1–2a; **41**:46; **46**:6–7; **47**:5–11, 27b–28; **48**:3–7; **49**:1a, 28b–33; **50**:12–13; *Exodus* **1**:1–5, 7, 13–14; **2**:23b–25; **6**:2–13, 26–30; **7**:1–13, 19–20a, 21b–22; **8**:5–7, 15b; **9**:8–12; **11**:9–10; **12**:1–20, 28, 37a, 40–41, 43–51; **13**:1–2, 20; **14**:1–4, 8–9, 15–18, 21a, c–23, 26–27a, 28a, 29; **16**:1–3, 6–24, 31–36; **17**:1a; **19**:1–2a; **24**:15–18a; **25**:1–**31**:18a; **34**:29–35; **35**:1–**40**:34; *Leviticus* **8**:1–10:20; **24**:10–23; *Numeri* **1**:1–4, 17–19; **7**:1–11, 89; **8**:1–22; **9**:1–23; **10**:11–28; **13**:1–3, 21, 25–26a, 32; **14**:1–2, 5–7, 10, 26–30, 34–38; **15**:32–36; **16**:1a, 2b–11, 16–17, 18–24, 27a, 35; **17**:1–28; **20**:1a, 2, 3b–13, 22–29; **21**:4a, 10–11a; **22**:1; **25**:6–19; **26**:1–4; **27**:1–23; **31**:1–54; **36**:1–13; *Deuteronomy* **32**:48–52; **34**:1a, 7–9.
3 The bulk of this paper is based on select parts of the introduction in my forthcoming thesis.

ment (first published in 1891).[4] In this publication, the scattered statements about suspected late lexicographic, grammatical and syntactic features that had started to appear in Hebrew grammars during the nineteenth century, were brought together and listed for the first time.[5] In addition to the lists of features, Driver notes that the general nature of the linguistic difference between SBH and LBH is a difference in frequency and distribution of a certain feature. Thus, "often observable in the Hebrew of the same age [i.e. post-exilic] is the *frequent* occurrence in it of a word or construction which occurs only *exceptionally* in the earlier Hebrew".[6] Of even more importance for the study of developments in the syntax of the verb is Driver's *A Treatise on the Use of Tenses in Hebrew*.[7] Above all, this study clearly shows that the developments in the use of verbal syntax in LBH are unequivocally connected to changes in frequency, i.e., increase or decrease in the use of certain verbal forms, or functions of these forms, in the post-exilic biblical compositions.

In the early history of the study of LBH syntax, the greatest landmark in terms of influence and recognition is the study of the linguistic features of the Chronicler by Arno Kropat from 1909.[8] Published in the same year, the largely overlooked dissertation of Rebecca Corwin on the use of verbal syntax in Chronicles, Ezra and Nehemiah is arguably an even more important investigation for the study of verbal syntax and sentence structure in LBH.[9]

The next major advance in the field of research came in 1927 with the publication of Moshe H. Segal's grammar of Mishnaic Hebrew.[10] In order to establish Mishnaic Hebrew as a linguistic stage in the historical development of Hebrew, Segal systematically compares it to Biblical Hebrew, with particular attention to the ways in which it is different to Biblical Hebrew. In this differentiation, Segal also provides many observations on the linguistic differences between SBH and LBH, with particular attention to the syntax of the verb.

The discovery of the Dead Sea Scrolls in 1947 produced further advances in the study of post-Biblical Hebrew, which also contributed to the understanding of the diachronic development of Biblical Hebrew. Outstanding among the early works is Eduard Y. Kutscher's magisterial treatment of the great Isaiah Scroll (1QIsa^a), which discusses practically every facet of phonetics, morphology, syntax and lexicon of the scroll in comparison to 'Basic' Biblical Hebrew, Late Biblical Hebrew

---

4 Driver, *Introduction*. This edition is the basis for the subsequent (unaltered) 7th–9th (1913) editions.
5 The first publication to propose a diachronic factor underlying consistent linguistic differences between earlier and later biblical books is that of Gesenius, *Geschichte*.
6 Driver, *Introduction*, 505.
7 Driver, *Treatise* [First published in 1874]. The legacy of Driver's *Tenses* in subsequent scholarship has primarily been the wide acceptance of Driver's 'aspect theory' as *the* explanatory model for the Biblical Hebrew verbal system.
8 Kropat, *Syntax*.
9 Corwin, *Verb*.
10 Segal, *Grammar*.

and Mishnaic Hebrew.[11] Another work of great importance is the posthumous publication of Kutscher's history of the Hebrew Language.[12] In addition to the linguistic treatment itself, this book contains Kutscher's classic formulation of the tripartite division between the diachronic stages of Archaic Biblical Hebrew (ABH), Standard Biblical Hebrew and Late Biblical Hebrew.

Avi Hurvitz, a student of Kutscher, is the most prominent scholar in the field of the historical development of Biblical Hebrew, on account of both the number and breadth of publications, since the early 1960s and onwards. It is widely acknowledged that one of the greatest contributions of Hurvitz's labour is his insistent effort to formulate an objective methodology for the diachronic study of Biblical Hebrew. Several publications by Hurvitz, together with the monograph by Robert Polzin, which have remained the most influential studies in the field of LBH studies in general, were aimed at determining the relative date of P from its linguistic profile.[13] In contrast to Hurvitz's focus on lexicographic features in P, Polzin considers features of grammar and syntax to be more objective criteria in the study of diachronic linguistic development.[14] The findings and conclusions of Hurvitz's extensive body of work on P may be summarized by the following quote: "The formative years which determined the shape of the Priestly corpus ought to be sought in pre-exilic times. This conclusion is borne out by the testimony of the language in which these texts are formulated; i.e., by P's linguistic profile, which reflects Classical BH at its best."[15] Polzin, on the other hand, concludes that "the grammatical/syntactic nature of P^g and P^s places them between classical BH and the LBH of Chronicles".[16]

The works of Hurvitz and Polzin have inspired a series of studies of LBH, which in most cases follow both Hurvitz and Polzin in their methodology and the selection of LBH features.[17] That is, most of these studies employ Hurvitz's method, include the features of grammar and morpho-syntax from Polzin, and select features from the lexicon isolated by Hurvitz.

---

11 Kutscher, *Language* [First published in Hebrew 1959].
12 Kutscher, *History*.
13 Hurvitz, "Usage"; idem, "Summary"; idem, "Evidence"; idem, *Study*; idem, "Studies"; idem, "Language; idem, "Dating"; idem, "Once Again"; Polzin, *Late Biblical Hebrew*.
14 Note that this is not to say that lexicographic features have no relevance or reliability in diachronic studies. On the contrary, evidence from the domains of lexicon, grammar and syntax should ultimately complement each other in diachronic linguistic studies of a particular text, in order to give a full picture of its linguistic profile.
15 Hurvitz, "Once Again," 190–191.
16 Polzin, *Late Biblical Hebrew*, 112. Polzin thereby finds that his study not only corroborates the source division of the documentary hypothesis, but also the traditional division between P^g and P^s (following Noth) and their suggested chronological relationship. "Such a situation I can only explain as exemplifying that frequent experience we all have had of something being right for the wrong reasons" (ibid. 87).
17 Guenther, *Study*; Hill, *Book of Malachi*; idem, *Malachi*; Bergey, *Book of Esther*; Wright, *Evidence*; Rooker, *Biblical Hebrew*; Shin, *Study*; Cohen, *Verbal Tense System*; Hornkohl, *Periodization*.

My diachronic study of the verbal syntax in P relates to the works of Hurvitz and Polzin in different ways. In particular, the principles of Hurvitz's method form the basis of the methodology of my thesis (see III, below), whereas the primary object of study – the P narrative – and the focus on syntax, overlaps more closely with the study by Polzin.[18] However, the approach of my thesis differs from that of Polzin with regard to which features of grammar and syntax that may be considered to give the most reliable results. That is, in contrast to the disparate collection of isolated 'grammatical/syntactic' features included in Polzin's study, the focus of my study on features of verbal syntax provides a means to get at the development of the linguistic system as such in LBH (see further II, below).[19]

Since the 1990s, several publications by Mats Eskhult and Jan Joosten have contributed to significant progress in the study of LBH, with a focus on the syntax of the verb in narrative prose. These scholars have advanced the description of the syntactic LBH features isolated by Driver, Kropat and Corwin around the turn of the twentieth century by incorporating contemporary linguistic approaches. In his PhD thesis, Eskhult devotes the final chapter to developments in LBH verbal syntax.[20] Following this publication, Eskhult has made several important contributions to the study of LBH verbal syntax that are of particular relevance to the present study.[21] In a recent monograph on the Biblical Hebrew verbal system, Joosten summarizes in a separate chapter many of the findings regarding LBH verbal syntax from his earlier studies.[22]

Over the past fifteen years or so, the study of the diachronic development of Biblical Hebrew within the traditional chronological framework of a development from SBH to LBH, has been questioned by a small but active group of biblical scholars. The strongest, most concentrated presentation to date of the case against the traditional chronological model, and the data on which this case is based, is the

---

18 However, since Polzin's corpus of the P narrative corresponds to the traditional delineation of P^g and P^s (outside Leviticus), it also includes comparatively large portions of legal and genealogical material. In the selection of the material for the corpus of the P narrative in my study, non-narrative material (e.g. laws, lists, and genealogies) is as a rule excluded. The following non-narrative passages in Polzin's corpora are not included my P corpus: (P^g): Gen 5:1–28, 30–32; 10:1a, 2–7, 20, 22–23, 31–32; 11:10–26; 25:12–17, 19–20, 26b; 35:22b–29; Num 1:5–16, 20–47; 2:1–34; 3:5–10, 14–25, 27–30, 32a, 33–39; 8:5–19. (P^s): Gen 46:8–27; Exod 6:14–25; Num 1:48–53; 3:1–4, 26, 31–32b, 40–43, 46–51.
19 To be sure, five of Polzin's nineteen LBH features concerns the verb, to some extent, but only two of them are connected to verbal syntax in any real sense of the word. Therefore, most of the LBH features found in Polzin's list of 'grammatical/syntactic' features are not of relevance to my study.
20 Eskhult, *Studies*, 103–120.
21 Eskhult, "Syntax"; idem, "Markers"; idem, "Traces"; idem, "Aspects"; idem, "2 Samuel".
22 Joosten, *System*, 377–409. See also Joosten, "Biblical Hebrew"; idem, "Pseudo-Classicisms"; idem, "Distinction"; idem, "Disappearance"; idem, "Syntax; idem, "Aspects"; idem, "History"; idem, "Evolution"; idem, "Imperative Clauses".

two-volume work by Ian Young, Robert Rezetko, and Martin Ehrensvärd.[23] Their main arguments (or 'new synthesis') may be summarized as follows; although SBH represents a typologically earlier stage of the language than LBH, and the pre-exilic Hebrew inscriptions demonstrate that the biblical language was formulated in the pre-exilic period, the Hebrew inscriptions cannot prove that any of the biblical books written in SBH must have been written in this period. The lack of extra-biblical Hebrew sources from the post-exilic period is used to argue the possibility that SBH could have continued to exist in the post-exilic period as an optional stylistic variation, parallel to LBH. The further implication is that relative dating of biblical texts based on the SBH–LBH distinction is no longer possible, since both forms would have been accessible to the writers in the post-exilic period. Arguably, the most important contribution of Young et al. is not their new synthesis but rather the renewed interest in the field of diachronic study of Biblical Hebrew, and the introspection of the field that it has provoked.[24] Above all, it has revealed several weaknesses in the traditional approach, and thus highlighted the necessity of incorporating theories and approaches from the wider field of linguistics in the continued study of the diachronic development of Biblical Hebrew.[25]

2. Theoretical Framework

In the field of historical linguistics, the primary object of study is the *linguistic system* of a language, as manifested at different stages of development in textual corpora. My study of the P narrative is focused on a central part of that system, namely, the *verbal system*. The diachronic development of the Hebrew verbal system is studied through observed change in the use of *verbal syntax* between corpora, which are representative of different chronological stages of linguistic development, on typological grounds. This further entails that the study of syntactic change is made from both a diachronic and a synchronic perspective, and concerns both the verbal system and the syntax of the verb.

In order to establish that syntactic change on the level of the text is indicative of diachronic development (as opposed to synchronic variation), syntactic change is

---

23 Young, Rezetko, and Ehrensvärd, *Linguistic Dating*.
24 Of particular importance is the demonstration that many of the traditional LBH features of e.g., Polzin are, in fact, chronologically irrelevant (and should therefore be abandoned in future studies in this field). However, it is noteworthy that the authors of *Linguistic Dating* still retain these features (after disqualifying them) in their own 'case studies'.
25 To be sure, this is rather a 'secondary effect' produced by the criticism of the principles and methodology of the traditional approach in Young et al., since this work is itself characterized by a complete negligence of the basic theories, working principles and approaches in the field of contemporary historical linguistics.

studied in my thesis with a focus on the diachronic grammaticalization processes involved in the renewal of the tense–aspect–modality (TAM) categories of the Hebrew verbal system. Because of the limited space of this paper, I will only touch briefly on some of the most central issues involved that I refer to in the following discussion (see III–IV, below).[26]

The process of grammaticalization is commonly viewed as occurring along universal diachronic *pathways*.[27] Diachronic pathways are universal in the sense that any grammaticalizations that begin with the same or similar source meaning can be expected to follow the same course of change, in a *unidirectional* and ordered development.[28] The process of grammaticalization typically creates a *layering effect*, which means that when a form acquires new functions, it often retains earlier meanings and functions. Thus, the older layers are not necessarily discarded, but may remain, to coexist with and to interact with new layers. Grammaticalization studies have shown that it is common to find more than one verbal form on the same grammaticalization path. The phenomenon that new structures keep being grammaticalized and entering the pathways of the system is usually referred to as *renewal*. In such cases, the older form and the younger form will have partly overlapping functions, and will compete with each other. The competition between an older and a newer form may eventually lead to the recession and complete loss of the older form.

With regard to the verbal system, the metaphorical notions of *core* and *periphery* may be applied both to individual verbal forms and to the system as a whole.[29] Thus, each individual form of the verbal system has values and functions that are considered more central (i.e. core), and values and functions that are more peripheral. At the same time, individual forms may be perceived of as either peripheral or core forms in the system at any given synchronic stage of the language. In either case, the distinction core/periphery reflects differences in the degree of grammaticalization and the degree of *frequency*. A distinction may also be made between *coming* forms (i.e. those which are invading the core area of the system), and *leaving* forms (i.e. those which have already achieved their functional culmination and are moving out of the centre back to the periphery). Combining the metaphorical notions of core/periphery, coming/leaving forms, and the empirically observable rates of increase/decrease in frequency, the verbal system in development may be schematized in the following way:

---

26 For an in-depth treatment and ample exemplification of all the issues involved, the interested reader is referred to the works of Dahl, *Tense*; idem, "Tense-Aspect Systems"; Bybee and Dahl, "Creation"; Bybee, Perkins, and Pagliuca, *Evolution of Grammar*.
27 Bybee, Perkins, and Pagliuca, *Evolution of Grammar*, identify four basic and universal pathways, which lead to the formation of verbal forms that feed TAM systems.
28 The basic assumption about unidirectionality is that there is a relationship between two stages A and B, such as that A occurs before B, but not vice versa.
29 See Dahl, "Tense-Aspect Systems," 14–15.

peripheral		core		peripheral
coming	→	coming → leaving	→	leaving
increasing		increasing → decreasing		decreasing

Studies in the field of comparative Semitic linguistics have shown that the ancient Hebrew verbal system, which has traditionally been viewed as anomalous and enigmatic from a synchronic view, may be understood and described in a diachronic, comparative, grammaticalization perspective.[30] In particular, previous grammaticalization studies of the Hebrew verb have been (largely) successful in associating the individual forms of the Hebrew verbal system with the universal pathways which lead to the formation of verbal forms that feed TAM systems.[31] Following these studies, the preliminary observation may be put forward that there are two oppositions in the core of the Hebrew verbal system.[32] Namely, that between two forms on different diachronic stages on the perfective → past pathway, and two forms on different diachronic stages on the imperfective → present pathway:[33]

---

30 Following Kuryłowicz, *Esquisses linguistiques II*, the seminal study by Cohen, *phrase nominale* treats the renewal of verbal TAM categories in the system of the Semitic language family in terms of grammaticalization processes. The large scale crosslinguistic grammaticalization studies by e.g. Bybee and Dahl, "Creation", and Bybee, Perkins, and Pagliuca, *Evolution of Grammar*, confirm the results of these early studies, and further establish far-reaching typological commonalities in the development of verbal categories in unrelated languages. More recent grammaticalization studies in the field of Semitic linguistics usually build (primarily) on the results of Bybee, Perkins, and Pagliuca, *Evolution of Grammar*.
31 See e.g. Andersen, "Evolution"; Cook, "Hebrew Verb"; idem, *Time*; idem, "Development".
32 As noted by Dahl, "Tense-Aspect Systems," 13–14, "[i]f one can talk about an 'opposition' between an older and a younger gram on the same path, it is rather a secondary effect of the relative positions of the grams. Indeed, due to the multidimensionality of the grammaticalization process, it may not be possible to establish a systematic semantic difference between two such grams".
33 Key to terminology used for the forms of the Hebrew verb in this paper:

qatal	perfect	*qatol*	absolute infinitive
yiqtol	imperfect	*qətol*	construct infinitive
wəqatal	perfect consecutive	*wəhaya*	perfect consecutive 3.m.s of the verb *hāyā*
wayyiqtol	imperfect consecutive	*wayhi*	imperfect consecutive 3.m.s of the verb *hāyā*
qtol	imperative	*qotel*	active participle

yiqtol (<*yaqtul*)	>	perfective → past path
qatal		
yiqtol (<*yaqtulu*)	>	imperfective → present path
qotel		

Further oppositions between the core (and peripheral) forms of the Biblical Hebrew verbal system may only be observed in actual usage (syntax) in different discourse types.

In my dissertation, the synchronic description of the verbal syntax in the main biblical corpora (i.e. the P narrative, SBH prose and LBH prose) is informed by a textlinguistic theory and approach. In contrast to traditional grammatical description, the textlinguistic approach views the verbal forms, as *clauses*, within the framework of the text. This means that verbal syntax is studied with focus on patterns or sequences of verbal clauses, rather than on individual verbs in isolated sentences. Textlinguistics is a firmly established discipline in the field of Biblical Hebrew linguistics, mainly focused on the description of narrative prose texts in the SBH prose corpus. In line with the majority of these studies, the syntactic analysis in my thesis is informed primarily by the semantic-functional approach to Biblical Hebrew syntax as outlined by Alviero Niccacci, and the cross-linguistic discourse pragmatic approach developed by Robert E. Longacre.[34] Of special importance to my study are Longacre's classifications of different *discourse types* within prose.

3. Methodology and the practical application of theoretical approaches

Hurvitz has developed a sound method for identifying late linguistic features in biblical texts.[35] I use the basic principles of his method as points of departure for detecting possible LBH features in the verbal syntax of the P narrative. The method involves four criteria. The first three criteria; (1) biblical distribution, (2) extra-biblical distribution, and (3) linguistic opposition, are used to determine if a particular linguistic *feature* is late. The fourth criterion, (4) accumulation, is used to determine

---

34 Niccacci, *Syntax*; idem, "Hebrew Verbal System"; idem, "Hebrew Syntax"; idem, "Basic Facts"; Longacre, *Grammar*; idem, *Joseph*; idem, "Discourse Perspective"; idem, "*Weqatal* Forms"; idem, "Proposal".
35 The presentation of Hurvitz's method is primarily based on Hurvitz, "Biblical Texts", in comparison with idem, *Transition Period*; idem, "Linguistic Criteria"; idem, "Continuity"; idem, "Debate".

whether or not the *linguistic profile* of a particular text is late, in other words, if it displays an accumulation or concentration of LBH features.[36]

Hurvitz (and most scholars following him and Polzin), has primarily used this method in order to identify late lexicographic and isolated grammatical features in particular texts. The method has not been applied in a systematic way to evaluate late features of verbal syntax.[37] Since the linguistic domains of lexicon, grammar, and syntax differ in many respects, the first three criteria of Hurvitz's method are adapted in my study in order to be applicable to the study of verbal syntax and diachronic syntactic change. The first three criteria represent practical 'steps' that are performed in the analysis of the diachronic features included in my investigation, whereas the accumulation of late syntactic features in the P narrative is evaluated in the summary and conclusions of my thesis (so also in this paper, see IV, below).

3.1 Biblical distribution

The first criterion of the method is defined by Hurvitz accordingly: "The linguistic element is attested within biblical literature exclusively, or predominantly, in acknowledged late compositions".[38] The feature should also be both common and of such significance that it indicates a potential linguistic development. As intended by the qualification 'predominantly', the feature may also be attested infrequently in the SBH corpus.

In applying this principle to an examination of developments reflected in the syntax of the verb, two further qualifications are necessary. Firstly, the core compositions of the LBH corpus (Chronicles, Ezra, Nehemiah, Esther, and Daniel) consist of narrative prose, and Hurvitz's SBH corpus comprises the entire SBH complex

---

36 The following example (adapted from Hurvitz, "Biblical Texts," 150–151) illustrates the application of the first three criteria in the identification of a late lexicographic feature:
Biblical distribution: Within the Hebrew Bible, the lexeme *ʾiggeret* 'letter' is attested x10 times. All attestations are found in the distinctive corpus of LBH: Esther (x2), Nehemiah (x6), Chronicles (x2).
Extra-biblical distribution: Outside the Hebrew Bible, *ʾiggeret* is frequently employed in Aramaic correspondence of the Persian period (Biblical Aramaic and Egyptian Aramaic *ʾiggərā*); i.e. in sources contemporary with LBH. The term is also widely documented in the post-biblical period – in both Aramaic sources (e.g. Bar-Kokhba letters, Palestinian Aramaic, Syriac) and in Mishnaic Hebrew.
Linguistic opposition: In SBH, the lexeme *ʾiggeret* is not attested, instead the term *sep̄er* is used to denote 'letter'. Additionally, *sep̄er* is attested in pre-exilic epigraphic Hebrew (in the Lachish letters), whereas *ʾiggeret* is not. A diachronic development is thus suggested by the fact that the earlier SBH term *sep̄er* was replaced in LBH by the later counterpart *ʾiggeret*.
37 A notable exception is Eskhult, who treats several important developments in LBH verbal syntax with specific reference to Hurvitz's method. See Eskhult, "Traces," 358 with n.13 and 359–370.
38 Hurvitz, "Biblical Texts," 148.

(SBH prose, SBH poetry and the Prophets – excluding only Archaic BH poetry). This approach is largely unproblematic with regard to lexicographical features, but it is not preferable when dealing with features of verbal syntax.[39] That is, in order to obtain methodologically proper comparison, late syntactic features of the LBH prose corpus must be evaluated primarily against syntactic usage in the narrative prose of the SBH corpus. For the same reason, the P corpus of my study (the P narrative) is restricted to include only narrative prose in order to be comparable to the SBH prose and LBH prose corpora.

Secondly, it is necessary to qualify what constitutes a late feature of verbal syntax. In contrast to lexicographic features, in which the mere appearance of a late word – as an item – may be considered a late feature in itself, syntactic features usually require more sophisticated analyses. Because it is essentially the same verbal system met with in SBH and LBH, in the sense that the verbal system of both corpora comprises the same set of verbal forms, late syntactic features are usually connected to the development or loss of specific *functions* of a verbal form in LBH in comparison to SBH. The increased or decreased frequency of a particular function (or several functions) performed by a verbal form usually leads to a corresponding increased or decreased frequency of the form itself.

All of the diachronic features included in my study involve observed changes with regard to frequency of the following verbs (or verbal clauses) in LBH, as compared to SBH:
- decreased use of the 'consecutive' syntagms *wayyiqtol* and *wəqatal*
- decreased use of non-past *qatal*
- decreased use of the absolute infinitive *qatol*.

In contrast to the majority of previous investigations, which have treated the decrease of these verbal forms in LBH more or less *en masse*, the textlinguistic approach employed in my study enables a treatment of each form, and its different syntactic functions, in the context of the appropriate discourse type. As a result, the decreased use of *wayyiqtol*, (*wə*)*qatal*, and *qatol* is studied in the context of seven different discourse types, in the form of fourteen different features of verbal syntax that may be considered indicative of a development from SBH to LBH (see further 3. below).

---

39 As duly recognized by Eskhult (e.g. "Traces," 354; "2 Samuel," 20) and Joosten (e.g. "Distinction," 329) in their treatments of Biblical Hebrew diachronic verbal syntax (see also Polzin, *Late Biblical Hebrew*, 1, 87). Unfortunately, this fundamental methodological premise is not adopted in most other treatments that include some features of verbal syntax alongside Hurvitz's and Polzin's traditional set of features from the lexicon and grammar. See e.g., Guenther, Study; Wright, *Evidence*, and most recently Young, Rezetko, and Ehrensvärd, *Linguistic Dating*.

3.2 Extra-biblical distribution

The second criterion is defined by Hurvitz accordingly: "The element can be shown to have been current in contemporary post-exilic sources outside the Hebrew Bible as well [as in LBH]".[40] This criterion ensures that a proposed LBH feature does indeed reflect late usage current in the linguistic milieu of the post-exilic era as a whole. Since this period (for the time being) lacks any extra-biblical Hebrew sources, the witness from the comparatively large corpus of contemporary Aramaic sources serves as the primary 'external control' for LBH. In Hurvitz's method, the criterion of extra-biblical distribution also includes attestations in the Hebrew and Aramaic sources of the post-biblical period. Occasionally, the pre-exilic extra-biblical sources may be invoked as additional 'external controls' for SBH usage, *after* the establishment of a linguistic opposition between LBH and SBH.

In contrast, the pre-exilic extra-biblical sources play a decisive role in the establishment of a linguistic opposition involving a feature of verbal syntax. Therefore, in my thesis, the description of SBH verbal syntax is viewed in a wider perspective, against the background of the earliest attested North-West Semitic (NWS) languages. In the approach taken in my study, the two main synchronic stages of Biblical Hebrew (SBH and LBH) are considered to form a diachronic linguistic continuum.[41] This linguistic continuum is studied within a wider diachronic continuum, as represented by the extra-biblical Hebrew and NWS sources, spanning from the middle of the 14th century BCE to the 2nd century CE:

---

40 Hurvitz, "Biblical Texts," 148.
41 Compare Givón. "Biblical Hebrew." Compare also the approach in Polzin, *Late Biblical Hebrew*, 88, 95, 101, 112, who seeks to establish a diachronic 'language continuum' between his SBH and LBH sources (JE → Court History → Dtr → Chr), in order to place his P^g and P^s corpora in this continuum.

Historical period	Corpus	Amount of words
1. Pre-biblical period	Amarna Canaanite	—
	Ugaritic	ca. 40.000
2. Pre-exilic (EBH) period	Phoenician	
	Old Aramaic and Early Official Aramaic	ca. 10.000
	Moabite (Mesha stele)	ca. 30.000
	Ammonite (Amman Citadel, Tel Siran)	512
		60
	Deir 'Alla (Combination I)	180
	Epigraphic Hebrew (excluding seals)	ca. 4.000
	Archaic Biblical Hebrew (ABH) poetry	ca. 2.900
Standard Biblical Hebrew prose	Genesis–2 Kings (excluding P and ABH)	ca. 158.000
Late Biblical Hebrew prose	Chronicles, Ezra, Nehemiah, Esther, Daniel	ca. 55.000
3. Exilic and Post-exilic (LBH) period	Egyptian Aramaic	ca. 43.000
	Biblical Aramaic	ca. 7.200
4. Post-biblical period	Ben Sira	ca. 16.500
	Qumran Hebrew and Aramaic	ca. 265.000
	Bar Kokhba Hebrew and Aramaic	—
	Mishnaic Hebrew (the Mishna)	ca. 265.000

In linguistic studies of modern language corpora, a 1000-word sample is considered adequate to reflect common grammatical and syntactic features reliably. In contrast, lexicographical research requires a corpus of a million words or more to adequately represent the range of lexical items (and various collocations of those items) within a language.[42] Each of the main corpora included in my study (the P narrative [ca. 23.000 words], SBH prose and LBH prose), are more than adequate for syntactic study in view of the requirement of a 1000-word sample. This also holds true for (most of) the extra-biblical Hebrew and NWS corpora used for comparison. This entails that the synchronic description of the linguistic system in each corpus provides a reliable basis for comparisons between these corpora, in order to trace diachronic syntactic change on typological grounds.

---

42 For references see Miller, "Methodological Issues," 285, n.14.

3.3 Linguistic opposition

The criterion of linguistic opposition is defined by Hurvitz accordingly: "SBH, which as a rule does not resort to the element being examined, is known to employ instead—in comparable contexts outside the LBH corpus—alternative linguistic modes of expression, commonly attested in the classical tradition of the language."[43] In other words, a proposed LBH feature should have a clear contrastive equivalent in comparable contexts in SBH. This criterion eliminates the possibility that a supposed LBH feature is missing in the SBH corpus, not because of its lateness, but perhaps, because the Hebrew Bible does not offer an occasion for its employment. Arguably, the criterion of linguistic opposition is to be considered *the* central principle of the methodology "by providing us with two distinct sets of rival elements— each characteristic of a different historical phase of BH—it confirms our conclusion that we are dealing with a genuine diachronic linguistic development".[44]

Now, in the diachronic study of lexical features, 'comparable contexts' naturally refers to content or subject matter.[45] In applying this principle to the examination of developments reflected in verbal syntax, 'comparable contexts' refers specifically to *discourse types*, which are not defined by content or subject matter. Instead, discourse types are characterized by their syntactic coding of mainline and offline constructions. Every discourse type has a constellation of several different types of verbal clauses, and this constellation is usually centred on one primary opposition between two types of verbal clauses. Regularly, the verbal clauses in the central opposition correspond to mainline and offline constructions in a discourse type, as illustrated by the following example of procedural (past-habitual) discourse in SBH:

---

43 Hurvitz, "Biblical Texts," 148.
44 Hurvitz, "Once Again," 150.
45 For example, Hurvitz compares the technical idioms and terminology of P to Chronicles, Ezra, Nehemiah and Ezekiel, since they "have close ties with priestly subjects" (Hurvitz, "The Evidence," 25). See also Hurvitz, "Continuity," which is a study of a formulaic idiom (the prostration formula) from the realm of the royal court, and its development in Chronicles as compared to Samuel and Kings (in comparison also to Ugaritic texts).

Procedural discourse (SBH)	Clause type	
and the people *used to see* the cloud-pillar standing at the tent door,	wəqatal	mainline
and all the people *would rise*,	wəqatal	mainline
and *worship*, each man in his tent door,	wəqatal	mainline
and YHWH *would speak* to Moses	wəqatal	mainline
–as a man speaks to his friend–	x–yiqtol	offline
and (afterwards) Moses *used to return* to the camp (Exod 33:10–11)	wəqatal	mainline

Most LBH syntactic features involve a decreased frequency of a particular syntactic function associated with a certain verbal form (or clause type) in a discourse type, in comparison to SBH usage. Since a development rarely happens in a vacuum, involving one verbal form in isolation, but typically affects another form in the same syntactic environment, the central criterion of linguistic opposition is fulfilled (almost by default) in every diachronic feature of verbal syntax.[46] To be more concrete, several syntactic LBH features involve a development in which a typologically younger verbal form takes on functions that were previously performed by a typologically older verbal form in SBH, thus resulting in a functional opposition between a younger and an older form. In a discourse context, this type of development is primarily detectable when there is a change in the syntactic coding of the textual mainline. Compare the previous example (above) to the following example of procedural (past-habitual) discourse in the LBH corpus:

Procedural discourse (LBH)	Clause type	
and the people of the land *would discourage* the people of Judah	wəx–qotel	mainline
and *make* them *afraid* to build	wəqotel	mainline
and *they used to bribe* officials ... (Ezra 4:4–5)	wəqotel	mainline

---

[46] It should be noted that this criterion has proven to be very difficult to fulfil in studies focused on lexicographic and isolated grammatical LBH features. According to Young, Rezetko, and Ehrensvärd, *Linguistic Dating*, I:88, only 2 of 37 features included in Rooker, *Biblical Hebrew*, meet the criterion of linguistic opposition (both are lexical features), and *none* of the 40 features included in Wright, *Evidence*, meet this criterion (excluding his discussion of 'Persianisms').

The example above shows that the active predicative participle *qotel* functions as a mainline construction in LBH procedural discourse, and thus encroaches on the functional domain of the SBH mainline construction *wəqatal* in this type of discourse. It should also be noted that predicative *qotel* is not used in the mainline of SBH procedural discourse. As a further consequence of this functional development, predicative *qotel* increases in frequency, and conversely, the syntagm *wəqatal* decreases in frequency in this discourse context in LBH. In fact, it has been questioned if *wəqatal* is attested at all in procedural discourse with this function in the LBH corpus.[47] The two examples from SBH and LBH procedural discourse (above) illustrate the type of opposition resulting from a direct functional 'competition' between a younger form and an older form in the verbal system. This kind of opposition I refer to as a 'direct opposition'.

Now, not all LBH features of verbal syntax involve developments that result in a direct opposition. Some syntactic LBH features involve loss of functions and concomitant decrease in textual (token) frequency of an older verbal form that are not conditioned by a 'competition' with a younger verbal form. In such cases, there are, as a rule, two old forms that share, and overlap each other, in the same functional domain in a certain discourse type in SBH. In LBH, when one of these forms in the process of grammaticalization loses its former function(s) and decreases in this functional domain, the other old form remains productive in that context. For example, in SBH hortatory discourse the absolute infinitive *qatol* is sometimes used with imperative force, as an equivalent of the regular imperative *qtol* in affirmative utterances directed to a 2nd person.[48] This function of *qatol* does not seem to be attested in LBH hortatory discourse, which only employs the imperative *qtol* in this context. Since the imperative *qtol* remained the default verbal form in this functional domain throughout the history of Ancient Hebrew, the non-use of imperatival *qatol* in LBH – and the resulting (marginally) increased use of *qtol* – is not depending on a functional competition between these two forms.[49] This kind of opposition I refer to as an 'indirect opposition' (indicated by square brackets in the table below).

A third type of LBH feature of verbal syntax does not involve any opposition (indicated by Ø in the table below). This concerns the rare case in which there is no renewal of a functional domain (occupied by one old form in SBH) by another form in LBH. In such cases, there is a loss of both form and function in LBH.

---

47 See Joosten, "Disappearance."
48 The infinitive *qatol* is also used in affirmative commands directed to a 2nd person in SBH (apodictic) juridical discourse. In this context however, the use of *qatol* is parallel to that of *yiqtol* with injunctive force rather than *qtol* (e.g., Deut 5:12: '*you shall keep* the Sabbath day' rather than '*keep*! ...'), which is never used in juridical discourse. Note that the related injunctive and imperative uses of *qatol* are treated together in the context of juridical discourse (see the list of diachronic features below) due to the distribution of these usages in the P narrative.
49 Rather, the non-use of imperatival *qatol* is connected to the overall decrease of *qatol* in most positions in LBH, as part of the general development towards the (practical) disappearance of the form from the Hebrew verbal system at the end of the post-biblical period.

In the analysis part of my thesis, I establish the SBH–LBH opposition in each syntactic feature within its discourse type, in order to compare the use of verbal syntax in the same discourse type in the P narrative. The diachronic features included in the study are listed below from the perspective of LBH as compared to SBH:

	List of Diachronic Features			
Discourse type		**Linguistic opposition**		
			Decrease	**Increase**
Juridical discourse	1	wəqatal in conditional structures		[x–yiqtol]
	2	paronomastic use of qatol		Ø
	3	injunctive/imperatival use of qatol		[yiqtol/qtol]
Hortatory discourse	4	mainline (and offline) wəqatal		[wə-volitive]
Instructional discourse	5	mainline wəqatal		(wə)qotel (wə)yiqtol
Procedural discourse (non-past)	6	mainline wəqatal		(wə)qotel (wə)yiqtol
Present discourse (actual present)	7	performative qatal		qotel
Predictive discourse	8	mainline wəqatal		(wə)qotel (wə)yiqtol
	9	macro-syntactic wəhaya		[w-prep-qətol]
	10	'prophetic perfect' qatal		[yiqtol]
Narrative discourse	11	mainline wayyiqtol		(wə)x–qatal
	12	macro-syntactic wayhi		[w-prep-qətol]
Procedural discourse (past)	13	mainline wəqatal		(wə)qotel
	14	macro-syntactic wəhaya		[w-prep-qətol]

It is important to note that all the features listed above do not carry the same weight. For example, features pertaining to functions of *wayyiqtol* and (*wə*)*qatal* that belong to the core of the SBH verbal system, carry more weight than features involving functions of *qatol*, which is a peripheral form in the system. To be sure, core verbal forms of the system may have *functions* that are peripheral (in relation to its core functions), e.g. feature (10) involves a peripheral function of *qatal*. Features pertaining to the use of the macro-syntactic markers *wayhi* (12) and *wəhaya* (9 and 14) carry less weight than features involving their predicative verbal counterparts (*wayyiqtol* and *wəqatal*) since they reflect developments on the textual level rather than developments in the verbal system. Thus, viewed independently, some features are less decisive than others. Viewed all together, however, these fourteen diachronic features show aspects of development that include and affect every verbal form at the core of the Biblical Hebrew verbal system.

4. Conclusion

The fourth criterion of the method determines whether or not the linguistic profile of a particular text is late. According to Hurvitz, "to linguistically assign a chronologically problematic text to the late biblical period, that text is required not only to stand the test of the three criteria outlined above; it must also satisfy a fourth criterion—that of Accumulation. It is only on the basis of a heavy concentration of late linguistic elements that a late dating may be securely established for texts of unknown age."[50]

Now, my study will show that the syntax of the verb in the P narrative does not display any form of accumulation – much less a 'heavy concentration' – of late syntactic features. In view of the unambiguous results of my study in this respect, it is safe to conclude that the syntax of the verb in the P narrative does *not* reflect LBH usage. The next question is whether the practical absence of distinctive LBH usage, in itself, indicates that the verbal syntax of the P narrative reflects SBH usage. The answer to this question depends on whether the absence of distinctive LBH usage in the P narrative may be explained as the result of (1) deliberate archaizing, and/or (2) conscious avoidance of features belonging to LBH verbal syntax. These two issues must be considered in the broader context of previous studies with a focus on isolated lexical and grammatical *elements* in LBH.

(1) The issue of archaizing has played a central role in Hurvitz's works on the linguistic profile of P due to the conception of P's 'archaizing style' as argued by Wellhausen.[51] Since Hurvitz has focused on identifying LBH features from the

---

50 Hurvitz, "Biblical Texts," 153.
51 Cf. Wellhausen, *Prolegomena*, 9–10: "it tries hard to imitate the costume of the Mosaic period, and, with whatever success, to disguise its own. (...) The Priestly code (...) guards itself against all reference to later times and settled life in Canaan (...) it keeps itself carefully and strictly within the limits of the situation in the wilderness, for which in all seriousness it seeks to give the law. It has actually been successful, with its movable tabernacle, its wandering camp, and other archaic details, in so concealing the true date of its composition that its many serious inconsistencies with what we know, from other sources (...) are only taken as proving that it lies far beyond all known history, and on account of its enormous antiquity can hardly be brought into any connection with it".

realm of the lexicon, the careful appreciation of the potential influence of archaizing in P is necessary, given that archaizing is a *stylistic* device, which concerns, first and foremost, choice of words, phrases, set expressions, or idioms. However, as pointed out by Hurvitz, it is only when both earlier and later modes of expression are found in one and the same composition that the older elements may be considered the result of an archaizing style.[52] Since Hurvitz does not find any clear imprints of late lexical-grammatical usage in P, its language is instead defined as genuinely 'archaic'. Considering that the verbal syntax of the P narrative does not attest to a mix of LBH and SBH usage, the absence of distinctive LBH verbal syntax in the P narrative is not to be regarded as the result of deliberate archaizing.

(2) Whereas an absence of late lexicographic elements may be explained by the possibility that an author in the LBH period consciously avoided (for whatever reason) use of late words or expressions (e.g. late Aramaic or Persian borrowings), an absence of late features of verbal syntax is not automatically explained by the same rationale. Firstly, in contrast to the use or non-use of items which belong to the linguistic domain of the lexicon, the use of verbal syntax is intimately connected to the domain of the verbal system. Because the verbal system belongs to the underlying level of the linguistic system as such, the use of verbal syntax is not governed by the same type of conscious choice on part of the author as the use of, for example, lexical items.[53] Secondly, these two domains not only belong to different levels of language, their diachronic development is governed by different rules. In particular, the development of the verbal TAM categories of the system is conditioned by the predictable, unidirectional and irreversible process of grammaticalization. In contrast, the semantic development of words, expressions, or idioms is neither predictable nor unidirectional. These two factors combined suggest that the possibility of an author in the LBH period consciously avoiding features of LBH verbal syntax – let alone having a complete mastery of SBH verbal syntax – would have been highly unlikely, if not non-existent.

Thus, it is safe to conclude that the syntax of the verb in the Priestly Narrative of the Pentateuch reflects Standard Biblical Hebrew usage.

---

52 See e.g., Hurvitz, *Study*, 163.
53 According to Fischer, *Morphosyntactic Change*, 33, "it is well-known that speakers are more aware of phonetic, and lexical, variation than of (morpho)syntactic variation, since the former concerns elements physically present, whereas the latter usually involves abstract structures".

Bibliography

Andersen, T. David. "The Evolution of the Hebrew Verbal System." *ZAH* 13 (2000): 1–66.
Bergey, Ronald L. *The Book of Esther: Its Place in the Linguistic Milieu of Post-Exilic Biblical Hebrew Prose: A Study in Late Biblical Hebrew*. PhD diss., Dropsie College for Hebrew and Cognate Learning, 1983.
Bybee, Joan L., and Östen Dahl. "The Creation of Tense and Aspect Systems in the Languages of the World." *SL* 13 (1989): 51–103.
Bybee, Joan, Revere Perkins, and William Pagliuca. *The Evolution of Grammar: Tense, Aspect and Modality in the Languages of the World*. Chicago: The University of Chicago Press, 1994.
Cohen, David. *La phrase nominale et l'évolution du système verbal en sémitique. Études de syntaxe historique*. Collection linguistique publiée par la Société de Linguistique de Paris LXXII. Leuven: Peeters, 1984.
Cohen, Ohad. *The Verbal Tense System in Late Biblical Hebrew Prose*. HSS 63. Winona Lake: Eisenbrauns, 2013.
Cook, John A. "The Hebrew Verb: A Grammaticalization Approach." *ZAH* 14 (2001): 117–143.
—. *Time and the Biblical Hebrew Verb: The Expression of Tense, Aspect, and Modality in Biblical Hebrew*. Winona Lake: Eisenbrauns, 2012.
—. "Detecting Development in Biblical Hebrew Using Diachronic Typology," in *Diachrony in Biblical Hebrew*. Edited by C. L. Miller-Naudé and Z. Zevit. Winona Lake: Eisenbrauns, 2012, 83–95.
Corwin, Rebecca. *The Verb and the Sentence in Chronicles, Ezra and Nehemiah: Part of a Dissertation*. Borna: Robert Noske, 1909.
Dahl, Östen. *Tense and Aspect Systems*. Oxford: Blackwell, 1985.
—. "The Tense-Aspect Systems of European Languages in a Typological Perspective," in *Tense and Aspect in the Languages of Europe*. Edited by Ö. Dahl. Berlin, 2000, 3–25.
Driver, Samuel R. *A Treatise on the Use of Tenses in Hebrew and Some Other Syntactical Problems*. 3rd ed. Oxford: Clarendon Press, 1892.
—. *An Introduction to the Literature of the Old Testament*. 6th ed. New York: Meridian Library, 1956.
Eskhult, Mats. *Studies in Verbal Aspect and Narrative Technique in Biblical Hebrew Prose*. Studia Semitica Upsaliensia 12. Uppsala: Acta Universitatis Upsaliensis, 1990.
—. "Verbal Syntax in Late Biblical Hebrew," in *Diggers at the Well: Proceedings of a Third International Symposium on the Hebrew of the Dead Sea Scrolls and Ben Sira*. Edited by T. Muraoka and J. F. Elwolde. Leiden: Brill, 2000, 84–93.
—. "Markers of Text Type in Biblical Hebrew from a Diachronic Perspective," in *Hamlet on a Hill: Semitic and Greek Studies Presented to Professor T. Muraoka on the Occasion of his Sixty-Fifth Birthday*. Edited by M. F. J. Baasten and W. Th. Van Peursen. Leuven: Peeters, 2003, 153–164.
—. "Traces of Linguistic Development in Biblical Hebrew." *HS* 46 (2005): 353–370.
—. "Some Aspects of the Verbal System in Qumran Hebrew," in *Conservatism and Innovation in the Hebrew Language of the Hellenistic Period: Proceedings of a Fourth International Symposium on the Hebrew of the Dead Sea Scrolls and Ben Sira*. Edited by J. Joosten and J-S. Rey. Leiden: Brill, 2008, 29–46.

—. "2 Samuel and the Deuteronomist – A Discussion of Verbal Syntax," in *Die Samuelbücher und die Deuteronomisten*. Edited by C. Schäfer-Lichtenberger. Stuttgart: Kohlhammer, 2010, 18–31.
Fischer, Olga. *Morphosyntactic Change. Functional and Formal Perspectives*. Oxford: Oxford University Press, 2007.
Gesenius, William. *Geschichte der hebräischen Sprache und Schrift: Eine philologisch-historische Einleitung in die Sprachlehren und Wörterbücher der hebräischen Sprache*. Leipzig: F. C. W. Vogel, 1815.
Givón, Talmy. "Biblical Hebrew as a Diachronic Continuum," in *Diachrony in Biblical Hebrew*. Edited by C. L. Miller-Naudé and Z. Zevit. Winona Lake: Eisenbrauns, 2012, 39–59.
Guenther, Allen R. *A Diachronic Study of Biblical Hebrew Prose Syntax: An Analysis of the Verbal Clause in Jeremiah 37–45 and Esther 1–10*. PhD diss., University of Toronto, 1977.
Hill, Andrew E. *The Book of Malachi: Its Place in Post-Exilic Chronology Linguistically Considered*. PhD diss., University of Michigan, 1981.
—. *Malachi: A New Translation with Introduction and Commentary*. AncB 25D. New York: Doubleday, 1998.
Hornkohl, Aaron D. *Ancient Hebrew Periodization and the Language of the Book of Jeremiah*. SSLL 74. Leiden: Brill, 2014.
Hurvitz, Avi. "The Usage of שש and בוץ in the Bible and Its Implications for the Date of P," *HThR* 60 (1967): 117–121.
—. "Summary of the Article: 'Linguistic Observations on the Priestly Term ʿedah and the Language of P'." *Immanuel* 1 (1972): 21–23.
—. *The Transition Period in Biblical Hebrew: A Study in Post-Exilic Hebrew and Its Implications for the Dating of Psalms* [in Hebrew]. Jerusalem: Bialik, 1972.
—. "Linguistic Criteria for Dating Problematic Biblical Texts." *Hebrew Abstracts* 14 (1973): 74–79.
—. "The Evidence of Language in Dating the Priestly Code: A Linguistic Study in Technical Idioms and Terminology." *RB* 81 (1974): 24–56.
—. *A Linguistic Study of the Relationship between the Priestly Source and the Book of Ezekiel: A New Approach to an Old Problem*. Paris: Gabalda, 1982.
—. "Studies in the Language of the Priestly Source – The Use of שְׁאָר and שְׁכָר in the Books of Leviticus and Numbers" [in Hebrew], in *Bible Studies: Y. M. Grintz in Memoriam*. Edited by B. Uffenheimer. Teʿudah 2. Tel Aviv: Tel Aviv University, 1982, 299–305.
—. "The Language of the Priestly Source and Its Historical Setting – The Case for an Early Date," in *Proceedings of the Eighth World Congress of Jewish Studies, Jerusalem, August 16–21, 1981, Panel Sessions: Bible Studies and Hebrew Language*. Jerusalem: World Union of Jewish Studies, 1983, 83–94.
—. "Dating the Priestly Source in Light of the Historical Study of Biblical Hebrew: A Century after Wellhausen." *ZAW* 100 (1988): 88–100.
—. "Continuity and Innovation in Biblical Hebrew – The Case of 'Semantic Change' in Post-Exilic Writings," in *Studies in Ancient Hebrew Semantics*. Edited by T. Muraoka. Leuven: Peeters, 1995, 1–10.
—. "Once Again: The Linguistic Profile of the Priestly Material in the Pentateuch and Its Historical Age – A Response to J. Blenkinsopp." *ZAW* 112 (2000): 180–191.

—. "Can Biblical Texts be Dated Linguistically? Chronological Perspectives in the Historical Study of Biblical Hebrew," in *Congress Volume: Oslo 1998*. Edited by A. Lemaire and M. Saebø. Vetus Testamentum Supplement 80. Leiden: Brill, 2000, 143–160.

—. "The Recent Debate on Late Biblical Hebrew: Solid Data, Experts' Opinions, and Inconclusive Arguments." *HS* 47 (2006): 191–210.

—. "Continuity and Change in Biblical Hebrew: The Linguistic History of a formulaic Idiom from the Realm of the Royal Court," in *Biblical Hebrew in Its Northwest Semitic Setting: Typological and Historical Perspectives*. Edited by S. E. Fassberg and A. Hurvitz. Jerusalem: Magnes Press/Winona Lake: Eisenbrauns, 2006, 127–133.

Joosten, Jan. "Biblical Hebrew *w^{e}qātal* and Syriac *hwā qātel* Expressing Repetition in the Past." *ZAH* 5 (1992): 1–14.

—. "Pseudo-Classicisms in Late Biblical Hebrew, in Ben Sira, and in Qumran Hebrew," in *Sirach, Scrolls and Sages: Proceedings of a Second International Symposium on the Hebrew of the Dead Sea Scrolls, and Ben Sira, and the Mishnah, Held at Leiden University, 15–17 December 1997*. Edited by T. Muraoka and J. F. Elwolde. Leiden: Brill, 1999, 146–159.

—. "The Distinction between Classical and Late Biblical Hebrew as Reflected in Syntax," *HS* 46 (2005): 327–339.

—. "The Disappearance of Iterative WEQATAL in the Biblical Hebrew Verbal System," in *Biblical Hebrew in Its Northwest Semitic Setting: Typological and Historical Perspectives*. Edited by S. E. Fassberg and A. Hurvitz. Jerusalem: Magnes Press/Winona Lake: Eisenbrauns, 2006, 135–147.

—. "The Syntax of Volitive Verbal Forms in Qoheleth in Historical Perspective," in *The Language of Qohelet in Its Context: Essays in Honour of Prof. A. Schoors on the Occasion of his Seventieth Birthday*. Edited by A. Berlejung and P. van Hecke. Leuven: Peeters, 2007, 47–61.

—. "Diachronic Aspects of Narrative *Wayhi* in Biblical Hebrew." *JNSL* 35 (2009): 43–61.

—. *The Verbal System of Biblical Hebrew: A New Synthesis Elaborated on the Basis of Classical Prose*. Jerusalem: Simor Ltd, 2012.

—. "Textual History and Linguistic Developments. The Doublet in 2 Kgs 8:28–29 // 9:15–16 in Light of 2 Chr 22:5–6," in *Textual Criticism and Dead Sea Scrolls Studies in Honour of Julio Trebolle Barrera: Florilegium Complutensis*. Edited by A. Piquer Otero and P. Torijano Morales. Leiden: Brill, 2012, 133–145.

—. "The Evolution of Literary Hebrew in Biblical Times: The Evidence of Pseudo-classicisms," in *Diachrony in Biblical Hebrew*. Edited by C. L. Miller-Naudé and Z. Zevit. Winona Lake: Eisenbrauns, 2012, 281–292.

—. "Imperative Clauses Containing a Temporal Phrase and the Study of Diachronic Syntax in Ancient Hebrew," in *Hebrew in the Second Temple Period: The Hebrew of the Dead Sea Scrolls and of Other Contemporary Sources*. Edited by S. E. Fassberg, M. Bar-Asher and R. A. Clements. Leiden: Brill, 2013, 117–131.

Kropat, Arno. *Die Syntax des Autors der Chronik verglichen mit der seiner Quellen: Ein Beitrag zur historischen Syntax des Hebräischen*. BZAW 16. Berlin: Walter de Gruyter & Co, 1909.

Kuryłowicz, Jerzy. *Esquisses linguistiques II*. Internationale Bibliothek für allgemeine Linguistik 37. Munich: W. Finck, 1975.

Kutscher, Eduard Y. *The Language and Linguistic Background of the Isaiah Scroll (1QIsa^a)*. StTDJ 6. Leiden: Brill, 1974.

—. *A History of the Hebrew Language*. Jerusalem: Magnes Press, 1982.
Longacre, Robert E. *The Grammar of Discourse*. New York: Plenum Press, 1983.
—. *Joseph – A Story of Divine Providence*. 2nd ed. Winona Lake: Eisenbrauns, 1989.
—. "Discourse Perspective on the Hebrew Verb: Affirmation and Restatement," in *Linguistics and Biblical Hebrew*. Edited by W. R. Bodine. Winona Lake: Eisenbrauns, 1992, 177–189.
—. "*Weqatal* Forms in Biblical Hebrew Prose: A Discourse-modular Approach," in *Biblical Hebrew and Discourse Linguistics*. Edited by R. D. Bergen. Winona Lake: Eisenbrauns, 1994, 50–98.
—. "A Proposal for a Discourse-Modular Grammar of Biblical Hebrew," in *Narrative and Comment: Contributions to Discourse Grammar and Biblical Hebrew*. Edited by E. Talstra. Amsterdam: Societas Hebraica Amstelodamensis, 1995, 99–103.
Miller, Cynthia L. "Methodological Issues in Reconstructing Language Systems from Epigraphic Fragments," in *The Future of Biblical Archaeology: Reassessing Methodologies and Assumptions*. Edited by J. K. Hoffmeier and A. Millard. Grand Rapids: Eerdmans, 2004, 281–305.
Niccacci, Alviero. *The Syntax of the Verb in Classical Hebrew Prose*. JSOT.S 86. Sheffield: Sheffield Academic Press, 1990.
—. "On the Hebrew Verbal System," in Biblical Hebrew and Discourse Linguistics. Edited by R. D. Bergen. Winona Lake: Eisenbrauns, 1994, 117–137.
—. "Essential Hebrew Syntax," in *Narrative and Comment: Contributions to Discourse Grammar and Biblical Hebrew*. Edited by E. Talstra. Amsterdam: Societas Hebraica Amstelodamensis, 1995, 111–125.
—. "Basic Facts and Theory of the Biblical Hebrew Verb System in Prose," in *Narrative Syntax and the Hebrew Bible: Papers of the Tilburg Conference 1996*. Edited by E. Van Wolde. Biblical Interpretation Series 29. Leiden: Brill, 1997, 167–202.
Petersson, Lina. *Syntax of the Verb in the Priestly Narrative of the Pentateuch – A Diachronic Study*. Studia Semitica Upsaliensia. Uppsala: Acta Universitatis Upsaliensis [forthcoming].
Polzin, Robert. *Late Biblical Hebrew: Toward an Historical Typology of Biblical Hebrew Prose*. Missoula: Scholars Press, 1976.
Rooker, Mark F. *Biblical Hebrew in Transition: The Language of the Book of Ezekiel*. Journal for the Study of the Old Testament Supplement 90. Sheffield: JSOT Press, 1990.
Segal, Moshe H. *A Grammar of Mishnaic Hebrew*. Eugene: Wipf and Stock Publishers, 2001.
Shin, Seoung-Yun. *A Lexical Study on the Language of Haggai-Zechariah-Malachi and Its Place in the History of Biblical Hebrew*. PhD diss., Hebrew University of Jerusalem, 2007.
Wellhausen, Julius. *Prolegomena to the History of Ancient Israel*. Translated by J. Sutherland Black and A. Enzies. New York: Meridian Books, 1957.
Wright, Richard M. *Linguistic Evidence for the Pre-Exilic Date of the Yahwist Source of the Pentateuch*. PhD diss., Cornell University, 1998.
—. *Linguistic Evidence for the Pre-exilic Date of the Yahwistic Source*. LHBOTS 419. London: T&T Clark International, 2005.
Young, Ian, Robert Rezetko, and Martin Ehrensvärd. *Linguistic Dating of Biblical Texts*. 2 vols. London: Equinox, 2008.

The Tabernacle and the Dating of P

Jan Retsö (University of Gothenburg)

The description of the movable sanctuary, the *mishkan*, 'the dwelling', or the *'ohel mô'ed*, 'the tent of meeting', is the central issue in the priestly writer's (P) version of the revelation on Mount Sinai. The divine instruction about its design followed by the account of its construction is the central piece to which the rest of P's Sinai pericope, the organisation of the tribes and the sacrificial cult relates.[1]

The existence of this sanctuary has been doubted by many scholars who have seen it as a late postexilic priestly speculation aiming at a Mosaic legitimization of the temple in Jerusalem. The understanding of the description has consequently been influenced by the description of that temple in 1 Kings 6–8/2Chronicles 3–8. There have been dissenting voices trying to relate the description to an earlier existing building like the temple in Shiloh or the sanctuary of David but no consensus has been reached so far.[2] The unrealistic setting of the construction (in the wilderness) as well as the programmatic character of the text remain relevant to many as objections to the traditional view of the tabernacle as a construction of real existence. At the same time the description has a very realistic flavour giving the impression that the writer actually has seen the construction or at least has had detailed information about an existing structure of a similar kind, and this gives some support to supporters of the traditional view.[3]

1. The *mishkan*

P in fact contains two descriptions of the tabernacle: the divine instruction to Moses for its construction and function (Exodus 25–31) and the account of the implementation of the instruction by Israelite craftsmen (Exodus 35–40). There are some discrepancies between these two descriptions and there are good arguments for seeing

---

1 I am obliged to Richard Averbeck for critical comments on the first version of this paper.
2 Cf. Cross, "Tabernacle," 63ff.; idem., *Epic*, 92f.; Haran, "Shiloh"; Rabe, "Identity".
3 Cf. the evidence for similar constructions presented by Kitchen, *Tabernacle*. For the utopian character of the sanctuary see Knohl, *Sanctuary,* 203.

the implementation account as secondary and dependent on the instruction.[4] We shall consequently concentrate on the latter.

P uses two designations for the building: *mishkan* and *'ohel mô'ed*. A close look at P's description shows that in the description of the sanctuary the *mishkan* is the term for the inner structure consisting of upright boards surrounding the holy objects screened off by the *paroket*.[5] This structure is covered by four large pieces of different cloths of which the inner one may belong to the *mishkan* structure but the three exterior ones are called *'ohel mô'ed*.[6] In the later instructions for the function of the building *'ohel mô'ed* is almost exclusively used. This goes together with the instructions for the sacrificial cult where *bnê 'aharôn*, 'the sons of Aaron' are the agents, not Aaron. The two designations thus parallel other differences which lead to the assumption that originally there were at least two different sanctuaries that have been amalgamated by P.[7]

The *mishkan* proper consists of 48 boards, *qrashîm*, standing on supports, *'adanîm*, made of silver. The construction is twenty boards in length and six boards in breadth.[8] The number of the upright boards is most likely not coincidental even if

---

4   *Pace* Albertz, "Beobachtungen," 50ff., who sees the implementation account as belonging to P ('der erste priesterliche Bearbeiter') whereas the instruction is a specific document received and used by him (cf. also Albertz, *Exodus*, 19–26.329ff.). The latter statement is likely to be correct (cf. von Rad, *Priesterschrift*, 181; Childs, *Exodus*, 535; Knohl, *Sanctuary*, 104 and 220ff., cf. also Levine, "Tabernacle," 308f.) but the arguments about the implementation remain doubtful. The ordering of the construction of the different parts of the sanctuary is different in the two accounts. The implementation account is shorter than the instruction. The former also shows several linguistic features pointing to a later date than the rest, cf. Popper, *Bericht*, 84–104; Wellhausen, *Composition*, 144–147; Noth, *Exodus*, 220–221. Neither Noth nor Albertz comment on the linguistic observations by Popper. It should be pointed out that of the building texts collected by Hurowitz, *House*, all except one contain only the implementation, i.e. a description of the actual construction process. The building commandment does not contain any details which also holds for the description of the building of Solomon's temple in 1 Kings 5–8. The only exception in Hurowitz' study is the text Samsu-iluna B (Hurowitz, *House*, 63–64 and Sollberger, "Samsu-Iluna"). P's description thus stands out. If the detailed implementation did not exist in P from the beginning, the need for such a text may have been felt, generating the text we have (Exodus 36–39). Possibly the original short implementation account is preserved in Exodus 40. One should observe that a more detailed instruction about the construction of the temple in Jerusalem is found in the Chronicler's version (1 Chronicles 28) where David shows a model of the building. Perhaps the temple vision in Ezechiel 40–48 belongs to this tradition. The missing detailed instruction of how to construct the temple finally emerges in the Temple Scroll from Qumrān.

5   Exodus 26:1–34.

6   For the differentiation between the two terms see Hendrix, "Miškān," and idem, *Use*. His observation that the two terms refer to different functions of the sanctuary points in the right direction although the full implications are not drawn.

7   Cf. Utzschneider, *Heiligtum*, 128 ff. who presents several convincing arguments. See also Haran, "Nature," 61–62 and n. 1 and Schmitt, *Zelt*, 253–255. For the whole discussion until the beginning of the 1970ies see Schmitt, *Zelt*, 175–253.

8   Since each board/frame has a breadth of 1.5 cubit, the length of the construction is 30 cubits and its breadth is 10 cubits. For the background of the number and arrangement of the boards (20 +

we cannot pinpoint the exact meaning. Suffice it to point out that the number 48 consists of 20 + 20 + 6 + 2. It is thus two times 24 or 4 times 12. None of these numbers are used haphazardly by P.

The term for the upright boards constituting the walls of the *mishkan*, *qrashîm*, is used as a designation of El's temple in the Ugaritic texts.[9] The term seems thus to have mythical connotations. Their design is not completely clear but it has, on good grounds, been assumed that they in fact consisted of two parallel strips joined together by shorter ones thus forming frames rather than boards.[10] This would make sense since otherwise the covering cloth with its embroidered cherubs would have been only partly visible. If the whole embroidered cloth could be seen from the inside it would indeed look like an image of the celestial abode of a god, fitting the Canaanite El as well as the Israelite YHWH.

2. The *paroket*

After the instruction of how to make the coverings (the *'ohel*) and the upright boards which obviously support the four coverings follows the instruction about the interior (Exodus 26):

v. 31: You shall make a *paroket*, blue and red purple, crimson and twisted [Egyptian] linen; webster's work one shall make it, *krûbîm*.

The syntax of the last sentence is awkward and obviously in disorder.[11] The word *paroket* is undoubtedly connected with the Akkadian *paruktum*, 'sail' etc.[12] The

---

20 + 6) see below notes 89 and 91.

9 *wyb'u qrš mlk 'ab šnm* (KTU 1.1.III l. 23–24) 'he [Kothar] entered the domicile of the king, the father of years'; Smith, *Baal Cycle* I:188–189 with references. Cf. Cassuto, *Commentary*, 322–323; Clifford, "Tent," 226;

10 See the reconstruction by Cross, "Tabernacle," 55, 57 and Propp, *Exodus,* 410–417. Cf. also Cross, *Epic,* 87; Fleming, "Public Tent," 486f.490f. referring to two texts from Mari (ca. 1800 BCE) mentioning *qersu* as part of a tent.

11 The ancient versions have had difficulties. The LXX and the Peshitta just follow the MT (*érgon hyphantòn poiēseis autò kheroubim*); *'abbāḏā ḏ-ummānā 'beḏīh krūḇā*. The Vulgate just ignores the *krûbîm*. Onqelos and Ps.-Yonathan interpret: *'ôbed ûmman ya 'bed yatah ṣûrat krûbîn* (O); *'wbd 'wmn y 'byd yth ṣyywryn krwbyn* (PJ).

12 Propp, *Exodus,* 417–418. The Hebrew *paroket* might well be an ancient borrowing from Akkadian (it shows the normal sound changes from a *parukt-. According to von Soden, however, it is an Aramaic borrowing in Akkadian (*Handwörterbuch* s.v. *paruktum*). From Parthian times we have at Hatra references to PRK' DY NBW, 'the PRK' of Nabu' and 'DN WPRK' D MRLH', 'the PRK' of Mar-allāhā'' (Hoftijzer/Jongeling, *Dictionary* s.v. 'DN and PRK'). The word PRK' looks related to *paruktum/paroket* but the context indicates a construction rather than a curtain and the word is rather related to the Akkadian *parakku(m)*. von Soden, *Handwörterbuch,* 827–828, gives the following meanings of *parakku*: Kultsockel, Heiligtum,

following description is of a textile composed of all the most expensive materials the ancient Orient knew.

v. 32aα: and you shall put (*natattā*) it on (*'al*) four columns of acacia.

The Hebrew is quite clear: the *paroket* is to be put on top of the columns. This is also how the ancient versions have understood it.[13] From what follows it seems necessary to assume that the columns stand in a square supporting the *paroket* which forms a canopy.

v. 32aβb covered with gold, whose *wawîm* are of [solid?] gold, [standing?] on four bases (*'adanîm*) of silver.

The *'amûdîm*, 'columns', in verse 32aα are characterized by three attributive phrases: a participle ('covered with gold'), the relative clause about the *wawîm*, and the prepositional phrase about the bases. The main problem in this passage is the word *wawîm*. W. Propp has suggested that the word is the name of the letter *waw* and that the object might have looked like the original form of that letter, reminiscent of our letter Y. He further assumes that the four Y-shaped posts (according to him standing in a row) carried a crossing pole to which the *paroket* was attached.[14] Columns with *wawîm* are mentioned also in connection with the fence surrounding the courtyard around the *mishkan* on which veils, *qla'îm*, obviously were fastened.[15] It is reasonable to assume that the *qla'îm* were hanging down like curtains attached to the columns but how they were fastened is not described. Nothing indicates, however, that they were attached to the *wawîm*. Besides, another object, *ḥashûqîm*, is also mentioned in the description of the fence which Propp suggests could have been crossing poles carried by the Y-shaped *wawîm* to which the *qla'îm* were fastened.[16] This is quite possible, but we should then notice that *ḥashûqîm*, whatever it means, are not mentioned in connection with the *paroket* and it is not said that the *qla'îm* are 'put' on the columns of the courtyard (the verb NTN is not used). The arrangement with the *paroket* of the interior of the *mishkan* is obviously different from that of the *qla'îm* of the courtyard outside it. The Septuagint translates *wawîm* in v. 32 by

---

Kapelle, Cella. The word is a borrowing from Sumerian BARAG, usually interpreted as 'dais' although it now seems that it might mean 'canopy' (Hurowitz, "Form," 144 referring to Jin Sup Kim: *Barag in Sumerian Literature*, Ph.D. diss. Annenberg Research Institute 1991). The meaning of the Hebrew *paroket* like the Akkadian *paruktum* seems to oscillate between 'cover' and 'Kapelle' and the two words may have influenced each other semantically, explicable if BARAG/*parakkum* may have the meaning 'canopy' as well.

13 LXX: *kaí epithēseis autò epì tessárōn stylōn*; Peshitta: *w-sîmay(hy) 'al 'arb'ā 'amûdê d-sîmā*. Onqelos: *w-tîttên yatah 'al 'arb'ā 'ammûdê šiṭṭîn*. Ps.-Yonathan: *wtsdr ytyh 'l 'rb'h 'mwdy šyṭyn*.
14 Propp, *Exodus*, 418–419, followed by Albertz, *Exodus II*, 179.
15 Exodus 27:9–10 (instruction), 38:9–20 (implementation). *Qla'îm* also means 'sails' (cf. Arabic *qilʿ*), thus the Hebrew equivalent to the Akkadian *paruktum*.
16 Propp, *Exodus*, 425–426. LXX translates *psallídes*, 'scissors'. The root ḤŠQ means 'bind', 'fasten', 'attach to', and the meaning of *ḥashûq* could well be 'hook' or the like.

kephalídes, 'capitals', which makes sense: the 'proto-Ionian' capitals found e.g. in Samaria have a kind of Y-shaped form which suits the arrangement of the *mishkan* quite well.[17]

v. 33aα: and you shall put (*natattā*) the *paroket* under (*taḥat*) the *qrasîm*.

The *qrasîm* are mentioned in connection with the making of the coverings of the *mishkan*. The interior covering is to be made of 10 separate pieces sewn together five by five into two larger pieces. These two are in turn provided with loops on one side and are then joined together by the *qrasîm* which thus must mean 'clasps' or the like.[18] The joint would thus have been visible from the interior, dividing the ceiling a little beyond the middle of the building. This is where the *paroket*, i.e. the canopy, should stand.

v. 33aβ: and you shall bring in there, inside (*mibbêt l*) the *paroket*, the box (*arôn*) of the *'edût*.

The main problem here is the expression *mibbêt l*. The phrase is a composite with the word *bayit* which can mean 'the interior', 'the inner part of' and with the *he locale* 'towards the interior.[19] The *min*, usually 'out from' etc. can also indicate location, like *mittaḥat* 'under', *miṣṣad* 'beside' etc. As a composite preposition *mibbêt l* must mean 'inside', which is not necessarily 'behind'. The expression is found in some other passages belonging to the P-tradition. In the description of the *yôm kippûr*-ritual it is said: 'he (i.e. Aaron) shall not at any time enter the holy, *mibbêt la-pparoket* towards (*'el*) the *kapporet* which is over the *'arôn*'.[20] Later it is said: 'And he shall bring in its (i.e. the sin-offering) blood *'el mibbêt la-pparoket*'.[21] 'And you shall keep your priestly service for every matter concerning (*l*) the altar and concerning *mibbêt la-pparoket*'.[22] In the description of the building of Solomon's temple it is said: 'And he built for him/it *mibbêt la-ddbîr* for the holy of holies'.[23] In another context it is said in connection with the deposition of queen Athaliah: 'Bring her to *mibbêt la-ssderôt*'.[24] The meaning of *mibbêt l-* is undoubt-

---

17 *Pace* Gooding, *Account*, 21. The Greek translator has probably had the correct understanding of the word. For a discussion of the translation of *wawîm* see Wade, *Account*, 95–97 esp. notes 82–84.
18 Exodus 26:1–14. Cf. the detailed analysis by Propp, *Exodus*, 406ff.
19 The word *bêt* in several passages has the meaning 'interior': Genesis 6:14; 1 Kings 6:15, 16, 7:25 (cf. 2 Chronicles 4:4); Exodus 28:26, 39:19. These passages belong to P, alternatively to the building of the temple. It could be compared to the *bêt* found in Syriac, derived from **bayn-t* (rather than *baynāt*) 'between', 'in the middle' (Brockelmann, *Grundriss I*, 498; Payne Smith, *Thesaurus syriacus*, 470f.). Ezekiel has the form *bênôt l* with the meaning 'between' clearly related to the meaning 'inside' (Ezekiel 10:2, 6, 7; cf. id. 1:27).
20 Leviticus 16:2, cf. v. 12.
21 Leviticus 16:15.
22 Numbers 18:7.
23 1 Kings 6:16.
24 2 Kings 11:15. The word *sderôt* is understood as 'row of columns', 'colonnade', viz. in the

edly 'inside', 'in the middle of'. As we can see the phrase is used in connection with the sanctuary of P, exceptionally also with reference to the Jerusalem temple. It is also connected with the word *paroket*.

> v. 33b: and the *paroket* shall divide for you between the holy and the most holy.

Here *paroket* evidently refers to the cloth that screens off the space between the columns from the rest of the *mishkan*.

> v. 34: And you shall put (*natattā*) the *paroket* on/over (*'al*) the box (*'arôn*) of the *'edût* in the most holy.

Undoubtedy the *paroket* must be a canopy over the *kapporet* and the *'arôn*. If it was a curtain dividing the hall it would be difficult to understand the phrase *natan 'al* 'put, place over'. Even if *'al* is interpreted as 'at', 'beside' which is one of its meanings, it does not make sense in this context. This understanding is supported by the passage at the end of the sanctuary pericope when Moses actually performs the order given here, an order which is repeated at the end of the pericope: *w-sakkôta 'al ha-'arôn 'et ha-pparoket* 'and you shall cover (SKK) the *'arôn* with the *paroket*'.[25] Then Moses performs the command: 'he put (*wayyasem*) the *paroket ha-mmasak* and made it cover (*wayyasek* from SKK) the *'arôn ha-'edût*'.[26]

Most modern translators and commentators have another view on the interior of the *mishkan* than the one given here: the verb *natattā* is rendered 'hang' which indicates that the *paroket* is fastened to the tops of the columns, hanging down in front of them, i.e. a curtain hanging down from four columns standing in a row dividing the *mishkan* in two.[27] The modern understanding of the description of the *mishkan* is

---

Temple. The idea is that the queen should not be killed in the temple building proper.
25 Exodus 40:3.
26 Exodus 40:21. The LXX: *kaì epéthēke tò katakálymma toû katapetásmatos kaì esképase tēn kibōtòn toû martyríou*. The verb *skepázō* as a rule means 'to cover', viz. 'with a blanket' (Liddell & Scott, *Lexicon,* s.v.). The Targums have *af'el* of ṬLL also meaning 'to cover'.
27 Cf. Haran, "Image," 194. This is how the Vulgate renders it: *quod appendes ante quattuor columnas*. The Hebrew word for 'hang' is TLY, *talā*, which does not occur in this context. That verb is, however, used by the tannaitic *Barayta de-mlekhet ha-mmishkan* (4:1) when explaining the passage. Josephus describes the *ádyton* like the *dbîr* in the temple, occupying the entire westernmost part of the 'tent', *skēnē* (*Antiquities* 3.122–125). He does, however, use the word *katapetánnymi*, 'cover', transitive (viz. the *kiónes*), probably understanding it as 'hide'. The Greek word used by LXX for *paroket*, *katapétasma*, is derived from this verb, thus meaning 'cover'. The designation in 35:12: *masak ha-pparoket* combines two terms from the instruction which refer to two different pieces: the cover of the *kapporet* on the four columns (*paroket*), and the curtain hung on the five columns at the entrance (*masak*). It is not unlikely that this reflects an early reinterpretation of the *paroket* from a canopy to a curtain, influenced by the arrangement in the second temple, which became the common view. The LXX uses *katapétasma* for both which might reflect the same interpretation of the *paroket* as similar to the *masak*. It may explain the description in the *Barayta de-mleket ha-mmishkan* (1:10) which confuses the columns of the entrance with those of the *paroket*.

clearly influenced by the tradition of the Jerusalem temple with its *Langhaus* divided in two parts, the rear part constituting the holy of holies. In the description of the temple in 2 Chronicles a veil or a curtain called *paroket* separates the choir (*dbîr*) from the main hall.[28] According to rabbinic and Christian tradition a similar curtain was found in the second temple.[29] In the book of Kings we instead have a door closing off the *dbîr*.[30]

This view is due to the idea that the tabernacle is a backward projection of the Jerusalem temple into the period of the desert wandering, a concept which seems difficult to get away from.[31] But a closer look at the description of that building shows that the parallels are not salient. If we for a moment forget the Jerusalem temple and read the text of P as it stands the design appears somewhat different.[32] The most important part of the *mishkan* seems to consist of four columns over which a cloth, the *paroket*, is laid which screens off the space on four sides. The result is a kind of pavilion or a canopy standing separately inside the walls of boards and not a screened-off section of the rear part of the whole construction like the *dbîr* of the Jerusalem temple.[33] The boards, *qrashîm*, and the coverings carried by them thus

---

28 2 Chronicles 3:14.
29 *Mishna Yômā* 5.1; Mark 15:38, cf. Hebrews 10:20. 2 Chronicles most likely reflects the second temple, not the first.
30 1 Kings 6:31–32. Josephus combines the traditions. According to him the *dbîr* was screened off by a door and a curtain (*Antiquities* 8:72). There is contradiction between the remark about the door of the *dbîr* and the statement in 1 Kings 18:6 according to which the *baddîm*, i.e. the poles for carrying the *'arôn*, are visible from outside the *dbîr*.
31 Classic statements in Wellhausen, *Prolegomena*, 37–38; de Vaux, *Histoire*, 435f.; Fritz, *Tempel*, 165f.; Albertz, *Religionsgeschichte II*, 524ff.
32 Cf. Haran, "Shiloh," 20.
33 Typical is the remark by Gooding, *Account*, 15: 'The Hebrew term *paroket* is applied to no other curtain'. The logic conclusion would be that the *paroket* is not a curtain. The only one who has suggested another solution is Friedman, *Exile*, 52; idem., *Tabernacle*, 295 (cf. the positive evaluation of this suggestion by Hurowitz, "Form," 144–146). In that context he refers to a Talmudic passage (*TB Sukkah* 7b) commenting Exodus 40:3: 'The *paroket* was a partition, yet the Scriptures call it a covering (*sukkah*). Consequently, a partition is meant in the sense of a covering. The rabbis say: It means that it is bent a little (at the top) so that it looks like a covering.' This shows that the rabbis clearly saw the problem: the discrepancy between the common opinion and the actual wording of the Torah-text, and tried to solve it in their own way. In three other passages (*TB Soṭah* 37a, *Menaḥot* 62a, 98a) they explain the preposition *'al* in Exodus 40:3 as 'near', 'close to' in accordance with settled opinion. But the fact that this had to be stated shows that they were aware of the problem. There are other problems with Friedman's reconstruction. According to him (*Exile*, 48 ff.) the tabernacle actually stood inside the first temple, in the *dbîr*, based on 1 Kings 8:4/2 Chronicles 5:5, cf. Hoffmeier, *Ancient Israel*, 200–201. The critical comments by Hurowitz, "Form," and Propp, *Exodus*, 707–708, should, however, be taken *ad notam*. The other passages adduced by Friedman are not convincing evidence but they might contain a reflexion of the fact that the *paroket* actually stood inside the *mishkan/'ohel mô'ed* (not the Jerusalem temple).

surround a canopy standing isolated inside. Neither the height of the columns nor the distance between them are given.[34]

3. The furnishing of the *paroket*

Inside the *paroket* we find three objects: the *'arôn*, meaning a box or a chest, the *'edût* and the *kapporet*, both with meanings not immediately recoverable from the context and not described in detail.[35] In the [first] Jerusalem temple it seems clear that an empty throne stood in the *dbîr* but the ensemble under the *paroket* in the *mishkan* was not primarily a throne.[36] This is not the place for a full analysis of the entire ensemble inside the *paroket*. Suffice it to point out that the *'arôn* and the *'edût* are also found outside P's description of the sanctuary with, as it seems, shapes and functions quite different from what is described by P. The historical relationship between the three objects is more complicated than usually assumed. For the purpose of this study the *kapporet* is the crucial piece. This object is to be placed 'on' (*'al*) the *'arôn*, 'above' (*milma'lā*).[37] It plays a role in the *yôm kippûr* ritual when blood is sprinkled on it but its most important function is as the place where YHWH will reveal himself: from (*me'al*) the *kapporet*, from between (*mibbên*) the two *krûbîm* who are part of the construction. He promises to talk to 'you' (Moses?) from between the two *krûbîm*, *me'al* 'from' the *kapporet*.[38] The measurements of the *kapporet* (2.5 x 1.5 cubits) are given indicating a rectangular shape. The fact that the measurements are identical with those of the *'arôn* with no indication of thickness has led to the assumption that because the *kapporet* is 'on' the *'arôn*, which is some kind of chest or box, it must be the upper cover or the lid of the chest. It has, however, been convincingly argued that this is not necessarily the correct interpretation.[39] The two *krûbîm*, closely connected with the *kapporet*, are to be made *miššnê qṣôt ha-kkapporet*, 'from' (or 'at'?) the two sides of the *kapporet*'. The impression is that the *krûbîm* are part of the *kapporet*, or, more exactly, part of the edge or margin

---

34 *Pace* Gooding, *Account*, 22. Only the height of the five door pillars is given.
35 Cf. Milgrom, *Leviticus*, 1014.
36 Cf. convincingly Hartmann, "Zelt," 225–232; Haran, "Ark," 32–34; Maier, *Lade*, 53–69.
37 The meaning of *'al* is not necessarily 'on' = 'above', 'on top of' (cf. Clines, *Dictionary*, 387f.). The present text, however, defines the meaning by the addition *milma'lā*. There is a consistent difference in the use of prepositions related to the *'arôn* and the *'edût*. The *'edût* is to be put *'el*, 'to' (?) the *'arôn*. The *kapporet* is to be put *'al* 'on' (?) the *'arôn*. This distinction, which is preserved in different ways by the LXX, the Samaritan text as well as the Aramaic ones (Targums, Peshitta), most likely mark some semantic distinction although it is not exactly clear which one, cf. Wade, *Consistency*, 34–35.
38 Exodus 25:22.
39 Janowski, *Sühne*, 274–276, esp. note 479; ibid. 347.

(*qaṣā*) of the *kapporet* (19b). Unfortunately we do not know what they looked like but this passage indicates that they represented some kind of beings with faces and wings.[40] They shall extend (PRS) their wings upwards (*l-ma'lā*) and cover (SKK) the *kapporet*, facing each other as well as the *kapporet*: *ûpnêhem 'îš 'el 'eḥayw // 'el ha-kkapporet yihyû pnê ha-kkrûbîm*: 'their faces towards each other // towards the *kapporet* shall the faces of the *krûbîm* be'.[41] It is worth observing that it is not said that they at the same time should look down (*l-maṭṭā*) on the *kapporet*, unlike what some modern translators think.[42] This would demand ocular acrobatics of a kind difficult to envisage. Neither is it said that they bow their heads or stand in a kneeling position.[43] This shows that the *kapporet* cannot be the lid of the *'arôn*.[44] The function of *krûbîm* in the Old Testament is clearly that of watchers or guardians.[45] If we get rid of the idea of the chest and its lid we are free to interpret the passage differently. The two prepositional phrases *me'al ha-kkaporet* and *mibbên ha-kkrûbîm* may be synonymous: YHWH will appear between the cherubim, from the *kapporet*. The preposition *me'al* is well documented with the meaning 'from' but not necessarily 'from above' but also 'from the side of' since the preposition *'al* often means 'at the side of'.[46] The *kapporet* is obviously an object between the *krûbîm* who face it.[47] If we assume that the *kapporet* does not lie horisontally but

---

40 Freedman and O'Connor, "Krûb". One should be cautious when drawing conclusions about the shape of the *krûbîm*, cf. Haran, "Ark," 35f. E.g. Kitchen's claim (Kitchen, "Tabernacle," 121*, cf. Maier, *Lade,* 53) that they were human-headed sphinxes has no direct support in the text (but see Maier, *Lade* 82!). Cf. the description in Ezekiel 1:5–18 which points in another direction.
41 So also LXX: *kaì tà prósōpa autōn eis állēla eis tò hilastērion ésontai tà prósōpa tōn kheroubîm*. The poetic structure of the passage should be noted.
42 E.g. Noth, *Exodus,* 165; Cassuto, *Commentary,* 335; Albertz, *Exodus,* 19–40:144. Beer and Galling, *Exodus,* 130, save the day by attributing the two 'contradictory' statements to von Rad's (*Priesterschrift*) two different layers of P: Pa and Pb. The explanation fails together with von Rad's hypothesis but the two scholars have the credit of having observed the problem.
43 Pace Milgrom, *Leviticus,* 1014.
44 Haran, "Ark," 32ff. realizes that the *'arôn* and the *kapporet* are two distinct objects. His claim that the *krûbîm* of the *kapporet* and those in the temple are identical is, however, not likely, neither is the *kapporet* a throne ("Ark," 36). Haran is right in rejecting the idea of the *'arôn* being a throne since it is not called so by P (*pace* e.g. de Vaux, "Arche," 268). But P does not claim that the *kapporet* is a throne either, neither are the *krûbîm*. It is more likely that the arrangement in the temple as described in 1 Kings 8 is quite different from that of P and also that of Ezechiel. The passage in 1 Chronicles 28:18 is obviously a harmonizing between the different traditions.
45 Genesis 3:14; Ezekiel 28:16; 1 Kings 6.
46 See Clines, *Dictionary,* 387f.396f. for examples.
47 Exodus 25:21–22. There is a slight contradiction between the two functions observed by Baentsch, *Exodus,* 225. An alternative understanding is that the verbs *nô'adtî*, 'I shall appear', and *dibbartî*, 'I shall speak', may originate from different concepts about the divine appearance: the first clearly is connected with the *'ohel mô'ed* tradition in which YHWH appears in a cloud, and the second could then be linked to the idea of the *panîm* reflected in Exodus 34:33–35 (cf. the use of the verb *dibber* in that passage; cf. the remarks by Schmitt, *Zelt,* 226ff.). Since it seems clear that P combines several sanctuary-traditions in his design, the slight contradiction

instead is standing up, things become more comprehensible. We get a standing rectangular plate flanked on both sides by two standing sculptured figures which are part of the plate itself with wings stretched above it as a cover.[48] One could imagine the *krûbîm* somewhat higher than the *kapporet* in order to be able to stretch their wings over it, thus facing each other as well as the *kapporet*. If we imagine the *kapporet* standing up, the blood of the *yôm kippûr* ritual is sprinkled on its 'face', i.e. directly 'forwards' and then in front of it, at its base.[49] It can be argued that the view of the *kapporet* as a standing object gives a comprehensible and possibly better understanding of the passage in Leviticus and it also puts the whole cultic arrangement described by P in a documentable religious context.

4. The *paroket*-canopy and its background

The question is whether the canopy with the objects inside, which seems to be the structure described as standing inside the *qrashîm*, is documented outside the Pentateuch and biblical tradition as well.

Monuments consisting of a central standing block, covered by a roof supported by surrounding columns are found at numerous sites in the Levant and adjacent areas. The first systematic study by P. Collart and P. Coupel in 1977 brought together evidence from a series of buildings from Lebanon showing these characteristics.[50] In some of them only a central cippus with niches with pictures of gods is preserved. Others still have remains of the surrounding columns. Two basic types were identified, one in which the central monolith reaches the ceiling and supports it, another where the monolith stands isolated without supporting function.[51] They usually stand on high fundaments. Their ground plan tends to be rectangular in the north but square in the south.[52] Usually a small altar stands in front of them. The preserved stone monuments are from the Hellenistic-Roman period (1st century BCE–2nd century CE). In spite of their resemblance to a Greek *peripteros* temple there is no doubt that they represent a local Levantine sanctuary tradition: they are much smaller than an ordinary Greek temple and they do not have a cella. Instead a

---

in Exodus 25:22 could reflect this. The *'ohel* and the *panîm*-traditions are combined in Exodus 33:7–11 where one should notice the contradiction between the divine appearance in the cloud and the function of the *'ohel*: Moses enters the *'ohel* in order to speak with the cloud which remains outside. Cf. Haran, "Nature," 55–56, who, however, gives a harmonizing reading.

48 Cf. Haran, "Ark," 36.
49 Leviticus 16:14–15.
50 Collart and Coupel, *Autel,* 77–90. The sites are: Mashnaqa, Kafr Dan, Ḥuṣn Nīḥa, Sfīreh, Qalʿat Faqra, Dayr al-Qalʿa, ʿAyn Ǧūǧ, the 'round temple' at Baalbek, and Ḥuṣn Sulaymān in Syria.
51 Collart and Coupel, *Autel,* 80–82.
52 Drijvers, "ḤMN'," 177.

monolith, on which images of a god or gods sometimes are found, stands in the centre. It is most likely that the stone in fact represents the divine presence. The original designation of these structures was identified by H. J. W. Drijvers in 1988 with the Aramaic term ḤMNʾ, *ḥammānāʾ*, found in inscriptions on similar monuments in Palmyra, especially the temple of Allāt.[53] He drew attention to the four large temples in Palmyra (Allāt, Bēl, Baʿal Shamīn, Nabū) and showed that they all contain traces of a *ḥammānāʾ* incorporated into a temple construction in Hellenistic style. Drijvers further noticed that this word occurs in the Old Testament designating a cult object.[54] In a final synthesis P. Xella in 1997 referred explicitly to the Old Testament parallel and pointed out that the word there usually appears together with the word *mizbeaḥ*, 'altar', designating some kind of sanctuary.[55] This shows that the cult is much older than the Hellenistic period. The term is documented already in Ugarit in the form ḤMN where it clearly designates some kind of small sanctuary.[56] The ḤMN was obviously part of a QRŠ, i.e. the palace of the god El.[57] Thus, in the Keret text it is told that he *ʿrb bẓl ḥmt / lqḥ ʾimr dbḥ bydh* 'he entered into the shade/covering of ḤMT / took a sheep for sacrifice with his hand'.[58] Especially interesting is the following passage in the Kothar wa-Xasis text: *ysq hym w tbth kt ʾil* 'he cast a ḤYM and a resting place for El'.[59] The ḤYM obviously is made of metal like the *kapporet* of P. From Ugarit we also have a personal name like ʿBD ḤMN, in vowel script Abdi Ḫamanu, a name that also is documented later on in Byblos.[60]

This leads to the association with the deity called BʿL ḤMN, who is mentioned for the first time in the Phoenician Kilamuwa-inscription at Samʾal, present-day Sıncırlı, in northern Syria from the 9th century BCE. BʿL ḤMN is mentioned together with BʿL ṢPN on an amulet from Tyre.[61] This deity is the main one in Carthage and other Phoenician colonies around the Mediterranean, well documented from ca 500 BCE and onwards.[62] Xella has pointed out that the cult of Baal Hammon is not linked to the city state but has a wider distribution.[63] The very name of the deity points to some kind of relationship with the sanctuary. Especially interest-

---

53 Drijvers, "ḤMNʾ," 170ff.
54 Ezekiel 6:4, 6; Isaiah 17:8, 27:9; 2 Chronicles 14:4, 34:4, 7; cf. Leviticus 26:30, Drijvers, "ḤMNʾ," 174.
55 Xella, *Baal Hammon*, 218–225.
56 Xella, *Baal Hammon*, 169–187; Olmo Lete and Sanmartín, *Diccionario* s.vv. *ḥmn*: 'capilla', 'templete'; *ḥmt*: 'tienda'; *ḥym*: 'dosel', 'baldaquín'.
57 Xella, *Baal Hammon*, 175, 177. As was pointed out above, this term is used for the boards of the *mishkan*.
58 KTU 1.14.III 52–58. + IV 1–8. The word *ẓl* means 'cover' and looks like a nice parallel to the *paroket* of P.
59 KTU 1.4.I 29. Cf. also KTU 1.112.3; KTU 1.106 12–13 (sacrifices to ḤMN).
60 Xella, *Baal Hammon*, 36.
61 Xella, *Baal Hammon*, 157.
62 Xella, *Baal Hammon*, 42–90.
63 Xella, *Baal Hammon*, 232.

ing is the mentioning in Punic inscriptions of BʿL ḤMN together with TNT PN BʿL, 'Tinnit, the face of Baal'.[64]

The term ḤMN with its derivations ḤYM and ḤMT could be formed from the root ḪYM, 'cover', 'protect'.[65] It would thus be a cognate of the Arabic *ḫaymat-*, 'tent'.[66] According to some Arab lexicographers, *ḫaymat-* among the pre-Islamic *ʿarab* was a construction of four wooden poles roofed with *ṯumām*-grass or palm-leaves.[67] It is worthwhile in this context to refer to a passage in Diodorus' *Bibliotheca*. He reports that, after having defeated Agathokles of Sicily in Libya in 307 BCE, the Carthaginians sacrificed at an altar close to a sacred tent (*hierā skēnē*) made from reeds and straw in their camp and that it burned down by accident.[68] There is no doubt that the sacrifice was performed for Baʿal Ḥammôn.[69] We do not know if this was at a *ḥammān* but it seems natural to suppose so.[70]

We find a similar design in the representations of the sanctuary of Zeus Kasios, i.e. *baʿal ṣapôn*, the deity dwelling on Mount Casius north of Ugarit. On coins from the Hellenistic/Roman period we see the temple of this god as a canopy with what looks like a textile covering resting on four columns. The walls are open so that the symbol of the god is visible in the form of a stone with some object on it.[71] The similarities between the Zeus Kasios canopy and the *ḥammān*-sanctuaries are salient. Even if the pictorial documentation is from the Hellenistic-Roman period the connection back to Ugaritic mythology is obvious.

---

64 Xella, *Baal Hammon*, 47ff., 192. The divine name is also found transcribed by Greek letters: *thenneith phenēbal*.
65 Xella, *Baal Hammon*, 170, 190. The Ugaritic evidence shows that the first consonant is Ḫ. The difference between Ḫ and Ḥ is not marked in the Phoenician script used for Hebrew and Aramaic, because the two consonants coincide in these languages. This makes Drijvers' suggested etymology as a derivation from ḤMY 'to protect' etc., most unlikely.
66 The earlier interpretations of *ḥammān* as 'incense-altar' (so still Milgrom, *Leviticus*, 2318) or referring to Mount Amanus (e.g. Cross, *Myth*, 26–29) are definitely rejected by Xella (*Baal Hammon*, 141–166), as it seems on very good grounds. Already Drijvers' study clearly demonstrates the proper meaning.
67 Lane, *Lexicon* s.v. *ḫym*. A similar construction is the *ʿarš*, *ʿarīš* (Lane, *Lexicon* s.v. *ʿrš*) described with the same terms as the *khayma*. The word is later used with the meaning 'throne', i.e. the seat of the (Islamic) ruler consisting of a canopy under which the ruler is seated, often with crossed legs without a chair. Remarkable is then the Arabic tradition that the 'tent' of Moses was an *ʿarš*, *ʿarīš* which is identified with the earliest Kaʿba which also is said to have been a *khayma*, see below n. 90 and Rubin, *Kaʿba*, 98–99.
68 Diodorus, *Bibliotheca* 20.65.
69 Cf. Diodorus, *Bibliotheca* 13.86.3; 20.14.4–6. The god is identified with Kronos, cf. Xella, *Baal Hammon*, 63.92.
70 Xella, *Baal Hammon*, 104–105.
71 It might be that the picture shows what was really there, not what it looked like to visitors to whom the holy symbol might have been screened off. Cf. the pictures in Egyptian temples which show all details in the holiest parts of the temple which hardly were accessible to ordinary visitors.

The cult of these *ḥammānîm*, which obviously was widely spread in Israel, is violently condemned by the Old Testament writers.[72] The condemnation is found in texts ascribed to writers working around 600 BCE or describing events around that date.[73] In spite of the condemnation the preceeding analysis suggests that the *paroket* and its equipment as described by P belong to this kind of sanctuary. It has further been pointed out that the description of the *paroket* points towards the image of YHWH as a storm god as described in Psalm 104:2–4 and 18:10–15 (= 2 Samuel 22:10–15).[74] In both theophanies we find the combination of pictures of thunder, lightning, and rainstorm with those of fire and smoke. This combination is also found in non-P's description of the theophany on the mountain.[75] We should observe the ties between the vocabulary of those theophanies and that found in P's description. The *krûbîm*, derivations from the root SKK, 'cover', the curtain, even the covering darkness establish an association. The theophanies seem to mix in images from a concrete sanctuary and natural phenomena. P's *paroket* contains symbols belonging to this theophany.

The theophanies point towards the apparition of the deity of rain and thunder, i.e. a Hadad/Baal figure. The deity on Mount Casius/Ṣapôn definitely belongs to this type. Apollodoros, in his rendering of the myth surrounding Mount Casius, describes the deity's theophany in terms reminiscent of the Israelite psalms.[76] Behind the name Zeus in the Apollodorus myth the local *baʻal* of the Casius mountain is hiding, i.e. the one whose sanctuary is shown on the coins mentioned.

From the analysis presented here it can be argued that the sanctuary described by P reflects an ancient Levantine tradition, representing divine presence through a cult object, usually a stone, under a canopy resting upon four poles. On the whole, several terms used in the description of the *mishkan* are connected with the mythology related to El and Baal in Ugarit and the Levant in general and thereby with the mountain of ṢPN. It is thus no suprise that the canopy inside the *mishkan* looks like the sanctuary of Zeus Kasios, i.e. *Baʻal Ṣapôn*. This would mean that P describes a sanctuary belonging to the 'god on the mountain', viz. Hadad/El/Baal/Zeus. The statement that the sanctuary is to be made according to a model shown on the mountain fits well into the scenario.[77]

---

72 In Hebrew the word occurs in plural only. It is most likely a borrowing (one would expect *ḥammôn*), possibly from Aramaic. If derived from the root ḤYM it should rather be *ḥamān.

73 Jeremiah, Ezekiel, the reform of Josiah. The Holiness Code has been dated to the same period (Milgrom, *Leviticus,* 1361–1364). Knohl (*Sanctuary,* 204ff.) associates it with the reforms of Hezekiah, i.e. around 700 BCE.

74 So Propp, *Exodus,* 387. Cf. Nonnos, *Dionysiaca* 1. 481ff.

75 Exodus 19.

76 Apollodorus, *Bibliotheca* 1.6.3: 'Having recovered his strength Zeus suddenly from heaven, riding a chariot of winged horses, pelted Typhon with thunderbolts and pursued him to the mountain called Nysa, where the *moîra* beguiled the fugitive'. The scene is developed into monumental dimensions and great detail in Nonnos' *Dionysiaca* 2.364–367; 391ff.; 414ff.

77 Exodus 25:9, 40; cf. 27:8.

An argument in favour of Zeus Kasios/*Baʿal Ṣapôn* as the most direct link to P is the fact that the *ḥammān* sanctuaries seem to be connected with another type of cult than that of the towns, linked instead to family, dynasty etc.[78] The theophany-elements in P's sanctuary and the psalms point towards the god of rain and storm.

So why the god from Mount Casius? Among the characteristics of this deity one is important here: he dwells on a border. It was pointed out long ago that the northern and southern borders of Syria are guarded by a deity named BʿL ṢPN.[79] Since there are weighty grounds to identify the mountain of revelation in P with the one at the southernmost border of the promised land, the function of the Canaanite mountain god which is relevant is that of guardian of the border.[80] Since P operates with a definition of the promised land that has its extreme points in the Negev and the northern slopes of Lebanon one should look for a location of the mountain of Hor (*Hor ha-har*) not only in the south (where it probably is identical with the mountain of revelation) but also in the north.[81] And a border mountain in Lebanon is a more natural home for a storm god than one in the southern deserts. P's version of the scouts sent out to investigate the promised land clearly refers to the border description that includes present-day Lebanon and southern Syria and that description most likely belongs to P.[82] There have been some different suggestions of the localisation of the northern Hor, none completely convincing.[83] A plausible candidate not suggested until now is the spectacular site of Sfīreh inland from Tarablus, the location of which suits the border description quite well and which, apart from the remains of at least three temples from Hellenistic/Roman times, also has traces of at least one construction which undoubtedly is a *ḥammān*.[84]

At the same time the mythology surrounding this god easily spread to the mountain in the south due to their parallel function as border-markings.[85] P's promised land is not the greater Syria from the northern Casius to Baʿal Ṣepôn at Lake Sirbonis but a smaller one encompassing the southern half of Syria from the Negev to northern Lebanon.[86].

---

78 Xella, *Baal Hammon*, 232.
79 Eissfeldt, *Baal Zaphon*, passim.
80 Retsö, "Petra," 126 ff.
81 Numbers 34:7.
82 Numbers 34:1–12; 13:4–17a, 22.
83 Simons, *Texts*, 98–102; Aharoni, *Land*, 65–67.
84 See Drijvers, "ḤMNʾ," 178 n. 42; Freyberger, "Funktion," 149–150. For a description of the site of Sfīreh see Butcher, *Syria*, 355–356, ibid. plate 5 and Freyberger, *loc. cit.*
85 We meet this god in non-P's version of the Sinai revelation (Exodus 19) where his appearance in thunder and lightning clearly shows who he is. This shows that the appearance of this deity on the mountain in the Negev is not the work of P but was a well-known idea.
86 I. e. the original Egyptian province of Kinahhu in the 13th century BCE. For this definition see Aharoni, *Land*, 61–70. For the attribution of the border-description to P see e.g. Driver, *Introduction*, 69; Gray, *Numbers* xxxix, 453; Eissfeldt, *Hexateuch-Synopse*, 195*. Noth *Exodus*, 214, attributes it to the late redactional layer uniting P and D.

It thus seems that P has integrated into his picture of the original sanctuary of Israel not only sacred traditions from the central highlands like the *'arôn*, and the *'ohel mô'ed*, but also elements from the cult of the god on the mountains at the borders of Canaan. At the same time it is the god of the southern mountain who is his primary concern. The prominence of this god and his mountain is a fact adopted by P and then developed in his own way. The tradition is consequently earlier than the composition of the Priestly Code. The question arising is then what it looked like when P started to work on it, or which elements in the P-tradition are earlier.

5. Final Remarks

The understanding of the sanctuary pericope of the priestly writer has been dominated by harmonizing readings apparent not only in modern critical scholarship but found already in Josephus, the ancient versions and rabbinic literature. The close relationship between the *mishkan* and the Solomonic temple has been taken for granted by most modern scholars. The *'edût* is identified with the tablets of the law; the *'arôn* of P is identical with the *'arôn ha-bberît* of Deuteronomy and the ark of David; the *mishkan* and the *'ohel mô'ed* refer to the same object; the layout of the interior of the *mishkan* coincides with that of the Solomonic temple; the *kapporet* is the lid of the *'arôn*; the space behind the *paroket* is the same as the *dbîr* in the temple etc. All this has led to the assumption that the *mishkan* has never existed outside the minds of some priestly writers who wanted to give the Jerusalem temple a venerable Mosaic predecessor.[87]

An element in this picture is that since P traditionally has been dated to the post-exilic period his sanctuary should reflect The Second Temple. Y. Kaufmann pointed out that there are details in the sanctuary description which do not fit the image of The Second Temple at all. In that building we hear nothing about the *'arôn*, the *kapporet*, tablets of law etc.[88] But the discrepancy is even more salient when it comes to The First Temple where most of the paraphernalia of the tabernacle are missing. The idea that the description of the tabernacle is dependent on either of the two temples in Jerusalem should be discarded. So what is/was the tabernacle?

This paper has tried to show that the central sacred object in the tabernacle, which is called *paroket*, is a specific Levantine sanctuary type, fairly well documented by texts and by archaeology. It is a palanquin, a piece of cloth or even a roof of wood or stone supported by four or more columns with a block of stone or metal

---

[87] Cf. Schmitt, *Zelt,* 228: 'Es darf das seit Wellhausen geschicherte Ergebnis der atl Forschung gelten, dass das von P in Ex 25ff. 35ff. beschriebene Heiligtum so in der Geschichte Israels nie existiert hat'.

[88] Kaufmann, *Religion,* 173–200 (*pace* de Vaux, "Arche," 273–274).

standing upright under it, indicating the presence of the deity. The standing block may have some pictorial element representing the god, which in the Hellenistic period develops into reliefs or even sculptures. As far as the proportion 20:6 of the surrounding *mishkan* is concerned it has been pointed out that it is actually found in concrete archaeological remains of sanctuaries in southern Judaea: Arad and Lakish.[89] It is difficult to avoid the conclusion that the proportions of P's *mishkan* in fact represent a concrete cultic tradition in this part of The Holy Land.[90] Even more remarkable is the parallel to another sanctuary, viz. the Ka'ba in Mecca. According to al-Azraqī's *Akhbār Makka*, 'the History of Mecca', written in the 9th century, containing a mass of traditional lore about the Meccan sanctuary, the original shape of the building was 20 x 6 cubits. The manuscripts of al-Azraqī's book even contain a plan of the building which thus, according to this tradition, was originally rectangular, not square as it is today.[91] The *Akhbār* does not show any acquaintance with the sanctuary tradition of the Pentateuch so it is very unlikely that the parallel is due to influence from P's description. It is also difficult to imagine that the rectangular shape is a late innovation since it goes against everything that is accepted knowledge in Islamic tradition about the Meccan sanctuary.

This shows that behind the image of the *mishkan* lies a sanctuary tradition documented archaeologically from southern Judaea and the Levant in the middle of the 1st millennium BCE but which might reflect a much wider complex stretching into North-Western Arabia. This raises the question anew whether the tabernacle of P

---

89 Aharoni, "Arad," 24f.; id., *Excavations*, 157 ff; cf. Fritz, *Tempel*, 57ff.86f.
90 Kitchen, "Tabernacle," refers to tents in Egypt which, according to him, show that the tabernacle is a construction of a kind that goes back to the Bronze Age. It is, however, worth observing that none of the Egyptian parallels adduced by him are identical with the *mishkan*, neither in design nor function. The technique of hanging cloths on a wooden structure creating protection from the sun etc., is of course widely spread all over the world. An important point illustrated by Kitchen's evidence is, however, that the *mishkan* is not a 'desert tent'. The tents of desert dwellers look quite different as is seen from the pictures of Arabs in Assurbanipal's palace. The design of the *mishkan* in Exodus 26 definitely points to the settled lands, where, as Kitchen shows, this kind of construction belongs, whereas the '*ohel môʿed* in Exodus 33:7–11 may well be compared to the *qubba* of the Arabs (cf. de Vaux, "Arche," 263 and n. 2 with references). Another conclusion from Kitchen's study is that the construction technique of the *mishkan* may be ancient.
91 Azraqī, *Akhbār*, 111–113. That this tradition is not without basis is shown by the description of the pilgimage performed by Muhammad just before his death. It is said that during the *ṭawāf* (the circumambulation of the Holy House) he stopped at the southern corner of the building, saluting the foundation stone there ('the White Stone'), then he proceeded to the eastern corner kissing the foundation stone there (the 'Black Stone'). But he ignored the two fundation stones of the northern and western corners of the building because they did not belong to the original foundation of Abraham (Bukhārī, *Ṣaḥīḥ*, Kitāb al-ḥaǧǧ bāb 42; Kitāb ʾaḥādīth al-ʾanbiyāʾ bāb 10 = ḥadīths 1583, 3368; cf. Wellhausen, *Reste*, 74). It follows from al-Azraqī's description that the area of the present-day *ḥiǧr* the semi-circular bench in front of the north-western wall, originally was incorporated into the building which, consequently, had a rectangular plan, not a square one as today, a plan whose proportions match those of the southern Israelite sanctuaries as well as that of the *mishkan* (see above note 56 and also Rubin, "Ka'ba," 101).

really ever existed. It is obvious that its main elements did exist which, however, is not the definite answer to the question. But it makes a positive answer less unlikely. Be this as it may, these insights may help us to read the text of P with fresh eyes, without reading into it things which are not there. A tentative conclusion is that the sanctuary of P is a combination of a southern Judaean temple type, the *mishkan*, and the *hammān/paroket* which is found in many places in the Levant. As far as the central piece of the sanctuary is concerned, the *paroket* and its furnishing, it has been shown here that it most likely represents a specific Levantine sanctuary tradition, the *hammān*.

If this is true it might be asked if an Israelite writer, priestly or not, would have imagined such a *sacrum* as the central piece of the original sanctuary of YHWH after the 7th century BCE. The *hammānîm* are violently condemned in texts that go back to the beginning of the 6th century. The condemnation is even found in the so-called Holiness Code (HC) which is probably pre-600 BCE and close to the P-tradition. I. Knohl has suggested that the HC is an integral part of the P layer, datable to the time of Hezekiah.[92] The arguments for the dating of the HC to that period are attractive but the final formation of the priestly account may be somewhat later, sometime in the 7th century. The relationship between the HC and the main priestly account would thus be similar to the relationship betwen the deuteronomic law corpus and the hortatory framework beginning in Deuteronomy 4:44. The image of the *paroket* given by P must be older and must have had a status of antiquity as a domestic cult object well established in the yahwistic religion. According to Knohl's analysis it is composed before the HC.[93] Unlike in the HC there is no polemic against *hammānîm* in P in general. But the total absence of the term in P might indicate that the traditional designation was becoming controversial. It should also be noticed that this *sacrum* is not a peripheral issue in the Priestly Code. It is the central piece in the whole P-work, carrying an essential part of the message of that literary composition. Another observation is that there is no trace of the catastrophe in 586 BCE in the P-work which is most remarkable if it was composed after this date – and even more if the sanctuary of P was a replica of the Jerualem temple. An unprejudiced reading shows that P's sanctuary is independent from the Jerusalem tradition. It can be argued that the few parallels that exist between the description of the tabernacle and the second temple are due to the fact that that the latter was influenced by the priestly sanctuary tradition, not vice versa. P's sanctuary is probably an alternative to the (first) Jerusalem temple while it was still standing, the cult of which was not acknowledged by some circles.[94] The image of the restored temple in

---

92 Knohl, *Sanctuary,* 204ff.
93 Knohl, *Sanctuary,* 220ff.
94 Cf. Fretheim, "Priestly Document". Utzschneider (*Heligtum* 57, 63ff.) dates P to the exile since he assumes that the construction of the sanctuary presupposes absence of the temple, a good argument but not decisive. A similar dating is claimed by Cross, *Myth,* 323f. Crawford "Shadow," 130f., argues for the time of Ahaz i.e. the end of the 8th century BCE. Haran, *Temple,* 146f., and Knohl (loc. cit) connect P with the time of Hezekiah, Ahaz' successor.

the book of Ezekiel may in fact be a Jerusalemite answer to the ideal sanctuary of P.[95]

Bibliography

Sources

Biblia Hebraica Stuttgartensia ed. K. Elliger/W. Rudolph. Stuttgart: Deutsche Bibelgesellschaft, 1977.
Biblia sacra iuxta Vulgatam Clementinam nova editio a A. Colunga & L. Turrado, 6 ed. Matriti: La editorial catolica, 1982.
The Old Testament in Syriac. Peshitta Version Part 1–2. 1b: Preface – Genesis – Exodus – Leviticus – Numbers – Deuteronomy – Joshua. Leiden: E. J. Brill, 1977–1999.
Septuaginta id est Vetus Testamentum Graece iuxta LXX interpretes Vol. I–II. Ed. A. Rahlfs. Stuttgart: Württembergische Bibelanstalt/Deutsche Bibelstiftung, 1935
Šišā sidrê Mišnā mefûrašîm bîdê Ḥ. Albeq ûmenûqad bîdê Ḥ Yalôn. Jerusalem: Bialik Institute/Dvir Co., 1959, repr. ibid. 1973.
Baraita de-Melekhet ha-Mishkan. A Critical Edition with Introduction and Translation by R. Kirschner. Cincinnati: Hebrew Union College Press, 1992.
Talmûd Bavlî 'im kol ha-mefarešîm ka'ašer nidpas mi-qedem. Yerûšalayyim. Hôṣa'at hatalmûd, s.a.
Targum Onkelos, hrsg. A. Berliner. Berlin: Gorczelanczyk & Co., 1884.
Pseudo-Jonathan (Targum Jonathan ben Usiël zum Pentateuch) hrsg. M. Ginsburger. Berlin: Calvary & Co. 1903.

---

[95] Not a few commentators have tried to identify many elements in the description of the tabernacle with cultic traditions from Egypt (cf. especially Hoffmeier, *Ancient Israel,* 193–222, cf. also Kitchen, *op.cit.*). This goes together with a conservative or 'maximalist' view on the biblical text which is seen as a quite trustworthy account of the events, e.g. the exodus from Egypt and the Sinai revelation (cf. Hoffmeier, *Ancient Israel,* 6–33). One does not have to be a 'minimalist' to be sceptical about this view. Suffice it to point out that the plethora of Egyptian elements in the cultic traditions of Israel according to Hoffmeier and his sympathizers creates a major problem: how do we account for the massive presence of 'pagan' Egyptian elements in the very centre of the yahwistic cult from the beginning? Not only Egypt but also her gods are totally condemned in the exodus account (Exodus 8:19; 12:12). The Egyptian connection is probably much exaggerated. This paper argues for an origin of the ancient Israelite sanctuary tradition in The Holy Land itself. This notwithstanding, there might still be some Egyptian elements in the Israelite sanctuary tradition, e. g. the names Pinhas and Hofni in the sanctuary at Shiloh and, perhaps, the design of the camp of the Israelites in Numbers (Hoffmeier, *Ancient Israel,* 206–208).

Apollodorus: The Library with an English Translation by Sir J. G. Frazer vols. I–II. Loeb Classical Library. Cambridge, Mass.,/London: Harvard University Press, 1921.
Diodorus of Sicily with an English translation by C. H. Oldfather I–XII. Loeb Classical Library. London/New York/Cambridge Mass. Harvard University Press, 1933–1967
Nonnos de Panopolis: Les dionysiaques t. I: Chants I–II ed. F. Vian. Paris: Les Belles Lettres, 1976.
Josephus with an English Translation by H. St. Thackeray/R. Marcus/A. Wikgren/L. H. Feldman Vol. V–IX: *Jewish Antiquities*. Loeb Classical Library. London/Cambridge Mass. Harvard University Press, 1961–1981.
al-Azraqī: Akhbār = F. Wüstenfeld (ed): *Die Chroniken der Stadt Mekka* I. Leipzig: Brockhaus, 1858.
Al-Bukhārī: Ṣaḥīḥ. Ṭabʿa ǧadīda maḍbūṭa wa-muṣaḥḥaḥa wa-mufahrasa. Aṭ-ṭabʿa l-ʾūlā Bayrūt: Dār Ibn Kathīr, 2002/1423.

Secondary literature

Aharoni, Yohanan. *The Land of the Bible. A Historical Geography*. London: Burns & Oates, 1967.
—. "Arad: Its Inscriptions and Temple." *BA* 31 (1968): 2–32.
—. "Trial Excavation in the 'Solar Shrine' at Lachish." *IEJ* 18 (1968): 157–169.
Albertz, Rainer. *Religionsgeschichte Israels in alttestamentlicher Zeit 1: von den Anfängen bis zum Ende der Königszeit. 2: Vom Exil bis zu den Makkabäern*. Göttingen: Vandehoeck & Ruprecht, 1992, 1997.
—. *Exodus Band I: Ex 1–18, Band II: Exodus 19–40*. Zürich: Theologischer Verlag, 2012, 2015.
—. "Beobachtungen zur Komposition der priesterlichen Texte Ex 25–40," in *Heiliger Raum. Exegese und Rezeption der Heiligtumstexte in Ex 24–40*. Edited by M. Hopf, W. Oswald, and S. Seiler. Stuttgart: Kohlhammer, 2016, 37–56.
Baentsch, B.: *Exodus – Leviticus – Numeri übersetzt und erklärt*. HK I,2. Göttingen: Vandenhoeck & Ruprecht, 1903.
Beer, G.: *Exodus mit einem Beitrag von K. Galling*. HAT 1:3. Tübingen: Mohr/Siebeck, 1939.
Brockelmann, C. *Grundriss der vergleichenden Grammatik der semitischen Sprachen I Band*. Berlin: Reuther & Reichard, 1908.
Butcher, K. *Roman Syria and the Near East*. London: The British Museum Press, 2003.
Cassuto, U. *A Commentary on the Book of Exodus*. Jerusalem: The Magnes Press, 1967.
Childs, B. S. *The Book of Exodus. A Critical, Theological Commentary*. OTL. Louisville/London: The Westminster Press, 1974.
Clifford, R. J. "The Tent of El and the Israelite Tent of Meeting." *CBQ* 33 (1971): 221–227.
Clines, D. A. ed., *The Dictionary of Classical Hebrew. Vol VI: samek-pe*. Sheffield: Sheffield Phoenix Press, 2007.
Collart, P. and Coupel, P. *Le petit autel de Baalbek*. Paris: Paul Geuthner, 1977.
Crawford, C. D. "Between Shadow and Substance: The Historical Relationship of Tabernacle and Temple in Light of Architecture and Iconography," in *Levites and Priests in Biblical History and Tradition*. Edited by M. A. Leuchter and J. M. Hutton. SBL 9. Atlanta: Society of Biblical Literature, 2011, 117–133.

Cross, F. M. "The Tabernacle. A Study from an Archaeological and Historical Approach." *BA* 10 (1947): 45–68.
—. *Canaanite Myth and Hebrew Epic. Essays in the History of the Religion of Israel*. Cambridge Mass./London: Harvard University Press, 1973.
—. *From Epic to Canon. History and Literature in Ancient Israel*. Baltimore/London: The Johns Hopkins Univerity Press, 1998.
Drijvers, H. J. W. "Aramaic *ḤMN'* and Hebrew *ḤMN*: Their Meaning and Root." *JSS* 33 (1988): 165–179.
Driver, S. R. *An Introduction to the Literature of the Old Testament*. London: Charles Scribner's Sons, 1898.
Eissfeldt, O. *Baal Zaphon, Zeus Kasios und der Durchzug der Israeliten durchs Meer*. Beiträge zur Religionsgeschichte des Altertums Heft 1. Halle (Saale): M. Niemeyer, 1932.
—. *Hexateuch-Synopse. Die Erzählung der fünf Bücher Mose und ded Buches Josua mit dem Anfange des Richterbuches*. Leipzig: J. C. Hinrichs Verlag, 1922.
Fleming, D. E. "Mari's Public Tent and the Priestly Tent Sanctuary." *VT* 50 (2000): 484–498.
Freedman, D. N. and O'Connor, P. "krûb," in *Theologisches Wörterbuch zum Alten Testament IV*. Stuttgart: Kohlhammer, 1984, 322–334.
Fretheim, T. E. "The Priestly Document: Anti-Temple?" *VT* 18 (1968): 313–329.
Freyberger, K. "Zur Funktion der Ḥamānā im Kontext lokaler Heiligtümer in Syrien und Palästina." *Damaszener Mitteilungen* 9 (1996): 143–161.
Friedman, R. E. *The Exile and Biblical Narrative*. Chico, Calif.: Scholars Press, 1981.
—. "Tabernacle," in *The Anchor Bible Dictionary Vol. 5*. Edited by D. N. Freedman. New York: Doubleday, 1992, 292–300.
Fritz, V. *Tempel und Zelt. Studien zum Tempelbau in Israel und zu dem Zeltheiligtum der Priesterschrift*. Neukirchen: Neukirchener Verlag, 1977.
Gooding, D. W. *The Account of the Tabernacle. Translation and Textual Problems of the Greek Exodus*. Texts and Studies VI. Cambridge: Cambridge University Press, 1959.
Gray, G. B. *A Critical and Exegetical Commentary on Numbers*. ICC. Edinburgh: T. & T. Clark, 1903.
Haran, M. "The Ark and the Cherubim: Their Symbolic Significance in Biblical Ritual." *IEJ* 9 (1959): 30–38.
—. "The Nature of the 'ohel mo'edh' in Pentateuchal Sources." *JSS* 5 (1960): 50–65.
—. "Shiloh and Jerusalem: the Origin of the Priestly Tradition in the Pentateuch." *JBL* 81 (1962): 14–24.
—. "The priestly image of the Tabernacle." *HUCA* 36 (1965): 191–226.
—. *Temples and Temple-Service in Ancient Israel. An Inquiry into Biblical Cult Phenomena and the Historical Setting of the Priestly School*. Winona Lake: Eisenbrauns, 1985.
Hartmann, R. "Zelt und Lade." *ZAW* 37 (1917/18): 209–244.
Hendrix, R. "Miškān and 'ohel mô'ed. Etymology, Lexical Definitions, and Extra-Biblical Usage." *AUSS* 29 (1991): 213–223.
—. "The Use of miškān and 'ohel mô'ed in Exodus 25–40." *AUSS* 30 (1992): 3–13.
Hoffmeier, J. *Ancient Israel in Sinai*. Oxford: Oxford University Press, 2005.
Hoftijzer, J. and Jongeling, K. *Dictionary of the North-West Semitic Inscriptions 1–2*. Leiden: E. J. Brill, 1992.
Hurowitz, V. A. "The Form and Fate of the Tabernacle: Reflections on a Recent Proposal." *JQR* 86 (1995): 127–151.

—. *I have Built You an Exalted House. Temple Building in the Bible in the Light of Mesopotamian and Northwest Semitic Writings*. JSOTS 115. Sheffield: Sheffield Academic Press, 1992.

Janowski, B. *Sühne als Heilsgeschehen. Studien zur Sühnetheologie der Priesterschrift und der Wurzel KPR im Alten Orient und im Alten Testament*. Neukirchen: Neukirchener Verlag, 1982.

Kaufmann, Y. *The Religion of Israel from its beginnings to the Babylonian exile*. Translated and abridged by Moshe Greenberg. New York: Schocken, 1960.

Kitchen, K. A. "The Tabernacle. A Bronze Age Artifact." *Eretz Israel* 24 (1993): 119*–129*.

Knohl, I. *The Sanctuary of Silence. The Priestly Torah and the Holiness School*. Minneapolis: Fortress Press, 1995.

Lane, E. W. *An Arabic-English Lexicon vol. 1–2*. London/Edinburg: Williams and Norgate, 1863, 1877.

Levine, B. "The Descriptive Tabernacle Texts of the Pentateuch." *JAOS* 85 (1965): 307–318.

Liddell, H. G. and Scott, R. *A Greek-English Lexicon N.E.* Oxford: Oxford University Press, 1940.

Maier, J. *Das altisraelitische Ladeheiligtum*. BZAW 93. Berlin: de Gruyter, 1965.

Milgrom, J. *Leviticus. A New Translation with Introduction and Commentary*. AB 3. New York et al.: Doubleday, 1991–2001.

Noth, M. *Das zweite Buch Mose. Exodus übersetzt und erklärt*. 4 Aufl. ATD 5. Göttingen: Vandenhoeck & Ruprecht, 1968.

del Olmo Lete, G. and Sanmartín, J. *Diccionario de la lengua ugarítica vols. I–II*. Barcelona: Editorial AUSA, 1996, 2000.

Payne Smith, R., ed., *Thesaurus Syriacus* I–II. Oxonii: Oxford University Press, 1879–1901.

Popper, J. *Der biblische Bericht über die Stiftshütte. Ein Beitrag zur Geschichte der Composition und Diaskeue des Pentateuch*. Leipzig: Heinrich Hunger, 1852.

Propp, W. H. C. *Exodus 19–40. A New Translation with Introduction and Commentary*. AB 2a. New York: Doubleday, 2006.

Rabe, V. W. "The Identity of the Priestly Tabernacle." *JNES* 25 (1966): 132–134.

von Rad, G. *Die Priesterschrift im Hexateuch. Literarisch untersucht und theologisch gewertet*. Stuttgart-Berlin: Kohlhammer, 1934.

Retsö, J. "Petra and Qadesh." *SEÅ* 76 (2011): 115–136.

Rubin, U. "The Kaʻba. Aspects of its ritual functions and position in the pre-Islamic and early Islamic times." *JSAI* 8 (1986): 97–131.

Schmitt, R. *Zelt und Lade als Thema alttestamentlicher Wissenschaft. Eine kritische forschungsgeschichtliche Darstellung*. Gütersloh: Gütersloher Verlaghaus Gerd Mohn, 1972.

Simons, J. *The Geographical and Topographical Texts of the Old Testament*. Leiden: E. J. Brill, 1959.

Smith, M. *The Ugaritic Baal Cycle Vol. 1: Introduction with Text, Translation & Commentary of KTU 1.1–1.2*. Leiden: E. J. Brill, 1994.

von Soden, W. *Akkadisches Handwörterbuch I–III*. Wiesbaden: Otto Harrassowitz, 1965–1981.

Sollberger, E. "Samsu-Iluna's Bilingual Inscription B: Text of the Akkadian Version." *RA* 61 (1967): 39–44.

Utzschneider, H. *Das Heiligtum und das Gesetz. Studien zur Bedeutung der sinaitischen Heiligtumstexte (Ex. 25–49; Lev. 8–9)*. Göttingen: Universitätsverlag Freiburg/Vandenhoeck & Ruprecht, 1988.

de Vaux, R. "Arche d'alliance et tente de reunion," in *A la rencontre de Dieu. Mémorial Albert Gelin*. Bibliothèque de la Faculté Catholique de Théologie Lyon. Le Puy: Xavier Mappus, 1961, 261–275.

—. *Histoire ancienne d'Israël des origines à l'installation en Canaan*. Paris: Librairie Lecoffre J. Gabalda, 1971.

Wade, M. L. *Consistency of Translation Techniques in the Tabernacle Accounts of Exodus in Old Greek*. Leiden: E. J. Brill, 2003.

Wellhausen, J. *Die Composition des Hexateuchs und der historischen Bücher des Alten Testaments*. 3 Aufl. Berlin: Georg Reimer, 1899.

—. *Reste arabischen Heidentums gesammelt und erläutert*. 2 Aufl. Berlin: Georg Reimer, 1897.

—. *Prolegomena zur Geschichte Israels*. 6 Aufl. Berlin: Georg Reimer, 1905.

Xella, P. Baal Hammon. Recherches sur l'identité et l'histoire d'un dieu phénico-punique. Roma: Consiglio nazionale delle ricerche, 1991.

A 'Samaritan' Pentateuch?

The Implications of the Pro-Northern Tendency of the Common Pentateuch

John S. Bergsma

(Franciscan University of Steubenville)

To play on a phrase once used of Karl Barth's *Romans* commentary, the day may come when it is said about Gary Knoppers monograph, *Jews and Samaritans*, that "it fell like a bomb on the playground" of Pentateuchal scholars. Whereas it has been common in modern scholarship to interpret the Pentateuch in its final form as the redactional product of the post-exilic Jerusalem priesthood with the intent to legitimize the Jerusalem temple and its cult,[1] Knoppers points out that a Yahwistic shrine was active at Gerizim from at least the mid-5th century (c. 450 BCE) on, meaning that "the place which the LORD your God shall choose" (Deut 12:5 *et passim*) could not simply be assumed to mean Jerusalem during the Second Temple period.[2] Knoppers argues instead that the Common Pentateuch[3] is a "compromise document" between the Judean and Samarian[4] establishments after the Judean exile, that allowed each community to interpret the text to support their own claims. Knoppers engages in an initial re-reading of the Common Pentateuch from the perspective of Samarian interests, showing how the various altar laws in the document could be construed in a way favorable to Samarian claims.[5] This paper continues Knopper's provocative re-reading of the Pentateuch from a Samarian (i.e. northern Israelite) perspective by surveying other macroscopic narrative elements from Genesis

---

1 E.g. Nihan, *Priestly Torah,* 614: "[The Priestly Document] is closely linked to the rebuilding of the Temple [and] the legitimation of the Second Temple community in Jerusalem. [. . .] The writing down of P also betrays the claims of the priestly class in Jerusalem." Similarly, Ziony Zevit, "Deuteronomy," 217, has described Deuteronomy as the work of a "Jerusalem Temple loyalist".
2 Knoppers, *Jews and Samaritans*, 11: "The Jerusalem Temple had a Yahwistic rival to the north significantly earlier than most scholars had assumed," i.e. from "the mid-fifth century onward."
3 By "Common Pentateuch" I mean the presumed *Urtext* from which the Samaritans developed their unique Samaritan Pentateuch, and the Judean tradition eventually developed the Masoretic Text.
4 Knoppers, following others before him, uses "Samarian" to describe the people and culture in the territory of Samaria prior to the schism between Judaism and Samaritanism due to the destruction of the Samaritan temple by John Hyrcanus c. 111–110 B.C.E.
5 Knoppers, *Jews and Samaritans*, 194–216.

through Deuteronomy, such as the locations dignified by patriarchal cultic activity, and the valorization of Judah and Joseph and their descendant tribes in the narrative. The pentateuchal portrayal of these issues is then contrasted with the approach of the *Book of Jubilees*, a second-century B.C.E. Judean rewriting of Genesis and Exodus. The contrast helps highlight the fact that the Pentateuch, even in its Masoretic form, lends itself better to the legitimation of Samarian/Samaritan claims than to Judean ones.

1. Sacred Sites in the Pentateuch

Genesis records at least nine different locations as sites of theophany or of worship by the patriarchs: Shechem (12:6; 33:18; 35:4), the midpoint between Bethel and Ai (12:8; 13:3–4), Hebron (13:18; 18:1; [also site of Sarah, Abraham, Isaac, Rebecca, Leah, Jacob's burials: 23:19, 25:9; 35:29; 49:30–31; 50:13]); Beersheba (21:33; 26:23–25; 46:1–4); an unknown mountain in the land of Moriah (Gen 22:2–18); Gerar (26:1–6); Bethel (Gen 28:17–21; 31:13; 35:1–15); Mahanaim (32:12); and Peniel (32:22–31). Of these, the four most significant locations are Bethel and Shechem in what later became Samaria, and Hebron and Beersheba in what later became Judah.

Notably absent from the text of Genesis is any explicit mention of Jerusalem or Zion. There are only subtle geographical links to Jerusalem in the text: the Gihon spring is mentioned in Gen 2:13 (cf. 1 Kgs 1:33); the enigmatic priest-king Melchizedek comes from "Salem" (Gen 14:18), possibly an ancient name for Jerusalem (cf. Ps 76:2); and the Aqedah takes place on a mountain in the land of Moriah (Gen 22:2) that later Jewish literature identifies with the Temple Mount (2 Chron 3:1 and *Jubilees* 18:13). It seems remarkable, however, that the presumed Second Temple priestly redactors in Jerusalem failed to intervene in the text with even a small gloss like הִיא יְרוּשָׁלָ͏ם[6] to clarify that the incident with Melchizedek and the *Aqedah* were tied to the sacred site of Jerusalem, especially since these are both attested interpretive traditions in the Second Temple period.[7] As a result of this apparent failure to clarify, the Pentateuchal connections with Jerusalem are not at all unambiguous. Antti Laato points out that "Salem" in Gen 14:18 could also be understood as another name for Shechem based on Gen 33:18, and the "Moriah" in Gen 22:2 could be a variant of Moreh, also in the vicinity of Shechem.[8] Thus, the text of the Com-

---

6 As is done in Joshua and Judges: Josh 15:8; 18:28; Judg 19:10.
7 For Melchizedek's association with Jerusalem, see Josephus, *Wars*, 6:438 and 1QapGen 22:15. For the mountain of the *Aqedah* as Jerusalem, see 2 Chron 3:1, *Jubilees* 18:13.
8 See Laato, *Cult Site*, 63–64. Genesis 33:18 can be read, "Jacob came to Salem, the city of Shechem," which is precisely how the LXX takes it (Gen 33:18 LXX). Thus Pseudo-Eupole-

mon Pentateuch leaves open the possibility that even these two subtle references to Jerusalem could actually be to Shechem instead. Therefore, without a single unambiguous reference to Zion or its vicinity, Genesis certainly does not anticipate that Jerusalem will one day become the sanctuary city *par excellence* of Abraham's descendants.

Of course, there is no explicit mention of Gerizim in Genesis, either. However, Gerizim benefits from its proximity to Shechem. Since Shechem lies in the valley between Mounts Gerizim and Ebal, either of these two hills provides an attractive location for a shrine associated with this city. And Shechem can at least claim to be the first site of patriarchal worship in the land of Canaan (Gen 12:7). Both Abraham and Jacob built altars there (Gen 12:7; Gen 33:20). According to Genesis 34, the city of Shechem is conquered by Israel already in the patriarchal period and "cleansed" of its pagan inhabitants: its males all slain and the women and children assimilated into the Israelite clan.[9] Thus Jacob speaks of having captured Shechem by his own sword and bow, and grants it to Joseph as an inheritance (Gen 48:22 MT). From the perspective of the narrative, it remains an "empty city" after the patriarchal period, awaiting Israelite settlement—Joshua will not need to conquer it. In Genesis 35, Jacob buries all his household idols under the oak at Shechem (=the Oak of Moreh; cf. Gen 12:6, Deut 11:30), which, far from defiling the site as some argue,[10] makes Shechem into a geographical symbol of the subjugation of Israel's idolatrous past to exclusive worship of the LORD, a motif that recurs in Joshua 24.

After Genesis, there are no references to sacred locations in the promised land again until the Book of Deuteronomy, where Moses designates the vicinity of Shechem as the location for the solemnization of the covenant between the LORD and Israel (Deut 11:30). Interestingly, he does not anticipate Israel having to overcome resistance from the Shechemites in order to perform this ceremony—perhaps because Shechem was regarded as already conquered (Gen 34:25–29; 48:22). The two mountains flanking Shechem—Ebal and Gerizim—will be used for the proclamation of the blessings and curses, a standard feature of ancient Near Eastern covenant rituals:

> And when the LORD your God brings you into the land ... you shall set the blessing on Mount Gerizim and the curse on Mount Ebal. Are they not be-

---

mos associates Melchizedek with "holy Argarizin" (=Mt. Gerizim; Kartveit, "Samaritan Temple," 89). Since Moriah is never identified or mentioned elsewhere in the Pentateuch, but Moreh has an important role (Gen 12:6; Deut 11:30; cf. Judg. 7:1), it is tempting to emend the text or take Moriah as variant orthography for the better-known Moreh.

9 The incident of Genesis 34 does not need to be read as anti-Shechem polemic (so Amit, "Shechem," 6). It can be interpreted, rather, as the first city in Canaan conquered by Israel, just as it was the first sacred site when Abraham entered the land. The pentateuchal narrative lends itself to such an interpretation.

10 So Amit, "Shechem," 6.

yond the Jordan, west of the road …over against Gilgal, beside the oak of Moreh? (Deut 11:29–30)

The Oak of Moreh is significant as a marker for the sacred precinct utilized by Abraham in his first act of cultic worship in the land of Canaan (Gen 12:7). As Abraham entered the land and immediately worshiped at Shechem, so Israel will enter the land and worship at the same location.

According to Josh 8:30–35, these Mosaic prescriptions were faithfully fulfilled under the leadership of Joshua after Israel had entered the land. Manuscript evidence suggests that the editors of the MT actually changed the location of Joshua's altar in Deut 27:4 (and Josh 8:30) from Gerizim to Ebal, demonstrating that later Judaism felt the force of this verse as evidence for the legitimacy of Gerizim as the best candidate for the site of the Deuteronomic central sanctuary.[11]

To summarize, Jerusalem is never mentioned by name in the Common Pentateuch, and Gerizim only twice, so the text does not reflect any aggressive redaction to support one or the other party in the Judean-Samaritan dispute over the location of the central sanctuary. Genesis, in fact, subverts the Deuteronomic emphasis on one central location by emphasizing the sacrality of several locations within the land, especially Bethel, but also Shechem, Hebron, and Beersheba.

Nonetheless, if one must build a case for the proper location of an Israelite central sanctuary from the text of the Pentateuch alone, by far the better case can be made for Gerizim rather than Jerusalem. At least Gerizim is mentioned, and designated as the mountain associated with the blessing of the twelve tribes in the context of covenant renewal (Deut 11:29; 27:12). Moreover, Gerizim is associated with Shechem, and Shechem is the first site of worship in Canaan by the patriarchs (Gen 12:7), the first site in Canaan conquered by Israel (Gen 34:25–29), the site of abandonment of idolatry and conversion to Yahwism (Gen 35:4; cf. Josh 24:19–24) and the area designated for covenant solemnization upon entry into the land (Deut 11:30 + Mss of 27:4). As Etienne Nodet has put it, "the Pentateuch, considered as a whole, goes better with Shechem than Jerusalem."[12]

If we extend our analysis to the Hexateuch, the case for Shechem only becomes stronger. There is no record of Joshua having to conquer Shechem (cf. Gen 34:25–29), but rather Joshua peacefully gathers the tribes there to solemnize the covenant (Josh 8:30–33), and re-convenes them there at the end of his life (Josh 24:1), when he recapitulates Genesis 35:4 by having them put away their foreign gods, renews the covenant with them (Josh 24:25), and sets up a sacred stone in the "sanctuary" (*miqdash*) of the LORD associated with the ancient oak that was there (Josh 24:26), probably the same known as the "oak of Moreh" (Gen 12:6; 11:30). It also becomes

---

11 Following Charlesworth, "Discovery"; idem, "What is a variant?", citing Old Latin Manuscript Codex 100, Greek manuscript Papyrus Giessen 19, and a recently recovered Dead Sea Scroll. See also Kartveit, "Samaritan Temple," 90–95; Ulrich, "4QJosh[a]," 145–146; Hjelm, "Northern Perspectives," 203; and Abegg et al., *Dead Sea Scrolls Bible*, 201–202.

12 Nodet, *Search*, 152.

the resting place of the remains of Joseph (Josh 24:32), the particular heir of the patriarchal promises (Gen 48:1–20). Thus, the final form of the Hexateuch concludes with a resounding endorsement of Shechem as a sacred site for all twelve tribes of Israel, and can be described as exhibiting a "from Shechem to Shechem" narrative arc (Genesis 12–Joshua 24) that can scarcely be dismissed as merely coincidental.[13]

2. The Characterizations of Judah and Joseph in the Pentateuch

2.1 The Patriarchs Judah and Joseph

The Samaritans claimed descent from Joseph, and research suggests that the Samaritan population was indeed largely composed of the descendants of the northern Israelites who had inhabited the territories associated with the Josephite tribes Ephraim and Manasseh in the First Temple period.[14] The Judeans, on the other hand, claimed descent from Judah.[15] Therefore, the valorization of these two patriarchs (Joseph and Judah) and their tribes in the Pentateuch could serve as a source of ethno-religious legitimation for these two communities in the Second Temple period.

Let us review the characterization of Joseph in the Pentateuchal narrative. Joseph is the favorite son of Jacob (Gen 37:3) the eldest son of Jacob/Israel's favorite wife (30:24). He has a prophetic gift, and dreams repeatedly of his entire family worshiping him (Gen 37:5–11). Although rejected by his brothers and betrayed especially by Judah (37:26–28), he rises to become the *de facto* ruler of the Near East as prime minister of Egypt (41:40). His sons Ephraim and Manasseh are born of a high-ranking Egyptian priestess (41:50–52), and are adopted directly by Jacob/Israel (48:5), who imposes upon them the patriarchal blessing handed down from Abraham (Gen 48:15–16). This blessing on Joseph and his descendants is re-iterated by Jacob/Israel in Gen 49:22–26, where Joseph receives the most effusive benediction of any of the twelve sons Jacob. There, Jacob/Israel denotes Joseph as the one who is

---

13 Hjelm, "Northern Perspectives," 188, comments: "Is it sheer accident that the Masoretic Hexateuch forms a continuum in its compositional form of 'promise (Genesis 12) and fulfillment' (Joshua 24), which may also be defined as "from Shechem to Shechem' (Genesis 12–Joshua 24), in which yet another continuum is included (Genesis 35–Joshua 24)?".
14 See Knoppers, *Jews and Samaritans*, 18–44; Hjelm, "Lost and Found", *passim*; Hjelm, "Northern Perspectives," 188–190.
15 Knoppers, *Jews and Samaritans*, 2: "Samaritans claimed to be descendants of the northern tribes of Joseph ... while Judeans claimed to be descendants of the southern tribes, most notably Jacob's progeny of Judah." Cf. Josephus, *Antiquities,* 11:340.

"prince" (Heb. *nazir*) among his brothers. Significantly, this effusive benediction of Jacob is repeated and expanded by Moses in Deut 33:13–17, near the close of the Common Pentateuch.

By contrast, Judah is the fourth son of Jacob/Israel's less favored wife, and appears to rise in leadership among the sons of Jacob largely because his older three brothers (Reuben, Simeon, and Levi) all fall under a paternal curse for various reasons (49:3–7). Judah has no prophetic gift or favorable omens about his future success. He is the betrayer of Joseph, the inventor of the plan to sell him into slavery (37:26–27). His procreative activities are scandalous. He marries a Canaanite woman (38:2) who gives him three half-Canaanite sons (38:3–5), the first two of which are so wicked they are slain directly by God (38:7–10). The large majority of Judah's descendants come not from his third and last son Shelah (1 Chron 4:21–23), but rather through Perez and Zerah (1 Chron 2:1–4:20), twins born to Judah's presumably Canaanite[16] daughter-in-law Tamar (38:27–30) after he engaged in illicit fornication with her while she was masquerading as a cult prostitute (38:12–19). More on this below. Nonetheless, in the course of the Joseph cycle, Judah does prove himself progressively to be a competent leader of his brothers (43:1–10) and defender of the interests of his father Jacob/Israel (44:18–34). In fact, Judah has the privilege of delivering the pathos-laden soliloquy at the climax of the Joseph cycle (44:18–34) that demonstrates his moral reformation and moves Joseph to uncontrolled weeping (45:1–3), thus opening the way to the resolution of the conflict between the brothers and the eventual reconciliation of the whole family. Jacob/Israel rewards Judah with a weighty blessing in Gen 49:8–12. But Jacob promises Judah leadership among the tribes (49:8) and the royal scepter (49:10) for only a limited time.[17] Significantly, at the end of the Pentateuch, Moses does *not* repeat the royal blessing given to Judah by Jacob, substituting instead a brief and perfunctory benediction for Judah (33:7) that pales next to those given to Levi (33:8–11) and Joseph (33:13–17).

Allow us to digress for a moment on Genesis 38, a truly scandalous text in light of the later rivalry between the Judeans and Samarians. It asserts that most Judeans are of mixed Canaanite descent through an illicit liaison between Judah and his own daughter-in-law, a union considered a capital crime by the Holiness Code (Lev 18:15; 20:12). Moreover, the patriarch Judah is shown as a cohabitor with Canaanite women who is not above frequenting pagan cult prostitutes. In the Second Temple period this text would have been absolutely devastating to the Judean pretensions of ethnic purity reflected in Ezra and Nehemiah (cf. Ezra 10:2–44; Neh 13:26–27), and

---

16 Tamar's ethnicity is not identified explicitly in Genesis, but by failing to provide a genealogy linking her to the patriarchal lineage, the text portrays her as a local woman unrelated to the sons of Israel, therefore presumably a Canaanite.

17 The text of Genesis 49:10 is a notorious crux. It appears to limit Judah's possession of the "scepter" by the phrase "until Shiloh comes." See discussion in Sarna, *Genesis*, 336–337: "Judah's hegemony over Israel will last until the secession of the north" (337).

must have provided the Samarians with a certain amount of *Schadenfreude* at the expense of their southern cousins. Clearly, if Judean priests in the post-exilic period had felt free to redact the text of the Pentateuch aggressively, Genesis 38 would have been removed. Certainly it was not a text *composed* by Judeans after the exile. We will see how *Jubilees* attempted to cope with this text below.

On the balance, then, the Pentateuchal characterization of the patriarchs Joseph and Judah grants the pre-eminence to Joseph. Judah does show moral development and leadership virtues, but his paternal blessing has a limitation on it and the scandal of his sexual unions and betrayal of Joseph weigh heavily on his character. By contrast, the narratives and oracles about Joseph are positive without exception. He receives divine prophetic dreams of his dominance over his brothers. He rises to become *de facto* ruler of the known world. He receives the patriarchal blessing from Jacob/Israel twice, and it is reaffirmed by Moses himself. The Pentateuch ends with every expectation that the future of Israel rests largely on the shoulders of Joseph's sons Ephraim and Manasseh (Deut 33:17).

2.2 The Tribes of Judah and Joseph (Ephraim and Manasseh)

Both the tribes of Judah and of Joseph (i.e. Ephraim and Manasseh) are portrayed favorably in the narrative from Exodus through Deuteronomy. The scouts from these two tribes—Joshua of Ephraim and Caleb from Judah—are the faithful spies who urge confidence in the LORD and immediate conquest of the land (Num 14:6–10). Nonetheless, Caleb is clearly a secondary figure to Joshua. This pattern of Judah second to Joseph is also repeated in the second census of the tribes in Numbers 26: the combined descendants of Joseph outnumber the descendants of any other patriarch by a large margin. The nearest competitor is Judah, who at 76,500 (Num 26:22), remains 8,700 short of Joseph's total (85,200; Num 26:34–37). This shows that the patriarchal blessing of fruitfulness and multiplication (Gen 28:3; 35:11) is experienced by Joseph above all others, as prophesied in Gen 48:1–20 and 49:22–26 (cf. 41:52).

Of great interest is the literary structure of Numbers and the emphasis that it places on the Joseph tribes. As is well known, Numbers can be divided literarily in two parts, each enclosed with an *inclusio*: Num 1–26, wrapped by two censuses (Num 1 and 26); followed by Num 27–36, wrapped by two narratives of the inheritance of Zelophehad's daughters (Num 27:1–11 and 36:1–13). The accounts of Zelophehad's daughters clearly belong together; yet they have been split in order to form bookends around the second half of the book of Numbers, probably by the final redactor. The theological and narrative effect of this literary structuring is to place focus on the promise of inheritance of the land for all the tribes, despite the ten rebellions that are recounted as having taken place in the wilderness (Num 11–25). Thus, the LORD's grace to Israel is highlighted: despite their sins, the sons of Israel will inherit God's good promise of the land. But notice: the recipients that Numbers chooses to highlight are daughters of Machir, son of Manasseh, son of Joseph.[18]

Now, Numbers is usually thought to be a book heavily shaped and redacted by P, and possibly forming the end of a Priestly Tetrateuch prior to the addition of Deuteronomy.[19] Yet the ending chapters of the two *inclusios* that form the bipartite structure of Numbers (chs. 26 and 36) are both pro-Josephite: in Numbers 26, Joseph has overtaken Judah as the largest tribe; in Numbers 36, the inalienable rights of the tribe of Manasseh to retain its inheritance is protected by Mosaic law. This concern Numbers shows for the enduring fulfillment of divine promises to the Joseph tribes (specifically the Manassites) is against the interests of Second Temple Jerusalem priests.[20] It could only tend to strengthen the claims of the Samaritans to be the descendants of the Joseph tribes still inhabiting the ancient tribal territories, especially Shechem and Gerizim, which were located in the traditional territory of Manasseh.

Thus, the Pentateuchal narrative from Exodus to Deuteronomy tends to valorize the tribe of Joseph above that of Judah.

This is all the more the case if we bring the entire Hexateuch under consideration. Moses transfers authority to Joshua, who is an Ephraimite. Joshua presides as the land is distributed to the twelve tribes, with the Joseph tribes receiving the central heartland (Josh 16–17), the other ten forming around them a buffer zone (Josh 14–15, 18–19). Joshua solemnizes the Deuteronomic covenant at Shechem (Josh 8) and renews it at the same location (Josh 24) apparently at the sacred precinct marked by the Oak of Moreh. Then he inters the remains of Joseph, the primary heir of the patriarchal blessings, at Shechem. Since Mt. Gerizim looms over Shechem, it shares in Shechem's dignity.

Thus, in the Second Temple period, the Samarians and later Samaritans could claim that their ancestor was *the pre-eminent son* of Jacob, to whom primary covenantal heirship was granted, the *nazîr* or "consecrated prince" among the sons of Jacob. Surely the central sanctuary belonged in or near the natural capital of their territory, Shechem, which Judges 9:37 calls "the navel of the land"!

---

18 Intriguingly, the Pentateuchal narrative shows unusual concern for this Machir: see Gen 50:23; Num 26:29; Deut 3:15.
19 See discussion in Levine, *Numbers 1–20*, 64–72, 101–103.
20 By the time of the Second Temple, the tribe of Manasseh had either been completely obliterated and/or exiled, if one follows 2 Kings 17; or else had become a component of the Samaritan people, if the claims of the Samaritans themselves were accepted. In either case, redacting the end of the Tetrateuch to emphasize the endurance of land inheritance to the clans of Manasseh (Num 27:1–11; Num 36:1–13) did nothing to serve the interests of the Judean Jerusalem priesthood.

3. The Contrast with *Jubilees*

The theological awkwardness of many Pentateuchal narratives for Second Temple Judaism can be perceived from the many ways the second-century B.C.E. *Book of Jubilees* alters the biblical story line while recounting it. The Pentateuch never mentions Jerusalem/Zion; *Jubilees* mentions it eight times (1:28 [3x]; 1:29 [2x]; 4:26; 8:19; 18:13). Already in its first chapter, *Jubilees* affirms the holiness of Zion and its eschatological role as a source of the new creation, elsewhere describing it as one of the four sacred places of the earth (4:26), the "center of the navel of the earth" (8:19), and the location of the *Aqedah* (Jub 18:13). Gerizim is never mentioned in *Jubilees*.

Jubilees does extensive "damage control" on the scandalous text Genesis 38, introducing the following changes to mitigate the effect on Judah's dignity:

1. Tamar is made a descendant of Aram (41:1), making her acceptable for marriage like fellow Aramaen women Rebekah, Leah and Rachel.
2. Er hates Tamar because he wants a Canaanite wife like his Canaanite mother, but (ironically) Jacob forbids Er to marry a Canaanite (41:2).
3. Tamar's marriages with Er and Onan were never consummated (41:27), leaving her a virgin when she conceives by Judah.
4. After the liaison with Tamar, Judah makes reparation through lament, confession, and earnest supplication, finally receiving forgiveness (41:23–25).
5. *Jubilees* holds in Judah's favor the fact that he intended to burn Tamar for her fornication (41:28), thus showing zeal for the law.
6. Readers of *Jubilees* are exhorted profusely *not* to follow Judah's example in sexual and marital matters (41:25–26).

Jubilees completely omits Jacob's blessing of Ephraim and Manasseh, and these two sons of Joseph are only mentioned once, in a brief genealogical notice (*Jub.* 44:24). Instead, *Jubilees* substitutes a narrative in which Jacob presents his two sons Levi and Judah to his father Isaac, who (in a scene clearly modeled on Genesis 48) bestows on these two an extensive priestly and royal blessing, respectively (*Jub.* 31:1–32). Levi is portrayed as already serving as a priest at the altar in Bethel (32:9), but later Jacob is warned not to build a temple at Bethel because it is "not the place" for an "eternal sanctuary" (32:22) despite all the valorization of it in Genesis.

Therefore, *Jubilees* reflects the discomfort Second Temple Judaism felt with many prominent features of the Pentateuch: the failure to mention Zion, Judah's scandalous sexual behavior, patriarchal worship at diverse shrines, and the emphasis on Joseph and the Josephite tribes. *Jubilees* is not the only text to display this discomfort. The LXX translation of Joshua relocates the scene of Joshua 24 in Shiloh, rather than Shechem, in what is almost certainly a Judean redaction aimed at reducing the legitimation that the Hexateuch provides for the Samaritan choice of Shechem/Gerizim as the place of the central sanctuary.[21] The Masoretic Text itself probably reflects an anti-Samaritan polemic in its reading of Ebal rather than Gerizim as the place for the altar used in the covenant solemnization ceremony specified in Deut 27:4 and Josh 8:30.[22] The authors of the Temple Scroll obviously felt compelled to compensate for the lack of Mosaic legitimation of the Jerusalem Temple in the Pentateuch by composing a new sacred document in which God reveals to Moses how the Jerusalem Temple should be built and operated. Thus, the author of *Jubilees* was not the only Second Temple scribe who felt the force of the Pentateuchal narrative as providing legitimation for the Samaritans.

4. Conclusion: The Problem of the Pro-Northern Bias of the Pentateuch

In this paper we have observed that the Common Pentateuch shows a pro-northern tendency to valorize Joseph and his descendants above those of Judah and his. In particular, the Pentateuch omits any mention of Jerusalem, Zion, or its temple, but does provide texts which support the cultic significance of Shechem. We may draw the following conclusions:

1. The attempt to read the Pentateuch as the redactional product of Second Temple Judean priests seeking to legitimize the Jerusalem Temple and its cult must be abandoned. Read in light of the polemical antagonism between Jerusalem and Gerizim beginning in the mid-fifth century B.C.E., the Common Pentateuch gives far too much support to the ideological claims of the Samarians/Samaritans to be the editorial product of their rivals to the south. In fact, at no time in history, from the Iron Age through the destruction of 70 C.E., would it ever have served the interests of the Jerusalem elite to promulgate a document like the Common Pentateuch, which valorizes Joseph and his descendants above Judah and his, and sanctifies the Shechem region with a noble sacred history while never once providing an unambiguous reference to Jerusalem.[23]

---

21 Laato, "Cult Site," 66; see also Hjelm, "Northern Perspectives," 188.
22 Kartveit, "Samaritan Temple," 91–93: "The change to 'Ebal' must have been made at the hands of Jews and could be a polemical alteration: an altar in the North was to be built on the mountain of curse. The conclusion is that the reading 'Gerizim' in Deut 27:4 is older than the reading 'Ebal' of the Masoretic Text (cf. BHQ)." See also Ulrich, "4QJosh[a]," 145; Abegg et al., *Dead Sea Scrolls Bible*, 201–202; Charlesworth, "Discovery," and "What is a Variant?"
23 As Hjelm, "Northern Perspectives," 202, puts it, "There is nothing Jerusalemite about the Pentateuch as such and were it not for tradition's assumption of a biblical Israel with a common past in which Jerusalem always had priority over against other Yahwistic cult centres in Palestine, no one would suggest that the Pentateuch had an origin in Jerusalem." Again, "Although

2. It is necessary to stop speaking of the Pentateuch as a Judean document that "accommodates" some northern traditions.[24] Rather, the Pentateuch is a predominantly northern document that accommodates some southern traditions. In fact, if only a single passage (Gen 49:8–10) were excised from the Pentateuch, Judah and the Judeans would be left without any pentateuchal justification for a claim to rival the role of Joseph within the idealized twelve-tribe nation of Israel. For this reason, too, it seems inappropriate to describe the Common Pentateuch as a "compromise" or "collaborative" project between Samarian and Judean interest groups, because there is no "compromise" present in the Pentateuch between Shechem and Jerusalem. Shechem, together with its mountains Gerizim and Ebal, plays a crucial and strategic role in the sacred narrative, while Jerusalem is never provided an unambiguous reference. If Samarians and Judeans did collaborate on the Pentateuch, all the compromise was on the part of the Judeans, and all the gain on the part of the Samarians. At best, the character of Judah is allowed to be rehabilitated after Genesis 38, but a limit is placed on his national leadership (Gen 49:10), and the primary inheritance is clearly to the descendants of Joseph (e.g. Gen 48), as we have seen.
3. Although the Common Pentateuch better supports the claims of the Samarians/Samaritans than those of the Judeans, in point of fact it shows no unambiguous evidence of an awareness of the controversy between these groups at all. If either group had redacted the Common Pentateuch from the time of the establishment of the rival Yahwistic sanctuary on Gerizim (c. 450 B.C.E.) on,[25] we would expect redactional elements that resolved the sanctuary controversy in one

---

Deuteronomy has an all Israel perspective, it nevertheless focuses on Shechem and Gerizim/Ebal ... which does not correspond well with an assumed origin in a Jerusalemite court at any time when looking at the book from a Pentateuchal perspective" (204).

24 E.g. Pummer, "Samaritans," 265: "The Pentateuch is accommodating toward the Samaritans ... besides Jerusalem traditions (Genesis 14, 22), traditions about Ebal and Gerizim are included." This is far too weak. It is remarkable that Pummer does not recognize the anti-Judean force of Genesis 38, for example. Furthermore, the Jerusalem connections with Genesis 14 and 22 are only indirect and of ambiguous significance, whereas the traditions concerning Shechem, Ebal, and Gerizim are explicit and forceful.

25 I follow Magnar Kartveit in seeing the *construction* of the Gerizim sanctuary (c. 450 B.C.E.) rather than its *destruction* (c. 111/112 B.C.E.) as marking the beginning of the Judean-Samaritan schism (Kartveit, "Samaritan Temple," 99). Since distinct Samaritan synagogues were being built around the Mediterranean rim by the second half of the third century B.C.E. (Pummer, "Samaritans," 239), a definite schism had already taken place prior to the destruction of the Gerizim Temple which prevented common prayer in shared synagogues. Indeed, the hatred of Samaritanism that motivated the destruction of their temple by John Hyrcanus presupposes the prior existence of a considerable animosity between the two groups. The effort to push the Judean-Samaritan schism back to the late second century B.C.E. is motivated (perhaps unconsciously) by a felt need to make space for a post-exilic (Jerusalem) Priestly redaction of the Pentateuch, itself an inheritance from Wellhausen's paradigm of pentateuchal composition. But Wellhausen's paradigm is based on principles (e.g. the prophets preceded the Law) which can no longer be defended (see n. 28 below).

direction or the other.[26] It is necessary, therefore, to look for the origin of the Common Pentateuch in the shared cultural traditions in an earlier (pre-exilic) period of the history of Israel and Judah.[27] This would agree well with the mounting evidence that the exilic prophetic books (Ezekiel, Jeremiah, Second Isaiah, and others) already knew and drew upon various pentateuchal texts and traditions.[28]

---

[26] The sanguine notion advanced by some that the priesthoods of the two groups collaborated on producing a Common Pentateuch regrettably overlooks the facts that (1) it is unrealistic to imagine the Judean priesthood conceding as much to northern interests as the Common Pentateuch actually does, and (2) a strong and explicit pro-Zion perspective dominates nearly all the Judean literature from the exilic, post-exilic, and Second Temple periods, among which we may mention Ezekiel, Jeremiah, Lamentations, Second and Third Isaiah, Daniel, Joel, Micah, Zephaniah, Zechariah, Amos, Obadiah, the Psalms, the Deuteronomistic History, the Chronicler, Sirach, *Jubilees*, the *Testament of the Twelve Patriarchs*, the Temple Scroll, and others. Scholars need clearly to confront the issue of whether it is realistic to think that the Jerusalem priesthood was selling out the exclusive claims of Zion in order to construct a Common Pentateuch with the leadership of Gerizim, at the very same time that the rest of religiously observant Judeans were studying, copying, redacting, or writing all these other pro-Zion sacred texts. Then, having produced the Zion-less Common Pentateuch in collaboration with the Samarians, the Jerusalem priesthood would somehow have convinced all those loyal to the pro-Zion sacred texts to accept this new Torah as the revealed Scriptures *par excellence*. Thus, scholars who argue for a Second Temple Judean-Samaritan "compromise Pentateuch" need to explain the absence of Jerusalem/Zion from the text, and provide a plausible means by which all branches of Second Temple Judaism could have been persuaded to accept a new, Zion-less sacred document as the foundation of their religion.

[27] Cf. Pummer, "Samaritans," 263: "Given the shared culture and longstanding substantial contacts, then, there is no reason that the interactions between the two communities should not have included participation in the development of some of the narrative and legal traditions that came to constitute the Pentateuch," and "the fall of the Northern Kingdom in the eighth century B.C.E. would have brought about a more concentrated effort to preserve the common patrimony ... in writing," quoting Blenkinsopp, *Pentateuch*, 234. Thus, Pummer seems to favor the late eighth century as a possible time for the compilation of much of the Pentateuch. But by this time, Zion theology was already well-established, even dominant, in Judah, and it is difficult to imagine the Jerusalemite priesthood cooperating with the composition of a sacred document that had the potential to undermine or delegitimize the choice of Zion as the place of the primary national sanctuary. The narrative shape of the common Pentateuch seems to demand a time of promulgation when there was a spirit of Israelite unity under Josephite primacy, before the rise of Zion theology. Obviously this is far removed from most current proposals, which generally pay inadequate attention to the implications of the narrative shape of the Pentateuch (and Hexateuch) as a whole.

[28] On Ezekiel's use of the *Torah*, see Levitt Kohn, *New Heart*, and Lyons, *From Law to Prophecy*. On Jeremiah's, see Rom-Shiloni, "Compositional Harmonization," Fischer, "Relationship," and Gile, "Deuteronomic Influence." On Second Isaiah's, see Sommer, *Prophet Reads Scripture*.

Bibliography

Abegg, Martin, Peter Flint, and Eugene Ulrich. *The Dead Sea Scrolls Bible*. San Francisco: Harper, 1999.

Amit, Yairah. "Shechem in Deuteronomy: A Seemingly Hidden Polemic," in *History, Memory, Hebrew Scriptures: A Festschrift for Ehud Ben Zvi*. Edited by Ian Douglas Wilson and Diana V. Edelman. Winona Lake: Eisenbrauns, 2015, 3–13.

Charlesworth, James H. "The Discovery of an Unknown Dead Sea Scroll: The Original Text of Deuteronomy 27?" [http://blogs.owu.edu/magazine/the-discovery-of-an-unknown-dead-sea-scroll-the-original-text-of-deuteronomy-27/].

—. "What is a variant?: Announcing a Dead Sea Scrolls Fragment of Deuteronomy." *Maarav* 16 (2009): 201–212, 273–274.

Edenburg, Cynthia and Reinhard Müller. "A Northern Provenance for Deuteronomy?: A Critical Review." *Hebrew Bible and Ancient Israel* 4.2 (2015): 148–161.

Fischer, Georg. "ותפשי התורה לא ידעוני – The Relationship of the Book of Jeremiah to the Torah," in *The Formation of the Pentateuch. Bridging the Academic Cultures of Europe, Israel, and North America*. Edited by Jan C. Gertz, et al. FAT 111. Tübingen: Mohr, 2016, 891–911.

Gile, Jason. "Deuteronomic Influence on the Book of Ezekiel." Ph.D. diss., Wheaton College, Ill., 2013.

Hjelm, Ingrid. "Northern Perspectives in Deuteronomy and its relation to the Samaritan Pentateuch." *Hebrew Bible and Ancient Israel* 4.2 (2015): 184–204.

Hjelm, Ingrid. "Lost and Found? A Non-Jewish Israel from the Merneptah Stele to the Byzantine Period," in *History, Archeology, and the Bible Forty Years after "Historicity."* Edited by Ingrid Hjelm and Thomas Thompson. Changing Perspectives 6. London: Routledge, Taylor & Francis Group, 2016, 112–129.

Kartveit, Magnar. "The Samaritan Temple and Rewritten Bible," in *Holy Places and Cult*. Edited by Erkki Koskenniemi and J. Cornelis de Vos. Studies in the Reception History of the Bible 5. Winona Lake: Eisenbrauns, 2014, 85–99.

Knoppers, Gary. *Jews and Samaritans: The Origins and History of their Early Relations*. New York: Oxford University Press, 2013.

—. "When the Foreign Monarch Speaks about the Israelite Tabernacle," in *History, Memory, Hebrew Scriptures: A Festschrift for Ehud Ben Zvi*. Edited by Ian Douglas Wilson and Diana V. Edelman. Winona Lake: Eisenbrauns, 2015, 49–63.

—. "The Northern Context of the Law-Code in Deuteronomy." *Hebrew Bible and Ancient Israel* 4.2 (2015): 162–183.

Laato, Antti. "The Cult Site on Mount Ebal: A Biblical Tradition Rewritten and Reinterpreted," in *Holy Places and Cult*. Edited by Erkki Koskenniemi and J. Cornelis de Vos. Studies in the Reception History of the Bible 5. Winona Lake: Abo Akademi University/Eisenbrauns, 2014, 51–84.

Levine, Baruch. *Numbers 1–20: A New Translation with Introduction and Commentary*. Anchor Bible 4. New York: Doubleday, 1993.

Levitt Kohn, Risa. *A New Heart and a New Soul: Ezekiel, the Exile, and the Torah*. JSOTSup 358. Sheffield: Sheffield Academic, 2002.

Lyons, Michael A. *From Law to Prophecy: Ezekiel's Use of the Holiness Code*. LHB/OTS 507. New York/London: T & T Clark, 2009.

Nihan, Christoph. *From Priestly Torah to Pentateuch: A Study in the Composition of the Book of Leviticus*. FAT² 25. Tübingen: Mohr Siebeck, 2007.

Nodet, Etienne. *A Search for the Origins of Judaism: From Joshua to the Mishnah*. Translated by Ed Crowley. JSOTSup 248. Sheffield: Sheffield Academic Press, 1997.

Pummer, Reinhard. "The Samaritans and Their Pentateuch," in *The Pentateuch as Torah: New Models for Understanding Its Promulgation and Acceptance*. Edited by Gary N. Knoppers and Bernard M. Levinson. Winona Lake: Eisenbrauns, 2007, 237–69.

Rom-Shiloni, Dalit. "Compositional Harmonization—Priestly and Deuteronomic References in the Book of Jeremiah—An Earlier Stage of a Recognized Interpretive Technique," in *The Formation of the Pentateuch. Bridging the Academic Cultures of Europe, Israel, and North America*. Edited by Jan C. Gertz, *et al*. FAT 111. Tübingen: Mohr, 2016, 913–941.

Sarna, Nahum. *The JPS Torah Commentary: Genesis*. Philadelphia: Jewish Publication Society, 1989.

Ska, Jean Louis. "Why Does the Pentateuch Speak so Much of Torah and so Little of Jerusalem?" in *The Fall of Jerusalem and the Rise of the Torah*. Edited by Peter Dubovsky, Dominik Markl, and Jean-Pierre Sonnet. FAT 107. Tübingen: Mohr Siebeck, 2016, 113–128.

Sommer, Benjamin. *A Prophet Reads Scripture: Allusion in Isaiah 40–66*. Stanford: Stanford University Press, 1997.

Ulrich, Eugene. "4QJosh[a]," in *Qumran Cave 4: IX: Deuteronomy, Joshua, Judges, Kings*. Edited by Eugene Ulrich *et al*. DJD 14. Oxford: Clarendon, 1995, 145–146.

Zevit, Ziony. "Deuteronomy and the Temple: An Exercise in Historical Imagining," in Mishneh Todah: Studies in Deuteronomy and Its Cultural Environment in Honor of Jeffrey H. Tigay. Edited by N. S. Fox, D. A. Glatt-Gilad, and M. J. Williams. Winona Lake, IN: Eisenbrauns, 2009, 201–218.

What's Money Got to Do with It?

Economics and the Question of the Provenance of Deuteronomy in the Neo-Babylonian and Persian Periods

Sandra Richter (Westmont College)

1. Preliminaries

This essay is dedicated to the age-old question of the social location(s) of the Book of Deuteronomy. As first addressed in "The Question of Provenance and the Economics of Deuteronomy," the culturally embedded economic features of the book have much to teach us regarding its provenance.[1] And whereas the usual reconstructions of *Urdeuteronomium* champion either the Hezekian or Josian political reforms set amidst the ongoing threat of the Neo-Assyrian Empire, the mechanisms of production, consumption and distribution inhabiting the book argue convincingly against either of these scenarios. Rather, the economic assumptions of the Book of Deuteronomy indicate that the best social location for *Urdeuteronomium* is the rural and isolated village life of the Central Hill Country – most specifically the expanding subsistence and reciprocal economy of the late Iron I/Iron IIA eras.[2] But as others have hypothesized that the largely barter-based, smallholder economy assumed in the book is best read as an exilic or post-exilic utopian work of imagination,[3] or as newer paradigms propose, a reflection of the Persian-period Judean/Samarian journey toward synthesis and compromise,[4] this current essay is dedicated to once again exploring *Urdeuteronomium* (roughly defined here as Deut 4:44–27:26[5]) via an economic lens. But this time the focus is on the Babylonian and Persian periods. I will first summarize the economies of the Hill Country during the Iron Age in order

---

1 Richter, "Question," 23–50. As the venerable Alfred Marshall states, economics provides us with a window into "the ordinary business of life" and therefore, as a discipline, "is on one side a study of wealth; and on the other, and more important side, a part of the study of man" (Marshall, *Principles*, 1).
2 Richter, "Question," 23–50.
3 Lohfink, *Studien*, 305–323; Crüsemann, " Bundesbuch," 29–30; Levinson, *Deuteronomy*, 50–52.135–136; Hölscher, "Komposition," 161–255; and Pakkala, "Date," 392–435.
4 See Knoppers, *Jews*; Nihan, "Torah".
5 Deuteronomy 27 is not typically included in *Urdeuteronomium*, and 28 often is. For my rationale see Richter, "Place of the Name," 342–366.

to establish the economic criterion for our discussion, and then survey the archaeologically reconstructed picture of the economies of the southern Levant in the Babylonian and Persian periods. Having identified and diagnosed the features of the Babylonian and Persian period economies in rural and urban areas in the southern Levant, we will then juxtapose these economic realities with the economic setting(s) assumed and portrayed in *Urdeuteronomium*. In this essay the role of *currency*, and its use in trade and taxation will play a critical role.

2. The Economy of the Central Hill Country in the Iron Age (c. 1200–586 BCE)[6]

The mechanisms by which a household, polity, or empire obtains wealth are essential to daily life and have distinct consequences for individuals on every level of society. As a result, it is wholly predictable that these mechanisms will appear in the literary artifacts of a society as well.[7] Archaeologically, these mechanisms may be tracked via material remains. Grinding stones, storage silos, faunal remains and carbonized seeds all speak to local production and consumption. Wineries, apiaries, and olive oil installations together with their written receipts of exchange help to map out distribution and trade. Booty and tribute lists and the final resting place of artifacts identify trade networks. During the Iron I (c. 1200–980 BCE[8]), the archaeologically reconstructed picture of the Central Hill Country demonstrates that the dominant economy was a village-based, subsistence economy, characterized by a mixture of pastoralism and diversified agriculture, and dependent on the limited patrimony of the often fragile extended family. The mechanisms for exchange in this era were poorly developed. Rather, the management of the household in order to diversify risk and optimize labor for the sake of survival was the preeminent concern of these Hill Country settlers. Minimal permanent architecture was present, and

---

6   Exactly when the transitions between the Iron I and Iron IIA, B, and C periods occur is debated. Much diversity emerges from regional distinctions, the scholars who specialize in those regions, and equally diverse approaches to cultural development. The transition from the Iron I to the Iron IIA is particularly difficult (see Finkelstein, "Archaeology Archaeology of the United Monarchy," 177–187; idem., "Stratigraphy," 170–184). This essay assumes Mazar's "Modified Conventional Chronology", affirming that the Iron IIA launches in c. 980 BCE and endures for approximately 150 years (see Ben-Tor and Zarzecki-Peleg, "Iron Age IIA-B," and Mazar, "From 1200 to 850 B.C.E."). The transition into the Iron IIC occurs in the north/Israel several decades before it occurs in Judah (see Gilboa, "Iron Age IIC: Northern Coast, Carmel Coast, Galilee, and Jezreel Valley," 301–344, and Gitin "Iron Age IIC: Judah," 345–366).
7   See Dever, "Bible," 1–22.
8   See note 7.

defense systems appear only toward the end of the period.[9] Metal of all sorts was scarce.[10] Thus, exchange was largely barter-based and non-monetary, and limited redistribution was facilitated by means of local social agencies (e.g., cult sites).[11] Silver as currency was present in the southern Levant, but extant hoards are limited to the great sea ports of Ashkelon (12th cent.) and Dor (11th–10th cents.), and the land trade centers of Bet Shean (12th–11th cent.) and Megiddo (11th cent.).[12] This distribution is understood to be the direct result of the growing trade relationship between the Arabian Desert caravans and the Phoenician port cities.[13] Hence, although *Hacksilber* as currency is moving through the southern Levant in the Iron I and early Iron IIA as a result of trade, taxes and tolls, the avenues of trade were such that it was moving *around* the Central Hill Country.

The Iron II period (980–732/701 BCE) sees significant population growth, agricultural intensification, and most importantly the onset of centralized power in the Central Hill Country. With the resulting mechanisms of redistribution (taxation and corvée labor in particular), surplus assets abound and public works proliferate: villages and cities are fortified; public storage buildings and water systems are constructed; and monumental architecture blossoms in urban centers.[14] Industrial production centers appear and multiply. Trade networks are secured and expanded as evinced by permanent markets, foreign goods, and the expansion of urban centers.[15] Most striking is that currency becomes the common medium of exchange—the "natural repercussion of a politically powerful center."[16] Whereas "low value" money such as grain or livestock could (and had) functioned efficiently in the local, non-monetized exchange of goods typical to the reciprocal economy of the Iron I, the broadly based, redistributive economy of the emerging Iron II required a fungible medium of exchange—silver.[17] The "bound silver" (Hebrew *ṣror késep*) collected from the Judahite citizenry for Jehoash's temple repair fund in 2 Kgs 12:9–

---

9 Richter, "Question," 26–29; cf. Meyers, "Family," 1–47; Faust, *Archaeology,* 7–27.145–151.255; Bloch-Smith and Nakhai, "Landscape," 62–92; Hopkins, "Life," 178–91; Rosen, "Subsistence Economy," 339–351.
10 Rosen, "Subsistence Economy," 343–346.
11 Finkelstein, *Archaeology of Israelite Settlement*, 205–234.
12 See Thompson, "Sealed Silver," 84 and 97–98, table 2 and appendix for the full list of sites and finds. Nava Panitz-Cohen adds to this list a small private hoard from 13th century Abel Beth Maacah (Panitz-Cohen et al., "Silver Lining," 22–23).
13 The two inter-related systems of long-distance trade in the Iron Age southern Levant were the shipping fleets of Phoenicia ("the Mediterranean 'superhighway'") and the camel caravans of the Arabian Peninsula (See Master, "Institutions," 501 and idem, "Economy," 20; Holladay, "Hezekiah's Tribute," 325–328; Younger, "Assyrian Economic Impact," 179–204; Eph'al, *Ancient Arabs*; and Walton, "Regional Economy," 281–284.
14 Richter, "Question," 29–32.
15 Master, "Economy," 81–97, n. 25; cf. Nam, *Portrayals,* 118–122.
16 Nam, *Portrayals,* 127.
17 Richter, "Question," 31–35.

10,[18] and the five separate descriptions of bullion-based tribute paid out by Israelite and Judean kings to foreign powers between 925 and 769 BCE make it clear that Iron II Israel and Judah were operating within a currency-based economy.[19]

With the Iron IIC period (c. 732/701–586 BCE[20]) Israel and Judah are incorporated into a world economy of "unparalleled economic specialization."[21] Catalyzed by a rapidly expanding Phoenician trade network and the rise of the Neo-Assyrian Empire, the result in the southern Levant was massive growth in Mediterranean maritime commerce, foreign sponsorship of local production, industrialization, and export.[22] This increasingly complex international economy is characterized by an official silver sale-weight system. *Hacksilber* and pre-portioned ingots were the standard medium of exchange, weighed out upon scales for local commerce (e.g. Micah 6:9–13 and Zeph 1:11),[23] bagged and bound for larger projects and purchases (e.g. Josiah's temple repair funds in 2 Kgs 22:1–6), or transported in enormous quantities as the internationally recognized vehicle for commerce and reparation (e.g. Menahem of Israel's tribute to Tiglath-pilesar III in 2 Kgs 15:19–20).[24] *Coinage* will not appear in Syria-Palestine until the 6th century.[25]

3. The Babylonian Period (604–539 BCE)

With the sixth century Judah suffers a tremendous blow in the aftermath of the Babylonian conquest. Urban centers were decimated such that Jerusalem and its environs appear to have been completely uninhabited.[26] Of the fifty late Iron Age rural sites excavated in Judah, only seven show possible continuity into the Persian pe-

---

18 Thompson, "Sealed Silver," 67–107. Thiele dates Jehoash of Judah to 835–796 BCE (Thiele, *Mysterious Numbers*, 217).
19 See Holladay, "How Much Is That In ...?," 207–222, especially Table 2.
20 See n. 7.
21 Nam, *Portrayals,* 130. See Walton, " Regional Economy."
22 See Richter, "Question," 35–38.
23 See Thompson, "Sealed Silver," 71–80 for images and descriptions; Master, "Institutions," 512–14 as well as Master, "Economy," 90–93; cf. Radner, "Money," 129.
24 Holladay notes that by Menahem's reign in the latter half of the 8th century it was apparently possible for an Israelite king to expeditiously assess one Mesopotamian *mina* of silver from *every* extended family in the Northern Kingdom: "there must already have been some established fail-safe system for gathering up and forwarding large quantities of wealth reliably to Samaria" (see Holladay, "How Much Is That In ...?", 212). Holladay concludes that bullion was the expected medium of tribute in the Neo-Assyrian period (Holladay, "Hezekiah's Tribute," 311–313).
25 See Betlyon, "Coinage," 1079–1084. For an updated discussion regarding the Southern Levant and Hill country see Zlotnik, "Samarian Coin Types" and Gitler and Tal, "Reclassifying Persian-Period Philistian Coins."
26 Lipschits, "Demographic Changes," 365. Cf. Stern, *Archaeology*, 309–310.

riod.[27] Lipschits reports that the settled area in Judah between the seventh and fifth centuries BCE declines by approximately 70%; the number of settlements decline by 83.5%; and the population declines by more than 70%.[28] In the words of Avraham Faust, this is a "post-collapse society" in which war and deportation has led to famine, disease, looting, and flight.[29] Master states, "[b]y the second quarter of the sixth century, most regions of Judah were virtually empty."[30] Indeed, the Babylonian conquest followed by its imperial absenteeism brought this "once-flourishing country to one of the lowest ebbs in its long history."[31] The resulting collapse of local infrastructure, kinship networks, state administration, and international trade left Judah and the remains of Israel a profoundly altered society. And although recent scholarship has attempted to substantiate a model of continuity as regards population and lifestyle,[32] the only real potential for such continuity is Benjamin in which the urban sector in particular remained largely intact.[33] Tell en-Naṣbeh (biblical Mizpah) became and remained the Neo-Babylonian provincial capital.[34] It is generally accepted that this site survived the 586 BCE destruction, and quite likely continued to function into the Persian period—although some decline (possibly after the assassination of the Neo-Babylonian governor Gedaliah reported in 2 Kgs 25:22–26; Jer 40–41) is evident.[35] The cities of biblical Gibeon, Bethel (Beîtin), and Gibeah (Tel el-Ful) show at least partial continued occupation beyond the Babylonian destruction of Jerusalem.[36] But Beîtin and Tel el-Ful, which offer the best-excavated picture of the region for this period, dramatically decline (or are destroyed and abandoned) as

---

27 Faust, *Judah*, 33–72.244.
28 Lipschits, "Demographic Changes," 332.355–357.364.
29 Faust, *Judah*, 167–180.
30 Master, "Comments on Oded Lipschits," 31–32.
31 Stern, *Archaeology*, 303. Stern states that "the most prominent feature left by seventy years of Babylonian domination in Palestine was the total destruction and devastation of all the main cities that had flourished during the Assyrian period" (ibid., 309).
32 See Carroll, "Myth," 79–93 and Barstad, *Myth*. Barstad categorically states: "The Judean state was then replaced with a Neo-Babylonian state. This would have but little effect on national production in Judah, where life fairly soon would have 'returned to normal'" (Barstad, "After the 'Myth of the Empty Land'," 3–4).
33 Betlyon, "A People Transformed," 6; cf. ibid., 23–26; Faust, *Judah*, 228–230. Stern hypothesizes that the governors of the previously Assyrian provinces transferred their loyalty to the Babylonians without resistance and therefore no conquest and no destruction resulted (Stern, *Archaeology*, 319).
34 Zorn, "Tell en-Naṣbeh," 415–445. Interestingly, whereas in the past the Phoenician coastal cities were preserved and protected for the sake of ongoing Mediterranean trade for whomever the new overlord might be, Faust states that "the long domination of Phoenicia (Tyre) in Mediterranean trade and its hegemony over the Phoenician colonies in the west came to an abrupt end during the first half of the sixth century, and many Phoenician colonies declined or were even abandoned" (Faust, *Judah*, 245; cf. 88–92).
35 Zorn, "Tell en-Naṣbeh," 415–445.
36 Blenkinsopp, "Bethel," 95–97; cf. Lipschits, "Demographic Changes," 346–355.

early as the second half of the sixth century.[37] The complete absence of Greek pottery in the region (pottery which circulated in large quantities around the entire Mediterranean during the sixth century BCE), indicates a catastrophic economic decline commencing just at the beginning of the Neo-Babylonian period.[38] Faust summarizes that "the Babylonians came to the west to sack, not to invest."[39] And although we can assume that surely thousands of people continued to live in some fashion in sixth-century Judah, particularly in territory of Benjamin,[40] the larger consensus is that these scattered survivors did not constitute intact families nor did they "form an organized society."[41] Rather, we are probably looking at squatters living amid the ruins of collapsed urban centers supported by subsistence level, diversified agriculture. Vanderhooft and Faust argue that the Babylonians, unlike the Assyrians, did not install any sort of effective imperial administration in the region, leaving the surviving Judeans with little infrastructure.[42] Moreover, as the Babylonians did not practice cross-deportation (transferring foreign populations into recently conquered territories), the mid-sixth century in Palestine is "characterized by sharp, if not total, demographic decline," one devoid of either local or imperial administrative structure.[43] Blenkinsopp attempts to find in this landscape, an operating (and unifying) central cult site. He proposes that the old Bethel sanctuary "obtained a new lease on life" by virtue of the destruction of the Jerusalem temple and Bethel's proximity to the Neo-Babylonian provincial capital at Mizpah; and argues that Bethel became the "official sanctuary of Judah, Benjamin, and perhaps also the central hill country" until at least 518 BCE.[44] He notes the prophetic texts of Jer 41:4–5; Zech 7:1–7; Hag 2:10–14 as potentially indicative of cult activity at Bethel

---

37 Contra Lipschits: Master, "Comments on Oded Lipschits," 31–32; cf. Faust, *Judah*, 73–92.
38 Faust, *Judah*, 188–193.245.
39 Ibid. 191.
40 Blenkinsopp summarizes "after the catastrophe of 586 BCE the center of gravity, politically, socially, and I believe, religiously, moved decisively northward from the Judean heartland to the region corresponding to the tribal territory of Benjamin" (Blenkinsopp, "Bethel," 96). Although not as optimistic as Blenkinsopp, Stern concludes that the region probably became a "haven for some of the refugees from other parts of Judah (Stern, *Archaeology*, 322). Master concludes, however, that even in Benjamin, "the sequences do not, at this time, support the contention that substantial portions of the Iron Age population continued unchanged into the fifth century," and the archaeological evidence is that all these cities in the territory of Benjamin were laid waste in approximately 480 BCE by as of yet unknown causes (Master, "Comments on Oded Lipschits," 32; Stern, *Archaeology*, 322).
41 "The Iron Age *bet av* and *mišpāhâ* ... became a thing of the past" (Faust, *Judah*, 9–10 n. 19; 234.248).
42 Vanderhooft states that the Neo-Babylonian royal inscriptions offer no evidence of any sort of coherent Babylonian administrative presence in the land of Judah after 586 BCE (Vanderhooft, *Neo-Babylonian Empire,* 235–262). Faust concurs: "There is currently not a single piece of evidence to indicate any form of organized political life during most of the Neo-Babylonian period" (Faust, *Judah*, 233).
43 Vanderhooft, "Babylonian Strategies," 247.256.
44 Blenkinsopp, "Bethel," 99.101.

during the Neo-Babylonian period (Zech 7:1–7 clearly being the most compelling). But even Blenkinsopp must conclude that the picture he is painting is unclear and at this point the evidence is far less than commanding.[45] Indeed, although it is broadly accepted that the city and its shrine were rebuilt toward the close of the 7th century BCE, Finkelstein indicates that the late 7th century BCE Bethel "was small and probably sparsely settled."[46] And whereas the excavators claimed that the site continued without interruption until the mid- or late-6th century BCE, Finkelstein counters that no unambiguous evidence indicates either a Neo-Babylonian or "full-fledged Persian-period" occupation.[47] Rather, "[e]vidence for activity at Bethel in the Babylonian, Persian and early Hellenistic period is very meager, if it exists at all."[48] Thus, the "closed economy" of the sixth century in the northern arena of the Central Hill Country in which the remaining Judahite populace returned to a simple, subsistence economy founded upon diversified agriculture with little to no outside economic contact could reflect that found in Deuteronomy. But the dispersion of the 586 BCE survivors throughout the region; the collapse of the *bêt 'āb* and larger kinship systems which created functioning villages and community-wide infrastructure, and most importantly, the lack of any known operating cult site as a center for in-kind based taxation and redistribution belies any real comparison with the economy assumed and portrayed in the Book of Deuteronomy.

4. The Persian Period (539–332 BCE)

When Cyrus the Great conquered Babylon in 539 BCE, the international policies of the new empire facilitated the resettling of the Judean exiles in Palestine. The post-collapse processes of the Syrian hinterland had permanently altered the identity of the surviving Judeans in "Beyond the River,"[49] and the Babylonian exile had equally transformed the profile of the returning refugees. But with (some of) the assets and authority of the newest empire at their disposal, the region began the slow process of reconstructing the infrastructure characteristic of an organized society. For the returning Judeans, this process included the daunting task of rebuilding the war-torn remains of Jerusalem and its environs with limited man power and resources; nearly

---

45 Ibid., 101.
46 Finkelstein and Singer-Avitz, "Reevaluating Bethel," 41; cf. Kelso, "Bethel," 192–194 and Stern, *Archaeology*, 321.
47 Finkelstein and Singer-Avitz, "Reevaluating Bethel," 42–43, cf. Table 1.
48 Ibid., 45. Stern concurs: "there are no sanctuaries or cult objects that can securely be attributed to the Babylonian period." (Stern, *Archaeology*, 347).
49 The appellative "Beyond the River" (Hebrew *'ēber hanāhār*) for the region of Palestine was derived from Assyrian administrative parceling of the region, known from at least the time of Esarhaddon (Stern, *Archaeology*, 366).

constant conflict with neighboring Samaritans, Ashdodites, Edomites, and Arabs; and the fact that the kinship structure that had preserved the economic and social well-being of Israel throughout the vagaries of the Iron Age was now profoundly altered as well.[50]

In place of the collapsed social and economic lifeways of the Iron Age and the economic vacuum of the post 586 BCE Neo-Babylonian period the imperial administration of Darius I emerged. Twenty Persian satrapies with their federally appointed governors, an imperial road and postal system defended by numerous fortified installations, a centrally administrated army, and a new system of tax collection will become the backdrop of the post-exilic, Judean narrative. Almost all of the resulting sites in Palestine have at least two major phases of occupation: early Persian, dating from 539-450 BCE; and late Persian, dating from 450-332/331 BCE.[51] In this mix, "Yehud was but one of about ten small administrative units that comprised Abar-nahara, a satrapy so large that it included at times the island of Cyprus as well as all those lands from just south of Cilicia in the north to the Negev in the south."[52]

Predictably, economic recovery occurs first along the Mediterranean coast—catalyzed by the empire's redeployment of the maritime expertise of the Phoenicians. As a result, Phoenician-influenced, Persian period occupational debris is extensive.[53] Acco evinces impressive administrative and commercial remains, and at least thirty-seven sites south of the Carmel range show Persian-period occupation: "[e]very conceivable place along the coast that could support an anchorage appears to have been utilized."[54] The Philistine cities of Ashdod, Ashkelon, and especially Gaza were clearly critical way stations within the Persian economic network and saw tremendous growth.[55] Sites located near these commercial centers and their well-

---

50 Vanderhooft states that the terms *mišpāhâ* and *bêt 'āb* has been redefined in the Chronicler's history identifying seismic changes to the Iron Age patriarchal system of Israelite society. Rather than identifying patrimonial identity, the *mišpāhâ* is now associated with "guilds," and the membership of the *bêt 'āb* is altered as well. Archaeologically this is evinced by the absence of the four-room pillared house and the group burials of the standard Judahite tomb (Vanderhooft, "The Israelite *Mišpaha*," 490–491). As Faust states: "When the *bet av* and the *mišpaha* dissolved, so did their archaeological correlates (*Judah*, 108).

51 Following the loss at Marathon and the great Egyptian revolts, Persia began focusing its attention on fortifying its western provinces and solidifying its relationship with the local populations by sponsoring and protecting industrial installations and local towns and cities. One result was the construction of fortresses in and along all major population centers and trade routes in ca. 460–440 BCE (Betlyon, "A People Transformed," 7.52).

52 Betlyon, "A People Transformed," 6.

53 Stager, *Ashkelon Discovered,* 23; cf. Stern, *Archaeology*, 370–372.379–422.

54 Betlyon, "A People Transformed," 31.

55 Although much of this vitality is attributed to Phoenician penetration, Stern goes on to note that Gaza also demonstrates strong Arabic influence, this city being the terminal port of all Arabian trade. Moreover, the Persians utilized these "Qedarite" tribal groups to protect the trade routes coming off the desert. In return, the Persian Empire granted them certain exemptions from taxation, and collected their taxes "in kind" as opposed to in currency (Stern, *Archaeology*, 407–

trafficked trade routes thrived under the Persian Empire as well.[56] The numerous Persian military and administrative installations designed to protect this trade network also prospered. Settlements designed to guard the coastal highway, gather taxes, administer infrastructure, and manage regional agricultural production saw a tremendous increase in settlement and local economic growth (e.g. Lachish, Tell Jemmeh, Tel Haror, Beer Sheba, and Tel Seraʻ).[57]

As regards the Hill Country, the Persian-period finds in Samaria and Wadi ed-Daliyeh indicate that Samaria was "one of the most important [cities] in Palestine" during the Persian period. Although the architectural remains of the Persian period city were apparently obliterated in the Hellenistic conquest and Herodian and Roman rebuilding, it is now clear that Samaria served as the local political and redistributive center for the now Persian province of Samaria, a role further illustrated by the fourth century "Samaria" and "Nablus" hoards.[58] The nearly 250 sites catalogued in the Samaria district with Persian-period pottery (particularly its western reaches) further illustrate the widespread Persian military and economic influence in the Province as well as its connection to the burgeoning Persian investments in Mediterranean trade.[59]

In the province of Judah, however, Persian occupational debris is nearly non-existent.[60] In the hill country we find a "marked process of attenuation of urban life" demonstrated by a lack of architectural remains, local power structures, and population.[61] Rather, throughout most of the Persian period, Palestine may be distinguished into two major economic zones. The first being the large, wealthy urban centers along the Mediterranean coast; the second, the rural and agricultural lifestyle of the hill country. Whereas the Assyrians had facilitated the expansion of their own coffers by encouraging the development of the Hill Country urban centers, the archaeological record demonstrates that "[n]either the Babylonians nor the Persians had any interest in encouraging and developing urban centers in the rural hilly regions on both sides of the Jordan."[62] Hence, along the coast we find grand, well-built, even Hippodamian cities characterized by wide-scale Phoenician influence, but in the hill

---

420; cf. Rainey and Notley, *Sacred Bridge*, 281).
56 Lipschits, "Achaemenid Imperial Policy," 26–29.
57 Betlyon, "A People Transformed," 9–14.51.
58 See Richter, "Archaeology," 304–337; cf. Stern, *Archaeology*, 422–428. The Samaria and Nablus hoards include 182 Samarian minted coins and silver jewelry (buried in 352 and 331 BCE respectively) (Stern, "A Persian-Period Hoard of Bullae from Samaria," 421–422). Metallurgical data further demonstrates that there was a high level of continuity in the production technology of all these pieces, probably indicating that the smiths were trained in the same workshop. Thus, it would seem that this technology was advanced and centralized (Ashkenazi et al., "Metallurgical Investigation").
59 Betlyon, "A People Transformed," 29.
60 Stager, *Ashkelon Discovered*, 23; cf. Stern, *Archaeology*, 370–372.379–422.
61 Lipschits, "Achaemenid Imperial Policy," 28.
62 Lipschits, "Achaemenid Imperial Policy," 26–29.

country we find little urban life.⁶³ Lipschits and others attribute this archaeological picture in part to two centuries of warfare and deportations, and in part to the region's continuing value to the empire as agricultural production areas.⁶⁴ The argument is that the only perceived economic value of the hill country in the Persian Period was to (1) utilize the land as fiefdoms gifted to Persian-approved officials such that rent and *ilku*-service might be collected; and (2) the collection of taxes to fuel the empire.⁶⁵ This testimony regarding the hill country in the early Persian period (539–450 BCE) is confirmed by Nehemiah's outcry regarding "the king's tax" (מִדַּה הַמֶּלֶךְ, Neh 5:4), and the corruption of the "former governors" in "the land of Judah" (פַּחוֹת, Neh 5:14–15; cf. 2:7, 9; 3:7).⁶⁶ As regards Jerusalem itself, it remained a small and sparsely populated city with scant architectural remains until the middle of the fifth century when the city's fortifications were restored and it became the *bîrâ* (capital) of Yehud.⁶⁷ As Stern reports, although the Persian stratum of Jerusalem is poorly preserved, the large quantity of small finds representing the entire range of known jar handle impressions from the era (and naming satraps such as Ahazai and Hananiah), indicate that Jerusalem was also inculcated into the Persian economic system.⁶⁸

Several exceptions to the somewhat vacuous picture of urban centers in Persian period Yehud include Tell en-Naṣbeh (see above), Nebi Samwil, Beth Zur, and Ramat Raḥel.⁶⁹ Recent publications indicate that Ramat Raḥel's role as a Neo-Assyrian royal administrative center continued into the Persian period.⁷⁰ The most compelling evidence for this ongoing identity is the more than 300 stamped jar impressions bearing the name *yhwd* which span the 6th–2nd centuries.⁷¹ The excavators conclude "that during the Persian and early Hellenistic periods the palace at Ramat

---

63 Lipschits, "Achaemenid Imperial Policy," 27–28. Tal notes activity at the fortress and agricultural estate of Har Adar and the agricultural estates of Qalandīya and Aderet (Tal, "Pottery," 266).
64 Lipschits, "Achaemenid Imperial Policy," 28.
65 See Fried, "Exploitation", 149–162; cf. Lipschits, "Achaemenid Imperial Policy," 30.
66 Betlyon, "A People Transformed," 51.
67 The agreement of the Persians to build fortifications in Jerusalem and to alter the status of the city to the capital of the province was the most dramatic change in the history of the city after the Babylonian destruction in 586" (Lipschits, "Achaemenid Imperial Policy," 41). Yet even with this dramatic transition, "at least until the 2nd century B.C.E., the settlement in Judah remained static; there was no strengthening of urban life" (Lipschits, "Rural Economy," 237). Few settlements in the Persian-period hill country were fortified with perimeters walls; Jerusalem is an exception (Betlyon, "A People Transformed," 38).
68 Stern, *Archaeology*, 435.
69 Ibid., 428–438; cf. Lipschits, "Rural Economy," 247.
70 Lipschits, Gadot and Freud, *Ramat Raḥel III*, 721.
71 Lipschits et al., "Palace and Village," 1–49. See the larger article for images and discussion of the stamp impressions that permeate this site. "We speculate that the lion stamp impression system is the 'missing link' in the administration that lasted until the beginning of the Persian period, at which point it was replaced by the *yhwd* stamp impression system" (Ibid., 33). Cf. Lipschits and Vanderhooft, "Forty unpublished *yhwd* stamp impressions," 409.

Raḥel was used in an administrative capacity for collecting wine and oil jars in Judah, probably as a levy."[72] They further hypothesize that the city eventually became the central government's *most* important administrative tax collection center in Judah.[73] Louis Jonker, working from Roland Boer's work, argues in contrast that Jerusalem "occupied a double economic position, acting as a buffer between the village communes of the rural areas and the allocative regime of the imperial center."[74] Working from either conclusion, it is clear that produce from the farmsteads and villages of Yehud, was being collected and stored for the purpose of redistribution as an aspect of imperial rule. Adding to this picture the known role of local Persian appointed officials to conscript militia for the Persian army, and we can safely conclude that the influence of the empire was seen and felt everywhere in "Beyond the River" during the Persian period.[75]

Of particular interest to this essay is that this new imperial system was facilitated by an equally new monetary unit—a 8.4 gram gold coin named for the emperor himself—the *daric*, first minted toward the end of the 6th century.[76] The introduction of coinage is a pivotal transition in the ANE.[77] The use of gold for currency is unusual as well. Radner confirms that although gold was used as currency in the Kassite period, it was not utilized in the Neo-Assyrian era, and did not return as a royal monetary standard until the *daric* of the Persian period, where the minting of this coin required the approval of the central government.[78] Hence, the discovery of the *daric* via literary or material remains is a significant historical marker.[79]

---

72 Lipschits et al., "Palace and Village," 34. Cf. Lipschits and Vanderhooft, "Forty unpublished *yhwd* stamp impressions," 409.
73 Lipschits et al., "Palace and Village," 35. Lipschits claims that there were three centers of the three districts in Persian period Yehud. Each served a different function: Jerusalem was the central and only cult center; Mizpah was the seat of the governor; and Ramat Raḥel was the collection center for agricultural produce (Lipschits, "Rural Economy," 257). Louis Jonker, working from Roland Boer's work, argues in contrast that Jerusalem "occupied a double economic position, acting as a buffer between the village communes of the rural areas and the allocative regime of the imperial center" (Jonker, "Yehud," 99. Cf. Eph'al, "Changes," 114–115).
74 Jonker, "Yehud," 99. Cf. Eph'al, "Changes," 114–115; Carter, *Emergence*, 216.
75 "Examining the names of the official title פחה in Samaria and Judah, we find that the Persian authorities tended to appoint members of the local ethnic groups to these positions (in contrast to the Assyrian names of the officials known to have served in the Assyrian province of Samaria) (Eph'al, "Changes," 106–119).
76 Stern, *Archaeology*, 557.
77 Definitions of "coinage," "currency," and "money" differ among scholars of various disciplines. The fundamental qualities of coinage, however, are broadly recognized as a piece made of metal, measured to a standard weight, and marked with a design or seal. It has long been held that coinage was first invented in Greco-Lydia by c. 560 BCE, but as Thompson states: "The enormous bibliography on the origins of coinage partly serves to highlight the continued absence of definitive answers to the fundamental questions of 'who, what, when, why, where?'" (Thompson, "Sealed Silver," 67, n. 2).
78 Radner, "Money," 132–34; Stern, *Archaeology*, 422–443.461–469.555–575; idem. Stern, "Hoard of Bullae," 421–437; Rainey and Notley, *Sacred Bridge*, 284–285.
79 Although "[g]old *darics* must have circulated in Palestine throughout the period of Persian

In the biblical text, the Persian *daric* is traditionally understood as the *'ădarkōnîm*. This coin is named in Ezra 8:27 as one of the precious items Ezra collects in Persia to adorn the temple in Jerusalem, and anachronistically in 1 Chron 29:7 where David seeks to accomplish a similar task.[80] The Hebrew term *darkĕmōnîm* is also a minted coin, but is typically translated as the Attic silver "drachma" (6 *obols*; 4.3 grams).[81] This coin is named as part of the contributions offered by the returning exiles for the purpose of restoring the temple, along with the silver *mina* (Hebrew *māneh*; Ezra 2:69 and Neh 7:70–71). The *mina* was already a unit of currency in the pre-exilic period, and particularly to the exiles as a Babylonian unit for silver currency (cf. Ezek. 45:12).[82] Additional Persian coinage included the *sigloi*—20 silver *sigloi* equaled one gold *daric* in value. Whereas the *daric* required imperial authorization, *sigloi* (after ca. 450 BCE) might be minted by local authorities in the satrapies.[83] Hence, the presence of coinage, especially *gold* coinage, in the Chronicler, Ezra, and Nehemiah are clear indications of the Persian-era provenance of these biblical books.

The use of coins increased rapidly with the return of economic prosperity under the Persians. Coins minted in Sidon, Tyre, Aradus, Byblos, and North Africa appear in Palestine in the 5th century; these are supplemented by coins from Greek and East Greek cities (Athens in particular) all of which became normative for trade in the region. An extensive collection of "Philisto-Arabian" coins from 450–333 BCE indicates that mints were established in Gaza, Ashdod, and Ashkelon as well.[84] The sub-satrapies of Samaria and Judah soon followed suit, and the "Yehud" coin—emanating from a mint in or near Jerusalem—made its first appearance soon after 400 BCE.[85] Coinage from sites along the major trade routes of Syria-Palestine and

---

domination," only two have been recovered from archaeological contexts—one from Samaria and one from the TransJordan (Betlyon, "A People Transformed," 48).

80 See Knopper's detailed note on the linguistic issues involved in the translation of this term in 1 Chronicles 29:7 (Knoppers, *I Chronicles 10–29*, 946–947). Cf. Williamson, *Ezra, Nehemiah*, 28–29.118–119, as well as his original piece, "Eschatology in Chronicles," 123–126.

81 Although the Attic drachma was typically silver, it is named in these texts as gold (Williamson, *Ezra, Nehemiah*, 28–29.118–119).

82 Silver ingots weighing a *mina* are known from Zinjirli inscribed with the name of Bir-Rekeb, son of Panamua as early as 710 BCE (Betlyon, "Coinage," 1079; and Williamson, *Ezra, Nehemiah*, 38). The silver *mina* weighed about 570 grams (King and Stager, *Life in Biblical Israel*, 199).

83 The silver *sigloi* were copied from East Greek manufacture and were used throughout the eastern Mediterranean (Betlyon, "Coinage," 1082).

84 Gitler, "Coins," 373–384; cf. Gitler and Tal, "Reclassifying," 11–22. As Betlyon details, the entire southwest coast was densely populated in the Persian period, with Gaza, Ashkelon, and Ashdod serving as important links in the Persian trade network—links that were heavily protected by the Persian military (Betlyon, "A People Transformed," 11–16).

85 The Samaria mint was first identified via the 1968 antiquities market discovery of the Samaria and Nablus hoards which contained an *obol* on which Frank Cross identified *šmyrn* (cf. Meshorer and Qedar, *The Coinage of Samaria*). All of these small silver coins were struck in the fourth century" (Betlyon, "A People Transformed," 49). Cf. Gitler and Tal who have re-

up and down the Levantine coast reflects a flourishing, redistributive, Phoenician-centered, Persian-sponsored, empire-driven economy indicative of Persia's policies of centralized economic planning and control.[86]

In sum, the picture which emerges of Judah during the Persian period is of a recovering, post-collapse society in which the population, and therefore kinship networks, are drastically reduced, with, initially, a corresponding dearth of family farms. But economic recovery launches with the investment of the Persian Empire and rapidly accelerates via Persian sponsored and Phoenician organized advances in Mediterranean trade. The logistical support of the Persian military stimulates and protects local economic growth, and "Beyond the River" at last experiences economic recovery. There is a significant shift in material culture from the "early" phase of the Persian empire (539–450 BCE) to the "later" and more established phase (450–332/331 BCE). Most significant to our discussion is that this new economy was fueled by monetary exchange in the form of coinage that facilitated international exchange while communicating the ideological and political identity of the Empire.[87] And although coinage was not the *only* medium of exchange, the redistributive elements of the Persian imperial economy rendered minted coinage (both silver and gold) ubiquitous as a medium of commerce and taxation on the coast and in the hill country (cf. Ezra 2:69; 8:27; Neh 5:1–9; 7:70–71; 1 Chron 29:7).[88] Commercial trade centers, provincial taxation capitals, and well-defended trade routes became normative as an aspect of Persian rule.

5. *Urdeuteronomium*

So how does this Persian economy compare to that portrayed in *Urdeuteronomium*? As I have argued previously, the Book of Deuteronomy assumes a populace living in small villages, dependent upon the *bêt 'āb* in which the main economy is a mixture

---

cently attributed additional *obols* from the Nablus 1968 hoard to Samaria, (Gitler and Tal, "Reclassifying," 11 n. 1; 20–21). As regards the *Yehud* coins: "The craftsmanship is poor. The die engravers copied Athenian types similar to those presumably copied in Gaza ... All of the coins are fractional silver denominations which functioned as small change to complement the larger silver coins of Gaza, Tyre, and Sidon" (Betlyon, "Coinage," 1083).

86 Some argue that these smaller local minters producing "small change" indicate an increase in local autonomy in the late fifth and the fourth centuries. But Betlyon argues the opposite—these are rather indicators of Persia's "policy of centralized economic planning and control" (Betlyon, "A People Transformed," 7–9).
87 Betlyon, "A People Transformed," 48.
88 As prosperity increased, so did a strong merchant class (Neh 13:15–21), a strategic new settlement pattern, and the mixed populace that came with it (Betlyon, "A People Transformed," 51–52).

of pastoralism and the diversified agriculture of crops native to the Hill Country.[89] *Urdeuteronomium* seems to know nothing of public works, international trade or its mechanisms, luxury items or imports.[90] Rather, civil law in the book assumes a robust, rural *bêt 'āb* as evinced by the *levirate* law (25:5–10), repeated concern for those outside the household (e.g., 10:18; 14:19–22, 28–29; 16:11–14, etc.), and the execution of incorrigible young adults (21:18–21).[91] The network of rural villages that make up this society are portrayed as the backbone of local judicial and notary action. Here the distinctive phrase "in your gates" communicates the public, communal village space essential to the gathering of the bounded community where the Sabbath, tithe, secular slaughter and charity toward the marginalized occurred (e.g. Deut 5:14; 12:12, 15, 17, 18, 21; 14:21, 27, 28, 29; 15:22; 16:5, 11, 14, 18; 24:14; 26:12).[92] The book knows little of kings, chariots, or horses. As Pakkala states: "*Urdeuteronomium* does not imply any state infrastructure or organization ... the monarch, the state, its structures, Judah, Jerusalem and the temple are completely missing in the document."[93] Most telling from an economic perspective is the conspicuous absence of coinage. In Deuteronomy commerce and taxation are described in terms of a simple, barter-based, "in-kind" exchange. Although *Hacksilber* is known, as I have argued elsewhere, it is utilized in the limited and predictable circumstances of an unstratified society moving toward a redistributive economy.[94]

Yet the archaeologically and biblically reconstructed picture of the Persian period indicates a highly complex local infrastructure designed to support a world economy. Here state-sponsored initiatives and wide-scale distribution are normative. As witnessed in the books of Ezra and Nehemiah, the imperial infrastructure of districts (פֶּלֶךְ of Neh 3:9, 12, 14–18), taxation and tribute (מִדַּה הַמֶּלֶךְ, Neh 5:1–7), the appointment of local Persian officials (פַּחוֹת, Neh 2:7, 9; 3:7; 5:14, 15, 18; 7:70–72; 12:26 and הַתִּרְשָׁתָא Ezra 2:63; Neh 7:65, 69; 8:9; 10:2), storehouses for the collection of wealth from the periphery for later redistribution (אוֹצָר, Neh 7:70), merchants and their imported items are well known in Palestine.

Even in the isolated hill country of Jerusalem we hear echoes of the same:

> And the men of Tyre who were living there (i.e. in Jerusalem) were importing fish (דָּאג) and all kinds of merchandise (מֶכֶר), and they were selling to the sons of Judah on the Sabbath, even in Jerusalem. (Neh 13:16)

---

89 Richter, "Question," 47–48.
90 Ibid., 38–40.
91 Caryn, *Enemy*, 4; cf. Fearon and Laitin, "Violence," 845–877.
92 Richter, "Question," 44–47.
93 Pakkala, "Date," 399. See MacDonald's rebuttal, "Issues," 431–435, and Pakkala's response "Dating," 431–436. As Nelson states: "[i]t is as though the context of state and temple does not even exist ... the burden of social support [is placed] entirely on the farmer, while ignoring artisans, merchants, and officials" (Nelson, *Deuteronomy*, 183).
94 Richter, "Question," 40–44.48.

Indeed, the "merchants" (רֹכֶלֶת and מֹכֵר) of international trade known to Ezekiel (17:4, 12, 13; 27:13, 15, 17, 20, 22–24) are found in this same narrative (Neh 13:15, 20) as is the queen of the Mediterranean superhighway, Tyre (Ezra 3:7 and Neh 13:16).[95] As discussed above, the coinage of the Persian Empire that facilitated this complex economy (the imperial *daric* and the coinages of the Aegean, Gaza, Samaria, Ashdod, Ashkelon, Jerusalem, and even Shechem)[96] is broadly attested via the material record and the biblical text. Moreover, the proliferation of this coinage and the stamped jar handles named above indicate that Jerusalem, Tell en-Naṣbeh, Ramat Raḥel, and Samaria were serving as Persian centres of taxation. Thus, whereas the Persian-sponsored Mediterranean port cities, their imports, the caravan trade routes that made them rich, and the imperial battalions that defended both local industrial centres and Persia's far reaching trade network (הַבִּירָה, Neh 2:8; 7:2) are well known in the Persian period, they are completely unknown in the Book of Deuteronomy. And so is the coinage that accompanied the Persian administration of Yehud.[97] As described above, the economy assumed in Deuteronomy is one in which the mechanisms for exchange were poorly developed, being primarily reciprocal and in-kind, with *Hacksilber* periodically appearing via Polanyi's "first general capacity" for money—payment for dowry, blood-money, or fines.[98] As Polanyi details, this category of currency is common to as-of-yet unstratified ancient economies and stands in contrast to more stratified societies which utilize currency for dues, taxes, and tribute.[99] As I have demonstrated elsewhere, the only utilization of *Hacksilber* for taxation or tribute is found in Deut 14:24–26 juxtaposed to an earlier "in kind" expression of the same law. I have proven on linguistic and economic grounds that this passage is an interpolation added to *Urdeuteronomium* at a later era in order to facilitate the new and expanding economic realities of the centralized Israelite monarchy.[100] The presence of *Hacksilber* in Deuteronomy as the medium for the tithe is significant because it demonstrates that the authors did incorporate evolving economic realities into the book on at least one occasion. This forces us to ask the question: if *Urdeuteronomium* were indeed located in the Persian period, how can we reasonably assert that authors who would update the "in-kind" requirements of Deut 14:22–23 to include the later realities of their own more mobile me-

---

95 Richter, "Question," 38–40. For the use of Hebrew רכל in international trade in the see Master, "Institutions," 513–514).
96 Richter, "Archaeology," 308–321.
97 Note that even the Jerusalem tithe has become a tax gathered by the Levites under the supervision of the priests for the Jerusalem temple (Neh 10:38–40). Knauf recognizes a similar dearth of money in the deuteronomic system in "Observations," 2–8, although his failure to address the larger economic picture of the southern Levant results in far different conclusions.
98 Richter, "Question," 43–44.
99 Polanyi, "Economy," 264–266.
100 Richter, "Question," 41–43.

dium of exchange in 14:24–26 not update the same to include coinage? Perhaps more telling, *could* a Persian author have managed to avoid the mention of coinage in his extensive discussion of prices, fines, penalties and tithes throughout the book? The fact that the Chronicler *failed* to accomplish this historiographic feat makes the claim even more unlikely. Indeed, in 1 Chron 29:7 David seeks to collect precious items for the adornment of the temple. Although in the first temple era coinage (and particularly the *daric*) has yet to be invented, the biblical writers record:

> Then the rulers (שָׂרֵי) of the fathers' households and the princes (שָׂרֵי) of the tribes of Israel, and the leaders (שָׂרֵי) of thousands and of hundreds, with the overseers (שָׂרֵי) over the king's work, offered willingly; and for the service for the house of God they gave 5,000 talents and 10,000 darics (אֲדַרְכֹנִים) *of gold*, and 10,0000 talents of silver, and 18,000 talents of brass, and 100,000 talents of iron.

Clearly, the Chronicler was unable to recreate the economy of a world long past without stumbling into anachronism. Rather, the economy of the historian's own day made its way into his treatment of the past. Historiography teaches us that this sort of anachronism is predictable when the subject of study lies beyond the author's own experience. In the Chronicler's case, the anachronism involved the Persian coinage of his day. Can we reasonably assert that the Deuteronomist would have been immune to the same impulse?

6. Conclusions

In sum, we have explored the economies of the Babylonian and Persian periods in the land once known as Israel, surveying the archaeologically and biblically reconstructed picture of these economies in rural and urban areas in the southern Levant, and have juxtaposed those economic realities with the economic setting(s) assumed and portrayed in *Urdeuteronomium* with a particular focus on *currency* and its use in trade and taxation. Per this investigation it is clear that the writers of *Urdeuteronomium* are writing against the backdrop of a far more functional economy than that of the post 586 BCE Neo-Babylonian era. In the "post collapse" society of the highlands of ancient Israel we see little of the Iron Age *bêt 'āb*, a kinship network, or the centralized tithe system of a functioning cult site so essential to the economy of *Urdeuteronmium*. As regards the Persian period, the archaeological and biblical record reports a highly complex world economy. And whereas coinage is ubiquitous in the Persian economic system, it is completely absent in *Urdeuteronomium*. The potential that a writer of a Persian period document as significant as Deuteronomy would choose to omit any interpolations incorporating the economy of his own day, or would succeed in flawlessly recreating an economy now centuries past in his quest to construct an utopian work of imagination, is unlikely at best. The possibility that he would do so without once falling victim to the same anachronisms as the Chronicler is even more unlikely. Rather, via economic lens, the data reviewed here compels us to conclude that the genesis of *Urdeuteronomium* cannot be located in the post-collapse era of the Neo-Babylonian period, the recovering early Persian period, or the complex economic realities of the late Persian period. Rather as my past study has indicated, the economic profile of *Urdeuteronomium* is best located in the transition period between the Iron I and Iron IIA period.

Bibliography

Ashkenazi, D. et al. "Metallurgical Investigation on Fourth Century BCE Silver Jewelry of Two Hoards from Samaria" *Scientific Reports* 7. Art number: 40659 (Jan 2017) [available at https://www.nature.com/articles/srep40659, accessed 28/2/17].

Barstad, Hans. "After the 'Myth of the Empty Land'," in *Judah and the Judeans in the Neo-Babylonian Period*. Edited by Oded Lipschits and Joseph Blenkinsopp. Winona Lake, IN: Eisenbrauns, 2003, 3–20.

—. *The Myth of the Empty Land: A Study in the History and Archaeology of Judah During the "Exilic" Period*. Symbolae Osloenses Fasc. Suppl. 28. Oslo: Scandinavian University Press, 1998.

Ben-Tor, Amnon, and Anabel Zarzecki-Peleg. "Iron Age IIA-B: Northern Valleys and Upper Galilee," in *The Ancient Pottery of Israel and Its Neighbors from the Iron Age through the Hellenistic Period*. Edited by Seymour Gitin. Jerusalem: Israel Exploration Society, 2015, 135–188.

Betlyon, John W. "A People Transformed." *Near Eastern Archaeology* 68,1-2 (2005): 4–58.

—. "Coinage." *ABD* 1: 1076–1089.

Blenkinsopp, Joseph. "Bethel in the Neo-Babylonian Period," in *Judah and the Judeans in the Neo-Babylonian Period*. Edited by Oded Lipschits and Joseph Blenkinsopp. Winona Lake, IN: Eisenbrauns, 2003, 93–108.

Bloch-Smith, Elizabeth, and Beth Alpert Nakhai. "A Landscape Comes to Life: The Iron I Period." *NEA* 62/2 (1999): 62–92.

Carroll, Robert. "The Myth of the Empty Land." *Semeia* 59 (1992): 79–93.

Carter, Charles E. *The Emergence of Yehud in the Persian Period: A Social and Demographic Study*. JSOT 294. Sheffield: Academic Press, 1999.

Crüsemann, Frank. "Das Bundesbuch: Historischer Ort und Instituioneller Hintergrund," in *Congress Volume: Jerusalem 1986*. Edited by J. A. Emerton. Leiden: Brill, 1988, 27–41.

Dever, William G. "The Bible as History, Literature, and Theology," in *What Did the Biblical Writers Know and When Did They Know It? What Archaeology Can Tell Us about the Reality of Ancient Israel* by idem. Grand Rapids: Eerdmans, 2001, 1–22.

Eph'al, Israel. "Changes in Palestine during the Persian Period in Light of Epigraphic Sources." *IEJ* 48,1/2 (1998): 106–119.

—. *The Ancient Arabs: Nomads on the Borders of the Fertile Crescent, 9th–5th centuries B.C.* Jerusalem: Hebrew University Magnes Press, 1984.
Faust, Avraham. *Judah in the Neo-Babylonian Period: The Archaeology of Desolation.* ABS 18. Atlanta: Scholars Press, 2012.
—. *The Archaeology of Israelite Society in Iron Age II.* Winona Lake, IN: Eisenbrauns, 2012.
Fearon James D., and David D. Laitin. "Violence and the Social Construction of Ethnic Identity." *International Organization* 54/4 (Autumn 2000): 845–877.
Finkelstein, Israel. *The Archaeology of Israelite Settlement.* Jerusalem: Israel Exploration Society, 1988.
—. "The Archaeology of the United Monarchy: An Alternative View." *Levant* 28 (1996): 177–187.
—. "The Stratigraphy and Chronology of Megiddo and Beth-Shan in the 12th–11th Centuries B.C.E." *Tel Aviv* 23 (1996): 170–184.
Finkelstein, Israel and Lily Singer-Avitz. "Reevaluating Bethel." *ZDPV* 125 (2009): 33–48.
Fried, Lisbeth S. "Exploitation of Depopulated Land in Achaemenid Judah," in *The Economy of Ancient Judah in Its Historical* Context. Edited by Marvin Lloyd Miller, Ehud Ben Zvi and Gary N. Knoppers. Winona Lake, IN: Eisenbrauns, 2015, 149–162.
Gilboa, Ayelet. "Iron Age IIC: Northern Coast, Carmel Coast, Galilee, and Jezreel Valley," in *The Ancient Pottery of Israel and Its Neighbors from the Iron Age through the Hellenistic Period.* Edited by Seymour Gitin. Jerusalem: Israel Exploration Society, 2015, 301–344.
Gitin, Seymour. "Iron Age IIC: Judah," in *The Ancient Pottery of Israel and Its Neighbors from the Iron Age through the Hellenistic Period.* Edited by Seymour Gitin. Jerusalem: Israel Exploration Society, 2015, 345–363.
Gitler, Haim. "Coins of the Fifth and Fourth Centuries B.C.," in *The Leon Levy Expedition to Ashkelon. Ashkelon I: Introduction and Overview (1985–2006).* Edited by Lawrence E. Stager, J. David Schloen, and Daniel M. Master. Winona Lake, IN: Eisenbrauns, 2008, 373–384.
Gitler, Haim, and Oren Tal. "Reclassifying Persian-Period Philistian Coins: Some New Identifications." *INR* 11 (2016): 11–22.
Holladay, John. "Hezekiah's Tribute, Long-Distance Trade, and the Wealth of Nations Ca. 1000–600 BC: A New Perspective," in *Confronting the Past: Archaeological and Historical Essays on Ancient Israel in Honor of William G. Dever.* Edited by Seymour Gitin, J. Edward Wright and J. P. Dessel. Winona Lake, IN: Eisenbrauns, 2006, 309–332.
—. "How Much Is That In ...? Monetization, Money, Royal States, and Empires," in *Exploring the Longue Durée: Essays in Honor of Lawrence E. Stager.* Edited by J. David Schloen. Winona Lake: Eisenbrauns, 2009, 207–222.
Hölscher, Gustav. "Komposition und Ursprung des Deuteronomiums." *ZAW* 40 (1922): 161–255.
Hopkins, David C. "Life on the Land: The Subsistence Struggles of Early Israel." *BA* 50/3 (1987): 178–191.
Jonker, Louis. "Yehud Economy in the Genealogies of Chronicles," in *The Economy of Ancient Judah in Its Historical* Context. Edited by Marvin Lloyd Miller, Ehud Ben Zvi and Gary N. Knoppers. Winona Lake, IN: Eisenbrauns, 2015, 77–101.
Kelso, James Leon. "Bethel," *NEAEHL* 1:192–194.
King, Philip J., and Lawrence E. Stager. *Life in Biblical Israel.* Library of Ancient Israel. Westminster: John Knox Press, 2002.
Knauf, Ernst Axel. "Observations on Judah's Social and Economic History and the Dating of the Laws in Deuteronomy." *JHS* 9/18 (2009): 2–8.
Knoppers, Gary. *Jews and Samaritans: The Origins and History of Their Early Relations.* New York: Oxford University Press, 2013.
—. *I Chronicles 10–29.* AB 12A. New York: Doubleday, 2004.

Levinson, Bernard M. *Deuteronomy and the Hermeneutics of Legal Innovation.* Oxford: Oxford University Press, 1998.
Lipschits, Oded. "Achaemenid Imperial Policy, Settlement Processes in Palestine, and the Status of Jerusalem in the Middle of the Fifth Century B.C.E.," in *Judah and the Judeans in the Persian Period.* Edited by Oded Lipschits and Manfred Oeming. Winona Lake, IN: Eisenbrauns, 2006, 19–52.
—. "Demographic Changes in Judah between the Seventh and the Fifth Centuries B.C.E.," in *Judah and the Judeans in the Neo-Babylonian Period.* Edited by Oded Lipschits and Joseph Blenkinsopp. Winona Lake, IN: Eisenbrauns, 2003, 323–376.
—. *The Fall and Rise of Jerusalem. Juda under Babylonian Rule.* Winona Lake, IN: Eisenbrauns, 2005.
—. "The Rural Economy of Judah during the Persian Period and the Settlement History of the District System," in *The Economy of Ancient Judah in Its Historical* Context. Edited by Marvin Lloyd Miller, Ehud Ben Zvi and Gary N. Knoppers. Winona Lake, IN: Eisenbrauns, 2015, 237–264.
Lipschits, Oded and David Vanderhooft. "Forty unpublished *yhwd* stamp impressions." In *Ramat Raḥel III: Final Publication of Yohanan Aharoni's Excavations (1954, 1959–1962).* Vol. 2. Edited by Oded Lipschits, Yuval Gadot and Liora Freud. Winona Lake, IN: Eisenbrauns, 2016, 409–436.
Lipschits, Oded, Yuval Gadot and Liora Freud. *Ramat Raḥel III: Final Publication of Yohanan Aharoni's Excavations (1954, 1959–1962).* Vol. 1. Winona Lake, IN: Eisenbrauns, 2016.
Lipschits, Oded, Yuval Gadot, Benjamin Arubas, and Manfred Oeming. "Palace and Village, Paradise and Oblivion: Unraveling the Riddles of Ramat Raḥel." *NEA* 74 (2011):1–49.
Lohfink, Norbert. *Studien zum Deuteronomium und zur deuteronomistischen Literatur 1.* SBAB 8. Stuttgart: Katholisches Bibelwerk, 1990.
MacDonald, Nathan. "Issues and Questions in the Dating of Deuteronomy: A Response to Juha Pakkala." *ZAW* 122/3 (2010): 431–435.
Marshall, Alfred. *Principles of Economics.* London and New York: Macmillan & Co., 1892.
Master, Daniel. "Comments on Oded Lipschits." Review of *The Fall and Rise of Jerusalem*, by Oded Lipschits. *JHebS* 7 (2016): 28–33.
—. "Economy and Exchange in the Iron Age Kingdoms of the Southern Levant." *BASOR* 372 (2014): 81–97.
—. "Institutions of Trade in 1 and 2 Kings," in *The Books of Kings: Sources, Composition, Historiography and Reception.* Edited by Baruch Halpern and André Lemaire. Leiden: Brill, 2010, 501–516.
Mazar, Amihai. "From 1200 to 850 B.C.E.: Remarks on Some Selected Archaeological Issues," in *Israel in Transition: From Late Bronze II to Iron IIa (c. 1250–850 B.C.E.).* Edited by Lester L. Grabbe. New York: T & T Clark, 2008, 86–120.
Meshorer, Y., and S. Qedar. *The Coinage of Samaria in the 4th Century BCE.* Jerusalem: Numismatic Fine Arts International, 1991.
Meyers, Carol. "The Family in Early Israel," in *Families in Ancient Israel.* The Family, Religion and Culture Series. Louisville, KY: Westminster John Knox Press, 1997, 1–47.
Nam, Roger S. *Portrayals of Economic Exchange in the Book of Kings.* Leiden: Brill, 2012.
Nelson, Richard. *Deuteronomy.* OTL. Louisville: John Knox, 2002.
Nihan, Christophe. "*The Torah between Samaria and Judah: Shechem and Gerizim in Deuteronomy and Joshua*," in *The Pentateuch as Torah: New Models for Understanding Its Promulgation and Acceptance.* Edited by Gary N. Knoppers and Bernard M. Levinson. Winona Lake: Eisenbrauns, 2007, 187–223.
Pakkala, Juha. "The Date of the Oldest Edition of Deuteronomy." *ZAW* 121 (2009): 392–435.
—. "The Dating of Deuteronomy: A Response to Nathan MacDonald." *ZAW* 123/3 (2011):

431–436.

Panitz-Cohen, Nava et al., "A Silver Lining at Abel Beth Maacah." *BAR* 42.4 (July/Aug 2016): 22–23.

Polanyi, Karl. "The Economy as Instituted Process," in *Trade and Market in the Early Empires: Economies in History and Theory.* Edited by Karl Polanyi, Conrad M. Arensberg and Harry W. Pearson. Glencoe, IL: The Free Press and The Falcon's Wing Press, 1957, 243–269.

Radner, Karen. "Money in the Neo-Assyrian Empire." *Trade and Finance in Ancient Mesopotamia*, MOS 1. Leiden: Nederlands Historisch-Archaeologisch Instituut te Istanbul, 1997.

Rainey, Anson F. and R. Steven Notley. *The Sacred Bridge.* Jerusalem: Carta, 2006.

Reeder, Caryn A. *The Enemy in the Household: Family Violence in Deuteronomy and Beyond.* Grand Rapids: Baker Academic, 2012.

Richter, Sandra. "The Archaeology of Mt. Ebal and Mt. Gerizim and Why It Matters to Deuteronomy," in *Sepher Torath Mosheh: Studies in the Composition and Interpretation of Deuteronomy.* Edited by Daniel Block and Richard Schultz. Peabody, MA: Hendrickson Publishers, 2017, 304–337.

—. "The Place of the Name in Deuteronomy." *VT* 57 (2007): 342–366.

—. "The Question of Provenance and the Economics of Deuteronomy." *JSOT* 42.1 (2017): 23–50.

Rosen, Baruch. "Subsistence Economy in Iron Age I.," in *From Nomadism to Monarchy: Archaeological and Historical Aspects of Early Israel.* Edited by Israel Finkelstein and Nadav Na'aman. Jerusalem: Israel Exploration Society, 1994, 339–351.

Stager, Lawrence E. *Ashkelon Discovered: From Canaanites and Philistines to Romans and Moslems.* Washington, DC: Biblical Archaeology Society, 1991.

Stern, Ephraim. "A Persian-Period Hoard of Bullae from Samaria," in *Exploring the Longue Durée: Essays in Honor of Lawrence E. Stager.* Edited by J. David Schloen. Winona Lake: Eisenbrauns, 2009, 421–437.

—. *Archaeology of the Land of the Bible, Vol. II: The Assyrian, Babylonian, and Persian Periods (732–332 B.C.E.).* ABRL. New York: Doubleday, 2001.

Tal, Oren. "Pottery from the Persian and Hellenistic Periods," in *Ramat Raḥel III: Final Publication of Yohanan Aharoni's Excavations (1954, 1959–1962).* Vol. 1. Edited by Oded Lipschits, Yuval Gadot and Liora Freud. Winona Lake, IN: Eisenbrauns, 2016, 266–271.

Thiele, Edwin R. *The Mysterious Numbers of the Hebrew Kings.* 3rd ed. Grand Rapids, MI: Zondervan/Kregel, 1983.

Thompson, Christine M. "Sealed Silver in Iron Age Cisjordan and the 'Invention' of Coinage." *OJA* 22/1 (2003): 67–107.

Vanderhooft, David. "Babylonian Strategies of Imperial Control in the West," in *Judah and the Judeans in the Neo-Babylonian Period.* Edited by Oded Lipschits and Joseph Blenkinsopp. Winona Lake, IN: Eisenbrauns, 2003, 235–262.

—. "The Israelite *Mishpaha* in the Priestly Writings, and Changing Valences in Israel's Kinship Terminology," in *Exploring the Longue Durée: Essays in Honor of Lawrence E. Stager.* Edited by J. David Schloen. Winona Lake: Eisenbrauns, 2009, 485–496.

—. *The Neo-Babylonian Empire and Babylon in the Latter Prophets.* HSM 59. Atlanta: Scholars Press, 1999.

Walton, Joshua T. "The Regional Economy of the Southern Levant in the 8th–7th Centuries BCE." Ph.D. diss., Harvard University, 2015.

Williamson, H. G. M. "Eschatology in Chronicles." *TynB* 28 (1977): 123–126.

—. *Ezra, Nehemiah.* WBC 16. Nashville, TN: Thomas Nelson, 1985.

Younger, K. Lawson Jr. "The Assyrian Economic Impact on the Southern Levant in the Light of Recent Study." *IEJ* 65.2 (2015): 179–204.

Zlotnik, Yehoshua. "Samarian Coin Types and Their Denominations." *INR* 11 (2016): 3–10.

Zorn, Jeffrey R. "Tell en-Naṣbeh and the Problem of the Material Culture of the Sixth Century," in *Judah and the Judeans in the Neo-Babylonian Period*. Edited by Oded Lipschits and Joseph Blenkinsopp. Winona Lake, IN: Eisenbrauns, 2003, 415–445.

Reconstruction the Social Contexts of the Priestly and Deuteronomic Materials in a Non-Wellhausian Setting

Pekka Pitkänen (University of Gloucestershire)

1. Introduction

As is well acknowledged, priestly (P/H) and Deuteronomic materials can be seen as significant textual and ideological building blocks in the Pentateuch, in addition to narrative (classically J/E) materials. Clearly there are enough stylistic differences to distinguish between the priestly and Deuteromic materials, and also see other narrative materials as a separate set, even when the distinctions may not always be hard and fast. In that sense, one can think that the early, pre-Wellhausenian scholarship, and also scholarship following him, has been on a right track, at least broadly so.[1] And, clearly, it seems reasonable to assume that the stylistic differences between the P/H and D codes, on which this paper focuses, suggest at the minimum a possibility of differing origins for them. In the Wellhausenian synthesis, the origins of the Pentateuchal law codes were essentially seen from a sequential perspective where each code followed its predecessor and built on it, sometimes developing and sometimes abrogating concepts relating to the predecessor. Such ideas about composition were also combined with an evolutionary concept of development from simple to complex, free-spirited to ritualistic and decentralised to centralised, with the process lasting for several centuries from the Covenant Code to Deuteronomy and then the priestly materials. In the final Pentateuch, the codes were ultimately seen as having been lumped together, with little consideration of their interplay in the context of the overall Pentateuchal narrative. Such neglect still remains one major drawback of Wellhausenian approaches.[2] While this issue is not the focus of this essay, it nevertheless highlights the question of to what extent the Pentateuch can be seen as a coherent piece of work and to what extent it may be a haphazard collection of materials. And, from the perspective of the legal materials within that context, is it right to assume an essentially separate and isolated provenance for them? In contrast

---

[1] Weinfeld, *Deuteronomy,* is one recent treatment that includes highlighting Deuteronomy's distinctive character from a stylistic perspective, also in relation to the priestly materials. Milgrom's three-volume commentary on Leviticus is an example that includes featuring the distinctive stylistic characteristics of priestly materials (P and H) in the Pentateuch.

[2] See esp. Kilchör, *Mosetora,* 1–30.

to the Wellhausenian views, the recent doctoral dissertation by Benjamin Kilchör has argued that Deuteronomy builds on both the Covenant Code and the priestly materials, with also minimum, if any, contention between the views of those legal materials.[3] Except for negating the essentials of the Wellhausenian scheme of the development of the Israelite religion,[4] such a view would build towards an idea of strong interconnections between the legal materials. When one combines this with the observation that Kilchör's analysis fits with a synchronic reading of the Pentateuch, one can infer at least the possibility of a more concurrent origin for the legal codes than that afforded by a Wellhausenian approach. But, certainly, the Wellhausenian approach already had implications for the possibility of a reasonably concurrent existence of reconstructed priestly and Deuteronomic schools,[5] as can for example be seen by a comparison of the date and overall style of the prophetic books of Jeremiah and Ezekiel, perhaps together with the postulated setting of the so-called Deuteronomistic history,[6] or at least the books of Kings, keeping in mind that Noth's theory and its derivatives are a disputed concept today.[7] More minimalist views about Deuteronomy and its provenance would seem to be in line with such concurrency to an even greater extent, this time more explicitly in the postexilic period. In this paper, I will build on these and other relevant observations (many of them made by people participating in the conference were this paper was presented) in order to suggest a plausible, or at least possible social context for the Priestly and Deuteronomic materials that does not follow a Wellhausenian approach. At the outset, one important related pair of presuppositions taken here is that the Covenant Code (and with it the Ritual Decalogue) is the earliest code on which both P, and especially D build,[8] and that H is a development on P.[9] I will also include considerations from my previous work that sees the Pentateuch, or, rather, Genesis–Joshua as a programmatic and essentially unified document of settler colonialism.[10] As part of a proposal for seeing Genesis–Joshua as a unified document in terms of its literary composition,[11] I have postulated that Genesis–Joshua were written by two authors together,

---

3 See ibid. But there nevertheless seem to be certain tensions between the codes; cf. Pitkänen, *Numbers*, passim.
4 Certainly, the views of such scholars as Weinfeld (esp. op. cit and *The Place of Law*), Milgrom (e.g. *Leviticus*, 3 vols.) and Joosten, *People and Land*, by dating the priestly materials before Deuteronomy, already implied problems for the Wellhausenian scheme of development from simple to complex.
5 Cf. e.g. Weinfeld, *Deuteronomy*.
6 Noth, *Deuteronomistic History*.
7 See e.g. Otto, *Deuteronomium 1,1–4,43*.
8 The plausibility of such a view is in my view demonstrated convincingly by Kilchör, *Mosetora*, which see for further details.
9 Nihan, *Priestly Torah*; Knohl, *Sanctuary*; cf. Frevel, " Book of Numbers," 1–37.
10 Pitkänen, "Pentateuch-Joshua," 245–276; idem., "Reading Genesis-Joshua," 3–31; cf. also idem., *Numbers*.
11 In line with a variety of sources for the Pentateuch (and Joshua), I see this unified work as having been composed of such sources, including the Priestly and Deuteronomic materials that,

with one author (A1) from priestly circles writing Genesis–Numbers and the other (AD) from Deuteronomic circles writing Deuteronomy and Joshua.[12] Such a dual authorship very strongly implies the concurrent existence of priestly and deuteronomic streams of tradition, if not schools or equivalent.

2. Social Contexts

2.1 Social Roles

It is generally postulated that the origin of both P/H and D is priestly, and this premise is followed here. The difference is that whereas P and H focus on priests, D attests lay theology.[13] Already considering that, in addition to Deuteronomy and Joshua being Deuteronomic in their theology,[14] much of the narrative in Genesis–Numbers is priestly, one can suggest that Genesis–Joshua as a whole is a priestly document, or at the minimum attests strong affinities with priestly theology. From a social scientific perspective, priests were well attested as an important social group in the ancient Near East. But, also from an (wider) anthropological perspective, priests can be seen to attest high status in a variety of societies across human history, in particular in the premodern era.[15] This is natural as premodern societies placed great emphasis on the divine and much of the purpose of the priestly profession was to act as a mediator between human and divine, certainly so in the ancient Near East.[16] In ancient Israel, the P/H corpus particularly emphasises the importance of priesthood. One area is the ritual system where priests administer practically all rites that relate to purity and expiation.[17] In addition, priests have best access to the divine, especially in the organised tabernacle cult. They also have access to sacrifices and offerings. And, they are separated from other Israelites based on a hereditary system (e.g. Lev 8–9; Num 16–18). All this at the minimum implies a high status for priests. However, there is a democratisation in that priests are not necessarily above reproach (e.g. Ex 32 and the golden calf narrative; cf. Num 20:1–3; 27:15–23). Also,

---

except for being most notably associated with the Pentateuchal legal materials, may also extend to other genres, especially narratives and genealogies.

12 Cf. Pitkänen, "Reading Genesis-Joshua"; idem., *Numbers*.
13 See e.g. Otto, *Das Deuteronomium im Pentateuch und Hexateuch*, 253.
14 See e.g. Pitkänen, *Joshua*; also building on Wenham, " Deuteronomic Theology".
15 See e.g. Lenski, *Power and Privilege*, esp. 256–266; Smith, *Ethnic Origins*, 42–43; Bell, *Ritual Theory,* 130–140.
16 See e.g. Pitkänen, *Central Sanctuary*; Hundley, *Gods,* which (as a later publication) interestingly takes many similar views as Pitkänen, even if often offering a more detailed treatment in a number of respects.
17 Two exceptions are Num 19 and Deut 21:1-9, but priests also play a role in these rituals.

in the view of P/H, and also D, priests and Levites, a (sub)category within the priestly group,[18] do not have landholdings and therefore cannot create excessive wealth (cf. the system of Levitical towns in Josh 21; repeated in 1 Chr 6). Also, local altars, where it would appear that lay people could offer sacrifices (Ex 20:22–26), are permissible in certain circumstances.[19] Deuteronomy's conceptualised placial network that encompasses the land is a further interesting issue.[20]

That Deuteronomy looks at society in a wider cross-sectional perspective (Deut 16:18–18:22), is in line with its overall characteristic focus on laity. It offers other parallel structures of society than just priests (and perhaps tribal leaders that are mentioned in both P/H and D). King is conceptualised in Deuteronomy (Deut 17:14–20) as someone who should be a humble person and is proffered as a potential future prospect rather than an actual reality.[21] Deuteronomy also presents judges and prophets as significant actors in society. All these features would suggest fairly careful egalitarian design by the authors of the documents, as has already been proposed in scholarship.[22] But, it is difficult to consider the egalitarianism of Deuteronomy as totalising or as utopian (however one might define the concept utopian).

---

18 The distinction between Levitical priests and non-priestly Levites does not seem an issue as such based on ancient Near Eastern parallels, cf. e.g. Taggar-Cohen, *Hittite Priesthood*.
19 See Pitkänen, *Central Sanctuary*.
20 See Parker, "Deuteronomy's Place."
21 The early Israelites seemed to be well aware of the rights of kings and the potential resulting social stratification that societies that exhibited kingship attested (1 Sam 8:11-17). This is completely in line with social stratification attested by agrarian societies throughout the world and through time, with ancient Israel clearly being an agrarian society (cf. Lenski, *Power and Privilege*, esp. 210–219; Nolan and Lenski, *Human Societies*; and cf. e.g. the characteristics of agrarian societies being attested in the ancient Near East [already] in the late 3rd millennium BCE in Foster, *Age of Agade*, 17 and *passim*). One of the brilliant conceptualisations of the early Israelite documents was seeing Yahweh as the king of Israel (see Deut 33:5; 1 Sam 8:7; cf. Foster, *Age of Agade*, 275 for an example of seeing the city god, Tishpak, as king of the city in Eshnunna at around 2010 BCE, even if the ruler, Shu-iliya did assume divine honours for himself, like with Naram-Sin, Shulgi and Shu-Sin). This analogy with kingship can for example be seen in the idea that Yahweh owned the land and could therefore give it to Israel (cf. Ex 3:3-8; Lev 25:23, 42; see Lenski, *Power and Privilege*, 216–217, 220–221 on such rights of kings; and see Harmanşah, *Cities*, 53–54 for an example of an Iron Age I ancient Near Eastern land grant in the northern Levant). Yahweh could then also equally take the privilege of land away (cf. Lev 26; Deut 28). Interestingly, one may ask if the authors could have imagined that Yahweh might eventually pardon a people whose land was taken away (by taking them away from it) and return them to it (Deut 4:29-31; 30:1-8)! All in all, in relation to such thinking by the ancient Israelites, one may also keep in mind that forced population transfers were demonstrably exercised at least by the Egyptian, Hittite and Middle Assyrian empires already in the late second millennium BCE (see e.g. Kitchen, *Reliability*, 301–302; Zadok, "Aramean Infiltration;" Younger, *Arameans*, 149). In the context of Yahweh being a king and the Israelites on the whole more or less egalitarian under Yahweh (cf. just ahead), it would at the minimum seem reasonably fitting for Deuteronomy to stipulate that a human king, if one were to be installed, should be a humble, non-ostentatious person who follows Yahweh.
22 See esp. Berman, *Created Equal*.

The existence of slavery, in particular in terms of non-Israelites, in Deuteronomy and also in P/H, is one clear aspect that mitigates against such notions.[23] Coming back to priests and Levites, Deuteronomy on the whole sees them (see below for further details on priests and Levites in Deuteronomy) as one strand of the institutions and power structures of society and particularly highlights the relative lack of landholdings by them. However, Deuteronomy is aware of their privileges and overall role in respect to the divine that, as we have just pointed out, cannot but imply a heightened social status (Deut 18:1–8). From such a perspective, one can suggest that the thought world of the P/H and D documents is at the very least broadly similar, even if the emphases are different. So, all in all, one can say that, across the P/H corpuses, social stratification clearly exists but is in many ways eschewed and flattened, and a variety of more or less parallel social institutions exist across the conceptualised society (elders, judges, prophets, priests, and possibly a king).

2.2 Date

Dating considerations cannot be avoided for reconstructing social contexts, even when some features of the texts could fit in more than one context, and certain contexts can at least potentially stay essentially similar for extended periods of time. Interestingly, in its narrative world, the books of Chronicles suggest that David reorganised the Pentateuchal system of worship for the newly built temple that took the place of the earlier tent of meeting. Clearly this, in addition to the Pentateuch itself, suggests a premonarchical setting for the P/H materials in the thought world of the ancient Israelites, even if the actual time of their production were to be deemed postexilic. As for D, the narrative setting is again Mosaic and thus premonarchic, however, in terms of the legal materials themselves, as such, they could fit a premonarchic, monarchic or even later setting. This includes the tentative presentation of a king in Deuteronomy (Deut 17:14–20) that could be read in both prospective and retrospective terms. In a non-Wellhausenian context, I have proposed a settler colonial reading of Genesis–Joshua. Such a reading sees that ancient document as essentially a blueprint for a new society that is settling in the southern Levantine area. In the process, the new society is to supplant existing indigenous societies, destroying them as societies and building a new society instead.[24] Such a reading suggests a time when the settler colonial process was ongoing. A further clue can be obtained by looking at an overall trajectory attested by the narrative of Genesis–

---

23 Deuteronomy's views against indigenous peoples are another issue; cf. below. An alternative expression to egalitarianism in Deuteronomy could be attenuated social stratification (and cf. e.g. Lenski, *Power and Privilege*; Nolan and Lenski, *Human Societies*).

24 See Pitkänen, "Pentateuch-Joshua." See also Parker, "Deuteronomy's Place," in regard to Deuteronomy, even when Parker's work does not directly address issues that relate to settler colonialism.

Joshua. It starts by creation and placing man in the garden where Yahweh is also present. However, due to disobedience, man is driven out from the garden. This state of affairs in essence ends with the setting of the tent of meeting as the dwelling place of Yahweh in the midst of Israel at Shiloh in the book of Joshua, preceded by the construction of the tent of meeting and the ancient Israelite cult at Sinai. The setting up of the tent of meeting at Shiloh can then be seen as a restoration of creation and is in line with overall conceptual settler colonial idylls.[25] Such a vision, then, would to me clearly seem to fit best to a time when Shiloh was prominent.[26] According to the biblical texts, this was the case until the disaster at Aphek at about 1050 BCE (1 Sam 4) after which, some 50–100 years later, Jerusalem became prominent through the building of the temple there. It would seem odd if Genesis–Joshua would promote Shiloh from that time on, including as Psalm 78 explicitly speaks for the replacement of Shiloh's conceptual status with Jerusalem.[27] But, of course, as such, I on my part would not be averse to other proposals for dating (and provenance) if they are able to attest explanatory power that can be deemed better. One should also keep in mind here that, including based on ancient Near Eastern parallels, one can very reasonably think that Genesis–Joshua would go through modifications as it was transmitted through time, so monarchic and potentially later features in it could have been added in after the composition of the main work,[28] in particular if such features are more or less isolated and not part of the main themes of the document.[29]

2.3 Writing

One objection to an early provenance is that it is often thought that the ancient Israelites could not write in the early period of their existence. However, writing in the ancient Near East was as such of course already some two thousand years old and alphabetic writing at least 500 years old by the time early Israel as a society appeared on the scene in the late second millennium BCE. While there is no direct positive evidence of Israelite writing from the premonarchical period, most notably, the recent finds at Khirbet Qeyafa are closely positioned in terms of time and geography.[30] It would seem reasonable that the Israelite documents were written on perishable materials, such as papyrus, and one could hardly imagine otherwise for a lengthy document such as Genesis–Joshua, considering that cuneiform would not appear to have been a popular medium in ancient Israel. Considering that writing

---

25 See Veracini, *Settler Colonialism*, 88–89.
26 On Shiloh in the premonarchical period, including from an archaeological perspective, see Pitkänen, *Central Sanctuary*, esp. 111–127.
27 Cf. ibid., esp. 127–158.
28 Cf. Carr, *Formation*; Pitkänen, *Joshua*.
29 For comments on Deuteronomy and urbanisation, see ahead.
30 Cf. Galil. "Inscription." For a summary of further related evidence, including e.g. the Izbert Sartah inscription, see Pitkänen, *Joshua*, 59–60.

was typically in the hands of scribes in the ancient Near East, I suggest here that there could have been separate scribes who codified the materials, or that priests could write, especially considering that this was an alphabetic script.[31] There is no need to necessarily assume widespread literacy for the period, in contrast to the later 8th–7th centuries,[32] even if writing would not have to be assumed to have been severely constrained at the (earlier) time either (cf. Judg 8:14, etc.). Of course Genesis–Joshua itself refers to writing, too. So, if writing was on perishable materials, there is no need to expect much evidence of it, in line with the present state of archaeological evidence. It should further be said that considering the premonarchical period as necessarily primitive, as is often done in scholarship, is at the very least arguably comparable to orientalism[33] and also an outlook that relates to modern Western attitudes towards preindustrial societies, whether such societies were past or present, especially if the societies cannot be classified under the category of a state. Such an approach was common in anthropology in the 19th century but was increasingly refuted in the 20th century (and into the 21st century). One may also keep in mind here that considerable literary compositions existed in the ancient Near East in the second millennium BCE, the most notable of them being the Gilgamesh epic, over twelve tablets (or so), that already reached its standard form by about 1100 BCE.[34] And, one should further note that the Merneptah Stele (ca. 1208 BCE) indicates that the Israelite settlement was well under way already before the collapse of the Late Bronze Age regional "system" in the early 12th century BCE (ca. 1177 BCE),[35] so one can expect that any technologies (and also thinking) in the Iron Age would be in continuity with the Late Bronze Age.

2.4 Other Archaeological Perspectives

Much of what is said in the biblical documents can clearly be seen to be a conceptual creation. Such conceptual creations ultimately reside in human brains and are therefore impossible to capture archaeologically unless they are, in one way or another, reified by humans into material objects. For analysis, it is also necessary that at least some of such material objects survive to the present when a large portion of the ancient world has been lost forever. Herein lies the difficulty for the archaeo-

---

31 Cf. also e.g. Cohen, *Scribes and Scholars* and comments made in Pitkänen, "Reading Genesis-Joshua," 17.
32 cf. e.g. Sanders, *Invention*.
33 Cf. Said, *Orientalism*, the afterword of the 1995 reprint includes responses to criticisms against his work, for example by Bernard Lewis. Note also the concept of hegemony as developed by Bruce Routledge (see Routledge, *Moab* and idem., *Archaeology*) based on concepts introduced by Antonio Gramsci, here in terms of Western scholarship.
34 See George, *Gilgamesh Epic*; Tigay, *Evolution of the Gilgamesh Epic*; cf. Carr, *Formation*, esp. 3–149.
35 Cf. Cline, *1177 B.C.*

logical discipline of trying to reconstruct the ancient world from material evidence (cf. e.g. issues outlined by Routledge and Schloen), or from material evidence only.[36] In addition, the biblical documents themselves indicate, or at least imply, that the system designed and also initiated by the ancient Israelites (cf. Joshua) did not work entirely well in practice, as attested especially by the book of Judges (more on that below).

But, there are also indications based on comparative ancient Near Eastern evidence that the ancient Israelites would in any case not have followed the rules and injunctions of the newly conceptualised society to the letter. For example, it is known that, in the ancient Near East, court cases hardly, if at all, quote the extant legal codes. That most Old Testament books, including the books of Samuel and Kings, are only loosely connected to the Israelite legal materials fits with such an idea. Accordingly, one does not, at the minimum as such, need to see the lack of references as indicating that the laws are a later creation, in contrast to what is suggested by Wellhausenian approaches. Also, with rituals, actual practice does not necessarily follow ritual manuals, and this is attested across human societies (cf. 1 Sam 2).[37] In addition, interestingly, Chronicles already indicates a system that is modified from the Pentateuchal legal materials since the time of David by the necessity of the changing setting of the newly build temple in comparison and contrast to the earlier tent of meeting for which the legal materials were at least ostensibly created. And, with apparently less than widespread literacy, as noted in the foregoing, at least before the 8th–7th centuries,[38] it is unlikely that many of the writers of the Old Testament texts should be expected to have known the legal codes and Genesis–Joshua as a whole. On the whole, the materials in Genesis–Joshua can be seen to have remained a vision of a small group of people who could not promulgate it across the society, whether through disseminating the ideas or through coercion, in line with sociological studies that suggest that such methods are necessary for social organisation.[39] From a slightly different but related perspective, the ancient Israelite ideas derive from ancient Near Eastern practice and thinking on the one hand and are tied with producing a narrative of common history (Egyptian slavery and exodus) and common descent (patriarchs, with genealogies particularly associated with priestly materials) on the other. These features link with producing a blueprint for the operation of the new (settler) society (cf. above). All this then can be seen in the light of aiming to produce a social hegemony, with reference to the 20th century Italian sociologist and activist Antonio Gramsci, particularly as interpreted and developed by Routledge, in effect as use of existing cultural resources for hegemonic

---

36 See Routledge, *Moab*, incl. p. 25; idem., *Archaeology*; Schloen, *House*, incl. 46.
37 See e.g. Bell, *Ritual Theory*, 137–140.
38 Cf. Sanders, *Invention*.
39 Cf. esp. the concepts and analysis of centrifugal ideologisation and cumulative bureaucratisation of coercion by Malešević, *Sociology*.

purposes.[40] In the ancient context, such concepts as ANE patrimonialism,[41] tribalism[42] and a sense of searching for freedom (cf. Exodus and liberation)[43] would be useful hegemonic building blocks and can be seen as having been fairly effective in the formation of the ancient Israelite society, as the (wider) biblical evidence seems to indicate. At the same time, other building blocks were not as easily digestible and it is therefore not entirely surprising that they were not internalised and put into practice easily by the ancient Israelites, again as the biblical evidence clearly seems to indicate (e.g. Judges, but also already Exodus–Joshua). This was the case despite of a strong rhetoric about following Yahwism and certain (related) patterns of behaviour, and despite seeking to implement certain social structures depicted in Genesis–Joshua. Malešević's comments about the failure of propaganda in the Soviet Union (and its success in the West)[44] and, from the perspective of ritual, Catherine Bell's discussion of the attempts at ritual innovation in the Soviet Union that were ultimately rather unsuccessful[45] provide interesting comparators. One should further consider that, on the assumption of an early date, the original documents already had to be adapted to changing circumstances from since the rejection of Shiloh and the choice of Jerusalem, and the establishment of kingship and its bureaucratic structures (1 Kgs 4; cf. 1 Sam 8:10–18) would have added to the difficulties with "literal" application.[46] In addition, it would seem that the original settler colonial vision would have become increasingly untenable with the loss of territories in the greater Israel from the ninth century on (2 Kgs 10:32–33), not to speak of the division of Israel into two kingdoms after the time of Solomon (1 Kgs 12).

But, overall there is some, and at least in my opinion clear, indication based on material evidence that a new entity arose in the area,[47] even if there is less certainty with the more specific archaeological detail. On such details, for example, there is certainly the issue of site identifications and such related issues as trying to match them with potential destructions that might be attributable to the Israelites. However, that discussion is covered elsewhere, to my view at the very least broadly satisfactorily, so I will not try and repeat it here.[48] All in all, again, one has to ask the question of to what extent human thinking can be captured in material remains that survive

---

40 See Routledge, *Moab*, esp. 27–40; idem., *Archaeology*, as already noted above, fn. 33.
41 At least aspects of it; cf. Schloen, *House*.
42 Cf. Pitkänen, "P/H and D".
43 Such search would be in the context of escaping the oppressive structures of agrarian societies; cf. Lenski, *Ecological-Evolutionary Theory*, esp. 147–168; Nolan and Lenski, *Human Societies*, esp. 198–200; cf. Pitkänen, "The ecological-evolutionary theory."
44 See Malešević, *Sociology*, 211–215.
45 See Bell, *Ritual*, 225–229.
46 Cf. comments in relation to Chronicles in the foregoing
47 See e.g. Finkelstein, *Archaeology*; Faust, *Israel's Ethnogenesis*; and cf. e.g. comments in Pitkänen, "Pentateuch-Joshua".
48 See e.g. Pitkänen, *Joshua*; idem., *Numbers*; idem., "The ecological-evolutionary"; Hawkins, *Israel*; cf. van Bekkum, *Conquest*. It must be said here that, under the present state of knowledge, Ai remains an issue.

and can be unearthed through archaeology, and one can in general ask the question of to what extent existing material remains should be reflected in the texts.[49] In this context, one may also keep in mind the wider discussion in archaeological theory that archaeological data requires interpretation,[50] just as is the case with textual materials, mutantis mutandis. And, interestingly, one should note that archaeological evidence from the Persian period in relation to the biblical texts is fairly limited[51]

---

49 An interesting example in this respect is the question of cities and Deuteronomy. It is often considered that Deuteronomy reflects an urban or urbanising society (e.g. Weinfeld, *Deuteronomy 1-11*, 36–37; this issue was drawn to my attention by John Bergsma at the conference where this paper was presented). To my mind, a main immediate issue to consider is the use of the word שַׁעַר (*ša'ar*, gate) in Deuteronomy. It seems that in a number of cases the word can be taken in a metonymical sense (see Deut 12:12, 18; 14:27; 16:11, 14; 18:6; 26:12). At the same time, the word gate seems to be more or less meant in Deut 6:9; 11:20; 17:5; 21:19; 22:15, 24; 25:7. Now, it is correct that the new settlements in the Palestinian highlands in Iron Age I were rural and unfortified, and this is in a number of ways comparable to for example developments in the northern Levant (cf. Harmanşah, *Cities*, 33–39). And yet, movement towards rural settlement did not at all mean that cities lost their overall significance, demonstrably so in the northern Levant (Harmanşah, *Cities*, e.g. 68–71), in fact, as Harmanşah points out, building cities was continually considered a feat in the northern Levantine cultural context in Iron Age I as well (see Harmanşah, *Cities*). Also, the situation was not quite the same in Transjordan as in the central Palestinian highlands. In Transjordan, both the biblical text and archaeological evidence indicate at least relative fortification (cf. Pitkänen, *Numbers*, 191–194; Routledge, *Moab*, 94–96). Similarly, Canaanite lowlands more or less remained fortified as is well known. In the context of the settler colonial orientation of the biblical documents, they visualised that Israel would take over and settle all of the highlands, lowlands and Transjordan. In this mix, Deuteronomy can be seen as talking about taking over towns that the Israelites did not build (Deut 6:10, in a future sense; cf. Deut 2:34; 3:4, 10, 12 in a past sense). It should be further noted that the legislation about Levitical towns in the P/H material can be read as indicating town planning in a programmatic settler colonial context (Num 35:1-8; cf. Pitkänen, *Numbers*, 204–209), and the Numbers passage (Num 35:4) indicates that such towns would have walls, at least in the imagination of the author. Moreover, the author of Joshua stipulates the practical implementation of Levitical towns (Josh 21), and I have argued that the same person (cf. in the foregoing in this essay) authored both Deuteronomy and Joshua, so this on its part further suggests that AD was aware of P/H materials (cf. Kilchör, *Mosetora*). Accordingly, and even if, as seems likely, the laws of Deuteronomy have a prehistory before being incorporated in the book of Deuteronomy and Genesis-Joshua as a whole, it would not be entirely impossible for Deuteronomy to speak in terms of towns and gates in its legislation already in Iron Age I (and, of course, assuming differing, even if collaborating and interlinked, authors and streams of tradition for P/H and D, they could on the whole use differing terminology). Rural communities, if thinking in terms of Deuteronomic legislation, would somehow have to substitute for (and adapt) the concept of gate in their local settings (and cf. the immediately apparent use of metonymy in the use of the term gate anyway as pointed out above). One should further note that the ancient Israelite society already started before Iron Age I (cf. comments in the foregoing). Otherwise, the centralising vision in Deuteronomy does not seem to me to necessitate an urban setting (cf. Pitkänen, *Central Sanctuary*). For considerations of what one might be able to say about the economic setting of Deuteronomy in interaction with archaeological data, see the essay by Richter in this volume.
50 Cf. e.g. Bintliff and Pearce, *Death*.
51 For a summary, see Lehmann, "Levant," 841–851.

but the (priestly) documents are nevertheless postulated to have been formed at that time in the Wellhausenian system, in that sense, the situation is hardly worse for the Early Iron Age.

2.5 P/H and D Personnel

We now return to some further details explicitly on the P/H and D materials. The intention here is to propose a possible way of accounting for the different views and perspectives between these two streams and suggest something about possible authorship. The differences in style in particular would seem to suggest the likelihood of a separate provenance for P/H and D in terms of the priestly personnel involved. One possibility, even if somewhat speculative, that I will propose here is that P/H was more or less produced by priests and D by Levites. A clue towards this can be obtained by looking at the construction of the system of priestly and Levitical towns in Joshua 21. In the vision that is attested by the chapter, priests are concentrated in the south (Judah, Simeon, Benjamin). Non-priestly Levites are placed in the north (and also in the East). If one looks at things from the perspective of ethnogenesis, one could also at least partially see this in the sense that a certain group of southerners are being defined as priestly cultic personnel and a certain group of northerners (and Easterners) as Levitical cultic personnel.[52] In the system, especially according to the book of Numbers, the Levites are involved in the service of the tent of meeting, assisting priests who themselves are also part of the Levitical tribe (Num 3–4, 18). With the setting up[53] of the tent of meeting, also as the central sanctuary, at Shiloh, a geographically very central location in the land, one can imagine that there would be both priests and Levites there in its service.[54] Thus one could assume that there would be a mixture of more southern based and more northern based personnel at Shiloh. Someone from the southern oriented contingent would then write Genesis–Numbers, and, equally, someone more oriented towards the north would write Deuteronomy and Joshua, also keeping in mind that Deuteronomy is often seen to be a document with at least northern influences (esp. Deut 27). If so, it would be natural to assume that the documents would attest some cultural and stylistic differences. Thus, the combination of P/H and D into Genesis–Joshua would then be a coming

---

[52] Cf. considerations in Pitkänen, "P/H and D." All in all, one should also note that the demarcation could have contributed towards forming the fault lines of the split of the United Monarchy (1 Ki 12). In addition, it is important to highlight that the Pentateuch indicates that the tombs of most of the patriarchs are in the south (Hebron), surely an important issue ideologically (cf. Pitkänen, "Reading Genesis-Joshua," 18, also noting that 1 Sam 10:2 particularly implies the possibility that the tomb tradition is early), and this could link with the south being associated with priests, already from earliest times.

[53] And maybe even construction; cf. Pitkänen, "P/H and D"; idem., *Numbers*.

[54] Some of these could at least theoretically be on a rotating basis (cf. apparently, or at least potentially, 1 Chr 23–26; also cf. Deut 18:6–8).

together of more southern and more northern traditions into one work, in the context of priests and Levites. If the author of Deuteronomy and Joshua were a Levite, he could be less concerned about priestly details in terms of terminology and on the other hand also e.g. focus on not forgetting the Levites (e.g. Deut 12:19). The speeches of Moses in Deuteronomy could then fairly naturally be seen as a fictional autobiography that would build on the tradition of Moses as a non-priestly Levite and then also attempt to construct a social hegemony through related legislation directly attributed to him (as with the P/H traditions in terms of legislation).[55] Other than this, perhaps a Levitical perspective could account for a wider focus on the land and its projected institutions as a whole, and not only on matters more directly related to priests. And, interestingly, the less than exact terminology of Deuteronomy (esp. the characteristic expression *hakohanim halewiyyim*) could be an attempt towards emphasising the ultimate equality of all Israelites for rhetorical purposes (cf. in slight contrast Num 17), and in that could also draw attention to priests being Levites, without needing to negate the importance of priests in cultic matters. As such, this proposal is building, but with a twist, for example on the work of von Rad who did already suggest Levites as being behind the composition of Deuteronomy.[56] Such a view could also help explain why there are two legal codes focused on the land in the Pentateuch, H (Lev 17–26) and D. Both have a vision of the land, but H is more focused on priesthood (esp. Lev 21–22; 24:1–9) and D on the wider society,[57] and H reflects a more southern[58] and D more northern context and basis,[59] even if the geographical focuses may be seen in the content of the codes themselves only intermittently and not necessarily overwhelmingly strongly in the context of the whole. All in all, Genesis–Joshua can then be seen as a work that unites two types of closely related traditions associated with two (or three) geographical regions into a single piece that emphasises the unity of the newly forming Israelite society in the context of settling the land and replacing indigenous societies under the rubric of promoting Yahwism. The JE style narratives that are also a part of the work can generally be seen in the context of tradition collected by the respective priestly and Levitical authors, with much of such tradition possibly

---

55 Cf. Longman, *Fictional Akkadian Autobiography*. On hegemony, cf. above.
56 See von Rad, *Studies in Deuteronomy*, 66–68, also referring to earlier work by Bentzen that von Rad had not seen, Bentzen, *josianische Reform*. Bentzen, pp. 60–65 suggests that Deuteronomy originates from country Levites. It should be noted that Bentzen otherwise follows the Wellhausenian framework of the development of priesthood and does not consider that priests had yet been distinguished from among Levites at the time when Deuteronomy came about.
57 I would like to thank my former student Lynn Underwood for suggesting that it would be useful to have materials addressed to ordinary people and not just priests.
58 E.g. Judah leads in the wilderness (Num 2) and Levitical towns for the priests are assigned from the South (Josh 21; cf. Lev 25:32-33). Num 7 could also be seen in this way.
59 Note also that the Transjordanians seem to be emphasised slightly more in the Deuteronomic tradition, with the priestly tradition tending to see the status of the land East of the Jordan as somewhat ambiguous; cf. Pitkänen, *Joshua*, 354–380; idem., *Numbers*, incl. on Num 32; and Weinfeld, *Promise*.

oral based. Finally, one could also assume that a copy of Deuteronomy could potentially be kept separately, in addition to a combined copy of Genesis–Joshua (Deut 31:24–26). In addition, one might be able to conceive that some excerpts from Exodus–Numbers could possibly have been kept as ritual manuals, even when it would seem that they were not followed completely in actual practice (e.g. 1 Sam 2), in line with what is known from ritual studies.[60]

3. Summary and Conclusions

This paper has outlined a possible way of looking at and reconstructing the social context of the priestly and deuteronomic materials in a setting that does not assume the main Wellhausenian scheme of development and dating of the Pentatateuchal materials. Such an examination is clearly, if not naturally, linked with dating and compositional issues that relate to this ancient document. Accordingly, I have outlined here how such an alternative reconstruction can link with the wider isagogical issues. I have above all suggested that priests and Levites as cultic personnel are responsible for creating Genesis–Joshua in the context of settling the Canaanite highlands and creating a new society there to replace existing indigenous societies. Such a reconstruction is certainly different from a Wellhausenian one, nevertheless it builds on the idea that a variety of sources were available to the authors from which they created the document. I hope this paper can stimulate further discussion about the Pentateuch in a context that is not limited to the Wellhausenian paradigm that in my view is a hindrance when trying to understand this amazing work from antiquity and the history of ancient Israel. Any new understandings may then also have related new ethical, religious and political implications for today (and also implications for academics). I believe that the above considerations, together with the other presentations at the conference that formed the basis of this volume, do present a plausible and credible alternative to the Wellhausenian approach that also at the minimum accounts very well for the related data as a whole.

---

60 Cf. above.

Bibliography

Bell, Catherine. *Ritual: Perspectives and Dimensions*. New York: Oxford University Press, 1997, with a new foreword in 2009.

—. *Ritual Theory, Ritual Practice*. New York: Oxford University Press 1992, with new foreword in 2009.

Bentzen, Aage. *Die josianische Reform und ihre Voraussetzungen*. København: P. Haase & Søns Forlag, 1926.

Berman, Joshua A. *Created Equal: How the Bible Broke with Ancient Political Thought*. New York: Oxford University Press, 2008.

Bintliff, John, and Mark Pearce, eds. *The Death of Archaeological Theory?* Oxford and Oakville: Oxbow Books, 2012.

Carr, David M. *The Formation of the Hebrew Bible: A New Reconstruction*. New York: OUP, 2011.

Cline, Eric H. *1177 B.C.: The Year Civilization Collapsed*. Princeton, NJ: Princeton University Press, 2014.

Cohen, Yoram. *The Scribes and Scholars of the City of Emar in the Late Bronze Age*. Winona Lake, IN: Eisenbrauns, 2009.

Faust, Avraham. *Israel's Ethnogenesis: Settlement, Interaction, Expansion and Resistance*. London: Equinox, 2006.

Finkelstein, Israel. *The Archaeology of the Israelite Settlement*. Jerusalem: Israel Exploration Society, 1988.

Foster, Benjamin. *The Age of Agade: Inventing Empire in Ancient Mesopotamia*. Abingdon, Oxon: Routledge, 2016.

Frevel, Christian. "The Book of Numbers – Formation, Composition and Interpretation of a Late Part of the Torah. Some Introductory Remarks," in *Torah and the Book of Numbers*. Edited by Christian Frevel, Thomas Pola and Aaron Schart. FAT II 62. Tübingen: Mohr Siebeck, 2013, 1–37.

Galil, Gershon. "The Hebrew Inscription from Khirbet Qeiyafa/Neta'im: Script, Language, Literature and History." *Ugarit Forschungen* 41 (2009): 193–242.

George, Andrew. *The Babylonian Gilgamesh Epic: Introduction, Critical Edition and Cuneiform Texts*. Oxford: OUP, 2003.

Harmanşah, Ömür. *Cities and the Shaping of Memory in the Ancient Near East*. New York: Cambridge University Press, 2013.

Hawkins, Ralph K. *How Israel Became a People*. Nashville: Abingdon Press, 2013.

Hundley, Michael B. *Gods in Dwellings: Temples and Divine Presence in the Ancient Near East*. Writings from the Ancient World Supplement Series 3. Atlanta: Society of Biblical Literature, 2013.

Joosten, Jan. *People and Land in the Holiness Code: An Exegetical Study of the Ideational Framework of the Law in Leviticus 17–26*. Leiden: Brill, 1996.

Kilchör, Benjamin. *Mosetora und Jahwetora. Das Verhältnis von Deuteronomium 12–26 zu Exodus, Levitikus und Numeri*. BZAR 21. Wiesbaden: Harrassowitz, 2015.

Kitchen, Kenneth A. *On the Reliability of the Old Testament*. Grand Rapids, Michigan: Eerdmans, 2003.

Knohl, Israel. *The Sanctuary of Silence: The Priestly Torah and the Holiness School*. Minneapolis: Fortress Press, 1995.

Lehmann, Gunnar. "The Levant during the Persian period," in *The Oxford Handbook of the Archaeology of the Levant c. 8000–332 BCE*. Edited by Margaret Steiner and Ann E. Killebrew. Oxford: Oxford University Press, 2014, 841–851.

Lenski, Gerhard. *Ecological-Evolutionary Theory: Principles and Applications*. London: Paradigm Publishers, 2005.

—. *Power and Privilege: A Theory of Social Stratification*. New York: McGraw-Hill Book Company, 1966.

Longman, Tremper. *Fictional Akkadian Autobiography: A Generic and Comparative Study*. Winona Lake: Eisenbrauns, 1990.

Malešević, Siniša. *The Sociology of War and Violence*. Cambridge: CUP, 2010.

Milgrom, Jacob. *Leviticus*. 3 vols. The Anchor Bible. New York: Doubleday, 1991–2001.

Nihan, Christophe. *From Priestly Torah to Pentateuch. A Study in the Composition of the Book of Leviticus*. FAT II 25. Tübingen: Mohr Siebeck, 2007.

Nolan, Patrick, and Gerhard Lenski, *Human Societies: An Introduction to Macrosociology*, 12th ed. Oxford: Oxford University Press, 2005.

Noth, Martin. *The Deuteronomistic History*. 2nd ed. JSOTSS 15. Sheffield: Sheffield Academic Press, 1991. (German original: *Überlieferungsgeschichtliche Studien. Die sammelnden und bearbeitenden Geschichtswerke im Alten Testament*. Vol. 1. SKG.G 18. Halle: Niemeyer, 1943).

Otto, Eckart. *Das Deuteronomium im Pentateuch und Hexateuch. Studien zur Literaturgeschichte von Pentateuch und Hexateuch im Lichte des Deuteronomiumrahmens*. FAT 30. Tübingen: Mohr Siebeck, 2000.

—. *Deuteronomium 1,1–4,43*. HThKAT. Freiburg: Herder, 2012.

Parker, Cynthia. *Deuteronomy's Place: An Analysis of the Placial Structure of Deuteronomy*. PhD diss., University of Gloucestershire, 2015 [available at http://eprints.glos.ac.uk/2259/, accessed 30/1/17].

Pitkänen, Pekka. *A Commentary on Numbers: Narrative, Ritual and Colonialism*. Routledge Studies in the Biblical World. London: Routledge, 2017.

—. *Central Sanctuary and Centralization of Worship in Ancient Israel: From the Settlement to the Building of Solomon's Temple*, reissue with a new introduction by the author. Piscataway, N.J.: Gorgias Press, 2014, first edition 2003, second publisher's edition 2004.

—. *Joshua*. Apollos Old Testament Commentary 6. Leicester: IVP, 2010.

—. "Pentateuch–Joshua: a settler-colonial document of a supplanting society." *Settler Colonial Studies* 4/3 (2014): 245–276.

—. "P/H and D in Joshua 22:9–34." *Biblische Notizen* 171 (2016): 27–35.

—. "Reading Genesis–Joshua as a unified document from an early date: A settler colonial perspective." *BTB* 45.1 (2015): 3–31.

—. "The ecological-evolutionary theory, migration, settler colonialism, sociology of violence and the origins of ancient Israel." *Cogent Social Sciences* 2/ 1210717 (2016): 1–23 [available at http://dx.doi.org/10.1080/23311886.2016.1210717].

Routledge, Bruce. *Archaeology and State Theory: Subjects and Objects of Power*. London and New York: Bloomsbury, 2011.

—. *Moab in the Iron Age: Hegemony, Polity, Archaeology*, Philadelphia: University of Pennsylvania Press, 2004.

Said, Edward. *Orientalism*. London: Routledge, 1978. Repr. with a new afterword 1995 and new preface in 2003.

Sanders, Seth L. *The Invention of Hebrew*. Urbana, Chicago, and Springfield: University of Illinois Press, 2009.
Schloen, J. David. *The House of the Father as Fact and Symbol: Patrimonialism in Ugarit and the Ancient Near East*. Winona Lake, IN: Eisenbrauns, 2001.
Smith, Anthony D. *The Ethnic Origins of Nations*. Oxford: Blackwell, 1986.
Taggar-Cohen, Ada. *Hittite Priesthood*. Texte der Hethiter: Philologische und historische Studien zur Altanatolistik 26. Heidelberg: Universitätsverlag Winter, 2006.
Tigay, Jeffrey. *The Evolution of the Gilgamesh Epic*. Philadelphia, Pennsylvania: University of Pennsylvania Press, 1982. Repr., Wauconda, IL: Bolchazy-Carducci Publishers, 2002.
Van Bekkum, Koert. *From Conquest to Coexistence: Ideology and Antiquarian Intent in the Historiography of Israel's Settlement in Canaan*. PhD diss., Theologische Universiteit van de Gereformeerde Kerken in Nederland te Kampen, 2010.
Von Rad, Gerhard. *Studies in Deuteronomy*, Studies in Biblical Theology 9. London: SCM Press, 1953 [German Original: *Deuteronomium-Studien*, Göttingen: Vandenhoek & Ruprecht, 1948].
Veracini, Lorenzo. *Settler Colonialism: A Theoretical Overview*. Basingstoke: Palgrave Macmillan, 2010.
Weinfeld, Moshe. *Deuteronomy and the Deuteronomic School*. Oxford: Clarendon Press, 1972 (with reprint Winona Lake: Eisenbrauns, 1992).
—. *Deuteronomy 1–11: A New Translation with Introduction and Commentary*. The Anchor Bible. New York: Doubleday, 1991.
—. *The Place of Law in the Religion of Ancient Israel*. VTSup 100. Leiden: Brill, 2004.
—. *The Promise of the Land: The Inheritance of the Land of Canaan by the Israelites*. Berkeley: University of California Press, 1993 [also available at http://ark.cdlib.org/ark:/13030/ft596nb3tj/; accessed 7/2/17].
Wenham, Gordon J. "The Deuteronomic Theology of the Book of Joshua." *JBL* 90 (1971): 140–148.
Younger, K. Lawson. *A Political History of the Arameans: From their Origins to the End of Their Polities*. Atlanta: SBL Press, 2016.
Zadok, Ran. "The Aramean Infiltration and Diffusion in the Upper Jazira, ca. 1150–930 BCE." Pages 569–579 in The Ancient Near East in the 12th–10th Centuries BCE: Culture and History. Edited by Gershon A. Galil, Ayelet Gilboa, Aren M. Maeir and Daniel Kahn. AOAT 392. Münster: Ugarit, 2012.

Index of Ancient Sources

Old Testament

Genesis
1–11	28, 38–40, 227
1:1–2:5	62
1:1–2:4	243
1:1–2:3	14, 16
1	9, 46
1:1	10
2:4–25	16
2:4	10, 13, 29
2:13	288
3	16
3:14	273
4	16
4:26	60
5–11	39
5	10, 39
5:1–28	246
5:1	29
5:22	10
5:24	10
5:30–32	246
6–9	8, *45–57*
6:7	*45–47*
6:9–11:26	62
6:9–22	243
6:9	10, 13, 29
6:14	269
6:19–20	45
6:20	47, 50
7:2–3	45, 47
7:6	243
7:7	45
7:8–9	50
7:10	49
7:11–12	48
7:11	47, 243
7:12	49
7:13	45
7:13–16	49, 243
7:15–16	48–49
7:16	49
7:17	49, 243
7:18–21	243
7:24	243
8:1–2	243
8:1	46
8:2	47–48
8:3–5	243
8:13	243
8:14–19	243
8:21	46
9:1–17	243
9:15	46
9:28–29	62, 243
10	10
10:1	29, 246
10:2–7	246
10:20	246
10:22–23	246
10:31–32	246
10:32	38
11	39
11:10–26	10, 246
11:10	29
11:27–32	10, 36
11:27	243
11:30	290
11:31–32	243
12–Josh 24	291
12–50	*27–31*, 38, 40
12–36	227
12	291

340   Index of Ancient Sources

12:1–3	33, 36	21:1	243
12:1–2	66	21:2–5	243
12:1	31	21:22–34	31
12:3	38, 40	21:23	288
12:4–5	243	22	36, 297
12:6–8	31	22:2–18	288
12:6	238, 288–290	22:2	288
12:7	289–290	22:15–18	36
12:8	288	22:19	31
12:10–20	10	22:20–24	36, 38
12:27	29	23	243
13:3–4	288	23:1–6	31
13:3	31	23:19	288
13:6	243	24	36
13:11–12	243	24:1–4	31
13:14–17	33	25:7–11	243
13:18	31, 288	25:9	288
14	238, 297	25:12–18	10, 35
14:2	238	25:12–17	246
14:3	238	25:12	29
14:5–7	239	25:19–20	243, 246
14:7	238–239	25:19	10, 13, 29
14:8	238–239	25:26	246
14:13–14	31	26:1–11	10
14:13	192	26:1–6	288
14:14	238–239	26:2–3	66
14:17	238	26:23–25	288
14:18	288	26:26–33	31
15	26, 67	26:34–35	243
15:1–20	33	27	35
15:12–16	26	27:46	243
15:13–16	237	28–32	36
15:16	12	28:1–9	243
16–17	35	28:3	60, 293
16	10	28:17–21	288
16:1	243	29:1–3	31
16:3	62, 243	29:24	243
16:15–16	62, 243	29:28–29	243
17	9, 14, 64, 66, 119, 243	29:31–34	35
17:1	60	30:4	243
17:6–7	120	30:24	291
17:19–21	120	31:3	66
18:1	31, 288	31:5	60
19:29	243	31:13	288
20	10	31:17–24	31
20:1	31	31:18	243
21	10, 35	31:39	87

31:42	60	40:15	192
32:12	288	41:12	192
32:22–31	288	41:40	192
33:7	292	41:46	243
33:8–11	292	41:50–52	192
33:13–17	292	41:52	293
33:18–34:2	31	43:1–10	292
33:18	243, 288	43:4–8	*86*
33:20	289	43:9	*86–87*
34	289	43:32	192
34:12	239	44:18–34	292
34:25–29	289–290	44:32–33	*86–87*
35–Josh 24	291	45:1–3	192
35	289	46:1–4	66, 237, 288
35:1–15	288	46:1	60
35:1–8	31	46:4	12
35:4	288, 290	46:5–7	31
35:9–15	64, 66	46:6–7	243
35:9–13	243	46:8–27	246
35:11	60, 293	46:9–26	63
35:15	243	47:1–6	31
35:16–21	31	47:5–11	243
35:22–29	243, 246	47:27–28	243
35:29	288	48–50	35
36	10	48	295, 297
36:1	29	48:1–20	291, 293
36:6–8	243	48:3–7	243
36:10	29	48:3	60
37–50	227	48:5	291
37	35, 38	48:15–16	291
37:1–2	243	48:19–20	37
37:1	31	48:22	289
37:2	10, 13, 29	49:1	243
37:3	291	49:3–7	292
37:5–11	291	49:8–12	292
37:12–17	31	49:8–10	297
37:26–28	291	49:8	292
37:26–27	292	49:10	292, 297
38	37, 292–293, 295, 297	49:22–26	291, 293
38:2	292	49:28–33	243
38:3–5	292	49:30–31	288
38:7–10	292	50	6
38:12–19	292	50:12–13	243
38:27–30	31, 292	50:13	288
39–48	38	50:23	294
39:14	192	50:24–26	237
39:17	192	50:24	67

50:25–26	26	3:22	63
50:26	235	4	63
		4:1	66
Exodus		4:9	212
1–15	14	4:19	66
1–4	26	4:23	212
1	26	4:27	63
1:1–7	63	5	63, 67
1:1–5	243	5:2	67
1:7	243	5:3	192, 194
1:13–14	243	5:4–5	67
1:15–16	192, 194	5:9	67
1:19	192, 194	5:11	67
2:1–10	8	5:15	67
2:6–7	192, 194	5:16	67
2:11	192, 194	5:18	67
2:13	192, 194	5:21	67
2:23–25	62–63, 243	5:23	67
2:23	66	6	*59–76*
2:24	31	6:1	67
2:25	64, 67	6:2–7:7	63
3:1–6:1	63	6:2–13	69, 243
3–4	10, 26, 60–61, 64–66	6:2–9	14, 62–64, 67
3	4, *59–76*	6:2–8	66
3:1–15	60	6:2–6	60
3:1	63	6:2–4	63
3:2	63	6:2	62, 64
3:3–8	326	6:3	67
3:3	63	6:4	67, 123
3:4	63	6:5–9	63
3:6	31, 63	6:5–6	67
3:7	63, 66	6:6	64, 67
3:8	63–64, 67–68	6:7	67, 123
3:9	66	6:8	63, 66–67
3:11–15	63	6:10–12	13–14, 64, 66
3:12	63	6:12–30	14
3:13–15	63	6:12	14
3:14–15	10, 69	6:13–25	64
3:14	60, 61, 68	6:14–27	13–14, 35, 63
3:15–22	63	6:14–25	246
3:15	63	6:16–20	14
3:16	63	6:26–30	243
3:17	63–64, 68	6:28–30	13–14
3:18	63, 192, 194	6:29–30	64, 66
3:19	63	6:30	14
3:20	67	7:1–13	243
3:21–22	63	7:5	67

Index of Ancient Sources

7:16	192, 194	16:1–3	243
7:17	67	16:1	62
7:19–20	243	16:6–24	243
7:21–22	243	16:31–36	243
7:28	125	17:1	62, 243
8:5–7	243	19:1–Num 10:10	231
8:9	67	19–24	7
8:15	243	19–20	25
8:27	67	19	277–278
9:1	192, 194	19:1–2	62, 243
9:8–12	243	20:1–25:9	83
9:13	192, 194	20:1–17	62
10:3	192, 194	20:22–26	326
11:4	67	20:24–26	103
11:8	67	20:24	180
11:9–10	243	21	189, 192–193
12:1–20	243	21:1–23:19	62
12:12	67	21:2–11	191–194
12:28	243	21:2	191–192, 194
12:34	125	21:5	194
12:37	62, 243	21:7–8	191
12:40–41	62, 243	21:12–14	180
12:43–51	243	21:13	180
12:51	62	21:14	180
13:1–2	243	21:26–27	192, 194
13:12	125	21:28–36	85
13:17	213	23:1–3	181
13:19	237	23:4–5	181
13:20	62, 243	23:6–8	181
14–15	7	23:20–33	118
14:1–4	243	23:25–27	125
14:8–9	243	23:25–26	117
14:9	212	24	*24–25*
14:13	212	24:1–17	*24*
14:15–18	243	24:1–11	118
14:21	243	24:3–8	62
14:21–23	243	24:11	24
14:23	212	24:12–18	*25*
14:26–27	243	24:15–18	25, 243
14:28	243	25–31	265
14:29	243	25:1–31:18	243
15	10	25:9	231, 277
15:1	212	25:21–22	273
15:12–16	67	25:22	272, 274
15:19	212	25:40	277
15:22–23	62	26	280
15:27	62	26:1–34	266

26:1–14	269	11	181
26:31	267	11:2–23	181
26:32	268	13–14	109
26:33	269–270	16:2	269
26:34	270	16:12	269
27:8	277	16:14–15	274
27:9–10	268	16:15	269
28:1	231	17–26	117, 135, 334
28:26	269	17	102, *103–106*
31:18	24	17:3–4	104
32	325	17:6	104–105
32:1	24	17:10–12	104
32:13–14	31	17:13–14	104–106
33:7–11	274, 280	17:13	104, 106
33:10–11	256	18–20	83
33:19	69	18:15	292
34:6–7	69	18:23	181
34:8–28	83	19:19	181
34:10–17	118	19:29	181
34:10–16	118	19:35–36	181
34:29–35	243	20:12	292
34:33–35	273	20:14	181
35–40	265	20:15–16	181
35:1–40:34	243	20:17	181
35:1–19	83	21–22	334
35:12	270	24–27	83
36–39	266	24	232
38:9–20	268	24:1–9	334
39:19	269	24:10–23	243
40	231, 266	25–27	232
40:3	270–271	25–26	151
40:21	270	25	120, 135, *189–205*, 232
40:34–35	231	25:1	232
40:34	231	25:8	199
40:35	231	25:9	199
		25:10	*194–198*, 200
Leviticus		25:13	195
1:1	231–232	25:19	120
3:1–17	105	25:22	120
3:16	105	25:23	326
3:17	104, 106	25:32–33	334
8–10	231	25:39–46	*194–198*, 202
8:1–10:20	243	25:39	192, 195–196
8–9	325	25:40	195
9:23–24	231	25:41–42	192
10	231	25:41	197
11–15	83	25:42	192, 195, 326

Index of Ancient Sources

25:46	195–196	26:26	127, 129–131, 134, 148, 154, 157, 159, 196
26	*115–175*, 195, 230, 326	26:28–33	125
26:3–45	126	26:28	158, 165, 167
26:3–13	119–120, 124, 126	26:29	127, 130, 146, 148
26:3	120, 122	26:30–31	129, 132, 154
26:4–6	121	26:30	134, 158, 167, 275
26:4–5	120	26:31	128, 134–135, 152–153, 156, 159
26:4	121, 123–124, 154	26:32	132, 148, 153, 156, 165
26:5	120, 130, 154, 159, 165–166	26:33	130, 132–133, 145, 148, 151–152, 154, 156, 158–159, 166
26:6–8	120	26:34–45	157, 168
26:6	121, 149, 152, 154, 165	26:34–35	154, 156
26:7	152, 159	26:34	153, 156, 160
26:8	159	26:35	153, 165
26:9–10	120	26:36–39	156
26:9	123, 153, 158, 165	26:36–38	156
26:10	120	26:36	152, 159, 166
26:11–12	120, 122, 124	26:37	166
26:11	154	26:38	159
26:12–13	123	26:39–45	122, 157
26:12	120, 122	26:39–43	158
26:13	120–121	26:39–41	156, 165
26:14–45	135, 163	26:39	116, 131–132, 152–153, 157–159
26:14–33	*125–129*, 135, 153	26:40–45	122, 154
26:14–17	125	26:40–41	156
26:14–15	142	26:40	130, 158, 160
26:15	130, 152, 158	26:41	156, 158, 168
26:16	126, 135, 143–144, 147–149, 151–153	26:42–45	156
26:17	144, 148–149, 151, 154, 157	26:42	31, 158
26:18–20	125	26:43	130, 153, 156, 158, 160, 165
26:18	165	26:44	152, 158–159
26:19–20	127, 151	26:45	158–159, 167
26:19	127, 130, 143, 148, 150, 154, 159	26:46	232
26:20	127, 148, 152, 154	27:34	231–232
26:21–22	125	*Numbers*	
26:21	165	1–26	293
26:22	128–131, 144, 148, 153, 159, 165	1	293
26:23–26	125	1:1–4	243
26:23	165	1:1	231–231
26:24	154, 165	1:5–16	246
26:25–26	153, 195–198	1:17–19	243
26:25	130, 135, 143, 148, 154, 166, 170, 196		

1:20–47	246	17	334
1:48–53	246	17:1–28	243
2	334	18	107, 333
2:1–34	246	18:1–2	110
3–4	333	18:7	269
3	107	19	325
3:1–4	246	20	181
3:5–10	246	20:1–3	325
3:14–25	246	20:1	243
3:26	246	20:2	243
3:27–30	246	20:3–13	243
3:31–32	246	20:22–29	243
3:32	246	21:4	243
3:33–39	246	21:10–11	243
3:40–43	246	22:1	243
3:46–51	246	25	35
7	334	25:6–19	243
7:1–11	243	26	293–294
7:89	243	26:1–4	243
8:1–22	243	26:22	293
8:5–19	246	26:29	294
9:1–23	243	26:34–37	293
10:11–28	243	27–36	293
11–25	293	27:1–23	243
12	109	27:1–11	293–294
13–14	9	27:15–23	325
13:1–3	243	31:1–54	243
13:4–17	278	32	334
13:21	243	33:50–55	118
13:22	278	33:52	134
13:25–26	243	34:1–12	278
13:32	243	34:7	278
14:1–2	243	35:1–8	332
14:5–7	243	35:4	332
14:6–10	293	36	294
14:10	243	36:1–13	243, 293–294
14:26–30	243		
14:34–38	243	*Deuteronomy*	
15:32–36	243	1:1–32:47	83
16–18	325	1–3	179
16	37	1:1–5	180, 182
16:1	243	1:5	102, 180
16:2–11	243	1:8	31
16:16–17	243	2:34	332
16:18–24	243	3:4	332
16:27	243	3:10	332
16:35	243	3:12	332

3:15	294	12:12	314, 332
4	139, *162–163*, 167, 185	12:13–19	105
4:6–8	140	12:13–14	105
4:9	218	12:15–16	106
4:23–28	162	12:15	105, 314
4:23–31	139	12:16	106
4:25–31	162–163, 183	12:17	314
4:25	162–163	12:18	314, 332
4:26–28	138–139	12:19	334
4:26–27	139	12:21	314
4:26	162–163	13:2–10	81
4:27	162–163	13:11	164
4:28	162	14	181
4:29–31	163, 326	14:4–20	181
4:29	162–164	14:19–22	314
4:30	162–163	14:21	214, 314
4:31	163	14:22–23	315
4:44–27:26	301	14:24–26	315–316
5:5	216	14:27	314, 332
5:12	257	14:28–29	314
5:14	314	14:28	314
6:5	161	14:29	314
6:9	332	15	*189–205*
6:10	332	15:1	191, 198
6:14	210	15:2	200
7	118, 124–125	15:3	214
7:2–4	217	15:9	199
7:7–11	31	15:11–12	192
7:13	124	15:12–18	*191–194*, 198
7:25	217	15:12–13	192, 194, 200
8:13	211, 217	15:12	191–195
8:14	218	15:15	192
10:12	161	15:16	192
10:16	161, 168	15:18	191–192, 194, 200
10:18	314	15:22	314
11:4	212	16:5	314
11:13	161	16:11–14	314
11:16	218	16:11	314, 332
11:20	332	16:14	314, 332
11:26	169	16:18–18:22	183, 207, 326
11:29–30	290	16:18	215, 314
11:29	169, 290	17	82, 214, 216
11:30	289–290	17:5	332
12–26	180–181, 207	17:14–20	*207–223*, 326–327
12	102, *103–106*, 181	17:14–15	210
12:5	287	17:14	214
12:8	216	17:15	210, 214, 218–220

348   Index of Ancient Sources

17:16–20	215	28–31	160, 162–163, 165–167, 169, 171–172
17:16–17	207–212, 215–219		
17:16	*209–214*	28–30	160, 162–163, 167, 169, 230
17:17–18	231		
17:17	*214–218*	28–29	169
17:18–19	218	28	81, *115–175*, 218, 301, 326
17:18	218		
17:20	210, 215, 218	28:1–14	*124–125*
18	183	28:1–2	124
18:1–8	110, 327	28:1	125
18:3–5	110	28:3–13	124
18:6–8	110, 333	28:3–6	124–125
18:6	332	28:3	124–125
18:9–14	210	28:4	124–125, 161
18:9	214	28:5	124–125
19	180	28:6	124
19:1–13	180	28:7–13	124
19:4	180	28:7	124, 136, 149
19:11	180	28:8	124–125
19:15–21	181	28:9–10	124
20:1	212	28:9	125
21:1–9	325	28:10	125
21:18–21	314	28:11	124
21:19	332	28:12–13	124, 137
22:1–4	181	28:12	124–125
22:9–11	181	28:13–14	124–125
22:15	332	28:14	152, 161, 165
22:24	332	28:15–68	*136–147*
23:18–19	181	28:15–44	137
23:21	214	28:15	142
24:8–9	*109–110*	28:16–19	136
24:8	110	28:20–47	136
24:14	314	28:20–44	81
25:5–10	314	28:20–25	137
25:7	332	28:20–22	136
25:13–16	181	28:21–22	141, 143
26:3–5	31	28:20	153
26:12	314, 332	28:21	140, 166, 170
27–28	142	28:22	148, 151, 154, 165–166
27	169, 180, 301, 333	28:23–42	137
27:4	290, 296	28:23–24	137, 151
27:12	290	28:23	136, 139, 143, 148–150
27:21	181	28:24	136, 143
27:22	181	28:25–26	137, 151, 195
27:23	181	28:25	136, 140, 144, 149, 195
28–32	160	28:26	136, 144, 149, 152–153, 165, 195, 199

Index of Ancient Sources

28:27–35	137	28:59–61	141, 151
28:27–28	136, 151	28:59	138, 152, 165
28:27	137, 140–141, 143, 154, 165	28:60	138, 154, 165–166
		28:61	138, 165, 169
28:28–29	137, 144	28:62–64	138–139
28:28	165	28:63–68	151
28:29	136–137, 165	28:63	138, 152, 161, 165–166
28:30–33	136–137, 151	28:64	138, 145, 152, 161, 163, 165
28:30	144, 165		
28:31	165	28:65	148–149, 166
28:32	145	28:66–67	165
28:33–34	137	28:66	123,
28:33	137, 140, 147	28:67	138
28:34	136–138	28:68	138, 150, 165–166, 170, 213
28:35–36	136		
28:35	137, 140, 165	29–34	183
28:36–37	137, 151	29–32	*160–169*
28:36	136–138, 140, 145, 152, 161, 165	29–31	115, 119, 160, 163, 171
		29–30	119, 160, *164–167*, 185
28:37	136–137, 140, 153	29	167
28:38–42	136–137	29:1–14	184
28:38–40	140	29:1–2	182
28:38–39	141	29:3	166
28:38	141–142	29:6	165
28:39–40	154	29:12	165
28:40	151	29:15–30:20	184
28:41	137, 145, 165	29:15	165
28:43–44	137	29:16	167, 217
28:44	137	29:18–20	160
28:45–47	137	29:20–21	169
28:45	137, 145	29:21–27	162
28:46–57	137	29:21–24	184
28:46	152	29:21	161, 165
28:47	137, 165	29:22	142, 154, 165–166
28:48–57	137	29:24	192
28:48–52	151	29:25	152
28:48	137, 140, 146, 153, 165–166	29:26	161
		29:27	161, 165–166, 169
28:49	140	30	163, 167
28:51	138, 141–142	30:1–10	162–163
28:53–57	127, 137, 146	30:1–8	326
28:53	153	30:1–3	165, 184
28:55	153	30:1	161, 165–166, 169
28:57	153	30:2	161, 163
28:58–68	138	30:3–5	164
28:58	138, 169	30:3–4	164
28:59–68	138	30:3	152, 161, 163–166, 168

30:4	165–166	14–15	294
30:5	161, 165–166, 168	15:8	288
30:6	161, 166–168, 184	16–17	294
30:7	161, 168	18–19	294
30:8–10	165	18:28	288
30:8	161, 163, 165	19:40–48	238
30:9	161, 166	21	326, 333–334
30:11	161	24	26, 289, 291, 294–295
30:17	161, 165–166	24:1–28	83
30:18	163	24:1	290
31	167	24:2–4	31
31:1–8	183	24:19–24	290
31:8	165	24:25	290
31:9–10	183	24:26	290
31:16–21	185	24:32	237, 291
31:16–18	162, 185		
31:16	152, 162, 165	*Judges*	
31:18	161	5	7
31:19	162, 169	7:1	289
31:20	152, 161, 165	8:14	329
31:24–26	231, 335	9:6	219
31:29	163, 165	9:37	294
32	7, 185	17:6	37
32:21	140	18:1	37
32:36	162	18:27–29	238
32:39	162	19:1	37
32:43	162	19:10	288
32:48–52	243	20:27	35
33:5	326	20–21	37
33:13–17	291	21:25	37
33:17	293		
34	3	*1 Samuel*	
34:1	243	1	179
34:7–9	243	2	330, 335
34:8	10	4:6	192
34:10–12	181, 185	4:9	192
		8:2–5	220
Joshua		8:5	220
3:14–17	140	8:7	326
4:1–2	140	8:10–18	331
8	294	8:11–17	326
8:30–35	290	8:11	211
8:30–33	290	8:19–20	220
8:30	290, 296	10:2	333
11:4	212	13:3	192
11:6	212	13:7	192
11:9	212	13:19	192

14:11	192	16:31–32	214
14:21	192	18:6	271
17:25	194	18:36	31
22:2	153		
24:2	238	*2 Kings*	
24:6	238	10:32–33	331
29:3	192	11:15	269
		12:9–10	303–304
2 Samuel		13:22–23	31
5:13–16	217	15:19–20	304
7:11–16	207	17	294
15:1	211–212	17:21	170
22:10–15	275	18:24	212
		22:1–6	304
1 Kings		25	180
1:5	211	25:22–26	305
1:33	288		
3–11	*216–217*	*Isaiah*	
3:10–14	217	2:7–9	209
3:13	216	2:7	212
4	331	9:19	134
5–8	266	10:27	165
5:6	211–212	17:8	275
6–8	265	22:18	210
6	273	27:9	275
6:15	269	30:1–7	209
6:16	269	30:2	209, 213
6:31–32	271	30:15–16	209
7:25	269	31	212
8	273	31:1–3	209
8:4	271	31:1	209, 212–213
8:58	216	36:8	212
9–11	217	58:6	192, 194
9:26–11:9	217	65:23	152
10–11	208		
10:21	217	*Jeremiah*	
10:25	210	2:8	17
10:26	211, 217	2:22	211
10:27	217	4:4	168
10:28–29	212, 216–217	5:15	140
11	216–217	5:24	123
11:1–11	214	6:23	212
11:1–9	216	7:33–34	152
11:1	214	7:33	153
11:2–4	216	9:15	152
11:8	214	11:10	152
12	331	14	134–135

352 Index of Ancient Sources

14:12	135, 140, 196	30:22	165
14:19	134–135	30:23	165
14:21	158	30:24	165
16:4	153	31:12	141
19	153	31:31–34	168
19:7–9	152	32	*164–167*
19:7	152	32:12	194
19:8	153	32:24	196
19:9	153	32:36–44	166–167
19:11	140	32:36–37	167
21:7	196	32:36	166–167, 196
21:9	196	32:37	166–167
22:13–17	209	32:39	166
24:9	140	32:40	166–167
24:10	196	32:41	166
25:11–14	164	32:43	166
25:11	160	32:44	166
27:3	213	33	167
27:7	160	34	*189–205*
27:8	196	34:8–22	189, *191–203*
27:13	196	34:8–11	189, 199–203
28:14	140	34:8	195, 197, 200
29–32	140	34:8–9	200
29	*164–167*	34:9–11	192, 194
29:10–14	164	34:9	191–196, 200–203
29:10	160, 164	34:10	193, 195, 199–202
29:13–24	164	34:11	195, 197, 199–202
29:13	164	34:12–22	189, 199, 201–203
29:14	164	34:13–14	202–203
29:17–18	196	34:13	192–193
30	*164–167*	34:14	189, 191–196, 200, 202–203
30:3	164, 166		
30:5	165	34:15–22	202–203
30:6	165	34:15–17	195, 197
30:7	165	34:15	197
30:8	165–166	34:16	192, 194, 197–198
30:9	165	34:17	153, 192, 195–197
30:10	165	34:20–21	196
30:11	165	34:20	153, 195
30:12	165	34:22	195
30:13	165	37:5–10	212
30:14	165	38:2	196
30:15	165	38:19	194
30:16	165	40–41	305
30:17	165	40:11–12	194
30:18	164–165	41:3	194
30:19	165	41:4–5	306

42:17	196	14:15–16	130
42:22	196	14:15	129–131
43:9	194	14:17	130
44:1	194	14:19	130
44:13	194	14:21	130–131, 196
51:64	236	15:7–8	157
52	236	15:9	132
52:28	194	16	158
52:30	194	16:3–5	158
		16:59–63	133, 158
Ezekiel		16:60	158
1:5–18	273	16:61	158
1:27	269	16:63	158
4	132	17:4	315
4:16–17	132, 157	17:12	315
4:16	131	17:13	315
4:17	153	17:15	209, 212–213
5–7	133	18:17–20	158
5	133	19:7	133
5:2	132	20:5–6	66
5:6	130	20:8–9	158, 167
5:8–17	131	20:9	159, 167
5:12	132, 140, 196	20:13	130
5:17	131, 196	20:16	130
6	132	20:24	130
6:1–14	132	20:30–44	158
6:3–6	132	20:33–44	158
6:3	130, 132	20:40–44	133–134
6:4	275	20:43	158
6:5	132	22:15–16	159
6:6	132, 275	24:15–27	134
6:11–12	196	24:21–24	159
6:12	140	24:21	130
7:15	196	24:23	131–132, 153, 157
10:2	269	25:7	159
10:6	269	25:19	120
10:7	269	27:13	315
11:8	130	27:15	315
11:14–21	158	27:17	315
11:17–19	122	27:20	315
11:20	120, 122	27:22–24	315
12:14	132	27:35	132
12:16	196	28:7	132
12:18–19	131	28:16	273
14	130	28:25–26	158
14:12–23	*129–130*	28:26	120
14:13	129–130	29:8	130

29:16	209	45:12	312
30:6	131		
30:11	132	*Hosea*	
30:18	131	1:7	212
33:2–3	130	2:10	141
33:10	131	2:24	141
33:11	131	4:9–10	153
33:28	131	4:9	153
34	121–122	4:10	134, 153
34:10	121	5:11	140
34:11–16	158	5:13	140, 213
34:22	121	8:9	213
34:23–31	158	10:8	134
34:24–30	121	10:13	209
34:24–28	*120–121*	11:5	212–213
34:25–30	121	14:4	209, 212
34:25	120–121		
34:26–27	120	*Amos*	
34:26	121, 123	4	153–155
34:27	120–121	4:6–12	153
34:28	120–121	4:6–11	153–155
34:30–31	120, 122	4:6	154
36	122, 133	4:7	154
36:8–15	158	4:8	154
36:9–11	120	4:9	154
36:11	120	4:10	154
36:15	140	4:11	154
36:23	122	5:21–22	134
36:24–28	168		
36:26	122	*Jonah*	
36:27	120, 122	1:9	192
36:28	120		
36:30	120	*Micah*	
36:32–38	158	5:9	212
36:33–35	133	6:9–13	304
36:34–35	133	6:14	134
37	121–122, 158	6:15	140
37:22	121		
37:23	120	*Zephaniah*	
37:25–26	121	1:11	304
37:26–27	120		
37:26	120	*Haggai*	
37:27	122	2:10–14	306
37:28	121–122		
40–48	265	*Zechariah*	
44	107–109	7:1–7	306–307
44:10–16	107	8	123

8:12	123	10:2–44	292
9:10	212	10:2	214
		10:10–11	214
Psalm		10:14	214
18:10–15	277	10:17–18	214
28:8	209	10:44	214
33:16–17	209		
33:17	209	*Nehemiah*	
72	207	2:7	310, 314
76:2	288	2:8	315
77:17–18	48	2:9	310, 314
88:6	194	3:7	310, 314
96:3	140	3:9	314
96:10	140	3:12	314
104:2–4	277	3:14–18	314
105	31	5:1–9	313
106:34–35	140	5:1–7	314
119:143	153	5:4	310
147:10–11	209	5:14–15	310
		5:14	314
Job		5:15	314
3:19	194	5:18	314
31:13	130	7:2	315
39:3	192	7:65	314
39:5	192, 194	7:69	314
		7:70–72	314
Proverbs		7:70–71	312–313
3:20	48	7:70	314
4:10	211	8:9	314
6:1–5	89	9:2	160
21:31	209, 212	9:7–8	31
22:16	211	10:2	314
27:13	89	10:38–40	315
31:3	214	12:26	314
		13:15–21	313
Ruth		13:15	315
4:18–22	31, 37	13:16	314–315
		13:20	315
Esther		13:26–27	214, 292
6:8–11	211	13:26	214
Ezra		*1 Chronicles*	
2:63	314	2:1–4:20	292
2:69	312–313	3:5–9	217
3:7	315	4:21–23	292
4:4–5	256	6	326
8:27	312–313	21:12	196

356   Index of Ancient Sources

23–26	333	3:1	288
28	266	4:4	269
28:5	207	5:5	271
28:18	273	14:4	134, 275
29:7–19	31	20:9	196
29:7	312–313, 316	30:6	3
29:23	207	34:4	134, 275
		34:7	134, 275
2 Chronicles		36:21	160
3–8	265		

Ancient Near Eastern Literature

Annals of Ashurbanipal		*Codex Lipit-Ishtar*	
	129	XXII 34–52	129
Assyrian King List		*Cuneiform Texts from Ugarit (KTU)*	
	37	1.1.III 1	267
		1.1. III 23–24	267
Baal Cycle		1.4.I 29	275
I:188–189	267	1.14.III 52–58	275
		1.14.IV 1–8	275
Codex Eschnunna		1.106.12–13	275
	88, 95	1.112.3	275
53–55	85		
		Deir Alla Inscription	
Codex Hammurapi		Comb. I	254
	81, 88, 95, *142–147*,	Comb. II, 10	128
	148	Comb. II, 12	128–129
XLIV 44–68	85		
XLIX 18–28	142	*Esarhaddon Succession Treaty*	
XLIX 53–54	145–146		81, 90, *141–147*, 148,
XLIX 66–67	146		150
XLIX 68–72	144	§38A–39	143
XLIX 74	145	§40	144
XLIX 80	145–146	§41	144
L 2–6	144	§42	144
L 64–71	143	§47	127, 129, 144
L 81–91	144	§59	144
LI 19–23	145	§63	143, 148
LI 50–69	143	§64	143
LI 84–91	143, 145	§69	129, 144
		§76	129

Gilgamesh Epic	8, 39	II 27	155
XI	*52–54*, 56	II 48	155
XI:98–103	47–48	II 59	155
		III 13	155
Kudurru of Merodach-Baladan I		III 38	155
SB33, III, 11–15	142	III 39	155
		V 61–62	156
Mesha Stele	254	V 90	155
		VIII 73	155
Sefire Steles	148	VIII 100	156
I 27	141	IX 20	156
I A 30	128	X 26	155
I A 32	128	XVIII 5	156

Tell Fekheriye Bilingual Inscription
         127–128, 141–142

I A 36	142		
II A 9	128	18–19 (Aram.)	141
		30–32 (Akkad.)	141
Sinuhe	37	37–38 (Akkad.)	142

Sumerian King List
    39–40

Treaty between Ashur-Nerari V and Mati'-Ilu   129

Šumma Izbu		
I 94	147	
II 3	155	*Treaty between Shatiwazza and*
II 6	155	*Shuppiluliuma I* 142
II 19	155	

Second Temple Jewish Literature

ben Sira	254	41:25–26	295
		41:27	295
Book of Jubilees	8, 293, *295–296*, 298	41:28	295
1:28	295	44:24	295
1:29	295		
4:26	295	*Genesis Apocryphon (1QapGen)*	
8:19	295	22:15	288
18:13	288, 295		
31:1–32	295	*Great Isaiah Scroll (1QIsa^a)*	
32:9	295		242
32:22	295		
41:1	295	*Josephus, Antiquities*	
41:2	295	3.122-125	270
41:23–25	295	8.72	271

11.340   291

Josephus, Jewish War
6.438   288

Temple Scroll (11Q19)
               8, 211, 298

New Testament

Mark
15:38   271

Hebrews
10:20   271

Rabbinic Sources

Baraita on the Erection of the Tabernacle
1:10   270
4:1   270

Mishna and Talmud
b. Menahot 62a   271
b. Menahot 98a   271
b. Sotah 37a   271
b. Sukkah 7b   271
m. Yoma 5.1   271

Greek and Roman Sources

Apollodorus, Bibliotheca
1.6.3.   277

Corpus Iuris Civilis
               79

Diodorus, Bibliotheca historica
XIII, 86.3   276
XX, 14.4–6   276
XX, 65   276

Dionysiaca
2.364–367   277
2.391ff.   277
2.414ff.   277

Gortyn Code   82, 90

Twelve Tables 82, 90

Index of Modern Authors

Aalders, G.Ch. 238, 241
Abegg, Martin 290, 296, 299
Achenbach, Reinhard 57, 61, 65, 69, 72
Aharoni, Yohanan 278, 280, 283, 319, 320
Aichele, George 3, 6, 18
Albertz, Rainer 72, 201, 213, 214, 219, 220, 266, 268, 271, 273, 283
Amit, Yairah 289, 299
Andersen, T. David 249, 261
Ankersmit, Frank R. 71, 72
Armgardt, Matthias 73, 75, 91, 99
Arnold, Bill T. 72, 74, 242
Arubas, Benjamin 319
Ashkenazi, D. 309, 317
Astruc, Jean 21, 62, 72, 74, 76
Auerbach, Erich 202, 204
Averbeck, Richard E. 24, 25, 26, 27, 28, 30, 31, 33, 34, 40, 70, 73, 265
Awabdi, Mark A. 67, 73
Baden, Joel S. 3, 19, 23, 24, 33, 41, 59, 64, 73, 101, 111, 179, 186
Baentsch, B. 273, 283
Balentine, Samuel E. 118, 126, 172
Baranowski, Krysztof J. 127, 172
Barstad, Hans 72, 73, 305, 317
Barton, John 24, 25, 41, 230, 241
Beckman, Gary 142, 172
Beer, G. 283
Bekkum, Koert van 67, 70, 72, 73, 338
Bell, Catherine 325, 330, 331, 336
Ben-Baraq, Zafrirah 219, 220
Ben-Tor, Amnon 302, 317
Benckert, H. 233, 241
Bentzen, Aage 334, 336
Bergey, Ronald L. 245, 261
Bergsma, John S. 153, 172, 189, 192, 195, 198, 204, 332
Berman, Joshua A. 8, 14, 18, 28, 41, 60, 73, 98, 99, 180, 186, 209, 215, 216, 217, 218, 220, 326, 336
Berner, Christoph 4, 6, 18, 69, 73

Betlyon, John W. 304, 305, 308, 309, 310, 312, 313, 317
Bintliff, John 332, 336
Blenkinsopp, Joseph 262, 298, 305, 306, 307, 317, 319, 320, 321
Bloch-Smith, Elizabeth 303, 317
Blum, Erhard 5, 18, 61, 65, 70, 73
Block, Daniel I. 31, 41, 108, 112, 174, 222, 223, 320
Borger, Rykle 142, 172
Botterweck, G. Johannes 220
Braulik, Georg 182, 186, 210, 216, 221
Brettler, Marc Z. 24, 41, 216, 221
Brockelmann, C. 269, 283
Brodie, Thomas L. 10, 11, 15, 16, 18
Brueggemann, Walter 216, 221
Brunner-Traut, Emma 16, 18
Burckhardt, Leonhard 82, 91
Butcher, K. 278, 283
Bybee, Joan L. 248, 249, 261
Cardellini, Innozenzo 189, 193, 204
Campbell, Anthony F. 22, 41
Cancik-Kirschbaum, Eva 94, 99
Cantrell, Deborah O'Daniel 211, 221
Carr, David M. 3, 11, 18, 22, 26, 27, 28, 41, 46, 47, 52, 57, 59, 61, 65, 66, 69, 73, 191, 204, 328, 329, 336
Carroll, Robert 305, 317
Carter, Charles E. 311, 317
Cassuto, Umberto 11, 56, 57, 267, 273, 283
Cathcart, Kevin J. 127, 134, 141, 142, 172
Charlesworth, James H. 290, 296, 299
Charpin, Dominique 93, 96, 99
Chavel, Simeon 189, 193, 196, 202, 203, 204
Childs, Brevard S. 266, 283
Cholewiński, Alfred , 104, 111, 182, 186
Chouraqui, André 15, 18
Clements, R.E. 216, 221, 263
Clifford, R.J. 267, 283

Cline, Eric H. 329, 336
Clines, D.A. 272, 273, 283
Cohen, David 249, 261
Cohen, Ohad 245, 261
Cohen, Yoram 329, 336
Collart, P. 274, 283
Colenso, John W. 63, 73
Cook, John A. 249, 261
Corwin, Rebecca 244, 246, 261
Coupel, P. 274, 283
Craigie, Peter C. 124, 139, 150, 172
Crawford, C.D. 281, 283
Crawford, Timothy G. 128, 129, 173
Cross, Frank M. 32, 41, 265, 267, 276, 281, 284, 312
Crüsemann, Frank 301, 317
Dahl, Östen 248, 249, 261
Dalley, S. 212, 221
Dever, William G. 302, 317, 318
Dietrich, Walter 6, 18
Dillmann, August 63, 74, 103
Dohmen, Christoph 69, 74
Dossin, Georges 215, 221
Dozeman, Thomas B. 57, 59, 61, 65, 67, 68, 73, 74, 75, 76, 179, 187
Dreytza, Manfred 236, 241
Drijvers, H.J.W. 274, 275, 276, 278, 284
Driver, Samuel R. 50, 57, 243, 244, 246, 261, 278, 284
Dutcher-Walls, Patricia 208, 215, 221
Ebach, Jürgen 86, 91
Ebach, Ruth 208, 221
Ede, Franziska 6, 19
Edenburg, Cynthia 299
Edzard, Dietz O. 97, 99
Ehrenreich, Ernst 160, 168, 173
Ehrensvärd, Martin 247, 252, 256, 264
Eichhorn, Johann G. 62, 74
Eissfeldt, Otto 76, 278, 284
Emerton, John 55, 57, 222, 317
Enns, Peter 69, 74
Eph'al, Israel 303, 311, 317, 318
Ernst, Wolfgang 98, 99
Eskhult, Mats 246, 251, 252, 261, 262
Fabry, Heinz-Josef 209, 220
Faust, Avraham 303, 305, 306, 308, 318, 331, 336

Fearon, James D. 314, 318
Finkelstein, Israel 302, 303, 307, 318, 320, 331, 336
Finsterbusch, Karin 124, 136, 173
Fischer, Georg 9, 10, 14, 17, 18, 19, 66, 67, 68, 69, 74, 108, 111, 140, 147, 152, 153, 156, 163, 164, 165, 166, 168, 173, 174, 183, 187, 189, 190, 192, 193, 204, 298, 299
Fischer, Irmtraud 10, 19
Fischer, Olga 260, 262
Fishbane, Michael 191, 204
Fitzmyer, Joseph A. 128, 141, 142, 173
Fleming, Daniel E. 30, 41, 267, 284
Flint, Peter 299
Florenskij, Pavel 16, 19
Foster, Benjamin 41, 48, 326, 336
Frankena, Rintije 81, 91
Freedman, David N. 196, 197, 204, 232, 241, 273, 284
Fretheim, T.E. 281, 284
Freud, Liora 310, 319, 320
Frevel, Christian 3, 5, 7, 9, 10, 15, 19, 20, 179, 187, 324, 336
Freyberger, K. 278, 284
Fried, Lisbeth S. 196, 197, 204, 310, 318
Friedman, R.E. 271, 284
Fritz, Volkmar 271, 280, 284
Gadot, Yuval 310, 319, 320
Galil, Gershon 220, 328, 336, 338
Ganzel, Tova 117, 158, 173
García López, Felix 209, 221
Garrett, Duane 238, 241
George, Andrew R. 48, 57, 241, 329, 336
Gerbrandt, Gerald E. 213, 221
Gerstenberger, Erhard S. 120, 126, 129, 131, 132, 154, 173
Gertz, Jan C. 19, 20, 41, 42, 51, 57, 59, 61, 62, 69, 72, 73, 74, 101, 111, 173, 174, 179, 186, 187, 204, 205, 299, 300
Gesenius, William 244, 262
Gilboa, Ayelet 302, 318, 338
Gile, Jason 298, 299
Gitin, Seymour 302, 317, 318
Gitler, Haim 304, 312, 313, 318
Givón, Talmy 253, 262

Glanz, Oliver 194, 195, 204
Glassner, Jean-Jacques 39, 41
Gooding, D.W. 269, 271, 272, 284
Gosden, Chris 32, 41
Graupner, Axel 9, 19, 209
Gray, G.B. 278, 284
Green, William H. 239, 241
Greenstein, Edward L. 3, 19
Grossfeld, Bernard 211, 221
Grünwaldt, Klaus 119, 120, 121, 126, 129, 130, 131, 132, 148, 154, 156, 173
Guenther, Allen R. 245, 252, 262
Gunneweg, Anton H.J. 107, 109, 111
Gutzwiller, Kathryn 230, 241
Hagedorn, Anselm C. 208, 216, 221
Hahn, Scott 60, 74
Hallo, William W. 8, 19, 42, 43, 48, 57
Halpern, Baruch 208, 209, 221, 319
Häner, Tobias 120, 121, 122, 130, 131, 132, 133, 158, 173
Haran, Menahem 110, 265, 266, 270, 271, 272, 273, 274, 281, 284
Harmanşah, Ömür 326, 332, 336
Hartenstein, Friedhelm 5, 19, 59, 74, 76, 179, 187
Hartley, John E. 119, 120, 129, 131, 132, 173
Hartmann, R. 272, 284
Hasel, Gerhard F. 160, 173
Hawkins, Ralph K. 331, 336
Hayes, John H. 22, 41
Helck, Wolfgang 221
Hendrix, R. 266, 284
Hieke, Thomas 13, 19, 119, 120, 123, 126, 131, 132, 135, 153, 156, 158, 159, 173
Hilgert, Markus 97, 99
Hill, Andrew E. 245, 262
Hillers, Delbert S. 151, 173
Hjelm, Ingrid 290, 291, 296, 299
Hoffmeier, James K. 41, 72, 74, 264, 271, 282, 284
Hoftijzer, Jacob 128, 129, 173, 267, 284
Holladay, John 303, 304, 318
Holladay, William L. 189, 193, 204
Hölscher, Gustav 301, 318

Holwerda, Benno 70, 74
Hood, Jared C. 70, 74
Hopkins, David C. 303, 318
Hornkohl, Aaron D. 190, 194, 204, 245, 262
Horowitz, Wayne 39, 41
Houtman, Cees 11, 17, 19, 68, 69, 74, 75, 101, 111, 228, 240, 241
Huddleston, Neil A. 218, 223
Hundley, Michael B. 325, 336
Hupfeld, Hermann 62, 63, 68, 70, 74, 179, 187
Hurowitz, A.V. 266, 268, 271, 284, 285
Hurvitz, Avi 107, 110, 111, 190, 204, 245, 246, 250, 251, 252, 253, 255, 259, 260, 262, 263
Ikeda, Yutaka 210, 212, 221
Jackson, Bernhard S. 84, 91
Jacob, Benno 11, 13, 19
Janowski, Bernd 272, 285
Jeremias, Jörg 154, 173
Johnson, J. Cale 95, 99
Johnston, Philip S. 219, 221, 222
Jonker, Louis 112, 311, 318
Joosten, Jan 103, 111, 190, 204, 246, 247, 252, 257, 261, 263, 324, 336
Kaiser, Otto 63, 74
Kartveit, Magnar 289, 290, 296, 297, 299
Kaufman, Stephen A. 127, 128, 141, 142, 173
Kaufmann, Yehetzkel 22, 108, 110, 112, 117, 279, 285
Kelso, James L. 307, 318
Kessler, John 153, 154, 155, 173
Kilchör, Benjamin 4, 19, 72, 73, 75, 99, 102, 103, 106, 110, 111, 169, 173, 180, 181, 182, 187, 232, 241, 323, 324, 332, 336
King, Philip J. 312, 318
Kitchen, Kenneth A. 79, 81, 82, 83, 84, 91, 265, 273, 280, 282, 285, 326, 336
Klostermann, August 107, 111
Knauf, Ernst A. 315, 318
Knobel, August 63, 75
Knohl, Israel 110, 265, 266, 277, 281, 285, 324, 336

Knoppers, Gary N. 207, 216, 221, 287, 291, 299, 230, 301, 312, 318, 319
Konkel, Michael 107, 108, 112
Kooij, G. van der 128, 129, 173
Koorevaar, Hendrik J. 118, 173, 228, 230, 231, 232, 235, 241
Koschaker, Paul 87, 88, 89, 90, 91
Krapf, Thomas M. 110, 112
Kropat, Arno 244, 246, 263
Krüger, Thomas 5, 12, 19
Kuenen, Abraham 5, 21, 63, 64, 68, 75, 101, 110
Kuhn, Thomas S. 21, 41
Kuryłowicz, Jerzy 249, 263
Kutscher, Eduard Y. 244, 245, 263, 264
Laato, Antti 288, 296, 299
Labuschagne, Caspar J. 209, 210, 216, 221
Landsberger, Benno 95, 97, 99
Lane, E.W. 276, 285
Lang, Brenden 28, 42
Lawrence, Paul 81, 82, 83, 84, 91
Lehmann, Gunnar 332, 337
Leichty, Erle 147, 153, 154, 155, 173
Lenski, Gerhard 325, 326, 327, 331, 337
Leuenberger, Martin 236, 241
Levin, Christoph 61, 65, 75, 101, 112
Levine, Baruch A. 126, 127, 128, 129, 130, 131, 132, 134, 147, 148, 149, 153, 157, 158, 174, 266, 285, 294, 299
Levinson, Bernard M. 46, 50, 57, 74, 103, 112, 180, 187, 189, 190, 193, 195, 196, 197, 201, 202, 203, 204, 205, 300, 301, 319
Levitt Kohn, Risa 107, 112, 117, 158, 173, 298, 299
Lichtheim, Miriam 38, 42
Liddell, H.G. 270, 285
Lipschits, Oded 304, 305, 306, 309, 310, 311, 317, 319, 320, 321
Lock, Gary 32, 41
Loewenstamm, Samuel 47, 48, 56, 57
Lohfink, Norbert 186, 207, 208, 212, 221, 222, 301, 319
Long, V. Philips 234, 242
Longacre, Robert E. 250, 264

Longman, Tremper 334, 337
Luhmann, Niklas 95, 99
Lundbom, Jack R. 189, 193, 204, 212, 213, 214, 216, 222
Lust, Johan 66, 75
Lyons, Michael A. 107, 112, 117, 119, 121, 122, 126, 130, 131, 132, 133, 155, 158, 174, 191, 196, 204, 298, 299
MacDonald, Nathan 107, 112, 314, 319
Maier, Christl 112, 189, 204
Maier, Johann 209, 222, 272, 273, 285
Malešević, Siniša 330, 331, 337
Mark, Martin 86, 91
Markl, Dominik 14, 17, 19, 20, 173, 174, 204, 223, 300
Marshall, Alfred 301, 319
Marx, Alfred 5, 14, 20
Master, Daniel 303, 304, 305, 306, 315, 318, 319
Mathys, Hans-Peter 103, 112
Mayes, A.D.H. 209, 213, 222
Mazar, Amihai 302, 319
McConville, J. Gordon 207, 210, 214, 222, 230, 242
McEvenue, Sean E. 9, 20, 50, 57
McKane, William 22, 42
Meshorer, Y. 312, 319
Meyers, Carol 303, 319
Milgrom, Jacob 110, 119, 120, 148, 173, 174, 204, 272, 273, 276, 277, 285, 323, 324, 337
Millard, Alan 37, 42, 220, 264
Millard, Matthias 238, 242
Miller, Cynthia L. 253, 261, 262, 263m 264
Miller, P.D. 196, 204
Milstein, Sara J. 40, 42
Miscall, Peter 3, 6, 18
Moberly, R.W.L. 67, 68, 70, 75
Möller, Wilhelm 238, 242
Morrow, Jeffrey L. 60, 75
Müller, Reinhard 299
Nakhai, Beth A. 303, 317
Nam, Roger S. 303, 304, 319
Nelson, Richard D. 208, 213, 214, 219, 222, 314, 319

Neumann, Hans 96, 99
Niccacci, Alviero 250, 264
Nicholson, Ernest 6, 10, 20, 214, 216, 219, 222
Niditch, Susan 31, 42
Nihan, Christophe 102, 104, 112, 181, 187, 188, 227, 242, 287, 300, 301, 319, 324, 337
Nodet, Etienne 290, 300
Nolan, Patrick 326, 327, 331, 337
Nöldeke, Theodor 63, 75
Noordtzij, Arje 126, 174
Noth, Martin 3, 20, 22, 64, 71, 75, 179, 187, 228, 242, 245, 266, 273, 278, 285, 324, 337
Notley, R. Steven 309, 311, 320
O'Brien, Mark A. 22, 41
O'Connor, B. 273, 284
Oeming, Manfred 319
Olmo Lete, G. del 275, 285
Oshima, Takayoshi 39, 41
Oswald, Wolfgang 6, 20, 283
Otto, Eberhard 221
Otto, Eckart 6, 20, 57, 61, 65, 75, 79, 85, 91, 93, 96, 99, 102, 104, 105, 110, 112, 139, 162, 168, 174, 179, 180, 181, 182, 183, 184, 185, 187, 208, 209, 210, 214, 218, 222, 324, 325, 337
Pagliuca, William 248, 249, 261
Pakkala, Juha 52, 57, 202, 205, 301, 314, 319
Panitz-Cohen, Nava 303, 320
Parker, Cynthia 326, 327, 337
Parpola, Simo 129, 142, 174
Paul, Mart-Jan 103, 112
Payne Smith, R. 269, 285
Pearce, Mark 332, 336
Peels, H.G.L. 69, 75
Peletz, Michael P. 32, 42
Perkins, Revere 248, 249, 261
Person, Raymond F., Jr. 31, 42
Petersson, Lina 70, 75, 243, 264
Petschow, Herbert 89, 91, 96, 99
Pfeifer, Guido 93, 94, 95, 96, 98, 99, 100
Pietsch, Michael 60, 61, 66, 75

Pitkänen, Pekka 103, 104, 112, 324, 325, 326, 327, 328, 329, 331, 332, 333, 334, 337
Polanyi, Karl 315, 320
Polzin, Robert 245, 246, 247, 251, 252, 253, 264
Popper, J. 266, 285
Porter, Anne 30, 42
Pritchard, James B. 142, 174
Propp, William H.C. 76, 267, 268, 269, 271, 277, 285
Prussner, Frederick C. 22, 41
Pummer, Reinhard 297, 298, 300
Qedar, S. 312, 319
Rabe, V.W. 265, 285
Radner, Karen 304, 311, 320
Rainey, Anson F. 309, 311, 320
Redditt, Paul R. 6, 20
Reeder, Caryn A. 320
Reimer, David J. 209, 213, 222
Rendsburg, Gary A. 54, 56, 57
Rendtorff, Rolf 22, 42, 61, 64, 65, 67, 68, 75, 101, 112, 241
Retsö, Jan 243, 278, 285
Reuter, Eleonore 103, 112
Rezetko, Robert 42, 247, 252, 256, 264
Richter, Sandra 301, 303, 304, 309, 314, 315, 320, 332
Ringgren, Helmer 220
Ritter, Jim 97, 100
Robson, James 215, 222
Rom-Shiloni, Dalit 74, 108, 112, 154, 174, 191, 204, 205, 298, 300
Römer, Thomas C. 11, 19, 61, 65, 67, 68, 71, 75, 105, 112, 173, 208, 213, 216, 222, 227, 241, 242
Rooker, Mark F. 245, 256, 264
Rosen, Baruch 303, 320
Roth, Martha T. 129, 140, 174
Routledge, Bruce 329, 330, 331, 332, 337
Rubin, U. 276, 280, 285
Rudnig, Thilo A. 107, 113
Rudolph, Wilhelm 59, 76, 282
Rütersworden, Udo 207, 209, 222
Said, Edward 329, 337
Samuel, Harald 107, 108, 110, 113

Sanmartín, J. 275, 285
San Nicolò, Marian 87, 91
Sanders, Seth L. 39, 41, 329, 330, 338
Sarna, Nahum M. 7, 11, 20, 193, 205, 292, 300
Schaper, Joachim 103, 107, 113
Schloen, J. David 318, 320, 330, 331, 338
Schmid, Hans H. 5, 20
Schmid, Konrad 5, 12, 19, 20, 22, 23, 26, 37, 41, 42, 57, 59, 61, 64, 65, 67, 71, 73, 74, 75, 76, 101, 111, 179, 187, 188, 204, 205
Schmidt, Ludwig 61, 76
Schmitt, R. 266, 273, 279, 285
Schwankl, Otto 7, 20
Schwartz, Baruch A. 3, 6, 57, 104, 113
Schwartz, Glenn M. 30, 42
Scott, R. 270, 285
Seebass, Horst 5, 11, 20
Segal, Moshe H. 244, 264
Seitz, Gottfried 209, 222
Seybold, Klaus 82, 91
Shedinger, Robert F. 21, 42
Shin, Seoung-Yun 245, 264
Shryock, Andrew 29, 32, 33, 34, 35, 36, 37, 42
Simons, J. 278, 285
Singer-Avitz, Lily 307, 318
Ska, Jean L. 9, 20, 24, 42, 46, 51, 57, 66, 67, 76, 188, 300
Skweres, Dieter E. 109, 113
Smend, Rudolf 62, 76, 112
Smith, Anthony D. 325, 338
Smith, Mark S. 267, 269, 285
Sollberger, E. 266, 285
Sommer, Benjamin D. 157, 174, 298, 300
Spinoza, Baruch 21, 59, 62, 76, 228
Stackert, Jeffrey 3, 23, 24, 26, 27, 41, 42, 66, 76, 101, 113
Stager, Lawrence E. 308, 309, 312, 318, 320
Steinberg, Julius 229, 242
Steinkeller, Piotr 40, 42
Stern, Ephraim 304, 305, 306, 307, 308, 309, 310, 311, 320
Stuart, Douglas 154, 174
Sweeney, Marvin A. 216, 222

Szuchman, Jeffrey 30, 42
Taggar-Cohen, Ada 173, 326, 338
Tal, Oren 304, 310, 312, 318, 320
Thiele, Edwin R. 304, 320
Thompson, Christine M. 303, 304, 311, 320
Tigay, Jeffrey H. 124, 136, 137, 150, 162, 163, 174, 210, 212, 213, 214, 215, 222, 300, 329, 338
Tooman, William A. 191, 205
Toorn, Karel van der 115, 174
Tucker, Paavo 67, 72, 76
Ulrich, Eugene 290, 296, 299, 300
Ungern-Sternberg, Jürgen von 82, 91
Ungnad, Arthur 87, 88, 89, 90, 91
Utzschneider, Helmut 6, 20, 266, 281, 285
Van Seters, John 5, 20, 22, 61, 65, 66, 76, 101, 113
Vanderhooft, David 306, 308, 310, 311, 319, 320
Vang, Carsten 197, 216, 222
Vanoni, Gottfried 164, 174
Vaux, Roland de 271, 273, 279, 280, 286
Veracini, Lorenzo 328, 338
Vogt, Peter T. 207, 210, 223
Volz, Paul 59, 76
Von Rad, Gerhard 22, 228, 242, 266, 273, 285, 334, 338
Von Soden, Wolfram 97, 100, 267, 285
Vriezen, Th.C. 61, 76
Wade, M.L. 269, 271, 286
Walsh, Richard 3, 6, 18
Walton, Joshua T. 303, 304, 320
Watts, James W. 7, 20
Wazana, Nili 208, 210, 212, 216, 217, 218, 219, 223
Weber, Max 94, 100
Weimar, Peter 14, 20
Weinfeld, Moshe 110, 201, 205, 209, 215, 217, 218, 223, 323, 324, 332, 334, 338
Wellhausen, Julius 5, 20, 21, 22, 23, 43, 63, 64, 70, 71, 76, 79, 101, 102, 103, 104, 106, 107, 108, 109, 110, 113, 179, 186, 189, 191, 205, 228, 240, 259, 262, 264, 266, 271, 279, 280,

286, 297, 322, 324, 327, 330, 333, 334, 335
Wenham, Gordon J. 11, 52, 54, 57, 118, 119, 129, 132, 136, 174, 325, 338
Westbrook, Raymond 94, 98, 100
Westendorf, Wolfgang 221
Westermann, Claus 11, 33, 34, 43, 54, 55, 57
Wette, Wilhelm M.L de 21, 22, 62, 68, 76, 79, 103, 112, 179, 187
Wiker, Benjamin 60, 74
Wilcke, Claus 94, 97, 99, 100
Williamson, Hugh G.M. 312, 320
Wilson, Robert R. 29, 33, 43, 111
Wolff, Hans W. 209, 223
Wray Beal, Lissa M. 216, 223
Wright, Christopher J.H. 209, 223
Wright, Richard M. 245, 252, 256, 264

Xella, P. 275, 276, 278, 286
Young, Ian 247, 252, 256, 264
Younger, K. Lawson, Jr. 28, 40, 42, 43, 218, 223, 303, 320, 326, 338
Zadok, Ran 326, 338
Zahn, Molly 52, 57
Zarzecki-Peleg, Anabel 302, 317
Zehnder, Markus 73, 75, 99, 117, 118, 124, 126, 130, 139, 141, 149, 150, 156, 157, 169, 170, 174, 175
Zenger, Erich 3, 5, 6, 20
Zevit, Ziony 261, 262, 263, 287, 300
Ziemer, Benjamin 8, 20
Zlotnik, Yehoshua 304, 321
Zobel, Konstantin 209, 210, 212, 213, 223
Zorn, Jeffrey R. 305, 321

Beihefte zur Zeitschrift für Altorientalische und Biblische Rechtsgeschichte

Herausgegeben von Eckart Otto, Dominik Markl und Guido Pfeifer

---

18: Dominik Markl
Gottes Volk im Deuteronomium
2012. XIV, 363 Seiten, 9 Diagramme, 3 Tabellen, gb
170x240 mm
ISBN 978-3-447-06763-8
⊙ E-Book: ISBN 978-3-447-19261-3   je € 84,– (D)

In seinen Abschiedsreden bereitet Mose das Volk Israel auf das Leben im Gelobten Land vor. Auf diese Weise wird im Buch Deuteronomium Israels religiöse, moralische, geschichtliche und rechtliche Identität formiert. Hinter Mose jedoch verbergen sich in der Endgestalt des Buches Deuteronomium Gelehrte der persischen Zeit (5./4. Jahrhundert v.Chr.), die die entstehende frühjüdische Gemeinschaft als Gottesvolk „Israel" etablieren.

Dominik Markl untersucht in seiner Studie erstmals systematisch die rhetorischen und literarischen Mittel, die im Buch Deuteronomium angewendet werden, um im Moabbund eine Glaubensgemeinschaft zu begründen, die nach der Katastrophe des Exils von Neuem erstehen soll. Dabei erweist sich das Buch Deuteronomium als Meisterwerk religiöser und politischer Rhetorik und Didaktik, in dem komplexe textpragmatische Mittel eingesetzt sind. Mose vermittelt, wer „wir" sind und fordert „heute" zu einer Entscheidung für den Bund mit Gott und für seine Tora heraus. Die Erzählstimme des Deuteronomium zeigt, wie Mose „dieses Buch" schreibt und wie das Grab dieses größten Propheten „bis heute" mysteriös verschollen bleibt. Nicht Moses Grab, sondern seine Tora bleibt Israels Erbe und so wird das „Heute" des Deuteronomium zum Geburtstag des Judentums.

19: Dominique Jaillard, Christophe Nihan (Eds.)
Writing Laws in Antiquity
L'écriture du droit dans l'Antiquité
2017. 170 pages, 1 tableau, relié
170x240 mm
ISBN 978-3-447-06894-9
⊙ E-Book: ISBN 978-3-447-19647-5   each € 58,– (D)

The present volume comprises various essays that examine the writing down and transmission of laws and legal collections in the ancient world, including Greece, Mesopotamia, Egypt, and Israel.

Using a comparative approach, the volume envisions the writing of legal collections as a complex set of social, political, economic, and religious processes, and seeks to trace a number of the key dynamics involved in those processes. Additionally, the volume gives special attention to the writing down of ritual laws, which are considered here as a specific yet nonetheless instructive instance of legal formulation in ancient societies.

In keeping with this methodological perspective, the first part of the volume ("Codes, Codification and Legislators") discusses the processes involved in the creation of legal collections as well as the relevance of the analytical categories used to describe these processes, whereas the second part ("Writing Ritual Prescriptions: Meanings and Functions") addresses issues related to the codification of ritual norms, especially in Greece and Israel. Overall, the volume aims to further the discussion on the writing of laws in antiquity with regard to a number of key questions, such as the relationship between written and unwritten norms, the function of written laws in the preservation and transformation of structures of authority, and the place of religion and rituals in processes of legal codification.

Beihefte zur Zeitschrift für Altorientalische und Biblische Rechtsgeschichte

Herausgegeben von Eckart Otto, Dominik Markl und Guido Pfeifer

---

20: Olivier Artus (Ed.)
Loi et Justice dans la Littérature du Proche-Orient ancien
2013. 274 pages, 9 tables, relié
170x240 mm
ISBN 978-3-447-10030-4 € 68,– (D)

What is the connection between law and justice in the literature of the Ancient Near East? Does justice always need the writing of laws? And what is the true purpose of the law collections of the Ancient Near East and of the Bible? To take the case of the Hammurapi code, does it represent an authentic legal text, or a work of royal propaganda, or rather a collection of case laws?
The volume edited by Olivier Artus gathers together conferences given on the occasion of two international colloques at the Catholic University of Paris (2010 and 2011) about this field of law and justice. The articles lead an investigation about the questions concerned from the legal texts of the Ancient Near East, particularly from Mesopotamian literature and from biblical legal texts as well as from wisdom biblical literature. The different studies try to set the legal texts in their historical situation and in the context of the political and theological debates of their time.

21: Benjamin Kilchör
Mosetora und Jahwetora
Das Verhältnis von Deuteronomium 12–26 zu Exodus, Levitikus und Numeri
2015. XVIII, 390 Seiten, 1 Diagramm, 110 Tabellen, gb
170x240 mm
ISBN 978-3-447-10409-8
⊙ E-Book: ISBN 978-3-447-19420-4 je € 98,– (D)

In den Büchern Exodus, Levitikus und Numeri tritt Jahwe als Gesetzgeber auf und übermittelt Mose die Tora. Im Deuteronomium spricht nicht mehr Jahwe, sondern Mose. Nach Dtn 1,5 legt Mose im Deuteronomium die Tora für das Volk Israel aus. Entgegen dieser Darstellung hat sich in den letzten 150 Jahren weitgehend die Meinung durchgesetzt, dass ein Großteil der Gesetze aus Exodus, Levitikus und Numeri jünger ist als das deuteronomische Gesetz und folglich im deuteronomischen Gesetz nicht ausgelegt sein kann.
Benjamin Kilchör vergleicht systematisch das gesamte deuteronomische Gesetz (Dtn 12,2–26,15) mit all seinen Parallelen in den Büchern Exodus, Levitikus und Numeri. Dabei zeigt sich, dass die Gesetze in Exodus, Levitikus und Numeri nicht nur auf der Ebene der Erzählung, sondern auch rechtsgeschichtlich im Deuteronomium vorausgesetzt sind. Das Deuteronomium greift diese älteren Gesetze auf, nicht um sie zu ersetzen, sondern um sie auf neue Situationen hin anzuwenden, zu ergänzen oder um Gesetzeslücken zu schließen. Eine wichtige Rolle für die Auslegung dieser älteren Gesetze spielen die Zehn Gebote, die dem deuteronomischen Gesetz seine Struktur und seinen Interpretationsrahmen geben.

VERLAG PUBLISHERS
HARRASSOWITZ